Praise for
Mike Nichols

"Terrific." —*San Francisco Chronicle*

"Anyone with an abiding love for film or theater will be fascinated by *Mike Nichols*, but even those with only a passing familiarity with his work are likely to find themselves taken in by this engrossing biography. Harris's book is a masterwork, endlessly engaging, and one of the best biographies of an American artist to be published in recent years." —NPR.org

"A superb new biography." —*Chicago Tribune*

"A pleasure to read and a model biography: appreciative yet critical, unfailingly intelligent and elegantly written . . . A shrewd, in-depth reckoning of the elusive man behind the polished façade . . . [Harris's] marvelous book makes palpable in artful detail the extraordinary scope and brilliance of [Nichols's] achievements."
—Wendy Smith, *The Washington Post*

"Gleaming . . . Fortified with a wealth of interviews that make the acknowledgments a red carpet roll call (Candice Bergen, Robert Redford, Meryl Streep . . .), *Mike Nichols: A Life* is a midcentury fairy tale of right place–right time–right crowd. . . . The rare large-scale biography without boring bits."
—James Wolcott, *The New York Times Book Review*

"Wonderful . . . [Harris] is in top form here. His command of the theater world and the film industry and his smart and engaging writing (he calls the profligate Nichols 'a rich man who enjoyed living like an even richer man') make the book a pleasure to read." —*The Christian Science Monitor*

"[A] crisp new biography . . . [Harris has] a gift for scene setting. He's at his best in *Mike Nichols: A Life* when he takes you inside a production. His chapters on the making of three films in particular—*The Graduate*, *Silkwood*, and *Angels in*

America—are miraculous: shrewd, tight, intimate, and funny. You sense he could turn each one into a book. . . . [Nichols] was a man in perpetual motion, and Harris chases him with patience, clarity, and care." —Dwight Garner, *The New York Times*

"Judicious and superbly well written . . . [Nichols's] peculiar gift was for making [actors] feel safe being precarious. The essence of life is that it unfolds chronologically and according to no script. Actors must capture this essence, then somehow transfer it into highly artificial situations. If Nichols played taskmaster, it was only to remind them that what is happening here has never happened before; you have no idea what others will say or do next, you must stay spontaneous and reactive— all while subordinating yourself to a larger story. That was, finally, the great, impossible neither/nor of his genius, as it is, too, of Mark Harris's wonderful book."
—Stephen Metcalf, *Los Angeles Times*

"Meticulous, deeply engrossing." —*Variety*

"May be the best biography of an artist in a very long time." —*The Wrap*

"I read this because I was such a fan of Mark Harris's first two books and wound up being fascinated by *Mike Nichols*. I found the book incredibly relaxing, in the same way going to the movies can be relaxing. I felt entertained and taken care of. It was an enormous treat." —Ann Patchett, via Instagram

"Harris, a proven scholar of Hollywood, writes brilliantly and gathers momentum with deeply researched, fascinating forensic passages about the challenges and conflicts of Nichols's great projects." —*USA Today*

"Fascinating, exhaustively researched, and utterly absorbing . . . A roller-coaster life that, no matter how challenging it might have been for Mike Nichols, makes a thrilling tale for the reader." —Vogue.com

"A monumental tribute to a singular talent . . . A cinderblock of a book whose weight is never felt in the reading . . . Getting [Elaine] May on the record stands as one of the book's major accomplishments, one that calls out for a full-fledged follow-up and affirms this most crucial of connections." —*The AV Club*

"Harris has produced a biography that transcends the prodigiously reported facts and wild-ride circumstances of Nichols's lives. The book pulses with a narrative energy equal to its subject. When was the last time you read a biography that also was a page-turner?" —*Theater News Online*

"Dazzling . . . A superb and definitive biography that Nichols and his fans deserve. Harris (*Pictures at a Revolution*) is part film historian, theater buff, and investigative reporter, which makes this rich, compassionate, and candid biography soar with fresh, firsthand anecdotes from Nichols's coworkers and Harris's astute observations about the director's work. . . . The ideal gift for anyone interested in the creative arts." —*Shelf Awareness*

"Sprawling yet intimate . . . Candid, colorful, and chock-full of detail, *Mike Nichols: A Life* is the biography that Nichols well deserves." —*BookPage* (starred review)

"A Mike Nichols credit always made the heart race with anticipation. So does *Mike Nichols: A Life*, an epic biography of an epic creative life . . . Engrossing."
—Douglass K. Daniel, Associated Press

"Mark Harris's biography is a must for every film and theatre buff. Every moment in Nichols's life and career comes vividly alive. . . . *Mike Nichols: A Life* is an invaluable contribution to the history of American theatre and film since World War II as well as a colorful portrait of one of its most celebrated and at times denigrated practitioners." —John M. Clum, *New York Journal of Books*

"Can't-put-it-down biography . . . Like his subject, its humor is sidesplitting, its behavioral insights keen, and its wit double-edged. . . . Harris's strength as a writer is not merely giving the reader a window onto how his subject put together a sketch, a play, a movie, a career, and a life, but putting her in the rooms where it happened. . . . Like all great biographies, Harris's book is a double portrait of an artist and his era." —Carrie Rickey, *The Forward*

"Such a wide-ranging professional life is the stuff of a major biography, and Mark Harris, author of *Pictures at a Revolution* and *Five Came Back*, two of the best books about film to come out in recent years, has delivered the goods. *Mike Nichols: A Life* is as fine a portrait of anyone in the performing arts as I have ever read. . . . Mark Harris's wonderful book, which comes seven years after [Nichols's] passing, will serve as his monument." —Terry Teachout, *Commentary*

"Fascinating for its exploration of a great artist's inner workings, as well as for its chronicling of an industry's evolution."
—*O, The Oprah Magazine* (Most Anticipated Books of 2021)

"Harris follows two outstanding works of film history (*Pictures at a Revolution*, 2008, and *Five Came Back*, 2014) with this robust biography of legendary director Mike Nichols. Harris's skill as a storyteller is on full view . . . with a novelist's feel for narrative. . . . Like the best biographies, Harris brings his subject's life and work together in a perfectly unified whole." —*Booklist* (starred review)

"The book is as smart and well paced as if Mike had directed it. It's *Virginia Woolf* brutal and *Birdcage* funny. I devoured the details of Mike's fascinating life, but I also marveled at Mark Harris's ability to lead us through it. The shaky wooden roller-coaster of collaboration, the serpent-tongued antihero's path to love, an artist's guide to not being trash, ten pounds of movie stars in a five-pound bag—this book has it all!" —Tina Fey

"Mike was many things to many people, a multi-talented man of many parts, who lived several lifetimes during his long, complicated roller-coaster of a life. But above all else, Mike was a great director, and Mark Harris has produced a clear-eyed, honest, enormously entertaining, deeply moving, and thought-provoking account of what a director's life is like and of what being a director means. His particular gifts, demonstrated in each book he writes, of combining objectivity with empathy and seriousness with delight, are precisely what make him Mike Nichols's ideal biographer. I can't think of any praise higher than to say that this book is worthy of its subject." —Steven Spielberg

"The rise and rise of Igor, the bald refugee kid from Berlin, is a Technicolor dream—a dazzling only-in-America story like something out of Horatio Alger. In this exciting biography, Mark Harris never loses sight of the sharper edges of Mike Nichols's success or the price he paid for it. But his deep love of his subjects—Nichols and the American performing arts—makes this an essential work for understanding our culture in the last century through one of its most outstanding, and most unlikely, protagonists."
—Benjamin Moser, Pulitzer Prize–winning author of *Sontag*

"Mike Nichols, born Igor Michael Peschkowsky, was something between a man and a self-made myth. Mark Harris's magnificent, mesmerizing biography honors both sides of the Nichols persona, conjuring his charismatic brilliance while probing the human complexity behind the impish grin. Virtuosic in style, deep in insight, at times convulsively funny, at times piercingly sad, this tour-de-force of reporting, storytelling, and analysis stands as a clear-eyed homage to an artist who willed his own golden age."
—Alex Ross, music critic of *The New Yorker* and author of *Wagnerism*

"There are so many lessons in Mike's nine-act tragedy and triumph of a life: the joy of collaboration, the thrill of finding collaborators and soulmates; the ups and downs of the creative process. Mark Harris introduces us to every version of Mike Nichols, and shows us how each one prepared the way for the next. It's an incredible achievement. Required reading." —Lin-Manuel Miranda

PENGUIN BOOKS
Mike Nichols

Mark Harris is the author of *Pictures at a Revolution: Five Movies and the Birth of the New Hollywood*, a *New York Times* notable book of the year, and *Five Came Back: A Story of Hollywood and the Second World War*, a finalist for the Los Angeles Times Book Prize for History. He has written for many newspapers and magazines, including *New York*, *Vanity Fair*, and *The New York Times*. He lives in New York City with his husband, Tony Kushner.

ALSO BY MARK HARRIS

Five Came Back
Pictures at a Revolution

Mike Nichols

A LIFE

Mark Harris

PENGUIN BOOKS

PENGUIN BOOKS
An imprint of Penguin Random House LLC
penguinrandomhouse.com

First published in the United States of America by Penguin Press,
an imprint of Penguin Random House LLC, 2021
Published in Penguin Books 2022

ISBN 9780399562266 (paperback)

THE LIBRARY OF CONGRESS HAS CATALOGED THE
HARDCOVER EDITION AS FOLLOWS:

Names: Harris, Mark, 1963– author.
Title: Mike Nichols: a life / Mark Harris.
Description: First edition. | New York: Penguin Press, 2021. |
Includes bibliographical references and index.
Identifiers: LCCN 2020016901 (print) | LCCN 2020016902 (ebook) |
ISBN 9780399562242 (hardcover) | ISBN 9780399562259 (ebook)
Subjects: LCSH: Nichols, Mike. | Motion picture producers and
directors—United States—Biography.
Classification: LCC PN1998.3.N54 H37 2021 (print) |
LCC PN1998.3.N54 (ebook) | DDC 791.4302/33092 [B]—dc23
LC record available at https://lccn.loc.gov/2020016901
LC ebook record available at https://lccn.loc.gov/2020016902

Printed in the United States of America
1st Printing

Designed by Amanda Dewey

For Tony

You don't know what's going to happen. Big things look like little things. Little things don't have big signs on them that say "This is a Big Thing." They look like everything else. Disaster can reorder our lives in wonderful ways, and you just go on to the next thing. I passionately believe that in art, and certainly in the theater, there are only two questions . . . The first question is: "What is this, really, when it happens in life?" Not what is the accepted convention . . . but what is it really like? And the other question we really have to ask is "What happens next?"

Mike Nichols

CONTENTS

Part One · What It Was Really Like

One. STARTING FROM ZERO *(1931–1944)*   3

Two. AGENT X-9 *(1944–1952)*   20

Three. A SENSE OF YOUR POSSIBILITIES *(1952–1955)*   36

Four. THE FIRST THING WE EVER DID
TOGETHER *(1955-1957)*   50

Five. THIS BOY AND GIRL *(1957–1959)*   69

Six. A NEW AND VERY STRANGE EXPERIENCE
(1959–1960)   88

Seven. THE MOST IMPORTANT PEOPLE *(1960–1962)*   103

Eight. PLAYING THE ROLE OF A FATHER *(1962–1963)*   120

Nine. OKAY, THAT'S GREAT, NOW LET'S TRY THIS
(1963–1964)   137

Ten. THE FUNNIEST DISTANCE BETWEEN
TWO POINTS *(1964–1965)*   155

Eleven. I WANT TO KNOW THIS PLACE *(1965–1966)*   170

Twelve. ONE CONSIDERABLE INTELLIGENCE *(1966–1967)*   188

Thirteen. PROVE YOU BELONG HERE *(1967)*   205

Fourteen. IT'S BEGINNING TO MAKE SENSE *(1967–1968)*   220

Fifteen. THE ONLY WAY TO LIVE YOUR LIFE *(1968–1969)*   238

Sixteen. COLD TO THE TOUCH AND BRILLIANT TO
THE EYE *(1969–1971)*   255

Seventeen. DOLPHINS ARE SMARTER THAN HUMAN
BEINGS *(1971–1973)*   273

Eighteen. MR. SUCCESS *(1973–1975)*   290

Part Two · What Happened Next

Nineteen. EVERYTHING GOES ON THE LINE *(1975–1977)*   311

Twenty. THE RAPTURE OF MY DEPTH *(1977–1980)*   329

Twenty-one. REUNIONS *(1980–1981)*   342

Twenty-two. AM I DOING THIS RIGHT? *(1981–1982)*   358

Twenty-three. OH, THIS IS TROUBLE *(1983–1985)*   372

Twenty-four. A SHOT ACROSS THE BOW *(1985–1986)*   391

Twenty-five. BORROWED TIME *(1986–1987)*   408

Twenty-six. PINOCCHIO AND CINDERELLA *(1987–1988)*   421

Twenty-seven. STILL HERE *(1988–1990)*   434

Twenty-eight. IT NEVER GOES AWAY *(1990–1993)*   452

Twenty-nine. THE BEST ROUTE TO REVENGE *(1993–1996)*   470

Thirty. SOMETHING SCARY *(1996–1999)*   488

Thirty-one. THE ULTIMATE TEST *(2000–2001)*   507

Thirty-two. MORE LIFE *(2001–2003)*   523

Thirty-three. BIG ISN'T TRUE *(2003–2005)*   537

Thirty-four. GOOD NIGHT, STARS *(2005–2009)*   553

Thirty-five. WAY OUT THERE IN THE BLUE *(2010–2014)*   572

EPILOGUE   591

Acknowledgments   595
Notes   601
Bibliography   647
Works by Mike Nichols   651
Image Credits   653
Index   655

PART ONE

What It Was Really Like

One

STARTING FROM ZERO

1931-1944

In the origin story that Mike Nichols liked to tell, he was born at the age of seven. The first image of himself he chose to conjure for people was that of a boy on a boat, holding his younger brother's hand, traveling from Germany to America. They were unaccompanied on that six-day crossing in 1939, their ailing mother still bedbound in Berlin. Their father was already in New York. His two small sons had not seen him for almost a year.

Nichols was not yet real even to himself. His name was Michael Igor Peschkowsky, or perhaps it wasn't. Decades later, his brother, Robert, looking into his family's history, told him that according to the ship's manifest and the petition for naturalization that was later filed by his father, his name was actually Igor Michael Peschkowsky. *Igor.* A horror-movie name. Nichols looked at him impassively. "Maybe," he said. "Maybe it was." It didn't matter. Whatever his name when he boarded ship, it was gone by the time he got to New York.

Nichols turned the transatlantic crossing into a story—his first self-revelation-as-anecdote, an approach that he would eventually refine into a shield and a disguise, but also into a style of directing, a means of conveying an idea or a feeling or a circumstance to an actor that he deployed with precision and finesse over a five-decade career in movies and theater. He first tried it out on journalists in his twenties, when suddenly everyone wanted to know who Mike Nichols was and where on earth he had come from. The story he told, droll and wry, with a slight undertow of despair, was that at seven he was packed onto the boat knowing only two sentences in what would become his new language: "I do not speak English" and "Please do not kiss me." In some tellings, he spoke no English at all and instead wore those two warnings on a penciled sign that was pinned to his clothes before boarding. It was this picture—the *New Yorker* cartoon version of his early life, with a punch line that hinted at both utter solitude and defiant standoffishness— that Nichols used to explain his personality to others, and to himself: a portrait of the artist as the Little Prince, alone on his planet and at home nowhere.

If the boy who had existed for seven years before that journey usu- ally went undiscussed in interviews, it was in part because Nichols's life before America was so hazy to him that he could retrieve little of it until adulthood. His childhood in Berlin—his years as either Michael or Igor—barely existed in his memory. As a youngster, he attended the Private Jüdische Waldschule Kaliski, an elementary school that, during Hitler's rise, became a Jews-only institution. Nichols's father, a doctor named Pavel Peschkowsky, was a Russian Jew, albeit so secular that he didn't even believe in circumcision. His mother, Brigitte Landauer, was a German Jew, wholly invested in and proud of her national heritage and also indifferent to her religion. Within their cultural circle, Paul and Brigitte were not atypical—as Lotte Kaliski, who founded the school Nichols attended, put it, "We all had to learn to become Jewish. Most of us came from very assimilated families and so did the children. But we understood that in order to give children a more positive atti- tude, they had to know something about their background."

Whatever that education was to be, Michael—or, as Elaine May later teasingly called him, "little Igor"—was not in the school long enough to absorb it. His memories of the Kaliski school were few, and mostly miserable. He recalled a group of German children in black shirts stealing his bicycle. And, more vividly, he could picture "with awful clarity a scene with my gym teacher and my mother, and realizing they were lovers. She was a beautiful woman, and I remember her quarreling with him, and he ripped a necklace off her and threw it out a window, and she went running after it." As an adult, Nichols spoke as if that moment were still raw, admitting, "I suppose I've spent a large part of my life trying to sort that out." But at other times, he pushed the door shut. "A Jew in Nazi Germany, parents always fighting," he would say, as detached as if he were musing about a stranger. "Aren't all childhoods bad?"

His ancestry—the "family legend," as he called it—was dramatic, filled with art and politics, wealth, loss, privation, and bloodshed. When he left Berlin as a little boy, he knew hardly any of it. His mother and his aunt had given him and Robert the good part—he was a cousin of Albert Einstein, no less, and thus had a famous relative already in America, a story he became so certain was prideful apocrypha that he was astonished when it turned out to be true. But they left out virtually everything else. He knew that his father was now a two-time emigrant; as a young anti-Bolshevik supporter of Alexander Kerensky, he had fled Russia, crossing the Gobi Desert into Manchuria and eventually resettling in Germany. But not until Nichols was almost eighty did he learn that a fortune in gold had helped Pavel Peschkowsky start his new life. "Jews with goldmines!" he marveled when, during a guest appearance on a TV genealogy show, he first heard the truth. One of his great-grandfathers, Grigory Distler, had taken possession of what was thought to be a depleted mine on Sakhalin Island and found an immense undiscovered trove of gold, enough to give his daughter Anna and her son—Nichols's father—seventy-five bars. The inheritance enabled their passage out of Russia and allowed Peschkowsky to set up a successful medical practice in Berlin. "I always had this picture of my father somehow working his way up," Nichols said. "They were rich! Who knew? I wish to God I had gotten to know my father better, because I had it all wrong."

His mother, Brigitte, came from unhappier circumstances. Her father, Gustav Landauer, was an intellectual polymath who studied metaphysics and translated Shakespeare into German. He was also a political firebrand, a committed believer in the philosophy of an anarchist, post-governmental agrarian utopia, and an agitator who served jail time for his insurrectionist articles in *Der Sozialist*. Bearded, oratorically fiery, and six and a half feet tall, he cut a formidable public figure. In 1903 he married Hedwig Lachmann, a poet and translator whose adaptation of Oscar Wilde's *Salomé* became the libretto for Richard Strauss's opera. Landauer was interested in religion as a field of research but had no use for it in his home, nor did his wife, despite being the daughter of a cantor. Brigitte grew up in Hermsdorf, a largely Jewish suburb of Berlin, in a house filled with literature and art. "I played with Jewish children," she recalled, "but we were the only ones who celebrated Christmas and Easter . . . an entirely secular Christmas, with presents, stars, tinsel . . . At school I was the only child who sat alone while the others studied religion and recited their prayers." Lachmann, who demanded near-constant quiet so she could work, and the stern, imposing Landauer were not natural parents. "There wasn't the family 'togetherness' one finds so often today," Brigitte said later. "We met at meals, but otherwise did little together."

What stability she had was shattered in 1918, when her mother became one of the first victims of the flu pandemic and died at fifty-two. Her father had just risen to become commissioner of enlightenment and public instruction during the very brief existence of the socialist Bavarian Soviet Republic, part of an ad hoc leadership cadre set up largely by poets and philosophers. In a matter of weeks, that interregnum fell to the German army, and Landauer became a hunted man. He made arrangements to hide Brigitte and her older sister, Gudula, in the home of friends and went on the run. In April 1919 he wrote, "My beloved children—Some of my friends were or are still imprisoned. But do not worry about me! I am looked after very well in every respect and I will be cautious. My greatest concern is that false rumors will reach and worry you . . . My second concern is that agitated bourgeois and peasants might harass you. I hope not. If it does happen, be wise and prudent . . . Do not forget to take the little bit of money that is in the house, as well as your and your mother's jewelry. I hope to hear from you soon!" Less than three weeks later, Landauer was murdered by members of the paramilitary Freikorps; he was beaten with gun butts and kicked to death, then shot in the head. Brigitte heard the news while riding in a Berlin streetcar. She was twelve.

In 1922, Peschkowsky, then twenty-two, arrived in Berlin, where he finished college, attended medical school, got his doctor's license, and set up a successful practice catering to artists, theater people, and fellow Russian émigrés. By then Brigitte was employed as a hospital social worker. They married in 1930. Michael, their first son, was born a little more than a year later, on November 6, 1931. A second son, Robert, was born in 1935.

A photograph of Michael gazing at his newborn younger brother shows a little boy with a full head of wavy dark brown hair. Soon after that, he was given an injection of whooping cough vaccine and, he was told, suffered an allergic reaction that resulted in a complete and lifelong inability to grow hair. He would grow up bald. It was, says his brother, "the defining aspect of his childhood."

At the beginning of Hitler's rise to power, Nichols's father did not think of leaving Germany, as many Jews did. But by 1938 it had become apparent that all Jews—even the wealthy, even the secular, even those who, like Brigitte, felt German to their core—were in grave danger, and he began planning an escape for his family. "One thing that I'm sure hastened his [departure]," Robert Nichols says, "was that . . .

Jews could no longer see any [non-Jewish] patients. They could function as practical nurses or orderlies, but otherwise, they could not
practice at all as of mid-1938." Returning to Russia, where two of
Peschkowsky's uncles had just been put to death for counterrevolution-
ary activities, was not an option. Instead, he would leave for New York
immediately; his mother, Anna Distler—Michael and Robert's only
living grandparent—would soon flee Berlin to return to Manchuria.
Brigitte and the boys would join Pavel in America as soon as he had
found work and a place for them to live. Under German law at that
time, he and his family were considered Russian, not German—because
he came from Russia, the boys were never technically German citizens,
and were therefore somewhat freer to travel. He secured the necessary
papers and left Germany that August.

Upon arriving in New York, he got work as an X-ray technician for
a local union. By the beginning of 1939, he had passed the state medical boards and was ready to set up a practice under the new name he
had chosen—Paul Nichols, a nod to his late father, Nikolai, who had
also been a physician. (Paul's patronymic was Nikolayevich.) "By the
time I spelled Peschkowsky," he joked to his sons, "my patient was in
the hospital." He was ready to have his wife and children join him, but
back in Berlin, a medical issue had arisen: Brigitte had been diagnosed
with deep vein thrombosis, a life-threatening condition in which blood
clots can travel to the lungs. At that time, extended bed rest was wrongly
considered to be an effective treatment. She was sent to a convalescent
hospital. Michael and Robert would have to make the journey alone.
Their aunt Gudula, who had been taking care of them in their mother's
absence, sewed 15 marks—about $40—into the lining of their clothes
and took them to the embarkation point of the SS *Bremen*, a luxury
ocean liner, for the trip, where she placed them in the care of a steward.
Their father would retrieve them at the other end. They set sail on
April 28, 1939.

In later years, Nichols would speak of his "unbelievable, undeserved, life-shaming luck" in being able to emigrate. Brigitte had a distant cousin in Connecticut—not Einstein, but someone who was willing to sponsor the family, a financial guarantee without which the United States was refusing the entry of most Jews from Europe. He and his brother left on the *Bremen* just two weeks before the ill-fated departure of another ship, the *St. Louis,* that came to be known as the "voyage of the damned," in which hundreds of Jewish refugees fleeing the Third Reich for Cuba were denied entry at one international port after another; many of them were returned to Germany and eventually killed in the Holocaust. "I remember everything about getting on the boat," Nichols said. "We were on the gangplank when everything stopped because of Hitler's speech . . . They had loudspeakers on every corner . . . I remember the sound but not the content."

But it was not, he took pains to say, a moment of fear. Nichols thought of himself as an immigrant but not as a survivor. He would reach his fifties having spent "years, decades, when I didn't think about it" before coming to realize how deeply a sense that "this is all borrowed time" resided within him. As a child, he saw the boat trip as an adventure. "I remember when we got to the end of the gangplank I jumped as hard as I could because I wanted to see the boat go up and down," he said. And the voyage itself wasn't scary. At seven, he was a self-contained, unsmiling child who had not seen his father for eight months and had gotten used to a mother who "was ill . . . and would be ill for much of the rest of her life." The only thing that could rattle him was the emotional display that the sight of a bald little uncared-for refugee boy holding a three-year-old's hand was likely to engender among adults. "Please do not kiss me" was an essential directive because "if you were alone people tended to kiss you," he said. "And I hated it."

During those few days, the boys had the run of much of the ship. There was a nursery with stuffed animals, and a nanny on staff to keep an eye on them during mealtimes and pack them off to their stateroom if they misbehaved. There were adults who found amusement in the beaky young boy with the serious demeanor. "I remember looking for the prow of the boat, or was it the bow?" Nichols said. "I remember asking a fellow passenger, in German, where was the tip? . . . He pointed to the tip of my nose. And I said, 'No, no, no, don't kid around!'" And there were movies, including the first one he ever saw, a dubbed German version of the 1938 Clark Gable–Spencer Tracy adventure *Test Pilot*—"test pee-lote," he said, sounding out the words on the screen. "That and another movie . . . I think it must have been *Gunga Din*. Because the army they were fighting was often shown in close-up, I thought they were fighting giants. I remember that I hadn't grasped perspective yet."

As promised, their father was waiting at the harbor to pick them up. "The first thing I saw getting off the boat was a kosher deli," said Nichols, "and in the neon sign were Hebrew letters. I said to my dad, 'Is that allowed?' And he said, 'Here, it is.' And from then on it was fun stuff. We'd never had food that made noise like Rice Krispies. Or drinks that were alive like Coke. And we just had fun." He also had a new name—one he hated. The short *i* with which both of his parents pronounced Michael—"Mick-eye-el"—made Michael Nichols sound like a nonsense name, or the start of a nursery rhyme. He shed it as soon as he learned that there was an American abbreviation. At home, he remained Michael. Everywhere else, he was, from the moment he could say it without an accent, Mike Nichols.

Nichols's recollection that they "just had fun" papered over a great deal of pain that began almost immediately upon their arrival in the United States. The reunion with their father did not last long. Paul Nichols had counted on a future in which Brigitte would arrive with the children and take care of them while he worked. Even if he had been ready to serve as a full-time parent to two little boys, he didn't have the disposition for it—the first bedtime story he ever told Mike was about the sinking of the *Titanic*—and he had not yet found an apartment suitable for a family of four. Within days of their disembarking, he sent Mike and Robert off to live on Long Island with two of his new patients, a well-to-do British couple with children of their own who had agreed to take care of his boys while he established himself in Manhattan. For the next several months, the two were essentially foster children. They rarely saw their father and lived in a home in which they were treated as second-class citizens. "They were awful," Nichols said of his caretakers. "They would kiss their own children good night, then shake our hands. We'd get a spoonful of milk of magnesia and go to bed."

It was nearly a year before Brigitte arrived and the family was reunited. The German-Soviet Non-Aggression Pact was still in place when she received permission to rejoin her Russian husband in America. She left Berlin in March 1940, her naturalization papers identifying her as Russian rather than German. Growing up, the boys were told that she was one of the last Jews to be allowed to leave Germany— that they had been saved from losing their mother by a matter of weeks, if not days. It was not precisely true—in fact, Brigitte would work hard for the next year and a half to bring her older sister over—but it was consistent with her sense that her well-being was terribly precarious, and it was close enough to accurate for Nichols to feel that "we had somehow miraculously walked through the flames and landed on West 70th Street . . . I almost felt guilty."

At the time the Nichols family settled in Manhattan, Jews represented a quarter of the city's population. No longer clustered on the Lower East Side, as their ancestors had been fifty years earlier, they had moved into, and reshaped, other neighborhoods. Still locked out of residential buildings on Fifth Avenue and Park Avenue, where "business and social references required" in real estate listings was a barely coded way of saying "No Jews allowed," they looked elsewhere. Many chose the Upper West Side, where poorer Jews lived in tenements with Black and Puerto Rican neighbors, middle-class families found apartments on West End Avenue or Riverside Drive, and the wealthiest lived on Central Park West. Other Jewish families had moved into Harlem, where, after thirty years, many of them were now leaving for the prettier streets of Morningside Heights or Washington Heights, or enclaves near Mosholu Parkway, in the Bronx, or Williamsburg or parts of Queens. Most New York Jews just before the United States entered World War II were not religious; a survey at the time showed that 72 percent of young Jewish men had attended no services in the past year. Of those who chose the Upper West Side, as the Nicholses were planning to, about half worked in clothing manufacturing; they liked the neighborhood because it was an easy subway commute a few miles south to the Garment District.

Paul Nichols soon found a place one block north of where he'd been staying—a new six-story building at 155 West Seventy-first Street where he could afford a first-floor office to see patients and two rooms on the fifth floor to live. It was neither a slum nor a luxury high-rise, just a modest apartment building on a middle-class street off Broadway where immigrant Jews could find a foothold and begin a new life. It was named, perfectly, Gatsby House. In 1941, Nichols and his family moved in.

Conditions were fine for the children, but cramped for the adults, especially two adults whose marriage had been tempestuous in Berlin, who hadn't seen each other for almost two years, and who were used to the privacy and autonomy that more space had afforded them. Here, the boys shared the bedroom and their parents slept on a hide-a-bed in the sunken living room; two steps up were a little dining area and a kitchenette. "It was a very small apartment," says Robert Nichols, "but I think we were comfortable financially. There was no sense of deprivation at all in our early childhood. Life was good, finally." As he had in Berlin, Paul Nichols was quickly able to build a word-of-mouth practice that attracted artists and musicians. Among his patients were the pianist Vladimir Horowitz and the music-and-concert impresario Sol Hurok, whose insignia, "S. Hurok Presents," was a familiar sight affixed to a recital or a performance. Sometimes there would be free tickets from grateful patients who found their new doctor witty and charming. (Hurok enjoyed Nichols's company but later told him, "You're not as funny as your father.") Paul Nichols was soon able to afford a Packard Clipper to get around the city for house calls.

Mike picked up English quickly. "I remember being on the school-bus," he said, and, seeing an ambulance, "saying 'What means EM-er-GEN-cy?' and then knowing it a couple of weeks later. And then the next stage, which all refugee kids remember, which is when you speak English and your parents speak German. They [speak] in German, you answer in English. And then there's this weird sort of bastardizing of language that also happens in a refugee family: 'Haster den room ge sweeped?'" His parents had initially enrolled him at Dalton, one of the best of the private schools in Manhattan that accepted Jews, and he was immediately advanced to the fourth grade. As a consequence, he missed the year in which his classmates had been taught cursive writing, and never caught up. "To this day," he said at thirty-five, "I have the hand-writing of an idiot."

"He printed everything, all his life," says the director Jack O'Brien, a longtime friend. "He couldn't make a cursive line. Those sweet sto-ries he tells about 'emergency' and learning the language are standard Mike, and they're lovely, but my feeling is, he was terribly cowed by America, and he didn't have the confidence in the pen that he had in his imagination, both visually and orally. I think that he didn't believe the written word was his métier. So he left it behind."

Dalton was the first of "a series of very chic . . . schools where we were taught French from playing cards and were served something every hour—second breakfast, mid-morning snack, hearty lunch, early afternoon cookies," said Nichols. He learned fast, but he still couldn't blend in. He spoke with an accent and wore a cap indoors to conceal his hairless head; his father would not get him a wig, believing that it was better for him to get used to his condition. "Children used to yell, 'Hey, baldy!'" says Robert Nichols. The playground was a nightmare. The best Mike could hope for, he later said, was to be "the most popular of the unpopular kids." One of his schoolmates that first year was Henry Zuckerman, who decades later would change his name to Buck Henry and become one of Nichols's most important collaborators. The two barely got to know each other. "The kid was as far outside as an outsider could get," Henry said. "I was a zero," said Nichols. "In every way that mattered, I was powerless."

Mike's parents had little time or inclination to coddle him. His father could be jovial—"What I loved him for," said Nichols, "even when he wasn't noticeably loving me, is that he had great vitality and joy." At his warmest, he would send Mike into fits of laughter by dancing around the apartment in his underwear. Socially, he was dapper, elegant, a wit and a storyteller, the life of every party. But he was often absent, and when he was at home, "he could rage" and would on occasion threaten to call the police when the kids misbehaved. "He had no idea what to do," said Nichols. And his mother was busy; soon after arriving, she started working at home as a typist, completing or translating letters and manuscripts for fellow immigrants. Being told to "go out and play" was, for Mike, like receiving an order to endure public humiliation. So he made his world smaller. He stayed home and played chess after school with Gordon Rogoff, a boy his age who sometimes came to the building to visit his aunt and uncle, and would show up only after being firmly nudged by them to go spend some time with Mike. "What I understood was that I was probably the only person his age who might be willing to play with him," said Rogoff.

And when Mike's parents would go out—sometimes together, sometimes separately—the older teenage girl they hired to babysit couldn't coax him out of the apartment. "He wasn't a happy child," says Mari-anne Mosbach, a German Jewish refugee who would come over, play with the boys, and do her homework after putting them to bed. "All the kids would make fun of him, and he would come home from school in a pretty bad mood. I was smart enough never to ask him 'How was your day?' because of the way he would stomp in." Instead of going to the park or the playground, they would make paper boats out of old newspapers and push them around in the sink until Mike got bored or irritated at losing an improvised race. Then he would putter around the small kitchen alone, making his own snacks and experimenting with food. "He would take leftover coffee and put it in the freezer to make cubes for iced coffee," says Mosbach. "His mother thought that was very clever." He warned Mosbach to leave him alone unless he needed something on a high shelf. He didn't want company.

"I was motivated then, and for a long time after, by revenge," said Nichols. That angry little boy remained embedded within, "saying 'Don't fuck with me.' And I can't stop him."

He didn't last long at Dalton. After a year, his parents moved him to the neighborhood public school, P.S. 87, where he was treated roughly and, for the first time since coming to America, encountered anti-Semitism from one of his instructors, who referred to him as "a Jewish kid" in a tone of manifest hostility. Mike knew that Hitler hated Jews, but it seemed to him that this teacher must have been talking about someone else, not a boy who was already used to Christmas presents and Easter eggs and had never seen the inside of a synagogue, who was, says Robert Nichols, "about as un-Jewish as it's possible for a Jew to be."

"I came home a little concerned, and my mother was great. She sort of put an arm around me . . . and she told me what it meant to be a Jew and what the problems were," Nichols said. "None of this had ever been spoken about before, or she wouldn't have had to have this little talk."

During the school year, Mike grew even angrier and became increasingly ungovernable, talking back at home, refusing to get out of bed in the morning, and sometimes cutting school altogether and hiding out in the cavernous Beacon Theatre, a 2,900-seat movie palace a few blocks away, with plenty of balconies and recesses where a kid could make himself scarce. "It was sort of my playground," he said. Mike loved the movies, but there was no thunderclap, no "This is what I want to do with my life" moment. The theater was just a comfortable refuge from an apartment where he felt "landlocked," caught between parents who, when they weren't mad at him, were at each other's throats, either about him or about things he didn't yet understand. Nichols's father was impatient, and his mother, who saw herself as being in a semi-permanent state of frail health, was now desperately trying to raise more than $1,000 to sponsor her older sister's emigration. (Those efforts would fail; Gudula would survive the war but spend it hidden in the house of a social worker outside Berlin.) "It was hard for them to have a fresh little kid around," said Nichols, "which I was." Finally, at a loss, they sent him away. At ten, he was enrolled in Cherry Lawn, a boarding school in Darien, Connecticut, about an hour from home. He would remain there for the next three years, returning to New York every weekend and for vacations and holidays.

The new school didn't lack bullies, including one who would routinely hold his head underwater. But as he entered junior high, Mike was a little less given to anger and sullenness. Instead, like many outsiders, he grew watchful. With his accent now all but gone, he was less of a target and more able to observe other kids from the sidelines. "I think there is an immigrant's ear that is particularly acute for 'How are they doing it here? What must I do to be unnoticeable, to be like them?'" he said. "You're forever looking at something as someone who just got here." Cherry Lawn had more options than his public school had offered, including a drama department, but Mike had little desire to put himself onstage—and, his teacher told him, little aptitude. She "said I was intelligent and not in any way suited to the theater. I think she was right," he would joke soon after his first directorial success. Instead he preferred to watch other kids, onstage and off. What did popularity look like? Or confidence? Or Americanness? How did kids behave with their friends? How did some people just naturally become the center of attention? And, conversely, who hung back? He learned to spot nervousness, vulnerability, diffidence—what it looks like when your joke fails, when you start to talk and nobody listens, when you boast because you're afraid of something. "You must learn to hear people thinking. Just in self-defense," he said, "you have to learn, where is their kindness? Where is their danger, where is their generosity?"

No longer trapped in two rooms seven days a week, no longer under the constant examination of his high-strung mother and his gruff father, Mike found it surprisingly easier to deal with both of them when he did go home. Family time was now a special occasion; weekends were treats, made bittersweet by the knowledge of how quickly he would be back on the train to Connecticut. Over one Thanksgiving holiday, his mother took him to Midtown for the premiere of *Casablanca* at the Hollywood Theatre. The opening was coincident with the Allied push into North Africa, and they sat near representatives of de Gaulle's Free French Forces, who sang along to "La Marseillaise." Sometimes they'd attend a Broadway musical like *One Touch of Venus*. Nichols was interested in plays as well; in the seventh and eighth grades, probably after seeing *Ah, Wilderness!*, he read every Eugene O'Neill play he could find, enthralled, as someone who had worked hard and quickly to master English, to discover that "you can be a very great writer without necessarily using words very well. That was a whole startling idea." As an audience member, "I liked the theater very much," he said. "But movies were where you could watch and not be you. You could be a lot of other people. I liked that. And it was always mixed with, oy, I'm gonna get sent away again."

By 1943, Mike knew, even though he wasn't home to witness it all the time, that his parents' marriage was in trouble. "As my mother later explained to me, Jews in Nazi Germany didn't have marital difficulties. It wasn't possible to concentrate on such luxuries," he said. But now, whatever his parents had long suppressed was exploding, and without much of a sense of discretion. When they fought, he would escape to the Beacon when he could—"'I'm going to the movies' became 'Screw this, and screw you,'" he said.

"There were a lot of problems," says Marianne Mosbach, whom Brigitte now had looking after Robert. "There was a lot of discord. His mother was absolutely beautiful. She had gorgeous skin and a beautifully shaped face and a very soft, seductive voice that she used to her advantage. At the time, she wasn't focused very much on her kids. Many men admired her and I think that after her time in Germany, she enjoyed the attention." She barely bothered to conceal her affairs, nor did Paul have the slightest interest in hiding his.

Mike had little doubt that his parents were heading for divorce when tragedy struck the family. Paul Nichols had been feeling tired and ill, and one day he went downstairs to his office, examined his own blood under a microscope, and diagnosed himself with leukemia. He believed it was a result of exposure to radiation in his first months in America, when he was improperly shielded from the X-ray equipment he was running.

"He had a sense of drama," says Robert Nichols. "One memory I have is . . . of him standing, when I was eight years old, at the threshold of our living room. He said, 'I have a terrible sore throat.' And he went downstairs and looked into the microscope." When Paul Nichols returned to the apartment, Robert says, "my mother, who helped him in the office, says he said [in German], 'You poor child. I have only two weeks to live.'"

His decline was shockingly swift. He was hospitalized immediately with what doctors assured him was mononucleosis rather than leukemia. "All his doctor friends said, 'Oh, no, it looks like it, but it isn't,'" said Nichols. "They told my mother to lie to him, and of course she couldn't." Mike was called home from school immediately. He sat by his father's hospital bed, looking at the bottle of urine being collected at its side, and at the stubble on his face, something he and his brother had never seen before. Paul Nichols died when he predicted he would, about two weeks later, in June 1944. He was forty-four years old.

"I wish I'd known him longer. We missed each other. We were just getting to the point when we might have found each other," said Nichols. "He died before he could see that he would be proud of me. I was actually more what he wished for than he thought."

Two

AGENT X-9

1944–1952

Soon after his father's death, Mike asked his mother for permission to be fitted for a hairpiece and false eyebrows. His first wig was cheap, with visible netting in front and an odd, too-short fit in the back—and it was blond, the better to look like an all-American boy. He had gotten what he wanted, but his prize came with a new set of struggles. The adhesive that attached the wig to his head was uncomfortable, and acetone, the solvent used to remove the glue at night, had a distinctive, unpleasant odor. "He would always refer to the wig as 'it,'" says his brother. "'How does it look? Is it all right?'" Like any awkward thirteen-year-old without many friends, he was self-conscious and nervous about his appearance. But even a just barely passable hairpiece was infinitely better than walking into school with no hair at all and becoming the instant target of stares, whispers, and worse.

Moreover, he would now have a chance to start fresh, with a group of classmates who didn't know what he used to look or sound like. His years at Cherry Lawn were done; his mother, now working nonstop to take care of herself and her two sons, wanted him at home, and needed him to contribute to the household by taking jobs after school and on weekends. He started ninth grade as a scholarship student at Walden, a progressive private school in Manhattan that was a twenty-minute walk up Central Park West from their apartment. Walden had a reputation as modern and almost experimental, with a multitude of art classes, teachers who allowed students to call them by their first names, and a lack of rigidity in the curriculum. In his years at Cherry Lawn, Mike had shed the last vestiges of his German accent. Now, for the first time, he had the chance to blend in.

The wig, inexpensive as it may have been, was nevertheless a luxury purchase, now a rarity for a family that had suddenly and unexpectedly fallen from middle-class comfort into poverty. "I have no figure for how much insurance my father may or may not have had. Ten thousand dollars is in my head," says Robert Nichols. "But whatever it was, it didn't last long . . . and [our mother] was left with the task of sustaining three lives without any clear profession or skills. She was reduced to trying any and all ways to scratch out a living." In addition to continuing to work as a typist, Brigitte started a word-of-mouth business selling leather goods and jewelry out of their increasingly cramped apartment, cluttering the living room where she slept with display tables. She found work in a bakery and a bookstore. Anything they needed was purchased on an installment plan; she even hung a good-customer certificate from the Household Finance Corporation on their wall, honoring her for always paying back what she borrowed.

For a time, it looked as if support would soon come from her older sister. Gudula had survived the war, and after it was over, Brigitte helped arrange a marriage of convenience between her and a homosexual pianist that would ease her move to New York. Mike and Robert both adored their doting aunt, who was fond of saying to them, "I love you heaps and loads." But in 1946, just weeks after her arrival, she was struck by a bus on Central Park West and killed.

It was one loss too many for Brigitte. Always anxious about her health, she was now afflicted by so many ailments, from migraines to asthma, that she sank into a depression and began to treat herself as a semi-invalid, lying on her unmade bed in the center of the living room, next to a makeshift night table with, Nichols said bitterly, "maybe a hundred and fifty bottles of medication, and the phone, on which she always was." Friends and neighbors tried to help by bringing over food, but the household suffered. Cockroaches infested the apartment, dishes piled up, cat hair was everywhere, and laundry went undone. "We weren't clean," Nichols recalled. And his relationship with his mother, which had become almost peaceful during the years he was at boarding school, now deteriorated into rancor, guilt, and caustic recrimination. "Everything wounded her," he said. "'I raised you so you could say that to me? Thank you very much, I deserve that.' It went on for hours, days."

"I don't think Mike ever granted her a pardon based on the unacceptable losses she had suffered," says Robert. "Mike and I were all she had left, and perhaps she clung to us too tightly and fearfully. It was mostly Mike who bore the brunt of her inability to cope. Nevertheless, she got the job done, despite our living in real poverty for years."

Not surprisingly, Mike tried to spend as much time outside the apartment as he could. Now a teenager, he was able to get a job as a children's riding instructor at the Claremont Stables, near Central Park—he liked the horses but had little patience for the kids. And high school was not the waking nightmare that his earlier education had been. There wasn't much bullying at Walden, and although he later insisted that he "never had a friend from the time I came to this country" until adulthood, that seems not to have been the case. At least one Walden faculty member recalled him as being reasonably popular with both teachers, who thought he was bright, if unmotivated, and classmates, who enjoyed his sense of humor. He didn't have the time or the means to socialize with other kids after classes—"I was in the position of going to expensive schools without having any spending money," he said. Inviting kids to his home was out of the question, and, by his own admission, he was too guarded and untrusting to make much of a connection with anyone.

"I was stranger than them in ways that I couldn't have pinpointed," he said. At times, he said, he felt like a human seismograph, recording "a thousand tiny victories and defeats in an ordinary conversation. I was so impaled on what people thought. I had to train myself away from that." He began imagining a future that would have no connection to anything he had experienced. "Mike often used the phrase 'When I'm rich and famous . . .' when he was young," says Robert, "perhaps even in his teen years."

As self-dramatizing as Mike's mother could be, she was also resourceful and determined to use whatever connections she had to improve her family's prospects. In her second year as a widow, she found a way to get herself and her sons out of their airless apartment during the sweltering city summers, partnering with another woman as the on-site manager of a couple of small hotels in the Catskills. These were not the resorts that were then so popular with relatively affluent Jewish New Yorkers, but inns that were smaller and catered to people like her—German or Austrian Jews who had fled Europe before the war. Mike and Robert went along, and Mike added to their income by working as a server or busboy. (He later told Edmund Wilson that he was fired at least once for "being too snappish with the customers in order to let them know that he was something better than a waiter.")

In the mid-1960s, in the course of a lengthy *Playboy* interview, Nichols claimed to have lost his virginity on the grounds of one of those hotels at fourteen. After a failed trip with some older busboys to a bordello that turned out to be closed, he returned to the hotel, "met this nice girl who was 18 and . . . took her up under a tree. I was a big reader and I expected to be disappointed, as in all the novels; but to my surprise, it wasn't disappointing at all." Unlike many stories from his childhood, this was not one Nichols repeated or referred to again. But a ready-made anecdote about the summer you lost your virginity to a kindhearted older girl was practically an obligatory response for a *Playboy* interview at the time, and, although Nichols gave readers what they wanted, including an offhandedly dismissive opener ("I'm afraid it wasn't very colorful") and a punch line ("The girl has since become a psychiatrist; make of that what you will"), this carefully shaped story— an attempt, a failure, and then an out-of-the-blue success that very day with a girl who isn't interested in the older boys—is not particularly consistent with the shyness, isolation, and trepidation that he more often said marked his early adolescence.

When she had any extra money, Brigitte found ways to expose her son to a wider world of culture. As a teenager, he once traveled with her to the music center Tanglewood, in western Massachusetts, where Leonard Bernstein, already becoming a celebrity in New York music circles, was conducting an opera. The sight of the handsome, beaming young maestro after the performance, aglow with perspiration and sur- rounded by cheering admirers as he hurried to his new convertible, left a vivid impression on Mike. "He looked golden," he said. It was his first intimate glimpse of celebrity, and of the life that went with it.

By the time he was sixteen, he had become more confident, and he even had a girlfriend. Her name was Lucy Halpern, and her parents, who liked him, were generous enough to pay for the dates. One night in December 1947, they handed Mike and Lucy a pair of tickets to see one of the first performances of Elia Kazan's Broadway production of *A Streetcar Named Desire*, with Marlon Brando and Jessica Tandy. Mike was interested in plays, and in Tennessee Williams—a year before, on his own and unable to afford a ticket, he had snuck into the second act of *The Glass Menagerie* to see Laurette Taylor's storied performance as Amanda Wingfield. But *Streetcar* was a transformative experience, one that shaped his understanding of theater in ways that would resonate through almost all of his work to come.

"It sounds very dramatic," he said, "but I never got over it. We never got up in the intermissions. We were poleaxed. Brando . . . first of all, you said, what is this? Who is this person who looks like a real person, not an actor? It was the only thing I've ever seen that was a hundred percent real and a hundred percent poetic, simultaneously. Kazan was, for many years, my hero of the theater, because he could really create life onstage." For Nichols, the drama that unfolded "was the opposite of what I think of as the most difficult thing about the theater, which is, you come in and you sit . . . and the curtain comes up and someone says [yelling], 'Mother came home last night and she doesn't yet know that the orphanage burned down,' and you think, *Oh, no, are they going to do this all night?* It was just alive. It was living in front of you."

Mike began seeing plays more avidly—Wendy Hiller in *The Heiress* also made a strong impression. A year later, when the Halperns handed him and Lucy tickets to Kazan's production of *Death of a Salesman*, he recalled being "totally devastated" by the power and artistry of what he saw—the story of a maybe Jewish family with two brothers, a father about to disappear, and a mother frantically trying to preserve some semblance of domestic life. But he had no particular idea of directing as a profession, or of how one pursued a career in the theater. His own life felt aimless, and his goals and ambitions were virtually nonexistent. In the spring of 1948, he graduated from Walden with a decent but hardly stellar academic record. Most of his classmates were headed to colleges or universities. He was not. "Lazy and disorganized" by his own description, he had not even bothered to take the college boards. He looked into enrolling at New York University but walked away in a fit of sullenness when he learned that incoming freshmen were required to memorize the school song. Instead, he began a year of drudgery in dead-end jobs—first as a stockroom worker for a life insurance firm, then as a shipping clerk for a costume jewelry company.

Despite their fraught relationship, Nichols stayed in New York, in part to be near his mother, who relied on him even as they tore at each other. But in 1949, five years after Paul Nichols's death, Brigitte met a man. Like her late husband, Franz Hausberger was a doctor—a research physician—and like Brigitte, he was a German émigré; he had been educated in Munich and had come to America after the war. He and Brigitte fell in love and arranged a move to Philadelphia, where he had a job as a professor. Once they married, she would work as his laboratory assistant, and her younger son would attend high school there. "The hard times dissolved," says Robert, who, like Mike, grew immensely fond of their new stepfather. "He became a long-standing professor at Jefferson Medical College. And she fell right into that non-Jewish life. She wasn't a practicing or believing Christian, but neither was she in any way a practicing Jew. In a social situation, my mother once said, 'I am of Jewish background,' and my friend muttered in my ear, 'And foreground.'"

With no reason left to stay in New York, Mike began to regret his decision to skip the board exams, a choice that, as he understood it, left him with only two options: Mexico City College (later renamed University of the Americas), which had become a four-year institution so recently that it hadn't yet given out its first bachelor's degrees, or the University of Chicago, which required only a placement exam. He applied to both, didn't get a response from Chicago, and was accepted by Mexico City College. He was about to leave for Mexico when he received a telegram of acceptance saying, "Show up at Mandel Hall"—in Chicago—"on Monday at 9 o'clock." He packed his bags, with warmer clothes this time, and got on the train.

"Yes, I had a tough childhood," he thought. "I had all those problems—but enough already. All the shit was in the beginning. Let's start now."

It's hard to know what surprised Nichols more when he arrived in Chicago for the fall term in 1949—that people liked him or that he liked people. "In high school you figure things are frozen forever in a certain pattern," he said. "There are a couple of guys you can beat up and a lot who can beat you up, and there are a few girls who'll go out with you and some more that won't, and that's the way the rest of life will be." For him, "the great discovery of college was that nothing was fixed and the world was wide open." On his first morning on campus, waiting in an endless line to register, he struck up a conversation with a fiercely bright and opinionated girl who was just sixteen but already enrolling as a transfer from Berkeley, eager to dig into the great books in Chicago's core curriculum. Her name was Susan Sontag. They became friends instantly.

The campus and its students were wildly overstimulating for him. In those years, the University of Chicago promoted itself as a bastion of secularism and free thought, with a rigorous slate of required reading and a proudly eccentric student body that forswore distractions like sports and fraternities in the ardent pursuit of knowledge. Here were people who wanted to read what he wanted to read, who loved classical music and could identify composers and their work by listening for a few seconds, who knew the name of his grandmother as soon as he said she'd written the libretto for *Salome*, who wanted to argue and compare notes and share experiences all night. "We talked about books, about feelings, about how to get free of our pasts," said Sontag. They did not become a couple; with studied offhandedness, Nichols told classmates, "I don't usually have alliances with lesbians," and she was thrown off by his wig. But most students didn't care what Mike looked like; if he was different, he was no more different than they felt themselves to be. "I wouldn't say [we were] misfits," said the musician Alex Hassilev, one of Nichols's first male friends at Chicago. "I would say we had unique ways of looking at the world. What drew us together was a kind of desire to be with others who were also a little strange."

The university "was paradise," Nichols said. "I began to see a world that I could fit in." It was also too much to handle. Tall, stooped, and baby-faced, Nichols knew his appearance was odd—"something out of a German Expressionist movie," according to his roommate, Aaron Asher. Overwhelmed by the effort "to be a *person* that many hours a day," he began to shut down, in part because the specific person he had decided to be was such a strenuous invention. Thrown off balance by everything around him, he responded by affecting a style of frosty, bored, hyper-cultured contempt for anyone or anything he found wanting in merit, seriousness, or intellect, and he expressed his scorn with such withering humor that his ability to destroy people with a sentence soon became the one thing classmates knew about him before they even met him. Nichols's hauteur—for the first time since immigrating, he decided to seem *more* European—was an anxious reaction to a kind of environment he had never before experienced. It was also a taxing performance. By the middle of his freshman year, he was staying in bed sixteen to eighteen hours a day. In the fall, he had signed up for a punishing course load of pre-med studies that he had chosen with the intention, almost by default, of becoming a doctor like his father and grandfather. Now he was skipping most of those classes. "A persona takes energy," he said. "I just needed a rest. Not to be anything in relation to anyone else."

At the time, the university's medical school offered undergraduates free sessions with psychoanalytic trainees. Nichols leapt at the chance to put himself on the couch, and, at a time when many people still viewed the process as faintly embarrassing, he wasn't shy about discussing it. "He was very outspoken," one of his classmates, Heyward Ehrlich, said. "Mike's therapy was at the top of his conversation. He publicized [it]."

Nichols discovered for the first time in his life that there was pleasure in being seen, in being understood, even in being found out. He was particularly taken with a humanities professor named Edward Rosenheim, who introduced him to Jonathan Swift and the principles of satire. It was one of the few classes for which he occasionally showed up. Not often enough, apparently: one day Rosenheim pulled him aside and said, "You know, Nichols, you're very charming and all that, but I really owe my time to people who do the work. Sorry."

"It threw me," said Nichols. "I was one of the millions of people to whom teachers always said, 'You could do so well if you only applied yourself.' I would sort of skate through and not work and do perfectly all right. It had never occurred to me that there was any other way. And this guy, whom I admired so much, made me realize, 'Maybe there's some pleasure in doing the work.'"

By his sophomore year, Nichols was more ready for the possibilities the university held for him, and he also knew that his future was not in medicine. After beginning psychoanalysis, he had thought of becoming a psychiatrist, but his spiraling grades made medical school unlikely. He was getting by, but just barely, with so little spending money that he would linger in the campus cafeteria after other students had left so that he could eat the leftovers off their plates. The gap between him and those classmates felt unbridgeable, and unjust. He wondered "why my rich friends didn't give me some of their money, since they had so much of it."

One day he struck up a conversation with one of the cafeteria's busboys, a student named Paul Sills. Sills was four years older than Nichols, but he had started at Chicago late and was, at twenty-four, just in his junior year. The son of the acting teacher Viola Spolin, whose galvanizing text on improvisational theater games would eventually become a mainstay of American acting classes, Sills was also an evangelist for her approach. In the last couple of years, he had become active in the university's undergraduate theater department. At the moment he met Nichols, he was involved in an internecine quarrel over his attempt to rewrite *The Duchess of Malfi* for a student production he was directing. Nichols was instantly captivated by him and started coming by regularly during his shifts to scrounge food—sometimes by entering through the back door as if he had already paid—and to "bullshit about theater." Sills, in turn, would come see Nichols at the hospital soda fountain, where he had gotten a job.

Nichols soon started attending Sills's informal weekly acting workshops. In those sessions, he got his first taste of life as a performer and also of his new mentor's approach to acting. Sills was not interested in pushing his actors toward the personal or internal exploration favored by adherents of Stanislavski. Rather, he believed that the games created or refined by his mother—which ranged from group touch exercises to word repetitions to physical stretches to something she called "developing organic response through gibberish"—were the way to engender trust and connection between performers, to shape power dynamics, and to teach actors to find the drama and meaning of any text. Sills's use of those games felt, to Nichols, both playful and radical. In one of his first exercises, he and classmate Zohra Lampert were asked to improvise a scene based on Thomas Mann's *The Magic Mountain* using only nonsense words.

Well before Sills founded Chicago's seminal improv troupe Second City, his eye for talent was already acute, and in Nichols he saw a quick and eager learner who neither looked nor sounded like anyone else in the school's drama subculture, someone who would be an ideal addition to the renegade campus theater company he was starting called Tonight at 8:30. It was, Nichols later said, "a 'revolutionary' group, which just meant the guys in 'Tonight at 8:30' didn't like the faculty head at the University Theater very much. All it really came down to was that you had a choice between doing a play at some little place and calling it 'Tonight at 8:30' or doing it on the big stage in Mandel Hall." Aware of Nichols's acid reputation, Sills cast him to type. He put together a reading of a dramatic adaptation of Nathanael West's *Miss Lonelyhearts* and had Nichols play the nasty, cynical newspaper editor Shrike. "I was extremely good," Nichols said. "I was a prick. And then I started playing snotty pricks." It was an easy fit. "I liked him," says

Ehrlich, "but . . . he was a pain in the ass. Mike Nichols was not Mike Nichols in those days. He was the person he came to satirize, and he wasn't laughing at it. He felt the world treated him cruelly, and the theater was his revenge."

"At the University of Chicago, Mike was a scary person," says his classmate and friend Joy Carlin, who signed up for Sills's new group at about the same time Nichols did. "There were plenty of people there who were really smart, and in that sense scary. But he was smart and had a truly wicked, sharp tongue. I was afraid to start a conversation with him, because I'd be skewered."

In the spring of 1951, Sills cast Nichols as Caesar in Tonight at 8:30's big production of the semester, Shaw's *Androcles and the Lion*. Nichols was eager to try his hand at directing, and Sills decided to give him a chance by adding a curtain-raiser—a staging of Yeats's short, two-character one-act *Purgatory*. "I was still always oversleeping," said Nichols. "The two actors would have to come get me and wake me up for rehearsals." One of them was Edward Asner, then a senior.

Initially, Asner was put off by Nichols's arrant snobbery. "There were times when I resented him," he says, "and thought he was acting too much the luftmensch. He was unusual—he was part of a coterie of would-be actors with a somewhat effeminate attitude. But it soon became very clear to me that he was the kind of man you had to watch your girl around—he dug women! His effeminacy was just that he had no beard, and he came off as something like a dilettante. But I think his direction was successful. He was having fun when he did it, and as time wore on, I realized there was a decent human being there."

By the time Nichols returned to the campus that fall, he was maintaining only the most tenuous connection to academic life—and would drop out before his junior year was over. Remaining enrolled as a student had become a means to an end, which was to keep working with Sills and Tonight at 8:30. Classes and grades were an afterthought; he spent more and more of his time traveling off-campus to go to the movies. In late 1951, he saw Montgomery Clift and Elizabeth Taylor in the film he would come to call his "bible"—George Stevens's *A Place in the Sun,* an experience he found as revelatory about movies as *Streetcar* and *Salesman* had been about theater. It is not hard to imagine what Nichols, at twenty, saw in Stevens's adaptation of Dreiser's *An American Tragedy,* the story of a lonely, ambitious young man, guilty about his widowed mother back home and eventually consumed and destroyed by the desire to move up in life and to belong. From its first scenes, the film is about the choking frustration of being an outsider who is so close to success and wealth that it is almost palpable.

But Nichols was now old enough to appreciate technique, and he was as gripped by the filmmaking as he was by the story. It was Stevens's deeply considered visual and structural sense, his way of framing shots, of staging action, of positioning and directing his cast, and of letting scenes unfold slowly that kept Nichols coming back. Throughout his life, *A Place in the Sun* would be the movie he would mine for inspiration—it was his core text when he prepared to direct Taylor himself in *Who's Afraid of Virginia Woolf?,* and the length of each shot and the stillness of Stevens's camera strongly influenced his approach to *The Graduate.* It was also the font of instruction to which, in later years, he would send novice directors, telling them, "Watch it twenty-five times. When you're done, let's talk." By his own count, he viewed the picture close to 150 times—many of them the year after it opened. "It just really got to me, like nothing else had," he said.

As an actor, Nichols was still learning on the fly. His only training came from Sills; otherwise he relied on guesswork and on-the-job experience. But there were limits to what he could teach himself—projecting an attitude, especially an unpleasant one, came naturally, but stage movement was so alien to him that he would often root himself to one spot and stay there during a scene, waiting for his castmates to come into his orbit. And he wasn't getting many opportunities to stretch. In 1952, when Sills took over from another student as the director of

Strindberg's *Miss Julie,* he again cast Nichols as an unsympathetic pos-
turer, the haughty, upward-striving valet Jean.

By then, Sills's productions were getting attention on campus and
even being showcased on the university's main stage. This time, to the
shock of everyone involved, they attracted the notice of a professional
critic, Sydney J. Harris of the *Chicago Daily News,* who wrote a rave
breathlessly comparing Sills's ensemble to "the highest possible level of
repertory in world drama" and noting that Nichols "exhibits an ease
and intelligence in the ambivalent role of the valet . . . His technique is
sometimes a bit ragged, but his emotional understanding . . . is more
than adequate compensation."

The production, which, like any other student show, had been
scheduled to run for just a couple of weekends, became a minor sensation and extended its run for two months. Nichols and his castmates,
who were certain the show was awful and didn't think much better of
their own work in it, felt both amused and mortified. "I can't tell you
how bad it was," he said. "One night, [the actress] who played my wife
came up—this was in the very last scene—and said to me, 'What are
you doing up so early, and with your hat on?' And I thought, this is
really interesting—I'm not wearing a hat. She had said that line for the
last two months, but she and I and the audience had been so bored that
we never noticed that I wasn't wearing a hat. That's how bad it was.
And we had to do it and do it and do it."

Nichols's misery was, in part, the result of a particular humiliation
he had experienced on opening night, when Sills brought a guest to the
show specifically to take a look at his work. She sat in the front row,
"about four feet away," and as Nichols walked through the role, he became acutely conscious of "this evil girl . . . with a sneer on her face . . .
this fascinating, beautiful, contemptuous girl." Her attention and her
expression didn't waver, and as the show dragged on, Nichols said,
"I knew she knew it was shit, and there was no way I could let her know
that I knew it also." Sills had set the table for her by saying, "I want you

to see the only person at the University of Chicago who is as hostile as you. You're both mean, and"—he added with mild derision—"both Method." He told her to keep her eye on Nichols. She seemed to be following his instruction to the letter.

"That was probably true," says Elaine May. "I was hostile. I couldn't believe that Paul said that to me—and I was dating him at the time! I've never forgotten it."

Nichols and May did not meet that night. But a couple of days later, he was walking down the street, a copy of the *Daily News* review in hand, and ran into Sills and his girlfriend. "Paul, look at this!" he said, and gave him the newspaper. Sills read it, but Nichols was interested only in May, who was reading over Sills's shoulder. She looked at the review. She looked at Nichols. Her expression was not a degree warmer than it had been in the front row. "Ha!" she barked at him and, without another word, walked away.

Years later, when Nichols and May became famous, they would be asked how they met by every interviewer who spoke to them. In response, Nichols told this story often, along with another, more cheerful one in which, either a few weeks or a few months down the road, he reencountered her at Illinois Central Station, the public transportation hub through which he would often pass on his way to a movie or as he headed back to his apartment. This time, May—poised, beautiful, unnervingly self-possessed—was alone. Nichols approached her with a comedy gambit, dusting off a version of his long-discarded German accent to say, "May I zit down?" "Eef you veesh," she replied, without batting an eye. "Vould you have a light?" he continued, taking out a cigarette. "Of course," she answered. "You are Agent X-9?" They took the train together and went on with the bit seamlessly. They had found, without even trying, a common language.

Nichols understood why the public wanted an explanation of this couple that wasn't a couple but looked and acted like one, this team that, with each appearance, was introducing the country to a completely new style of acutely observant, seemingly off-the-cuff comedy. More than May, he was expert at crafting anecdotes that satisfied a craving while sealing off further inquiry. Did either of those encounters happen precisely as described? They could have, although both were so embellished by decades of retelling that it's impossible to know. Nichols himself, at eighty, put it more simply, if paradoxically, when he said, "I met Elaine several ways." But what is clear is that, however they first encountered each other, it felt momentous. Something was beginning. "I knew then that she was the best girl I ever met," he said. Or, to put it another way: He was in love.

Three

A SENSE OF YOUR POSIBILITIES

1952–1955

Nobody at the University of Chicago knew what to make of Elaine May when she first showed up. She and Nichols could not have been a less likely match. May was born in Philadelphia, where her father, Jack Berlin, was a performer and director of Yiddish theater; her mother, Ida, sold tickets and made the programs. They first put May onstage when she was a baby. Eventually they moved to California, where their daughter dropped out of ninth grade, married and divorced a man named Marvin May at sixteen, and by nineteen had studied acting with Maria Ouspenskaya, worked as a private investigator, and decided it might be interesting to go to college. May had also become a mother; she and her ex-husband had a toddler named Jeannie, whom she left with her mother before hitchhiking to Chicago to get an education at one of the only American universities that didn't require its students to have a high school diploma.

On campus, May came off as a sharp, tense, and wary woman among children. She didn't bother to register for classes; she just showed up in seminars and lecture halls, already apparently conversant in every piece of literature anyone could mention, or able to fake it with such sang-froid that others fell silent. She would usually vanish before students or professors could get a bead on her. The night she saw Nichols for the first time, she said she "loathed [him] on sight."

May could be somewhat forbidding at first glance—she wore a near-constant frown and had long dark hair through which she only occasionally thought to run a comb. Boys were wildly attracted to her; she couldn't have had less use for their leering and jesting. One day, when she went into a coffee shop looking windblown and unkempt, a couple of guys laughed at her. "Hi, Elaine—did you bring your broom today?" one yelled. "Why?" she snapped. "Do you want something up your ass? Tired of each other?" Male students learned, if not to keep their distance, to approach her with caution and respect.

But she and Nichols had something in common besides the hostility that Sills had pointed out. "We were both seductive," Nichols said, "and we were both very much on the defensive with other people. We both had big chips on our shoulders—chips that we in different ways whittled away at during the course of our lives and reduced in size." In addition, they shared "reputations on campus as being dangerous to vicious depending on the stimulus, and so we were both interested in each other from that point of view."

If, given the rather dramatic sense of themselves they shared, they were destined to become romantically involved, they did not remain so for long. David Shepherd, the cofounder of the Compass Players, the theater that was soon to become their training ground, referred to their liaison as "the three days that Mike lived with Elaine." And a decade later, in response to press questions, Nichols would either joke it away ("We live very quietly and we date occasionally—right now, we are seeing Comden and Green," he told *Time* magazine) or take what was already shrouded in mystery and render it even murkier. Did they sleep together? "No," he told *Playboy*, "we never did . . . Maybe we did once or twice." Whatever it was, he said, lasted "only sort of for a minute."

Soon after they met, May, who could not have been less interested in domesticity, took him back to her place on the South Side, where they both lived, made him a hamburger with cream cheese and ketchup— one of the only things she could cook—and showed him her copy of the Kama Sutra, which she thought was a potentially interesting tool for improv. He was smitten. So, in her way, was she. That the two of them, both just twenty years old at the end of the school year, were too young and combustible to sustain themselves as a couple was hardly a shock. What was more surprising was how quickly they realized it and decided they wanted, perhaps even needed, to cling to each other as friends. After their stab at romance, Nichols knew they had found something deeper: He believed they would always, from then on, exempt each other from their cruelty. "She could, God knows, defend herself when attacked. But her toughness was an illusion," he said. May saw in Nichols someone who could lift her spirits—"I'm a much more negative person than you," she told him after a lifetime of work and friendship, "and I always have been: I the darkness, you the light." And in May, Nichols saw something he had never found before. He felt early on, he said, that they were "safe from each other forever. We can't do each other any harm or say anything wrong to each other." And he also sensed that "she wouldn't lose interest and move on. I knew instantly that everything that happened to us was ours."

Their creative partnership would have to wait a little while. May was there to study; she had not been able to stand the regimentation of high school for more than three weeks, but she loved to read, and with the benefit of a couple of years at Chicago, she said, "I thought I would become extremely educated." Nichols, however, had no interest in finishing his four years, and soon after he and May met, he dropped out to pursue acting full-time. He took whatever nearby jobs he could find, working just enough to get by. He was a clerk at Sears and a post office truck driver during the Christmas rush. At night he managed a tree nursery. And whenever possible, he continued working with Sills, who was now conducting formal classes in acting technique and theater games. Nichols loved them. "Once every [so often] you would . . . be possessed and speak languages you didn't speak," he said. "Like doing twenty minutes of iambic pentameter that we had not thought of but just came pouring out. That was thrilling. You'd be drained and amazed afterward, and you'd have a sense of your possibilities."

Sills was ready to take the next step. He had gone as far with Tonight at 8:30 as he could; he wanted to start a semi-professional company. In 1953, he, Shepherd, and Eugene Troobnick founded the Playwrights Theatre Club on North LaSalle Street, in downtown Chicago, in a storefront that had last housed a Chinese restaurant. The company couldn't afford to pay its members a living wage. What little money there was came from Shepherd, an owlish, serious-minded twenty-nine-year-old Harvard grad with an M.A. in theater from Columbia who came from a wealthy family. Shepherd knew little about acting but was full of lofty ideas about creating political theater for the proletariat, and he was impressed by Sills's work. The two envisioned a repertory company that would perform Brecht and Cocteau and Büchner but also plays by its own founders; the shows would be rehearsed for a week or ten days and then given a bare-bones staging with minimal costumes and props over a weekend. The troupe Sills assembled included many of the actors from his classes, a couple of recent graduates like Ed Asner, and some new arrivals—including Tom O'Horgan (later the director of *Hair* and *Jesus Christ Superstar*) and Barbara Harris, a teenager who showed up one day, saw that a group of people were putting on a play, and said, "Can I be in it?" They gave her a job sweeping up. "She just wandered in and turned out to be a genius," Nichols said. "That's how Paul was. He said, come and do it, you'll be okay—anybody that wanted to."

May was one of the only members of the acting company who could also write, and Sills created a children's theater program within Playwrights so he could stage her version of *Rumpelstiltskin*. Nichols was around a little less. He had just gotten a job that was turning him into a minor local celebrity, working as the DJ of a classical music program at WFMT, a mom-and-pop radio station. His roster was thoughtfully curated, but it was his droll, anarchic patter between selections—his engineer, Cal Herrmann, remembers him ripping a teletype off the machine, then urgently announcing, "There is no news tonight!"—that built him a cult following in the area. Sometimes friends and fans would even come to the studio to watch him work. Soon WFMT let him start a new weekend show, *The Midnight Special*, an eclectic hour of folk music, oddities, and LP cuts determined entirely by his own taste and whims. "There was a lot of folk, but there were also songs by Charlotte Rae and Flanders & Swann, and Wally Cox singing 'There Is a Tavern in the Town,'" says the writer Deborah Eisenberg, who, as a kid in the Chicago suburbs, listened regularly and found herself transfixed by the amused, polished sound of the man whose references seemed limitless without being intimidating. "[Mike's] voice was so reassuring, so natural, so *actual*. It all suggested a big world that existed elsewhere."

The radio gig was Nichols's first real taste of attention, but it locked up his Friday and Saturday nights, which meant he had to turn down Sills and Shepherd's offer to become a full-time member of Playwrights. When he could—and sometimes even when he couldn't—he would sneak away to join them, to the ongoing consternation of the couple who owned the station. "He was funny and knowledgeable but totally unreliable," said Aaron Asher. "They fired him a number of times."

Like many enterprises founded and run by creative people in their twenties, Playwrights was inherently, almost comically unstable and quarrelsome. From the moment of its founding, it was in a state of churn, contention, and high-minded dispute. Sills was performer driven; he wanted a theater where actors would feel "liberated," often via improvisation, to construct a "shared reality" that would "raise the consciousness of the community." Shepherd cared very little about technique; he wanted plays and productions that would change the world and speed the revolution.

But both men imagined a theater that could serve as a finger in the eye of an increasingly uptight and conservative society. At the time, Sills said, "the main thing we experienced was the repression of any kind of deviant behavior under the guise of anti-Communism." None of them could understand why there weren't more people, especially artists, fighting it. "A pall of McCarthyism lay over the land," said Bernie Sahlins, a producer at Playwrights, "and all you heard on TV were mother-in-law jokes." Playwrights was originally envisioned as a savage, destabilizing cultural counterthrust. But it took less than a year for Shepherd to become utterly disillusioned by the work they were doing and by the audience it was attracting. "I have built a miserable, self-centered arts club which talks over the heads of its bourgeois members at the same time it licks their feet for support," he fumed in his journal in May 1954. "For a brief moment last fall . . . Paul and I saw that the goal of our theater should be a riot in the audience. How could we forget it?"

By that point, Nichols was ready to move on. He had been acting in Chicago on and off for three years, and he had dipped in and out of productions at Playwrights, appearing when he could. But he didn't share Shepherd's ideological fervor; like most of the group's actors, he had one eye on his own career, and he no longer felt he was making progress, either professionally or creatively. The theater scene in Chicago was growing every year, but it still had nothing like the national reputation it would eventually acquire; it was a breeding ground for committed amateurs and little more than a whistle stop for touring stars from New York. Nichols's ambition was considerable; when a road production of Lillian Hellman's play *The Children's Hour* arrived in Chicago, he had sought out its star Patricia Neal to ask her to record a Roald Dahl story for their theater. Neal agreed to do it, but when he told her of his desire to become an actor, she looked at the yearning, ungainly young man in the ill-fitting toupee and gently tried to push him away from show business.

Nichols wasn't dissuaded, but his confidence in his own abilities was waning. "At some point at Playwrights Theatre Club," says troupe member Joy Carlin, "we looked at each other and I said, 'I don't know how to act.' And he said, 'No, I don't either. What do we do?'" It didn't take him long to decide. He quit his job at WFMT and said goodbye to May, Sills, and the company. In the summer of 1954, after almost five years away, he moved back to New York City.

Nichols had almost no money—a condition that now felt permanent to him—but he did have a plan: He wanted to study with Lee Strasberg, the director and teacher who had, a couple of years earlier, taken charge of the Actors Studio. Strasberg had become something between an instructor and a mystic for performers who wanted to learn the Method—a process that combined psychology, technique, and disciplined use of emotional memory to elicit deep feeling and naturalistic, fully inhabited performances. Brando was Method personified; by 1954, when *On the Waterfront* opened, every actor wanted to be him. Nichols couldn't afford to enter the official Actors Studio program, but Strasberg also taught actors on the side, in groups of twenty, and admitted Nichols to his twice-weekly class.

With his mother and brother long settled in Philadelphia, Nichols, at twenty-two, was truly on his own in New York for the first time, ready to begin what he thought would be his adult life. He got a job behind the counter at a Howard Johnson's in Greenwich Village and moved into the last bad Manhattan apartment he would ever occupy, an eight-dollar-a-week, one-room third-floor walk-up with a communal toilet at the end of the hall, in a West Eighty-seventh Street brownstone near Riverside Park. Joy Carlin moved into a much nicer apartment across the street, sharing it with two young women.

To join the ranks of New York City's aspiring actors in the mid-1950s was to be suspended equidistant between opportunity and starvation. Sixty or seventy new shows opened on Broadway every season and, farther downtown, smaller, more adventurous and experimental theaters were sprouting in any vacant spot big enough to hold a stage and fifty seats. There were radio serials and fifteen-minute daytime soaps, and a booming local TV production industry that kept the three major networks regularly supplied with sixty- and ninety-minute dramas, often telecast live. Scouts from the studios would sweep through regularly to eye the new talent. To Nichols and his friends, success looked as simple as an agent or a manager or a producer pointing a finger and saying "You." An actress struggling with a scene in Strasberg's class one week could land a role on TV or Broadway the next and be gone, only to return, unemployed again, six months—or sometimes six days—later. They all knew about his student Paul Newman, who would still sit in once in a while and had gotten regular TV roles and even a movie contract. Making it big felt alternately imminent and impossible, and the sudden luck of a classmate was both celebrated and obsessively picked to pieces: Had they sold out? Had they really earned their shot? Was it because they were Lee's favorite? Weren't there people right in their midst who were so much more deserving? Yes, Newman was handsome, but was he really that good?

Nichols had little to his name but a bed and a TV, which he would watch night after night in search of a single role that he could imagine himself playing. He had come to New York believing that he was a castable type—"nervous young man" was the category he imagined for

himself—but as he watched *Philco Television Playhouse* or *Producers'
Showcase* or *General Electric Theater,* he said, "I couldn't find any part
that was right for me."

Initially, his work in Strasberg's classes gave him some hope. The
room was full of young talent—Gene Hackman would show up, and
Carroll Baker, just a year away from being cast by Kazan in *Baby Doll,*
and Inger Stevens, a beautiful, fragile nineteen-year-old from Sweden
whom Nichols started dating casually—and they were all impressed by
him. It was obvious that "he was exceptionally gifted," Baker wrote.
"While the rest of us were making an effort just to place one foot in
front of the other without tripping, Mike was showing signs of being a
brilliant comedian." His work with Sills in Chicago was paying dividends. "He could make even a simple exercise hysterically funny in an
absolutely genuine way."

But Baker declined to work with Nichols in class—"he'd end up
directing you," she said. When paired with another actor, he would
find himself steering and modifying the scene almost unconsciously.
"What I didn't really understand," he said later, "was that [Strasberg]
was not only teaching acting, he was teaching directing. I didn't understand that I was listening to the director part. I never knew it." In fact,
he had no thought of directing at all. "I keep thinking, we can do what
we want to do," he wrote to a friend that year. "I better reconcile myself
to keep trying to be an actor. Nothing else will do."

"Strasberg . . . said the best thing about acting I've heard to this
day," Nichols said. "A girl was doing a scene and he said, 'What were
you working for?' And she said, 'Oh, spring, and just the feeling of
longing.' He said, 'Do you know how to make fruit salad?' She said
yeah. He said, 'How?' She said, 'I take some apples and peel them and
cut them up, and take a banana and peel it and cut it, and an orange . . .'
He said, 'That's right. That's how you make fruit salad. You can sit in
front of it for weeks, saying, 'Fruit salad.' But you will never have fruit
salad until you pick up each piece, one at a time . . . It's the most useful

metaphor I've heard for working on a play. You do the first job as neatly as you can: He comes in. Then: He sees her. And so on."

More than anything, Nichols wanted to learn "how to be in the course of your life [and] performing a play" night after night, making it new and real each time. He liked Strasberg's notion that the director creates the events of the play, but he was even more drawn to Kazan's conviction that psychology onstage is best illuminated when it is made manifest in physical behavior. He felt he was growing in skill every week; if he couldn't get cast in great roles right away, he told a friend, maybe he would eventually age into a career as a comic character actor, like Robert Morley. But as the months went by, he couldn't help but notice how quickly his contemporaries seemed to be moving ahead while he stood still. His Chicago classmate Zohra Lampert, who had also come east, was now in the cast of a daytime soap opera called *Hawkins Falls.* Carroll Baker got a Robert Anderson play on Broadway. And his casual girlfriend Stevens "hit the jackpot," he wrote to Carlin, who had left New York to go on her honeymoon in Mexico. "She had a lead on Philco three weeks ago and from then on she was in . . . She had her picture in Time magazine . . . The caption was 'From Sweden, big eyed silences' and the article said as how she was hauntingly attractive and her silences were more eloquent than all the speeches of the other actors . . . Well, she's been on a TV show every week since then . . . and may get a cover story on Life. She is being great about the whole thing," he said, remarking sourly, "I am continually astonished at the minimum of acting ability that is required, once you're in a little bit."

Nichols was getting nothing, and he was increasingly unable to afford even the modest tuition that Strasberg required. Howard Johnson's fired him for mouthing off to a customer. (Asked what the cafeteria's ice cream flavor of the month was, he had snappishly replied, "Chicken.") For a while, he worked as a runner for the spoken-word label Caedmon Records, which, like every other employer he encountered in the city, seemed remarkably unimpressed with his potential.

"I would get terrific ideas like, 'Let's have Robert Frost reading his own work,'" he said, "and they would say, 'Take this package to 105th Street.'"

Joy Carlin's husband, Jerry, who had come with her from Chicago, was also a friend of Nichols's; the newlyweds would sometimes meet him in Greenwich Village, then walk five miles uptown to Eighty-seventh Street, winding through the Theater District, chatting earnestly about their futures. They knew Nichols was suffering; during his time at Howard Johnson's, he would pocket ketchup and mustard packets, then walk over to the Horn & Hardart Automat, get a cup of hot water, mix the free soda crackers on the table into it, and squirt in the condiments. Sometimes that would be dinner; sometimes it would be cheese he stole from the grocery store; sometimes, when he was lucky, Joy and her roommates would bring leftovers to his small, disheveled room, where, she said, "the smell of acetone"—the wig-glue remover he used—"would just hit you in the face. He was really struggling. It was horrible."

At one point, the Carlins, seeing Nichols losing a battle with his circumstances, urged him to get on the phone with Sills and consider returning to Chicago and Playwrights Theatre Club. But Nichols's time with Strasberg had caused Sills to tumble in his estimation; he had come to believe that Sills "castrated his actors" and had "no method with which to communicate with" them. Besides, he said, "right now I feel I can't go home again."

But he was out of options. "I was in class, and I was doing good," he wrote to Joy. "Like, I cried during the song exercise and all that. But . . . I'm getting farther behind and all, and one day Lee says to me . . . there'll always be a place for me in class but maybe I better drop out for a while until I can get back on my feet, and I allowed as how this seemed the only thing to do."

Then he got lucky: A man to whom he had applied for a radio-hosting job months earlier told him there was an opening in Philadelphia. The position came with a good salary and hours flexible enough to allow him to commute to New York twice a week for Strasberg's classes. In December 1954, Nichols essentially moved home. "The idea," he told Carlin, "is to save till I have paid my debts and accrued enough backing to return and tilt at New York again. In the meantime I go to bed at nine every night, get up promptly at four thirty in the morning . . . drive out in the family car, which is mine to use, and work till twelve or one. I live in a beautiful room . . . near my family with whom I eat dinner. I have eighteen clean white shirts. I go into New York most weekends to see the gang. It's a regular metamorphosis."

For several months, Nichols enjoyed his new life in Philadelphia as a morning DJ—he played classical music and poetry and even got an acting job as, of all things, an Italian immigrant on the radio station's apparently terrible local soap opera, *Rittenhouse Square*. But his heart was in New York, and, according to Jerome Toobin, a co-worker at the station with whom he became friendly, he didn't last long. "Like all little stations with frugal bosses, ours was a one-man operation at sign-on time," Toobin wrote. "Mike would arrive at, let us say, 7:14 a.m. and sign on cheerily with a 'Good morning, it's seven o'clock!' Sometimes he arrived earlier—7:08—sometimes later—7:21—but he always said seven o'clock. None of the brass knew—for a while. One morning the owner happened to hear Nichols announce that it was 7 a.m. on his car radio, looked at his watch, drove to the station and fired [him] on the spot." Nichols didn't seem particularly upset—or if he was, he put on a brave face, saying that he "couldn't stand Philadelphia anymore."

On one of his weekend visits to New York, Nichols agreed to meet with Sills and Barbara Harris, who had just gotten married. The Playwrights Theatre Club—which, despite its name and the intentions behind it, had not succeeded in commissioning any production-worthy new work—had outlasted David Shepherd's disillusionment with it by only a few months. It had been forced to move twice and had fallen apart for good in February 1955, when its latest venue failed a fire code inspection. Shepherd regrouped and made plans to form a new theater company in Chicago called the Compass Players, which he intended to be driven by new writing, preferably about issues of the day; he would populate it with many Playwrights alumni, including Sills. But the loose, fluctuating group of fifteen or twenty would-be actors, producers, writers, and directors who had constituted the nucleus of Playwrights had reached an awkward turning point, with some committing to careers in the theater and others drifting away from what had been a hobby and moving toward families and steady jobs. Much of the remaining troupe was still so young that the Compass's ranks had shrunk noticeably with the start of the school year in September.

Sills and Shepherd still didn't see eye to eye on the group's mission: Shepherd envisioned a slate of "newspaper plays," a rotating set of one-acts that would be inspired by the day's headlines and form the Compass's core repertoire. Sills was more interested in spontaneity and improvisation. But both agreed that, this time, they needed a group of professional, fully committed actors. Like many of the leaders of the just barely budding Chicago theater scene, Sills viewed New York talent with some skepticism—he didn't want anyone to think his work needed to be legitimized by out-of-town recruits. But Nichols was different—they had worked together before, and Sills couldn't dismiss the fact that he had studied with Strasberg. Sills himself had won a Fulbright scholarship and was leaving Chicago for six months in Europe with Harris; after discussing it with Shepherd, he agreed to stop in New York long enough to try to talk Nichols and a couple of other actors into returning to Chicago. As an incentive, Shepherd offered them a modest but workable salary of $28 a week.

Nichols wasn't sure how to play it. With friends in Philadelphia, he was airy and offhand; he went over to dinner at the house of a friend named Herbert Gans, told him he had saved some money, "and said, 'I am either going to buy a new car or go back to Chicago.' A funny choice," recalls Gans, "but I didn't ask." On the other hand, Nichols knew what it would look like to his New York pals: a retreat by an actor who had tried to make it and not only failed, but failed after having been fired even from the jobs he had taken in order to scrape by. Nichols knew how to put on a good front—he'd been doing it every day since he first arrived in Chicago, six years earlier. But he wouldn't lie to himself. "If I'd stayed in New York with Lee Strasberg, who was very important to me, and just tried to be an actor, nothing would have happened," he said. "I slunk back to Chicago."

Privately, Nichols was enthusiastic, even a little excited. He had, after all, finally been offered full-time work as an actor, which was what he wanted, although not where he wanted it. Sills had characterized the new venture as a "cabaret," which sounded promising. And Elaine May would be there. They hadn't been in touch, but Nichols felt they were not through with each other yet. He couldn't stop thinking about "her and that train station and those hamburgers she made me in her apartment, and what came with them." His feeling that there was more for them to explore—perhaps as a couple, perhaps not—was decisive. He took the job.

Four

THE FIRST THING WE EVER DID TOGETHER

1955-1957

The Elaine May whom Nichols encountered when he returned to Chicago was no longer the campus terror he had first met three years earlier but an intensely focused theater artist. By the fall of 1955, May had become indispensable to the newly formed Compass Players. For one thing, the group tilted male, which meant, she said, that she "got all the parts that called for a girl who could wear a trenchcoat and a beret." It also meant that many of the men she worked with wanted her, something she had learned to navigate in a way that would preserve her growing status without demolishing guys who could then punish her for rejecting them. ("If I kiss, I fuck, and I don't want to fuck," she told one potential suitor pleasantly.)

The group's younger members were dazzled and baffled by her. "Elaine was very much into thought, and very sophisticated, and very smart," said Barbara Harris. "[But she] was so . . . well . . . incompetent in terms of being able to get her clothes on. I was somehow more able to iron my clothes." The idea of putting things away or tidying up was utterly alien to her. "Physical reality," Nichols said later, "does not interest her."

To Sills, May had become an adviser, counseling him on casting and pushing him to notice talent he might otherwise overlook. And Shepherd knew the group needed her in order to succeed—something the men of the Compass conceded only with great condescension. At first they patronized her as a kind of savant. "She knew everything about the theatre and psychoanalysis," said James Sacks, who dated her at the time. "She didn't know about anything else. She didn't know if Eisenhower was a Republican or a Democrat." But they understood that without May, the whole fragile enterprise might collapse. Playwrights Theater Club had relied largely on staging the classics, but Compass shows were supposed to consist of new material, and May was one of the few performers who could not only act and direct but write. Time and again, she would save them; they could barely bring themselves to thank her. "Every time she came in with material," said Compass member Mark Gordon, "it was 'Oh, my God, it's awful, it'll never work' . . . Then we'd do it for people . . . and the audience would be hysterical loving it. And then somebody maybe would say, 'Oh, I guess it's all right.' But there was never a recognition that Elaine's stuff was fantastic."

That summer, Shepherd had found a space for the Compass's performances in Hyde Park, a nightspot called the Hi-Hat Lounge. Drinks were served at a long bar on one side; performances took place on the other. Their first efforts had a casual, seat-of-the-pants quality that its members valued, "a kind of generosity of energy and spirit," Harris said. "We were pursuing something that we didn't know would work. It wasn't very down-to-earth." At first, "we were guided by David's political ideals. He would bring newspapers to work and choose what to deal with—what was happening with atomic bombs . . . whatever the political issues of the time were."

"David was the sociopolitical point man," said Ed Asner. "He wanted his People's Theater . . . whereas Paul was the communicator to actors, the director, the inspirer." The two men soon realized that they were facing the same dilemma: What good was a theater group if it had nothing to perform? Shepherd took out ads in New York trade papers offering $100 for any producible script. None arrived that met his standards—and the "newspaper plays" had too short a shelf life to sustain the group. So he came up with a different solution. By the time Nichols arrived to start work, Compass was relying on what Shepherd called "scenario plays"—a set of ideological one-acts that he and like-minded members of the company had contrived. "They all seemed to have a theme in common—how society molds people into the shape it wants them to take," said Compass member Roger Bowen. "Compass was David Shepherd's personality."

Nichols was less interested in what he was going to play than in who he was going to play it with. From his first day back, Shepherd said, "he latched on to Elaine and that was the end of it. He was resolute." Fred Wranovics, who ran the Hi-Hat, recalled seeing Nichols and May sitting in a back room. "It was like a summit meeting," he said. "The two of them sat on these stools, testing each other's ad-lib ability and spontaneity. Everyone was watching. It was like the Actors Studio versus the local fast gun. I guess they hit it off."

Improvisation began at the Compass not because Shepherd had a taste for comedy: He was "not a man with a natural sense of humor—he [could] see the irony in things but not the joke," said the playwright and improv historian Jeffrey Sweet. It was, rather, a way to make the shows long enough to justify charging admission. The first half of every Compass performance would be rehearsed playlets and sketches—some combination of the scenario plays, the news of the day, and anything else that someone, usually May, had gotten into performable shape. Then, after a break, the players would come back with a couple of scenes based on audience suggestions that had been solicited at the start of the evening—not pure in-the-moment improv, but as close as they had yet come. May, fast and confident, had a knack for it; Nichols didn't, and found himself flailing. "He didn't seem well," said Shepherd, "didn't seem healthy." And he certainly didn't seem like an actor worth importing from New York.

In his first days onstage, Nichols would try to shake things up, only to be thwarted by May's desire to keep it all real, to respect the premise they had set up and see where it went. At one point during a sketch, he shoved a hand in his pocket, then whipped it out and aimed an imaginary gun at her. "Why are you pointing your finger at me?" she said, without missing a beat. It was embarrassing, and, he knew, his own fault. "I was horrible, the worst improviser anybody ever saw, for weeks if not months," he said. Nor was he any better in the written sketches, where his persistent discomfort with physical action—sometimes because he was worried about his hairpiece—became a severe limitation. "One night we were doing Hansel and Gretel and Mike was playing the witch," said Compass member Andrew Duncan. When the other actors "popped him into the oven"—a door with a slatted opening—"you heard this 'Argh!' . . . he had broken his collarbone." Nichols became so nervous that he started smoking onstage—ostensibly as a character choice, but really to hide his shaking hands. He gravitated toward roles in his comfort zone—the know-it-all, the dandy, the snob—and, as had been the case since he first worked for Sills, he would barely move. "He would root himself in a chair and smoke," said Duncan. "You could always tell when a Mike Nichols scene had been done, because afterward the stage would be littered with Kent Micronite filters."

Every Compass performer saw May as their ticket to more stage time. Severn Darden, another actor Sills had lured back from New York, was a lightning-fast improviser with prodigious language skills; he could easily have paired with her. Shelley Berman, a more seasoned thirty-year-old comic, had primarily worked as a solo act, but he wanted in on sketches, too. Now that Barbara Harris was abroad with Sills, May was one of only two women regularly appearing in the shows. If you wanted to do anything about romance or dating or marriage or sex, a partnership with her was the way in.

But she stuck with Nichols, trusting their connection the same way he did. They would sit on the floor of her apartment and swoon over the same music, engaging in a kind of quasi-carnal intellectual frottage that they would eventually spoof on a famous track from their first album, or they would talk about the Russian novels they were both obsessively reading. "We were in a kind of ecstasy over literature," he said. A line from *The Brothers Karamazov*—"All my life you will remain a wound in my soul and I in yours—that's how it should be"—seemed to sum up their self-romanticizing feelings perfectly. Then they would eat—"cholesterol food," May says, "flat food. Cheeses and flat steaks were the only food I could hide under my coat and steal. I couldn't steal bread, because it was too bulky, so I would make sandwiches out of two steaks and some cheese. That would be our dinner. And then we would work on a scene and hang out."

They both knew they were good for each other, even essential. May drew him out; she understood that if the lacerating wit he showed her in private could be brought out onstage, he would be unstoppable. And Nichols, in turn, knew how to help May tame her volatility and wariness without being too controlling. "One night," she recalls, "Mike said, 'We're going to see my dear friends the Minnerles. Please don't be mean. They're nice people.' So we go downstairs to the Minnerles, who lived in a basement. They had a parrot. She was beautiful; she was from Brazil; I remember he was tall. I was so bad at chat, and she said something about the weather, and I was alarmed immediately. I had no idea how to respond. I forget what I said, but it wasn't good. When we left, Mike said to me, 'Why are you so rude? Why? People talk about the weather—that's how they begin things! Why do you go out on a date and say before you buy dessert, "I want you to know I'm not sleeping with you"? Why are you like that?' And I thought, *Why* am *I*? I became aware that people were saying what they had to say just to begin a conversation. They'd say, 'How are you?' and I immediately thought, *They don't care!* So I thought, *I'm going to learn to say things like 'Why, yes, it is hot'* or whatever it is you're supposed to say. Years later I said to Mike, 'You know, that night with the Minnerles changed my life.' And he said, 'Who are the Minnerles?'"

At first, May tried Nichols out in one of the scenario plays. "The Fifth Amendment" was a heartfelt tract about a man who gets a letter saying that he's blacklisted and goes from friend to friend—the better to give every actor a role—asking them what to do. Repetitively structured, devoid of characterization, and brandishing its politics on its sleeve, it was the diametrical opposite of something May would have written, but in those days, she says, "anybody who didn't go out to coffee at the right time had to direct," and this time the task had fallen to her. The play had been plotted, but no dialogue was on paper; that was for the actors to come up with. Nichols braced himself. "I'm not funny," he told her. "I can't be funny." So instead he decided to be extremely serious.

The result was a disaster. "At first," May says, "he pantomimed opening this letter with Bobbi Gordon, who played the wife, and he looked at it and burst into tears. This was at the first rehearsal! She waited and waited while he cried, and then she got furious and said, 'So what's in the letter?'"

May reeled him in a bit, but by the night of the first public performance, she says, "he was nervous again, his energy was up, and he opened the letter, looked at the audience, and burst into tears. Again. Bobbi said, 'What does it say?' and he kept sobbing. Finally she had to say, 'Let me see it' and read him the letter." In the following scene, Nichols was supposed to arrive at a friend's house and ask four pals for advice. "One of them was Alex Hassilev, who was a wonderful guitar player," says May. "What the scene was going to be was that he would talk to them and sing some songs. But Alex opened the door and Mike was still sobbing and couldn't talk. He literally sobbed his way through the whole thing because he was so prepared, so Method. Afterward he apologized to everyone."

The first time he and May tried to conceive their own scene was, if possible, even worse. "Mike said, 'You know how when you're going to break up with someone and they're crazy about you, you think, *Oh, I can't, I don't want to hurt them*? And you do it, and then you see them with someone else and gradually you want them again?'" May recalls. She sparked to the feeling instantly. "Why don't you call me," she suggested, "and the phone is busy, and you call again and it's still busy, and you think, *Who is she talking to?* and then you call a third time and the phone just rings and I'm not there?"

Not until they got onstage to perform the sketch in front of a paying audience did they discover—at the same grisly moment—the trap they had built for themselves. They entered, sat on two cubes positioned on opposite sides of the stage, and said . . . nothing. "We suddenly realize," May says, "that we have thought of no way to dramatize this. There's no one for him to talk to, and then I'm not there. Both of us thought only in concepts—it had never occurred to us that we needed a way to tell the story.

"There were dial phones then—it's still so humiliating to think about it. He had to pantomime dialing and make a dialing sound and then make a little busy-signal sound. I could see him deciding to do it. And there was nothing I could do, because I was on the phone on the other side of the stage! How could we be this dumb? Then he had to hang up—I don't think he even said anything, because he would have just been talking to himself. Then he had to do it again. *Again* he made the busy-signal sound. To hear him make that sound . . . it was so demeaning to him. And the third time, he made the ringing sound."

May couldn't help him, because the concept of the scene was that this time she was gone and the phone would just keep ringing. She was supposed to walk offstage as soon as he started to dial. But, feeling both embarrassed and protective of him, she couldn't bring herself to leave him alone—they had plunged in heedlessly together, and together they would suffer the consequences. So she stayed onstage, retreated into a corner, and waited as he made sad little ringing sounds. "Finally he hung up," she said. "And the guy on lights just had to gradually fade us out. We just stood there. I never forgot it. It was the most painful thing I've ever done onstage. And it was the first thing we ever did together."

If anything, that terrible performance cemented their bond. They were now a team, for better or worse. "For a month I was a disaster," Nichols said. "I cried in scenes because that's what I thought I'd learned from Strasberg." And when called upon to improvise, "I was desperate, I was boring, I couldn't think of anything." The moods that Nichols was able to access spontaneously—anger, whininess, arrogance, resentment—had served him well in his acting class. In sketches, however, they were often dead ends.

"But if you keep at it," he said, "suddenly the light switches on." One night he and May were onstage playing with an idea they had started to develop about two Brits together on a bridle path. Once again, they hadn't quite thought it through; May says that it wasn't until they were performing that "we realized I would have to be both me *and* the horse." But in that moment, something from Nichols's past as a teenage riding instructor clicked, and so did their shared affection for British movies. They swung into a routine, with May cantering in circles around Nichols. It worked. The audience started to laugh. One of the Compass actors taking a break at the bar was so surprised that he yelled to the rest of the actors, "Come quick—Mike has a character!"

"What is implied in that story—and it was true for the first time in my life—is affection," Nichols said. "I began to understand that I could be kidded, and people could be fond of me, and that this would all be a pleasurable thing." After that, with remarkable rapidity, Nichols and May started to find their groove. The instant audience feedback connected with a ruthless instinct they shared about what worked and what didn't. In this case, they discarded the troublesome gimmick—the riding—and kept the gold: perfect pitch in re-creating the movie dialogue of stoic, gallant, and desperately bland Englishmen and Englishwomen in a doomed romance. "Our work was all about [shared] references and context," he said. And "the referential joke was [about to become] the highest currency." The sketch they developed from that night's seedling was a version of *Brief Encounter* reset in a dentist's office, with Nichols as the dentist and May as the patient, both coolly discussing their torrid passion in the most banal context imaginable. "There, I've said it," said Nichols at the climax. "I do love you. Let's not talk about it for just a moment. Rinse out, please." It was the first of six or eight scenes that would, over the next several years, carry them to New York nightclubs, national television appearances, and Broadway. Almost every one of the sketches that made Nichols and May famous was incubated at the Compass.

The moment Nichols felt accepted, he started to loosen up. Even failure didn't upset him as much as it used to. By then, the Compass had moved to another venue—a place called the Dock, where, he said, "if you screwed up, you could run down to Lake Michigan"—which was just across from the theater—"and jump in and run back and do another scene." The range of characters he could create on the spot became greater, and the audience suggestions—an element of the evening that soon became the most popular part of Compass shows—now energized rather than terrified him. "With Elaine, I got rather good at improvising," he said. "And in some way, I began to really use what I learned with Strasberg—not acting, but what scenes are made of."

Together they came to realize, he said, that "you have to create a situation, an event . . . or you're just sitting there making up lines." Nichols also came to respect and value the imperative of the audience. "When you're making up a scene for people who have a lot of beers in their hands, you learn in a painful and memorable way what the audience expects," he said. "The audience says, 'Why are you telling me this?' and you have to have an answer. One is, 'Because it's funny.' But that's not enough because you're only going from laugh to laugh and in between, there's this terrifying vacuum with no purpose. The additional answer is, 'This is about you. This is about your life. Or the life we all have together' . . . And if you do it right, somehow they will say, 'Yes! How did you know? Look at that! I know that man! I am that man!'"

In the mid-1950s, sketch comedy tended to be situation comedy—and the situations were generally so timeworn that audiences knew where the laughs would come before a word was spoken. The first few years of network television had made the setups numbingly familiar: the door-to-door salesman who won't take a housewife's no for an answer, the randy boss chasing Miss So-and-So around a desk, the mad scientist and his dumb-blonde lab assistant. Comedy was, in some ways, less about character than about character types, whether the immigrant with the funny accent, the put-upon schnook with a catchphrase, or the exasperated blusterer forever on the verge of exploding.

To a form that was in serious danger of going stale, Nichols and May brought something slyer, sharper, and wholly new—a comedy rooted in deep observation of the tics, vulnerabilities, insecurities, vanities, and pretensions of others, and of themselves. Once they knew what they were doing, they found that their strengths complemented each other perfectly. May had a genius for turning an idea into a narrative—she told Nichols that everything they did together should be a fight, a negotiation, or a seduction and added, "When in doubt, seduce." And he turned out to be a natural editor who understood that changing one word could gain them or lose them a laugh; he also had a faultless sense of when to move from one beat in a scene to the next.

Throughout the first half of 1956, Nichols and May developed a core repertoire that became the Compass's main attraction. The troupe had started as an ensemble; now it had stars. "Shelley Berman was great right away," said Nichols. "But I was better with Elaine. And soon we had a body of work together."

Their first triumph grew out of an emotionally brutal, far-ahead-of-its-time scenario May had written called "Georgina's First Date," about an overweight teenage wallflower who is escorted to her prom by a college boy as part of a fraternity prank and then raped by him at the end of the night. The scene ended with her returning home in shock and murmuring to her ecstatic mother, "I had a wonderful time." That searing one-act was way too hard-edged to become a recurring piece at the Compass, but she and Nichols took an element of it—the fragility of a teenage girl trying to decide whether to lose her virginity—and changed the boy from a smug rapist into an awkward, alternately boastful and bumbling but fundamentally decent high school jock, a type Nichols had observed throughout his teens and could replicate down to the nasal honk and mannered drawl. The scene, now a short two-hander known as "Teenagers" and set entirely in the front seat of a car, became one of their best-loved routines, incorporating everything from physical comedy to a heartbreaking dip into tenderness and vulnerability for May to a final emotional swerve that makes it clear that Nichols is as scared as she is. Audiences howled with laughter, but it was the laughter of personal recognition. "Elaine and I had a rule," Nichols said. "Never try for a laugh. Get the laugh on the way to something else. Trying for it directly is prideless and dangerous, and the audience loses respect."

Together they scavenged culture, high and low, for ripe targets, and they could be merciless. Tennessee Williams became "Alabama Glass," a flamboyant, florid southern playwright. (One of his characters turns to "drink, prostitution, and puttin' on airs" after her husband commits suicide in response to an accusation of "not bein' homosexual.") They took a Chicago radio personality named Jack Eigen, whose show was broadcast live from a local nightspot called Chez Paree and who liked to boast about the famous people he was friends with, and turned him first into "Jack Fagan" and then into the preening and unctuous "Jack Ego," interrupting his own interview with a starlet, played by May, to observe, "Bertrand Russell was on. Bert is a heck of a good kid. He's not like a lot of your philosophers. By that I mean he's not pushy, and that is a terrific thing to see, we're all crazy about him—whaddaya say, sweetheart?"

Not only could May keep up with him, but, to his manifest delight, she could leave him gasping in the dust. Nichols recalled one moment during the Jack Ego sketch:

I thought I'd throw Elaine something new: "I understand your new picture, 'The Brothers Karamazov,' will be out soon," I said.

"Yes, Jack," she said coquettishly. "It was a great opportunity for me. I don't swim in this one at all. I was just fortunate enough to get to record the title song."

"Really," I said. "How wonderful. Could you sing some of it for us?" I asked, mean and curious.

"Surely," said Elaine. And the lyric that she ad-libbed is engraved forever in my memory:

There was dashing Dimitri, elusive Ee-vahn,
And Alyosha with the laughing eyes,
Then came the dawn,
The brothers were gone,
I just can't forget those wonderful guys.

Nichols burst into uncontrollable laughter. "People would drive miles to see Mike and Elaine tear apart Jack Eigen," said Shepherd.

One of them was Patricia Scot, a Chicago jazz and pop singer who also appeared on a local variety TV program called *In Town Tonight* (meaning "Who's in town tonight from New York or Los Angeles?"—

a measure of the degree to which Chicago still saw its own cultural life as essentially provincial). Scot's associate producer, Joe Goldberg, had heard about the couple at the Compass that everyone had to see, and took her along one evening. "I was flabbergasted," she says. "I was amazed. I said to Joe, 'My God, they're doing with acting what we're doing with music.' I was just enthralled by the whole group. The TV show was over at ten thirty every night, and I'd hightail it out to the place, this little hole in the wall on the South Side. At the time, it embarrasses me to say it, but I was kind of a star in Chicago, a personality. I had a show and pictures on billboards, that kind of thing. So eventually I was able to go backstage and meet all of them. And of course, it didn't take very long to discover Mike's special brilliance. I've always been attracted to brains."

Scot, then twenty-four, was a sultry, auburn-haired former model who, as more than one person at the Compass noted, bore a distinct resemblance to May. She and Nichols hit it off instantly, and, to the goggle-eyed shock of the men in the Compass, Mike the misfit, of all people, had not only become one of the stars of the show but now had a glamorous girlfriend who lived in a fancy apartment, "with wall-to-wall carpeting and an Eames chair," one said, while "we all lived in walkups with bare floors and roaches."

By the summer of 1956, when Sills and Harris returned from England, they barely recognized the scruffy, threadbare company they had left behind. It wasn't just that the Compass had now moved to a larger, fancier nightclub-style space called the Argo Off-Beat Room. "They had made something different out of it, much more professional-looking, more groomed," Harris said. The actors now wore jackets and ties—the Argo had a dress code—and were earning three times what they used to ($75 a week, a decent income at the time). And the show itself seemed tidier, more formal, more grown-up. "For one thing, the long scenarios were pretty much gone, and two-people scenes had taken their place," Harris said. "Nichols and May were the dominant talents, and Shelley Berman would do his single scenes . . . It was a surprise."

Sills was furious—this was far from his vision—but his complaints had little impact, because he had been gone for most of the Compass's existence. And Shepherd was, once again, disillusioned. Nichols no longer wanted anything to do with his political plays. "Mike hated the whole idea of the scenarios," said company member Larry Arrick. After "The Fifth Amendment," "he found the form constricting, pretentious, and boring. He would rather do how hard it is to get a ticket at the airline."

Within a few months of Sills's return, the Compass was starting to fly apart. Shepherd quit, then came back, Sills intervened with a heavy hand, then stepped away, and both came to realize that the eventual fate of their brainchild would have less to do with either of their concepts for it than with the two performers who were now filling the house night after night. Nichols and May were continuing to develop new material and building what was essentially a show of their own within the Compass. Not everything they did worked—they both wanted to come up with a nagging-mother-and-unhappy-son sketch that was rooted in their own pasts, but their first try, an update of *Hamlet* set in a Jewish deli, with Nichols as Hamlet, May as Gertrude, cutting meat behind the counter, and Berman as "Uncle Claude," never quite landed the way they wanted it to.

But at their strongest, they took themselves and Compass audiences into new and more formally daring territory. Late in 1956, they developed a long, complicated sketch known as "Pirandello" that, true to its namesake, played explicitly with notions of performance, reality, absurdism, and metatheatricality as it wound through several beats that had to be calibrated perfectly to create the level of discomfort and anxiety in the audience that they were after. The scene began with Nichols and May as two small siblings in a burping contest. "Mike would say, 'I can belch louder than you.' He was a great belcher," says May. "It would bring the house down. And then somehow the game went into, we started imitating Mommy and Daddy." Seamlessly, without tipping audience members as to exactly when the shift happened, Nichols and May glided from playing kids acting like their parents to playing the parents themselves, in an escalatingly personal and ugly fight. "And then," May says, "we became . . . not really *us*, but we made it sound like we, the performers, were fighting. At some point, I found something to say within the fight that had something to do with his being impotent. And he would walk offstage. When he did that, there was *sort* of a laugh, because they still thought it was part of the sketch, and I would laugh, too, and say, 'Is it something I said?' in the way that one performer would say something to cover for another."

As Nichols and May developed the sketch, they dared themselves to take it even further. Nichols would return to the stage, they would exchange some ugly words, she would turn away from him dismissively, he would grab her arm angrily to spin her around and, in doing so, tear her blouse, and she would start to cry. As the audience gasped, Nichols and May would face front simultaneously, announce, "This is Pirandello!" and bow, as if to say, "Fooled you!"

"The audience didn't give a shit when we did that," says May. "Sometimes they still didn't believe we'd been acting." They would perform and refine the sketch for the next five years—it was a dance they did together based, as much as anything, on their own awareness that they were capable of hurting each other and their desire to see how close to the edge they could get. It was unforgettable to those who saw it—but you had to be there; "Pirandello" was the only major Nichols and May routine that they chose never to film or record.

By the end of 1956 the Compass was over, a victim of changing career priorities. Once Nichols, May, and Berman decided to go out on their own, there was basically nothing left to disband. Berman pitched a three-way act to Nichols and May, but by then Nichols, who had himself become prickly and territorial, couldn't bear Berman's jittery competitiveness. "Shelley is the first person at Compass who had to count who had how many sketches, and I still think of it as the first bite of the apple," he said later. Aside from that, Berman's style of comedy—insistent, hustling, unembarrassedly Jewish—represented every fear Nichols had ever had about how he might come off to strangers; being Berman was what he had worked to avoid.

In 1957, Nichols and May started performing in a club on Chicago's North Side as a solo act. During their nights off, she would write and he would act elsewhere, first in a production of *Lysistrata* directed by Sills, which critics trashed, and then as Lucky in a well-received staging of *Waiting for Godot* in a 1,200-seat theater that he called "as happy an experience as I ever had. I had white makeup and the first girl backstage burst through the door very excited and said, 'Oh my God! Mike! How did you get your tongue so pink?'" His bold, committed performance, in a cast that also included Harvey Korman and Louis Zorich, startled colleagues who still remembered the awkward, almost immobile performer who had arrived in Chicago just eighteen months earlier. "I [had] never seen Mike so physical," said Andy Duncan. "He played it like a dog. Slavering. He would sit up and pant. He really threw himself into it. I was amazed."

Nichols and Pat Scot were still seeing each other and getting more serious. It was a match that puzzled people who knew them, and sometimes bewildered Scot herself. "I was not in his league intellectually," she says. "I was this little girl from Milwaukee, kind of from the sticks. Graduated from high school, never went to college, and here I was, thrown in with . . . Well, once, in Chicago, we were at a party, a gathering of a lot of book-reading people. I was standing alone and Mike came over and said to me, 'What's the matter, honey—are you boring?' It was a joke on me, but I had to laugh at it, because I was. I didn't have anything to say to anybody and they didn't have anything to say to me. It was very obvious I was in the wrong world."

Nevertheless, Nichols appeared to be in love, and by spring he and

Scot were engaged. "I remember going to a furrier and helping them pick out a fur coat," says Joy Carlin. "He must have had some money by then." The two married on June 8, 1957, in the chapel at the University of Chicago. May attended, and although she had been politely supportive, could not resist remarking to a friend, "Isn't it a beautiful first wedding?" Nichols and Scot left for New York for two weeks, on what Scot refers to as "our so-called honeymoon. We spent a week in New York and then a week with his mother and her husband somewhere in a resort area. And talk about his mother! Oy, God. Can you imagine being on your honeymoon with your mother-in-law in the next room? Oh, it was terrible. She looked like Greta Garbo—even older; she was absolutely beautiful. She took one look at me and thought, *Oh my God, what has he done?* I hadn't brought proper shoes for the sandy walking around, so she loaned me a pair of sneakers for the week. At the end, I gave them back and said, 'Thank you so much, I was really glad to have these.' And she said, 'You are welcome. Of course, I could have used them.' Jesus Christ."

What followed was a final, brief, and deeply awkward episode with the Compass, or a version of it. David Shepherd was trying to reconstitute the theater in other cities—first in St. Louis and then, if everything worked out, in New York. May needed a job and, to Nichols's apparent chagrin, said yes to Shepherd's offer to go down to St. Louis to work for the summer, where she would be in partnership with Del Close, a young former member of the Chicago troupe. Nichols and Shepherd were barely speaking by then—he had spent many of his last months at Compass expecting Shepherd to fire him—but he couldn't risk losing May to another partner. Just weeks after he and Scot had found an apartment in Chicago's Old Town, he left for Missouri.

Nichols and Close detested each other. "We just weren't mature enough to treat each other properly," Close later said. And during that summer in St. Louis, for the first time since they started working together, Nichols and May found themselves at odds. His marriage had thrown her off balance, as did their new living arrangements; she and Nichols shared an apartment, and Scot would commute from Chicago to see her new husband every weekend. Perhaps in response, May started working more regularly with Close; Nichols became jealous, and Scot got the worst of it. "I'm flying down on Friday and flying back on Sunday, just in tears," she recalls. "From the beginning, it was difficult. There was such a chasm between us. You could see that he felt, 'Who is this woman? Why is she here?' It was really not a good thing. We kind of tried, but you can just feel that horrible coldness, that distance. Poor Mike, poor baby. He really didn't want to get married. Why did he?"

By late August, Nichols's professional marriage was foundering just as badly. There were rumblings about Nichols and May going to New York to launch the Compass there, and the two were even dispatched east for a brief visit to meet with a potential backer. But something was rupturing between them, largely, Nichols later said, as a result of his own bad behavior. Del Close had strong ideas about the troupe's work that would eventually form the basis of much of modern improvisation technique; that summer in St. Louis, he and May started to articulate some basic principles of performance: Always make the active rather than the passive choice, justify every action that you're playing, and, most important, never deny verbal reality—a tenet that came to be known as the "Yes, and . . ." rule. (Example: If two actors are improvising a divorce scene and one says, "What about our children?" it's cheating to say, "We don't have any." You say, "Yes, the children will suffer, and . . .") But Nichols couldn't, or wouldn't, function in a place where someone else—least of all an upstart twenty-three-year-old like Close—was setting the rules. "I persecuted the shit out of Del," he said. "Nothing could stop me."

How it all ended in St. Louis was, over the decades, the subject of varyingly self-serving accounts from everyone involved. At first, Nichols and May said they had made a joint decision to seek their fortune in

New York. The reality may be more complex, if not much clearer than Shepherd's diary entry for August 25, 1957, which read "Mike and Elaine crisis all day and all night." Nichols told what may be the truest version in the late 1980s: "I was basically fired for being such a pain in the ass. It had to do with Elaine and me, and who she was spending time with," meaning Close. "But I was finished." Others said it was May who, at the end of her rope, demanded that Nichols be fired—or it was May who, at the end of her rope after his firing, demanded that he be rehired. In any event, Nichols left amid a storm of bad feeling, with Shepherd warning him that he and Compass owned all of the material Nichols and May had developed in their time there. (They didn't, as Shepherd soon found out. "You can't copyright improvised work," he said. "Shtick is not permanent. That's what the outcome of that was.")

Nichols flew to New York. May stayed in St. Louis. He started calling her, entreating her to come. Within a week or two she realized that, as impossibly as he had behaved, she didn't want to be stuck in St. Louis without him, working on yet another version of someone else's idea for a theater. When he called one weekend in September and said, "I might have a gig for us," she got in her car. Three days later she was in Manhattan.

Nichols and May didn't have plans for the future; they barely had plans for the next two weeks. They had never operated out of anything other than his belief that performing "was a lot of fun *for now*. It was something you did until you started your life as a grownup. Eventually we would find out what we were going to do, and do it, and have lives like normal people," Nichols said.

"This did not happen."

Five

THIS BOY AND GIRL

1957–1959

Nichols had one phone number in his pocket, and it was all he needed. He and May were in New York City with $40 in borrowed money, the names of a couple of friends willing to let them sleep on their sofas, and a single contact. An actress he had known from his Strasberg days was married to an associate of Jack Rollins, a talent manager who could book singers, comedians, and novelty acts into any club in town. They got an appointment, visited Rollins in his small office, and did fifteen or twenty minutes of material. First they showed him "Teenagers," then they tried out an idea they had started to develop in Chicago. They asked Rollins to suggest a first line and a last line and told him they would invent a scene for him on the spot. May riffed; Nichols moved her along when he sensed the time was right. "Elaine would go on forever if you let her," said Rollins. "She was insanely creative but had no sense of when to quit. Mike [was] Mr. Practical." They won him over. "[I thought] my God! I am finding two people who are writing hilarious comedy on their feet," he said. "They did things that were taboo in those days . . . they would uncover dark little niches that you felt but never had expressed. They expressed it for you."

It was done. They were in. "They were remarkable," Rollins said. "They were complete. I knew they had something odd and wonderful, but I didn't know whether to laugh or cry." That day he took them out to lunch at the Russian Tea Room and signed them. They were relieved when he picked up the check.

In the late 1950s, supper-club culture was still a thriving New York scene, with full houses, big names, and a cadre of columnists covering every up and down, and Rollins got them an audition at one of the most popular of the East Side cabarets, the Blue Angel. The owner, Max Gordon, was as impressed as Rollins had been, and offered them a booking in two weeks. Politely, Nichols explained that they needed money sooner than that. So Gordon gave them a second, temporary gig—starting right away, they could play his downtown club, the Village Vanguard, until the spot at the Blue Angel opened up.

The venues couldn't have been more different. The Vanguard had been a mainstay of the West Village for almost twenty-five years, a casual watering hole for a young crowd of locals, beatniks, poets, potheads, and anyone else who liked jazz combos, blues singers, and cheap drinks. The acoustics were rough, and the chairs scraped noisily on the floor when anyone moved. The Blue Angel was dark, plush, and self-consciously swank, a long, narrow space with gray velour and pink rosettes covering the walls, thick carpeting, a well-dressed clientele crowded at small black tables, and, in the back room, a stage so tiny that the singer and actress Dorothy Loudon once said it was "like trying to perform on top of a cocktail napkin."

The Vanguard, which bore a close resemblance to the bars Nichols and May had played in Chicago, was a comfortable place for them to warm up. They started there in early October as the opening act for Mort Sahl, whose style of casually delivered topical humor—the equivalent of a live late-night monologue—had brought him a measure of success in the previous few years. Every night, Sahl would stroll out onstage, usually in a red V-neck sweater and with a folded newspaper under one arm, and riff on the day's events. It wasn't Nichols's style, but he saw how effectively Sahl worked the turf; he packed the Vanguard every night, and thus guaranteed his two novice openers a big audience. They came up with a short set tailored to the small space—nothing that required props or a lot of physical action would work, but "Teenagers," set in a parked car at night, could be done with just two high stools on which they sat side by side. The radio-host-and-starlet sketch might also play well, or perhaps "Telephone," a reliable routine they'd worked up with Nichols as a young man desperate to make a call from a pay phone and down to his last dime and May voicing a series of operators ranging from bored to extravagantly solicitous.

After "Teenagers" and maybe one more sketch (or not, depending on Sahl's level of impatience), they would do what they'd done to impress Rollins: They would ask the audience for line suggestions—and for a particular literary style, from Shakespeare to Tolstoy to Clifford Odets—and, for their big finish, they would improvise a scene in that writer's style. The laugh when they got to the last line, with the audience delighted to discover how they'd made their way there, was a perfect high on which to end. "The trick was, we had both read everything," May says. "The toughest thing was if they gave us an easy one, because we hadn't read the easy ones. But they would try to stump us, and the more they did that, the easier it got. Greek plays were easy. Ibsen was easy. Harold Robbins would have been hard, because we hadn't read him." The improv invariably showcased the two of them at their most relaxed and connected. Nichols would have to fight to keep from breaking character and cracking up, a habit he'd gotten into in Chicago, sometimes to get an audience on their side but more often because he just couldn't help it. "This will sound simple-minded, but we both thought the same things were funny," May says. "We found each other hilarious."

Downtown, they were an instant sensation—so instant that the audience on the second night already included repeat visitors. Sahl was in danger of being upstaged, and he knew it; in the second week of their Vanguard run, he stepped in a couple of times just as they were about to go on and canceled their set, telling them the crowd was already primed enough for the main attraction.

They hurtled toward their opening at the Blue Angel with barely a moment to rearrange their lives. At the Vanguard, Nichols and May could wear trousers and turtlenecks, but when they left St. Louis, neither of them had taken along anything dressy enough for a Midtown nightclub. "Jack bought Mike a new shirt, and Jack's wife took Elaine out and bought her a dress," recalled Rollins's partner, Charles Joffe. Both of them were trying to find apartments—May would soon be able to move both her mother and her daughter to New York to live with her, and Nichols was on the phone to his wife, trying to get her to tie up loose ends in Chicago and join him. Otherwise, they hadn't touched base with anyone, a fact of which Nichols was reminded when the phone rang and the voice at the other end, with icy precision, said, "Hello, Michael. This is your mother speaking. Do you remember me?"

"I said, 'Mom, can I call you right back?'" Nichols remembered. "And I called Elaine and said, 'I have a new piece for tonight,' and I told her the first line. She said, 'Oh! Say no more!' We did it that night. We had talked about it no more than that and the way we did it stayed forever. I told my mother it was Elaine's mother, she told her mother it was my mother . . . it was very liberating!" The sketch, known as "Mother and Son," was a six-minute phone conversation between Nichols, as a brilliant rocket scientist in the middle of a launch, and his emotional assassin of a mother. ("Arthur, I sat by that phone all day Friday and all day Friday night and all day Saturday and all day Sunday. Your father finally said to me, 'Phyllis, eat something, you'll faint.' I said, 'Harry, no. I don't want my mouth to be full when my son calls.'") It was a superb showcase for May, who made a feast out of lines like "I'm sorry I bothered you when you were so busy—believe me, I won't be around to bother you much longer" and "[My doctor] said, 'Mrs. White, I have been a doctor for thirty-five years and I have never heard of a son who's too busy to call his mother.' That's what he said to me, Arthur, and that man is a *doctor*.")

The mother as underminer was not a new comedy invention, and there was a measure of Eisenhower-era misogyny in the notion that all women eventually emasculate their sons—Nichols's character literally becomes a babbling toddler by the end. But the barbs were so well aimed and the passive-aggression so specifically and personally observed that it all felt as fresh to audience members as if Nichols and May had somehow unearthed their family secrets. With Nichols graciously teeing up one punch line after another for her, the scene became an instant staple of their act and one of their most frequently requested sketches.

For the Blue Angel they created a set list that included "Teenagers," "Mother and Son," "Disc Jockey" (the Jack Ego sketch), and "Pirandello" and ended with the audience-prompted improv. They gave their first performance in mid-October; they were initially a late-night act, for those who didn't mind staying up and staying out. Two weeks later, Rollins said, "they were the hottest thing in the city."

As hyperbolic as that sounds, it wasn't much of an exaggeration. Within days of Nichols and May's Blue Angel opening, it became a badge of cultural cachet to say you saw them first, you saw them twice, you saw them in Chicago, you saw them downtown. On October 24, they got their first review, from the *New York Journal-American*'s Gene Knight. "A large crowd gathered on the sidewalk in front of 152 E 55th St. Something happen? Yes. This was the Blue Angel at midnight and Mike Nichols and Elaine May, sensational young comedy team, were about to go on. These people outside were trying, more or less unsuccessfully, to get in. I was among the fortunate . . . Mike and Elaine certainly pack 'em in. Without any waste of time, this boy and girl went to work on their disk jockey bit. I've heard them do it before, but they stage sketches you enjoy seeing again and again . . . The lines (they write their own sophisticated stuff) are the cleverest heard at any club in town. The pace leads to laugh after laugh . . . There is nothing funnier in the niteries." (*Variety*'s critic wasn't as sure; he called them "hipsters' hipsters" and warned, "in average . . . spots the act will have trouble finding its mark.")

Gordon realized that he'd stumbled upon gold; he quickly signed Nichols and May to a six-month contract. By December they had landed in the pages of *The New Yorker*. "Taking shelter from the damp one recent night, I wandered into the Blue Angel and caught their act. I enjoyed it so much that I've been back a couple of times since," Douglas Watt wrote in his Tables for Two column. "Mr. Nichols, a fair youth with an alert and friendly mien, and Miss May carry on little dialogues . . . with something of the same delightful interplay characteristic of that splendid vaudeville team the Lunts; the bantering tone, the repeated phrases, the artful covering of each other's lines—all these devices are present, and well-mastered." Watt raised a skeptical eyebrow at the improv sketch, remarking, "I suspect . . . that they have situations prepared for these invited little emergencies, but I still couldn't help being impressed by the ease with which they slipped into and out of them. On one of my visits they took off on Euripides (with no props at all), and I'm sure that the Greek theatre was never more fun."

"New York is not only fashion-driven but fashion-obsessed—and we were stunned to become a fashion," Nichols said. "We'd just been in Chicago, where people laughed if it was funny; if it wasn't, they didn't. [But] once [Watt] said we were like the Lunts, they laughed when we came out on stage." Audiences were fascinated by the pair: Male-female comic duos were unusual enough, and this one seemed not to fit any template. Unlike almost all comic actresses of the time, May was glamorous and self-possessed rather than goofy or clownish, and Nichols, with his affable, cagey grin and pleasant, high drone of a voice, appeared so ordinary that his sharpness came as a series of jolts. He "looked pale and soft, like the boy who never played ball," Betty Rollin wrote in *Look*. "Except the eyes. They have played ball."

At the end of the year, Rollins got them an audition for Jack Paar, the new host of NBC's *Tonight Show*. Paar agreed to try them out in front of a full studio audience during a rehearsal—essentially a camera test. It went poorly. The audience was used to stand-up comics, but not to the sly observational role-playing that had won over clubgoers. Nichols and May went into a routine, and when Paar sensed that they were starting to lose the crowd, he pulled the camera off them midsentence and said, "Do an improvisation, kids, and make it snappy." They stumbled through an attempt, but they were rattled and thrown—and not invited to appear on the show.

Undeterred, Rollins booked them on the competition—ABC's *The Steve Allen Show*—and on December 29, 1957, Nichols and May made their national television debut. Allen introduced them as "a youthful duo . . . two young folks who [are] a pair of bright lights on the comedy horizon. Very clever," and then the camera cut to them in their newly bought clothes—a jacket and bowtie for him, a long-sleeved black dress for her—sitting on stools in front of a microphone. They had chosen to do "Disc Jockey," their most flexible piece: The sophistication of the references in the DJ's name-dropping could be dialed up or down depending on the audience, as could the double entendres and allusions in the starlet's responses. Both were visibly nervous, and Nichols had been given the deadly task of explaining the joke in advance, telling the audience, "Elaine and I have been listening to some of the big disc jockeys, and we've found that they're playing less and less records and they're talking more and more. A lot of them seem to know everyone in the whole world, which we think is kind of terrific, considering that they never get out of the studio." He waited for a laugh that never came, took a breath, looked down at his cards, and soldiered on.

Once the sketch started, and he introduced May as "Barbara Musk, in town publicizing her latest picture, *I Was a Teenage Brain Surgeon*," they were on safer ground. He got some chuckles with a riff about his close friendship with Bernard Baruch, and she got louder laughs with her inane, vamping answers ("Bernie, for me, is a real great guy . . . For me, a pushy philosopher is always a drag"). The bit wasn't a home run, and a final joke about "Tristan and Isolde—a great team" fell flat. But over the course of its seven minutes, one can feel the audience gradually warming up as it catches on to a rhythm and style it hadn't seen before. The two of them, relieved to be done, took their bows as Allen, in his businesslike way, said, "Elaine May and Mike Nichols, real great. We'll have 'em back soon."

Three weeks later, their lives changed forever. On Tuesday, January 14, 1958, NBC's popular program *Omnibus* aired a two-hour prime-time special called "Suburban Revue," a series of routines, sketches, and songs built around a unifying theme. The show's producer liked what he had seen on Allen's show, and he gave Nichols and May two slots. This time, the framework allowed them to be presented as sketch artists rather than stand-up comedians. "I made a deal that they do two pieces, and that nobody had the right to do any editing," said Rollins. The first was a slightly self-censored version of "Teenagers" (May didn't take off her blouse to reveal the top of a slip, as she sometimes did onstage) that the show introduced as "The Dawn of Love, or The Moon Also Rises in an Automobile." The second was "Telephone," the desperate-caller-and-operator scene.

The special was a mess that never quite recovered from the irrelevance of its opening, a flapper-era song-and-dance skit called "The Gladiola Girl" that dragged on for eighteen minutes with barely a smile from the audience. But Nichols and May were standouts; the laughs built steadily in both of their appearances, with the biggest of the night coming in "Teenagers." Over the years, they had worked out their only extended bit of physical comedy—a long car-seat kiss during which all four of their arms flail and interlock as they negotiate the holding of a cigarette; after a long time, May pulls her lips away from his to exhale a cloud of smoke. When they did it on *Omnibus,* the audience exploded with laughter—as it did when, a few moments later, Nichols said to May, with imploring urgency, that if she let him go further, "I wanna tell you right here and now that I would respect you *like crazy.*"

By the end of the telephone sketch, when the audience howled at May's throaty, heartfelt "You go ahead and cry—Bell Telephone understands," it was clear they had stolen the show, and they knew it—but amid the program's general dreariness, had anyone noticed? Nichols got up in the middle of the night and headed for the newsstand to find out. The first review he saw was from *The New York Times,* whose critic Jack Gould wrote, "The only two interludes of distinction were provided by Elaine May and Mike Nichols in two good sketches . . . each item had style and freshness." The other papers followed suit, and in a column that ran that Sunday, the *Times* reiterated its praise—particularly for May, who it said "should go skyrocketing in the musical comedy world." *Time, Life,* and *Newsweek* all weighed in as well, with *Time* echoing the unanimous verdict that their "satiric thrusts were fresh, inspired stuff."

Tens of millions of people watched that episode of *Omnibus*—not just watched, but paid attention. "Everyone had said to Rollins, 'Nobody will get them, they're too intellectual,'" says May. "Well, everyone got us. We couldn't believe it." Nichols and May had had a "Who are *they*?" moment in front of mainstream America: They were literally an overnight success. "We did twenty minutes and just like that, we were famous," said Nichols, who knew it had happened the second he read the first review. (He immediately woke May and said, "What do we do now?") The trajectory that Rollins had mapped out for them—perhaps a few more appearances on Steve Allen's show if they were lucky, plus steady work at the Blue Angel—was scrapped. In one step, they had cut straight to the finish line. They were no longer up-and-comers; they were stars. Rollins started planning an LP and a national tour; he would still put Nichols and May on TV, but now he was demanding $5,000 for each appearance—more than either of them had made in total during their last year at the Compass—and getting it.

For the rest of his professional life, no moment would disorient Nichols as profoundly as the sudden, simultaneous arrival of wealth and celebrity did in the first months of 1958. He was twenty-six years old, less than six months past being fired from a minor comedy gig in Missouri, and had only recently been able to afford a new and slightly better toupee. The self that he would painstakingly compose in front of the bathroom mirror—"It takes me three hours every morning to become Mike Nichols," he later told the actor George Segal—was a struggler, a striver, someone who had to put great daily effort into making himself just passable enough to blend in. Now, he said, "I had sharkskin suits and Jack Rollins calling us the hottest team in showbiz." At the time, Nichols insisted that he saw "nothing operationally different in my life." It couldn't have been further from the truth.

Suddenly, people—young, talented people doing interesting things—wanted to know him. The *Village Voice* cartoonist Jules Feiffer, already a brilliant social anatomist at twenty-eight, had turned on *Omnibus* that night and thought, "*Oh my God—they're me, but they're better.* They'd gone further and perfected it. I was afraid to laugh, because I might miss something. When they were doing 'Teenagers,' I could not believe what I was looking at. Everything was unprecedented. All I could think was *I have to know them, I have to meet them, I have to let them know about me.* The only social part of my existence was when I turned in the cartoon and spoke to everybody at the *Voice.* Other than that, going out at night, getting drunk, and trying to get laid was about it. So I went to see them at the club and worked up the nerve to go backstage and discovered that they were fans of mine. I started hanging out with them, because it was a lonely world out there if you were doing the sort of work we were doing."

Another early visitor to the Blue Angel was Stephen Sondheim, then twenty-seven, whose new show *West Side Story* had opened on Broadway the week Nichols and May started at the Village Vanguard. Sondheim was a decade younger than his collaborators Leonard Bernstein, Arthur Laurents, and Jerome Robbins, and when he was dragged backstage to meet Nichols and May by a friend, he felt an instant connection to a fellow wunderkind. "Mike and I just hit it off," he says. "I'm smart, he was smart, and we were both sly—he was slyer than I. With him, nothing was just on the surface—there was always some little undercurrent that made you either apprehensive or giggling. Always something funny and always something surprising."

By then, Nichols and May were no longer the midnight show at the Blue Angel; ten weeks into their run, they were headliners, and other comics were vying for the chance to open for them. But Rollins cut their stint short; he promised Max Gordon they would fulfill the rest of their contract later in the year, but right now there were too many opportunities; there was too much money to be made. He moved them to a higher-paying run at a club in the Duane Hotel, on Thirty-seventh Street, called the Den in the Duane, and started fielding offers. Steve Allen wanted them back; Dinah Shore invited them on her show, and Perry Como on his. And Paar had changed his mind; with breathtaking chutzpah, he complained that, having discovered Nichols and May, he now had to pay through the nose to get them.

It frustrated May that the demands of their schedule now left little time to develop new sketches—they probably had no more than ten reliable performance pieces—but to the networks, eager to put them on the air, it didn't matter: They wanted "Teenagers" again, or "Mother and Son," or "Telephone." For Nichols, each new appearance was an opportunity to calibrate a line or laugh or gesture a little more finely; everything about "Teenagers" on *The Perry Como Show* was slightly more polished than it had been a few weeks earlier on "Suburban Revue" and, accordingly, they got more laughs. "The bigger the night-club we were in, the bigger the television show we were on, the more pressure there was to have the sketches we did be the best we had. And we found ourselves doing the same material over and over," Nichols said. "This took a great toll on Elaine." But, he said, "early on . . . we discovered that pieces that seemed boring to us because they were com-pletely set were tremendous successes on television."

In Chicago, Pat Scot was reduced to writing her husband a plaintive song:

> *Do you recall*
> *A chapel small*
> *The eighth of June*
> *I stood with you*
> *And listened to*
> *A wedding tune*
> *And then we went on our honeymoon*
> *Remember me?*

She went to work every evening at WBBM, then came home to see if her husband was on television. "I thought, *What the hell? This is stu-pid*," she recalls. "So I got out of my contract and flew to New York. It was surreal. I slept for three days, just trying to escape from it all. Mike used to say to me, 'You're out of touch with reality,' and of course, he was right. We both were when we got married, and then comes the dawn."

For a while, they thought they could make a go of it. They found an apartment on East Fifty-eighth Street, a duplex that was nicer than any place Nichols had ever lived. He bought them a Mercedes convertible, and Rollins got her a singing gig at the Den in the Duane, opening for Lenny Bruce—"a sweet, gentle man," she says, "who used to massage my feet between shows." Nichols made it a point to watch her perform— and then to stay and watch Bruce, whom he admired. They bought nice furniture and got a Saint Bernard puppy and tried their best to act the way they thought a young, up-and-coming married couple would.

May moved to a large apartment in a quiet neighborhood across town on Riverside Drive, where she, her mother, Ida, and her young daughter, Jeannie, eventually settled in, and although she was dubious about the marriage, she tried to give Nichols and his wife a wide berth. It didn't help. "I felt very left out because of their twosome-ness," says Scot. "I was jealous. Because she was incredibly beautiful, in that zaftig Jewish way. She was *ripe*. Here's the thing: If they had been having sex, which they hadn't—maybe they had one time, but who cares?—it would have been one thing. But they were so much closer than just sexual partners. There was no way to compete with that." And when Nichols would take Pat to parties, more often than not he'd strand her. "It was a whole different world—his world of celebrity—and I was not fitting in at all. 'Intellectual' started to be a dirty word to me. I got tired of being put down subtly. I was at a party that [the actor and restaurateur] Patrick O'Neal and his wife, Cynthia, were hosting. Norman Mailer came over and we were chatting, and after a while he said, 'Sit down. Let's see if you've got anything on the ball.' And I said, 'Fuck you!' I still remember the shock on his face. He came back a little later to apologize. But I just wasn't interested in passing his IQ test."

In the spring, Rollins sent Nichols and May to Los Angeles for a couple of TV appearances, some network meetings, and an engagement at one of the city's biggest nightspots, the Mocambo, which was then in its last months of operation. The gig was a bleak affair. "I remember one performance in which absolutely no one laughed. At the end they clapped heartily, but nobody laughed," said May. "I also remember there was a huge glass wall with tropical birds flying around inside. Every night during our performance, one of the birds would die. We would learn this because the next night the old wardrobe woman would come to me and say, 'Well, another bird died last night.'" Nichols found himself disliking club work more and more. People "go there to drink, or to impress a girl or a client—a lot of reasons that have nothing to do with the show," he said. "They're terribly distracting places to work in. Nobody's paying attention, the waiters are always bouncing crockery around."

In the months that followed, Nichols and May started to learn what to avoid—sometimes the hard way. The lure of television was overwhelming, and he was faster to say yes than she was, becoming the business-decision maker for both of them. An appearance in a CBS presentation of a creaky Victor Herbert operetta called "The Red Mill" was their first and only TV acting job as a team—they played a pair of spoiled, vapid Hollywood celebrities, and as soon as the director told them, "You don't have to hold to the script—say anything you want, kids," they knew they were in trouble. Nichols later said, "There's no such thing as a brilliant production of a nonexistent play." At one point, they were required to ride a horse onto the set. The result, Nichols said, "doesn't bear thinking about."

A turning point came when Desi Arnaz and Lucille Ball, whose jointly owned company Desilu had become, in the wake of *I Love Lucy*, a major TV production entity that would go on to launch some of the most successful hour-long dramas of the 1960s, made Nichols and May an offer that would have reshaped both of their careers—the chance to develop and costar in a comedy series. The two went over to CBS and, on the precipice of signing a contract, looked at each other. "Maybe we shouldn't," May said to him. Nichols giggled. "I don't think I will," he said, and put down the pen. They laughed and flew back to New York.

By July 1958, when they resumed their run at the Blue Angel to work off the last three months of their contract, they had a somewhat better sense of what they excelled at and what they disliked. Radio appearances and print interviews were fine; they sat down to talk to Mitch Miller for his radio show and to Mike Wallace for his newspaper column. ("I had this big revelation one day," Nichols told Wallace. "I always thought the guys in the Jaguars and the little caps were different from me. And then one day I looked at one, and I realized he's just a guy like me who bought a Jaguar and a little cap.") They knew that regular TV appearances were essential exposure, but, when possible, they preferred not to get roped into more than a brief role in anyone else's sketches. During one segment of *The Dinah Shore Chevy Show* in which he and May had to act like they were at a cocktail party and sing "Well, Did You Evah (What a Swell Party This Is)" alongside the hour's other guests, Nichols was briefly flooded with an urge to quit show business altogether.

As soon as their run at the Blue Angel ended, he threw himself into further work. Rollins had gotten them a record deal with Mercury, and in the fall they recorded a set of eight two-person vignettes, spoken over background instrumentals, that they called *Improvisations to Music.* The tracks showcased an aspect of their work that had often gone unremarked during their club and TV appearances: Both Nichols and May had become so skilled vocally that they could nail their characters even when nobody could see them. To do so, they drew on their own history: That first encounter years earlier at Illinois Central Station when they'd both gone into a spy routine became "Mysterioso," with the two of them as a pair of Boris-and-Natasha agents exchanging cryptic messages aboard a railroad until it slowly becomes clear that they're just a couple on a commuter train heading home to a Connecticut suburb:

He: Listen very closely . . . Ven you go . . . tell zem I asked for no starch in the collar.
She: It's impossible! It can't be done.

He: It *must* be done.

She: What about the cuffs?

He: Never mind the cuffs, fool!

Their *Brief Encounter/*dentist sketch worked beautifully as an audio track, as did a couple of scenes that expressed May's "When in doubt, seduce" maxim. "Cocktail Piano," in which a boss who encounters his secretary at a bar tries to get her to come home with him, was an ideal showcase for one of Nichols's improv specialties—libidinous panic expressed as placidly as possible. And the album's masterpiece was "Bach to Bach," about two sophisticates lying on a bed who essentially talk each other to the point of intellectual orgasm over their love of music while listening to Bartók.

She: I can never believe that Bartók died on Central Park West.

He: Isn't that *ugly?*

She: Ugly, ugly, ugly . . . Oh, I love this part—

He: Yes, here, here, here.

She: Yes! Yes, yes, yes, yes.

He: Almost hurts . . . I know *exactly* what you mean! . . . I don't
  know how to say this, but for the whole last two hours I've
  really had my anxiety allayed.

At the end, they smoke a cigarette. The perfect placement of "allayed" was pure Nichols; the uncanny ear for loftiness that veered into lunacy ("Too many people think of Adler as a man who made mice neurotic—he was more, much more") was pure May. "I had never actually heard someone deliver irony in the tone of their voices, and sarcasm, and satire. [It] was very, very new," said Steve Martin, who discovered the album as a teenager.

Improvisations to Music wasn't like other comedy albums: From the first, it was about the possibility of sex, the mores of flirtation, the telltale signs of desperation, the current of carnal hunger that ran through ordinary life. "Most of the time, people thought we were making fun of others when we were making fun of ourselves," Nichols said. "Pretentiousness. Snobbiness. Horniness." The tracks weren't parodies, but Nichols and May assumed that their listeners read the same magazines, saw the same movies, and listened to the same newscasts they did and were just waiting for someone to come along and point out their absurdities. This was the first work by the duo to which people could return whenever they pleased, and they did: The album, which reached *Billboard*'s top forty and won them a 1959 Grammy nomination, was practically memorized by a generation of comedy aficionados. To its fans, finding someone else who loved *Improvisations to Music* created an instant kinship.

Public curiosity about the pair reached new heights, aided by their unwillingness to give very much away. The biographies they wrote for the album jacket epitomized their calculatedly teasing approach. "Mike Nichols is not a member of the Actors Studio, which has produced such stars as Marlon Brando, Julie Harris, Ben Gazzara, Eva Marie Saint, Carroll Baker, and others too numerous to mention. He has never toured with *Mr. Roberts* and has never appeared on such television programs as the *Goodyear Playhouse* and the *Kraft Theatre*," it read. "Miss May does not exist."

Even as the album started to take off, Nichols was increasingly unsure of what their future should look like. Were they recording artists now? Could they be dramatic performers? Regulars on TV panel shows? Were they comics, as Milton Berle, an almost obsessive guest at their shows who watched them perform at the Blue Angel sixty times, said they were? Or were they, as Mitch Miller had suggested to them, "actors who don't rely on jokes but . . . character and situation"? ("No Fooling, They're Actors" insisted the headline of one 1958 interview, an idea Nichols fully endorsed.) As he and May continued to draw crowds, he found himself wondering if what they were doing so well was a kind of trap that would turn out to be the only thing he would ever be suited for.

He grew testy, impatient. A nasty story started circulating that when someone asked him if it was true he was an immigrant, he snapped back, "Not anymore!" But Nichols wasn't ashamed of his roots so much as he was bewildered to be entangled in them once again, back in the city in which he had grown up and suffered, the toast of a town that just three years earlier had spat him out. He wasn't embarrassed; if anything, he felt so vengeful he couldn't hide it, telling a gloating story to *TV Guide* about his wife's singing coach, a woman who had treated him rudely in Chicago "because I didn't have a big shiny car. Well, the other day I was at NBC when someone comes up to me and says, 'I have love and kisses from a very old and dear friend of yours.' That foolish woman. You wish that the people who couldn't see you before would have the good taste to be that way now. But they don't."

Nothing satisfied him. The apartment he and Pat had moved into, which he had hoped would feel like the start of his new life, now seemed an irritating reminder of everything he had once wanted to escape. "This was a neighborhood where everyone was out on the street," Scot recalls, "sitting on stoops and talking and yelling across to each other. He came out one morning and said, 'We've *got* to get out of here—it's like living in Italy!' Oh, he was a snob—but a funny, brilliant snob."

One afternoon, they drove out to the suburbs with their new dog to visit friends whose grown Saint Bernard had just given birth to a litter. "They let her come in, and she just got our puppy by the throat and killed her," Scot recalls. "Oh, my God, it was horrible. Mike and I just sobbed and sobbed." As bereft as they felt, it was also a moment of true emotional connection between them. There weren't many. They bought another puppy, desperate to find something that would bind them to each other. The new dog turned out to have a serious illness. A sense of futility began to overtake them.

Nichols was never intentionally cruel to his wife, but his obliviousness could feel punishing. Their fights kept looping around the same track. She felt depressed, out of place, and ignored; he would try to convince her that she wasn't seeing things clearly; when that didn't work, he would pull away, leaving her feeling more isolated. "Once we were in the hallway after *The Jack Paar Show,* and Mike and Paar were talking," she says. "I'm standing there like a bump on a log, and Paar looked at me, acknowledging my presence. The conversation ended and we walked away, and I looked at Mike and said, 'Thanks a lot.' Then he said, 'Oh, my God. Oh, Mr. Paar, Mr. Paar—this is my wife.' It was so embarrassing. Because what he meant was 'This is my after-thought. This is that woman I wish had stayed in Chicago.'"

Six

A NEW AND VERY STRANGE EXPERIENCE

1959-1960

Nichols and May were in Los Angeles, back on TV, doing "Disc Jockey" once again, this time for a crowd that already knew what was coming. "In the short period of two years, Mike and Elaine have become the biggest comedy team in show business!" Dinah Shore announced exultantly. "Since their last appearance on our show, they've done things that have brought them recognition in many new areas. They were the first comedy team ever to play New York City's Town Hall—of course they were a smash—and now they have, of all things, a hit record album!" That night on Shore's show, they put themselves dutifully through their paces. Los Angeles audiences, they now knew, didn't yelp with knowing pleasure at the names Bernard Baruch and Bertrand Russell the way New York club crowds did, and a joke about Levittown drew blank stares on the West Coast. But it didn't matter: They were winners now, their familiar punch lines applauded and their occasional missteps forgiven or ignored. "The more we became the talk of the town," Nichols said, "the more I was afraid to try something new, when we had . . . things that worked so well. After all, other performers repeated their act. Why the hell should we have a new one every night?"

If Nichols was feeling alternately complacent and anxious, it was because he knew that their few blunders were more his fault than May's. When offers came along, he would jump at anything that looked like an interesting opportunity; she was warier. A few months earlier, they had met with Charles Strouse, an aspiring Broadway composer who had an idea for a musical about modern teens called *Love and Kisses*. Perhaps because of their "Teenagers" sketch, he thought Nichols and May might be good choices to write the book. May heard the pitch and, Strouse said, "simply didn't show up after our very first meeting." But Nichols banged away at a draft, only to realize glumly and after too much effort that he was getting nowhere. (Strouse moved on to another writer; the result was *Bye Bye Birdie*.)

Then Nichols and May were offered a weekly spot on a new NBC game show hosted by Dick Van Dyke called *Laugh Line,* a laborious concept in which four celebrity panelists would spend endless time moving a group of costumed actors around a stage, tell them to hold the pose, and then compete to write the best caption for the living cartoon they had created. The money was right; the show was a complete misfire. Nichols didn't even bother to hide his contempt, telling an interviewer at the time, "What do you want me to say—that I hate it, that it's a big nothing, or what? . . . We wouldn't have taken it if we thought it was gonna bomb, right? . . . We don't expect to stay with it forever." They quit that week.

Had they been less successful, Nichols might have faced consequences for trashing a series he was being paid to do, but the industry was too infatuated with them to mind. A few weeks later, they were invited to perform on the eleventh annual Emmy Awards. May approached the podium and said, with deadpan earnestness, "There will be a lot said here tonight about excellence, and the creative, the artistic, and the skillful will all be recognized and rewarded. But what of the others in this industry? Seriously, there are men . . . who go on, year in and year out, quietly and unassumingly producing garbage." The audience roared as Nichols, playing "Lionel Glutz," bounded onstage to kiss May passionately and accept a trophy for "Most Total Mediocrity." "I'm very proud that you have shown your faith in me for sticking to my one ideal: money," he said. "I'd like to say briefly how I did it—no matter what suggestions the sponsor makes, I take 'em!" They were a smash with the invited audience; if anything, to work in television and submit willingly to their mockery was a sign of self-awareness and good taste.

And their Town Hall appearance was, as Shore had said, historic: back-to-back sold-out shows in a 1,500-seat theater that, *The New York Times* wrote, "broke new ground for concert hall attractions." "From the throng of pilgrims on Forty-third Street the passerby might have guessed that Segovia was giving his farewell concert," one report noted. The performances were basically a longer version of their club set, including the unnerving "Pirandello"—cited by the *Times* as "a scene that not only is extremely funny but that also involves a steady, subtle and, climactically, shocking shift of focus." For the final improv, "the [requested] style was that of Jack Kerouac," the reviewer noted, "and between the opening line, 'Dear Mr. Anthony, I have a problem,' and the closing 'It was better in the laundry,' they created a scene that was no less funny than the set pieces in their program."

In the summer of 1959, Nichols and May finally took a breather from club dates and variety shows. They signed a deal to write and voice animated commercials for Jax Beer and another to record a series of off-the-cuff improvisations for the NBC radio show *Monitor*. The contracts were so astonishingly lucrative that by the end of the year, Nichols's annual income was projected to be close to $500,000.

For the first time since coming to New York, they could stop performing for a while and think about what might come next. May began writing a play, a contemporary comedy called *The Better Part of Valor*, which was to star the two of them. And Nichols left her alone until the fall, when he got an offer he didn't think they should pass up. The photographer Richard Avedon had called to ask if he and May would be interested in writing a sketch for Marilyn Monroe, who was considering an appearance on an upcoming CBS special called *The Fabulous Fifties*.

Nichols and Avedon had not met, but Avedon, who was eight years older and already deeply entwined in the worlds of fashion, publishing, and show business, had been fascinated by him ever since he first saw them at the Blue Angel. He returned several times, bringing high-profile guests like Leonard Bernstein and his wife, Felicia Montealegre, or Betty Comden and Adolph Green, but he always left when it was time to go backstage. This was his first overture, and the beginning of what would become Nichols's first close male friendship.

Avedon invited them to his Park Avenue apartment for a brainstorming session. Nichols and May walked in, sat down on what he described as "a big white couch covered in a field-of-poppies fabric," and started batting ideas back and forth with him. "At the end of the visit," Nichols said, "he put his arm around me and walked me to the elevator. He said, 'I have the feeling we're going to be friends for life.'" The following week, the three of them went to the Sutton Place apartment Monroe and Arthur Miller shared to pitch their idea; Miller listened politely and said, "I don't think it's for Marilyn." But something between Nichols and Avedon had been sparked—a charged and complicated kinship that, over the decades, would be tinged with envy, need, and longing.

Avedon had come into Nichols's life just as his marriage to Pat Scot was irretrievably disintegrating, and he wasn't shy about saying what he saw. "He took me and [Pat] out to dinner a lot," Nichols said. "He told me he could see that she and I weren't each other's time of day. [We] split up right around then."

"This is really hard to explain," Pat Scot says, "but once a month Mike would have a talk with me to try to get me back in touch with reality. It got to be so that I felt someone was pounding me into the ground. Finally I said, 'Who needs this shit? I'm outta here.'" They separated, and she moved to a new apartment a few blocks away. "But in New York," she says, "if you're blocks apart, you might as well be in different countries. One time, we found ourselves on Seventy-fifth Street, both trying to get a cab, and said, 'Hello. How are you?' We were strangers. So I moved to Alabama and got a divorce, and that was that. I was not good for him, and he was not good for me, and it was time to go find my own way. Eventually you forgive him and you forgive yourself. Because what's the point? We were young, we were stupid, and we were unsuited. That doesn't mean you can't be nice later."

Avedon and his wife, Eve, swept the newly single Nichols into their lives and made him their project and their pupil. At the beginning of 1960, they took him on an extended vacation to Jamaica, where he got a crash course in two subjects that preoccupied and fascinated him: how to be rich and how to be a celebrity. "Being famous was a new and very strange experience for me," he said. "Dick had been famous for a couple of years and he was the perfect cicerone." Nichols was full of questions: "Do celebrities only know other celebrities? Do they go to the theatre only on opening nights? Do they spend the winters only in Montego Bay?" Avedon had not only experience but a seductive level of self-assurance—Nichols was still deeply impressionable about New York's high life, and when Avedon told him who should decorate his apartment or where to buy the best caviar, his pronouncements had the ring of foundational principles, and Nichols absorbed them all. His extended stay with the Avedons—who had also invited William and Babe Paley and Truman Capote—was not only his introduction to a style of luxe, indolent socializing that he came to love, but a finishing school for him, an education not only in "the right things to eat . . . and how to order in a restaurant, and how to travel, and where to travel, and how to dress," but in how to comport oneself in a roomful of people whose wealth, background, or accomplishments might intimidate him.

Avedon "said to me, 'Just ask them about themselves and they don't stop talking.'"

When Nichols returned to New York, he and May, for the first time in a long while, wrote a new full-length scene, a bright, caustic riff on the game-show-rigging scandal that had been front-page news two months earlier, when Charles Van Doren, whose cheating had been exposed, testified before Congress. The sketch's topicality was a departure for them, but it was a huge success when they performed it as two co-workers standing by a water cooler on *The Fabulous Fifties* in a segment directed by Norman Jewison.

> **Nichols:** Thank heaven for the investigation.
> **May:** Oh, yes. They're *getting* him.
> **Nichols:** When I feel worst, I say to myself, "At least the government has taken a firm stand."
> **May:** Well, they can't fool around with this the way they did with integration.
> **Nichols:** No.
> **May:** This is a . . . something—
> **Nichols:** A moral issue.
> **May:** *Yes! Yes!* It is a moral issue.
> **Nichols:** A moral issue!
> **May:** And to me, that's always so much more interesting than a *real* issue.

The routine was so popular that *Life* magazine reprinted it and reported that "the day after the show they had 28 offers of high-priced work." But Nichols was already doing what he wanted—developing new material with May. During their biweekly recording sessions for NBC's radio show *Monitor*—three hours in a studio in the RCA Building at Rockefeller Center, with May and Nichols across the table from each other in a sound booth and a producer listening but rarely interfering—they generated hundreds of comic vignettes ranging from more than ten minutes to less than thirty seconds; only the best made it to air.

The *Monitor* sessions, with Nichols and May unfiltered and thinking on their feet, offer a rare glimpse into their process. In some scenes, they gave each other equal room to fly. With a savage ear, he plays Laurence Olivier doing Hamlet, with May, as the representative of a beer company, tweaking his performance: "If you could substitute something for 'this too too solid flesh,' which I think implies fatness or grossness . . ." A lot of their exchanges are miniature absurdist vignettes—a man comes home to discover that just before a party for eighty, his wife has painted all the doorknobs and drawer handles. Nichols was especially good at providing premises that gave May room to expand, resist, or complain. "Lily, look what I've brought you," he would say out of the blue. "It's a box with twelve hundred frogs." Or "Laura, if I got us a cow, would you make us butter and cheese?" No, she says. He persists: "You're like this with everything I bring up. You wouldn't let me get the loom, either." Her: "Let's get a really good girl and teach *her* to churn and weave." And often, Nichols would choose to play an impatient character—someone who wants or needs something urgently—as a way of keeping May moving.

When they ran out of ideas, they used whatever was at hand—in one segment, May pretended to interview the RCA window washer. Sometimes a great run would be derailed by his laughter, in which case they'd rerecord it. And because the sessions weren't live, they didn't worry if the scenes got too raunchy. In one, Nichols played an old man trying to tell his equally old wife that maybe she shouldn't wear the bikini she's proudly modeling for him—it's too immodest for the beach. She's determined to show it off; he finally gives in. His priceless, concerned last line: "Is there a top to it?"

Almost no type of embarrassment was off-limits, and it was a measure of Nichols's unshakable trust in May by this point in their partnership that he let her go where they had never gone before—toward gentle jests about the pain and embarrassment of his hairlessness. In one scene, she plays a woman who announces she's bald to her date. Nichols, seemingly caught off guard, starts to giggle.

May: It doesn't prevent serious relationships.
Nichols (*encouragingly*): Why would it?
May: Well, the hat gets in the way.
Nichols: I think it's probably in your mind. Look, take off your hat
    and let's forget about it.
May (*tentatively*): All right . . . I just wanted to tell you first . . .
Nichols: (*gasps*).
May: Another drink?
Nichols (*trying to recover*): Wha . . . uh . . . pardon me?
May: Shall we have another drink?
Nichols: Yeah . . . uh . . . listen . . . are you getting hungry? I'm
    kinda hungry! PUT ON YOUR HAT and let's go to dinner!

In another sketch, she reprised Barbara Musk, the movie star from "Disc Jockey," and revealed her condition to a cabdriver gamely played by Nichols.

May: It was a childhood disease. I lost my hair.
Nichols: Well, what do you care, right? . . . I wouldn't worry about
    it if I were you.
May: Well, thank you. I *have* worried about it, but I won't any-
    more. In fact, may I have your number? I'd like to repay you.
Nichols: Well, you could tip me.
May: No. Not only am I bald, I'm also cheap.

May was still writing her play when, in the spring of 1960, the producer and impresario Alexander Cohen approached them with a proposition: He wanted them to turn their club act into a Broadway show. A year earlier, Cohen had had some success putting Flanders & Swann, a British duo who specialized in comic songs, on Broadway for a brief run under the umbrella *The Nine O'Clock Revue* (so named because it aimed for a younger and livelier crowd by starting an hour later than most Broadway productions). He wanted *An Evening with Mike Nichols and Elaine May* as the next installment. The production, which he estimated would cost $50,000 to mount, would be a gamble: As popular as they were, there was no guarantee that they could fill upward of six thousand seats per eight-performance week. But Broadway felt like the top of the mountain—the destination to which five years of work had been leading. They couldn't say no.

A part of Nichols had never fully abandoned the dream of becoming a serious actor, and just before he and May began the months of preparation that their show would require, he indulged his fantasy one last time. "Journey to the Day" was just the kind of job he had longed to get while living in a one-room walk-up and going to Strasberg's class— a part on an episode of the dramatic anthology television series *Playhouse 90,* directed by a talented up-and-comer, John Frankenheimer. The story was about a Brazilian doctor running a group therapy session in a psychiatric ward; Nichols and May both took roles as patients. He lost the twenty or so pounds of post-divorce weight he had gained and started preparing for his role as a manic-depressive actor. May was to play a catatonic woman with one line of dialogue. "Elaine quit when the director asked her to assume a fetal position under a table," Nichols said. "I stayed and cried and carried on." He got good reviews for his role in the earnest, talky piece; nevertheless, he said, "I just would have liked to take me out of it—it would have been better still." It would be his last dramatic role for almost twenty years.

As soon as Nichols's work on the show was done, Cohen sent him and May to San Francisco for a week to test material—a trial run that would give them a sense of how their comedy played in a large house (the 1,550-seat Geary Theater) that wasn't packed with New Yorkers who already knew their routines inside and out. Billed as *An Evening of Mad Fun with Mike Nichols and Elaine May,* the weeklong engagement got a divided reception; the *San Francisco Chronicle* loved it, but *Variety's* review complained that "the impression was that the show has been thrown together in order to cash in on the comics' TV popularity" and warned that, at the end, "the pair dragoon the audience into what they call an 'improvisation,' which is all very well for a nightclub."

For Cohen, who was trying to sell investors on $1,000 buy-ins to the show, the review came as an early heads-up that there was no guarantee Nichols and May were going to have a smooth ride. They would have to work on their presentation and woo the Broadway community. When they returned to New York, Cohen sprang into action. He hired Avedon to do their publicity shots, scheduled a lunch for theater-party bookers at the "21" Club and told Nichols and May to go in and work the room, set up a pre-Broadway tour in three out-of-town theaters, and, perhaps most important, gave his two stars something they had never before had, or needed: a director. Arthur Penn was a decade older than Nichols and May, and he was respected for his work on television dramas and, increasingly, on Broadway, where he had two hit plays running simultaneously. Nichols and May were only casually friendly with him, but they admired his work enough that, six months earlier, they had attended a rehearsal to watch him shape his production of *The Miracle Worker,* which had since opened and become a breakout success, with a movie adaptation on the way.

Penn proved to be the new pair of eyes they needed. "We had to have someone who would stage it as a show, not just as an act," says May. "We never got off our stools or changed anything, but he brought in a curtain and two men to close it and bentwood furniture—I remember he said, 'Bentwood will make it seem less nightclubby!'—and lighting. And suddenly it felt like a play. That's what he did, and he did it beautifully." Penn also gave the show a shape it hadn't always had at the Blue Angel: He put in an intermission and told them to end the first act with "Pirandello," their most complicated piece and one that, because it played so riskily with the engagement of their audience and veered into a kind of savage, mutual sexual taunting toward the end, they could never have done on television. For the more established sketches, he did little more than watch, listen, and gently nudge the two of them whenever a moment felt rote or unshaped. "Because he's a very good director, he kept leading us back to ourselves and our initial impulses, how these pieces had come about and what they were," said Nichols. "It was material we had done for years. [But] he [had] an intelligence that we could trust absolutely."

With their pre-Broadway run scheduled to begin in August, Nichols took off for Venice on another vacation with his new friends. "I was still very much the Avedons' student, learning how you do all this social shit," he said. "One night they took me to dinner at some palazzo on the Grand Canal . . . where there were fucking Giottos on the walls and a footman behind every chair . . . I was put next to Nancy Mitford, who didn't say a word, only made unintelligible British sounds—just sort of little moans . . . On our way back to the hotel I said to Dick and Evie, 'You two may like this stuff, but I can't stand these counts and princesses, it's too much for me,' to which Evie replied, 'You're so full of shit, Mike—you love it, admit it' . . . And of course, she was right . . . I developed a serious crush on her . . . But what could I do? I was already Dick's best non-strategic friend."

By then, Cohen told Nichols, the show was "totally capitalized and I am listening to constant complaints from people who can no longer have a piece." There were endless details to take care of—physicals for both of them so the show could be insured ("We are trying to get Elaine examined, and if you think that's easy . . ." he wrote Nichols), a publicity campaign, and, most urgently, the hiring of musicians for an onstage jazz quartet that could swing with the improv sketch no matter what direction it took. Nichols and May settled on a young musician named William Goldenberg who could, on three seconds' notice, undergird whatever literary style they were spoofing. As they improvised, Goldenberg learned to listen for a throwaway line of dialogue—"He's not with us"—which was code for *He's gone off in the wrong direction.*

In the middle of August, seven weeks before their scheduled Broadway opening, Nichols and May took their show on the road. The first stop was a week at the Falmouth Playhouse, on Cape Cod. The influential Boston critic Elliot Norton wrote, "With his hands in his pockets, and a broad smile on his face he looks like a kindly undergraduate from the Farm Belt. This façade is phony; he is neither kindly nor naïve, but preternaturally alert and observant and much of the time magnificently malicious . . . In action, she is a tornado of mischief, of guile and of sly wickedness." Cohen, watching their first performances, had notes: He was happy with the order of Act I—a popular routine they had long done about adultery in different countries, followed by "Mother and Son" (the rocket scientist sketch), "Disc Jockey," and "Pirandello"—but he thought the ending of "Pirandello," in which Penn had experimented with having two stagehands come out and break up their fight, still needed work. About the final improv, he wrote, "It would be helpful if the encores were 'requested' . . . Mike might say, 'You've been just lovely and Elaine and I would like to do . . .' Audiences, as we know, love the feeling of getting something that isn't billed."

They got it, and then some, on one scary evening when the show moved to Westport, Connecticut. Nichols and May were, by this point, feeling the pressure, and it was increasingly emerging in "Pirandello," a scene that had always depended on their total immersion in order to succeed. It was high-wire work: If they couldn't convince the audience that it was witnessing a battle between two characters turn into an ugly subtextual fight between two actors, the scene wouldn't land. "The piece created hostility," said Nichols. "Without even knowing it, we drew on real things, and we argued and fought about that scene all the years we did it. How long this beat was, when to start the next beat—we could never leave it alone. We tortured ourselves over it, and all that time, it never occurred to us that what was really happening was that the scene was taking us over. And it went very far. When we were in Westport, I must have blanked out or something, because I was hitting Elaine, back and forth on both sides of her face, and she had clawed open my chest, which was pouring blood, and we didn't know how we had got there."

The moment was sobering for both of them. They weren't kids anymore; however charged the history between them had become, there was too much at stake to let things fly apart this way, with their Broadway opening less than a month away. "They brought the curtain down and we burst into tears and embraced and sort of controlled it after that," said Nichols. "It was scary. It really got away from us."

They set box office records in Westport and moved on to the Paper Mill Playhouse, in Millburn, New Jersey, for a smooth fortnight of fine-tuning. On October 8, 1960, they opened at Broadway's John Golden Theatre.

In an era when a new show or two opened on Broadway every week, the arrival of *An Evening with Mike Nichols and Elaine May* was nonetheless an event. Cohen closed down Shubert Alley for a midnight "block party" that included a working Ferris wheel and invited celebrities to man every concession. Tennessee Williams was in the audience, tickled to see himself sent up as "Alabama Glass." Ethel Merman came, as did Gypsy Rose Lee. Harry Belafonte, Lucille Ball, Sidney Lumet, Jackie Gleason, and Gloria Vanderbilt were in attendance, too, eager to be the first to see a show that would turn into a celebrity magnet, attracting big names from Los Angeles to London throughout its run. The performance itself was slightly rocky. After the Westport incident, the two of them were handling "Pirandello" with extreme care, and on opening night it felt tentative, leading the critic Walter Kerr to note that "they have been known to bring it off so that your hair stands on end" and wonder what went wrong. May, uncharacteristically, almost broke during "Disc Jockey." And Cohen's insistence that they give the opening-night crowd a bonus by ending with two improvs instead of one felt, to some, like too much of a good thing.

To old-guard theater critics, Nichols and May were interlopers—cabaret performers or, even worse, television personalities who had no business on a Broadway stage. The initial *New York Times* review expressed only qualified approval. "The preponderance of what the team does is amusing," Howard Taubman wrote. "They are attractive comedians whose years in night clubs have not given them a hard sheen . . . [But] in certain places . . . Miss May or Mr. Nichols seem to be reaching for the next move. Such hesitations are discomfiting: they rob a scene and its characters of definition; they give professional work an amateurish vagueness." But most other critics heard those pauses and false starts differently—as the carefully captured rhythm of human speech. They are "laureates of the fatuous," *Life*'s critic wrote. "Their humor depends on catching the exact tone, the hemming and hawing and terrible illogic of ordinary conversation. They hold the human race on a pin and make it laugh at itself while it squirms." In *The New Republic*, Robert Brustein called them "the voice of outraged intelligence in a world given over to false piety, cloying sentiment, and institutionalized stupidity," who use "extraordinary powers of observation to locate clichés of conventional middle-class life," stripping them "to their essential absurdity." Brustein placed them alongside Jules Feiffer and Lenny Bruce as part of a group he designated "Comedians from the Underground."

With that declaration, battle lines were drawn: In the critical discourse, the audience for *An Evening with Mike Nichols and Elaine May* would be divided into those who got it and those who, humiliatingly, didn't. Their show was essential theatergoing, and Nichols and May became the avatars of a generational shift from the cheerful sitcom brightness of the previous decade to something truer, more troublesome, and more cutting. By the end of 1960, even Taubman had come around, celebrating them as a needed counterpoint to the season's old-fashioned boulevard comedies—plays like *Under the Yum-Yum Tree*, *Send Me No Flowers*, and *Critic's Choice*—that "accept mannerisms for originality, wisecracks for wit, and caricatures for people." No reviewer, after all, wanted to be on the wrong side of comedy history.

By the end of its first month, *An Evening With* was selling out regularly. Each of its stars was taking home about $3,000 a week—a modest sum compared with the $75,000 they had made from a single beer commercial, the $30,000 they now commanded for one variety show appearance, or the $160,000 apiece they would make for a series of TV specials they had agreed to star in for producer David Susskind if they could find the time, but still enough to place them among the best-paid entertainers in New York.

Shortly before the inauguration of President Kennedy in January 1961, the production went into profit. May wondered if the new presidency was a sign that the culture was moving past the 1950s conformity, awkwardness, and repression that they were making a fortune mocking. "I told Mike," she said, "there was no way we could top ourselves." At the time, he didn't take it as a warning.

Seven

THE MOST IMPORTANT PEOPLE

1960–1962

After almost every performance of their show, May would go home and Nichols would go out. Although she had learned to fake her way through small talk, she was not a natural socializer. "If somebody came toward us in a restaurant waving," she says, "I would look at him blankly and Mike would say softly, 'You slept with him for two weeks. He's part of the Socialist Party. You had a big fight. When he left, he broke all the dishes. His name is Bert.'" Whenever possible, she opted out of the late-night festivities that were a cherished post-show release valve for many Broadway performers. But each evening brought a fresh luminary or two to the stage door, and Nichols took to his new status as the celebrity everyone wanted to know with unashamed glee.

There was always someone new to meet. The essayist and critic Edmund Wilson went to see *An Evening With* four times and made it his business to get close to them. "Even after I had ceased to laugh very much," he wrote, "I was fascinated by their ability to take the stage and hold it and to create a dramatic tension in every one of their sketches."

Another ardent admirer, Lillian Hellman, went backstage specifically to gush over Nichols; a month later, he met her again when they both attended a birthday party for Leonard Bernstein at which a portrait of the maestro was unveiled. As the guests murmured their admiration, Hellman spluttered, "What the hell is everybody talking about?! It makes Lennie look like a middle-aged fag—I think it's the worst mess I've ever seen in my life." Bernstein's homosexuality was known to enough of the attendees—though not, apparently, to Hellman—that a mortified hush fell over the room. As Bernstein's wife ushered the other guests away, Hellman covered her face and muttered, "Now look what I've done." Nichols came up, put his arms around her, and said, "Will you marry me?" They were friends thereafter; Hellman felt they both "pretend[ed] to be hopeless about the world and ourselves when we really have rather hopeful natures."

Not everyone was a fan. At a dinner party, Norman Mailer called Nichols a "royal baby" and told him he was too comfortable being surrounded by sycophants. ("Mike said he didn't mind Mailer's characterization because it was kind of true," says his friend Peter Davis.) And when the critic Kenneth Tynan brokered what he hoped would be a meeting of the minds between Nichols and Peter Sellers, the result fizzled. "Nothing that Peter said amused Mike; nothing that Mike said amused Peter," he wrote. "The sly, pragmatic, New York Jewish sense of humour meant nothing to Peter; and the giggly-facetious, whimsical fantastic . . . jokes of Sellers seemed merely embarrassing to Mike."

But within the theater community, almost everyone was intrigued by Nichols. When Avedon threw him a surprise twenty-ninth-birthday party at a Chinese restaurant, Tynan, the Bernsteins, Sondheim, Comden and Green, Lauren Bacall, and Jule Styne all came, as well as May and her new boyfriend, *Fiddler on the Roof* lyricist Sheldon Harnick. Avedon made sure New York's society and entertainment columnists knew that Nichols was now at least an honorary member of a clique of creative artists that Sondheim memorialized as "The Blob":

The bodies you read about
The ones who know everyone
That everyone knows . . .
They're the most important people
In the most important city
In the most important country
In the you-know-what!

Nichols forged his closest bond during the show's run with the people right next door. Two months after *An Evening with Mike Nichols and Elaine May* opened, the musical *Camelot*, with Richard Burton and Julie Andrews, arrived at the Majestic Theatre, the stage door of which was right next to the Golden. Andrews had recently married Tony Walton, an aspiring production designer; each night, as he waited for the curtain to fall on the very long musical so he could pick up his wife, he made a point of arriving early enough to sneak into the back of the Golden and watch the improv scene, new each time, that ended the show. Walton and Nichols, who were about the same age, became pals, and Walton drew him into the orbit of Andrews and, by extension, Burton, whose dressing room was the site of an ongoing all-star party at which alcohol and gossip flowed abundantly. "Sometimes Elaine would come, too," says Walton, "but mostly just Mike and Julie and I would sit and schmooze for a while." Nichols and Burton, who had seen his show before *Camelot* opened and had great admiration for his talent, struck up a friendship as well. Burton was more intimidated by May, whom he found "too formidable, one of the most intelligent, beautiful, and witty women I had ever met. I hoped I would never see her again."

Alexander Cohen was working hard to keep May and Nichols on a tight leash; the stage manager's log for their Broadway run includes terse notations like "late" or "tipsy" whenever either of them showed up less than fully ready to perform. Nichols himself was, by his own description, becoming increasingly petulant and ill-tempered. "For him the slightest detail, until it's solved, has the importance of the Geneva Convention," said Cohen. One evening, during a scene with May, Nichols looked up from the stage and saw that one of about thirty lights on the balcony rail was out. He fumed throughout their performance, then called Cohen at home in what the producer described as "a cold, white fury," said, "The theater is in *total darkness*," and hung up. "I was narcissistic," Nichols said. "I would get mad. I bitched about our billing. I did all the things I dislike. Comedy is the only work in the world in which the work and the reward are simultaneous. Comedians get it on the spot. It's very corrupting to your character."

The release of a hit album with about thirty minutes of material from the show—a recording that reached *Billboard*'s top ten and would win them a Grammy the following year—only increased demand for tickets. Cohen realized that if the show was to stay on track, there could be no distractions. He told their manager, Jack Rollins, to turn down all benefits, TV appearances, and outside engagements for the duration of the run. "Their health is at stake," Cohen wrote. "They are the only two performers in a long and arduous show . . . With the compliments of the management . . . offer to each charity that you must decline to help a pair of tickets which they may use as a door prize." May, the more politically active of the two, insisted on two exceptions— one for the New York party celebrating Kennedy's inauguration, and one for a benefit for the Congress of Racial Equality.

As the number of performances climbed past 150, staying focused became a struggle and, on some nights, a test of discipline that they couldn't pass. They had never imagined doing exactly the same show over and over on a rigorous schedule with no end in sight. Early in the run, the intensity of Nichols's emotional connection had sometimes rattled May, especially when she played the innocent, vulnerable girl in "Teenagers." "During that sketch, I would say to him before I undressed, 'I really like you,'" she recalls. "And as I was saying it, tears would fill his eyes because he felt so bad for me. I finally said, 'It's hard for me to do that—to see you in tears when I'm submitting myself to you.' And he said, 'I can't help it.'"

That was no longer a problem. Instead, Nichols found himself tripping up over his propensity to break into laughter mid-sketch, especially if anything went wrong; May would sometimes succumb as well. "One night in 'Teenagers,' he grabbed me to kiss me and our teeth hit each other, and we broke," she says. "We kissed for a long time, trying to get control of ourselves, because we were afraid we'd break again. We separated, but somehow or other, seeing each other caused us to break *again*. This went on for a while, and the audience laughed, too, and then we broke up again. Something happened to us that night. We broke up throughout the show, every third line—and after a while the audience did not find it that amusing. We barely got a laugh.

"The intermission came, and Mike said, 'This is so irresponsible.' I said, 'It is.' He said, 'We're acting like children. These people have spent money to come here. They've probably gotten babysitters.' I said, 'And they expected a good evening.' We gave each other this really adult pep talk. And the lights went on, we went onstage, and before we even spoke, we broke. We just went to pieces. What I remember was that it was the most responsibly we'd ever spoken to each other. And we meant it! But it was just too adult a conversation for us."

They had long since stopped changing the dialogue in their sketches, a choice that troubled May, who wanted every moment to be fresh, much more than Nichols, who wanted every moment to be perfect. The three exceptions were a sketch called "PTA Fun Night," in which May frequently extemporized during her introduction of Nichols as Alabama Glass, "Pirandello," where the exact wording and pacing were never quite locked, and the final improv scene. Many who saw the show, including critics, liked to speculate about just how spontaneous those closing sketches were; they wondered if the line suggestions came from audience plants, or if the literary styles were chosen from a small repertoire of about a dozen. Neither was the case. Although some writers came up often—Shakespeare more than fifty times, Tennessee Williams more than twenty, and Chekhov, Noël Coward, and Brendan Behan (whose play *The Hostage* was then on Broadway) more than a dozen each—Nichols and May took ninety different style suggestions during the run of the show, including Jane Austen, Ingmar Bergman, Ray Bradbury, Chaucer, Dick Tracy, Gilbert & Sullivan, James Joyce, Kabuki, Molière, Richard Nixon, the Old Testament, Poe, Proust, Gertrude Stein, and the Yiddish Art Theater. Nor did they ever reuse an opening or closing line—even in January, when, for a while, almost every suggestion was about the Kennedys. When the audience got playful or belligerent, Nichols and May would go right along. "Why don't you start the show on time?" someone yelled one night. On another, a patron demanded, "Finish the last scene!" And on another: "Will you do the next act of the 'Teenagers'?" They just laughed and used all three as first lines.

By the spring of 1961, the work was taking its toll. Cohen was losing patience with the chronic tardiness of both performers, which, combined with May's appetite for playing out all the possibilities of an improvisation, was threatening to push the show's end past 11 p.m., triggering union overtime charges. "WE ARE THE ONLY SHOW IN TOWN THAT GOES UP CONSISTENTLY LATE," he told his stage manager in a furious memo. "Under no circumstances . . . is this show to run into overtime and if you think it is going to come within one minute of running into overtime, cut the encores."

And Nichols and May themselves were no longer bothering to conceal their growing tension. A *New Yorker* writer who profiled the two noted that "there is little carefulness . . . in the way they talk to each other privately during practically every intermission. In fact, these colloquies are often conducted in such injurious terms that the team sounds like a married couple on the way home from a particularly disorderly cocktail party; how-dare-you-treat-me-this-way is a recurrent theme." In an interview she and Nichols had done a few months earlier with Mitch Miller, May had drily remarked, "We don't speak, except onstage," and Nichols had said, "She resents those two hours." It was no longer clear if either of them was joking.

May had always let Nichols handle the business side of their partnership; he dealt with the details of their finances, contract issues, and publicity. (Cohen once estimated that while the show was on Broadway, he talked to Nichols four times a day and May once every two weeks.) But now Nichols started to try to run the show itself. What had been a productive dynamic—"Elaine would fill sketches, and I would shape them," he often said—became a contentious one. During her introduction of Alabama Glass, he would stand in the wings, gesturing at her to move it along; she would spot him out of the corner of her eye and continue, furious. He grew afraid of the final improv sketch; for her, it became the only part of the evening she enjoyed. "She got so bored," he said. "All comedians want to change at a certain point. Your act becomes your enemy. She was more interested in taking chances than in being a hit. I was more interested in making the audience happy."

But Nichols was growing frustrated, too; he felt that his performance had become "rote and dehumanized," and, partly to shake himself out of a depression, "I would start playing games like, 'Let's see how fast I can make it go,'" he said. "I had to push the sketch ahead, because I couldn't invent as she could." He later expressed deep regret for his behavior during the last months of the run. "She was a real actress, and I was beginning to be a real pain in the ass to her," he said. "I was very controlling—'You were a little too slow tonight.' Once that happens, you're in very bad trouble. We could not recover."

Onstage, Nichols and May had always represented their partnership as a kind of challenging quasi marriage. They weren't George Burns and Gracie Allen, or Lucy and Desi, kidding and squabbling throughout but hugging and kissing at the end, but rather two spiky, sharp, neurotic people in an ever-evolving contest of wills, who, especially in "Pirandello," would turn the tenuousness of their bond into a public storyline every night. They had never imagined their act would reach its climax with them doing the same thing week after week, month after month. Nor had they anticipated how much it would fray the connection between them.

Finally May had had enough. A clause in their contracts allowed either performer to quit on four weeks' notice, and after she and Nichols talked it over, she told Cohen she was leaving, writing a formal letter in which she said, "I have enjoyed my association with you, but I do not wish to continue in the Play as it is too great a strain upon my strength and time." *An Evening with Mike Nichols and Elaine May* closed on July 1, 1961, after 311 performances. It had more than doubled its investors' money.

For the first time since they had come together six years earlier, they had no particular goal for the next stage of their performing career. "We'll be writing separately and writing together," Nichols said. "Elaine has been working on a play for us . . . [but] this will be the first break we've had in many years." There had been talk of a second show—an all-new assemblage of sketches that they would contrive out of their recording sessions for *Monitor.* Nichols quashed that speculation unambiguously. "We're not going to do the revue type of thing again." Cohen had gotten them to agree to bring *An Evening With* to Toronto for a week at the end of the year, but for the six months until then, there would be no urgent need for them to work together, and they kept a respectful distance. "He felt guilty that he had been mean to me, and I felt guilty that I had left the show," says May.

"Elaine pulled back from the high life," said Nichols. "She wanted to stay [home], she was writing, her daughter had joined her. And I was going through the things that happen after [divorce], dating and so forth." Their sudden awkwardness felt inevitable to him. "When you do a show for a year . . . you can't be best friends anymore," he said. "It's like you've lived with somebody and fucked each other's brains out and you're so sick of them, you just have to get out of the house."

Nichols was, in every sense, single again, and he soon had someone new in his life—an actress named Joanna Brown, who had recently divorced the writer Harold Brodkey and who, like May, had a little girl. Brown had become disenchanted with performing after a couple of roles on Broadway and had taken a job in Avedon's office; he thought she and Nichols might be right for each other and introduced them. To those in Nichols's circle, the relationship had the feel of a rebound—but they weren't sure from whom. "She is very good-looking, but it is perhaps not a good sign that she gets herself up like Elaine," wrote Edmund Wilson, who hosted a lunch for Nichols and Brown that became considerably more strained when they were joined by May and Harnick. As soon as Brown was out of the room, Nichols started disparaging her intelligence. "[Mike] is evidently still in love with [Elaine]," Wilson observed. "Their relationship is so peculiar, both alienated and incredibly close, that it must make their relationships with other people precarious. This is perhaps not surprising."

While May worked on the play, she kept him at arm's length until he got tired of calling and decided to get out of New York. He packed a box of books he'd been meaning to read, rented a big house with a pool in Stamford, Connecticut, across the street from Sondheim, installed himself there with Brown and her daughter, and started to spend more time with Leonard and Felicia Bernstein, who had a house in nearby Fairfield, becoming a sort of fun young uncle to their three children. Sondheim would drop by once in a while to lounge by the pool, "not for dinner or anything, just swimming and sitting on the lawn. I knew him well enough to do that, but we weren't really friends yet."

By the fall, Nichols and Brown had become serious; they rented an apartment in Manhattan, planned to move in together, scheduled a wedding, and sent out invitations. "I love this girl—I just hope she'll be happy," May told a reporter when she and Nichols went to Toronto to do five performances at the beginning of December.

But other friends were alarmed at Nichols's impetuosity—including Avedon, who started to rue the match he had made and worked to convince Nichols he was making a mistake. At the very last minute, they broke off their engagement, returned the gifts, and ended the relationship. "She told a story to me about being in a taxi with him and having a conversation where it became clear to her that she would never be more important to him than his career," says Brown's daughter, Temi Rose. "She was old-fashioned, and I think that what he was to her, she knew she wasn't going to be to him. My mom went to Radcliffe, but she was a girly girl, closer in spirit to the fifties than the sixties. She was from a wealthy family and a class of person that a Jewish man in America at that time would have considered very desirable. I don't think she was the right person for Mike—she wasn't intellectually up to him. But I don't think she was even close to in love with my father the way she was in love with Mike. She loved him forever."

"It was unwise. We were both smart not to get married," said Nichols later. "The young lady was much better off."

At the beginning of 1962, Nichols felt pleasantly adrift. He was thirty, unmarried, and, for the first time in his life, rich enough not to work unless he wanted to. He could travel as he pleased, idle when he felt like it, while away the time as a charming weekend guest or extra man at his friends' dinner parties. With May, he became almost courtly; he felt that throughout their partnership, he had always been the one to push them forward, and now it was time to take his cues from her. In January, she told him that her play, which she had retitled *A Matter of Position*, was complete. The piece had originally been commissioned by Fred Coe, the producer of *Playhouse 90*, as a television production; when Nichols read it, he told May it belonged onstage. Nichols agreed to star, Coe would produce it, and a November Broadway opening was scheduled.

That gave Nichols almost a year to dabble, and he did, making tentative forays into writing and directing, mostly at the suggestion or invitation of his new friends. He signed on as the co-writer of what turned out to be an immensely successful TV special that paired Julie Andrews with Carol Burnett at Carnegie Hall, contributing a novelty song called "You're So London" and polishing their banter. And he agreed, on a lark, to direct a summer-stock evening of one-acts by Jules Feiffer; he assumed his job would require no more than the type of light, advisory touch-ups that Arthur Penn had contributed to their act.

That spring, very suddenly, May and Sheldon Harnick got married, a surprise that, Nichols said, "really threw me for a loop." He was used to seeing her through brief relationships—and used to being the friend to whom she would always return. Shaken in ways he hadn't anticipated, he left town. He and Brown had planned to marry in Rome; Richard Burton and his wife, Sybil, who were living there while he filmed *Cleopatra*, had volunteered to serve as their hosts. But just as Nichols was ending his engagement, Burton was beginning an affair with Elizabeth Taylor; rumors had hit the gossip columns with seismic force, and their lives were now in chaos. Burton called Nichols, told him not to fret over the canceled wedding, and insisted he come anyway. The *Cleopatra* shoot was already so far behind schedule that he now had to travel to Paris for a week to film scenes for another movie, *The Longest Day*. He knew that Taylor would be penned inside their Rome villa by paparazzi, and he wanted a trusted friend to show her a good time and distract her. Nichols got on the first flight he could. What could be more fun than serving as the temporary escort of the world's most beautiful woman?

In Rome, he met Taylor for the first time and was unexpectedly touched by her openness and warmth. "I can't leave the house," she said. "We're surrounded." He told her to "put a thing on your head, a kerchief . . . come out the back way, and we'll drive somewhere." They got in his rented VW and spent a calm afternoon at the Villa d'Este, interrupted only when a tourist pointed at the two of them and said, "That's Mike Nichols!"

"She never had a life of her own," said Nichols. "Every movement had always been public. But where most people would have developed a shell, she didn't. She said a startling thing to me during those days in Rome, when we were at some horse show and everyone was walking past to stare at her. I asked her if it was ever a pain in the ass being so beautiful. And she looked at me and said, 'I can't wait for it to go.'" Just as Burton returned to Rome, the scandal reached an even higher pitch, with the Vatican publication *L'Osservatore della Domenica* publishing a letter accusing Taylor of "erotic vagrancy" and calling her an unfit mother. In just a few days, Nichols had become the kind of friend with whom she could cry, and she did. She also went to *Cleopatra*'s hairstyle designer, Paul Huntley, and said, "Do you do personal wigs? Because I have a dear friend who's a comic in New York, and he wears one of the worst wigs I've ever seen." From that point on, Nichols's toupees would be impeccable.

From Rome, Nichols flew to Paris, where he found himself in the exceedingly strange position of being asked to parody the life he had just lived for the past ten days. Avedon had invited him to participate in an extended photo shoot with the model Suzy Parker that he had conceived as a "gag on Richard Burton and Elizabeth Taylor in *Cleopatra*." He had been assigned to shoot the new fall collections for *Harper's Bazaar* and had the then-unprecedented idea to do it tabloid-style, as if he were photographing the public embraces, spats, and scandalous outings of a famous couple. He wanted Nichols to write a scenario for him and then to play Parker's consort in a ten-page photo essay, saying, "I need you to help me use fashion to send up the whole culture of fame—so go write a burlesque of Liz and Dick."

"Well, they were certainly nothing if not spoofable," said Nichols.

For a week, he and Parker dressed up and Avedon shot them all over Paris: "One scene I wrote had him throwing a glass of champagne in her face during a squabble we were supposedly having at dinner at Maxim's," he recalled. "And Dick photographed all that shit as if he were covering it for *Paris Match* rather than *Harper's Bazaar*."* It would not be the last time Nichols enjoyed the position of insider/outsider, someone who could serve as a detached, wry commentator on excess even while being a knowing participant in it.

By the time he returned to New York, May's impulsive marriage was all but over—barely a blip in the memory of either party to it. (Asked more than fifty years later about the long-forgotten nuptials, Harnick said, "Elaine and I were never married—well, yes, we were, my goodness! It was very unfortunate. She initiated divorce proceedings a couple of months later.") On May 19, 1962, Nichols and May performed new material together for the first time in almost a year, at a birthday salute to President Kennedy at Madison Square Garden—the show at which Marilyn Monroe famously sang "Happy Birthday, Mr. President." They read fake congratulatory telegrams they had written ("If things had been different, tonight would have been my birthday—Richard Nixon") and met the president later that night at a party at the home of film executive Arthur Krim and his wife, Dr. Mathilde Krim. "We were on the dance floor," Nichols said, "and [Bobby Kennedy] and Marilyn danced past us, having met that night. And I actually heard her

---

* In the 2017 Avedon biography *Something Personal*, Avedon's former assistant Norma Stevens asserts that Avedon, who was either bisexual or homosexual, told her that he and Nichols had a romantic relationship that lasted ten years, quoting him (via Stevens's memory) as saying, "At one point we even thought about running away together. Eloping, we called it—leaving our wives and our lives and moving to Gay Paree . . . We chickened out, but we were together for years." Rumors of Nichols's bisexuality persisted throughout his career and were a subject of speculation by some of those who knew him, and he and Avedon certainly could have had an affair. But nothing in the circumstances of Nichols's life suggests they had anything like a long sexual relationship. The notion of two well-known, careerist men in 1962 discussing "eloping" feels anachronistic. And the remarks the book posthumously attributes to Avedon—"He's above me intellectually, but I'm the artist, so it evens out . . . We're equally corrupt. We were made for each other"—owe more to *All About Eve* than to reality. In researching this biography, I remained open to any information about Nichols's history with men that was specific and/or confirmable; I found none. If I had, I would not have considered it to be embarrassing, scandalous, or necessary to suppress—nor was I ever asked to.

say—it's so bizarre—I heard her say, 'I like you, Bobby.' And he said, 'I like you too, Marilyn.' Who would write this dialogue for the night they met?"

The World of Jules Feiffer, on which Nichols worked that June and July, had the feeling of a casual summer project with friends—an extension of his social life—rather than the prelude to a major career shift. "It was Mickey and Judy—'Okay, we've got the barn next Saturday: You do the costumes, you do the songs, we open on Monday,'" says Sondheim. "Mike said, 'Do you want to write a little one-act musical? We have two weeks.' I said, 'Mike . . .' He said, 'Oh, now, Steve, it's easy, it doesn't need a lot . . .' It was fun, and it was the thing that pushed us from acquaintanceship to friendship." The show, a trio of vignettes that was to play for just six days at the Hunterdon Hills Playhouse, in Union, New Jersey, was an ideal match for Nichols's sensibility. One of Feiffer's short pieces, "Crawling Arnold," was an almost exact companion to Nichols and May's routine about the rocket scientist infantilized by one phone call from his mother; it depicted a middle-class man in his thirties who, "as soon as he returns home, reverts to crawling, for all sorts of reasons that are explained in the play, which was about atomic bomb testing and Black nationalism," says Feiffer. "It was anarchic and political and sexy, and it was written in twenty-four hours, and it was my only foolproof piece of theatrical work."

A version of the show, which also included a *Cinderella*-inspired gloss on celebrity called "Passionella," had been staged in Chicago by Paul Sills, who had originally commissioned the work from Feiffer. But Nichols reworked and reshaped it, added two songs and some background music by Sondheim, and cast his friend Dorothy Loudon, a talented singer-comedienne with whom he'd worked in New York clubs, as the lead. Feiffer was impressed. "At one point while we were rehearsing, Mike said, 'Look, I'd like you to leave the room for a while.

There's something I don't want you to see while we're doing it.' I went out and after about twenty minutes, he called me in, and they played the scene. He had somehow changed everything I thought I had intended and made it more interesting, deeper, better, funnier. I looked at him, stunned, and said, 'Where did this come from?' And he pointed to the script and said, 'It's all in there.' That was the moment I understood what he was going to become." It was also the only time that Nichols, who became known for being exceptionally collaborative with writers, was shy enough about his process to ask the author not to watch.

The show got a positive review in *Variety* and, given the involvement of Nichols and Sondheim, might well have continued its development and found a path to New York. It was Feiffer who hit the brakes. "As the work advanced, I retreated," he said. "I didn't belong there. Sondheim had written some lovely songs, fresh, funny, touching, and original. And Mike's production was obviously the creation of a soon-to-be-brilliant theater director . . . who hadn't quite put it all together yet." But, he said, "this was more their show than mine, and it had my name on it. I was not ready to confront the conflicting emotions and certain humiliation of putting it on . . . [They] could not have been more gracious."

Nichols was uneasy about his return to work with May from the moment he turned his attention to *A Matter of Position* in September. The play was to have a trial run in Philadelphia, then another in New Haven, where any kinks could be worked out before Broadway. Nichols was happy about that, but deeply concerned about two other decisions. One was that May no longer planned to costar with him; the other was that Arthur Penn, who had agreed to direct, had dropped out, frustrated by her reluctance to make cuts. May had replaced him with the show's accommodating producer, Fred Coe, who would now do double duty. The decision, Nichols said, "didn't work for me, it didn't work for her . . . If we had had Arthur, or somebody who knew how to work on a play, it might have helped us."

Then there was the play itself. Nichols started to have a queasy sus-
picion that a piece that had originally been written for him had somehow turned into a piece *about* him—and not a flattering one. The main
character, a stubborn man who bends others to his will by planting
himself in his bed and refusing to budge, seemed like an attempt "to
make him ridiculous, to express some kind of contempt . . . She had
made him a moral monster whom the audience couldn't like," he told
Edmund Wilson.

The relationship between Nichols and May had been shaky in the
year since their show had closed; once they started work in Philadelphia,
it ruptured fatally. "It was pretty much an unmitigated disaster," said
Nichols. "We, who had always been together, were now in an impossible situation in which I was performing and she was in the audience
sitting next to the director watching, and it just imploded under that
pressure." As an actor, Nichols said, "I was, God knows, inadequate."
Nonetheless, he felt stung by her judgment; she felt unsupported by the
one person she thought she could trust and knew the producers were
not on her side. From the first performances of *A Matter of Position*,
"there was something about the play itself that nobody liked," says May.
"It went so badly that at intermission I went out in the lobby and heard
someone say, 'Who can I write to about this?' It was tough. I didn't like
what he was doing, and that had never happened to us before—that we
were at odds." Even in times of stress, they had always been a unit;
now, Nichols said, "as soon as we weren't in balance, great angers arose.
We flew apart."

What followed was a bitter and ugly power struggle. Coe and the
play's other producers urged May to cut forty minutes; she insisted she
could get the time down by working with the actors herself and essentially stepped in as director. Nichols grew so angry that he threatened
to quit if she didn't make the cuts he wanted; she went to the producers
and told them to replace him. The producers sided with Nichols, shoved
May aside, and made their own cuts. May said publicly that they had

taken a play that had "something to do with the realities of human be-havior" and "emasculated it." When it opened, one critic wrote, "those members of the audience who had not already beat a hasty retreat be-fore the final curtain, as many did, were left with a sensation of numb-ness that was too far down to be attributed to heartburn." *A Matter of Position* closed in Philadelphia. The Broadway run was canceled.

Nichols and May would eventually make peace. Over the next five decades, they would perform together, collaborate many times as writer and director, act opposite each other, and heal their relationship. Nich-ols would never direct a movie without showing her the script; she would rely on his judgment just as much. But their romantically charged, pas-sionate, two-against-the-world intimacy, the dangerous dynamic that had fueled their work and their art through the better part of ten years, would not return. "We stayed in each other's lives," said May. "But it wasn't the same. We had seen each other every day, we knew each oth-er's lives, we made fun of each other's dates. But after this, we were careful of each other's feelings as we had never been before. There was a formality between us that only happens when you hurt someone. He would never turn me down, and I would never turn him down, and I was very careful about asking him to do anything . . . In memory, I thought our estrangement was longer than it was. But we were estranged in that forever we felt guilty."

"It took years for Elaine and me to come back to each other after that," said Nichols. "And what happened in those years is that we be-came two individual people rather than Nichols-and-May."

Eight

PLAYING THE ROLE
OF A FATHER
1962-1963

They kept the breakup a secret for almost a year. In November, a few weeks after May's play had been scheduled to open on Broadway, they gritted their teeth and got through a benefit performance for the New York Philharmonic to which they had long been committed; they barely spoke except onstage. A third hit album, *Nichols and May Examine Doctors,* was compiled out of their *Monitor* sketches and won them another Grammy nomination; they avoided doing publicity. Their contract to star in eight television specials was quietly undone by lawyers. Nichols had felt injured and angry when he realized that the character May had written for him in *A Matter of Position* was a synthesis of what she saw as his worst traits. But in the wake of their split, he did exactly what the character he had just played would have done. "He went to bed. Period," said his agent, Robert Lantz. "He really wasn't functioning."

Nichols was in what Lantz described as a "state of deep depression," a condition with which he would struggle, intermittently, for the rest of his life. He could find nothing to hold on to. "In a way, it was the worst time in my life," he said, "because not only had I lost my best friend, but I had lost my work—it was who I was." He frequently referred to himself as "the leftover half of a comedy team." He knew what the press would say when the news finally broke—that he was an affable and skilled comic actor, but May was the truly incandescent talent of the two. He did not disagree. "I felt for a long time that what I was able to do came from my special connection with Elaine," he said. "Without her, there was not much." Even the friends who tried to give him pep talks couldn't hide their uncertainty. "Oh, Mikey," said Leonard Bernstein after a long, consoling walk along Park Avenue. "You're so good! . . . I don't know at *what*."

Should he start auditioning? Should he try to write? Nothing felt like a good fit; everything reminded him of her. He went to see the new play everyone was talking about, Edward Albee's *Who's Afraid of Virginia Woolf?*, which had opened on Broadway the week that May's play was supposed to start previews. He felt "enormously jealous, having just been in a play that didn't work at all," but also overwhelmed by the war of wills he saw onstage. He was uncomfortably familiar with the way "the two main characters compete in recruiting the audience to their side" and with how "they enjoy each other's prowess . . . They're often quite amused by the terrible things they say to each other," he said. "It's a fairly accurate portrayal of two people . . . who really do love each other and have allowed things to get in the way of the relationship surviving." Watching Uta Hagen's Martha and Arthur Hill's George slash at each other, first playfully and then lethally, he couldn't help but think of the "Pirandello" sketch. What was *Virginia Woolf* if not the story of a long and dangerous improv?

A couple of years earlier, he had met Albee, who had, in his "austere and restrained" way, been complimentary about their show. After he saw *Virginia Woolf*, Nichols called to offer his congratulations. He couldn't get the play out of his head—he later said it was the most powerful experience he had had in a theater since seeing *A Streetcar Named*

Desire as a teenager—but he had no particular thought of trying to attach himself to it, or to anything else, as a director. Richard Burton wanted to work with him on, of all things, *Othello*, in a proposed off-Broadway production in which he would play the Moor and Nichols would play Iago. They got as far as one reading. "As Richard and I read together," said Nichols, "my voice got higher and higher, and more midwestern. Iago became a squeaking Chicagoan. At the end, I closed the book and said, so long, everybody." (Burton wisely thought better of the plan and instead went to Broadway in an acclaimed production of *Hamlet* directed by John Gielgud.)

Lantz urged Nichols to try something, anything, that might help him shake off the doldrums, and convinced him to spend part of the spring of 1963 at the Vancouver International Festival, staging a short run of *The Importance of Being Earnest* while playing the Dauphin in *Saint Joan*. Nichols acquiesced—he had nothing better to do—but he wasn't happy, and phoned Lantz every night, saying, "Get me out of this!"

The call that would change his career came without fanfare. Lantz told him that a producer named Arnold Saint-Subber—he used only his last name professionally and was "Saint" to his friends—was looking for someone to direct a still-unfinished play by Neil Simon called *Nobody Loves Me* at the Bucks County Playhouse, in Pennsylvania. Simon had been a staff writer for *Your Show of Shows* in the 1950s and had turned from television to theater at the age of thirty. His first Broadway show, the moderate success *Come Blow Your Horn*, had recently closed; his second, the book for the Cy Coleman–Carolyn Leigh musical *Little Me*, was struggling. He had written only the first act of the new play, a comedy about a young New York couple in their first week of marriage trying to get used to living with each other, and he had sketched a quick outline of Acts II and III.

Nobody Loves Me already had its leading lady. Elizabeth Ashley, a young actress with a quick wit and a distinctive catch in her husky voice, had won a Tony Award a couple of years earlier as the ingenue opposite Art Carney in a throwaway father-daughter comedy called *Take Her, She's Mine*. The play had been directed by George Abbott, a venerable Broadway force whose bright, surehanded style had been a much-imitated hallmark of New York stage comedies and musicals for more than thirty years. Ashley wanted Abbott for this job, but he was well into his seventies. "Stark Hesseltine, my agent, said no, they wanted to make it—I remember this phrase—'a new comedy,'" she says. "Somehow, in my contract I had director approval—I was, what, twenty-three? That's nuts."

When Nichols's name came up, she loved the idea. "I was a little smarter than just being starstruck," she says. "I just knew that, although it seemed like an outside-the-box idea to the grown-ups, it was right. There was a school of Broadway directors—Garson Kanin was typical— who all directed big hit comedies the same way"—with actors smirking, mugging, and halfway facing the audience as they delivered their wisecracks. It didn't have to be believable as long as it got laughs. Like Nichols, Ashley had studied with Lee Strasberg. "For my crowd," she said, "the kind of work that we trained in and were pursuing was diametrically opposed to the school of acting favored by Broadway comedy directors. If they really wanted to put someone down, they'd say, 'Oh, he's a Method actor.' They hated that. That, primarily, was why the idea of Mike Nichols thrilled me. He wasn't part of that Broadway comedy establishment."

Simon—"Doc" to his colleagues—was not as convinced. Congenitally nervous, driven, insecure, and quick to see the downside in practically anything, he was skeptical when Saint-Subber suggested Nichols. "He's not a director, he's a comic," he protested. But when Nichols called him, told him he loved the first act, and said he "wanted to meet with us as soon as he was through Dauphining— Mike would talk like that," the playwright agreed to get together with him in New York.

Saint-Subber arranged a meeting at his East Side brownstone. It had been a long time since Nichols had had to audition for a job, but he charmed both the unfamiliar producer and the unconvinced writer in minutes, telling them he would direct the play in Bucks County, and after that, if he or they felt unsatisfied, they could part ways with no harm done. *Nobody Loves Me* still lacked a leading man, and Saint-Subber and Simon both suggested George Peppard, a handsome, WASPy actor more than a decade older than Ashley who had recently signed a Hollywood contract. "At the time, my attitude was, 'Why do you want to go with somebody who's gone off to be a movie star?'" said Ashley. "What about my buddy Bob?" "Bob" was Robert Redford, a twenty-six-year-old actor with whom she had worked in a 1959 Broadway play called *The Highest Tree*. In the past year or two, he had been getting regular gigs on television dramas, and Nichols remembered being impressed by him in an episode of *Alcoa Playhouse* called "The Voice of Charlie Pont," in which he played a struggling writer. "I experienced that frisson you get when you're surprised by someone," he said. "It wasn't 'Gee, he was interesting.' It was more 'Where the hell did he come from?' I just thought, he's gonna crack it."

Redford was not part of Ashley's coterie of vibrant, social young Broadway actors. He was a private, taciturn man who had sworn off theater since his last stage appearance, in a flop called *Sunday in New York*. "There was always this thing about Redford that he didn't really want to be an actor. He wanted to be a painter," says Ashley. "My friends were rag-ass, dope-smoking Greenwich Village types. Bob was a little finer—he was an artist, and we were showbiz trash. There was a sense that he was acting to pay the rent." When Ashley and Redford first worked together, he had been a young newlywed whom she watched endure a tragic loss. "He and [his wife] Lola had a baby, and when we were in that play, the baby died—crib death," says Ashley. "I remember Bob didn't even have enough money for the funeral."

Although television had allowed Redford to make a decent living, often playing bad guys, Hollywood had not yet come calling, and he was on nobody's short list for romantic comedies. "When I got word that Nichols wanted me to be in the play," he recalls, "I thought, *Why is he choosing me?*" The part of Paul Bratter, a staid young professional gradually getting used to his free-spirited wife, Corie, and realizing that he would have to change his life just to keep up with her, seemed on paper like a straight-man role without a lot of opportunity. When Redford met Nichols, he asked, baffled, "What do *you* see in this?" Plenty, said Nichols, who knew how much could be made of the push-and-pull between an uptight man and a smart, alluring woman who alternately attracted him and drove him crazy. "It's a battle," Nichols told him. "These two are in a full-scale war."

"It felt slightly perverse," Redford says, "in a way that fascinated me. As soon as he said that, I thought, *His idiosyncratic sensibility could make this really fun.*" He was reluctant nevertheless; he and Lola had recently moved to Utah, where they were building a house and raising their two young children. "I didn't want to get back in the race," he said. He told Nichols he would commit to the short run in Bucks County but not to anything more. "It was half-assed," he said, "but it was the best I could do, given where I was at emotionally."

Nichols walked into the rehearsal room, looked around, and said genially, "Is it possible there are no doughnuts? There's no point in rehearsing if there are no doughnuts!" There were three weeks until *Nobody Loves Me* was to begin its Bucks County run, and it didn't take long for him to size up what he had to work with: a reticent leading man, a high-strung leading lady, and a writer so convinced his play was awful that when they started reading it aloud for the first time, he excused himself to go sit in the hall. Simon came back in when he finally heard a big laugh, only to discover that the cast had taken a break and Nichols was cracking them up with a story about working with May.

When Simon asked, "Can we get out of the Bucks County booking?" he recalled, "Mike looked at me as if I were insane. [He said,] 'Didn't it occur to you that the actors were nervous?'"

They were. Nichols was not. In one day of work, he said, he had discovered exactly what he wanted to do for the rest of his career. He was struck by two revelations. The first was that, rather than acting, "this was the job I had been preparing for without knowing it," he remembered. "All the Strasberg, all the studying, all the yakking at night over one cup of coffee driving the people in the restaurant crazy was for this." The second discovery was more personal. "If you're missing your father, as I had all during my adolescence, there's something about playing the role of a father that is very reassuring," he said. "I had a sense of enormous relief and joy that I had found a process that . . . allowed me to be my father and the group's father."

He now realized that performing—the thing he had thought he wanted most—"made me unhappy. It brings out [my] childishness. Directing encourages the adult portion of your character." As he looked at Simon and the actors, he knew not only that his job was to help them, but that he could. "Look at this! *Look at this!*" he thought. "This is my job! I knew instantly what I wanted them to do, what *we* would do. It was perfectly clear." Not wanting to overwhelm Simon with suggestions, Nichols told him to calm down about the play. "Once they're relaxed in rehearsal, you'll change your mind. I'm not positive it's good but I think it is. Anyway, it'll be fun trying." Then he told his jittery writer to think about a new title. Simon came back with one the next morning: *Barefoot in the Park.*

His play was brisk, funny, almost overpacked with one-liners, and shrewdly constructed, complete with a secondary plot that mirrored the main story, in which Corie's widowed mother, played by the veteran Mildred Natwick, learns to loosen up when she is wooed by the Bratters' eccentric European neighbor. Simon was a fast rewriter, and his characters were equally fast talkers, batting his banter at one another so rapidly that it could easily become tinny and false. The first thing Nichols did was tell his cast to play the material as if the characters had no idea it was supposed to be comical. "Let's do it as though we don't know what's going to happen," he said. "As if the people were alive. I didn't want to keep tipping the comedy, having the actors running downstage, yelling, slamming doors, things like that." Play it as if you think it's *King Lear,* he told them.

Nichols's approach drew on everything he had learned with Strasberg about rooting performances in psychological truth, and on everything he and May had discovered about getting laughs by refusing to chase them. The result, when Ashley and Redford got on their feet and started to play the scenes, surprised even their author. Standing next to Nichols at the back of the theater, watching the play's first big fight, Simon recalled, he "began to see what Mike had done. He had turned the play from artifice to believability." As the fight went on, Simon whispered to Nichols, "I don't think we should be watching this . . . It's too private. Too intimate. I feel like I'm eavesdropping." "Good," Nichols said. "Then it's working."

Nichols wasn't shy about using his personal experience to motivate his actors—he told funny, embarrassing stories about the rocky start of his marriage to Pat Scot and their terrible honeymoon. But the cast got a more vivid glimpse of his romantic life when the woman who would soon become his second wife arrived in Bucks County. Margot Callas was a tall, stunning twenty-eight-year-old who had, until a few years earlier, lived with the much older British novelist and poet Robert Graves, who referred to her as his muse, "the white goddess." The company of *Barefoot in the Park* was dumbstruck when she swept into Bucks County. "Mike would bring people as presents for us to play with— interesting, fabulous people," says Ashley. (Among them: Stephen Sondheim and Susan Sontag.) "And one of them was Margot. She was just earth-shatteringly beautiful. If I use the word 'trophy,' I don't intend it to be derisive. It was almost like a Scott Fitzgerald thing—the most beautiful woman and the smartest, most creative man. What better merger could there be?"

Ashley herself was in the middle of a romance that would complicate her work on the play considerably—she was now dating Peppard, the actor whom she had dismissed when he was suggested for Redford's part a few months earlier and a man who, it turned out, was bent on undermining her.* "George would always have some question," she says. "It was subtle. It was 'Nichols, yeah, he had that comedy show, big success, but he may not know what he's doing.' And 'Redford—well, he's good, but can he carry a show?' So what Mike Nichols got when he got me was this girl who was overly successful with this movie-star boyfriend and heavy-duty agents who would come in and give their notes."

As the first performance neared, Nichols's main worry was about his cast. "I knew they were all solid," he said, "all good at getting the 'bounce' in the thing. If I had reservations it was with Bob and Liz's mindset." Ashley was game but emotionally volatile and had to be urged to shake off both Peppard's interference and some bad habits picked up from past plays. "I don't want you being cute when you're upset," Nichols told her. And Redford could be almost too laid back; Nichols soon discovered that he was funniest when the play gave him something to be angry about. "He was pissed a lot in those days," he said, "so that was great electricity for Paul Bratter. Once Bob got those elements by the neck, he was off and running."

By opening night in Bucks County, Nichols felt he had the cast and play in good working order. Simon did not agree; after a deadly dress rehearsal, he approached the stage manager and asked, "Have you ever had anything worse than this?" The laconic reply: "Maybe a couple of things." "That's it," Simon told Nichols. "We're not opening the play."

"I said the first grown-up thing of my life," Nichols recalled. "'Why

---

* Peppard and Ashley were married from 1966 to 1972.

don't we wait until tomorrow to see what it's like with an audience?' And we did, and they laughed their asses off."

Barefoot in the Park finished its brief run in May, and Saint-Subber announced that it would open at Broadway's Biltmore Theatre in October. The Biltmore's owner groused to him that Ashley's character was underdeveloped and that the play still didn't have a workable third act—a hard problem to solve, given that Simon hadn't come up with any conflict more dramatic than two people getting married, briefly experiencing cold feet, and then deciding to give it a go anyway. Nichols wasn't worried; he would have all summer to figure it out.

He had started dividing his vacation time between Connecticut and Martha's Vineyard, where a year earlier he had become friendlier with the Bernsteins and also with the writer William Styron and his wife, Rose. "Lennie and Mike would turn up and we would play word games all the time," she remembers. "Then Mike and I would play tennis." In the summer of 1963, he surprised the Styrons—and everyone who knew him—by arriving with a new wife. He and Margot Callas had quietly married—on their wedding day, Robert Graves, who had met Nichols, had sent him a telegram, half wounding, half warning, that read "KEEP YOUR HAIR UP." By the fall, Callas would be pregnant. "My memory is of her standing at the net when Mike and I played tennis," says Rose Styron, "wearing white gloves, touching the post at the net, and keeping score." Nichols and Callas had known each other for only a short time; she was emphatically not a part of his New York circle, and if friends raised their eyebrows at Nichols's marrying a second time at thirty-one, they noted that at least his depression had lifted and kept the rest of their thoughts private.

By September, Nichols had regained enough confidence to go public about the dissolution of his partnership with May, in a carefully handled news story that noted that "Elaine will continue to write, Mike will continue to direct, and they'll both perform together whenever they feel the urge." The piece added that they had "just improvised" a fourth comedy album, to be titled *Men, Women, and Children*. (This was an apparently inaccurate reference to an attempt to get a second LP out of their *Monitor* sketches; it was never released.) Nichols was much more eager to talk about directing, telling his interviewer, "I learned that things you plan cold-bloodedly are not as funny as what happens when you're actually doing a scene. I want to create an atmosphere of freedom for my actors. I haven't blocked the script."

That wouldn't be true for long. Nichols was, and always would be, open to suggestions from his cast and to his own on-the-spot impulses—"Do you think you could have a cold?" he asked Redford at one point and watched, delighted, as the actor's instant adjustment invigorated the scene. But in the two-month run-up to Broadway, Nichols worked out every piece of movement, beat by beat. *Barefoot in the Park* was set entirely in Paul and Corie's sixth-floor walk-up, and he was determined that the snappy, rapid-fire dialogue be undergirded by comically naturalistic physical action. Redford and Ashley would never be standing at center stage, nose to nose, trading zingers—that was a style of Broadway boulevard comedy that, to actors and directors of Nichols's generation, had come to feel false and trite. Instead, while Paul and Corie talked at (but rarely to) each other, she would be unpacking cardboard boxes and checking herself in the mirror, and he would be looking for one shoe and using a dictionary to press a wrinkle out of his tie while he was still wearing it. And Nichols turned each character's entrance through the front door into one of *Barefoot*'s best running gags—a can-you-top-this sequence of gasps and heaves after racing up five flights of stairs. Meanwhile, Simon hammered away at a new draft of the ending. "I could wake [Mike] at two in the morning and say, 'I've figured out what's wrong with the third act,' and he would curse me and then come meet me to listen to it," said Simon. "It was the joy of discovering things together."

During the long break after Bucks County, Ashley had gone to California to make her movie debut in *The Carpetbaggers*, a lurid, high-profile melodrama about a thinly disguised version of Howard Hughes that was designed to launch Peppard as a movie star. She returned to the rehearsal room with her agents scolding her that she was wasting her time doing a play. "I was conflict walking," she recalls, "a perfect caricature of the fucked-up overnight success." Nichols and Redford had developed a close working relationship—"I had some of the best times of my life working with Mike," Redford says. "As soon as I understood that he saw the play as a contest of wills, things really got terrific and enlivened the whole experience for me." As Ashley watched them work, she became certain that the show was slipping away from her.

"The play would not have become the huge hit that it was if not for what Mike and Redford did in inventing Paul," says Ashley. "Mike was like a ferret, burrowing into the marrow of that character in every line, every second. But my character was a general everygirl." And when Peppard—"a misogynist, a control freak, and a deeply twisted man," she says—would swing by the rehearsal room, "what he fed to me was 'Nichols is handing the play to Redford. They're stealing it from you.'" Her distress became evident to Nichols, who was well-meaning but not initially helpful. "He said, 'Let's have a sit-down. I hear that you feel neglected!'" she remembers. "I started to cry, which is every director's nightmare—to have the chick in the show start to cry. I said, 'I don't know who I am in the play!' And Mike took my face in his hands and said, 'You're just a girl! That's the magic of the play! She's just a girl!' And I remember sobbing. 'But I don't know how to *play* that!' Mike had a sort of funny smile and internal laugh. And he said, 'You don't have to play her, don't you understand? You are the girl everyone wants. You're the girl every girl wants to be.' And I said, 'But I'm *not* that girl!'"

Nichols finally heard her, and as they started to block the first scene—a moving-in vignette with a repairman coming and going that devolves into a why-did-we-get-married fight—he realized that he had to make her character as idiosyncratic as Redford's. Merely patting her on the head wouldn't serve her performance or the play. "He said, 'Look, I want you to stand downstage left and play one thing only: Say the lines, but do not move, no matter what happens,'" says Ashley. "'You are Joan of Arc at the stake, and God is with *you*, and they may be putting the torches to the kindling, but you will not lose faith, because you are with God. I don't care what Redford does—that's what you play, no matter who comes onstage or who leaves, until you hear me say okay!' He framed it as an exercise. So I thought, *I'll just say my lines to God.* And it went on and on and on, and finally he said, '*O-kay!*' And I found out all kinds of things about my girl. What I learned from Mike was, even if you want something to be universal, you make every detail unique to that person, that circumstance, that character's history. I suddenly realized I was playing the girl who feared her husband was turning into a middle-aged white-shoe country-club fart. Sometimes you just know a director's right. Don't question. Just do it. By the very act of doing it, you will find out everything you've been trying to discover. That was Mike. He would just say, 'Let's try it.'"

Redford's own meltdown came soon after, when the production moved to New Haven for its first out-of-town tryout, and it became evident that a newly confident Ashley was now walking away with the play. "I behaved badly. I did not want to be there and I did not cooperate," Redford said. "I had agreed to do the play, but part of me was resisting everything. My head was still in Utah. When we opened in New Haven, I basically lay down. I thought, *I'm going to show everybody why I shouldn't be in this play—I'm going to be so bad they'll have to get rid of me.* And I was." Reviews called Ashley sparkling and suggested that Redford tended to recede into the background. Nichols took him to lunch and said, "Look, I know how two people onstage can be. You can't win the battle until you acknowledge it's a battle," Redford recalled. "I know what you're doing, but it's not going to work. I'm not going to replace you." Redford dug in; when the play moved to

Washington, D.C., his performance was still lackadaisical and uncommitted.

So Nichols tried another approach. "He said, 'I think you're somebody who probably has some secrets that you keep hidden,'" Redford remembers. "'Why don't you search yourself? Search for the things you hide. What if you use that for the character—the idea that you carry all these secrets around?' I had never been aware of that, but he had a deep sense of psychology. So that night when I went on, I didn't say my lines. I just whistled. The audience didn't know what the fuck was going on." Ashley was unnerved as well. "I whistled and whistled, and suddenly I felt so comfortable that I was doing what I wanted to do that I came alive. Mike just kept plugging away until he finally hit the nerve that freed me up." The battle had been joined. "When we did the show that night," Nichols said, "Liz became invisible. He pulled out every trick and knocked her off the planet. That's when we really took off . . . As we headed for Broadway, Bob challenged her, and she gave him a run for his money."

With every performance, Nichols balanced them more effectively, until, Ashley says, "the audience would not stop fucking laughing." At the start of one rehearsal, she remembers Nichols telling the cast, "'There will be no squealing, whining, crying, or screaming, because we're going to be cutting. But nobody should throw away the pages we are tearing out. You should put them in a safety deposit box, because you will all have hundreds of thousands of dollars' worth of gag lines.' Doc Simon was in the back of the theater, pale and shrunken. But we had to get the show down in size."

By the time a shorter version of *Barefoot in the Park* arrived in New York, it lacked only the tweak that would complete its third act—and that was solved by a question from Lillian Hellman, who had seen the play and, at a dinner with Nichols and his new bride, said that she was confused about whether Corie's mother had actually consummated an affair with the older man she had met. "I said, 'Can you excuse me for about an hour?'" said Nichols. He left the table and called Simon. Until that point, the act had been dragged down by a scene in which the two older characters tried to describe what had happened between them. "It was so boring," said Nichols. "We tried this and that . . . and after a whole day, I said, 'What if it seems funny to you as you recollect it? What if you start to laugh at what happened last night?' They tried it, and we had solved it . . . I then came to appreciate that this job that I so loved, that I was going to be okay at, needed the unconscious just as much as it needed improv."

With just one show, Nichols had come to feel at home in his work. The insecurities and vanities of actors didn't irritate him; he delighted in helping them to the finish line. He greeted the anxieties of writers with serene optimism. And the sound of an audience—or even its silence—only made him feel more in control. He found he could walk into the theater at any point during a performance and "in five seconds I know how it's doing. It has nothing to do with laughs. You *hear* it. I hear what people are thinking."

On October 23, 1963, *Barefoot in the Park* opened on Broadway. Just before his extremely nervous cast took the stage, Nichols gathered them for a final pep talk. "Everybody relax," Redford says he told them. "You know your positions, you know your laughs, you know your lines, you know where the comfort zones are. So enjoy yourselves, and remember: *Everything depends on tonight.*"

On the page, *Barefoot in the Park* reads as a fairly standard romantic TV-style sitcom of its era; in fact, it became one seven years later. It can be hard to understand why its arrival on Broadway dazzled not only critics but a generation of young comedy aficionados like Lorne Michaels, who believes the work that Nichols did with Neil Simon in the 1960s was "revolutionary."

"Doc Simon owed more to Nichols than he could ever acknowledge," says Ashley. "He turned that play into something real." What critics saw onstage that night was a comedy of the kind they had been trudging to for a decade or more, but this time played with effortless verisimilitude—the acutely funny lines were combined with a rare glimpse at how people go about their lives in the privacy of their own homes, their physical tics, their tiny irritations, the odd habits that you never realized everyone shared until someone revealed them to you on-stage. It was the Nichols touch, honed by his years of working with May and getting the audience to say, "Yes! How did you know?"

The reviews were raves. "Mike Nichols—you can call him director Mike Nichols after this one . . . doesn't busy his actors for the sake of busyness alone," wrote Walter Kerr in the *New York Herald Tribune*. "Mr. Nichols's eye is a restless absolute, as his ear has perfect pitch." Critics knew the plot was flimsy; it didn't matter. "Ah, what the actors, paced by genius Nichols, make of this familiar charade!" the reviewer for *Cue* magazine wrote. "If you haven't heard by now, [he] leaps into a leading position as a director of comedy." They particularly loved what Nichols had done with the escalating stakes of the entrances, capped by a scene in which a drunken Redford bursts through the door carrying Mildred Natwick and reels across the room to the couch, a laugh that stopped the show for a full minute. "These entrances could become classics of a kind as exercises for students of advanced acting," said *The New York Times*. Summarizing the reaction, the *New York Post*'s Richard Watts wrote, "Every reviewer in town recognized the deftness, inventiveness and sureness of touch with which Mike Nichols staged the comedy, and thereby he stepped immediately to the top of the class."

In 1963, there was only one way to get tickets to a Broadway show: Go to the theater and line up outside the box office. The day the reviews for *Barefoot in the Park* ran, crowds at the Biltmore were so big that the *Times* sent a photographer to shoot Nichols and Simon, Broadway's new dream team, grinning in front of the throng as it waited hours to secure seats to the blockbuster hit. By the end of the day, the play had advance sales of $350,000—the equivalent of nine sold-out weeks. Saint-Subber guessed, with wild enthusiasm, that it was on its way to a three-year run. It would run for four.

The show would not make Nichols much richer than he was; he had been paid just $4,000 to direct it, and his royalties for the run would amount to somewhere between $500 and $1,000 a week. But *Barefoot in the Park* had transformed his life. An out-of-work actor had become the hottest director in New York. And he was already thinking ahead—to his next play, and his first movie.

Nine

OKAY, THAT'S GREAT, NOW LET'S TRY THIS

1963–1964

Two weeks after *Barefoot in the Park* opened, Nichols celebrated his birthday with Margot and six or eight friends at their apartment. (His mother called during the party and said, "Well, thirty-two years ago I can tell you I wasn't having such an easy time of it.") In the year that followed, he would commit to directing three plays and three movies, become a father, end his marriage, begin a new relationship, make a lucrative television deal, and reunite with Elaine May. He was not manic, heedless, or overconfident; if anything, he was afraid. His debut as a director had brought him a new kind of celebrity, and the sudden opportunities it afforded him felt fragile and transient. "I think people try to become famous because they think, 'If you can get the world to revolve around you, you won't die,'" he remarked at the time. But his dry detachment was a posture—the only acceptable mode of self-presentation for a young man who wanted a great deal but had, since his first day at the University of Chicago, taken great care never to look or sound too excited about anything.

He learned fast that Broadway shows didn't stop needing a director's attention once they were up and running. At the play's opening-
night party at Tavern on the Green, he had watched with growing
irritation as Peppard tried to drag Ashley away before any publicity
photos could be taken; Nichols had had to intervene and had barely
controlled his temper. Ashley's misery was apparent to everyone in the
production. The raves did not boost her confidence; they "only made it
worse," she wrote. "The next day we were taken to lunch at '21' to celebrate my being the hottest little piece of ass in show business for that
five minutes. I was so stoned and miserable and spaced out I didn't even
know where I was." She became, by her own description, "bitchy" to
Redford and Natwick, and so combative with Neil Simon that he said,
"Elizabeth, you're the most defensive girl I've ever known!" (Nichols,
standing behind him and seeing the shock on her face, murmured, "It's
not a *bad* thing . . .")

The play was a month into its run when news broke of the assassination of President Kennedy. In shock, Ashley left her apartment and
headed for a newsstand, looking for the afternoon papers. Instead she
saw her own face staring back at her from every corner. Shortly before
Barefoot opened, a photographer from *Life* had made the rounds to
shoot a portfolio of up-and-coming Broadway talent. Nobody told her
she had made the cover. It was more than she could handle. She almost
walked into traffic.

A few days later, sitting at her makeup table before a performance,
she started to shake uncontrollably and was unable to speak. Alarmed,
the stage manager phoned Peppard, who got her admitted to Manhattan's high-end psychiatric hospital Payne Whitney. The production put
out a press release saying that she had hurt her back. "But I had cracked
up," she said. "I was ignorant of so much about myself and the world
and relationships, and it was coming at me from all directions."

Nichols himself was still reeling from the news of Kennedy's death.
Two days after the assassination, he and Margot, who was pregnant,

were walking on Fifth Avenue near their apartment and ran into Stephen Sondheim. "Come on up," Nichols said to him, "and we'll watch the news." They went into the bedroom, turned on the TV, and sat on the edge of the bed. "The three of us together saw Jack Ruby kill Lee Harvey Oswald," said Sondheim. "Our jaws dropped with a clang. That's my memory of Mike at that time—us in their perfectly nice upper-middle-class young person's apartment, just sitting on their bed in disbelief."

When Ashley returned to the play a week or so later, she felt ashamed and humiliated. Shortly before she was to give her first performance since being released from the hospital, Nichols visited her in her dressing room. "Mike, I've got to tell you," she said. "I don't feel like I know any more now than I did before I went in there. I don't know if I'm going to go crazy again or what."

"It's okay," he said. "I've been there. We've all been there. Look at me. I'm still crazy, I never know from one day to the next if I'm going to make it." She believed him. In Nichols she saw someone who had worked tremendously hard not to come apart and had succeeded. "Mike was the opposite of a control freak," she says. "The only thing he demanded that he maintain absolute control of was his invention of himself. And that self was so much a product of the self he had left behind." His kindness helped her get through nine more months of the play's run. "Mike was one of the first people I met in the theater who had a kind of humanity about art and artists," she recalled a decade after leaving the play. "I regret that I worked with him at a time when I had so many demons in my head."

That November, Nichols and May gave their first major performance together in two and a half years. Long ago in Chicago, after they had gone out on their own, they had developed a sketch about a bereaved young man and a funeral-parlor saleswoman who was trying to hard-sell him on all the extras she could think of. The result was so bleak that the club owner warned them "that if we ever did it again, they'd . . . throw us out," said Nichols. But in the summer of 1963, *The American Way of Death*, Jessica Mitford's scathing book about manipulative funeral-home practices, had become a bestseller and the subject of national discussion; comedy mores had changed enough that their daring sketch now felt prescient, and they decided to refine it and perform it on NBC's *That Was the Week That Was*. Nichols played "Charles Maslow-Freen," May was "Miss Loomis, your grief lady":

May: Would you be interested in some extras for the loved one?
Nichols: What kind of extras?
May: Well . . . how about a casket?
Nichols: Isn't that included in the funeral?
May: No.
Nichols: We have to have a casket!
May: Yes. It looks better.

The sketch reminded Nichols and May of how much they enjoyed working with each other. Over the next year, they would perform at benefits—for Nichols's old high school, Walden, which May's daughter was now attending, and for the American Yiddish Theater—and, for a great deal of money, they would make half a dozen appearances on Jack Paar's show, a kind of greatest-hits reprise of their best-loved sketches that they appear to have filmed in one day, with virtually no interaction with Paar. Publicly, Nichols made it clear that their joint appearances did not signal a return to full-time performing. "Miss May and I cannot do material together without a lot of time which I can't spare," he said, adding, "I don't think I'll ever miss acting." But privately, he was happy to have May back in his life. "Once we got over being mad at each other, we could come together for this or that ratfuck"—Nichols's favorite word for any event that involved a lot of well-known and/or well-heeled people. "And that was fun . . . We had created a body of work, and there it was. God knows we presented it enough."

A magazine profile of Nichols would soon assert that "things have reached such a monkey-see-monkey-do situation that it is now incumbent upon anyone who has written a funny play or novel, or who has the rights to such and wishes to produce same, to send the work to Nichols with a note exhorting him to direct it." The first request had come days before *Barefoot in the Park* opened, when Neil Simon told him he was working on a new comedy, a kind of bookend to *Barefoot* about "rehabilitation after divorce." "He's calling the notion 'The Odd Couple,' [and] has a loose outline of the characters involved," *The New York Times* reported. Nichols signed on before the play was finished.

The requests had turned into a deluge as soon as *Barefoot*'s reviews hit the papers. The next one he accepted came from an old friend, Richard Burton's ex-wife, Sybil. Nichols had stayed close to both Burtons after their divorce earlier in the year, and Sybil, who had set up a small off-Broadway theater called the Establishment, was hoping he would direct a hit British comedy called *The Knack*, by the young writer Ann Jellicoe. It was a surprisingly modest choice for the follow-up to a big success—a three-character piece set in a one-room flat—and it would play not on Broadway but in a 199-seat theater on the Upper East Side, just a block from the Blue Angel. "The audience can appreciate the outlandish things that happen only if they get involved in that confined apartment where everyone gets in each other's way," Nichols insisted. "That's what makes *The Knack* fun."

Nichols's choice for his first film was similarly small-scale. Peter Shaffer's *The Public Eye*, was, like *The Knack*, a one-set British sex comedy, with a clever plot about a suspicious husband who hires an eccentric detective to tail his much younger wife, only to learn a few weeks later that his wife has fallen in love with the mysterious man she has noticed is following her all over London. The action, which takes place entirely in the detective's office, did not seem particularly cinematic, but it had the feeling of a well-developed Compass Theater scenario, and it was a style of droll, absurdist, performance-driven comedy that Nichols knew he could handle. The play had moved to Broadway just before *Barefoot in the Park* opened, and both productions had been noticed by Ross Hunter, a film producer at Universal who kept an eye out for rising New York talent. Once he learned that Paramount had already grabbed the film rights to *Barefoot,* he saw an opportunity to pair its hot young director with the new comedy that was playing just two blocks away. He called Nichols and asked if he could buy him the film rights to Shaffer's play.

For much of the past decade, Hunter, a former musical-comedy actor who adored ostentatious lavishness both onscreen and off, had been responsible for keeping Universal well stocked with "women's pictures," from Doris Day comedies to Douglas Sirk melodramas. To Nichols, he embodied both the pretension and the vulgarity that, for a young generation of East Coast artists, characterized the Hollywood movie business. "I was Mister Theater and he was this unbearable silly queen, was the short of it," Nichols said. "But I'd seen the play in London with Maggie Smith, and I had liked it, and suddenly, I seemed to be signed up to make this movie."

Nichols committed to *The Public Eye* in January 1964, but it was not scheduled to begin production until November. Still unaware of how quickly Hollywood plans could be upended, he mapped out the rest of his year. After *The Knack,* he would spend the summer working with Shaffer on the *Public Eye* screenplay, launch a London production and a U.S. tour of *Barefoot in the Park,* and then direct another play in New York in the early fall. "I'm laid out for years," he happily announced to the press.

His calendar now included a second film to which he had agreed almost as an afterthought. An aspiring producer named Lawrence Turman had spent $1,000 to buy the rights to a first novel by Charles Webb, a writer just two years out of college. Webb's book, *The Gradu-*

ate, was written largely as a series of dialogue scenes; to Turman, it felt easily adaptable to the screen. He had loved Nichols's work on *Barefoot*, but what resonated just as much, he says, was "the funny nervousness of his performances with Elaine May," which suggested an affinity with the anxious, hyperserious demeanor of Webb's protagonist, Benjamin Braddock. Turman thought Nichols might enjoy the novel, despite what one critic had complained was a failure to answer "questions about the psychological motivation of its hero" and "a preposterous climax."

"It seemed to me totally unoriginal," Nichols said, "but a good old gag. Kid, older lady, that's how everyone got started." He said it reminded him of *The Catcher in the Rye* and also of the French novel *The Devil in the Flesh*, about a married nurse during World War I who has an affair with a seventeen-year-old. The next day, he left Turman a phone message saying he was in.

With that, Nichols promptly put both movies out of his mind; he had more pressing work. Less than a year earlier, he had undertaken *Barefoot* as the new kid, the untested commodity. On *The Knack*, a comedy by a fledgling playwright with a youthful ensemble of four, he was, for the first time, the senior talent in the room, and he played it that way, striding into the first day of rehearsal wearing expensive imported leather boots and a top-of-the-line tailored British dress shirt. His cast included George Segal, a thirty-year-old improv actor whom he had first auditioned a couple of years earlier for the "Crawling Arnold" segment of *The World of Jules Feiffer*. "I remember crawling around on the floor," says Segal, "and Mike having this attitude toward me of *Okay, hotshot, Elaine speaks highly of you, but let's see what you can do*." Segal hadn't gotten that part, but Nichols thought he was right for the role of Tolen, *The Knack*'s sexually confident ladies' man who competes with two flatmates for the attention of a girl who wanders by their first-floor window.

In twenty-first-century terms, Tolen would be seen as a potential date rapist, and *The Knack*'s many discomforting jokes about a young woman who passes out and wakes up convinced that she has been assaulted—a twist that becomes the entire plot engine—have made it all but unrevivable. ("You think you're pretty clever! . . . Mr. Smartie! Mr. Tight Trousers!" she shrieks before fainting at the end of Act II; in Act III, Tolen announces, "She has fabricated this fantasy because she really does want to be raped," and tries to convince one of his friends to do the job.) But in 1964, nobody involved with the play raised an eyebrow at its sexual politics, nor did critics or audiences, who saw it only as a refreshingly frank comic peek at swinging London that was less prim about sex than its American counterparts.

It's possible that what drew Nichols to *The Knack* was that he recognized a younger version of himself in all three male characters—Colin, the awkward lad who can't connect with girls; Tom, the detached, wry onlooker; and Tolen, the self-invented expert. But it seems likelier that he was attracted by the staging challenge—the play is set entirely in an almost bare apartment and is essentially a blank canvas for a director to color in with stage business and movement. Nichols found himself serving as choreographer almost as much as director, and he manifested so little interest in the characters themselves that, at one point during rehearsals, Segal blew up. "I remember saying, 'There's no depth here! You're keeping him at arm's length!' And after that, he gave me a little more room. It was one of those actor-director fights that was more bonding than separating," he says.

Nichols wasn't sure any of it was working, and Margot, who would come to rehearsals, did nothing to boost his confidence. Tony Walton, who was beginning a decades-long association with Nichols as his set designer, remembers an especially hard day during which Nichols labored over the timing of *The Knack*'s most elaborate set piece, a lengthy near-slapstick attempt to shove a large bed through a narrow doorway. "Mike was in deep distress," Walton says. "He thought he'd stopped the momentum and destroyed the show. Everyone came up to him and reassured him that not only was it fine, but what he had done with the bed was brilliant. Margot waited until everyone was done and then came up and whispered, 'They're lying.'"

On May 24, the Tony Awards were handed out in a low-key ceremony at the New York Hilton that lasted just an hour and was telecast only on a local TV station. At that time, the nominees and winners were selected largely by theater journalists. Nichols, Simon, and Ashley were all up for awards. Nichols put on a tuxedo, went to the dinner, and came home with his first trophy—he had won the Tony for Best Direction of a Play. Three days later, *The Knack* opened, and critics seemed to affirm that they had made the right choice. "Give Mike Nichols a virtually empty stage . . . and he fills it not with furniture but with laughter," Howard Taubman wrote in *The New York Times*. "Mr. Nichols . . . is going to be our most gifted director of comedy if he isn't careful." Nichols himself felt that he "never quite solved the problems of *The Knack*," and kept going back after it opened to tweak a gesture or a bit of byplay. But audiences loved what one reviewer called "a restless, ceaseless quest for extraction of every gram of fun and frolic"; the play settled into a run of nearly seven hundred performances.

By the time *The Knack* opened, Nichols's marriage to Margot was over, almost as soon as it had begun. She had given birth to a daughter, Daisy, and soon after, she took her to live in Europe. Few of his friends knew what had happened; some had never even met her. Nichols himself called the marriage "disastrous" and "catastrophic." Decades later, when the writer Aaron Sorkin asked him, "Where, in an eleven-month marriage, do you discover that this isn't going to work?" his dark reply was "When she pulled a knife on me." That may have been an exaggeration; although a few people remember Nichols alluding to some sort of physical confrontation as the last straw, most who knew Nichols in the early 1960s say they have only hazy memories of his and Margot's relationship or its end.

The collapse of his marriage to Pat Scot had not embarrassed him; the fact that he was headed toward his second divorce at thirty-two did. He decided to lie low for a while. Nichols had learned well from Avedon; he knew how to live the life of a rich man now, and he started to spend money like someone who believed it would never run low. Over the past few years, his work with May on *Monitor* and in a series of commercial endorsements had afforded him a reliable six-figure income. Soon after he gave up the Fifth Avenue apartment he and his wife had shared, he bought an aerie high above the city, a triplex penthouse in the Beresford, an imposing Central Park West building that overlooked the park and the Museum of Natural History. He also purchased, for what he said was "a small fortune," a colt he called Max, and became interested in buying and breeding Arabian horses, a hobby, investment, and obsession he would pursue for the next thirty years. For part of the summer, he retreated to Martha's Vineyard. And, as he often did in times of depression or stress, he spent a staggering portion of each day asleep. Peter Shaffer, in New York to work with him on the *Public Eye* script, got used to arriving at the Beresford for their noon work sessions only to see Nichols stumble from the bedroom in a daze, wondering who could be interrupting his rest so early in the day.

"I was still in my first mode, doing what I did in college," said Nichols. "Peter used to get very pissed off at me for oversleeping. But he was so funny. I'd say, 'What will we do about Ross Hunter?' And Peter would say, 'I'll take care of him.' He started doing things like writing 'She appears at the top of the stairs' in the script, and then he would say, in parentheses, 'beautifully gowned.' He'd put in a lot of that shit to keep Ross Hunter happy."

Nichols's enthusiasm for *The Public Eye* started to fade over the summer—he thought Shaffer's script was "nice . . . it was all right," but not more; it felt nowhere near a final draft, no casting had been discussed, and he hadn't even met Hunter face-to-face. Moviemaking was still abstract to him—he had no firm grasp of how a deal translated into an enterprise involving hundreds of people for weeks or months on end, nor was he sure how directing a film even worked. He saw himself as a man of the theater, and that September he turned his attention to his next Broadway show.

Nichols had had nothing to do with the writing of Murray Schisgal's play *Luv*—an American comedy that had already opened in London to mixed reviews. But when it was announced that he would direct it, the choice was seen as the epitome of a Nichols project—a bleak, off-kilter one-set urban adult comedy about contemporary love and marriage. Not only did the play have the spiraling-toward-insanity quality of the best Nichols and May sketches, but two of its three characters could easily have been played by Nichols and May themselves. Instead they would be played by the married actors Eli Wallach and Anne Jackson; *Luv*'s producer, Claire Nichtern, had been pursuing Nichols to direct them since the moment she read the reviews for *Barefoot in the Park*. Wallach, who urged Nichtern to "always grab the hot director," took an active hand as well, asking, "Should I write to Mike and tell him how happy we'd be if he could work *Luv* into his crowded schedule?" He and Jackson were thrilled when Nichols agreed to oversee the rewrites that they all felt Schisgal needed to do. "Mike will be diagnostician, friend & surgeon—all in one . . . & we trust him absolutely," Wallach wrote to his producer.

In *Luv*, Wallach and Jackson would serve as two points of an improbable romantic triangle. For months, they had sought Walter Matthau for the third role, a sad sack who, as the play opens, is about to jump from the bridge that serves as the main set, and ends up stealing the wife (Jackson) of the onetime classmate (Wallach) who comes along just in time to talk him down. Matthau had toiled for a decade on television and in movies, mostly in dramatic roles, but in 1962 he had won a Tony for a French farce called *A Shot in the Dark*; now he was determined to make the most of his breakthrough and stalled the *Luv* team with endless demands. His insistence on top billing was the last straw. "Walter is a wonderful actor," Nichtern told Wallach, "but he has a tremendously exaggerated sense of his own importance right now, and it makes him a trouble-maker. He's shot his mouth off all over town, and frankly, his competitiveness frightens me in terms of working out a team of three."

Instead, Nichtern went to Alan Arkin, who had gotten his start in the Second City improv troupe a few years after Nichols left Chicago. Like Matthau, Arkin had recently won a Tony, for his performance in an adaptation of a book by Carl Reiner called *Enter Laughing*; unlike Matthau, he used the award to torture himself rather than others. "Doing what you've hoped to do all your life is frightening," he said. When rehearsals for *Luv* began in September, Nichols's apparent detachment seemed the worst possible match for Arkin's dour, burrowing angst. "I was going through the tortures of the damned," he said, "and he was as calm as a cucumber." Arkin, increasingly enraged, finally stopped mid-rehearsal and said to Nichols, "Why are you so uninvolved in this experience?"

He soon realized that although Nichols "has a way of speaking that avoids passion . . . He feels very deeply." By this point, on his third show in a year, Nichols's unflappable demeanor, which had started as a carefully calibrated defense against a potentially hostile world, was becoming second nature. Actors could have their breakdowns and flare-ups, their tantrums and dejections. He would not; he would, if necessary, bring them to heel by way of his impenetrable, unshakable air of steadiness and certainty. ("I only knew I'd done something wrong during rehearsals, when, from far back in the theater, I heard a very quiet 'Um,'" said Richard Benjamin, who starred in the national tour of

Barefoot in the Park.) Nichols's refusal to overreact—or, at times, to react at all—also bought him time to think. "It's only when rehearsals start, and the characters begin to be people, that I see what's happening and what has to be made stronger," he said. "That's when I begin to have my ideas."

Nichols tackled *Luv* with an almost forensic sense of inquiry, searching scene by scene and sometimes line by line for ways to turn the play from dialogue into real life. Often he would find a way to pair a line with an action that would deepen or complicate its meaning. A scene in which Jackson tells Arkin that she thinks their marriage is in trouble and Arkin replies, "*Our* marriage a *failure?*" didn't work until Nichols told Arkin to say the line while sitting in her lap; it then became the play's biggest laugh. What critics came to see as "the Nichols touch" was, to him, simply how any director should approach his work. "Style," he said, "is a way of doing everything in a play so that all the things called for by the author can actually happen." It was particularly apt for the stage comedies that made his reputation, which can read as arch or artificial; he sought any moment that would allow theatergoers to recognize themselves or others, even fleetingly.

"In *Luv* there's a scene with a woman talking about being lonely as a child, reading, going deeper and deeper inside herself," Nichols said. "If she stands there and says it, it's just a woman talking. If she takes a guy's arm and they walk along the bridge and offstage, and then they come back and she's still talking, what you've seen is a woman who can't *stop* talking about her past and herself. You've seen it physically. That's what I look for, and I wish I found it more often. You must find it for every moment in a play. Every moment must be physically comprehensible—you must see people trying to do things that are not expressed in words. Very often they are the direct opposite of the words." Nichols insisted that he would never suggest a line to a playwright—"from the moment you read a play and like it, you know that the author knows more than anyone in the world about how the characters should speak. You can only question him and punch away in the weak places . . . The same goes for acting. I never want to show them how to do it . . . because the right actor can do it better."

Shortly before his work on *Luv* started, Nichols had begun dating again. His new girlfriend was an up-and-coming freelance magazine journalist who had recently ended a relationship with Robert Benton, then the art director at *Esquire*. Nichols invited her to sit in on some of *Luv*'s rehearsals, and as she watched him work, she was impressed by the way his guidance reshaped the play. "He wasn't dictatorial," says Gloria Steinem. "It was never 'That's wrong, do it my way.' It was 'Okay, that's great, now let's try this.' The play was very insubstantial, but I was entranced, because I had seen it develop. And I was also entranced by the world that he provided a window on." Nichols was deeply attracted to Steinem's intelligence and wit, and, she says, "he was incredibly smart and fun to be with. He got every joke, and that was important to me. And he was appreciative of talent, so he always had interesting friends—Adolph Green and Betty Comden, Julie [Andrews] and Tony [Walton]. I remember wandering around the Village singing on the street with Julie. I mean, I like to think that maybe I was interesting as an individual, but my life was not that interesting then!"

Steinem's career was beginning to move into higher gear, with better assignments and a staff gig on *That Was the Week That Was*, but they both knew, she says, that "at a party or an opening, he was the person people wanted to talk to. And he knew that it was not always sincere. Once we were in the lobby of a theater and there was somebody who was waving at Mike, clearly trying to demonstrate that he knew him. Somehow, in an instant, you knew that this was not a friend, this person yelling, 'Mike, Mike, we have to get together!' across a noisy crowd. Mike waved and smiled and yelled, 'I wouldn't dream of it!' I only once had the nerve to do that myself, but I never forgot it."

Nichols felt strongly that *Luv* was "not a play that everyone is going to like . . . It's a little like those new [European] movies, appealing to the unconscious. You can have a very strange experience watching them. Suddenly you fall into the movie and it becomes your own life and personal experience." When it began performances at Broadway's Booth Theatre, he was not surprised to see about sixty walkouts every night. Older theatergoers were particularly put off. "I was friends with John Kenneth Galbraith and I encouraged him to go," says Steinem. "That was an error, to put it mildly."

"Then [critics] said it was okay to laugh," said Nichols, "and we stopped losing them." The reviews heralded *Luv* as "a delicious spoof on . . . love, marriage, loneliness, lost identity, homosexuality, suicide, housekeeping—you name it." Nichols was hailed by the *New York Post* as "one of the best comedy directors in the world." "He not only knows what is funny," said the *Saturday Review*. "He also knows how to persuade actors to perform it with the right mixture of precision and abandon." Schisgal had to grit his teeth at the many reviews that credited the play to Nichols more than to him. "It is almost a new play," insisted Harold Clurman, who had given the London production a tepid review. Thanks to "Mike Nichols's inventive fancy . . . the gags become cunning notes of imaginative statement, comparable to a fine flourish of ballet movement."

Luv became a standing-room-only hit—Nichols's third concurrent sellout success in New York—and would run for more than two years, its director taking home 3 percent of the box office, or about $1,000 a week. *Barefoot in the Park* had shown critics how Nichols could freshen an old-fashioned comedy; *Luv* was something different—a mordant expression of adult existential despair that did not seem to owe anything to the 1950s—and Nichols's expert stewardship of it marked him as the master of a new comic sensibility. It was a role he was happy to embrace. "I would rather do *Luv* and have some people say, 'I don't get it' than do *Hello, Dolly!*, which offends no one," he said.

In November, *The New York Times* dispatched one of its reporters, Sam Zolotow, to Nichols's apartment. "Joe would like a piece for tomorrow's paper on Mike Nichols, pegged to the great notices received by 'Luv,'" said the assignment memo. "The piece should point up that he has three hits now running—Barefoot, The Knack, Luv—has a couple of movies in the works. Has he been inundated with offers since he's such a hot property? What are his plans? Also, a little personal stuff about him." Nichols obliged. "Is a perfectionist, no tantrums, has a sense of humor that dissolves crises into laughter," Zolotow wrote while talking to him. And beneath it, he scribbled a quick rundown of his priorities: "1) The Odd Couple 2) The Public Eye for Universal 3) The Graduate."

The Odd Couple sat atop the list by default; the script felt close to ready, and Nichols had an available slot. Movies happened more slowly than he thought they would—*The Public Eye*, which had been slated to start filming right after *Luv*'s opening, was now postponed until at least the spring of 1965, and *The Graduate* didn't even have a screenplay. Lawrence Turman had, however, secured a distribution deal for the film—not with a major studio but with Embassy Pictures, an independent company run by Joseph E. Levine, an outsize huckster who had gained a foothold in Hollywood primarily by importing and redubbing *Hercules* films from Italy and selling them with lurid ad campaigns. "I never quite knew that Larry had been to every studio, every outfit," and had been turned down by all of them, said Nichols. "I was still so naive. I certainly knew, though, that in every possible sense, Joseph E. Levine was scraping the bottom of the barrel."

A few weeks later, Nichols added one more project to the list. Jack Warner had bought the film rights to *Who's Afraid of Virginia Woolf?* and hired Ernest Lehman, the veteran screenwriter of *The King and I, North by Northwest,* and *West Side Story,* to write and produce the picture. Warner had wanted Bette Davis—who is the main subject of conversation in the play's first scene—to star with James Mason, but

Lehman wanted Elizabeth Taylor, and Taylor wanted to do it. When she first showed Burton the script, he told her, "Maybe you don't have the power [for the role]. But you've got to play it to stop anybody else from playing it."

"People know how Uta Hagen played it," Lehman told Warner. "They certainly know how Bette Davis would do it. But they wonder how Elizabeth Taylor will do it." Edward Albee protested that the actress, then thirty-two, was "twenty years too young" for the blowsy middle-aged harridan Martha, but he had taken $500,000 from Warner Bros. and signed away creative control and casting approval. The part was Taylor's.

Nichols wanted in, badly. For the first time in his career as a director, he didn't wait for an offer—he went after the job, calling Taylor's press agent and saying, "Tell her I should direct this." "I'm amazed that I had the balls," he said. "And he called me back and said, 'She agrees with you.'" Taylor's desires carried considerable weight with Lehman, who knew that entrusting the decade's most significant play to an untried film director was a risk but also knew that forcing an unwanted choice on Taylor was a greater one. Burton was already hovering around the role of George, and unless he and Taylor got who they wanted behind the camera, Lehman warned Jack Warner, "they'll eat our director alive." By agreeing to Nichols, Lehman knew he could lock in the other half of the world's most famous couple. And Nichols thought Burton was the only choice for the role. "The people in the play loved each other, as they did, and had some complications, as they did. They're there already," he said. Once Burton heard that Nichols was on board, he agreed to costar without hesitation.

On December 12, 1964, Nichols—"our popular hero," as *The New York Times* referred to him when it broke the story—got the job. He would be paid $250,000, a news-making sum for a first-time director. *The Public Eye* and *The Graduate* would have to wait. Nichols would leave for Hollywood right away for two weeks of talks and meetings, come back to New York to direct *The Odd Couple,* and then begin production on *Virginia Woolf* in the summer of 1965. Until recently, he had been garrulous and accessible in interviews. But now, facing a job that daunted him, he retreated once again behind a mask of opaque serenity. All he said was "I'm almost certain it will turn out all right."

Ten

THE FUNNIEST DISTANCE
BETWEEN TWO POINTS

1964–1965

Nichols had always viewed Hollywood with a measure of amused snobbery. He often said that the first spoken line in *The Graduate*—"Ladies and gentlemen, we're about to begin our descent into Los Angeles"—was an intentional encapsulation of its entire theme. To him, L.A. was an oasis of tacky luxury and seductive schlock, a fun place to parachute into for a variety show appearance or a nightclub performance, but only if you left before it started to nibble away at your values. This trip was different; he was there to learn. "I'm more anxious to do films than anything else," he said. "Movies are the best things we have, part of everybody's experience—something you can really share with others." Like a lot of young film buffs, he had little use for the bloated spectacles that the studios were then manufacturing as a bulwark against the popularity of television and felt that the most exciting new work was coming from overseas. "There are movie directors whose toes I couldn't touch in a million years," he said. "Truffaut! Fellini! It's mysterious. They're always reaching for something new."

He arrived in California intending to start a new career, at a moment when the industry's caution about outsiders was just beginning to give way to a hunger for newcomers. Although he was welcomed, he knew, he said, that "if I foul up on the first movie, they'll send me right back." He wasn't embarrassed to ask for guidance, and he got plenty: Veteran filmmakers, most of whom in 1965 were no more excited about current studio product than he was, were eager to meet the upstart from New York whose stage work they had heard so much about, the kid who had gotten a top-tier assignment that everyone thought would go to an eminence like Fred Zinnemann. The actor Norman Lloyd was told by his friend Adolph Green that Nichols felt "fully in control of what he wanted to do with the story [in *Virginia Woolf*], but not of technique." Lloyd responded by setting up a lunch for Nichols with the revered master Jean Renoir, who was then seventy and all but retired. "Don't worry about the technical stuff," Renoir advised. "Stick with the story and the actors—the cameraman will take care of all the rest." "He told Mike how to get through it without committing suicide," says Lloyd.

Billy Wilder reached out to Nichols and invited him to lunch with Joseph L. Mankiewicz and Otto Preminger. Together, the three directors schooled him on everything from the artistic to the strategic to the mundane. Wilder was especially generous with his time. "He was my mentor," Nichols said. "When I got to California, I was worried about what to wear on the set. He said, 'Go with windbreakers and blue jeans.' *Then* I got into 'What is a camera?'" Wilder also gave him a piece of advice about how to allow a narrative adequate space to unfold onscreen, telling him, "Don't forget to leave some string for the pearls." Nichols never forgot it. "It was the most useful thing anyone ever said to me. He meant, connect your masterpiece scenes—tell the fucking story!"

Nichols also met with a filmmaker his own age—Norman Jewison, an affable Canadian who had directed him and May in the quiz-show-scandal sketch for *The Fabulous Fifties* several years earlier and had since become a successful director. Jewison was several months from starting production on *The Russians Are Coming! The Russians Are Coming!* and had questions for Nichols about Alan Arkin, whom he wanted to star in the comedy once his *Luv* contract was up. After they compared notes, Nichols mentioned that he was making lists of actors who might play the young biology professor Nick and his alcoholic wife, Honey, the other two roles in *Who's Afraid of Virginia Woolf?* Jewison suggested that he ask Haskell Wexler, a cinematographer who had a gritty, non-Hollywood visual aesthetic and had recently shot *America America* for Elia Kazan, to film screen tests and possibly be the movie's director of photography.

Just how much sway Nichols would have in choosing the creative team for *Virginia Woolf* was very much in doubt. Early on, he realized that he would be up against both Jack Warner, the aging autocrat who had cofounded the studio forty years earlier, and Ernest Lehman, whom he handled with wary respect in their first meetings but soon came to regard as a kind of surrogate studio executive. (Nichols later referred to him as "the writer-producer who was neither producer nor writer.") In addition, *Virginia Woolf* presented formidable content problems. The Production Code Administration, the industry board that had governed the content of all studio movies for decades, had been on alert ever since Warner Bros. purchased the play. Albee's profane, scabrous language had been a jolt even to sophisticated theater audiences; in mainstream movies, the words his characters tossed around so casually had never been heard. In a memo to the studio, a PCA representative had annotated the playscript and, starting with "Jesus H. Christ," on page 1, flagged every "goddamn," "angel tits," "son of a bitch," and "hump the hostess" as unacceptable. And any off-color language that the Code could be persuaded to let slip would surely run afoul of its religious counterpart, the National Catholic Office for Motion Pictures (long known as the Legion of Decency). A rating of "condemned" from the Church or the denial of a seal of approval from the Code would render a movie version of *Virginia Woolf* unplayable for most theater chains and unreleasable in many cities. Nichols encouraged Lehman to stand firm and defend every epithet but noticed that he was dutifully changing "you bastard" to "you lousy . . ." and doubted he was up to the fight.

One last meeting remained on his schedule: an evening with Ross Hunter, his *Public Eye* producer. Nichols suspected they would be a poor match, and when Hunter proudly told him of his insistence that not a speck of dirt appear in his movies, he barely knew how to respond. Hunter had set up a screening of Jewison's latest picture, the Doris Day–Rock Hudson comedy *Send Me No Flowers,* one of Day's few films in recent years to have been made without Hunter's detail-and-decor-oriented supervision. The two men sat and watched in silence. When the lights came up, Hunter said, "As a producer, I was very offended by it." Nichols replied, "I don't understand, completely." Hunter said, "Well, as a producer, I wanted to rush up to the screen and just rip every bow off her dress."

"I thought, *This is a gag. They're kidding me. I can't possibly work with this guy,*" Nichols said. He calmly returned to his hotel, called his agent, Robert Lantz, and told him to get him out of his contract. "I mean, it would be terrible. It would be hopeless," he said. "I knew I would kill him." Lantz did his job—"There was something unpleasant, a deal in which I owed Universal a movie, one of those things that studios do and then never collect on," Nichols said. "And I think it cost me money, too. But anyway, it was over." He flew back to New York, relieved.

Nichols barely had a moment to relax before beginning work on *The Odd Couple,* which had its first rehearsal on December 28, 1964. Neil Simon had sold him on the inherent comedy of a mismatched pair of middle-aged divorced men in New York City becoming roommates. (His pitch: "They start to treat each other the way they treated their wives.") He had also sold Walter Matthau, who read the script and told his wife he thought it could run for ten years. Matthau was an inveterate and heedless gambler who swung between fortune and serious debt; to him, the play felt like such a sure bet that he told Simon he would invest as well as star—but rather than play the disheveled, ill-tempered Oscar Madison, he wanted to stretch himself by taking on the tidy, neurotic Felix Ungar. "Walter, do me a favor," said Simon. "Act in someone else's play. Do Oscar in mine." For Felix, Simon and Saint-Subber had recruited Art Carney, who had turned to Broadway after a run on television in *The Honeymooners* that had won him three Emmys.

As had been the case with *Barefoot in the Park,* Simon had gotten off to a roaring start without figuring out how to resolve his premise. *The Odd Couple*'s first act—built around a raucous poker game interrupted by the arrival of Felix, whose wife has just kicked him out—was full of laughs, as was its second, which focused on Felix and Oscar's double date with their British neighbors, the Pigeon sisters. But even after several drafts of the third act, Simon hadn't yet found the play's comic boiling point. Nichols assured him he had time; they would try out *The Odd Couple* in Delaware, Boston, and Washington, D.C., before reaching Broadway. That gave Simon almost three months, and he was already rewriting so compulsively that Nichols had to tell him to slow down and at least let the actors try his new material before he decided it wasn't good enough.

At a party on the eve of the first rehearsal, Simon told Nichols he was worried that the play wasn't ready. Nichols, by now accustomed to his forecasts of apocalypse, told him to postpone any judgments until the next morning's read-through.

The Odd Couple was the first play on which Nichols worked with two well-established stars. Carney, who was struggling mightily with alcoholism and his own failing marriage, was a bundle of nerves. Matthau was grouchy, resentful, and certain he knew best about everything. They were perfectly cast. "Art Carney was a saint," said Nichols. "Walter Matthau was not a nice man." When Simon and Nichols gathered their cast of eight to read the play aloud, the first two acts went smoothly. The third, according to Simon, was "unimaginably bad." He and Nichols exchanged glances as "the room grew strangely quiet . . . now we knew where the trouble was."

Matthau announced that the play was "god-awful" and said he was thinking of quitting. Nichols, in no apparent distress, told the ensemble that it "just needed a little tinkering" and suggested that, rather than read the whole thing a second time, they break for lunch, come back, and start working on the first scene. "What do we do?" Simon asked him once the actors had left. "Well, I'm going out to lunch," Nichols said. "You go home and write a new third act."

While Simon wrestled with the ending, Nichols dove into one of the greatest challenges of his career as a theater director: figuring out how to turn a group of men sitting around a table playing poker—one of the most unphysical and inherently untheatrical group activities imaginable—into a tour de force that could carry most of the first act. "One of the things he said that was very valuable was 'At moments when Felix and Oscar are arguing, I don't want the audience to think you've stopped talking to each other at the poker table,'" says Paul Dooley, who understudied Felix and played one of the poker players as well. "'I want them to feel a real game is going on, so deal the cards, and put your bets in, and keep it real.'" The scene became an obsession for Nichols, who, at that point in his young directing career, enjoyed having technical problems to solve—he filled it with gestures, grimaces, and muttering, added and then removed a baseball game playing on TV in the background, layered in jibes, comebacks, and cross talk, phones and doorbells, the lighting of cigars, the making of sandwiches, and the spilling and spraying of beers until he had turned Simon's scene into a hilarious group character study and an intimate portrait of a male ritual. As they refined the scene, he spent half the time on his feet, often running to whisper a note into an actor's ear. When Carney entered, Nichols told him a version of what he had told his *Barefoot in the Park* stars: "I don't want you to think about playing jokes, enhancing jokes, finding something which might be a joke and trying to make it as good as you think it should be," he said. "If there are any jokes, it's because of Neil Simon, and they'll take care of themselves. They don't need you to push. Just play it."

The stakes were high; Nichols himself was so sure of the upside that, for the first time, he had put his own money into a play. And Simon still couldn't find an ending. Two weeks into rehearsal, he returned, triumphantly brandishing a fresh draft of the last act. It was even worse than before. "Go home and try *anything*," Nichols told him. "Try something bad, who knows, it might be good. Something will come. And we have those three and a half hours on the train to Wilmington to talk."

Just before *The Odd Couple* began its Delaware tryout, Nichols took a brief break and went with Steinem to Washington, D.C., for the inauguration of Lyndon Johnson; he and May had agreed to perform at one of the parties. The increasing demands on his professional life had left him with little free time, and his relationship with Steinem had become strained. In Washington, things only got worse. She and Nichols were staying in the same room; when she tried to order food and gave her last name, the operator insisted that she couldn't have anything delivered to Nichols's suite unless she was his wife. Steinem finally had to state that she was, in fact, "Mrs. Nichols" in order to get lunch. When the room service waiter arrived, he smirked at her and said, "Congratulations." It was too much, too shaming. Nichols, who was separated from Margot Callas but not divorced, was already being urged by friends to propose to Steinem; she was not interested in marrying. She felt she and Nichols should break up, but rather than confront him, she started seeing other men. "I somehow began to go out with another friend without being honest about it, and was not truthful," she says. "I regretted that."

Nichols worked with Simon on the train to Delaware, read yet another version of Act III, and said, "I like it. It's not there yet . . . but it's better than what we have now." Simon assumed that they would wait until they got to Boston to try performing it. Nichols surprised him by gathering the cast in Wilmington and telling them he wanted the new material in right away. "Why do a bad third act well when we can do a good third act badly?" he said. "It'll get better each night."

In rehearsals, Matthau had mostly behaved himself, despite grumbling to Louis Zorich, his understudy, that "there were so many changes that at any given time, with the wrong cue I would have been in *Macbeth*." But now, about to perform the play before its first audience, he blew up. "I've never been unprepared in my life and I'm not going to start now," he said. Nichols was amiable but wouldn't budge. "All right, you bastard," Matthau eventually conceded. "I'll go out there and make a fool of myself. But at the curtain call, I'm going to say to the audience, I did my best. Blame this shit on Nichols and Simon."

For the first time, Nichols began to betray some stress. Briefly, he wondered if the poker game—*The Odd Couple*'s one surefire sequence—belonged in the play at all. And he seemed uncharacteristically embarrassed by a scene in which Matthau was onstage without his pants. "Mike was in some ways a very conventional guy," says Ann Roth, his longtime costume designer. "I put Walter in undershorts in Wilmington, and Gloria Steinem was sitting there, and I think he thought, *Why is this man in underwear in front of my guests?* He wasn't as relaxed as he got to be."

The new third act still wasn't right, but audiences clearly liked what they saw well enough that Matthau could keep his curtain-call speech in his pocket and the creative team could exhale. "The play had a different ending every night," said Nichols. "Neil Simon and I, that was the most fun we had."

Carney, who had approached his role studiously and with a great deal of anxiety, began to relax once he knew it was working. Matthau, however, started to chase laughs. "For twenty-five years I've been a serious actor," he said. "Now I want to be a popular actor." Nichols had never before directed a performer who didn't give a damn about his purported genius or the writer's wishes; Matthau was going to do things his own way and would stop at nothing to get the audience on his side. One flashpoint was a scene in which Simon had written the stage direction "Oscar looks to heaven" in exasperation before saying about Felix, "Why doesn't he hear me? I know I'm talking. I recognize my voice." In Boston, Matthau decided it would be funnier to deliver the line to a lady in the second row. During the notes session that takes place after every preview of a play, Nichols said, "Walter, don't do that. Sure, you get a bigger laugh than you would have gotten, because you've broken the fourth wall. But unless the play is full of moments where we break the fourth wall, one time looks really odd, and it takes ten minutes to get the audience back." Matthau nodded, then did it again the next night. Nichols gave him the same note. Matthau glared at him and said, "Well, maybe I'm just not a good enough actor to resist doing that."

"He never stopped," says Dooley, "all the way up to the opening in New York. He never listened to what Mike said, but he had a lot of bullshit answers. I must have heard Mike give the note ten times, until it finally became 'Oh, and Walter: No.' It was Mike's way of telling him, 'I haven't forgotten this point, and you haven't exactly won.' But Matthau did win. He was saying, in effect, 'Look, I'm gonna do this, I'm the star of the show, and once this thing is on Broadway, you'll be leaving.'"

In Boston, almost by accident, Simon came up with what may have been the single best-received joke in his entire body of work, a moment that went halfway to solving the third act. During the climactic fight that results in Felix's departure, he had Oscar say, "You leave me little notes on my pillow! I told you a hundred times, I can't stand little notes on my pillow. 'We're all out of cornflakes. F.U.' . . . It took me three hours to figure out F.U. was Felix Ungar." The laugh the almost dirty line got from a customarily prim Boston audience the first night was so long that even Matthau, who was used to milking every moment, had nothing to do but stand there until it died down.

It was a critic who gave Simon the third-act fix that *The Odd Couple* needed. In the *Boston Record American,* Elliot Norton raved about much of the play, and about Nichols's work as a "cunning manipulator who makes every situation pay off at its comic maximum." But Norton also wrote that "in the third [act] it runs down and out despite the . . . stunning performances of Walter Matthau and Art Carney," a verdict shared by most out-of-town reviewers. In the version of *The Odd Couple* the Boston critics saw, Oscar takes in Felix, kicks him out, realizes he wants him back, and reconciles with him so that at the end Felix can leave on his own terms. It imbalanced the play, which became about Oscar's dilemma, not Felix's—and Norton, who was not averse to giving a playwright or director a note or two, had a private suggestion: He told Simon and Nichols to bring back the Pigeon sisters, the ladies down the hall who had witnessed Felix fall apart just before their blind date in Act II. The idea clicked for Simon right away—"A lightbulb did not go on above my head," he wrote. "It was a two-mile-long neon sign." Felix would get his own happy ending by moving in with the sisters, and Oscar would return to his normal life a slightly better man thanks to his ex-roommate. "Let's play poker!" he barks at his friends in the play's last line, then adds, "And watch your cigarettes, will you? This is my house, not a pig sty."

With a viable third act finally in place, and the cast getting through it with increasing confidence, *The Odd Couple* sailed through its

Washington, D.C., tryout and into New York. But Matthau wasn't done causing chaos. He would throw off the poker players by muttering during their lines. When Nichols cut a moment Matthau liked, he snapped, "Mike, you're emasculating me. Can I have my balls back now?" ("Props!" Nichols yelled in response.) And Matthau saved a special punishment for his insecure costar just before the Broadway opening. "I was restaging something, just a little something, and I said, 'Art, I like it when you come downstage and do this,' and Matthau said, 'Mike, don't you think Art is a little *faggy* when he does that?'" Nichols recalled. "And I [thought], *Thanks for fucking up our opening night.* That was his approach."

The Odd Couple opened at the Plymouth Theatre, next door to *Luv*, on March 10, 1965. *Barefoot in the Park* was still riding high well into its second year, and *The Knack* hit its first anniversary with no signs of slowing. Nichols had his fourth hit in eighteen months. The poker game was hailed as a master class in staging—Walter Kerr wrote that the Moscow Art Theater, then in New York, could learn a lot from its specificity and verisimilitude—and, as Nichols suspected he would, Matthau had unsettled Carney just enough to walk off with the reviews. (The play would win Matthau his second Tony; Carney would not be nominated.)

Most of the notices hailed Nichols as "a sorcerer, a wizard, a prestidigitator." But a few sounded a note of skepticism about patterns they had started to notice. "All of Nichols's trademarks are on exhibition: if a can of beer is opened, it is sure to spritz everybody in sight; if spaghetti appears, it will inevitably wind up on the wall; if someone has to cross a crowded room, the funniest distance between two points is always a straight line—over furniture, laps, and other actors' lines. What Nichols . . . does with great skill is keep his performers' timing at the most precise pitch," but ultimately, *Newsweek*'s review argued, he "imparts muscle to what he touches, but not soul."

———

To some degree, Nichols may have shared that dissenting assessment. It had been a frantic and pressured two years, and his face-offs with Matthau had made *The Odd Couple* a markedly less pleasant experience than the three plays preceding it. Although he was full of compliments for his stars in the interviews he did, when a reporter told him that Matthau had announced his intention to trade parts with Carney, he no longer bothered to hide his impatience. "It is a bad idea," he said. "I thought it was a bad idea the first time he broached it, I will continue to think it is a bad idea, and by no means will I allow them to switch roles next year."

Nichols's depression started to loom again, as it sometimes did at moments of respite, and became more and more public. "I'm bored in the theater, at other people's plays and my own," he told *Newsweek* soon after the opening. And to the *Times* of London: "Why is my pleasure gone?" He said he felt numb. "Here I am with plays on Broadway and money and an apartment," he told Steinem. "Why don't I feel anything? Maybe I should throw it all away, turn my back on it." Her tart reply: "You know, all this bitching you do . . . is just a safety valve that allows you to keep doing it. You don't have to throw it away. You just have to keep doing things that scare you."

Nichols had a chance to test that premise soon after *The Odd Couple* opened, when May called him and told him they should go to Alabama to perform for the civil rights protesters who were marching from Selma to the state capital in Montgomery. The marches had been going on for two weeks, and the brutality with which state troopers and local racist militia had reacted was filling national newscasts. Nichols had been scheduled to leave for Hollywood to start preproduction on *Who's Afraid of Virginia Woolf?* He called Ernest Lehman, who warned him to stay away from political controversy.

May didn't ask for much, but when she did, she meant business. "I said to Elaine, 'He won't let me.' And she said, 'You're going.' So I had to go," said Nichols. "Mike was aware of the violence, and he was a bit concerned," says Steinem. "But I remember him deciding to go."

In Alabama, Nichols, May, and the other celebrities who had traveled from New York and Los Angeles—Sammy Davis Jr., Harry Belafonte, Leonard Bernstein, James Baldwin, Shelley Winters, Anthony Perkins, Peter, Paul, and Mary—"were met by a guy," Nichols recalled, "who gave us each a dime to call the FBI in case anything went wrong. Really? Calling the FBI from a pay phone? Is that the best way to be safe?" That night, on a makeshift outdoor stage in sweltering heat, Nichols and May, scripts still in hand, performed a version of their telephone sketch, this time about Governor George Wallace, played by Nichols, trying to get past a bored operator to reach President Johnson:

Nichols (*as Wallace*): It costs a lot of money to keep all those people in jail.

May (*repeating*): Costs a lot of money . . . to keep all those people . . . in jail.

Nichols: Not to mention the upkeep on the billy clubs . . . and the cattle prodders . . . and the bullwhips . . .

May: Bullwhips?

Nichols: Bullwhips is right.

May: Is that two words or one?

Nichols: It's one.

May: One word. Yes, sir.

Nichols: And the police themselves cost a lot of money . . .

May (*repeating*): Police cost money . . .

Nichols: Even though some of them take very little and just do it for the sheer love of the work!

When Nichols got back to New York, he turned his attention to the last two roles in *Who's Afraid of Virginia Woolf?* For Nick, the jockish, always-a-beat-behind teacher who becomes Martha's lover during the long night in which the play's action unfolds, Nichols approached Robert Redford, and was jolted when the actor turned him down flat. It's possible that, having suffered the loss of an infant, Redford found the idea of an evening of cruel psychological gamesmanship about an invented baby profoundly unappealing. Nichols's take was that he didn't want to play a character whose weaknesses made him a target for scorn and mockery. "I was never a fan of the play," Redford says. "At that point I felt, *This is not an honest play, and I don't want to be in it.* I was wrong on many levels, but that was my standpoint at the time."

Nichols then turned to George Segal, who seemed "close enough to the young god he needed to be for Elizabeth, and witty enough and funny enough to deal with all that humiliation." Taylor had casting approval, so Nichols set up a private performance of *The Knack* for her. "Elizabeth and [her ex-husband] Michael Wilding sat on two folding chairs to watch, and that's how I got the part," Segal says. Taylor's next stop was a Broadway comedy called *Any Wednesday,* one of many plays Nichols had been offered after *Barefoot in the Park.* The show's star, Sandy Dennis, had never come close to a major movie role, but she had won Tony Awards for two years in a row, and her stage work was strong enough to move her up Nichols's list past Barbara Harris, whom he had wanted to work with again since his Compass days, and Melinda Dillon, who had originated the role onstage. Warner Bros. was not as certain. Dennis was not conventionally pretty ("her stomach protrudes," Ernest Lehman complained), and she had an eccentric, halting delivery; onstage, if she didn't like the way a line sounded as she was saying it, she would simply start again. But Nichols took Jewison's advice and hired Wexler to shoot her screen test. Lehman and Warner were convinced that she could play the "mousey little thing with no hips," as Martha refers to her. *Virginia Woolf*'s cast was complete.

While Nichols was on the road with *The Odd Couple,* he had, at Avedon's urging, hired the interior decorator Billy Baldwin to furnish his penthouse. He now had the showplace apartment he had always wanted, and no time to spend in it. As soon as casting was finished, he packed up and moved across the country to Tower Grove, the Spanish-style mansion in Benedict Canyon that he had rented from David O. Selznick. Over the next nine months, he would be too immersed in moviemaking to spend any time in New York. He would make a quick trip back in the spring, but only to collect his second consecutive Tony Award for Best Director of a Play, this time for his work on both *Luv* and *The Odd Couple.* He thanked his casts and his scenic and lighting designers, whom he said were collectively "responsible for most of my distinctive director's touches." "By the way," the announcer said as Nichols quickly exited the stage, "he's directing a movie, *Who's Afraid of Virginia Woolf?* He's hard at work on it at this very moment!"

By then, after a month in Los Angeles, Nichols had overruled his writer-producer, fired his first cinematographer, and told the head of the studio he was quitting unless he got what he wanted—all before a foot of film had been shot. Decades later, he would wonder at his own bravado. "I was so sure I knew what to do," he said. "I never was again."

Eleven

I WANT TO KNOW
THIS PLACE
1965-1966

In his first days working on *Who's Afraid of Virginia Woolf?* Nichols felt very much alone. His four stage productions had been group efforts, and he loved the creative churn and hum of a rehearsal space full of actors and designers; he would take a good suggestion from anyone in the room. But there was no such room on *Virginia Woolf,* nor was there a team. Elizabeth Taylor and Richard Burton would not arrive in Los Angeles until just a couple of days before rehearsals. Until then, Nichols would have to contend with the vaguely menacing abstraction of a movie studio, and with the various unfamiliar professionals—cinematographer, production designer, costume designer, editor—who were being urged on him. It was hard to tell friend from foe.

That was true even when it came to Ernest Lehman, who presented himself as an eager ally but who sometimes seemed to want to make an altogether different movie than the one Nichols was envisioning. Lehman's earliest draft of the *Virginia Woolf* screenplay included a change intended to placate that portion of the theater audience that the play had bewildered or annoyed. He had gotten rid of the nonexistent child

George and Martha pretend to have in their game of "Get the Guests," a chimera George ultimately uses against Martha in a climax that lays bare the ways in which shared fictions can both sustain and destroy a relationship. In Lehman's reworking, they were now the parents of a real son who had hanged himself in a closet that they then boarded up as a representation of everything repressed and unspoken in their lives. What had been a symbol of the ineffable bond in their broken relationship had become the kind of thuddingly literal "dark secret" that melodramas had trafficked in for decades.

"I, first gently and then not very, explained that that wasn't going to be possible," said Nichols. "It was immaterial whether it was criticized [onstage] or not. What you see when you find out about the imaginary child is how much they love each other . . . You can't take all that out." Nichols wrested the script from Lehman and systematically restored as much of Albee's text as he could.

Lehman felt insulted—he had wanted to produce the film because he "was sick and tired of having someone else always take over my baby . . . and Mike Nichols promptly took over my baby. Becoming a producer is a false solution to a writer's ego problems," he concluded. Nichols's attitude didn't help. "I didn't have the patience," he admitted. "I would get pissed off . . . more than I needed to be." They quarreled over everything from Lehman's idea that the movie should open with a scene of two dogs having sex ("This must be beautifully shot," he had noted optimistically) to whether Burton should wear eyeglasses. "Ernie was whining, 'I don't like his glasses,'" said Sam O'Steen, the film editor who would become one of Nichols's closest creative partners. "Mike said . . . that they fit Burton's character. So Ernie said, 'Well, what if it comes to the last day and we have to go one way and I don't want him to wear glasses?' 'Well,' said Mike, 'I'll kill you.'"

To his credit, Lehman, who was so worried about the movie that he took to popping prescription methamphetamines to get through the day, never turned against Nichols, in part because he recognized that they were similar. Both men were taking on roles with unfamiliar responsibilities, and both were hypersensitive to public displays of respect or perceived slights. In June of 1965, they flew to Massachusetts to scout locations—although the play unfolds entirely during a long, boozy night at George and Martha's house on a college campus, they wanted to open the action out to include the backyard as well as a local roadhouse. On the way back to the airport, Nichols opened up for the first time.

"He told me when he got into the car that he was slightly loaded, and I could really detect the fumes," Lehman wrote in his diary. "He said he felt a few little wisps of bad feeling between us. He had heard rumors that I was upset about all the publicity he was getting and wanted to assure me that he didn't seek publicity. I assured him that it was neurotic of me to be upset . . . He also brought up the fact that he has been going through some slightly neurotic feeling about, oh, things that happen when we arrive at airports . . . Mike has been feeling slighted because of possibly five percent more attention being paid to me by the person who met us to handle the baggage . . . It was a pretty weird conversation."

While he awaited his stars, Nichols retreated into himself. He screened movies obsessively—*A Place in the Sun,* to convince himself that Taylor could manage a difficult role, Truffaut's *The 400 Blows,* to remind himself of what a novice director could do, *A Streetcar Named Desire,* for proof that a play could work on film, and, most often, Fellini's *8½.* Four times during preproduction he returned to the portrait of a director as romantic antihero, both solitary and besieged, connecting to nothing but his own creative instincts. For a while, he believed it was the best movie ever made.

One of those screenings precipitated his first serious showdown with Warner Bros. By 1965, black-and-white movies were all but extinct; the advent of television had hastened a shift to color, and only a handful of directors—Billy Wilder, Martin Ritt, Stanley Kramer, Sidney

Lumet—were still insisting that black-and-white was the best aesthetic choice for serious films. From the start, Nichols knew *Virginia Woolf* had to be in black-and-white, for reasons both practical—the makeup required to age Taylor would look garish in color—and artistic. "Here's the thing about black-and-white," he said. "It's not literal. It is a metaphor, automatically . . . and that's the point: A movie *is* a metaphor. If it's in black-and-white, it's partly solved—it's already saying, 'No, this is not life, this is something *about* life.'"

Jack Warner wasn't interested in metaphors. To him, color meant modernity and, more to the point, revenue—and he had given Nichols a cinematographer who he thought would bring him around. Harry Stradling had won Oscars for his work in both black-and-white (for *The Picture of Dorian Gray,* in 1945) and color (for *My Fair Lady,* just before being assigned to *Virginia Woolf*). Nichols respected his experience— after all, he had shot *A Streetcar Named Desire*—but not his taste. He invited both Stradling and Haskell Wexler to watch *8½* with him, and after the movie ended, Stradling, "in his usual candid way, said, 'I think that film was a piece of shit.' Nichols was very upset," said Wexler, "and he looked over at me." The final straw was Stradling's pitch for a compromise: They could shoot *Virginia Woolf* in color and print it in black-and-white, an idea Nichols knew meant that Stradling was working primarily in the interests of the studio. The trepidation he had felt when he got to Los Angeles a few weeks earlier, when he had told Lehman he was "absolutely overwhelmed with anxiety," had given way to a determination not to be thwarted. "Oh, Harry," he said. "I'm so sorry. I have to fire you."

Nichols and Lehman ended up in Jack Warner's office, where he told them, "Boys, I'm sorry, but the movie has to be in color." Nichols said, "The sets are built. The costumes are made. The makeup would never hold up." Warner held firm. Nichols replied, "Well, you do it then. I like it at home. I'll just go home."

"I was perfectly happy not to do it, and he could see that, and he said, 'All right, all right, all right,'" said Nichols. Warner told him he could hire Wexler and shoot *Virginia Woolf* in black-and-white. "I was a real snot," said Nichols. "That's how I started out. I have no idea why. But when dealing with studio heads, there's nothing wrong with that."

When Taylor and Burton got to Los Angeles, they were embroiled in the latest installment of a worldwide soap opera that they professed to loathe even while feeding it with every move. In the two years since *Cleopatra*, each new movie they made together played as a self-consciously teasing window on their relationship, a chance for audiences to see them enact fictional elements of the real-life melodrama in which they seemed permanently and consensually engaged. In the latest install-ment, the glossy melodrama *The Sandpiper*, Taylor played an unwed mother and free-spirited artist in Big Sur who attracts her young son's headmaster, an anguished Episcopal priest played by Burton. As they arrived, the film was just opening, to scornful reviews.

Taylor told Lehman that she and Burton thought the picture was "a pile of crap, and that they had done it only for the money." Both actors knew that *Virginia Woolf*, a behind-closed-doors portrait of two mar-ried people locked in combat that was sometimes performative and sometimes real, ran the risk of playing as yet another commodification of their (barely) private lives. If so, Burton said, at least audiences would "stay, not run out of the theater the way they're doing at *The Sandpiper*." They hoped Nichols would not only keep them on track but, when necessary, stand up to them. "I have actually seen people shiver as they cross the room to be introduced to Elizabeth," Burton wrote in his diary. "What the hell is it? . . . I know that we are both dangerous but we are fundamentally very nice. I mean we only hurt each other."

Nichols was closer to Burton than to Taylor, but in the years since he first visited her in Rome during *Cleopatra*, he had seen them to-gether often enough to understand what he was facing. She was a movie star desperate to be seen as an actress; he was an actor who craved stardom but who "wasn't pleased with himself for the way he ended up as part of an international marriage scandal that was perpetual," Nichols said. While Lehman handled the elaborate niceties to which they had become accustomed ("I could have written one-half of a screenplay with the creative energy that went into the . . . notes that I enclosed with the fruit baskets or champagne gifts or flower arrangements," he said), Nichols began to feel his way toward a working relationship with Taylor. He developed a light, jokey rapport with her, and came to admire the way she was willing to turn "the world's most beautiful eyes [into] those of a tired woman who drinks a great deal, whose makeup smears and mascara runs."

Nichols was still uncertain about the technical basics of filmmaking and was too embarrassed to ask rookie questions of Wexler, who could be witheringly dismissive. "I did my investigating on the most childish level," Nichols said. "I was friends with Tony Perkins, and . . . I said, 'There's nobody else I can ask. I know I want to start with them coming through the door, coming at the camera, and I know I want to be very close to Elizabeth when she comes in and then to Richard. But won't the door hit the camera?' This was my level of sophistication. And then he reminded me about lenses, and I said, 'Oh, yeah, right, right, of course.'" In just three days, Nichols said, "he explained the principles of photography to me."

Nichols was more comfortable with production design—something for which, at least, an analogous job existed in theater. Steinem recommended that he hire her friend Richard Sylbert, an art director who, like Nichols, had grown up in New York in a Jewish family of modest means and reinvented himself as a man of impeccable taste and no apparent origins. They became fast friends and would work together for the next decade. Nichols's conception of George and Martha derived in part from memories of his own parents' fights—although those weren't "as searching, or vicious," he said—and in part from a Chicago couple he had known who were prone to horrific brawls. It was their house that he wanted Sylbert to put onscreen: "I said . . . 'You gotta have these bookshelves, with the bricks, and the boards on the bricks . . . I want to know this place.'" Sylbert not only understood; he chose every volume on George and Martha's headboard shelf, including, as an inside joke, a copy of *Summerhill: A Radical Approach to Child Rearing.* "The titles were all very pertinent and even witty," says Sylbert's former wife, the writer Susanna Moore. "All those details that Dick attended to regardless of whether anyone would notice them or not—that was something Mike esteemed." (In a wink to his best friend, Nichols made a design contribution of his own, adorning George and Martha's living room and bedroom with Avedon's portraits of Marianne Moore and Isak Dinesen.)

Three days before rehearsals began, Nichols went to a Fourth of July party thrown by Jane Fonda and Roger Vadim, who had opened their Malibu home to both old and new Hollywood and invited the Byrds to play. He knew few of the guests personally. As he wandered between the house and the beach, he spotted a few people he had met in New York, including Warren Beatty, who had asked Nichols to direct him in the comedy *What's New, Pussycat?* But he was shy about approaching the industry lions—Henry Fonda, Gene Kelly, William Wyler—who had gathered indoors, away from the noisy oceanside rock and roll. A few years earlier, Nichols might have viewed the Hollywood ritual unfolding before him with ironic detachment. That was largely gone. He was not starstruck, but he was star-conscious, and everywhere he turned, another famous face reminded him that, to the extent he was now on Hollywood's A-list, it was entirely on spec—almost alone among the partygoers, he was a man without a movie credit to his name, and with a great deal to prove.

By the night before the first rehearsal, his practiced air of calm had deserted him. At Lehman's house, sitting beside his pool, Nichols railed at him for not following Jack Warner's instinct and casting Bette Davis. Taylor was too young, too soft, not enough of an actress. "It's like asking a chocolate milkshake to do the work of a double martini," he complained. Lehman was too preoccupied to talk Nichols off the ledge. Warner was paying the Burtons huge sums—$1.1 million for her, $750,000 for him, a combined fee that equaled the entire budget of some movies—and the studio had instructed Lehman to treat them like royalty. Their custom-built "dressing room" on the lot was essentially an entire private house—each of their suites included its own kitchen and piano, with a common living room. Burton's side was stocked with cases of champagne, Scotch, and cognac; Taylor's was to be regularly resupplied with white roses and lilies of the valley. (An assistant to Burton hilariously warned Lehman to keep everything "moderate and in good taste.")

"I've never seen people treated like that," says George Segal. "There was a list that went out, a sheet that was distributed to all personnel at Warner Bros., titled 'How to Treat the Burtons.' Number 10 was 'Don't greet the Burtons unless they greet you first.' In other words, don't talk to them."

Burton and Taylor were by then so familiar with the level of barely suppressed panic their fame caused that they knew it was their job to put everyone at ease. They arrived casually dressed and with no entourage; Burton made small talk while Taylor, proudly overweight, showed off her belly to Sandy Dennis. Nichols had insisted on three weeks of rehearsals and was stunned when Taylor told him that in twenty years and three dozen movies, no director had ever asked her to rehearse. That morning, Nichols, Lehman, and the actors sat down, poured Bloody Marys, and read the script aloud from beginning to end.

Taylor took to the new experience avidly; she loved the process, even though Burton didn't hesitate to upbraid her—her voice was too high, she didn't understand a transition, she was missing the point of the scene! "They had a real student-teacher relationship," says Segal. "He had her reciting E. E. Cummings and Dylan Thomas." It was sometimes hard for those in the room, including Nichols, to tell if they were witnessing two actors getting into character or the fracturing of a marriage. "Elizabeth and I were quite frightened," Burton admitted after the film wrapped. "However much we tried to be logical or pragmatic and say, 'It's just a job' . . . I went into it with . . . dread that something would happen between [us] because of the nature of the piece."

Taylor, however, was nobody's doormat. While Burton provided acting lessons, she offered a tutorial in stardom. Before the movie's press day, when the cast was to be introduced before sixty photographers, she told Lehman, "You must be sure to tell the press that you and Mike ordered me to get fat, to stuff myself and drink malted milks between meals for the realism of the role. I don't want them to get the idea that I'm overweight and sloppy simply because I don't know any better." She refused Nichols's request to wear rubber prosthetics under her eyes to give her bags. And eventually, she became confident enough to confront Nichols and Lehman about the roadhouse scene, which she felt was a violation of the intentional confinement of the play. When Lehman dismissed her objection as "intellectual," she replied, "Why, thank you, Ernie, for calling me an intellectual." She didn't get her way on that point, but "politically, she ran the production," Segal says, "and she made it comfortable for Mike."

Because Burton sometimes treated her roughly, Nichols played good cop, reassuring her, teasing her, making it an adventure; once he had the cast rehearse all night so they would know how the characters felt on their midnight-to-dawn journey. Booze and food were constants: While Burton's and Taylor's appetites did not derail rehearsals, they certainly reshaped them. Over the three weeks, the 9 a.m. start time rolled toward 10 a.m. and, if hangovers were severe enough, later; it was understood that "lunch hour" was a euphemism for a period during which the Burtons would entertain visitors and possibly demolish much of the afternoon, depending on which eminence happened to be in town. "He would yell at her, she would cry, and then the Duke and Duchess of Windsor would come to the set and take them to lunch, and they'd come back hours late," said Nichols. There were days when little progress was made.

Nevertheless, rehearsals proved as valuable for Nichols as for his stars. "It gave me a chance . . . to understand what the keys to *them* were," he said. "Elizabeth is very, very physical. What helps her is to know where she'll be, what she'll be wearing, and so forth—the business. And I'm good at business—it's what I used to do for Neil Simon . . . Richard is about the sound. He would say, 'How should I say it? Say it for me' . . . We found each other through rehearsals." Nichols also made some important decisions about the movie's tone and pacing. "In *Virginia Woolf*, there's a laugh about every 20 seconds," he said, "and part of the problem of seeing it onstage is that it's broken up into little pieces. To a great extent, emotion and tension are discharged in laughter. [But] you don't stop or slow down for laughs in movies. Therefore, the movie would have to be far more emotional than the play. The recruiting of the audience as a participant in the battle was no longer possible . . . That prizefight element of the play was gone, which left me with the heart of it."

On the morning of July 28, 1965, he stood next to Wexler behind the camera, so tense and braced that Taylor finally said gently, "I can't act until you say 'Action.'" With that, his career as a movie director began. "You prepare your ass off," Nichols said, "and then when you're ready to shoot, you throw it all away and see what has stuck."

From the minute the camera rolled, any tentativeness Taylor had evinced in rehearsal was replaced by a confidence that surprised Nichols. She "can keep in her mind fourteen dialogue changes, twelve floor marks and ten pauses," he said. Taylor seemed to inhabit Martha with ease; she developed what she called a "stumpy walk" for the character that changed her entire body language and threw herself into Martha's high-volume belligerence without faltering. She also knew how to protect herself: Every morning, she would tell Wexler, "I know I'm not supposed to look good, but don't go *too* far," and give him a long, warm hug. "I had my light meter on my belt and I'd say, 'You're crushing my light meter,'" said Wexler. "And she'd say, 'You keep doing well by me and I'll crush it every morning.'"

Segal proved a generous and flexible scene partner, and it was clear from the start that Dennis was doing exceptional work as the awkward, chattery, ever more intoxicated Honey. "She was brilliant at extreme states," said Nichols. "The glory of Sandy was whatever she was playing, she was funny at least part of the time. Because of Elaine May, I used to define great acting as somebody being inside a person and out at the same time—they could make a case for the person but also discreetly point out some of the flaws. Anything that was alive, she would go with, which for movies is great." Of the four, it was Burton who now felt the most reliant on his director's guidance. But Nichols loved doing the kind of specific, text-based work he wanted. "His behavior, his manner, are silky soft," said Burton. "He appears to defer to you, then in the end gets exactly what he wants. He conspires with you rather than directs you . . . He'd make me throw away a line where I'd have hit it hard . . . and he was right every time."

The contracts for both stars stipulated that, except for night shoots, they wouldn't work before ten or after six; their epic meal breaks, which continued from rehearsal straight through the film's production, would eventually drive *Virginia Woolf* hugely over budget and thirty days over schedule. The delays incensed Nichols—"He'd walk around saying, 'Cocksuckers, I hate their fuckin' guts,'" said O'Steen. But for the most part, he greeted their idiosyncrasies with strategic equanimity. "We never got a shot before lunch," Nichols said. "The Burtons are immensely powerful. If they want to come on the set at 12:30, there's very little you can do. There were times when I wanted Elizabeth to do retakes. She could have said no. Instead, she'd say, 'Goddamnit, do I have to do that whole thing again?' I'd say, 'Yes, I screwed up,' and she would." Nichols also kept a watchful eye on whether his stars started to critique each other. "I [knew] from having had a partner, that's a great danger," he said. But once shooting began, "they [didn't] . . . get into each other's performances."

Many aspects of the job still flummoxed him. Initially, O'Steen said, "Mike just wet his pants. He was sweating it out." He had decided to shoot *Virginia Woolf* in sequence as much as possible, and at first nothing worked. He planned an opening-credits montage of Taylor and Burton walking home across campus in long shot; audiences would not see their faces until they entered their house, a moment Nichols wanted to have the impact of a star entrance onstage. The opening shot of them coming through the door took Wexler four hours to set up; only then did Nichols realize he had had Sylbert put the door hinges on the wrong side for the shot he needed. "I wanted to cry," Nichols said. "I thought, oh my God, here I am making a film and I can't even get them through the front door. I turned to [Wexler] and said, 'Get me out of this hole.' And he did."

Just before production, Billy Wilder had told Nichols to have Doane Harrison, an editor since the silent era, on the set to tell him what angles he would need to cut a scene together. Within a week, "he left because I didn't follow his scheme," said Nichols. "What he didn't know is I didn't *understand* his scheme. I could only shoot what I knew was happening, and it seemed to me there was only one place the camera could be." Instead Nichols turned to O'Steen, who edited scenes every weekend and also taught him how to shoot overlapping dialogue, which was not part of Albee's play but which Nichols felt was necessary to keep the film moving.

Every morning, Nichols tried to remind himself that he was the general and the film was a campaign. "Wake up!" he would bark at himself in the mirror. "You're directing a picture with the Burtons!" That rarely worked; he had never been sharp early in the day and was lucky that his two stars bought him time by arriving late as often as they did. His need to indulge them left him with little patience for anyone else's slackness. In theater, failures were affordable; every day offered a new opportunity to do it again, to do it better, to find a solution. "A week later I say, 'Let's take these lines out,' or the actors find something to add, or the playwright says, 'Listen, let's have him do so-and-so.' There's a reassuring feeling that you have time," Nichols said. "[On a movie] you have to do it *now*, and then move on."

As difficult as their habits made them, Taylor and Burton proved staunch protectors of his interests. Nichols often told a story that, at the end of the first week, he heard an assistant director mutter, "Oh, well, it's just another picture" after a bad take and fired him on the spot. In fact, it was Taylor who heard the remark; she had been watching the AD undermine Nichols to the rest of the crew for days and believed Nichols was unaware of it. She went to Lehman and told him that she and Burton wanted the AD off the picture immediately. Lehman, treating it as "a major emergency," did as she said.

"I had done films before," said Wexler, "but they hadn't seemed to put this emotional or psychological or professional pressure on me . . . I believe that I helped somewhat in framing and saying what shots were necessary . . . but every day, Mike would learn more than some directors learn in years of shooting." Nichols's sense that he was taking a risk—pushing two stars past their limits with raw, angry, often ugly material—became one of his prime motivations. When Lehman asked him why he wasn't shooting alternate, milder versions of scenes with lines like "Screw you" that would never pass the Production Code, Nichols said, "Because if I do, you'll use them." And with time, he became more adventurous with the camera. Wexler would try anything—overhead shots, handheld work, extreme close-ups, long takes in constant motion. Once he even roped himself to Burton for a scene in which George spins around the living room while dancing.

In August, the cast and a crew of sixty flew east for what was supposed to be two weeks (it became four) of night shooting on the Smith College campus, a location Steinem had suggested to Nichols. Lehman had chartered a plane for the trip. By then, Nichols had started to learn the political necessity of camaraderie with the crew. "There was a first-class section for Elizabeth, Richard, Ernie, me, and Sandy and George, and then a curtain," said Nichols. "I said, 'Ernie, what have you done? You have kicked this production in the balls and we're not even off the ground. Now open the fucking curtain and let's go in the back.'" Public curiosity about the movie was so fevered that in Northampton it took seventy security guards to keep onlookers away from 8:30 at night to 5 a.m. One evening, Taylor slipped off to the movies; "Elizabeth's gone to see *What's New, Pussycat?* with ten policemen," Burton told a reporter.

"They tried to tell me I could have done it all on a back lot," Nichols said. "I was too stupid to know that we could've." But in truth, he was happy to be three thousand miles from the Warner executive suite and to enjoy a temporary end to the stream of studio notes telling him that the dailies looked too dark or grim or shaky. At first, the shoot felt familial. There were cookouts and parties; Nichols shared a house with Segal and his family, and Burton and Taylor had four of their children with them. But soon enough, it became an ordeal. They were slowed by rain, by fog, by perfectionism, by Taylor's sudden illnesses and Burton's frequent benders. Neither star was used to the rigors of one all-night shoot after another, and Nichols, with every beat of the movie already taking shape in his mind, drove them through take after take until she was weeping and he was shaking. Burton's alcoholism was so severe that there were nights, Nichols recalls, when he said, "I can't act," and they would have to shoot around him. "When Richard was drinking, he was difficult," Nichols said. "But he wasn't vicious, he was unhappy." Taylor, too, was pushed to her limits. During a fight scene in a parking lot outside the roadhouse, Burton shook her so hard that she hit her head on the roof of the car she was leaning against and nearly blacked out. Nichols kept it in the movie.

Lehman felt out of his element and grew more paranoid by the week. There was endless waiting as the setups were lit—Wexler's deliberation and exactitude, though it yielded extraordinary results, was slowing the process so much that Nichols swore he would never work with him again. "He became my nemesis," he said. "I really, really disliked him." Dennis and Taylor would pass the time with belching contests. And Nichols would while away hours playing long rounds of anagrams with Segal and whoever had come to visit—Steinem, Sondheim, Tony Perkins. One night Lehman arrived on location late and asked Nichols, who was playing memory games with three Smith students, if anything had gotten done yet. "They wouldn't shoot without telling you," one girl assured him. "This bunch would not only shoot it, they would edit it, cut it, premiere it, distribute it, and sell it to television without telling me," Lehman replied in front of a visiting reporter and walked off. "Ernie's a lot of fun," Nichols remarked once he had gone.

After watching dailies with O'Steen in the wine cellar of the Northampton Inn, which they used as a cutting room, Nichols would end some workdays at dawn, slumped in a diner, as exhausted as his stars. "I'd like somebody from another planet to come down and adopt me, to give me toys, to clean up after me," he moped. He turned to a waitress and said, "That cake over there, you see the one? Well, I'd like just the frosting off it." He had gained ten pounds. Of the crew, he told a reporter, "You will notice that all of them are watching my every move. They are waiting for me to screw up. And I will."

Burton got more frightened as his personal Everest neared—a long confessional monologue to Nick about a tragedy involving a teenage boy that Nichols had set in the backyard of their house. In the play, it is the only sustained passage during which George appears to drop his guard. It was a challenge Burton dreaded. Lehman objected to the slow, dialogue-free shift to the yard that Nichols planned to precede the speech; Nichols insisted on it, understanding that at that point—which coincided with the play's first intermission—audiences would require a stretch of silence, a brief respite from listening.

The closer Burton got to shooting the speech, the more certain he was that he couldn't do it; the greater his fear, the more he drank. Nichols knew how hard it would be, and he gave Segal his direction in advance in order to be sure that Burton would have his undivided attention during filming.

"We did it over and over, with Nichols watching and maybe giving a little nudge to Burton now and then," Segal said.

"Richard was not so great at remembering long things at this point," said Nichols. "He was terrified, and I didn't let on, but I was terrified, [because] I knew it should be in one [take] . . . Richard stumbled around and he did a few takes and then the thing happened that you pray for— he did this perfect, beautiful, very moving version. He just did it perfectly. We were thrilled, and I kissed him and said, 'God bless you.' Well, the next day, it turned out that Haskell had miscalculated the exposure . . . It looked like high noon. And I said, 'Haskell, he's not gonna ever do it again as well as that. You've got to just dupe it and dupe it and dupe it [in order to darken it], whatever you need to do.' Which he did, and it's not bad . . . That's one of the things I learned: If you said, 'This is it, sorry,' there was recourse."

Sondheim was on the set that night, and after the shoot, Nichols invited him to watch some footage they had shot earlier, in an impromptu screening room they had set up with a white sheet in a nearby school. "You won't believe how great Elizabeth is," Nichols told him. "Richard is fine, he always is, but she is fabulous."

"We watched the first five minutes of the film, sitting side by side," Sondheim said. "I did not open my mouth or move my body. The lights came up and he read my mind. He turned to me and said, 'She's terrible, and he's terrific, right?' His sensitivity to people around him was so keen. Believe me, I didn't do anything to give away what I was thinking. I had intended to say, 'Wonderful, wonderful, my God, how exciting for you.' But he knew."

In Nichols's theater circles, skepticism about whether Taylor could pull off such a difficult role had run deep since her casting was announced. Nichols himself oscillated between optimism and despair, and knew he had asked for trouble by showing Sondheim the first scene he had shot, when both he and Taylor were still finding their way. When the cast and crew returned to Los Angeles to finish the movie, he felt shaken. The performances in the original stage production were never far from his mind, and after listening one time too many to Uta Hagen and Arthur Hill on the Broadway cast recording, he called Lehman and said, "I'm very depressed . . . Here's what I think is going to happen . . . Sandy Dennis is going to be fine . . . George Segal is going to be fine. Richard is absolutely going to walk away with the picture . . . but I just don't think Elizabeth is going to make it." Lehman tried to reassure him, saying, "There's a lot of film still left to be shot." But he, too, was worried, writing that he feared Nichols's mood crash was "an ill omen" and possibly "the first crack of doom for the picture." Taylor herself told Lehman that she expected "to get blasted by reviewers."

"I told her I didn't think she would be," Lehman wrote, "but she said they always blast her. I said, 'Why don't you screen the reviews and not read the bad ones?' She said, 'No, I won't do that. I'm not a masochist but I do want to read everything that they say about me, even if it's bad.'"

Taylor's determination helped pull Nichols through the rest of the shoot. He felt her work had improved with every scene, as had his own—"I think you can actually see me learning during the course of *Who's Afraid of Virginia Woolf?*" he later said. The more sequences he and O'Steen edited, the more he came to appreciate her performance. "Here were four stage people—Richard, George, Sandy, and me—and we were all awed by Elizabeth's knowledge of film acting," he said. "[We] watched her very closely and learned from her. The main thing that Richard learned was to do as little as possible. I have hundreds of thousands of feet of Richard listening in scenes. On the floor, over and over, I'd say after take eighteen, 'Okay, I guess that's it, there's not going to be any more, thanks, Elizabeth,' and I'd see it the next day and it was 50 percent better. All these things that you couldn't see standing six feet away were there. When I was editing, I realized she even left room for the score in some semiconscious way. Her essential nature informed so much of it." By the end, Taylor's main worry was whether she would be able to cry on cue—especially because, throughout the shoot, Nichols had told her to hold off any tears until the end. "She finally did it, just perfectly, this thing that had so frightened her, and then, in the middle of the scene, there was snoring. Some crew member up on a catwalk had gone to sleep and was snoring so loudly that I had to cut. And the first thing she said, the only thing, was 'Please don't fire him!'"

The shoot went so long that the wrap party took place while Nichols, Burton, and Taylor were filming the last moments of the movie; the crew, deliriously happy to be done, had to be quieted for the last few takes. Nichols didn't know whether he had pulled it off. But "I did know," he said, "and this is very rare for me, that it was something I could never use up, that [making movies] was going to be endlessly fascinating and exciting. It was a process the tools and possibilities of which are infinite . . . and over a very long time, it can become as simple as your own grammar. One of my problems is that I do wear things out and want to go on to something else . . . [But this] was something I knew I could never tire of."

One month later, Jack Warner fired him.

Twelve

ONE CONSIDERABLE
INTELLIGENCE
1966-1967

At the beginning of 1966, an aloof thirty-four-year-old who "had two marriages that went phffft" and was now spending his days with "Jackie [Kennedy] and Lee and Stas [Radziwill] and Truman and Lennie and Felicia" was the subject of a *New York Times* profile. Nichols had returned to New York for a weekend to be interviewed by Vincent Canby, in what Canby described as "the triplex apartment with the five telephones and God knows how many rooms" on Central Park West. The story, titled "The Cold Loneliness of It All," was perfumed with disdain, and an implication that its subject was rapidly becoming his own worst advertisement. A few months earlier, *The New York Times Magazine*, in a widely read article called "The In Crowd and the Out Crowd," had identified him as part of a group of celebrities who were supplanting old-guard New York society. Nichols, who was not shy about discussing money and had started to parade his world-weariness a little too visibly—he chose ANOMIE as a vanity license plate—found himself playing into the hands of those who agreed with Mailer's verdict that he was a "royal baby." He told one reporter that he had spent $300,000, including "taxes and alimonies," in the past year and had just traded his Lincoln Continental for a Rolls Silver Cloud III, then told NBC he had sold the car to buy a painting; he already owned a Picasso and a Matisse. *Newsweek* joked that he "could live on a loaf of bread but would need a staff of ten to keep the loaf." And when he sat for a *Playboy* interview in "his large, imposingly baronial home in suburban Brentwood," the writer commented that his amiability was occasionally "broken by an off-putting, glacial stare . . . that could shatter a producer's sunglasses at fifty paces—and someday quite probably will."

When Canby asked Nichols what was next, he kept one big undertaking to himself: He was already in discussions to direct a film version of Joseph Heller's *Catch-22*. But several other projects would come first. He planned to start filming *The Graduate* in September and was talking to Lillian Hellman about directing a revival of her 1939 play *The Little Foxes*. In addition, he and Elaine May were discussing a collaboration on a script "somewhere in the distant future." But Nichols was primarily engaged in finishing *Who's Afraid of Virginia Woolf?* and insisted that "he was never bothered by the Warner Brothers front office at all."

That was about to change. By the time the story ran, the studio had kicked him out of the editing room. Jack Warner, who often removed directors during postproduction, had run out of patience and wanted him gone. The ostensible reason was Nichols's insistence that Andre Previn be hired to score the picture instead of the studio's choice, the older and more traditional composer Alex North, but beyond that, Warner now viewed Nichols as expendable. He had been indulged as the shooting of *Virginia Woolf* ran over schedule because there had been no choice; Warner knew that to take him on would have meant a showdown with Burton and Taylor that the studio was in no position to win. But since the end of production, Nichols and Warner had clashed over *Virginia Woolf*'s greater-than-expected profanity—"My God, we've got

a $7.5 million dirty movie on our hands," the seventy-two-year-old stu-
dio chief had said the first time he saw it. Warner had also become
livid at Nichols's insistence on flying back to New York every weekend
to record radio spots with May, an ongoing gig for which they were very
well paid. "Is he doing that or is he doing this?" Warner snapped. Just
as Nichols and O'Steen were about to start work on the sound mix, "he
was thrown off the lot," O'Steen said. "He yelled about it, but there was
nothing he could do. The guards were told not to let him in. Warner
would have given him at least a little more time if he hadn't been pissed."

For a month, Nichols seethed in New York, raging to friends like
Hellman while he and O'Steen worked in secret via daily long-distance
calls during which Nichols would listen to the mix over the phone and
say, "Can you bring the music down there?" or "I don't think we need
that sound." "That's where O'Steen proved he was the man he was,
aside from his great editing," Nichols said. "But at a certain point I said,
'I can't do it this way anymore.'"

For nine months, Nichols had worked on the movie almost nonstop.
He had left four plays behind, and some of them were suffering without him. *The Knack*, after a long and profitable run, became the first of
his productions to close. And *The Odd Couple*, which he and Simon had
hoped would serve as their nest egg for a decade, was struggling. Shortly
after the play opened, Nichols had told Walter Matthau, "You're a good
actor, but a bad man." Once Nichols was gone, the show had deteriorated rapidly. Matthau started adding words and changing lines to keep
himself interested and, not incidentally, to unsettle and upstage Art
Carney. The other actors in the play grew so angry that, while Nichols
was busy in Los Angeles, the stage manager had had to call a cast
meeting to defuse tensions. It didn't work. "The problem is that Walter
keeps fucking up the play every night!" Paul Dooley said. "Well, if
people think I'm interfering with the success of the play, I could always
withdraw," Matthau replied. Carney started drinking again, missed
twelve performances in a month, and, one night in October, was so

shaken that he walked offstage after the curtain call, drove to Connecticut, and checked himself into a psychiatric hospital, where he spent more than a month. He never returned to the show, and Matthau left soon after, finished with Broadway for good. Their replacements, Eddie Bracken as Felix and Jack Klugman as Oscar, were not pulling in crowds. *The Odd Couple* was still doing decent business, but as a phenomenon it was over, and much more quickly than anyone had anticipated.

Nichols had no interest in returning to theater right away. He didn't even want to be in New York. His heart and head were still in *Virginia Woolf,* and he approached Jack Warner with a proposition. If Warner would let him back into the editing room, he would enlist a powerful ally to get the movie past the onetime Legion of Decency. Nichols promised that he would arrange for Jacqueline Kennedy to join the eighty judges at the National Catholic Office for Motion Pictures for their screening, sit directly behind the primary decision makers, or, as he put it, "Monsignor What's-His-Face," and, when the lights came up, say, "What a beautiful movie. Jack would have loved it."

Warner was ready to bargain. In early 1966, the gossip columns were full of rumors that Nichols and Kennedy were dating. They weren't; although he later acknowledged that he had something of a crush on her, she had made it clear there would be no romance. But their friendship was real; he was one of a small number of escorts she could be certain would never embarrass her at a time when she was reemerging into society after two years of widowhood. Nichols had recently taken her to Arthur, an East Side discotheque in which he had invested. "They did the Watusi and the Frug—and got jostled by other people," the *New York Post* reported. "They stayed about 90 minutes . . . and Jackie stood waiting, like other girls, while her date waited for his coat . . . Then off into the frosty night." Warner took the deal, and Nichols went back to Los Angeles to finish the film.

The work was painstaking. Nichols and O'Steen made a thousand tiny cuts, going through the dialogue track line by line, sometimes grabbing a word or even a vowel sound from elsewhere in the picture to improve Taylor's line delivery, to fix Burton's Latin, to heighten dramatic moments, or to soften lines they now knew they couldn't get away with. Martha's "Screw you!" (unacceptable) became "God damn you!" (possibly acceptable), even though Taylor wasn't available to redub it; they brought in another actress to imitate her and cut away from her face for the first two words so moviegoers wouldn't see her mouthing "Screw."

The film passed its first test in late February, when it won the approval of Edward Albee, who, when he first found out that Nichols was to direct it, had said, "My play is not a farce." Albee had kept his distance during production, in part, he said, because "I kept getting reports about terrible things happening—like their dropping the imaginary kid from the script." When Nichols showed him the movie, "part of my pleasure was relief," Albee said. "I found out that he had a pretty good idea of what the play was about. There was at least one considerable intelligence at work." Albee didn't like the addition of the roadhouse scene or the "sentimentalized" score (Warner had gotten his way about the music), and for decades he would remain annoyed by Lehman's writing credit, at one point telling him, "It's my play fucking word for word." But he was happy enough with what he saw that Nichols and Warner Bros. knew he would make no trouble.

With the opening still four months away, Nichols went on the run. New York did not, at that moment, feel welcoming. The end of his relationship with Steinem, though long in coming, was painful—when she passed by his table in a restaurant a couple of years later, Nichols muttered to his companion, "I almost killed myself for her." He started dating again immediately, taking the twenty-one-year-old actress Mia Farrow to Italy to visit Burton and Taylor, who were there working on Franco Zeffirelli's film adaptation of *The Taming of the Shrew*. Neither star knew quite what to make of the new relationship. "That M. Nichols really gets the girls," Burton wrote in his diary, after a lunch during which he said that Farrow was "forever apologizing . . . for her silly little ability not to know anybody in theatre or films before her time—which she [implied] was last week. [They] appear to be in love and register in hotels as Mr and Mrs N. . . . I wish Farrow would put on 15lbs and grow her hair."

That spring, Nichols also made a more private trip—one he had resisted all of his adult life: He returned to Berlin for the first time since 1939. He wandered through the changed city as a tourist, seeing as many plays as he could at the Berliner Ensemble, immersing himself in productions of Brecht and Shakespeare. And he took an afternoon to walk to the house where he had spent his first seven years, in a neighborhood of what was now West Berlin. It was gone. A modern apartment building stood in its place.

From there he flew to see his daughter, Daisy, who had just turned two. Margot Callas was still living in Europe, and since she and Nichols were still married, he had no ability to formalize a custody-sharing arrangement in American courts. Visits with Daisy were, at that time, infrequent and tensely negotiated, and when Nichols spoke of himself as the parent of a toddler, he sounded brittle and emotionally distant. "Children survive extraordinary things and fail to survive literally tiny details," he told an interviewer who asked him about being an absent father. "People who say, 'I'm staying to hold the family together' are really saying, 'My children are the only things that touch me and I'm not going to leave their presence.' I love my child and she touches me, but she's not the only thing that touches me, which is better for me and definitely better for her." He finished his travels in Jamaica, where he rested and wondered where and when he might next feel at home.

Until just days before its release, there was still serious doubt about whether *Virginia Woolf* would be able to play in movie theaters without cuts that Nichols—and Warner Bros., which was now ready to fight for the film—was refusing to make. Jacqueline Kennedy had done exactly what Nichols had vowed she would—"It's the only time in my life I've ever used a friend in that way," he said—and it had worked. The Catholic Office agonized over the movie's language, but rather than rate it C ("condemned") or B ("morally objectionable in part for all"), they gave Warner Bros. a clean win by rating it A-IV ("morally unobjectionable for adults, with reservations"). "We put *Virginia Woolf* in what we call our 'think film' category" alongside *8½* and *La Dolce Vita,* one rater explained, saying, "I've never heard those words on a screen before, but I've heard them at Coney Island."

That still left the Production Code. Although its influence was waning, its oversight was still in place, and in May, PCA head Geoffrey Shurlock told Warner that he had no choice but to withhold a seal of approval. Warner fought back on two fronts—he announced that the movie would be the first of his studio's releases ever to carry a "For Adults Only" label in advertisements, and he appealed the ruling to the Motion Picture Association of America. On June 11, just eleven days before the movie's scheduled opening, the MPAA overruled Shurlock, dealing a blow to the Code that would prove fatal within the year. *Virginia Woolf* would be shown in the form Nichols intended. Its language, MPAA head Jack Valenti predicted, would "hit the American public like an angry fist."

At the film's premiere, at Los Angeles's Pantages Theatre, "Mike was a basket case," said O'Steen, who sat beside him in the back row. Ten minutes after it began, Nichols sat bolt upright in his seat, alarmed that the second reel of the print they were showing was too light. "I thought I was going to have a heart attack. I went running into the projection booth. [The next day] people went nuts [for the movie] in the papers. I thought, 'Yeah, yeah, yeah, *but that reel* . . .'" It's a way to protect yourself from worrying about the real things," Nichols said. "It took me years not to be that kind of asshole."

The film's reception was overwhelmingly positive. Although *The*

Village Voice's Andrew Sarris complained that Nichols had "committed all the classic errors of the sophisticated stage director let loose on the unsophisticated movies . . . in his search for visual pyrotechnics," most notices came closer to *The Hollywood Reporter*'s assertion that "the screen has never held a more shattering and indelible drama . . . and the greatest credit . . . must go to the director." In *The New York Times*, Stanley Kauffmann called *Virginia Woolf* "one of the most scathingly honest American films ever made" and wrote, "Mike Nichols, after a brilliant and too-brief career as a satirist, proved to be a brilliant theatrical director of comedy. This is his debut as a film director, and it is a successful Houdini feat . . . He was given two world-shaking stars, the play of the decade and the auspices of a large looming studio. What more inhibiting conditions could be imagined for a first film, if the director is a man of talent? . . . The triumph is just to come out alive. Which Mr. Nichols has done." Kauffmann noted that the play's stage origins limited what Nichols could accomplish but argued that "he has . . . made the most of the two elements left to him—intimacy and acting" and called Taylor's performance "the best work of her career, sustained and urgent." The *Times*'s veteran reviewer Bosley Crowther concurred, calling it "an example of daring that inspires admiration and hope."

The reviews, combined with Burton's and Taylor's drawing power and the headline-making controversy over its content, were enough to make the film a smash. *Who's Afraid of Virginia Woolf?* would end 1966 as the year's third-highest grosser, behind only the James Bond movie *Thunderball* and David Lean's *Doctor Zhivago*. The film also affirmed Nichols as a central figure in a rapidly shifting culture; for the first time, he found himself on the covers of magazines. A few months earlier, when his involvement in *Catch-22* had been announced, it sounded like just one more doomed attempt to get the movie version of a novel widely regarded as unfilmable off the ground. Now it seemed more possible. In the last five years, *Catch-22* had been to American literature what *Who's Afraid of Virginia Woolf?* had been to American theater. Who better to take it on than a director who had proved he could wrestle with dark, sardonic source material and emerge victorious? "You are without a doubt this year's number-one celebrity!" Barbara Walters crowed when she landed him for an NBC interview. "How does this explosion of fame affect you?" "It's nice," he said, adding, "What I'm sometimes afraid of is that you do get a little insulated."

Nichols was well aware that his status as a public figure had practical limits; he certainly couldn't use it to spark any momentum for *The Graduate*. Charles Webb's novel had vanished from public discussion right after it was released. It had been almost two years since Nichols agreed to direct the movie, and only now did he and Lawrence Turman have a script they liked. One year earlier, at Jane Fonda's Fourth of July beach party, Nichols had sought a cool spot under a tree, away from the dancing. A slight, sharp-eyed young man spotted him and said, "Are you having a good time in L.A., Mike?" It was Buck Henry. Nichols knew him by reputation—"He had been an improvisational comic, but at the Premise [New York City's first major improv group], not the Compass like me," he said—but they hadn't met since Nichols's one sad year at the Dalton School, where Henry remembered him only as a shy, sullen fourth grader who never took off his cap unless a teacher made him.

Just as he had done when he stumbled upon Elaine May in a Chicago train station, Nichols kindled their friendship by starting a comic bit and seeing if Henry would pick up on it—an overture that was also a test. "Yes," he replied. "Here, under the shadow of this great tree, I have found peace." Henry laughed and kept it going. They connected.

By then, *The Graduate* was on its third screenwriter, Calder Willingham, a southern novelist whose witty, laconic style had seemed to Turman a good match for Webb's terse, barely inflected dialogue. But the book was proving difficult to adapt—Benjamin Braddock, so earnest in its pages, was coming across as a high-minded prig in the scripts, and the wit Nichols had enjoyed was getting lost. He found the screenplays "in every way unacceptable." Soon after the party, Nichols asked Henry if he'd like to take a crack at screenwriting. After reading the novel and visiting Nichols on the *Virginia Woolf* set, he signed on. "It didn't take more than ten pages to see that this was really interesting," he said. "Larry and Mike and I all thought that we were the protagonist of the book. We were all roughly the same age, we'd all gone to the same kind of schools, we all laughed at the same jokes. But hiring me was a leap of faith on Mike's part. He was really just going on personality and *Get Smart*," the hit sitcom that Henry had cocreated with Mel Brooks.

Henry wrote two drafts alone, eliminating some of the novel's odd detours, including a long sequence in which Benjamin becomes a firefighter in the California forests, and zeroing in on the sexual tension, generational angst, and social comedy. "The book is filled with all of the stuff you can wring out of the upper middle class," he said. "That hadn't been very evident in American films for a long time." Henry preserved the best of Webb's dialogue almost verbatim, added many of his own droll touches, and discovered a way to explore Benjamin's self-seriousness without endorsing it. "I have a feeling that in real life, Benjamin Braddock was not a person you'd want to know. He's a bit of a prick—he doesn't give anybody much of a chance," he said. The Benjamin whom Henry created was still the WASP athlete of Webb's novel, but more vulnerable and more easily caught off guard.

Once Nichols started working through the screenplay with Henry, it "was more fun than anything I'd done since Elaine," he said. Early on, Henry had landed on the movie's most reliable laugh—"Plastics," the solemnly intoned one-word piece of career advice Benjamin receives at his welcome-home party—then almost took it out. He thought, "Are we too old-fashioned with what was a sort of fifties society way of complaining about falseness? But I couldn't ever think of anything that was a better word for him to say."

Nichols now had a screenplay he loved—"I knew it was a perfect plot," he said, "and I knew what it was about, which usually takes me forever." But by the time *Who's Afraid of Virginia Woolf?* opened, it was clear that *The Graduate* could not begin production in September and would have to wait until 1967. Nobody was cast, and nobody was close. To play Mrs. Robinson, the bored, prowling Southern California woman of leisure with whom Benjamin begins an affair, Nichols approached Patricia Neal, an actress he had long admired. But Neal had had two severe strokes and was struggling with a limp and with memory problems. Nichols offered to work around both issues, but she told him she just wasn't up to it. He also went to Jeanne Moreau, ready to reimagine the character as French; she, too, turned him down, a decision she later regretted. And he toyed with the idea of Doris Day and Ronald Reagan as Benjamin's parents, but Martin Melcher, Day's husband and manager, wouldn't even show her the script. As for Benjamin, Nichols had no candidates whatsoever, in part because in his mind the character still stood at an uneasy midpoint between the standoffish young hero of the novel and the script's more awkward underdog. "It's the hardest thing I've ever tried to cast," he said.

Shortly after that, Nichols met Dustin Hoffman. Their first encounter was not auspicious. With no movie to shoot, Nichols had agreed to spend the fall directing a Broadway musical for the first time, an omnibus of three one-acts, with music by Jerry Bock and lyrics by Elaine May's ex-husband Sheldon Harnick, called *Come Back! Go Away! I Love You!* The show, their first since the huge success of *Fiddler on the Roof,* had been trudging along a rough path to Broadway— Jerome Robbins had considered directing it, then walked away after a year, a book writer had come and gone, and one of the three stories Bock and Harnick had chosen had already been dumped. Once Nichols came in, he worked swiftly: He changed the title to *The Apple Tree* and insisted on replacing another of the one-acts with a new version of Jules Feiffer's "Passionella," the showbiz-Cinderella spoof he had done in summer stock four years earlier. He also cast Barbara Harris "without an audition," according to producer Stuart Ostrow. Harris had come far since the Compass; she had just won a Tony nomination for *On a Clear Day You Can See Forever*. But her singing voice was a source of great insecurity for her, and her emotional health was precarious; she suffered from bouts of uncontrollable stage fright. Nichols had dealt with shaky performers before; he thought he knew how to handle Harris and started looking for two leading men to play opposite her. One of the actors who read for him was Hoffman, an unprepossessing twenty-eight-year-old who had gotten some attention for an off-Broadway play called *The Journey of the Fifth Horse*. "I think I should tell you," he said well into the audition, "I don't sing." With what Ostrow called his "signature-chic-ridicule delivery," Nichols replied, "Then why are you here?" Hoffman didn't get the part.

To play opposite Harris, Nichols cast Alan Alda, who had worked with her before and knew how to put her at ease. Nichols had him read a scene from what was to be the opening playlet, an adaptation of Mark Twain's "The Diary of Adam and Eve." "I improvised a little moment as Adam—trying to fish out a fish from a river—and I heard Mike laugh. My agent reprimanded me on the way home," Alda said, "but I got it."

Bock and Harnick—who said he "threw up all over the Beverly Hills Hotel" the day Nichols told him he wanted them to replace their final act with "Passionella"—had to work very quickly, and Nichols never seemed satisfied with the result. He loved the version that Feiffer had written back in 1962 and the song that Stephen Sondheim had composed for it. At one point he called Sondheim and said, "I'm sorry to bother you, but I'm having trouble with Sheldon and Jerry."

"Mike," Sondheim says he replied, "you will never like what they write for 'Passionella,' because you liked what I wrote. They could write a symphony and you would still say, 'It's not right,' because your first lay is the great lay." Nichols responded, "'Thank you very much' and that was that."

As work got under way, Nichols, at first, felt very much back in his element, once again pushing his actors to stay true to life and engaged with one another. "He was an actor's director," says Alda. "Once when Barbara and I were rehearsing, he said this thing that has aided me all my life. He didn't feel we were connecting to each other, and he said, 'You kids think relating is the icing on the cake. It's not. It's the cake.'"

"Like all good directors, he was a total collaborator, and asked wonderful questions," says Harnick. "One of the first things Mike did in rehearsal—and I think Alan and Barbara were delighted—was that when they were playing Adam and Eve, he had them switch roles. Alan was Eve and Barbara was Adam, and they both learned something about the script."

Ostrow had arranged for *The Apple Tree* to try out in Boston. Once the company got there, Nichols realized how unready he was for the challenge of mounting a musical. Harnick felt that the lineup of stories, originally intended as a triptych about the push and pull between men and women, had changed so often that it now played as "three more or less disconnected musicals . . . The audience had a good time, but not a wholly satisfying time." And Ostrow became convinced that he had "hired a terrific comedy director who froze every time the music started." Nichols himself had never felt so hemmed in. When he directed plays, anything that didn't work could be rewritten almost on the spot, but re-orchestrating and re-choreographing was another matter entirely. Replacing a song took weeks, not days. He couldn't conceal his uncertainty; at one point he brought the director and choreographer Herbert Ross, a close friend, up to Boston to work on the musical numbers. (The final, unusual credits read "Entire Production Directed by Mike Nichols, Additional Musical Staging by Herbert Ross.") "I admired very much his openness about it being his first musical," says Alda. "Sometimes as he was about to make a decision, he'd be in the audience and we'd be onstage and he'd call out, 'How would we do this if this were a *real* musical?'"

Ostrow started to worry. For "The Diary of Adam and Eve," Nichols had had Tony Walton design an elaborate and beautiful stained-glass garden of Eden. "They were light boxes, lit from behind," says Walton, "flora and fauna in various colors. It was a technique that hadn't been tried at the time and hasn't really been since," and it created a stunning effect as the curtain rose for the first act on a stage full of line drawings that slowly deepened into three-dimensional renderings filled with color and light. As Nichols prepared to rehearse on the new set for the first time, the lights went up, and he snapped at Jerry Adler, then a veteran Broadway stage manager who had not yet become an actor, "Where are Barbara and Alan? How could you take the curtain up without the stars on the stage?"

"They're on the stage," Adler replied.

"Alan is supposed to be in the tree!" Nichols insisted.

"Alan *is* in the tree," Adler said.

The backlighting had rendered both stars completely invisible. Nichols turned to Ostrow. "Stuart, I'm about to make you a famous producer," he said. "We're going to throw out all the scenery." The set, which had cost more than $100,000, was scrapped; "The Diary of Adam and Eve" would be performed on Broadway in the style of "poor theater," with just a stepladder and a bare minimum of props.

As the Boston tryout neared its end, Nichols's faith that he could pull the show together had all but evaporated. After Jerome Robbins went to see it and, at Nichols's invitation, gave him and the cast more than two hundred notes, he took Nichols aside for a blunt heart-to-heart. "Is there any chance you could stay out of New York another two weeks?" Robbins said. Nichols thought for a moment. "No, I don't think so," he said. "I think we would lose Barbara."

"He was very worried," Harnick says. "We all were. She was so delicate psychologically that we were afraid something might happen."

The Apple Tree opened at the Shubert Theatre on Broadway in October 1966; it was the first show Nichols directed that was not a major hit, though it ran for a year. Reviews were warm for Harris but mixed for the show itself; "mildly pleasant" was typical of the faint praise, and for every critic who called it charming or entertaining, there was another who found it "flaccid and maladroit." For some reviewers, "Passionella," which featured a dazzling quick change for Harris as a charwoman who is magically transformed into a movie sex symbol, was the highlight; for others, it wasn't worth the wait. "The myth of Director Mike Nichols, invulnerable up to now, has been that he could bust a comic rib with an onion-thin script," said *Time* magazine, "but *The Apple Tree* is too thin even for his nimble touch."

The show was far from a disaster—it received seven Tony nominations, including one for Nichols (his third)—but the experience was not a happy one. Feiffer saw what Nichols had done with "Passionella" and left feeling that the show "had emasculated the satirical thrust I had in mind . . . What they got onstage was 'Passionella' with all the bite removed. I've never said this, but I didn't like it. Mike's work was wonderful, but I didn't see onstage what I wanted. I may have said something to Mike at the time. I pissed him off, and I was pissed off." Harris won the Tony for her performance, but it would be her last work in theater. At one point, when Alda left briefly to make a movie and an unfamiliar scene partner stepped in, she walked out onstage and started naming people she recognized in the first few rows instead of the animals in Eden. Another night, she said her opening lines, then looked at the audience, muttered, "I can't do this anymore," and walked off. "Broadway scared the hell out of her," says Adler. "She started smoking pot before the show, she got into cocaine in order to get herself out on the stage. It was just awful. I'd hear her in her dressing room with Warren Beatty [her boyfriend at the time] and she was sobbing—I finally had to kick him out of the theater. She'd go on half-gassed just to get through the two hours. She was destroying herself. She couldn't wait for the run to be over."

Nichols's own distress was becoming more manifest. Self-loathing had never been far beneath his painstakingly composed surface; now he could barely conceal it, and didn't seem to want to. Every joke he told about himself was a carefully polished expression of misery. He said he arose every morning with the words "'Thank you, God, for another perfect day,' uttered in a tone of absolute despair." He started a production company he called Icarus, "as a reminder to myself not to get too cocky," and, perhaps sensitive about how little time he was spending with his daughter, sneered at people who name production companies "after your children" as a display of parental love "and never see [them] again." He was enraged by a quote attributed to him in *Newsweek*'s cover story—"I'm doing it better than anyone and I can't do it at all—I'm a fraud"—and sought a correction, insisting that he had never said it and that it represented "such a bizarre combination of arrogance and truckling that I must try to set it right." It was a disorienting moment for him—a minor misfire just as year-end honors for *Virginia Woolf* were starting to pour in, but one that seemed to confirm his worst suspicions about himself. For the first time, his work had inspired condescension from his own cadre of tastemakers. Robert Brustein complained that he was "becoming famous directing precisely the kind of spineless comedies and boneless musicals that he once would have satirized." And his old friend Susan Sontag said to a *Newsweek* interviewer, "The question is, how ambitious is Mike willing to be? He's one of the few people in this country who could direct Brecht properly."

Of everyone in Nichols's many social circles, Sontag was the most natural fit to play the scolding conscience on his shoulder, urging him away from commerce and toward art. In one breath, she could ask for a loan; in the next, she could reprove him for the way he had earned the money he was handing over. He didn't seem to mind it. "My friends

have never especially liked any of the things I've done," he said in response. "I suppose that's why they're my friends." It was a brave face to
put on, but Nichols couldn't wait to get out of New York and back to
moviemaking. "I find myself talking about it day and night," he said.
"I'm afraid that this is what I want to do for the rest of my life." As 1967
began, he spoke of his desire to form a repertory company that would
include Jane Fonda, Sandy Dennis, Anne Bancroft, Robert Redford,
and Alan Arkin; and, perhaps stung by the critique that he was coast-
ing, he talked of his ambition to direct Chekhov, Beckett, and Pinter.
(He would direct all three, although it would take him forty-eight
years to cross the last name off the list.) He seemed eager to put *The
Apple Tree* behind him—with one exception. He couldn't stop thinking
about the actor he'd passed on during auditions, the short one who said
he couldn't sing and who kept doing tiny off-Broadway plays and running away with them.

"I've discovered this terrific young guy," he told Jerry Adler. "I'm
going to put him in *The Graduate*."

"Who?" Adler said, surprised. "The no-name? You're really gonna
use him?"

"I really am," Nichols said.

Thirteen

PROVE YOU
BELONG HERE

1967

It came down to a screen test, one that dragged through an entire day in such slow-motion embarrassment and humiliation that after every take, Nichols looked at Hoffman and thought, *I can't do it. This will never work.* Without knowing why, he had gradually been moving away from the notion that Benjamin and his parents should be what Buck Henry called "the Surfboards"—tall, lean, hard, blond, all-American. Originally, "Mike and I never thought that a short, dark guy with a big nose" should be the lead of *The Graduate,* Henry said. "Sand in the genes, the roar of the ocean. Robert Redford and Candice Bergen, the ideal couple—that's what we were thinking." Redford wanted the part badly, and he and Bergen tested together. "It certainly would have been a different way to go," she says, laughing. Afterward, Redford went over to Nichols's rented house in Beverly Hills and got the bad news over a game of pool. "You can't play a loser," Nichols said. "Look at you. How many times have you struck out with a woman?"

"And he said, I swear to you, 'What do you mean?'" said Nichols. "He didn't even understand the concept. That's how I learned Benjamin can't be a winner." Nichols also tested Tony Bill, a handsome, dark-haired actor who was known as a Warren-Beatty's-younger-brother type, and Charles Grodin, whose quiet, deadpan style felt close to what he wanted. And he considered Alan Alda, but Alda was thirty-one and looked it. Nichols had already cast Anne Bancroft, who, at thirty-six, was a decade too young for Mrs. Robinson; he and Dick Sylbert, who would again serve as his production designer, were planning to put a gray streak in her hair and use makeup to create the leathery tan of a middle-aged woman whose empty days left her with too much time to lounge by the pool. But Benjamin needed to look credibly postcolle-giate, and Hoffman came close enough that Nichols thought he was worth flying out to Los Angeles and testing with Katharine Ross, a young actress with a few years of television experience who reminded him of his first wife.

"I didn't want to read for it," Hoffman says. "I reacted against it: I was right, Nichols was wrong, I was not in any way right for that part. I thought, *Are these people having a breakdown?*" Things were going well for Hoffman in New York; after years of striving, he was landing steady work off-Broadway. "*I'm not going to screw it up by making a Hollywood movie and being miscast*," he recalls thinking. "I said, 'This character's so WASPish.' And Mike said, 'Maybe he's Jewish inside.'"

A few days later, Hoffman found himself in a makeup chair, being blended and daubed and cleansed and trimmed while Nichols peered at him as if he were an art project, and said, "What can we do about his nose? What can we do about his eyebrows?" Hoffman was so nervous, he started to perspire before he walked onto the soundstage, which was empty except for a bed on which he and Ross were to do a ten-page scene that he had barely memorized. "I couldn't get through it," he says. "I remember at one point patting [Ross] on the back and saying, 'Come on,' and giving her a gentle little pinch on the tush. And she went, 'Don't you *ever* do that.'" At the end of the day, Hoffman reached into his pocket and a handful of coins flew out. A stagehand retrieved a subway token from the floor and said, "You'll need this." It is safe to say that no one involved thought they would see him again.

Not until the next afternoon, when Nichols watched the screen test on film, did he know he had found Benjamin. "He had this thing I'd only seen in Elizabeth Taylor, and that I'd certainly not seen in any of the other tests," Nichols said. "That secret. That deal with Technicolor where you do nothing and it turns out you were doing everything. He was compelling and hilarious and impassive. It was startling. That's what a great movie actor does. They don't know how they do it, and I don't know how they do it, but the difference is shocking."

Hoffman flew home to New York, waited a few days in the Upper West Side apartment he shared with his girlfriend, Anne Byrne, and then, on a Sunday morning, called Nichols. "He said, 'Well,' pause, 'you got it,'" says Hoffman. "I didn't say a word. Maybe 'Oh,' or 'Thank you.' There was another pause, and he said, 'You don't seem very excited.' I said, 'Oh, no, yeah, thanks.' All I knew is that I was working with the greatest director around, and that he was about to make the biggest mistake. I hung up, and I looked at my girlfriend and I said, 'I got it.' There was this terrible sad moment. And she said, 'I knew you would.' It was heavy. Laden with potential regret that that was going to break us up."

In everything he had directed until *The Graduate,* Nichols had succeeded on the basis of his ability to create a warm, director-as-nurturing-papa gestalt with his actors, an approach that inspired them to do their best work for him. The success of *Virginia Woolf* had hinged on his decision to form an us-against-the-world bond with his cast of four, taking their hands and promising to lead them safely into unknown territory. But as production of *The Graduate* neared, Nichols retreated into himself. On this film, there was no studio to strong-arm him; unlike Warner Bros., Embassy was merely a distribution company without design, sound, or music departments, and Joe Levine was a proudly crass financier and salesman who would have nothing to say until he watched the first cut, at which point he offered Nichols his highest praise: "I smell money." Free to make his own choices, Nichols brought aboard the two *Virginia Woolf* alums he trusted completely—Sylbert and Sam O'Steen. They, along with Buck Henry and the crusty cinematographer Robert Surtees, would collectively serve as a kind of cabinet for Nichols. But more often, he kept his own counsel. During preproduction, he spent mornings alone in his house, mapping out shots, annotating each line of the script, and listening over and over to *Sounds of Silence,* the Simon & Garfunkel album that his brother, Robert, now a doctor, had sent him, until one day he came in and told his team he had found the music for the movie.

The actors, who had assembled to rehearse in Los Angeles in March 1967, awaited Nichols's every pronouncement. There weren't many, and initially, some of them thought there was nothing much worth discussing. This was not *Virginia Woolf,* a play that everyone had seen and analyzed and argued over for years before Nichols brought it to the screen. That film, which was still playing across the country, had just received thirteen Academy Award nominations, including Best Picture, Best Director—Nichols was only the seventh filmmaker to get a nomination for his debut movie—and acting nominations for all four cast members. To some in the *Graduate* ensemble, as excited as they were to work with him, this movie seemed certain to be a comedown; they thought it read as little more than a "completely unoriginal" young-guy-older-woman comedy, as Nichols himself had called it. "I don't think anyone sensed it was going to become a classic," says William Daniels, a theater actor who, at thirty-nine, was playing Hoffman's father. "We had all seen *Barefoot in the Park* and we thought, *Here's a New York director who does light comedies.* We assumed it was a light comedy about Anne Bancroft and the young boy." It wasn't until Nichols played them the music, Daniels says, that they realized "this was all going to be told through Dustin's eyes," and that it might be "a significant film."

The Apple Tree was still fresh in Nichols's mind. It was the first time he had ever been caught underprepared, and he was so determined not to let it happen again on *The Graduate* that he overcompensated by scheduling three weeks of rehearsals. That had proved useful on *Virginia Woolf,* a densely written adaptation of a three-hour play with a tiny cast. But the dialogue scenes in *The Graduate* were relatively brief. Nichols had his actors run their lines and hit the marks he had taped to the soundstage floor as if a curtain were about to go up the next night. But there was little to rehearse. From the opening-credits shot, with Benjamin standing on a moving sidewalk at the airport, to the five-minute montage that Nichols and Henry had started to work out, shot by shot, to show him sliding into an aimless, joyless affair with Mrs. Robinson, to the climax, in which he drives frantically to stop Elaine's wedding, many of what would become *The Graduate*'s signature scenes didn't have a word of dialogue.

The biggest performance adjustments Nichols wanted to make were accomplished very soon after the group read-through on day one. That first pass, as the actors sat around a table warily assessing one another, their director, and the screenplay, was bogged down by the inclusion of several extraneous scenes that never made it into the finished film. That morning, "the movie just fell right on its ass," says Hoffman. To some of his costars, the performance of their unknown leading man seemed barely to register, but Nichols was unperturbed; he understood that Hoffman's work would bloom on film rather than in the rehearsal room. As for Bancroft, her lusty, earthy Mrs. Robinson was entirely wrong—it lacked boredom, brittleness, and hauteur. "I wasn't seeing upper middle class," said Henry. "I was seeing lower middle class, or upper lower class."

But Nichols, who had briefly dated Bancroft long before she married Mel Brooks, knew how to steer her. "Do you like [what I'm doing with] my character?" she asked him early on.

"No, not at all," he said. "She's much too nice."

"*Why* isn't she nice?" she said.

"I don't know why," he said. "But I can tell you how she sounds. I can do it for you." Nichols almost never gave line readings, but in a chilly, detached, almost entirely uninflected tone, he said, "Benjamin, will you drive me home?"

"Oh!" Bancroft said, her entire characterization clicking into place. "I can do that. That's *anger.*"

One actor didn't make it past the second week. For the role of Mr. Robinson, Nichols had cast Gene Hackman, who had come up in New York stage and television and was friends with Hoffman. (They had studied acting together under Lee Strasberg.) One morning before rehearsals, both actors were in the men's room, and Hackman said to Hoffman, "I think I'm getting fired. He doesn't like what I'm doing." By the end of the day he was gone. The reasons were never clear: Nichols, who liked Hackman personally and would go on to work with him several times, took the blame, saying he had simply miscast him and that, at thirty-seven, he looked too young for the role. (His replacement, Murray Hamilton, was forty-five.) Hoffman believed that Nichols felt Hackman couldn't handle the comedy. Elizabeth Wilson, the stage actress playing Benjamin's mother, thought Nichols was angry that, unlike the rest of the cast, Hackman hadn't yet learned his lines. And Buck Henry, who was present throughout rehearsals and had agreed to play a small, funny role as the desk clerk at the hotel where Benjamin checks in for his first assignation, was caught completely off guard. "I thought, *Oh, God, is this the beginning of everything coming apart?*" he said.

It wasn't, but it was the start of what became a lifelong practice for Nichols: sacrificing an actor early on when something felt wrong. Sometimes the performance or attitude was actually the problem, sometimes it wasn't, but almost always, the decision came abruptly and served as a jolt of adrenaline, a reminder to everyone involved, and sometimes to himself, that the business at hand was serious. In this case, it also helped Nichols realize that he had come to the end of a process. He and the actors had gotten everything they could out of working on the scenes; he now knew his cast's strengths and idiosyncrasies. He called them together, told them they were doing good work, and said, "Listen, this is silly—I'm acting like this is an out-of-town tryout." He canceled the final week of rehearsals, told them to get some rest, and sent them home.

Nichols used the extra time to work with Sylbert on the final details of a visual scheme that would mark *The Graduate* as one of the first modern-looking mainstream American movies of the 1960s. Freed from the single-set constraints of *Virginia Woolf* and working in color for the first time, he and Sylbert came up with a palette—shiny blacks, animal prints, and wildly overgrown garden foliage for Mrs. Robinson's lair (Sylbert and Nichols called her "the beast in the jungle") and sunbaked whites for the Braddocks' home, with its shimmering blue swimming pool serving as a status symbol for the Braddocks, and womb and refuge for Benjamin.

At the time, Nichols, who was acutely aware of how much his own life had become about buying whatever he wanted, and of how little pleasure it gave him, started to see *The Graduate* as the story of a young man suffocating beneath a surfeit of material goods while he himself is treated as a prized possession. "He comes home and is almost catatonic from the bombardment of *things*," he said, noting that when Mrs. Robinson first asks what's bothering him, he replies, "I'm just sort of disturbed about things." Accordingly, Nichols wanted the film's look to be "cold, glassy, plastic" at the beginning and give way to more diffused shots and natural light once the Robinsons' daughter, Elaine, comes into Benjamin's life. Trapping him against glass, water, or both would be a visual motif, from the opening, in which he sits glumly before the fish tank in his boyhood bedroom, to the shot in which he spreads his arms, Christlike, against the transparent wall of an ultramodern church. "The picture is entirely from Benjamin's point of view," he reminded his team. "Nothing happens that doesn't happen to him or through his eyes."

At first, Nichols wondered if Surtees, who had been shooting movies since the early 1930s, would be a generational naysayer schooling an upstart director on what could and could not be done. He had won three Academy Awards, most recently for *Ben-Hur*, but nothing on his résumé suggested an affinity with the sleek, modernist look Nichols was after. He had just come off the creative miasma of 20th Century Fox's misbegotten *Doctor Dolittle* and was exhausted; Nichols knew that spending the next five months trying to light giant panes of glass without having them glare would test any cinematographer's sanity. But "he was glorious," Nichols said. "I loved him. From the first moment, I asked for really weird things, and he fell all over himself to do them."

Instead of an adversary, Surtees became a partner, one who was happy both to learn new tricks and to teach Nichols everything he had spent a career mastering. When Nichols wanted to use a long lens for a scene between Benjamin and Elaine in a tiny dorm room, Surtees told him to rip out a wall; they could shoot it from a city block away if necessary. He also helped Nichols fine-tune the atmosphere for *The Graduate*'s initial sexual encounter, in which Benjamin famously says, "Mrs. Robinson, you're trying to seduce me," then adds a frightened "Aren't you?" The through-the-leg shot of Benjamin, which became the film's poster, was easy, and O'Steen, whom Nichols kept on set for the entire production, knew exactly what shots he would need in order to do the rapid cutting that would convey Benjamin's mounting panic in the bedroom. But it was Surtees who showed Nichols how lighting could subtly change the film's mood. The bedroom sequence is bracketed by two scenes at the wet bar in the Robinsons' den. In the beginning, when Benjamin and Mrs. Robinson enter, the lighting is cozy and inviting; later, when he runs downstairs just as Mr. Robinson gets home, Surtees had somehow transformed it into "a dark, scary place, [because]

Mr. Robinson is scary and drunk, and she's *really* scary when she comes in," said Nichols. "The lighting is different. Surtees said to me, 'It's all right. You can do that in movies. How the lights were when they left the room is beside the point.' I learned so much from him."

For the first time, Nichols started to view film technique not as a burdensome code he needed others to crack for him but as a tool in his arsenal; now his attitude was that if it could be done, it should be done, and money and time were no object. *The Graduate* began production shortly before the Academy Awards were handed out; although Nichols lost to Fred Zinnemann for *A Man for All Seasons*, the five Oscars won by *Who's Afraid of Virginia Woolf?*—including statuettes to Elizabeth Taylor for Best Actress and Sandy Dennis for Best Supporting Actress—were an affirmation that gave him license to insist that things be done his way. If the Robinsons' house, which Sylbert had built on a soundstage, had a hallway too narrow for the camera to follow Benjamin, Nichols would tell his crew to rebuild it. When they said it would take days, he replied, "We'll wait."

At the center of it all was Hoffman, who began almost every shooting day wondering in what new way he was going to fail the script, Bancroft, Nichols, himself. He was, in many ways, Nichols's kind of actor—intuitive, inquisitive, perfectionistic, and willing to engage with anything his director threw at him. In the first phase of their work on *The Graduate*, Nichols peppered him with questions to keep him alert to every possibility: Do you think Benjamin is a virgin? (Hoffman didn't.) What do you think frightens him? Where did he learn about sex? Hoffman knew he had succeeded when Nichols would ruin a take by laughing, and he wasn't afraid to try anything. During a rehearsal for his first sex scene with Bancroft, he boldly put one hand on her breast, over her brassiere. When it came time to shoot the scene, Nichols said to him, "Do that again, but don't tell her you're going to—I want to see what she does." The cameras rolled and, after Bancroft took her sweater off, Hoffman did it. Without breaking character for a second, she glanced at his hand, barely curious, then, much more interested, noticed a spot on the sweater she was still holding and started to pick at it. Hoffman was so close to breaking into laughter at her perfect improvisation that he removed his hand, turned away from the camera, walked over to the hotel room wall, and started rhythmically banging his head. Nichols, no stranger to fighting the urge to laugh in the middle of an improv, made it part of the movie. (He was also willing to filch from his own repertoire for a laugh: A shot in which Mrs. Robinson exhales a cloud of cigarette smoke after Benjamin kisses her came straight from "Teenagers.")

The three of them spent days working on the film's longest dialogue scene, a tense, sad, winding conversation in bed, during which Benjamin coaxes Mrs. Robinson to reveal details about her past, learns that she had to marry because she was pregnant and that she had once studied art history, then turns on her and calls her a "broken-down alcoholic." Henry had written the scene as a fully shaped fifteen-minute one-act play—it begins with Benjamin telling Mrs. Robinson they should talk more and ends with his defeated line "Let's not talk at all." The scene was important, revealing her vulnerability and his capacity for cruelty, but it also had the contours of a classic Nichols and May sketch, and offered Nichols a chance to do the kind of granular, character-based work he most enjoyed. As they shot, he realized with dejection that only a fraction of it could be used—as much as he loved the scene, it played as a piece of theater in the middle of a movie. He and Henry came up with a device—switching the lights on and off—that broke it up into fragments and would make cutting easier when the time came.

When Hoffman got stuck, Nichols's instincts were unerring—he knew when to fill him up with a story or an analogy and when to draw him out about his own life. In the scene in which Benjamin checks into the Taft Hotel for a tryst, Hoffman couldn't find the right combination of determination and shame. He and Nichols took a break and talked for a long time about embarrassment. Hoffman remembered trying to buy condoms as a teenager; Nichols told him to imagine that the desk clerk, played by Henry, was a female pharmacist. They shared an emotional vocabulary—every slight, mortification, failure, or misstep from Hoffman's past was cataloged in his memory, waiting to be unlocked by Nichols. Hoffman had an older brother; Nichols, five years older than his star, *was* an older brother. It was an ideal dynamic.

Except when it wasn't. Although Nichols could be encouraging and generous, finding just the right words when he thought Hoffman was in danger of being overcome by the feeling that he was in over his head, he could also be tough, caustic, and dismissive. "Go clean the inside of your nose," Nichols would tell Hoffman again and again before takes. "Oh, I'm sick of that shirt off," he remarked to the crew as Hoffman started to undress for a scene. "We've got to have him dressed once in a while. It's not like he's Bardot." When he didn't like Hoffman's approach, his wit hardened into ice. "What were you doing?" he asked after one take.

"Well, I made a choice . . ." Hoffman started to say.

"I see," said Nichols. "Well, the next time you get a thought, do the opposite."

At times, Nichols's behavior verged on sadistic. He insisted on shooting fifteen takes of a scene in which Elaine slaps Benjamin, and the slaps weren't faked. The next day, blood poured out of Hoffman's ear; he had torn his eardrum.

To those who witnessed their evolving relationship, Nichols's alternately benevolent and withholding demeanor felt tactical—a calculated move by a director who wanted to render his novice leading man just anxious and off balance enough to keep him in character. But it was also a by-product of ill temper at what was becoming a difficult, overbudget shoot. As filming of *The Graduate* rolled through spring and into the suffocating heat of July and August, nobody was happy. Early in rehearsals, the journalist Betty Rollin had come to the set to report a piece for

Look magazine. Her first impressions were that Bancroft was "languid," Hoffman "jumpy," and Ross "unsure." That held true throughout the shoot. "Annie wasn't Mrs. Robinson," said Nichols, "but she had this tremendous anger—that was real, that was her power." Twenty-five years later, she reminded him that, for her, the making of the movie "wasn't such a wonderful time." She had cramps and hangovers and fainting spells, and days when she felt disconnected from her character. At home, she had to handle her husband's persistent kvetching about her bedroom scenes with her younger costar—Brooks was still annoyed that Hoffman had turned down an offer to star in *The Producers*. And at work, she had to contend with the fact that Nichols, afraid she would become insecure about how old he and Surtees were making her look, wouldn't even let her see dailies. Ross struggled with her part to the point that Nichols snapped at O'Steen, "She's driving me fucking crazy, she can't do it, she doesn't have it." And Hoffman, who put in the longest days of any actor, then dragged himself back to his hotel room at the Chateau Marmont each night to work on the next day's scenes before falling into bed exhausted, eventually became so emotionally frayed that when "they had me do all the stuff in the Alfa Romeo at the end, and they said, 'Pass every car,'" he grew convinced that nobody on the set "really cared whether I lived or died after a certain point."

The shoot left Nichols almost no time to decompress. Not until *The Graduate* moved to Berkeley for the scenes in which Benjamin arrives on campus to try to win back Elaine did he find himself with a free evening to spend with an old friend—Joy Carlin, the girl with whom he had left Chicago for New York a dozen years earlier. She was eager to cook dinner for her now-famous pal. "I think I was trying to impress him—I had oysters and steak," she says. Halfway through the meal, Nichols mentioned that he had been driven there in a limousine by a chauffeur who was parked outside. "Invite him in," Carlin said. Nichols shook his head as she started to argue. "No, no," he said, explaining the rules of his new life. "You don't understand—you don't do that. That's not how it's done."

By the last weeks of production, Nichols's imperiousness was starting to wear on everyone. "Sometimes Katharine and I would look at each other and say, 'Is he in a bad mood? Did he see the rushes? Did we do something wrong?'" Hoffman says. As they were grabbing a quick shot on the Sunset Strip of Benjamin and Elaine walking toward a club where he deliberately humiliates her, Nichols realized, for the first time, how much his irritability and condescension were poisoning the experience for those around him. It was a moment he would remember for the rest of his career and try to head off whenever he caught himself doing it again. A shot had gone wrong, and "I said something snotty, as I often did to the crew. And Surtees—I heard him say to them, but it wasn't for me—said, 'It's okay. It's not much longer,'" Nichols recalled. "I thought, *Oh man*. How could I have been such a shit that this man that I revere feels that way about me? But I was. And he did.

"Part of me must have known what I then had no real inkling of, which is that I would never get material . . . so suited to *me* again," Nichols said. But "when you know exactly what you want to do, it doesn't make you particularly nice. Sometimes just the opposite: 'Don't you get it? Don't do *that*—do *this*. God, doesn't anybody understand me?' It's so revolting. But on this picture, I was not a nice guy. I was a nightmare."

The moment brought Nichols up short; he didn't realize how unhappy he was, or how much he had taken it out on everyone. He had recently begun living with Penelope Gilliatt, an English writer and critic who had ended her marriage to the playwright John Osborne and moved to the United States. "Remind me when this is over," he told her, "that I'm not enjoying this. And of course, she did."

Much later, Nichols would come to understand more of what was behind his charged, intimate, punishing relationship with Hoffman on *The Graduate,* and the degree to which, as he put it, "my unconscious was making this movie." For the first time in his career as a director, he had found something he hadn't known he was looking for and wasn't sure he wanted: a doppelgänger who solved the riddle of a character and a movie while at the same time inflaming every private insecurity Nichols had—about his personality, about his physical appearance, about his place in the world. When Hoffman couldn't get something right, Nichols felt like he, too, was failing; when a pretty extra flirted with him, Nichols thought, *Why not with me?*

One morning toward the end, Hoffman came in looking so drawn that Nichols pulled him aside and asked what was wrong.

"I'm tired," he said.

"Well," said Nichols, "this is the only chance you're ever going to have to do this scene for the rest of your life. When you look back, do you really want to say 'I was tired'?"

"He doesn't say it," Hoffman said at the time, "but soon you realize that he's asking for your peak every minute. So you give it—not out of fear but out of respect." But more than high standards were at play in Nichols's approach. He was saying, *Prove you belong here.* And just as clearly, *Prove I belong here.* The story of an alienated young man cosseted by privilege, smothered by the comforts that surround him, and determined to listen to himself had come to feel personal in a way he had never imagined.

"It was there from the very beginning, when I was choosing him," Nichols said. "Dummy! Who was the Jew among the goyim? And who was forever a visitor in a strange land?" It had not even occurred to him to examine the resonance of his decision to make a romantic comedy that culminated with the hero seeing his first love slip just out of his reach as he shouts, "Elaine! Elaine! Elaine!"

In the movie's last shot, Benjamin and Elaine, exhilarated and adrenalized, flee her wedding. (The novel had Benjamin reach her just before the vows were completed; Nichols and Henry changed it to just after.) They race for a bus, jump on board, and are carried off into their new lives, the joy on their faces slowly giving way to ambivalence. Generations of audiences would ask what happened to them, and be unsatisfied by both Nichols's answer ("They become their parents") and Henry's ("They get off the bus, ultimately"). Nichols liked to say that he simply told Hoffman and Ross to get on the bus and grin madly, then never yelled "Cut," waited until the smiles faded from their faces, and used the result. It wasn't true; for the final shot, one of the last things to be filmed in the movie, he got back to his first principles as a director. There was no tyranny and no petulance; he told them, "Sit down and take a ride, and we'll see what happens."

For much of the shoot, "there was a kind of tension of, we're working with a master and he's not cutting corners, so we'd better get it right," says Hoffman. "But he was open. He got on the bus with us at the end, with a handheld camera, and talked. He said, 'Okay, look back. Now look ahead. Now each of you think of the most painful memory you have. Now think of a really great moment in your life. Now just look— don't think of anything. He knew he'd build it in the cutting room."

In August 1967, *The Graduate* wrapped. Nichols wasn't sure he had a movie, let alone a good movie. But he wasn't especially worried. "If I'm terrified and mystified and feel, 'I'm lost, this is the one that's going to destroy me, I'll never figure it out and it's not about anything, how could I have made that mistake?'" he said, "I'm fine. That terror is the life of it."

Fourteen

IT'S BEGINNING TO
MAKE SENSE

1967–1968

Y ou can't do this, Mike," Sam O'Steen told him. "You're killing
everybody."

As he edited *The Graduate*, Nichols was, he said, "in the
grip of something" that was testing the forbearance of even his closest
colleagues. First, he decided that the movie wasn't finished. He called
Elizabeth Wilson and William Daniels, who had completed their work
and returned to New York, and told them he had decided to add a couple of scenes. Wilson wasn't surprised—"the whole experience had been
many, many, many takes, as if they had all the time in the world," she
said, "so it seemed like a movie that would never be done." They
dropped everything, flew to Los Angeles, and checked into the Chateau Marmont, only to get a call from Nichols, who sheepishly said he
had changed his mind. "Goddammit, I just flew three thousand miles!"
said Daniels. "Okay, okay," said Nichols, "I'll do it." The next morning
they walked onto a giant, unrealistic dining room set that Daniels said
"looked like something out of a German Expressionist film" and shot
the new scene. Nichols looked so stricken that Wilson joked, "Well,

you always said you wanted to be a director." "Ha, ha, ha," he muttered. The scene was never used.

Now, back in New York, Nichols was holed up in an editing room above a Midtown strip joint, hovering and fussing until O'Steen told him to get out and give him a chance to finish the sound mix. He agreed, even though at that point *The Graduate* felt to him like a series of problems only he could solve. Chief among them was the music. Nichols couldn't get Simon & Garfunkel out of his head; when the shoot was almost over, he asked them if they would consider scoring the movie. "They were, as they were about everything then, unenthusiastic," he said. "But Paul consented to write a few songs."

But by then, Nichols had boxed himself in. He and O'Steen had already shaped one of *The Graduate*'s most striking sequences—a wordless montage in which Benjamin drifts from his own room to Mrs. Robinson's bed, from hotel encounters to his parents' kitchen, from pillow to pool—a perfect representation of a young man wafting through summer in a nihilistic trance. It ended with Benjamin thrusting himself upward onto a pool raft and, with one cut, onto Bancroft in bed, so that when he turned over, he would see his father looking down, seemingly frowning on both activities at once. Nichols and O'Steen had scored the montage with the two Simon & Garfunkel songs Nichols had been listening to for months—"The Sound of Silence," which had become a hit a year and a half earlier, and "April Come She Will." He had always planned to replace those tracks with new music. Now he found that nothing else worked.

"It was the only thing to do," he said. "'Hello, darkness, my old friend' was what was happening in Benjamin's head. It's a characteristic of movies that at a certain point, they decide what you need. You're not doing it anymore—you are possessed by them and you do what the movie wants." Nichols also included two more old Simon & Garfunkel songs, "Scarborough Fair," which he deployed intermittently over an eleven-minute stretch in which Benjamin starts to realize he's in love with Elaine, and "The Big Bright Green Pleasure Machine," which he used on a jukebox as background music. When he told Simon he didn't like either of the new songs he had written for the film, Simon played him a tune he had been working on called "Mrs. Roosevelt." Nichols thought it suited the movie beautifully, but it was just a fragment with no completed lyrics. What's heard in the film is an embryonic version of the song that eventually became "Mrs. Robinson," but ironically, it's used only once Benjamin is finished with her, and the lyrics on the soundtrack are mostly nonsense syllables that Simon & Garfunkel were using as placeholders.

Joe Levine had been planning to sell *The Graduate* with music and sex, and now he felt deprived of both. The idea of using pop songs that people already knew seemed to him like an admission of defeat—and Nichols's plan to play "The Sound of Silence" twice—first over the opening credits and again forty minutes later—felt almost defiant. Nor was Levine getting the cooperation he wanted from Bancroft's and Hoffman's representatives. He was used to marketing art movies as if they were lurid trash—the leering, cleavage-filled ad campaigns he had masterminded for *Marriage Italian Style* and Jean-Luc Godard's *Contempt* had put a lot of money in his pocket. For *The Graduate*, he wanted Hoffman and Bancroft naked in the poster. "He was thinking, *All this movie's ever going to be is an art-house release, and if people think there's nudity, maybe they'll come*," says Hoffman. "Anne wouldn't do it, but the one who *really* wouldn't do it was Nichols."

By October, Nichols and O'Steen had pared *The Graduate* to a lean 106 minutes, removing anything that strayed from Benjamin's perspective and ending on just the right expressions of contentment, ambivalence, and trepidation on Hoffman's and Ross's faces. Finally, even Nichols felt he had done everything he wanted to do with the film. With the release set for December, he turned to Lillian Hellman's *The Little Foxes*, which he had agreed to direct on Broadway in its first revival since the original staging in 1939. In some ways, he had contrived the production as an extension of his work on *The Graduate*—Bancroft would star as Regina Giddens, the cold-blooded center of a rotting turn-of-the-century southern family who wrests a fortune from her conniving brothers and ailing husband, and he hired Elizabeth Wilson as her standby. He even tried to persuade Hoffman to join the cast as Leo Hubbard, Regina's doltish, thieving nephew. Depleted from the long shoot, Hoffman said no; Nichols hired Austin Pendleton instead.

The Little Foxes offered Nichols a chance to restart his theater career on new terms. Earlier in 1967, *Luv* had closed after more than two years. *Barefoot in the Park* and *The Odd Couple* had both ended their long runs while he was filming over the summer, *The Apple Tree* was closing in November, and film versions of *Barefoot* and *Luv*, by other directors, had just opened across the country. Nichols had had no interest in making those movies himself—"They were dead for me," he said. "There was nothing to discover." But he was also aware of the criticism that he was too content to linger in the shallows of popular comedy, and this moment, at which he had gone from having four plays on Broadway to none, felt like an opportunity for reinvention. *The Little Foxes* would be his first stage drama, his first revival, and the first time his name alone would guarantee an all-star cast. Besides Bancroft, he signed Margaret Leighton, a frail, respected British actress who had won Tonys for Terence Rattigan and Tennessee Williams plays, E. G. Marshall, and George C. Scott, a dynamic, volatile talent who had quit his last Broadway production, a play by Ira Levin that he had agreed to direct, after just five days.

Hellman had tried to persuade Nichols to direct her work for years, but as *The Little Foxes* began rehearsals, some in its cast wondered if he would ever get the chance. "I wanted him to do it," she said, but "I had real worries about . . . the rigidity that so often comes when you try something, anything, for the second time . . . Can the second husband ever be the saint the first husband never was?" During an early read-through, Hellman sat beside Nichols, smoking and taking notes, then began a long talk about what the script meant and how it should be played. "She was delightful and terrible," says Pendleton. She seemed to have no intention of leaving. As rehearsals continued, she would dictate notes to her assistant about the actors' deficiencies in a gravelly rasp loud enough to carry from the back row of the orchestra to the performers. When she took to striding through the theater, eyeing the stage from various angles and barking commentary to Nichols about what he was doing wrong, he told her she couldn't come back until previews began.

Nichols was aware that, for all its internecine savagery, *The Little Foxes* risked looking like an antique in its depiction of race. Its two Black characters, Cal and Addie, were house servants who were seen more than heard, and he was dusting off the play at a time when new works by James Baldwin and Lorraine Hansberry made Hellman's approach look even more dated. Even movies were fitfully trying to grapple with American race relations in less perfunctory ways. Norman Jewison's *In the Heat of the Night* had just opened, and Beah Richards, the actress and activist Nichols had cast as Addie, had just finished playing Sidney Poitier's mother in Stanley Kramer's interracial-marriage comedy *Guess Who's Coming to Dinner*, which was due to open the same week as *The Graduate*.

Through five stage productions and two movies, Nichols had yet to direct a single Black performer. He had grown up in an era in which Black actors rarely appeared in studio movies except as comic housekeepers, feckless sidekicks, or musical specialty acts, but he was not oblivious to the ways in which Hellman's use of Black characters as sentimentalized embodiments of decency and rectitude had aged poorly.

Hellman was not about to rewrite the parts, so Nichols decided he would at least place the two servants in the foreground; as *The Little Foxes* began, with the Hubbard and Giddens families squabbling and backbiting, he would have Richards's Addie come to the lip of the thrust stage at Lincoln Center's Vivian Beaumont Theater and repeatedly shake her head in disgust, in an attempt to create complicity with the audience. It was a stretch—one that would delight some critics, infuriate others, and frustrate Nichols himself. He later said that he felt he had "screwed up" and wished he had found a better way to present the play's Black characters.

The Little Foxes had too many other problems for Nichols to give the issue his full attention. Hellman kept hammering at him about Bancroft's performance, until he began to lose confidence in his own judgment. "I think it was a sexual thing, a kind of jealousy," says Pendleton. "She felt there was a closeness he had with Anne Bancroft, and she would not let up on him." Leighton, who suffered from multiple sclerosis, struggled physically. "She was brilliant, and fragile, and I would watch her propel herself out onto that stage every night, just holding herself together," says Maria Tucci, who played Regina's daughter Alexandra. Nichols was happy with George C. Scott, but the weekend breaks between the matinee and evening performances, when the actors would gather at Patrick O'Neal's popular restaurant the Ginger Man, across from Lincoln Center, were perilous, and on at least one occasion Scott got so drunk he told his castmates, "You go back to the theater. I'm not doing it." The next day, he made the rounds backstage, apologizing. Most of his costars shrugged the incident off, but Leighton could not forgive him for walking out on the job. "How dare you," she said.

Nichols was even tougher on Pendleton than he had been on Hoffman, telling him on the second day of rehearsal, "You know you're totally wrong for this part, don't you? Don't worry, we'll work on it." They did, to little avail. "In those days, my mind was so literal," says

Pendleton. "He gave me every direction he could think of, but I couldn't figure out how to turn what he wanted into stage acting." After one run-through, he had notes for everyone else in the cast but him. "Like an idiot, as they all left, I said, 'So I guess you're getting happy,'" Pendleton says. "And Mike said, 'How can I be pleased with a performance that is wrong from beginning to end? You haven't addressed it at all.' He was pissed off." Pendleton became Nichols's scapegoat in the production, and it was Bancroft who probably saved his job. "It's the way you walk," she said, pulling him into her dressing room. "You lead with your head, because smart people lead with their heads. Leo has been told he's stupid since he was two. So you should lead with your crotch. I want you to go in tomorrow and don't think about anything but that, and don't tell Mike I told you." Pendleton did as she said, "and a few minutes in, Mike said, 'Okay! Now it's beginning to make sense!' After that he was totally supportive."

Nichols never distanced himself from a production he thought wasn't working, but flailing in the course of mounting a Broadway play was new to him, and unnerving. Before *The Little Foxes* opened, he gave his cast the pep talk he reserved for tough times, telling them, "This is the best company I've ever worked with," rather than using the sardonic "Remember—everything depends on tonight" line that he had come to favor when he knew he had a hit. Then he steeled himself for excoriating reviews.

He got a few, but they were exceptions. Most critics enjoyed the production, which played for a couple of months, then transferred, with a few cast changes, to another Broadway theater and went on to a national tour. No one contended that it was his best work, but the debate focused on the play itself, and its most heated critics took greater issue with what they saw as the heavy-handed self-righteousness of Hellman's writing than with Nichols's adherence to it. If his goal had been to prove that he could direct serious drama, the jury instead became engaged in a side argument about whether Hellman's work qualified.

She had always been a lightning rod, and the quarrels the production sparked in places like *The New York Review of Books* were more about her work than his. Nichols, for his part, believed he had gotten off lucky. "He told me on the set of *Catch-22* that he regarded *Little Foxes* as the one production he was ashamed of," says Pendleton (who directed its next Broadway revival many years later). "He did the play for Lillian, and she hated it."

Nichols felt he had never fully engaged with the material, in part because his mind was still on *The Graduate*. He had reason to worry. With the opening weeks away, buzz was not good. "The first people who saw the movie had only derogatory things to say about Hoffman," Buck Henry said. "'Oh, it's wonderful, Mike, so beautiful to look at—a shame about the boy.'"

"I remember," said Nichols, "like people who remember the one vicious line when they had raves, a screening at the Directors Guild of America" at which he sat directly behind Elia Kazan. "I heard him say to [the screenwriter] Budd Schulberg, 'I don't know, I was taught to have a *worthy* adversary.' And I thought, really? You don't think Mrs. Robinson was worthy?" said Nichols. "[Kazan] was my hero. And there was a lot of rolling of eyes. I was so sad." Even some of *The Graduate*'s actors were indifferent or worse. When he invited Elizabeth Wilson to an early screening, "it didn't hit me the way I thought it was going to," she recalled, "and I couldn't cover my disappointment. I must have said something to Mike, and he got angry." William Daniels took his wife to a screening and was so annoyed at how much of his work had been cut that he skipped the after-party. "I didn't make any judgment about the movie," he said, "but I probably had a chip on my shoulder."

A few people were encouraging. Jules Feiffer had been furious at Nichols for more than a year, ever since Nichols had passed on directing his play *Little Murders*. He went to a *Graduate* screening "hoping it would be a great flop," he says. "I just wanted bad things for Mike. And it took my breath away. I inhaled it frame by frame. By the time it was on for ten minutes, I knew I was seeing something revolutionary, and all I kept thinking was 'Don't sell it out, don't fuck it up.' When I got home, I wrote a love note to Mike, saying just how remarkable I thought the film was. My grudge didn't matter anymore." Nichols, feeling he would need every friend he had, messengered back a grateful reply, and their rift ended.

Nichols didn't understand what *The Graduate* was going to become until the film had its first public preview, on Manhattan's Upper East Side. Hoffman sat in the back row of the balcony with Anne Byrne. He found the experience "excruciating" and had no sense of how the movie was playing until its climax, when he heard noise, walked down to peer over the edge of the balcony, and saw the young audience on its feet, cheering for Benjamin and Elaine to escape. "We were speechless," said Nichols. "We didn't understand why people were going nuts . . . [It] never crossed our minds that it would have such a shocking reaction."

The Graduate opened on December 20. Critics were, at first, divided—Pauline Kael sneeringly called the film "a television commercial," and John Simon railed against its "rock-bottom" music and "obviousness, pretentiousness . . . and sketchiness." But *The Graduate* got a rave from Bosley Crowther, the veteran *New York Times* reviewer who, in his final piece before retiring, called it "one of the best seriocomic social satires we've had from Hollywood since Preston Sturges was making them." The film became not only an instant hit but a cultural milestone that was widely seen as Hollywood's first great exploration of the generation gap, a subject in which Nichols—who, at thirty-six, belonged to neither generation represented in the movie—had little interest. "The film demonstrates a youth movement that can be cheered or jeered, enjoyed or criticized," said the *New York Post*. "The point is that Nichols has come through with something distinctly new under the movie sun." Everyone had an opinion, and as often as not an angry one. David Brinkley called it "frantic nonsense," then admitted that his son and his friends, who were Benjamin's age, thought it "was absolutely the best movie they ever saw." *Life* magazine labeled *The Graduate* "the latest symbol of the battle cry, 'Don't trust anyone over thirty,'" and *Saturday Review* noted that older audiences "almost felt personally attacked" by the film. It didn't matter. Soon after *The Graduate* opened, the studios got the startling results of a study revealing that almost half of American ticket buyers were under twenty-four. It was an audience that Hollywood had either ignored or taken for granted for decades. The aging men who ran the studios had long assumed that their target audience was Benjamin's parents. *The Graduate* showed them it was Benjamin.

Two months after it opened, the film received seven Academy Award nominations, including Best Picture and Best Director. Henry's script and Surtees's cinematography were also recognized, as were Hoffman, Bancroft, and Ross. By then, *The Graduate* was, as *The New Yorker* put it, "a nearly mandatory movie experience, which can be discussed in gatherings that cross the boundaries of age and class. It also seems to be one of those propitious works of art which support the theory that we are no longer necessarily two publics—the undiscerning and the demanding—for whom separate kinds of entertainment must be provided." By the time it completed its run, two full years later, *The Graduate* had become the third-highest-grossing film in history, behind only *Gone With the Wind* and *The Sound of Music*. Moreover, it had arrived just as film programs were sprouting at American universities, where students not only debated the movie's themes and cultural politics but paid obsessive attention to its technique, examining every cut in the musical montages, every zoom in the film's second half, and every moment when Nichols and Surtees managed to film Benjamin against so much glass without ever catching reflections. Nichols, after just two movies, had turned into a filmmaking hero to an emerging crop of novice directors who, according to a *New York Times* report, "speak with a special fervor about . . . *The Graduate*."

I t was not a role he relished. Nichols had no appetite to become a generational spokesman. He had assumed that the result of nearly a year's work would be a tepidly received comedy that would mark him as what *Time* magazine's dismissive review called "a victim of the sophomore jinx" and assumed the best medicine would be to have returned to work by the time the movie opened. Neil Simon's play *Plaza Suite* was, on paper, exactly the kind of easy, often broad comedy that *The Graduate* seemed to render irrelevant. Nichols was delighted by the format—four unrelated short plays set in the same New York hotel room—and he thought Simon's goal to present "a drama, a satire, a comedy, and a farce" in one evening, all played by the same two leading actors, would allow him to do the kind of detailed work with performers and staging that he loved.

The play's setting also attracted him. Nichols had spent much of the preceding three years in hotels, whether on location with movies or on the road with plays; he understood the ways in which unfamiliar surroundings can allow for a suspension of the rules or bring tensions to the surface. In some ways, the domesticity of home was no more familiar to him than a rented room was. He and Penelope Gilliatt were now living together in his penthouse; she was starting a new job as co–lead film critic for *The New Yorker* and flying to and from England to finalize an ugly divorce from John Osborne, who was livid that she had moved in with Nichols and missed no chance to be cruel about it. (Gilliatt told Edmund Wilson that Osborne tore the hair off their young daughter's dolls "to show what Mike Nichols's head was like.")

According to some newspaper columns, Nichols was ready to embark on his third marriage just as soon as Gilliatt's papers came through; "Jacqueline Kennedy's brace of eligible bachelor escorts is diminishing by the day," said one. It wasn't true; Gilliatt was mercurial, and Nichols worried that she was too invested in him—when he was working on *The Apple Tree*, she had shown up for rehearsals so often that he complained "she was like a ghost hanging around." "You sometimes meet couples and think, 'Oh my God, they're so in love.' I didn't feel that with Mike and Penelope," says Wallace Shawn, who first met Nichols around that time. "They lived up in that magnificent tower on Eighty-first Street, and she was very witty, and very passionate, very emotional, but I don't remember thinking, *They can't get enough of each other.*" Nichols had scheduled out-of-town tryouts for *Plaza Suite* in New Haven and Boston, and he was planning to go alone.

He began rehearsals with George C. Scott and Maureen Stapleton two days before *The Graduate* opened. Like Scott, Stapleton was an alcoholic—during the run of *Plaza Suite*, Simon would write *The Gingerbread Lady*, a comedy-drama about an actress just home from a rehab clinic, with her in mind. Unlike Scott, she drank when the curtain came down, not before it went up. Later in his career, Nichols would institute what he called the "no assholes" rule. It was based on his conviction that one bad personality could sour a production, a lesson he learned partly from Walter Matthau. But for him, actors with substance abuse issues didn't fall into that category; Nichols viewed addiction as a fact of people's lives, one to be worked around or through but always approached with empathy. His awareness of Art Carney's struggles, of Richard Burton's, and even of Scott's, only made him understand how much harder they had to work; he thought his job was, in most cases, to give talented actors whatever support they needed, not to judge them.

Like many of his contemporaries, Nichols believed that Scott was one role away from being widely recognized as a great American actor. And Scott, who was embarrassed by his behavior during *The Little Foxes*, was grateful for his director's unflappability. "Inside he may be going through the [tortures of the] damned," he said, "but it never shows. He creates an atmosphere for an actor to work in that is so easy you can't believe it."

At Nichols's urging, Simon eliminated one of the four playlets early in rehearsal. What was left was equal riches for both leads. The first play, "Visitor from Mamaroneck," a dramatic piece about a middle-aged woman on her second honeymoon who realizes how little the marriage means to her husband, was a showcase for Stapleton; the second, the broad sex comedy "Visitor from Hollywood," allowed Scott to own the stage as a movie producer eager to get a starstruck old love into bed. The closing act, "Visitor from Forest Hills," was pure farce, with the two stars getting equal time as a couple whose about-to-be-married daughter locks herself in the bathroom and refuses to come out.

"Mike was a behaviorist," says Bob Balaban, who was cast as a bell-boy. "He always went back to 'Where did you come from? What space are you in? What are you doing in this scene?' You had to have both an emotional and a physical life, even if you were a star. So for the first three or four hours, they got used to the room and thought about 'Well, do you hang your coat up first? Do you look to see if there's ice?' and they tried out some of the lines as they moved around." Simon decided to watch Nichols in order to learn "his style, his tricks, his attack on the art of directing . . . After ten days, I realized I had learned nothing. He had no tricks," he wrote. "What he had mostly was his intelligence, his knowledge of the world outside the world of the theater, his keen, sharp eye for the manners and behavior of people."

Everyone seemed happy until two weeks in, when Scott didn't show up. Nichols spent the afternoon working around him. The next morning Stapleton came in. "Is the Pussycat here?" she asked. He was not. By the afternoon of the second day, Nichols asked Scott's understudy to rehearse with her. That afternoon, Scott walked in mid-rehearsal, glowering. His volcanic temper was known to everyone working on the play. The room froze, braced for a blowup, wondering how Nichols would handle it. Finally Nichols looked over and said, "Hi, George. We're on act one, scene two. You're on the phone calling this girl in New Jersey." "There was a silent moment," Simon wrote, "where no one moved or breathed, then George slowly walked to the bed, sat down, picked up the phone, dialed, thought for a second, and called out 'Line.' The stage manager quietly gave him his line, and George picked up his cue and proceeded with the scene as though he had never been gone."

Whether out of fear or pragmatism, Scott's moods were endured, his whims indulged, his ideas entertained. At one point he announced to Stapleton that he thought it would be a great idea for them both to play most of one act in a bathroom where they would be heard but not seen. "Okay," said Nichols, "we'll try it that way tomorrow." Scott left for the day, and Stapleton said, "There is no way that I'm going to play an entire act offstage."

"I have to give George enough rope," Nichols told her. "You watch— he'll come in tomorrow and say it can't be done."

"The next day," Stapleton said, "George marched in rather solemnly and said that he'd thought it through and felt we should do the scene the old way."

Things only got worse. In New Haven, Scott complained that his second-act costume made him look like a "faggot" and stormed out of the theater. In Boston, angry at something Stapleton had done, he grabbed her mink coat and shoved it into a toilet. Stapleton was tolerant of what she called "the little glitches in our relationship that were usually fueled by alcohol." "George had a vicious, terrible, difficult drinking problem," says Balaban, "but onstage, he and Maureen were both wildly professional. For all the difficulties, the play was proceeding like a dream." On opening night in Boston, audiences and critics greeted the play with enthusiastic laughter. By then, the company was tightly bonded—they were staying in the same hotel; there were long meals and rounds of word games, and Scott, at his best, was the life of any party. During the post-show celebration, Stapleton, well into a bottle of vodka, told the stage manager, "Wake me at noon, take me to the theater, and have someone remind me what play this is." Scott called his wife, Colleen Dewhurst, and said, evidently delighted, "I'm finally in a goddamn hit, can you imagine that?"

At 3:40 a.m., Nichols showed up at Simon's hotel room, looking shattered. He had just spent two hours with Scott. "George wants to quit the play," Nichols said. "He said something was coming over him. He can always feel when it's happening. This one's a tornado, he said. He doesn't want to hurt Maureen or you or me." Nichols ordered ice cream from room service.

"You're going to eat ice cream *now?*" Simon said.

"You mean if I don't eat ice cream, maybe he'll come back?" Nichols replied.

Nobody knew where Scott had gone. His understudy went on the next day. Simon and Nichols started batting around possible replacements—Hal Holbrook, José Ferrer—but by the third day they were discussing canceling the Broadway run. "There was no obviously visible terror," Balaban says. "It was just very quiet. Nobody ever said the words 'He went on a bender because of the pressure.' He had never appeared to be nervous or scared about anything." After four days, Scott returned. "Mike came around and had to say to us, 'Here's the drill. Don't say *Welcome back,* don't ask how he is. Make it be like he was here yesterday, no references to anything out of the ordinary,'" Balaban says. "And the play went on."

Plaza Suite opened on Broadway on Valentine's Day 1968, for what would become a tremendously profitable run of almost three years. The play made Nichols considerably more money than any of his previous theater work. One-sixth of the show's $150,000 capitalization had come from him, entitling him to a large share of the profits; in addition, instead of the then-standard director's royalty of 3 percent, he got

7 percent—5 percent for his directing and 2 percent for "consultation"—an acknowledgment of how instrumental he had become to Simon's work. For the first time, the warm reviews were tinged with a kind of nostalgia. Harold Clurman wrote in *The Nation* that the play was "reminiscent of the shrewd Nichols-and-May pieces of yesteryear." "His direction on its own has sweep and great feel for comedy," another critic wrote, but "here and there, one detects an echo of the Nichols and May era, of the smooth and inventive patterns they made on a stage, the little thrusts and parries that illuminated their routines."

Era. Yesteryear. It was a jolt for Nichols to see his first career discussed as part of a distant past, a reminder of a style of comedy that was beginning to give way to something angrier, more topical, more political. In movies, he was now seen as a torchbearer for a new age; in theater, he was becoming regarded as a kind of preservationist who used his sure touch to elevate comfortable comedy for a bourgeois Broadway audience.

By the time *Plaza Suite* began its run, Nichols was beginning to collect awards for *The Graduate*; he had won the Golden Globe and the Directors Guild of America prize and was expected to take the Academy Award as well. He didn't give it much thought; the age of intense, extended Oscar campaigns had not yet begun, and the ceremony was disdained by younger New York theater and film people as a vulgar, self-satisfied Hollywood rite that rewarded mediocrity and sentiment. "It used to be straightforward—if you had been sick that year, or were a shiksa playing a whore, you won," he said. "Everybody knew the rules."

Nichols's friends had pulled him into Eugene McCarthy's campaign for the 1968 Democratic presidential nomination, and in late March he went with the Bernsteins, Comden and Green, and Paul Newman and Joanne Woodward to stump for McCarthy in Wisconsin. A few days later he returned to New York. On April 4, he and Gilliatt were at his apartment having dinner with Arthur Penn, who had directed the year's other major critical and cultural sensation, *Bonnie and Clyde* ("We loved *Bonnie and Clyde*," he said. "Who wouldn't?"), when news broke that the Reverend Dr. Martin Luther King Jr. had been assassinated.

The Oscars were scheduled to take place four days later. "I said, 'I won't go,'" said Nichols. "And Arthur said, 'I won't go either.'" As other performers and presenters, including all of the Black people who were scheduled to appear, demanded that the ceremony be postponed in the wake of the national tragedy, the Academy, which had first responded to the news with "The show must go on," realized it had misread the mood of the nation and of its own industry, and agreed to wait two extra days.

Nichols attended the tense and subdued evening, which was hosted by an awkward Bob Hope, and he won the Academy Award. After Leslie Caron handed him the statuette, he said, "Until this moment, my greatest pleasure in *The Graduate* was making it. It's a picture made by a group, and we cared for each other, and we cared for what we were doing. So this award quite literally belongs to them at least as much as it does to me. I'm grateful to them, and to the Academy, and to the movies themselves. And I'd also like to wish my mother a happy birthday. Thank you."

Onstage, Nichols was charming and modest. Inside, "I was Mister Anhedonia," he said. "I think there may be people who can enjoy the Academy Awards, but I'm just not one of them. I was completely blank. I had no pleasure in it. I had nothing. The way I put it is, you end up at the Beverly Hills Hotel at midnight feeling empty. To me, that's what the Academy Award was. But I think I was (a) very spoiled, (b) very neurotic, and (c) I had a very impaired sense of reality."

"If you're ever the golden boy, which I seem to be at the moment," he had said a couple of years earlier, "it's going to change. You don't go through your professional life without having it flip over suddenly . . . Even as you do well, energy is being stored up for the attack . . . I have a realistic view about doing well, so I won't be destroyed when I make a mistake some day—as I must."

That moment hadn't yet come. But a year later, Nichols repeated the warning, bracing everyone, and perhaps himself. "Wait!" he said. "You're going to see such failures, you wouldn't believe it!"

Fifteen

THE ONLY WAY TO LIVE
YOUR LIFE

1968–1969

By the Sunday after the awards, Nichols was back in New York with Gilliatt and her young daughter. Edmund Wilson had recently published a glowing "open letter" in *The New York Review of Books* in which he implored the young prodigy on whom he doted to flee "the fleshpots of Hollywood steeped in which so many fine talents have foundered." But after all, he had just won an Oscar, and who would pass up a chance to see one of those up close? Wilson and Arthur Schlesinger Jr. came over to the penthouse to offer their congratulations. While they were there, they stood at his window for a while and gazed down at Central Park, where a memorial march for Martin Luther King Jr. was slowly moving along the paths.

"He is living in more or less luxury," the apparently perplexed Wilson wrote when he got home. "[He] has a large young Great Dane bitch and a little fuzzy white dog that belongs to the rather odd-looking small butler, perhaps a Puerto Rican."

Nichols had only a few days in New York and was trying to cram in as much as he could. Later that afternoon, he went to see Stanley

Kubrick's *2001: A Space Odyssey,* which had just opened. He was awed. He immediately called Buck Henry and told him he had to go. He was thinking big, ready at last to give his full attention to the film that would consume him for the next two years. Playwrights, including Neil Simon, sent him their new work; he turned them all down, telling them he anticipated being busy on *Catch-22* until the end of 1969. Henry was at work on the screenplay, and Nichols was planning a film the scale and cost of which would dwarf anything he had directed. The following Sunday, he won his third Tony as Best Director, for *Plaza Suite,* but he was gone; he had flown to Rome to scout locations. With him were Dick Sylbert, who had come to serve as a kind of overall visual consultant for him, and *Catch-22*'s producer, John Calley, with whom Nichols would forge one of his closest lifelong friendships.

On its surface, the story Joseph Heller told in *Catch-22* was simple: Yossarian, his protagonist, is a bombardier in an Army hospital in Italy during World War II who is caught between two strategies: insisting that he's too crazy to fly and trying to complete enough missions to be permitted to stay on the ground—a threshold that keeps being raised so that it's always just out of reach. In the novel, which was promoted with the advertising tagline "What's the Catch?" when it was first published, Heller defines "Catch-22" as the paradox that any flier who refuses dangerous missions on the grounds of insanity is by definition sane enough to undertake them. The only way to prove you're unfit to fly is to fly.

Catch-22 had received several admiring reviews when it came out in the fall of 1961—in *The Nation,* Nelson Algren called it "the strongest repudiation of our civilization, in fiction, to come out of World War II"—but it did not reach bestseller lists until a year later, when a seventy-five-cent paperback edition was released. Within a few months, the novel had sold more than a million copies, the title had entered the vernacular, and Hollywood had bought the film rights and signed Heller to write the first draft of a screenplay.

But in the years since then, the project had stalled; Heller had no idea how to turn his novel into a movie, and neither did anyone else. *Catch-22* presented an array of nearly insurmountable problems for any director or screenwriter who dared to tackle it. The novel runs to five hundred pages and features more than fifty characters. Its narrative proceeds on two braided time tracks between 1942 and 1944, repeatedly looping backward to a bomber crash that, by degrees, explains part of Yossarian's existential dilemma. Heller's storytelling is both repetitive and episodic, with so many barely connected vignettes illustrating different absurdly comic aspects of the futility and despair of life during wartime that Norman Mailer complained, "One could take a hundred pages anywhere from the middle . . . and not even the author could be sure they were gone." Still more daunting for a screenwriter was what Mailer had identified as the novel's own Catch-22: The "surprisingly powerful" last fifty pages couldn't work without the excess that preceded it. "Heller," he concluded, "is carrying his reader on a more consistent voyage through Hell than any American writer before him . . . It's the rock and roll of novels." Paramount's attraction to Nichols was natural, as was his own attraction to the material—the book can be read as a series of sketches, something with which he had ample experience both as a performer and a stage director.

Henry was too smart to try to create a "greatest hits" version of *Catch-22* by simply stringing together its most extreme and widely discussed episodes—an extended interaction between a GI named Huple and his possibly homicidal cat, a ceremony in which Yossarian shows up stark naked to accept a medal from General Dreedle, the recurring appearances by a deranged assassin known only as "Nately's whore." Instead, he chose a more punishing approach: He mapped the novel on hundreds of index cards that noted every plot point, character, entrance, and death, arranged them into an exact chronology he could reshuffle as he pleased, and wrote a draft that encompassed the entire book. His first attempt at a screenplay ran to 385 pages—the equivalent of a six-and-a-half-hour film.

While Henry rewrote, Nichols started feeling his way toward a vision for the movie. "*Catch-22* is about dying," he said as he began work. "That's really all I know right now. It presents terrific technical problems—25 bombers, 60 speaking parts. But that doesn't worry me as much as finding the proper metaphor—what the experience is of either knowing or not knowing you're dying . . . It's something that happens with Vietnam, that it becomes an abstraction—some think, 'Those aren't real people getting killed' . . . Everybody on television is getting killed and people can possibly no longer distinguish between the ones that will rise again for next week's segment of the series and the Vietnamese, who will not . . . I think it changes the idea of death, and I think the only way to live your life is to know all the time that it's going to end."

Nichols thought *Catch-22* would have to feel "somewhat dreamlike, not quite real—either something remembered or a nightmare. That's very hard to do with living actors with pores and noses, because they're so definitely there." Together, he and Henry made their first important decision—that the fever dream of the hospitalized Yossarian would lead to many of the flashbacks and that, as Henry said, "the picture [would] be cut as if Yossarian's delirium were cutting it." With that idea as their north star, they worked on three subsequent drafts until they had cut two hundred pages and eliminated thirty characters.

Eventually they had a script they felt was viable—but nowhere to shoot it. Nichols's scouting trip to Rome had been a bust. He, Sylbert, and Calley had gone on to Sicily, Corsica (where Heller had been stationed during the war), and Sardinia for a visit with Elizabeth Taylor and Richard Burton, who were there filming *Boom!*, one of several ill-advised projects they had taken on since *Virginia Woolf.* Everywhere, the story was the same. "We asked in our failing Italian, 'Where is

World War II?'" Sylbert said. It was gone. The highways, factories, and apartment buildings of the new Italy made it impossible to simulate wartime conditions.

The production needed a town that looked untouched by time but had space to build an airstrip big enough to house the vintage planes the team was acquiring. By June, they had found a remote patch of land—"10,000 desolate acres of scrub and cactus," Henry called it— twenty miles outside of Guaymas, a small city in northwestern Mexico, about 250 miles south of the Arizona border. Gilliatt warned Nichols that it would be hard flying in and out of such a remote location, but Nichols worried that if they didn't make a decision soon, the movie would stall—cameras were now unlikely to roll until January 1969— and Paramount seemed willing to throw money at any problem. By the time production started, the studio had spent $180,000 to build a highway from Guaymas to the location, $250,000 to create a working mile-long landing strip that would serve as a major outdoor set, and $200,000 to assemble a squadron of vintage B-25s from various private collectors.

Paramount also spent $1 million up front to secure Nichols's services for the duration, with a promised share of profits on the other side. It was an unheard-of sum for a director with a two-film résumé. Nichols spent much of that fall preoccupied with casting. Over the years, Heller had been approached by everyone from Jack Lemmon to Zero Mostel, but Nichols wasn't taking requests: The ensemble he put together was a combination of friends (Buck Henry and Anthony Perkins), people he had worked with (Richard Benjamin, Austin Pendleton, Bob Balaban, and Art Garfunkel, who had never acted but whose baby face and innocent demeanor Nichols thought would be right for Nately), and a handful of up-and-comers, among them Charles Grodin, Stacy Keach, Martin Sheen, and, in the showy role of the hyper-capitalist entrepreneur Milo Minderbinder, Jon Voight—a part Dustin Hoffman, Voight's costar in the forthcoming *Midnight Cowboy*, also wanted. And John Calley got Orson Welles, then short on money, to

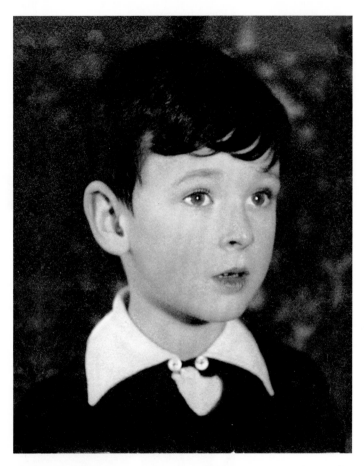

"I suppose I've spent a large part of my life trying to sort that out,"
Nichols said of his early childhood. Berlin, circa 1936.

With his mother, Brigitte Landauer, before the family left Germany for the United States.

"I wish I'd known him longer," Nichols said of his father, Pavel Peschkowsky (in Berlin with Brigitte). "We missed each other."

Nichols (top center) with members of Chicago's Compass Players, where he first started acting—and improvising.

The Compass Players, circa 1955. From left: Severn Darden, Larry Arrick, Elaine May, Shelley Berman, Mike Nichols, Rose Arrick, and Barbara Harris, whom Nichols later directed to a Tony Award in *The Apple Tree*.

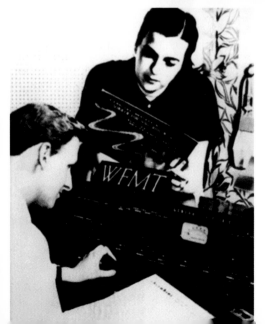

At twenty-two, Nichols started *The Midnight Special*, a popular program of folk music on WFMT, a Chicago station co-founded by Rita Jacobs Willems (standing).

"I knew she wouldn't lose interest and move on," Nichols said of Elaine May. "I knew instantly that everything that happened to us was ours."

Nichols's first wife,
Patricia Scot.

Nichols rehearsing a rare dramatic appearance in the *Playhouse 90* episode *Journey to the Day* with Elaine May (who quit) and Mary Astor.

Nichols and May rehearsing the all-star TV special *The Fabulous Fifties* with (from left) Shelley Berman, Maria Karnilova, Dick Van Dyke, Betty Comden, Henry Fonda, Adolph Green, Julie Andrews, and Rex Harrison.

Nichols and May hit Broadway. "They hold the human race on a pin and make it laugh at itself while it squirms," *Life*'s critic wrote.

Lucille Ball was among the guests at the carnival-themed opening-night party in Shubert Alley for *An Evening with Mike Nichols and Elaine May.*

Robert Redford and Elizabeth Ashley in Nichols's Broadway directorial debut, *Barefoot in the Park.* "Bob challenged her, and she gave him a run for his money," Nichols said.

Nichols with Neil Simon, celebrating the raves and long lines the day after *Barefoot* opened for what would become a four-year run.

Art Carney, who was, according to Nichols, "a saint," and Walter Matthau, who was, according to Nichols, not, backstage at *The Odd Couple*.

Matthau and Carney (covering his face) take a final piece of direction from Nichols in rehearsal at Broadway's Plymouth Theatre.

May and Nichols perform for supporters and activists the night before the final day of the march from Selma to Montgomery, March 24, 1965.

Nichols with Richard Burton and Elizabeth Taylor rehearsing *Who's Afraid of Virginia Woolf?* "He conspires with you rather than directs you," Burton said. "And he was right every time."

Marlene Dietrich, one of the many celebrities to visit Taylor and Burton during the *Virginia Woolf* shoot.

Nichols's *Woolf* quartet: George Segal, Burton, Sandy Dennis, and Taylor. "I was so sure I knew what to do," Nichols said. "I never was again."

Nichols and Taylor behind the scenes. "I think you can actually see me learning during the course of *Who's Afraid of Virginia Woolf?*" he later said. Moviemaking, he knew, "was something I could never use up."

Cinematographer Robert Surtees (left) and Nichols rehearse Dustin Hoffman and Katharine Ross on the set of *The Graduate*.

"Sometimes Katharine and I would look at each other and say, 'Is he in a bad mood? Did he see the rushes? Did we do something wrong?'" said Hoffman.

Nichols lights a cigarette for his date, Jacqueline Kennedy, at the Right Bank restaurant in New York City, March 29, 1968.

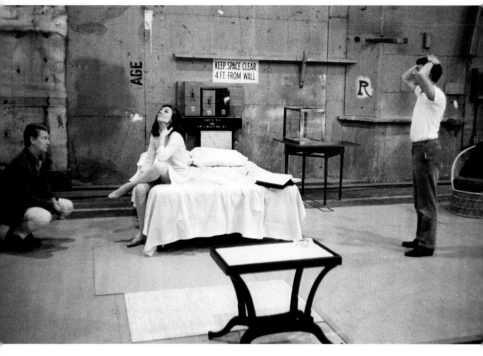

Nichols rehearsed *The Graduate*'s bedroom scenes between Anne Bancroft and Hoffman as if he were staging a play and encouraged both actors to improvise.

Leslie Caron hands Nichols an Academy Award for his direction of *The Graduate* on April 10, 1968. Under the frozen smile, he said, "I was Mister Anhedonia."

"You need a buddy to find the nonrealistic true things": Nichols with his friend and frequent collaborator, the writer Buck Henry.

Nichols on the set of *Catch-22* in Mexico during the two weeks when Orson Welles (seated, center) came to the shoot, an experience that brought the rest of the cast close to mutiny.

Nichols with Candice Bergen, Art Garfunkel, and Jack Nicholson on a break during the *Carnal Knowledge* shoot.

Nicholson with Nichols and May when they reunited for the Stars for McGovern rally at Madison Square Garden, June 14, 1972.

Lee Grant and Peter Falk in Nichols's Broadway staging of Neil Simon's *The Prisoner of Second Avenue*.

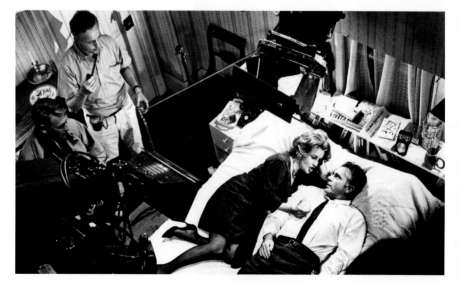

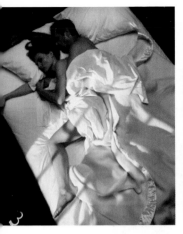
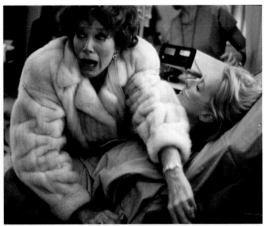

"I think maybe my subject is the relationships between men and women, without much of anything else, centered [on] a bed," said Nichols. "I don't know how to narrow it down any more." Top (from left): *The Fortune, Silkwood, Wolf, Postcards from the Edge.* Middle (from left): *The Graduate, Primary Colors, Heartburn, Closer.* Bottom (from left): *Who's Afraid of Virginia Woolf?, Angels in America.*

Nichols at home in New York, 1964.

play General Dreedle. (Nichols joked that in his fantasy, "he'd start to say a line and then instantly I would say, 'No, no, no, Orson!'")

"We saw loads of actors," says Alan Shayne, the movie's casting director. "He was wonderful with everyone—he gave them space, he encouraged them." Nichols could switch from sleeves-rolled-up director to pampered prince in a blink; Shayne says they "would stop suddenly if Calley would arrive with a beautiful leather or suede jacket for Mike to try on, or he would rush out to go look at a new Mercedes convertible." But most of the time, he kept his mind on the job.

Nichols didn't get everyone he went after—he was high on Al Pacino, a young New York theater actor with no movie experience, but they never connected, and George C. Scott, who already had *Patton* in his sights, read Henry's script and turned Nichols down flat, saying, "No way . . . It's just awful!" For Yossarian, Nichols resisted the studio's suggestions to pursue Paul Newman and instead cast Alan Arkin. Their working relationship on *Luv* had not been easy, but "Arkin was in my mind from the beginning," Nichols said. "Yossarian is the little guy caught in the middle, and [he and] Arkin's deliberate witty inexpressiveness seemed to go together so well." Arkin himself called Yossarian "the only part I've ever worked on that didn't demand a conception, because there isn't much difference between me and Yossarian."

As production neared, Nichols returned to *Plaza Suite*, making sure no moment in the play got slack or sloppy. He had no intention of letting it fall apart the way *The Odd Couple* had. At one point, Maureen Stapleton said, "I lost a solid built-in laugh. I tried everything I knew to get it back, but it wouldn't come. I called Mike and asked him to . . . see if he could figure out what I should do. Mike came to a performance and afterward said, 'Just take the second half of the line an octave lower.' I did what he told me and like music to my ears, the laughter rolled over the footlights."

"Mike was the conductor of those laughs, and that roar from the audience became part of your expectation as an actor," says Lee Grant, who replaced Stapleton on Broadway before starring in the play's Los Angeles production. "And you couldn't deviate with a word—Neil's writing was almost rigidly musical. When I was first rehearsing, I went through a scene and Mike said, 'Of! But! Two! For!' Those were the words I had left out, and it shocked me. But once I had it down, it was total freedom."

Nichols needed the show to be rock solid. He expected to be gone a long time. Before heading south, he and Henry flew to California and visited the Orange County airfield where the B-25s were being refurbished and stunt fliers were being hired. He climbed into an old bomber and crawled around, taken aback by how cramped the interior was and how hard it would be to film in a space that small. It was a taste of how little on *Catch-22* would go according to plan. "I think it'll work," he finally said to Frank Tallman, the flying supervisor. "Look—we mount the camera here, in the entrance to the cockpit. We can shoot across Garfunkel in the pilot's seat and [Peter] Bonerz in the copilot's seat. There's just enough room for the camera crew back there—and I can lie down here on the floor between the camera and the actors." Tallman looked "puzzled," said Henry.

"Something wrong with that idea?" said Nichols.

"Uh, Mike . . ." said Tallman. "Who's going to fly the plane?"

On January 2, 1969, the cast and crew of *Catch-22* flew from Los Angeles to Mexico to start work. At 8 a.m. on January 11, after a week of rehearsal, production began. Nine hours later, production wrapped for the day. Not a single foot of film had been shot. The count remained the same: 187 pages and 445 shots to go. David Watkin, the British cinematographer Nichols had hired based on his work for Tony Richardson on *The Charge of the Light Brigade*, had spent much of rehearsal week "lying on his back and staring through a dark filter at the sky," Henry wrote. He had "the disarming habit of, when being asked a direct question, answering with, 'Well . . .' and then leaving the room," but he had a plan Nichols loved—to shoot the entire movie with backlighting. On the first day of filming, he told Nichols what that would mean: No exterior shots would be possible between 11 a.m. and 2 p.m., when the sun was high. "I loved him," said Nichols. "He wasn't the guy that I need[ed] as my partner, but he was a wonderful man."

At first, Nichols, who would weather every setback on the film with a despairing smile, as if he had become one of the novel's characters, was "kind of amused," says Richard Benjamin. But after the first week, he called Benjamin over and said, "Here's a little secret. I haven't seen anybody's face. Watkin says it's all there, but with the projection equipment we have down here, we can't see anybody." That weekend, Nichols and Calley had to drive hours to the nearest airport, fly to Los Angeles, drive to Paramount, and run the dailies in a screening room to confirm that Watkin was, in fact, correct: The actors' faces were visible. They flew back to Mexico to begin week two.

That was the first indication of just how long *Catch-22* was going to take. The second came a week later, when Nichols announced that he was throwing out everything they had shot so far and starting again. By then he had been diagnosed with a hernia, Sylbert had contracted hepatitis and flown home, the plane shuttling the dailies to and from Los Angeles had been delayed at least once, one of the B-25s had lost control on the runway and sent the extras in its path scrambling for safety, and, according to Henry, Arkin was "lapsing into a coma-like depression." None of those issues were the problem; Nichols just hated all the footage he had filmed. Originally, says Peter Bonerz, "the idea was to fill up the background with young airmen. So he got hundreds of extras from Tucson or somewhere. I was at dinner with Mike and Buck—they'd just come back from the rushes, and Mike said, 'You know, there's something wrong here.'"

"I was really scared," said Nichols. "I knew it was a screwup and that it wasn't working. It looked like an Air Force movie." Clive Reed, his first assistant director, said, "What if we didn't have the extras?" Within days, Nichols sent them home. (It hadn't helped that the local government, which both resented the Hollywood intrusion and knew how much money was to be made from it, threatened to arrest any extra found in possession of marijuana, which in 1969 was basically all of them.)

"Mike said, 'It's not supposed to look real. It's Yossarian's version of reality,'" Bonerz says. "'And in a dream, or a nightmare, you don't have extras.'"

"As soon as they were gone," Nichols said, "it began to be *Catch-22*." By then he had also fired one of his actors—Stacy Keach, who was to play Colonel Cathcart, the ambitious functionary who keeps forcing Yossarian to fly again. As with Gene Hackman on *The Graduate*, Nichols blamed himself, saying Keach, at twenty-seven, was too young for the role; he replaced him with Martin Balsam, who was more than twenty years older.

But Keach and many of his castmates felt something else was at play. *Catch-22* was a shoot with endless downtime, and a hierarchy had swiftly been established; actors like Arkin and Perkins and Benjamin, who felt comfortable shooting the breeze with Nichols, who were versatile enough to improvise and play word games to pass the hours, were in favor. They "would sit around doing bits to make Mike laugh," said Keach, who was furious about his firing. "He digs that sort of game. But I couldn't make that scene."

As the weeks in Guaymas rolled on, some actors found it more bearable than others. "Sitting around in Mexico on camp chairs with Mike and Buck was the time of my life," says Bonerz. "I got a salary plus a per diem. What the fuck is wrong with that? Buck and I would invent games—picking up pebbles and tossing them into coffee cans. I played a lot of tennis with Arkin. And there was a lot of drinking." But many of the actors felt trapped. "The nearest airport was in Hermosillo, which was then a [long] drive away," says Balaban. "There were literally three flights a week, so it wasn't like you could say, 'Oh, I'm not working for a few days—I'll go to L.A.'"

"All that waiting, all those delays—it was very debilitating," said Perkins. "There's nothing worse than a bunch of actors with nothing to do but sit around and talk about all the work they're not doing. The drinkers all drank, and the nondrinkers wished they could cultivate the habit."

"We make bets," Bob Newhart told Nora Ephron, then a young reporter who came down to observe Nichols for *The New York Times Magazine*, "on who's going to go insane or has already gone insane . . . We have no norm here. We have no way of judging."

When the boredom was interrupted, it would be for such a high-stakes shot that sometimes the actors themselves couldn't believe what they were doing. Nichols relished every chance to try to pull off the miraculous, including what may have been the most elaborate shot in his entire body of work. "Martin Balsam walking down this airstrip in Mexico, me talking to him," said Jon Voight. "This plane was supposed to come in behind us, its undercarriage in flames, pass by out of camera, crash and we'd go on walking, pass it still talking, get in a jeep, sweep out, there's an explosion off camera where the plane really went up, then we'd go off down the airfield. All in one shot. We did it twice. The man who flew the plane was risking his life and we were in danger, too. I got very nervous. What happens if I go up on my lines? . . . It was crazy stuff."

"It's such a powerful memory," said Nichols. "*Catch-22* was a nightmare to make, physically. And everybody on it was unhappy except me. All the actors kept bitching because they couldn't leave. I was as happy as a clam. I had the sixth-largest air force in the world. I didn't think it was going very well—it wasn't my kind of picture—but I was happy anyway." Gilliatt came and went; like most visitors, she was so exhausted by the logistics of getting there that by the time she had recovered, the trip was over. Nichols didn't mind; he had begun an affair with a young woman he had met on the set. "She stayed," he said, "and I was so happy with her."

For Nichols, *Catch-22* was a chance to drop out of his own life at just the moment his post-*Graduate* celebrity had become overwhelming. He was almost desperate to escape; serving as the symbolic leader of a fake army in a foreign country felt easier to him than, say, managing his calendar. "It was good to be away from phones and traffic and dinners and acquaintances," he said. "And I had something to concentrate on the whole time . . . It's impossible to make a picture without tensions, angers, fears and all the strong emotions and technical crises that go into it. It's simply that I would rather do it than not do it."

His seeming serenity baffled even those closest to him: Did he believe everything would work out, or was he in so far over his head that he had given up and could only shrug? Or was he high? The last was a real possibility; drug use on sets had, by then, become a matter of course. Some of the actors were regularly dropping acid, and Nichols, on *Catch-22*, became a fairly avid user of marijuana and, for the first time, cocaine.

"When Nichols is unhappy," Henry wrote in his somewhat sanitized set diary, "he lights another of the cigarettes that he chain-smokes, stares vacantly into space for a while, whistling softly, then begins wandering about the set, tripping relentlessly over whatever cable, rope or wire lies in his path . . . Sam O'Steen . . . swears he once saw Nichols trip over the shadow of the microphone boom."

"I'm certain he felt the pressure," Bonerz says. "Every once in a while John Calley would fly down with a bunch of guys with big briefcases, and they'd go and huddle. You sort of knew that was about money."

"I couldn't get ahold of the scenes the way I usually do," Nichols said. "It was a trancelike thing where you just moved forward and trusted the scheme of the overall action. It was very hard. Arkin was unhappy because I spent so much time with the technical aspect of it, plotting the planes going past him. He said, 'You could have spent a little more time with us,' and he's right. But the technical stuff was very daunting."

When Orson Welles arrived, the cast's mood changed from weariness to open revolt. Welles stepped off the plane with a small entourage (including Peter Bogdanovich, who was interviewing him) and a large chip on his shoulder. He immediately asked to be taken to wardrobe and given his general's uniform, which he wore on and off camera for the duration of his stay in Mexico. Unbeknownst to Nichols, Welles had tried and failed to secure the rights to *Catch-22* several years earlier; now, almost thirty years after *Citizen Kane*, he was to be directed by someone who had come out of the gate with a big hit that he immediately followed with a bigger one. Welles did not handle the moment graciously.

"He did his best to utterly sabotage those two weeks," says Pendleton, who played the general's son-in-law and shared all of his scenes. "He was a terrible lens hog," says Bonerz. "Whenever Mike did a master shot"—a take in which all actors in a scene are visible—"Orson would mess up his lines so that they would have to be done in close-up. Not only that, but sometimes he would look at the camera in the middle of one of his own lines and say, 'Mike, I'm sure you'll be on someone else here, let's just move on.'"

"Day after day, he told fascinating stories," Ephron wrote. "He also told Nichols how to direct the film, the crew how to move the camera, Sam O'Steen how to cut the scene, and most of the actors how to deliver their lines. Welles even lectured Martin Balsam for three minutes on how to deliver the line, 'Yes sir.'" He insisted on multiple takes of the medal-of-valor scene, despite Arkin's evident embarrassment at appearing nude, except for a modesty pouch, in front of a large cast and crew. He couldn't remember his lines. And when Nichols asked for alternate takes, Welles would decline, saying that he didn't want to give "some drunken editor" the chance to choose badly. "Who the fuck is this fat asshole," O'Steen thought, "who hasn't made a good picture since . . ."

At one point Nichols said, "Okay, in this take, Orson, you get out of the jeep because it's a better cut—"

"What do you mean, 'it's a better cut'?" said Welles. "You think I haven't cut pictures before?"

After a few days with him, many of the actors were barely concealing their hostility. When Welles turned to Pendleton after one take and said, "Are you sure you want to say the line that way?" Pendleton glared at him and snapped, "Yes."

"The Welles situation . . . was almost identical to what was written in the script," said Bonerz. "We were all under the thumb of this huge, cigar-smoking general. The discomfort we were feeling was real."

Nichols never lost his temper or evinced a hint of annoyance. "Not only was he forced to take a part because he needed money, but he was being directed by this pipsqueak, and he was humiliated. He was a pain in the ass on the set," Nichols said. But "I was very moved by Welles . . . Where the camera is and what it does [was] so much a part of his life— how is he suddenly supposed to ignore it? If you know that much, what are you supposed to do with it?"

Welles rebuffed all of Nichols's overtures until the end of his time in Mexico, when he accepted his invitation to dinner. "He said beautiful, startling things," Nichols said. "He said, 'You know, I've always thought lives are either an ascent from where you started or they start on a high and are just a slow descent. Obviously mine is the second kind, and I wouldn't have it any other way.'" He couldn't resist leaving Nichols with a warning about success: "Better late than early."

Reporters came and went, including Ephron, who bonded with Nichols over the treats he had flown in weekly from Zabar's and Greenberg's in New York. The logistical nightmares of the production were detailed in stories that ran more than a year before the film's planned release. The cost rose from $11 million to $15 million, and then to $20 million. The mood on the set became so toxic that people started calling the production "Kvetch-22." Nichols did take after take of a grisly scene in which a plane cuts a man standing on a raft in two and his legs stand there for a while before falling over. "It was this wonderful, ghoulish thing," says Balaban, "but every time the plane did it, the impact of the piano wire on the dummy caused a puff of smoke to come out of him. He must have shot it a million times."

It took two long nights of work just to get a single shot of Arkin running toward a burning building as a B-25 landed—a moment that took up one-sixteenth of a page in the script. "That was good terror, Alan!" Nichols said at 4 a.m. on the second night. "That was *real* terror, Mike," Arkin replied. On another evening, after eighteen thousand sticks of dynamite detonated on cue and an actor blew his lines, Nichols calmly said to Henry, "You carry on. I'm taking my life tonight." At the beginning of the shoot, some of the actors had believed that Nichols must have had the whole movie in his head. Now they doubted it; more than one had heard him say, after watching the dailies, "My God. It just sits there."

Word drifted back to Hollywood about a production careening out of control. Some people were hungry for a comeuppance. To those outside Nichols's orbit, what was happening in Mexico sounded like arrogance. At one point, John Wayne, who was looking to buy property adjacent to the location, came to visit. Wayne was, at that point, viewed by the emerging New Hollywood generation as the embodiment of reactionary, pro–Vietnam War hawkishness. He expected a star's greeting; instead, not a single actor came out to meet him. Wayne was angry and hurt; alone in the local hotel bar, he drank himself into a fury and trashed the place until he toppled over and broke a couple of ribs. At the time, Henry responded dryly, "We are trying to make up for it by getting a print of *The Green Berets* and showing it to the crew. In the meantime, we've just been sitting around here, watching the days go by and waiting for him to come back and bomb us."

"We were such prigs," said Nichols later, "such righteous schmucks when he landed. Buck and I were both furious at ourselves for years and years."

Principal photography in Guaymas ended in late April; there was still a month of aerial stunt shooting needed, but Nichols was so far behind that he left the task to his second unit director. His main aerial cameraman was John Jordan, a forty-four-year-old daredevil who had lost a leg three years earlier when he fell into a helicopter blade while filming a stunt for the James Bond movie *You Only Live Twice*. A month after Nichols and the actors left, Jordan, who refused to wear a harness, was leaning out of one airplane in order to film another, lost his grip, and fell to his death in the Gulf of Mexico.

Nichols was in Rome by then, shooting a few street scenes with Garfunkel; Paul Simon, waiting for him to be done so they could finish their next album, had grown irritated by "the presence of Mike Nichols" as a "disconcerting" figure who kept interrupting their real careers, and finally, tired of waiting, drafted "The Only Living Boy in New York," a song about his sense of abandonment, for their next album, *Bridge Over Troubled Water*. Rome was, said Nichols, "like a holiday," in part because David Watkin told him there were only two hours a day when the light was right for filming. It took them two months to shoot a relatively small portion of the movie.

Catch-22 would wrap with what was supposed to be a month of work on a Hollywood soundstage; by then, nobody was surprised when it turned out to take twice that long. They spent two weeks just trying to figure out how to hang a partial replica of a B-25 from the ceiling so that Nichols could film the crucial recurring "Help him! Help the bombardier!" flashbacks that punctuate the movie. In late June, Nichols fell twenty feet off a ladder on the soundstage and dislocated his shoulder. Paramount executives, increasingly angry, would come down to the set and say to Sam O'Steen, "Can't you do something?"

"He finishes when he finishes," O'Steen replied.

Jon Korkes, the young actor who played the maimed and mangled bombardier, spent several days with Arkin in the plane; Nichols put him in a flight suit torn open so that he could be covered in sheep intestines that were kept refrigerated and immersed in chemicals most of the day. "Mike would not let me see it beforehand," he says. "I guess he was afraid I would get squeamish, but I was having the time of my life. Every time we did a portion of that sequence, I'd be covered with chemical blood and crap. They would unhook me and pick me up and take me over and change me and clean me off and get me a new flight suit and then I'd go lie down again. I think they had thirteen flight suits for me in all."

"We worked on the front-projection stuff for four weeks," said Nichols. "And my strange obsession with staying in one shot and not cutting, of course, made it even more of a nightmare."

In late August, *Catch-22* wrapped production. Nichols expected editing to take almost a year. In interviews, he started to sound like he was out of his mind. "Simplicity," he announced to a UPI reporter as the seventh month of shooting ended. "One basic fact has come home to me. Simplicity. And that's the direction you're down to as you progress." To another, he talked with aimless grandiosity of "how I want to live—I'm going to get rid of myself in stages . . . there are so many things that we must do for one another to make sure that we continue to live on this earth." But privately, Nichols was crashing hard, telling colleagues, "I feel like I'm pregnant with a dead child."

"The thing about directing a movie," he said toward the end of his life, "is that every day you think, *Oh no. This time I'm fucked. I cannot get out of this corner. This scene is awful. She's awful, he's awful, I'm awful, the writing is awful. There's one small chance. Maybe if we put her over here and cut this and put this line first, well, that could almost work.* And you talk your way out of the end of the world. You shoot one more scene and you're saved again. That's an ordinary day, and it's *every* day in some way or another. And it's very addicting. You can save yourself one more time. *Not* all the time."

Sixteen

COLD TO THE TOUCH AND
BRILLIANT TO THE EYE

1969–1971

At the end of 1969, Nichols came under the influence of a pop psychologist described by Stephen Sondheim as "completely unethical and a danger to humanity." Nichols first heard about Mildred Newman from Tony Perkins during the *Catch-22* shoot in Mexico. Perkins and his longtime boyfriend, Grover Dale, had both become convinced that their homosexuality was obstructing their happiness and wanted to restart their lives with women. Newman and her husband, Bernard Berkowitz, were not conversion therapists, but like many old-guard Freudians of the time, they clung to the belief that male homosexuality was a form of arrested development, and made a small fortune convincing willing clients that it was an impediment to getting what they wanted.

Nichols didn't imagine that Perkins was suddenly going to become heterosexual, but he was interested when the actor, who had grown so insecure about his talent that he had begun to lose jobs, told him that Newman had restored his confidence. Richard Benjamin's wife, Paula Prentiss, who had a small role in *Catch-22*, also swore by Newman's methods. And when Nichols heard that Neil Simon and Nora Ephron were seeing her as well, he decided to pay a visit to her Greenwich Village office.

Newman and Berkowitz employed a lax-unto-nonexistent code of conduct—they would sometimes cold-call famous people and say, "I hear you might need my help," and were so interventive that when an artist was in conflict with someone else, they would contact the offending party themselves. Eventually they gathered their precepts into the bestselling "Me" Decade totem *How to Be Your Own Best Friend*, complete with blurbs from Simon, Ephron, and Perkins. Their fifty-six-page book's happiness-first gospel encouraged readers to love themselves and expel from their lives anyone who might undermine them, a message with irresistible appeal to ambitious creative professionals who wanted permission to put their own needs ahead of anyone else's. Newman was, at that moment, a perfect fit for Nichols, who had recently telephoned Penelope Gilliatt, told her he had been living with another woman for a month in Los Angeles, and asked her to move out of their apartment.

By the end of production on *Catch-22*, Nichols had become a big target—a symbol of unchecked brashness and self-regarding excess. He complained that the press caricatured him, but he couldn't stop it. There were now people openly rooting for his failure, and going after him publicly had become a form of self-credentialing. François Truffaut sniped that Nichols had practically ruined *The Graduate* with his "constant interruption of the drama with all that music." And Dennis Hopper said, "I resent Mike Nichols spending $15 million or $23 million or whatever it cost to make *Catch-22*. But of course Nichols doesn't care if Paramount falls apart."

But what stung most was a sustained attack by the novelist and screenwriter William Goldman. In his 1969 book *The Season*, a gossipy, knowing account of a year on Broadway, he devoted an entire chapter to trashing Nichols. Contemptuously titled "Culture Hero," the section derided him as a slick hypocrite draped in false modesty. Seething that "no one in the art world has moved as fast in five Octobers," Goldman called Nichols's production of *The Little Foxes* "execrable"; contended that he had "castrated" Richard Sylbert, Sam O'Steen, and Robert Surtees by thanking them in an acceptance speech for *The Graduate;* dismissed his tendency to have "characters walking off stage while talking, or talking to other characters who are off stage" as "self-serving direction, and no one is better at it"; and concluded that he was an apt icon for a benighted era: "brilliant and trivial and frigid." Goldman was a walking compendium of grudges, resentments, and omniscient appraisals, and his attack was so outsize that in a review, Walter Kerr mused that it "may require another book to explain" what was behind it.

Nichols tried to keep his head down and work on *Catch-22,* but he sensed that the film would confirm the worst opinions of his detractors. The edit was exceptionally difficult. Buck Henry had structured his screenplay so tightly that the last line of one scene flowed directly into the first line of the next, and the solution—to cut from the middle of scenes—only muddied a narrative that they already suspected movie-goers would have trouble following. Nichols had originally planned to return to the gory, traumatic "Help the bombardier!" flashback in its entirety five times; O'Steen warned him that audiences "will start saying, 'Oh, Jesus.'" When a test screening proved him right, they came up with a more effective structure in which more of the sequence would be shown each time, until the final, horrific reveal of exactly what had traumatized Yossarian.

There were moments when Nichols's optimism surged. Three months into editing, he called John Calley and said, "I want you to come and look. I think I love it." But for most of *Catch-22*'s postproduction, his mood was grim. Once it was cut to two hours, "almost everybody in the movie was unhappy with his role, which to me was a kind of tribute to Nichols, [who] would not let any actor take over the picture," said Joseph Heller.

In January 1970, *M*A*S*H* opened, and the day Nichols and Calley saw it, they realized that *Catch-22* was doomed. Robert Altman's movie was what Nichols intended his own to be—a depiction of the madness of Vietnam refracted through a different war. Moreover, Altman had changed the vocabulary of war films by inventing a loose, free-associative, casually profane style that Nichols's tightly controlled *Catch-22* would never achieve. "When the lights came up," Calley said, "we looked at each other, and we knew that Altman had gotten the essence of what we had wanted to do, and had done it in a much simpler way."

"I almost passed out," Nichols said. "It was brilliant and alive and it put us to shame. Certainly everybody else thought so and I secretly did too. [It had] everything that *Catch-22* couldn't have—freedom and wildness and a half-assed improvised quality—[and] made us seem even more stately." The release of his own film was still five months away, but Nichols knew that every critic would compare the two and find his wanting: In his *New York Times* review of *M*A*S*H*, Roger Greenspun had referred to *Catch-22* as "the legendary unfinished movie."

The trudge to the finish line became a death march. "I saw it at an invited screening, and when the credit 'A Mike Nichols Film' appeared, there was a terrible slow clap," says Pendleton. "It was awful." Some questioned Nichols's decision not to have an original score, a choice that made the film feel persuasively stark but, at times, toneless. One of the only music cues—a wink at *2001* using "Thus Spake Zarathustra" as the camera leers at a voluptuous Italian woman—felt uncharacteristically obvious. ("People begged me not to do [it]," Nichols said. "It was tasteless and vulgar and there was almost no excuse for it, and I just couldn't let it go.") When Kubrick attended a screening, he ignored the joke, offered some kind words, and told Nichols, "I think you're gonna have problems with the narrative."

"And of course, we did," said Nichols. "People were confused." As the lights went down for the first public preview, *Catch-22* seemed to announce its solemnity right away, with a three-minute white-on-black credits sequence that slowly faded into a shot of mountains against water. The first lines weren't spoken for more than five minutes, and deliberately rendered inaudible by the noise of airplane engines. In the first scene, Yossarian is stabbed. And what follows is less funny than icily ironic, with every exchange crafted to make a point about either the dehumanizing experience of war or the ritual strangeness of military life. Nothing about the film's look—the backlit actors, the drab palette, the austere shot composition, which bore Kubrick's heavy influence, the overt Fellini homage in Rome—suggested it was a comedy. "It was the first preview I ever had where I thought, *Something's wrong,*" said Nichols. "There was a sense that it was not completely connecting."

"We saw the audience not knowing whether to laugh or to be serious or to cry," said Henry. And suddenly, he said, a simple fact that had been obscured beneath Henry's strenuous effort to find a structure for the screenplay and Nichols's overwhelming attention to logistics in Mexico announced itself with brutal clarity: The movie was "not about human behavior," Henry said. "That's one of the things that drove Mike crazy. He had no behavior to work with, just attitudes."

That diagnosis came too late. *Catch-22*'s reviews were not unanimously negative—*The New York Times*'s new critic Vincent Canby called it "the best American film I've seen this year . . . as close to being an epic human comedy as Hollywood has ever made." But even he conceded, "I'm not sure that anyone who has not read the novel will make complete sense out of the movie's narrative line." His review was by far the kindest. *The Hollywood Reporter* called it "possibly the biggest, most hopeless, nihilistic picture ever to go out" from a studio. Andrew Sarris pronounced it "a bomb" and launched a savage attack on "Michelangelo Nichols . . . getting a million dollars and throwing his weight around and puffing himself up to be canonized on the cover of *Time.*" *Time* did indeed put Nichols on the cover and called the movie "cold to the touch and brilliant to the eye" but shrugged that "anti-war films have become faddish." And in *New York*, Judith Crist wrote, "What it lacks is cohesion, a style, an essential mood . . . We are on the outside, watching, seldom feeling, observing a careful technical job . . . Where is all the joyous collaboration between director and actors that we read about? Nowhere is that air of spontaneous improvised lunacy . . . that distinguished *Dr. Strangelove* or *M*A*S*H* . . . This might make us consider a reappraisal of the Wunderkind directorial abilities of Mike Nichols."

The final blow was, inevitably, delivered by *Mad* magazine:

—Help him! Help the Bombardier!
—I'M the Bombardier! I'm okay!
—Then help HIM!
—Who? Help who?
—Help HIM! Help the director!
—What seems to be his problem?
—He doesn't understand the movie!

If *Catch-22* was a victim of expectations, of hype, and of an appetite to take Nichols down at long last, it was also a movie that Nichols often said was not to his own taste: a virtuoso demonstration of everything he had learned about the camera, but not a film with characters for whom he had any passion. At the time, he was understandably defensive, insisting that "I never intended anything to be unclear . . . It seems to me that things that are mysterious to some degree can be valuable in art." But "I never found the heart of *Catch-22*," he later conceded. "I could have scored it. I could have used a warmer actor more connected to the audience for Yossarian, like Dustin. Most of all, I could have made it for half of what it cost, not been so ambitious with the airplanes. There's certainly arrogance in all that . . . I would like to have been a little more aware of taking the audience by the hand and leading them through this series of very confusing events . . . Some of the time

I sacrificed clarity for style." He had, he said, taken care of "the despairing and surrealistic aspects of it, but discouraged the comedy."

"I'd had all these hits," he said, "and this was my first failure. I remember thinking it would be terrible. But it wasn't bad. I was thrilled that it didn't dash me. It had to come eventually. And when it did, I thought, *What's the big deal?*"

There would be times to come when a public disaster would send Nichols plummeting into depression and fear. The disappointment of *Catch-22*—which did not bankrupt Paramount but came nowhere close to making back its money—was not one of those times. Nichols was glad to have the movie out of his life, and he had already made plans to move ahead. While he was still editing, Jules Feiffer had sent him a playscript he'd written called *True Confessions,* a comedy-drama about, as Feiffer put it, "the fact that heterosexual men don't like women." Nichols found it raw and cruel, but also unsettlingly believable; he recognized his worst self in the attitudes expressed by Feiffer's two main male characters, friends who devolve from collegiate horniness youth into a rancid and misogynistic middle age. He knew them intimately; he understood the anger and sourness that could reshape a man's personality once he reached his post-prodigy years. Nichols himself was nearing forty. He was, for the first time in almost a decade, not romantically involved with anyone. The culinary indulgences that were a part of every production he worked on had given him a paunch that hung over his belt buckle, and he had become a chain-smoker. He had a string of failed relationships and a daughter he saw only when, after communiqués, quarrels, and reversals, Margot Callas—to whom he was still legally married—would bring her to New York for a visit. Feiffer's play was about "a kind of adolescent narcissism that many men . . . persist in holding onto against all odds, [even if] it doesn't make them happy." It started as a version of one of the awkward scenes that had helped make Nichols and May famous—an almost gentle depiction of a posturing man, an earnest, searching woman, and an exchange of attitudes as a kind of foreplay—and then took the scenario to its darkest possible conclusion. The script read as a warning to him: *It would be so easy to become one of these men. Maybe you already have.*

He told Feiffer he wanted to direct it—but as a movie. "It had to do with the expression in people's eyes," Nichols said. "I wanted to be very close to them, especially to the men, when they did these monologues about how often they did or did not have sex. It seemed to me that the despair at being trapped in this macho role could best be expressed when you were right into those faces."

"I said, 'What about the language?'" Feiffer recalls. "And he said, 'We can do anything we want.' Because he was now the director of *The Graduate,* and he knew that he had the power to get it on the screen."

In practical terms, the movie business had changed immensely in the few years since Nichols had fought for a handful of mild profanities in *Who's Afraid of Virginia Woolf?* and inserted a flash cut of a bare breast in *The Graduate.* There were no longer any serious restrictions on sex, nudity, or language. But Nichols was attracted to the project as a way of embracing limits, not testing them. *Carnal Knowledge*—as Feiffer provocatively renamed it—was not a shoot that could spin out of control. The budget was a modest $4 million. There were no stunts or special effects or complicated locations. Like *Virginia Woolf,* it had just four principal roles—two men and two women—and a series of long, well-shaped dialogue scenes that would allow him to dig deep into character.

When he thought *Carnal Knowledge* would end up onstage, Feiffer had offered the role of Jonathan, a cocky, cynical ladies' man at the start of the story and a bitter mess by the end, to Alan Arkin. "Arkin didn't like it," says Feiffer. "And after *Catch-22,* he was dead on the film and dead on Mike. I didn't get why, but maybe their difference in personality was just too great." Nichols wanted to sign Jack Nicholson on the basis of his scene-stealing supporting role in *Easy Rider*. He had not yet carried a studio movie, and Feiffer was skeptical that "this guy with a kind of hillbilly drawl" could play "a Jewish boy from the Bronx." Nichols told him he was wrong and said that Nicholson was "going to be our most important actor since Brando."

"We never talked about it this way," Nichols said, "but it seemed very useful that Jack *wasn't* Jewish, because Jules and I of course are, and I didn't want to limit it even more, to Jews of a certain generation. Pretty soon it would just be about Jules and me. Jack broadened it." To play the sweeter, more conventional Sandy, Nichols reenlisted Art Garfunkel—"there was this thing about Artie, he was so sweet and beautiful, but there was something else, something a little unnerving, a little malicious, a little other, and that's what I wanted." And as Susan, the Smith College beauty in whom both men are interested, he cast Candice Bergen, with whom he had become friends while shooting *The Graduate* in Los Angeles. Bergen's main acting experience had been in Sidney Lumet's indifferently received adaptation of Mary McCarthy's *The Group*. "Can she act?" Feiffer asked. Nichols replied, "She'll act for me."

The most difficult role to cast was Bobbie, the model Jonathan pursues as a trophy, only to turn on her when he discovers he can't handle her sadness and vulnerability. The role was a potential tour de force, but one that required nudity, deep emotional spirals, and a willingness to be on the receiving end of Feiffer's most punishing lines. They went to Jane Fonda first. "Mike Nichols just offered me the part of a girl with forty-inch boobs! I turned it down," she told a reporter. "I'd give anything to work with Mike, but can you imagine me with forty-inch boobs?" (She chose *Klute* instead.) Nichols looked at Karen Black, Ellen Burstyn, and Raquel Welch. Then Ann-Margret's agent, Sue Mengers, called. At twenty-nine, her client had aged out of sex kitten parts, couldn't get seen for a serious role in Hollywood, and had been doing cut-rate action films in Europe. She wanted the job badly enough to fly to New York, audition, and screen-test. "Just don't humiliate her," Mengers told him.

"It was, like, they knew that she was an actress," said Nichols, "and if [they] could just get her an acting part, everything would change. And she *was* an actress."

Nichols reassembled his team—O'Steen, Dick Sylbert, costume designer Anthea Sylbert (Dick's sister-in-law)—and added a new collaborator with whom he had long dreamed of working: cinematographer Giuseppe Rotunno, who had shot films for Fellini and Visconti. Joe Levine would serve as executive producer and distributor—he had signed Nichols for two films after *The Graduate*, each with a million-dollar salary—but he had agreed to write the checks and stay out of the way. "Nichols will be the boss—the director and producer—for the first time," he announced in a burst of exuberance that, notably, came before the opening of *Catch-22*. "And he richly deserves it." Nichols went into the movie with a strong visual strategy. "I knew exactly what I was going to do as soon as I read it," he said. The men, he understood, could easily dominate the film, but, he said, "I wanted to see those who were not talking—the women. I wanted to do a movie that was [also] about the listener." As for the talkers, Nichols wanted very little cutting, with the screenplay's monologues and exchanges shot in sustained medium close-ups and two-shots and sometimes delivered almost directly to the lens, as if the characters were living versions of the searching, hyperarticulate, self-defeating adults who populated Feiffer's *Village Voice* comic strips.

Carnal Knowledge began shooting in September 1970 in Vancouver, after three weeks of rehearsals, a luxury Nichols had not had on *Catch-22*. He often described the production as the most relaxed experience he'd ever had making a movie. From the start, he was in full, cheerful command. He told Nicholson and Garfunkel to hang out with each other before production and suggested they room together on location. He also, pleasantly but firmly, told Nicholson and the other actors to refrain from smoking pot during filming. "We had all taken a vow," said Nicholson, who had, by his own estimation, gotten high every day for fifteen years before quitting for *Carnal Knowledge*. "Mike felt, properly, that grass slows down your tempo a little bit. Without it, he felt there would be more vitality, especially in the earlier college sequences," which were set not long after World War II.

Nichols had not lost his immigrant's ear for the eccentricities of American speech, and he had always been drawn to writers—Neil Simon, Murray Schisgal, Edward Albee, Buck Henry—whose dialogue was heightened or non-naturalistic. Feiffer was no exception—the lines he wrote were spare, and intentionally devoid of *um*s and false starts. It was Nichols's task to make his largely inexperienced actors comfortable with the script's ten-degrees-off-normal syntax. "He worked very hard with Jules to bring it out of the cartoon format," Bergen says. "And he wanted us to play it for truthfulness and to avoid any glibness." As the cast got to know one another, everyone was impressed by the way Nicholson's commitment manifested itself. He took Garfunkel under his wing and sang James Taylor's "Fire and Rain" with him every day as they were driven to the soundstage, harmonizing as a way of keeping their characters in sync, and suggested that they spend a night or two sleeping on the college-dorm set so that they would feel what it was like to live in that space. And Nicholson's rented house became the nexus of a never-ending party to which everyone was drawn.

"First of all, Jack had a hot tub," Nichols said. "And I don't have to say any more. Artie was over there all the time. At the time, he had a girlfriend that we were all terrified of. But he didn't have her that long, because Jack somehow took care of that, too. There was more and more fun, and everyone got closer and closer."

"It was a picture about fucking," said O'Steen, "and everybody on the crew was fucking like a bunch of apes. There were a lot of girls around."

"When you take a film out of one's home city, you force closeness and intimacy," says Bergen. "That's always better for whatever you're shooting. *Carnal Knowledge* was the most sensuous set I've ever been on. Mike decided he wanted to work French hours, so nobody had to get up early. You'd start shooting at eleven and leave at four or five. There was always a groaning board of food, but it wasn't just roast beef and ham—it was lobster and pâté and fresh Vancouver seafood, so you were eating all the time. It was like a really exclusive camp."

Nicholson's impact on Nichols during the *Carnal Knowledge* shoot— they became instant friends, calling each other "Nick" and "Nick"— was profound. Nichols, says his longtime assistant director Mike Haley, was "not a crew guy"—he could be high-handed and impatient with the combination of bustle and dragginess that characterizes most sets. In Nicholson, he saw a different approach to life on a soundstage: courtliness, generosity, seduction. Nicholson "was the first actor I knew who needed to be connected to everyone on the set—a hundred people," Nichols said. "They're all his friends. And so, when he started a scene, everybody's love just lifted him. I'd never seen anybody quite so gifted at using whatever was around to do what he needed." Even when he had to appear nude—his character's constant need to shower is one of the film's motifs—Nicholson concentrated on relaxing the crew. "He said, 'All right, everyone, stand back, 'Steve' is coming out!'" said Nichols. "It was just an ordinary dick, but he treated it like other guys would commit suicide and women would fall to their knees." When he told Nicholson how impressed he was, the actor levelly replied, "Well, everybody has to do it their own way. For you, it works being a little mean."

Working with a tiny cast—*Carnal Knowledge* has only six speaking parts—Nichols kept his caustic side in check and developed an approach he would use on many films to come: He would get the actors in the right mood, then let that mood carry them directly into the action. With Nicholson, who had worked on every beat of the script, he had little to do but ask for slight variations in tone. With Garfunkel, he worked as he had with Dustin Hoffman, sidling up, kidding him, prompting him with analogies: "Remember how you felt when . . ." and "It's as if . . ." "He brought you up to your best smart self," said Garfunkel, "and kept it light and funny." His job with Bergen was to get her to relax, particularly in one daring shot during which Jonathan and Sandy try to charm her with jokes and Rotunno's camera holds on her laughing so long that it finally becomes clear that her character is also performing for them. Nichols invented word games and puns for Nicholson and Garfunkel to tease her with; he would wait for her to laugh, start shooting, stop whenever she did, and immediately have them start a new cascade of jokes. "Finally, she was completely hysterical because she realized they were never going to stop," he said, "and then she lost it, and I had what I wanted."

He faltered only once, just before shooting the extended argument in which Nicholson's Jonathan goes after Ann-Margret's Bobbie, who has become a homebound depressive. "You have such contempt for me," she says, weeping. "Kid, you worked hard for it! You'll do anything you can to ruin my day, won't you? I got up feeling so good!" he replies. The fight had, for Nichols, uncomfortable echoes of the collapse of his marriage to Pat Scot, and it contains some of Feiffer's sharpest writing:

> **Bobbie:** The reason I sleep all day is that I can't stand my life!
> **Jonathan:** *What* life?!
> **Bobbie:** *Sleeping all day!*

The exchange reaches its nadir when Jonathan shouts, "*Please* leave me! For God's sake, I'd almost marry you if you'd leave me!" and calls her a "ball-busting, castrating son of a cunt-bitch." It was a word that had never been heard in a major movie, and a kind of unsparing evisceration that had rarely been seen.

Nichols wasn't sure he or his actress could pull it off. Ann-Margret, who had rented a house in Vancouver with her husband and avoided the festive scene around Nicholson, had gained weight for the role, was taking sleeping pills to get through the night, and had crossed "the psychological line that separated fantasy from reality. I became Bobbie, this pitiful woman, this doormat for abuse," she wrote in her autobiography. "I spent hours at night pacing the bathroom, depressed, teetering on the brink of a breakdown."

The night before work on the scene was to start, Nichols told Feiffer, "I don't think we can shoot it. It's too awful and too strong, and the audience will hate [Jonathan] from that point on."

"I had the instinct, and the intelligence by that time, not to fight with Mike," says Feiffer. "If I became the opposition, it would deepen his position. So I was just gonna let him talk this out. He talked and talked in his office, and then we got in the car to go to dinner, and he talked some more and I said nothing but 'Uh-huh' and 'That's interesting.' By the time we arrived at the Chinese restaurant, he said, 'No, we have to shoot it, because that's what would happen.'"

Nichols filmed the scene in alternating close-ups of Nicholson and Ann-Margret, "as a way to express their separation. My fear was that Ann-Margret didn't have the experience to sustain such a long, emotional scene . . . Up to that point, she hadn't done anything that demanding. It took us time to find the way for her to approach [it]," he said. At first he suggested that she have a few drinks, "but that just pulled the timing apart." The next day, she tried it sober. During her takes, Nicholson stayed just off camera. "He started screaming insults, horrible things about Bobbie that caused me to burst into tears instantly," she said. It was a genuine attempt to help her stay in character, but a punishing experience for both performers.

"Jack had no voice when I turned around" to do his close-ups, Nichols said. "It was gone. He'd been screaming at her—and for her—for a week."

Eventually she became too numb to cry, and Nichols stepped in, working with her a line at a time until he got what he needed. "I sat on the edge of the bed," she said. "I felt exposed and jittery. My breathing was heavy as I waited for Mike to get everything set up. He walked beside me, studied me for a moment, then put his hand very gently on top of my head and held it there for an instant—a simple, comforting gesture." It made her cry. As soon as she did, he called "Action."

Even Nichols felt depleted at the end of that week, declining to look at dailies and telling O'Steen to pull together the best takes. He couldn't wait to get away from it. As soon as *Carnal Knowledge* wrapped, he flew to Poland to look at Arabian horses. The diversion that he had taken up a few years earlier as a rich man's hobby had grown into an obsession. His Connecticut horse farm was now a refuge, the only world where he could be alone with his thoughts.

In the spring of 1971, he screened a rough cut for some of his New York friends, "all of the literary and upscale theatrical people he knew," says Feiffer. "It was a mess—awful and long and boring. I was shocked, because I had been there for the shoot, and this was not the film I thought we had made. I went home and called Mike and said, 'You've got too many soft-focus fade-outs, and it takes too long to begin and too long to end. You're telling the audience all the way through that this is a classic, a serious and important movie, and you can't do that. Let them find out for themselves.' He was really pissed off, and I started writing a long memo, scene by scene, of what he could cut. By the time I finished, he had another screening. I went, and everything I was going to tell him, he had already done. In just four days, he had turned it into essentially the film that was released."

The warmest initial praise for *Carnal Knowledge* came from Nichols's fellow directors, but even that contained notes of caution. After a DGA screening, William Wyler, who had just made his final movie, came over to shake Nichols's and Feiffer's hands. "Uncompromising!" he said. John Frankenheimer told them, "It was like open-heart surgery." Feiffer leaned over and whispered to Nichols, "We're dead." Some of their own friends were appalled. "It's a picture that so demeans relations between men and women that I can't talk about it," said Lillian Hellman, who told Feiffer the film made her "very, very angry."

Calley was more encouraging, and when Nichols showed the movie in Los Angeles, he invited Calley's assistant, Annabel Davis-Goff, to attend. Davis-Goff was twenty-nine, an Irish-born aspiring writer who worked as what was then called a script girl in British television and on a few movies. Calley had introduced them a year earlier at a *Catch-22* screening and they had become phone friends. This time, something sparked; Nichols and Davis-Goff fell hard for each other, and although their relationship was complicated and sometimes stormy, they would remain together for the better part of the next fifteen years.

*C*arnal Knowledge* opened on June 30, 1971, and its reception was explosive—divided and furious in precisely the way that Nichols and Feiffer hoped it would be. Vincent Canby called the film "a nearly ideal collaboration of directorial and writing talents," with performances that were "spectacularly right," and noted that, "more than any other film Nichols has made, [it] reminds me of his stage work at its best." Thus began a summer during which *The New York Times* seemed to run a new essay on the movie every week. Many were unflattering. "There is not one moment of tenderness or exuberance or passion or even simple lust in all the movie's scenes of sexual exploitation and failure . . . *Carnal Knowledge* is . . . youthful sex seen through the eyes of sour, jaundiced old men," Stephen Farber complained. "Do Men Really Hate Women?" asked the artist and writer Rosalyn Drexler in the title of her broadside. "I'm not sure a picture like this isn't harmful," she wrote. "Instead of being an object lesson of depersonalization punished, it provides immediate identification for the corrupt." John Simon was so livid at what he called the film's "unconscious vindictiveness," "unbreathable monomania," and "unending sequence of close-ups and tight two-shots" that he titled his piece "An Appalling Plague Has Been Loosed on Our Films." And the director and acting teacher Kristin Linklater, in a letter to the *Times*, wrote, "I was profoundly hurt and angered by the callousness and brutishness of the script . . . Had I had the liberated courage of my female convictions, I would have thrown a bomb (if I had happened to have one handy) at the celluloid." For every critic who condemned the film for seeming to endorse the reprehensible behavior of its two main characters, there was another, like Pauline Kael, who condemned it for *condemning* those characters. It was "show business fundamentalism," she sniffed, that "never let[s] them win a round."

That reaction was, as Joe Levine would have put it, money in the bank. *Carnal Knowledge* was a solidly profitable hit—it played for twenty-five weeks at Manhattan's most desirable movie house, the Cinema 1 on Third Avenue and Sixtieth Street, before Levine, never one to miss an opportunity, booked it into a two-screen softcore porno house in Times Square. By then, the film had become a mandatory cultural touchpoint, a *Tonight Show* punch line, a fight starter, and even a joke on the TV season's most polarizing new comedy, *All in the Family*, when Edith Bunker obliviously takes Archie to see it. ("I thought it was a religious picture—'Cardinal Knowledge!'" she says. "One of the dirtiest pictures I've ever seen," Archie complains. "Hormones are flying all over the screen!")

Every indignant complaint about the movie made people more determined to see it for themselves. "What we have here is the phenomenon of a movie thriving on bad word-of-mouth," wrote Roger Ebert, who called it Nichols's best film to date. "*Carnal Knowledge* will come up in a conversation and nearly everyone present will have seen it (because of the big hype, because of the word-of-mouth, because of Nichols, because 'everyone else' has seen it, etc.) . . . Women will say their husbands didn't like it. Men will say their wives 'aren't like that.'

Everybody will agree that the characters in the movie 'aren't real' . . . It has been attacked because it is chauvinistic, because it presents sex lives that are without joy; because it is really a story of the homosexual friendship between the two men . . . because it is 'just like a Feiffer cartoon'; because it is 'just like a Nichols-and-May sketch' . . . Feiffer and Nichols have hit a nerve. They have approached a truth. They have been almost cruelly accurate in getting down on film what men sometimes say to each other about women—and how they say it."

Carnal Knowledge received only a single Academy Award nomination—for Ann-Margret's performance—but it didn't matter. By then, an Albany, Georgia, theater manager had been arrested on obscenity charges for showing the movie; Louis Nizer had agreed to represent him, and the case was headed for the Supreme Court (which, after a private screening, would rule unanimously that "nothing in the movie [is] material which may constitutionally be found 'patently offensive'"). The film was now front-page news. The demise of *Catch-22* no longer mattered. Nichols had gotten a do-over. And he was back at the center of the action.

Seventeen

DOLPHINS ARE SMARTER
THAN HUMAN BEINGS

1971–1973

Nichols's first comeback proved to be far more destabilizing than his first failure. In 1971, he turned forty and, for the first time, took his eye off the ball. In the next few years, he would marry for a third time and have two more children; for a while, his new life would, to his surprise, achieve a benign equilibrium he had never experienced. At the same time, many of his professional decisions would derive from a combination of impulsivity and caution, recklessness and magical thinking. He would work with the right people on the wrong things and with the wrong people on the right things, feeling invincible one day and talentless the next, until, after one misstep too many, he would limp away, so hollowed out that he couldn't imagine standing behind a camera again. More than once, he'd struggle to make sense of his own behavior during these years. At one point, he would go to an analyst seeking counsel and end up diagnosing himself. All the time, the effort, the sheer exhausting work of self-creation was costing him too much. "I've gotta tell you," he said, "I really am tired of being Mike Nichols. Get me out."

Nichols hadn't directed a play for almost three years when, shortly before the opening of *Carnal Knowledge*, Neil Simon asked him to take a look at *God's Favorite*, a modern-day retelling of the Book of Job, about a beset Jewish patriarch on Long Island. Nichols didn't think the wobbly little parable was ready for Broadway—and after *Catch-22*, he was leery of any script in which the characters were symbols or stand-ins for ideas rather than fully developed people. He asked Simon if he was working on anything else, and Simon told him he was just finishing the first act of a comedy-drama about the misery of middle-class Manhattan life called *The Prisoner of Second Avenue*. The main character, a married man who retreats to his high-rise apartment and has a breakdown after losing his job, bore some resemblance to the part Nichols had played in Elaine May's *A Matter of Position*. He was intrigued enough to tell Simon he would direct it on Broadway that fall.

Eight years after *Barefoot in the Park*, Nichols's reputation in the theater had evolved from boy wonder to something narrower—he was an acclaimed stage director who essentially worked with only one playwright. His partnership with Simon had changed the way comedies looked and sounded, but to his critics it had come to represent an almost willful desire to please the audience without challenging himself. Going from the R-rated ferocity of *Carnal Knowledge* to another of Simon's ingratiating, metronomically timed laugh machines may have struck some as a retreat. But for Nichols, it was a way of reconnecting with the basics: out-of-town tryouts, nightly rewrites, and filigree work to give any moment that felt pat or synthetic the underpinnings of closely observed realism.

And even if one more collaboration with Simon felt like a revisitation of past glories, Nichols genuinely loved their partnership. "The only questions he asks are: Does it work? Does it fit together? Is it clear? Are the people doing what people do?" he said of Simon. "If something doesn't work, the only person he blames is himself, and he immediately does something about it." Simon, in turn, depended on

Nichols as a sounding board and an editor. "Mike did not write one single word in the play, yet he is as responsible for the final shape of it as I am," he said. Setbacks that others found alarming were now second nature to both men; after the first read-through, they walked off to one side of the rehearsal space, huddled for twenty minutes, then calmly told their cast that the third act was out, to be replaced by a better version down the road and probably *on* the road, either in New Haven or Washington, D.C. They'd been there before.

The two leads were willing to roll with it. Peter Falk and Lee Grant had worked together several months earlier on a TV mystery movie called *Ransom for a Dead Man* that NBC liked enough to turn into a series built around Falk's character, Lieutenant Columbo. Falk had just shot *Columbo*'s first season; the series premiered on the second day of rehearsals for *The Prisoner of Second Avenue* and turned him, almost instantly, into one of America's biggest TV stars. Grant, a victim of the blacklist, had fought her way back into a career, first in television, winning an Emmy for *Peyton Place*, then in movies like *In the Heat of the Night*. She was now looking, she said, "to knock it out of the park on Broadway. I had Neil Simon, I had Mike Nichols, and my attitude was 'Watch out, here I come.'"

But Grant was taken aback on day one, when she realized during the read-through what she had not understood when she first looked at the play—that it was going to be Falk's show all the way. Simon had given his character the emotional journey and the biggest laughs; she was the helpmate, the reactor, the support. "Mike turned to me and said, 'You are the gardener. He is the flower,'" says Grant. "And I thought, *What the fuck? Did I leave my house in Malibu and come here to be the* gardener? My mission was, at last, to be the flower! I thought very seriously of going home." And a couple of weeks later, Falk walked out in anger when Nichols sat in the back row of the theater and repeatedly told him he was inaudible. The next day, he returned in such a foul temper that Nichols had to take him aside and tell him, "You're having an anxiety attack." "I never heard of that," said Falk. Nichols handed him a Valium. Falk asked what it was for. "He explained," the actor wrote in his memoir. "I eventually took the pill, and wow! He was right. I got mellow, took a nap, and woke up relaxed."

During rehearsals, Nichols helped Grant realize that, as she put it, "two actors cannot have nervous breakdowns on the same stage." He also got Falk to calm down. "I was running around . . . like a hyena, energy passing for truth," he said. "Then you try to correct it, and pauses and a low voice pass for truth. All bullshit. That's where a guy like Mike comes in. He understands pain. He understands fear."

It took more work to make Grant and Falk's marriage believable. "Our only intimacy was onstage," she says. "Offstage, we had no relationship at all. He didn't want it. He would go to the Art Students League and paint every day. That's what he had plunged into as a way of keeping himself alive in New York." To bring them together, Nichols reached back to an acting exercise from his Chicago days. "He made Peter and me lie down together on a cot backstage," Grant says. "We lay there, close to each other in the dark, and went through the entire play line by line," with a prompter standing by in case one of them couldn't remember the words. "It was brilliant. You know, lying there, you feel somebody breathe and you feel them cough. You hear when their nose is stuffed. We had to become a couple, and Mike helped us do that."

The Prisoner of Second Avenue was warmly received, although a few critics compared it unfavorably to Jules Feiffer's *Little Murders,* a much darker look at existential despair in New York City, and a play Nichols had declined to direct. (He apologized to Feiffer once he saw it, saying, "I was wrong. I just didn't get it.") Simon's comedy opened the same week as David Rabe's dark Vietnam War play *Sticks and Bones* and Harold Pinter's *Old Times,* and it was hard for some to see it as anything but a safe choice for Nichols, the confirmation of Buck Henry's recent complaint that in theater, he "only takes a risk on things he knows he can do better than anyone else." His direction was praised by Walter Kerr as "immaculately restrained" and by Clive Barnes as "perfect for the play because it trades in . . . heightened naturalism. It concentrates on that style of cabaret acting—made indigenous to America by television—where caricature is transformed into a stylized gesture of truth." Come spring, Nichols won his fourth Tony Award for directing in nine years—and he had barely broken a sweat.

During the summer of 1972, Nichols presided like a country squire over a large home in Bridgewater, Connecticut, that he had recently bought, renovated, and outfitted in decidedly non-rustic luxury. He had gone house hunting with Rose Styron and found a property where, she says, "everything was purple—the Naugahyde furniture and the wallpaper and the curtains. I thought, *This will never do,* and he bought it and made it into one of the most beautiful places I'd ever seen. Then he built a stable for all his horses. He would have his movie friends come over and ride with him, and he had a wonderful life there." The house was at the bottom of a large, hilly piece of land, and the property included an old tobacco barn that he converted into a three-story outbuilding that included a screening room, a large kitchen with a fireplace, enough guest bedrooms and bathrooms to sleep five, and two editing and postproduction suites in which his editors could sequester themselves. Within a couple of years, Nichols would sell his Beresford triplex—for just two or three hundred thousand dollars, well before New York's real estate boom. The buyers were the producer David Brown and his wife, *Cosmopolitan* editor Helen Gurley Brown, who had, several years earlier, defined her magazine's prototypical readers as "girls who have never heard of Mike Nichols."

There was a time when that statement might have hurt; now it didn't, partly because it was no longer true, but also because Nichols felt no pressing need to be bigger, more known, more successful. His

professional ambition seemed to slacken slightly; for a while, his drive
gave way to domestic contentment. He and Davis-Goff were now
serious enough about their new relationship that he was introducing
her to his friends. "Living with one woman after another. In a house.
Every woman but me," Lillian Hellman grumbled. "The idea that
you can find that many people you want to live in a house with is absolutely bewildering. I think it shows a kind of contempt." But Nichols
was committed to Davis-Goff, and eventually even Hellman came to
adore her.

Whatever damage *Catch-22* had done to his reputation, *Carnal
Knowledge* had repaired. Nichols was offered everything—and turned
everything down. He had a girlfriend and a Broadway hit and a pair of
national-horse-show champions on which he lavished endless attention,
and he felt no particular eagerness to leave it all behind for a job. Jack
Nicholson wanted them to make another film. "We're waiting for a script
that Robert Towne is now writing for us," he told journalists after *Carnal
Knowledge* opened, "a story with a variety of adventures—you might call
it a detective story. The setting will not be contemporary—it's to be a
period piece." The movie was *Chinatown*; for reasons he never discussed,
Nichols passed. He also passed when Calley, now an executive at Warner
Bros., offered him *The Exorcist*. "I didn't like it," he said. "And why spend
four months doing that to a little girl?" Nichols's daughter, Daisy, was
then seven; he said he "couldn't imagine going to work, saying, 'Today is
the day that you vomit blood, and here's what you say . . .'"

Instead, Nichols made the first sloppy decision of his career. In later
years, he would refer to *The Day of the Dolphin*—or, as he called it, "the
fish movie"—as "a terrible mistake" and a "pretty horrible experience"
and offer various explanations for his choice to take it on. He sometimes claimed he made the movie as a favor to Roman Polanski, who
had been preparing to direct it when Sharon Tate was murdered. In fact,
Nichols didn't get involved until three years after the Manson killings;
it was Franklin J. Schaffner (*Patton*) who stepped in for Polanski, tried

to redevelop the movie, and gave up. At other times, Nichols described the film as a contractual obligation, and technically it was—he owed Joseph E. Levine one last picture—but there is no evidence that Levine pressured him into this particular project. Buck Henry, who signed on to write the script, remembered it as a game of brinkmanship that Nichols lost: "At one point Mike said, 'I'm gonna propose, because I've got to get him to dump this contract, that we do [the opera] *Der Rosenkavalier*. Surely Joe Levine is not going to be interested,' he said. So he proposed it and Joe immediately said, 'Let's get to work!' This horrified Nichols, so he searched frantically . . . He was stuck. He couldn't take another job until he finished this contract. *Day of the Dolphin* came up and everybody went for it."

The rationales were evasions of a truth that Nichols probably found embarrassing: He thought the movie would be fun. Years earlier, when he and Elaine May were improvising sketches for *Monitor* that sprang off whatever captured their interest at the moment, he had begun one by announcing, with clear delight, "Dolphins are smarter than human beings! They communicate! They have a whole language, they can learn English. I'm not making it up!" His enthusiasm left May at an uncharacteristic loss for a response.

The movie's source material was a 1967 French bestseller called *Un animal doué de raison*, by Robert Merle, that blended sardonic social satire with warnings about humankind's bent for heedless destruction. The heart of the film's narrative—the attempt to teach two dolphins human speech—derives from the novel, but on the page, it's buried beneath discursions on dolphin biology, Marx, Engels, imperialism, anti-Semitism, American exceptionalism, nuclear war, Vietnam, and the Warren Commission. In the book—unlike the movie—the dolphins speak fluently, making remarks like "I am not a fish. I am a cetacean. How many times do I have to say it?" and "We cannot withdraw from Vietnam. That would encourage aggression." Merle's novel, said Henry, was "a giant, sprawling mess. The government was going to put mines on the backs of dolphins, which they would then go and plant under a Chinese aircraft carrier, blow it up, and start World War III." It sounded like an episode of his show *Get Smart*, but played in deadly earnest.

Henry wisely lowered the stakes—the bomb-toting dolphins were no longer deployed to precipitate the end of the world, and rather than discuss the existence of God at a press conference, they spoke in mono-syllables ("Fa love Pa"), which Henry himself would spend the film's production grimly voicing in falsetto off camera. "I thought it was a stupid book," he said. "I tried to move it in the direction of a less stupid film." The screenplay, a science-oriented thriller set at a research facil-ity in the Caribbean, pleased Levine, who offset much of the $8 mil-lion budget by preselling the film to NBC for a Christmas 1976 telecast. It also satisfied Nichols, who saw it as his chance to make an action blockbuster. He then made the inexplicable decision to cast George C. Scott, who had been so difficult on *Plaza Suite*; in a one-for-commerce, one-for-art tradeoff, Nichols got him to agree to star in *Uncle Vanya* on Broadway as soon as production on *Dolphin* ended. *Patton* had finally turned Scott into the movie star Nichols predicted he would become. He was still drinking, and he had just divorced Colleen Dewhurst for the second time and married the much younger Trish Van Devere. In his dark moments, he would refer to her as "the worst actress of all time." On happier days, he would announce that she really should co-star in the movie. His director had little choice but to say yes.

That summer, Elaine May briefly came back into Nichols's profes-sional life. They had long been on friendly terms, checking in regularly and showing each other scripts; May had just directed her second movie, *The Heartbreak Kid*. But they had not worked together before a large audience in almost a decade. Now, on a whim, they thought about coming together again as performers—so much time had passed! maybe it would be fun!—and even went so far as to book ten nights at Chicago's Playboy Club, where they planned to test new material for a special on NBC. It was a startling reversal for Nichols, who had long insisted that his performing days were over—and just a week after agreeing to the deal, he got cold feet and canceled it.

Nichols and May both felt that, as he said, "the rhythm and tone of the world have changed. There's a lot to be said for letting the past be the past. What I love most is that when we stopped, we stopped. We haven't kept trying to reopen that part of our lives." But in June, they reunited for one night before an audience of thousands at Madison Square Garden, at a fundraiser for George McGovern's presidential campaign. The theme of the evening was "togetherness," and—in what *The New York Times* called "a coup of historic proportions"—Warren Beatty, who was producing the event, had gotten them to agree to appear alongside Peter, Paul and Mary and Simon & Garfunkel, two groups that had recently split up. From the Garden stage, Nichols joked to the audience, "We feel we are laboring at a disadvantage in comparison with the other[s] on this program. They quarreled viciously and broke up only a few months ago, but we have not spoken for 12 years!" They talked about McGovern's Vietnam policy ("I've always wanted to get out of Vietnam," said May, "even before we got in"), made fun of Hubert Humphrey, and did a variation on their old caller-and-operator sketch with some pointed contemporary additions about phone tapping. "We were just stunned [McGovern] didn't win the election," May joked years later. "Our concert went so well."

The Day of the Dolphin was not scheduled to start production until the end of the year; Nichols would spend the autumn in Connecticut and New York glumly attending openings, plays, and parties—"Is this the whole thing? Talking about where you were last week and where you're going next week?" he complained. His half-heartedness as he prepared for the shoot was evident. Sylbert had reluctantly scouted locations in the Bahamas—"he never thought that Mike should do the movie," says Susanna Moore.

"Mike never really wanted to do it," said O'Steen. "He kept thinking they would cancel it, that he could wave a wand and it would go away." At any other time, Nichols might have called his agent, Robert Lantz, with instructions he had given more than once: *Make this go away*. But he had only recently settled a lawsuit with Lantz, in part over the huge commissions the agent was collecting on the movies in Nichols's deal with Levine. No escape hatch presented itself. Even Roman Polanski was amused: Just before production began, he sent Nichols a jar of gefilte fish with a note that read "If only it could talk."

"He was very unhappy," says Alan Shayne, who cast the movie. "I got a call he wanted me on the island [Great Abaco] where they were shooting. I was to go immediately from New York to Florida, and a private plane would take me to the island. Mike wanted to discuss some small parts. So I took my Players' Guide and went down to see him. I arrived in the morning, went to Mike's cottage, and Annabel cooked me breakfast. I said, 'Well, Mike, you want to discuss some casting?' He said, 'Oh, I don't know. I don't think it's really necessary. They're just day players. Have you got some ideas?' I showed him some pictures and he said 'Fine,' and I went back to New York. It was very Hollywood, which he hadn't been a couple of years earlier."

Two weeks before production, Nichols lost a major cast member when Jason Robards had a near-fatal car accident in California. Until then, "Mike was going to have two of the biggest drunks in New York on an island running around together going crazy," said Jon Korkes, who acted in the film. Now there was only Scott, his new wife, and his anger. Just before shooting began, Nichols assembled his cast in Miami to read the script. Scott looked frustrated when they got to the last page and told Nichols that the ending made no sense. "Mike instantly answered," said Korkes. "George listened and asked another question. Mike had answers for everything. George nodded and said, 'Oh, yeah, okay, all right.' And he left. Someone said to Mike, 'What did you say to him?' And Mike said, 'Oh, I just made something up.' He pulled it out of his ass. It was bullshit, but for him it was effortless—he was one of the great improvisers, and George didn't want to admit that he didn't understand a word of it."

At one point, Scott asked, "What if a circus kidnapped the dolphins?" "His narrative ideas were not so hot," said Henry, "but then, neither were anyone else's . . . He could do an awful lot with an awful little, and he proved it time and time again."

From the start, Scott asserted himself as a fearsome and unpredictable force. When Van Devere showed up to shoot her first scene in a bathing suit, Nichols and O'Steen asked her to shave her armpits, and she did. When Scott found out, he exploded—at her, not at them. "George dragged Trish out of the trailer—her feet didn't even touch the ground—and threw her in this big Cadillac. Then he got in the car and took off," said O'Steen. "The next day they didn't come back. We thought George had killed her." The cast and crew stayed in a hotel or small cottages on Abaco; Scott and Van Devere lived on a yacht. "It was like a cruise ship for Aristotle Onassis or something," said their costar Fritz Weaver—and they barely socialized. Things were no warmer on the set, where Scott was seldom seen without "two terrifying German shepherds," said Nichols. "He called them 'Gog' and 'Magog.'"

"Those dogs were dead inside," said Korkes. "They recognized George and Trish, but no one else was human as far as they were concerned." A pair of former NYPD cops also loomed near Scott at all times. "Bodyguards?" Weaver asked him. "Who's attacking you?" "No, you don't understand," Scott replied. "They're protecting other people *from* me."

During production, innumerable delays were caused by the dolphins, who tended to make a game out of rearranging the underwater lights once they had been set up. Even the crew would laugh. "What can I tell you—sometimes we had a good time!" said Henry. "They'd do everything that was called for perfectly," Nichols said. "Then we'd roll the camera and they wouldn't do it. Then we'd cut and they'd do it . . . You'd get furious at them, and then you'd be sitting on the crane with your legs in the water, and they'd rub their bellies on your feet and nibble your toes, like saying, 'Come on, don't be mad.'" Scott's behavior was no more predictable, and somewhat less endearing; he would disappear on benders for days at a time, then show up worn-looking and contrite.

The Day of the Dolphin soon ran over schedule and over budget, and Nichols, trapped on an island making a movie he knew was going badly, was more than willing to spend Levine's money. He insisted that Levine build him a state-of-the-art kitchen on the island so he could fly his personal chef down from New York. At one point, he sent an airplane on a round trip to Miami just to bring him some copies of *The New York Times*. "We were on location for a long, long time," said Edward Herrmann, who had a supporting role as a marine researcher. "He'd get really interesting people to come down—Richard Avedon, Mary Ellen Mark, these brilliant New York people . . . and that would take the sting out of it for a while." Rose Styron and Lillian Hellman visited; so did Tony Walton. "One morning George called up," Walton recalls, "and said he needed to come over because he'd come to the conclusion that this acting business was no job for a grown man and he would like to leave the movie. It was not an easy time."

Scott could be expansive, funny, and collegial one day, angry and harsh the next, and his behavior left its mark on several cast members who didn't have the standing to push back. Only Mike Haley, a young assistant director who would become a mainstay of Nichols's films for the next forty years, knew how to keep him amused and in check. Late in the production, Scott tried to mend fences by inviting a half dozen of the actors to dinner on the yacht. "It was strange," says Korkes. "They took us in a launch out to his giant boat. We had this amazing buffet and ended up sitting around a big coffee table piled with dessert and booze." Scott, steadily emptying a bottle of Courvoisier he held in one fist, began a stream-of-consciousness monologue, interrupted only by short bathroom breaks, about every injury and injustice he had suffered, starting with the time Dame Judith Anderson snubbed him. As his captive guests started to eye their watches nervously, he remained oblivious; he finally released them at 4 a.m. and called in sick the next day.

At the beginning of the shoot, Nichols asked each cast member what they thought *The Day of the Dolphin* was about, and talked earnestly of the idea that if dolphins could speak, the words would be so pure that it would be like listening to God. A couple of months later, he said to the actors, "Tell me why I'm doing this film." They reminded him of what he had said, and he replied, "Yes, I know, but . . . what *else?*" "It was very hard on [Mike]," said Henry, "because if George was being particularly temperamental, he bore the brunt." For the first time in his career, Nichols all but gave up. "You can't imagine what it's like," he said, "to be directing a thing like that, and you're halfway through this enormous edifice of a job, and you realize it's not going to be any good." He got so brusque with the crew that toward the end, he told his cinematographer, William Fraker, that he wanted to apologize to his team for the way he had behaved. Fraker shook his head. "It's too late for that," he said. Nichols had had a similar warning five years earlier from Robert Surtees on *The Graduate,* but this time, "it took my breath away," he said. He had violated his own "no assholes" rule. "It made me realize that I had to put the brakes on completely," he said. "Because nobody can fight back, the director has an absolute obligation to treat people decently."

By the time principal photography ended in April 1973, Davis-Goff was pregnant—a development that she and Nichols had neither planned nor expected—and they wanted to get back to New York quickly. Nichols left it to O'Steen to tell the second unit what dolphin footage they still needed. "I'd send notes," O'Steen said. "'Get me something so that it looks like they're saying, Help, help.' Stuff like that."

Buck Henry stayed in the Bahamas "until the bitter end," the final moment that Ginger and his namesake Buck, the two dolphins playing Fa and Bi, appeared on camera. "The last day of the shoot, we did three takes of Buck and Ginger swimming off. After take three, they never came back," Henry said. "We were always haunted by that. If only we could get certain actors to swim out to sea and not come back."

With no break, Nichols began rehearsals for *Uncle Vanya,* a limited-run production he knew was being viewed by some as a test of whether he was a serious theater artist or merely a proficient stager of comedies. Ticket sales were not a concern; the casting of Scott as Astrov and of Julie Christie as Yelena would ensure a sellout, and this production also boasted Barnard Hughes and two beloved veterans, seventy-nine-year-old Lillian Gish and eighty-four-year-old Cathleen Nesbitt. People were calling it "the all-star *Vanya*" with the combination of skepticism and curiosity that had long characterized the New York theater press.

Nichols had thrown a stick of dynamite into the center of the play by casting the title role with Nicol Williamson, a Scottish actor who had stepped into *Plaza Suite* five years earlier after Scott injured his eye, and one of the few performers whose alcohol consumption and temper rivaled his costar's. Perhaps Nichols thought that, as with Robards, having a comrade in arms might neutralize Scott. That was not the case; instead, Williamson's presence inflamed a competitive instinct in Scott that threatened to derail the production. Rehearsals were mostly smooth, although when Nichols tried a large-scale version of his lying-down technique—he brought eleven cots into the Circle in the Square and had the cast run the play—Scott got restless, sat up, and started doing a crossword puzzle while the other actors were talking. The rest of the cast loved the process so much that Nichols, who presided over the read-throughs while lolling on a couch that Williamson thought looked like it belonged in "an ornate Viennese psychiatrist's office," repeated it before each performance to which critics were invited. Gish and Nesbitt placed handkerchiefs over their eyes to aid their concentration, and Williamson pronounced the read-through "worth its weight in gold, it induced such a state of relaxation."

Nichols saw *Vanya* as a play about feeling "left out of life . . . everyone feels that life is happening to the others but not to themselves." This was the first time he had directed a major play without a writer by his side; he had worked on the adaptation himself, and he took every actor by the hand and encouraged them to dig into the truth of the text, forgoing props and physical staging until the words became second nature. They all let him lead—from Nesbitt and Gish, who had first appeared on Broadway in 1911 and 1913, to Christie, who was making her first (and, it turned out, only) appearance on a New York stage and was so terrified that she wouldn't even let the understudies watch rehearsals. Only Scott resisted; he didn't care for Chekhov and admitted that "there was an ugly period during rehearsals when I didn't think much of the characters." When he suddenly disappeared for three days, leaving his costars in the lurch, Nichols could no longer even feign surprise.

Williamson's connection to Nichols was deeper, in part because Nichols himself identified with what he called Vanya's "satirical impatience." Vanya, he said, "may be ineffectual, but he's very concerned with getting things centered around him. He does what self-dramatizing neurotics do—he gets attention through his problems. One of the tools he uses is humor . . . and when that does not work, he starts yowling." In Scott's Astrov, Nichols saw another Russian doctor, his late father: "He is an entertainer," he said. "He tells stories. So much of Russian life is talking around the samovar."

By opening night, tickets were in such demand that the New York attorney general's office opened an investigation into whether the theater's box office was colluding with scalpers. *Uncle Vanya* received positive reviews—the play had not been seen in New York in seventeen years, and most critics were pleasantly surprised (though some were annoyed) by how funny they found it. "The play is full of soliloquies and Nichols has directed them so that, for once, they seem as if the characters were talking to themselves rather than confiding in an audience," *Newsday*'s reviewer wrote. "He has made *Vanya* a comedy instead of a comedy-drama, an accomplishment that I believe Chekhov would have applauded." Critics were divided about whether the production was sufficiently moving—*The New Yorker*'s Brendan Gill felt it had "more than its usual power . . . We are left in a state of exalted emotional dishevelment," while *The Christian Science Monitor* dismissed it as "Chekhov without tears" and defined the Nichols touch as "more laughs, less sensibility."

Reviewers also split on whether the night belonged to Scott or Williamson—*Time* called their scenes "mano a mano contests between bullfighters." Antipathy between them grew every week. Nichols became concerned enough to deputize his friend Tony Walton, who had designed the show, to keep Scott sober between matinee and evening performances. "It went okay," says Walton, "up until one evening when he was certainly not sober. Nicol, at that point, was at his peak as an actor, and he liked to experiment. He'd do Vanya differently on different nights, and that night he did it lying down in a hammock. I had designed these old oak garden benches, and George was so angry that he picked one of them up and went at Nicol—it looked like he meant to kill him. Nicol squirmed out of there at the speed of light and ran for his life. He got a taxi to the airport."

Scott quit the next day. The play shut down while Nichols persuaded Williamson not to fly home to Scotland yet and frantically called Richard Burton to see if he'd step in for Scott for the rest of the run. After a few fruitless days, he summoned both Scott and Williamson to his apartment—"I hope George doesn't throw me out a window," he told Walton—and ordered them to work it out. The two actors glowered at each other, walked onto Nichols's balcony, and returned to his living room some time later with their arms around each other, singing.

They finished the run amicably, but not before an incident that turned out to be the last straw for Nichols. Scott, drunk, called him late one night, woke him from a sound sleep, and snapped, "Nicol is out of his fucking mind again."

"I'll come see the matinee tomorrow," Nichols said groggily.

"You'd better," said Scott. "Slap on your wig and get your ass down to the theater."

Nichols's hairpiece was not a secret. Over the years, he would some-times mention it to colleagues with a casualness that was actually the result of careful judgment; most people understood that his references to his hair, when they came, were a sign of trust. Some years later, when his son, Max, was a preschooler, Nichols shocked and delighted one of his casts when he told them that over the weekend Max had crawled into his parents' bed and, seeing the back of Nichols's head, screamed, "Where's Daddy's face?" He could also be open about how vulnerable it made him feel; around this time, he told his friend Peter Davis, the director of the Vietnam documentary *Hearts and Minds,* that the film's producer, Bert Schneider, had said, "You'll never really be the fullest artist you can be until you take off your hair." Nichols could handle the thoughtlessness of remarks like that. But what he would not tolerate was callous sneering or deliberate injury. After three plays, a movie, and countless accommodations to Scott's own vulnerabilities, Nichols had had his fill of him. "I never forgave him for that insensi-tivity," he said. They never worked together again.

Eighteen

MR. SUCCESS

1973–1975

On July 28, 1973, *Uncle Vanya* closed at the end of a sold-out two-month run. The revival had all the contours of a success; the following year, both Scott and Williamson would be nominated for Tonys for Best Actor, and Nichols would receive his sixth nomination for directing. None of it mattered to him; during his work on the play, he had spiraled into what he called a "severe depression."

"When my failures come up," he said, "[the discussion] tends to begin with *The Day of the Dolphin*." But to him, it was his work on Chekhov—the first fulfillment of a promise he had made to himself to test his abilities—that overwhelmed him with humiliation and despondency. "I literally did not know what I was doing, nor did I care," he said, "and, for the most part, it did not seem to matter." What had started as an unsettling sense of alienation ended two years later as a plunge into hopelessness.

Nichols hid his feelings from most of his friends and colleagues. "With the exception of a few people associated with the production," he said, "no one thought things were off. I don't think anyone looked at what I was doing and wondered into which dark wood I had wandered." Even the handful of bad reviews *Vanya* received were, Nichols said, "no different than the negative reviews of productions on which I *did* know what I was doing, of work of which I was proud." But this time he could not shake the certainty that he had embarrassed himself, let down his cast, and failed the play. He believed his ineptitude had been laid bare and that, at forty-one, he had discovered himself to be the shallow poseur his most hostile detractors claimed he was.

The December opening of *The Day of the Dolphin* sat on his calendar like a time bomb. He could not rouse himself to micromanage the edit, as he had done on every previous film. A lush score by Georges Delerue—the first extensive orchestral music he had ever used in a movie—was draped over the aquatic scenes without any protest from him. The ad campaign's awkward tagline—"Unwittingly, he trained a dolphin to kill the president of the United States"—gave away a plot twist that the movie kept secret for over an hour. He didn't care.

Davis-Goff was away in England for several months working as script supervisor on the Robert Redford–Mia Farrow version of *The Great Gatsby*, and Margot Callas, who was living in Switzerland, had allowed Daisy to come to the United States for her first extended stay with her father. That summer, he hunkered down in Connecticut with his nine-year-old daughter and experienced his first real stretch as a full-time parent. The Bridgewater house seemed a safe place to hide, so much so that he decided to go in with his neighbors Philip Roth, William Styron, and producer Lewis Allen on two hundred acres of farm country adjacent to their properties for the sole purpose of making sure nobody else could build on it. A no-man's-land protecting him from the rest of the world was starting to feel essential.

The Day of the Dolphin opened just two weeks after Annabel gave birth to Max. Nichols felt detached from the thumping the film took. He didn't care much about the fate of a movie he himself thought was a dud. The reviews were what he knew they would be: *The New York*

Times called *Dolphin* "a Flipper film for adults" and wondered what had moved Nichols and Henry to "work (sometimes desperately) in several genres that are not their own." The *Daily News* dismissed it as "*Lassie Come Home* for fish," and Pauline Kael derided it as "the most expensive Rin Tin Tin picture ever made." Critics who had long admired his work, like the *New York Post*'s Archer Winsten, shrugged and admitted that "it's hard to relate this picture to the prior respective geniuses of Mike Nichols and Buck Henry," adding, "May they soon return to the fields of human foible and humor they have worked so well." And those who had long been gunning for them now went in for the kill: "If Mike Nichols and Buck Henry don't have anything better to make movies about than English-speaking dolphins in assassination attempts," Kael wrote, "why don't they stop making movies?"

They did, at least with each other. Earlier in 1973, Nichols and Henry had decided to collaborate on an adaptation of F. Scott Fitzgerald's unfinished novel *The Last Tycoon* for producer Sam Spiegel, the seventy-two-year-old showman behind *The African Queen* and *Lawrence of Arabia*. After the *Dolphin* reviews came out, Henry quietly left the project. "We were targeted to a certain extent as 'that hotshot New Yorky café society team,'" he said. "So I think we thought, *We should end this now. We'll get back together someday, but let them have other targets.*" They never made another film together, but they stayed friends. "It was nothing ever but a pleasure for me to work with Mike," Henry said. "We always had a good time."

Nichols was acutely sensitive to fluctuations in his standing in Hollywood, and it was a gut punch when, two weeks after *Dolphin*, William Friedkin's *The Exorcist* opened to far better reviews and grosses. The next time Nichols flew to Los Angeles to talk about new projects, John Calley drove him past the theater where the movie was playing, made sure he got a good look at the blocks-long line, and told him he had missed a chance to set himself up financially for life, a goal that would eventually become a fixation. "You personally lost $30 million by not making this movie," Calley said. When Nichols called Elaine May to lick his wounds, she laughed and told him, "Don't regret anything. If you directed *The Exorcist*, it wouldn't have made money at all!"

Nichols knew *The Last Tycoon* was not going to turn him into a rich man, but it was an opportunity to work with Harold Pinter, whom Spiegel had hired to replace Henry. Spiegel "adapted Jewish-mother practices to business," Nichols said. "Sam was not capable of guilt . . . but he did know how to use guilt . . . He'd mix it all up so that whenever I said no to Sam, I felt I was saying no to my uncle or someone in my family. He was a master of that." Spiegel was also famously imperious, summoning Pinter and Nichols to his London apartment to work on the script and watching them while they did it, leaving the room only when his masseuse arrived or he needed to pee. "Sam was so controlling that Harold's and my best work on the screenplay was when Sam was in the bathroom, literally," said Nichols. "Finally, I said, 'I can't do this. I can't work, think, or live in his rhythm.'"

"Mike couldn't take it," said Pinter. "Sam made him very nervous indeed." After a year of work, Nichols quit, "quite carefully," he said. "Sam was paying me relatively modest amounts every six months [about $25,000], and I took great care to tell him that I was going to withdraw before the payment was due." Things did not end well between them. Elia Kazan replaced Nichols, and when *The Last Tycoon* opened in 1976, Spiegel publicly accused Nichols of having quit because he was "bogged down" editing his next movie, *The Fortune*, "knew that he had an unsuccessful picture and . . . was in a state of depression." Nichols stiffly replied, "At the time I informed Mr. Spiegel that I would not direct *The Last Tycoon* it was, as Mr. Spiegel knows, some months before I began shooting *The Fortune*. I do not wish to bore the layman with abstruse details of film technique; suffice it to say that it is technically impossible to edit a film before it has been shot. I write lest some neophyte—or even Mr. Spiegel, who has worked with so many great filmmakers—should attempt to reverse the classic order. He would surely bog down."

*T*he Fortune began as a lark, a chance for Nichols to reunite with Nicholson (who had just finished *Chinatown*) and to work with Warren Beatty (who had just finished *Shampoo*). Both actors were at the early peak of their stardom, and their decision to team up made the movie an instant big deal, even though Nichols saw it as a toss-off, a Jazz Age scam comedy about "a time in America when people sat on flagpoles and had breath-holding contests and dance marathons . . . In the '20s, news clippings were about love nests, famous murders. There was a grand feeling in the country that you could do anything you wanted." At the studios, in the wake of *The Sting* and *Paper Moon*, Prohibition-era whimsy was being talked up feverishly as the next sure-fire genre. *The Fortune* was a sly and nasty variation on the theme; while its dark plot, about two con men trying to seduce and eventually murder the oblivious heiress of a sanitary-napkin empire, owed a debt to Alec Guinness movies like *Kind Hearts and Coronets*, Nichols saw its true antecedents as Laurel and Hardy—or Tom and Jerry if they joined forces to take on Tweety Bird.

Nichols also viewed *The Fortune* as his chance to cash in with a crowd-pleaser—"which of course God always punishes you for imme-diately," he said. "Even for a moment if you think something so stupid, it's over, [and] it will cost you a lot of money." He had only an incom-plete and very rough first draft of a script. Ever since *Carnal Knowledge*, Nicholson had been urging him to commit to a screenplay titled *The Mousebed Heiress*, by his friend Carole Eastman. Nichols had taken the script with him to Poland when he went horse shopping and thought it was funny but far from ready—it was crazily overlong, and Eastman had yet to come up with an ending.

As it turned out, she never would. Eastman was, according to Henry, "severely strange"—a high-energy chain-smoker who was phobic about planes, elevators, and cameras, not to mention instructions from directors. She had written *Five Easy Pieces* for Nicholson and had his enthusiastic support, as well as, for a time, Beatty's amorous attention. What she did not have was an ability to write her characters out of the situation she had put them in. For Nichols, who had worked only with writers who were both cooperative and swift, her intractability came as a shock. If he said, "You're being completely unprofessional, Carole," she would reply, "I like being an amateur."

The film wasn't going to be cheap. Nicholson and Beatty were each getting $1.5 million, and Nichols was paid close to that. They saved money by casting an unknown female lead, after a great deal of looking. Nichols wanted Bette Midler, but she declined to read for it. Cher, at the time still a variety show star, was interested, but Nichols told her, "There are two kinds of girls in the world, the kind you want to fuck and the kind you don't," then explained that she was the former and the character was the latter. And Anjelica Huston, who would later say she had been "a bit on my high horse about accepting stuff I didn't feel I'd earned" at the time, said no when Nicholson, who was dating her, offered her an audition. Stockard Channing had never had a major role in a movie when she came in to help out during a read-through. "For all they knew, I was an office temp," she said. "I'd never even seen a real movie star before. Jack was in dark glasses and a mink-lined Levi jacket . . . Warren came in sunglasses and they were rapping about a party and using everybody's first names . . . I was sitting there on the couch and no one paid any attention to me. I wanted that part more than anything, but I was getting more depressed every second." Channing rallied herself and blazed through what turned out to be a five-hour reading of the massive script. Nichols gave her the role and paid her $20,000.

By the time the shoot started, he and Eastman had virtually stopped speaking. "The script was 345 pages and had no ending," said Nichols. "I had to carve a story out of those pages, sort of like a butter sculpture at a wedding." *The Fortune* would mark the last time that he began a movie without a completed script, and he regretted it instantly. In a series of contentious meetings at the Beverly Hills Hotel, "he kept cutting all the good stuff out," said Polly Platt, who had been hired to design the movie. "[Eastman] would suffer over it, but she couldn't do anything about it." She later wrote that Nichols was "surrounded by yes-men."

Nichols fired Platt soon after that—she was too clearly on Eastman's side—and replaced her with Dick Sylbert. He was without some of his usual allies on *The Fortune*; O'Steen was trying to start his own directing career, and cinematographer John Alonzo, who had shot *Chinatown*, was Nicholson's pick. In the absence of a writer with whom he could partner, Nichols was more isolated than he had been since the first days of *Virginia Woolf*. "I had to do what I could," he said. "But I think you could say it was underprepared."

Beatty, who said he "didn't read *The Fortune* until the day I showed up" and did it "to work with Mike and Jack," remembers the film as an easy shoot—a "silly story about silly idiots" on which he and Nicholson had a good time "misbehaving, as if we were not kindergarteners but perhaps junior high schoolers." But Nichols later said that throughout filming he had that "little tickle in the back of your mind that something isn't quite right." For one thing, everyone involved was working in a different comic register: Nicholson, who had permed his hair so that it would stick out from each side in wings, was going for played-to-the-rafters clowning. Channing was drawing inspiration from fizzy screwball comedies like *My Man Godfrey*. Eastman, who had envisioned Three Stooges–style slapstick, lurked at the periphery of the set in dark glasses and occasionally whispered with Nicholson. And Beatty, who had imagined a more character-driven project, was knocked back on his heels and stuck playing the thankless role of the snobbish straight man. For his part, Nichols couldn't, or wouldn't, choose a consistent tone. He laughed at—and acceded to—everything that Nicholson did. He would worry about how the pieces fit together later.

There's no doubt that Nichols enjoyed himself through much of the shoot. The atmosphere was convivial, even familial; Nichols and Nicholson took pleasure in each other's company, and Davis-Goff, whom Nichols had hired as script supervisor, was there every day. But sets can be too happy; part of the grand time apparently had on *The Fortune* was the high-flying, tunnel-vision, manic cheer of Hollywood sets at the beginning of the cocaine years. "I heard the word 'wonderful' more times in ten days than I had heard it in my entire life," wrote Frank Rich, who, as a twenty-four-year-old reporter, was invited to the lot. "Everything was 'wonderful' and some things were 'very wonderful' or even 'extremely wonderful.' When Nichols finished a take, he was more likely than not to deem it 'wonderful.' If people had been to a party the night before, that party was 'wonderful'; the rushes screened each morning were invariably 'wonderful' . . . It never would have occurred to me or anyone else that all the wonderfulness might produce a movie like *The Fortune*."

On the set, nobody could agree what the point of the film was—or face the fact that two criminals conspiring to kill a young woman might not be the most natural material for a comedy. In Rich's analysis, Nichols himself was the cause of palpable uneasiness. "[He] works almost too hard at maintaining a cool and breezy front," he wrote. "After a while, his success at keeping his feelings in check can become peculiarly rattling . . . There were instances . . . when technical snafus ruined takes or scenes just refused to come alive, and Nichols always kept his feelings in tight control. His response to calamity was to drift off into an edgy silence, light another cigarette and stare intently at the bustling technicians around him."

Nicholson's energy was deflated by two blows the actor suffered during production. The first was the death of the Mamas and the

Papas singer Cass Elliot, a close friend, on July 29, 1974. "He was weeping in the makeup chair during lunch," said Nichols. "I said, 'Jack, do you want to go home? Won't you feel better?' and he said, 'I don't want to feel better.' That's very much him." The second was a call Nicholson received from a *Time* reporter who, while preparing a story on *Chinatown,* had been researching his family. The reporter told him what he had discovered: The woman he thought was his older sister was his mother, and his father, whom he had been told was dead, was alive. Nicholson was so devastated that he couldn't discuss it; he told Nichols only that he had had some rough personal news and would need to be watched closely in case his performance faltered.

Nichols had lent his New York apartment to Peter Davis after his wife, Josie, a close friend of Annabel's, was struck and killed by a taxi on a city sidewalk, leaving him a young widower with two children. He and Nichols had become friends; Davis was one of the few people Nichols could talk to about his past, his Jewishness, his nagging feeling that he would never fully belong. "One time we were at the Kennedy compound in Hyannisport," says Davis. "He saw some very WASPy people coming over and said, 'Of course, there are certain things they'll never discuss in front of me. You know, *pas devant le* kike.'" Nichols was always generous—with money, with recommendations, with help. He told Davis to stay in the penthouse with his children until he got his bearings again. That turned out to be four months. So in the fall, when the *Fortune* shoot was over, Nichols retreated to Connecticut and tried to pull the movie together.

He soon realized how much of it didn't work. *The Fortune* didn't look like a comedy: He had chosen to shoot long, studied, slightly languorous takes, with the intention of doing as little cutting as he could, for no particular reason other than that it had worked for *Carnal Knowledge.* The result lacked visual energy—the bungalow Sylbert had designed for the main characters to share was true to the period but drab and claustrophobic for a comedy, and much of the action was set in its small rooms. *The Fortune* also had little momentum. Nichols, whose credo throughout his career was "if it *can* be cut, it *must* be cut," discarded scene after scene that failed to land, and when he strung together what remained, the movie came in at ninety-five minutes, and it still felt stretched at times. "I remember going up to his Connecticut estate to screen the movie," says David Shire, who oversaw the score. "Watching with Mike and his editor sitting behind me was indeed an unnerving experience. I found the movie very entertaining, but I wasn't reacting in any visible or audible way. So when the lights came up, the first thing Mike asked was whether I really wanted to work on the picture . . . Mike clearly thought I hadn't liked the film very much. And [my] being one of the first outsiders . . . to see the cut, this was clearly unnerving to him."

Shire stayed overnight, got a tour of the ever-growing horse farm, and met the requisite famous houseguest, a "somewhat sleep-disheveled Lillian Hellman." Nichols had come to enjoy playing lord of the manor so much that when Avedon came to visit, he took his onetime protégé to task. Avedon was never at his happiest when Nichols was in a romance—and after a visit to Bridgewater, Nichols said he complained "that I had far surpassed my teacher in the art of living well and that he wasn't comfortable in my world anymore, that it was all big-name and big-money people. He attacked me—affectionately—for collecting horses and Morandis and for not decorating my places spontaneously enough." When Nichols told Avedon that he had arranged for them to have lunch with the New York socialite Slim Keith and dinner with Bill and Rose Styron, he cut his planned weekend short and left immediately.

In December 1974, ten years after she and Nichols had separated, Margot Callas returned to the United States for divorce proceedings, which unfolded somewhat seriocomically in a small courthouse in Litchfield, Connecticut. "Mike asked me if I would be the witness," says Rose Styron. "I sat in the front row in case they needed to call me. Mike was very worried. Margot came from New York looking gorgeous in high heels and a beautiful dress. She had a very tall, distinguished lawyer with her. Mike, who was much heavier at the time, came in wearing a Chinese suit with a high neck and brass buttons down the front, looking quite round and spiffy. And following him was his very small, thin, dark-haired lawyer from Waterbury, wearing exactly the same outfit. I burst out laughing. The judge and the people of Litchfield were just country bumpkins, watching this ceremony. They were all one hundred percent in favor of Mike, and zero percent in favor of stylish New York Margot and the lawyer. The judge ruled in favor of Mike and said he didn't have to give Margot anything. Mike was so embarrassed that he agreed to give her quite a bit of money and to make sure, because she and Daisy were living in Paris, that they could come once a year to New York and he would have Daisy for a summer month or two."

In the cocoon of his country life, Nichols could tell himself that everything was going to be all right. When Shire started working on the score, Nichols told him that *The Fortune* was "about the American dream gone sour." He still believed that, for all its inconsistencies, the movie would emerge as a cohesive and pungent social satire about capitalism, personal ambition, and greed. By the time it had its first preview, a few months later, his perspective had grown more pragmatic. When a reporter asked what the film was about, he replied, "It's about 'If we don't get a laugh every thirty seconds, we're in the toilet.'"

The Fortune did not get a laugh every thirty seconds. Nichols may not have fully understood what kind of movie he had made until he saw an industry audience react to its misanthropy and cynicism. Without intending to, he had turned the film into a transposition of *Carnal Knowledge* to a different genre—another story in which the woman is an exasperating hysteric, always crying and making noise, and the primary relationship is the competitive, slightly homoerotic tug-of-war

between two men. No amount of editing could give *The Fortune* a stable comic mood, or solve the disconnect between Beatty, evidently ill at
ease and trying to find the charm in his character, and Nicholson, ever
louder in his hunt for laughs. Nichols had paced the movie to play like
a knockabout romantic comedy for most of the first half, making the
introduction of the murder scheme feel particularly chilly, an announcement that the characters the audience has been led to care about
are, in fact, awful.

"I meant *The Fortune* to be a small, happy, funny movie," he insisted. "It's about people so innocent they don't know when you kill
someone, she dies." Shaken, he retreated to safer ground. He had just
been offered Judith Rossner's *Looking for Mr. Goodbar* and turned it
down—the last thing he wanted to immerse himself in was yet another
film about a woman being brutalized. Instead he got in touch with his
two most loyal collaborators, Elaine May and Neil Simon. He asked
May to work with him on radio ads for *The Fortune*—he eventually
discarded them because, Nichols said, "they seemed to me to be commercials for Nichols and May rather than for" the movie. But their reconnection did yield an idea that would bear fruit several years later:
They started to discuss acting together onstage as George and Martha
in a revival of *Who's Afraid of Virginia Woolf?* And he told Simon, who
had been begging him to do so for years, that he wanted to direct his
next movie.

Nichols was already indirectly responsible for Simon's new screenplay. The idea for *Bogart Slept Here,* about a struggling off-Broadway
actor whose marriage is destabilized when he's offered a potential
breakthrough movie role, sprang from Dustin Hoffman's story about
the moment Nichols called to tell him he had been cast in *The Graduate*
and he and his then girlfriend looked at each other and thought, *We're
in trouble.* Simon had written *Bogart Slept Here* for Marsha Mason,
whom he had recently married, and he and Nichols both wanted Robert De Niro, who was in ever-growing demand after *The Godfather:*

Part II, to play her boyfriend. Nichols hoped to be in production by the time *The Fortune* opened in May 1975, but De Niro was so busy—he was in the middle of shooting Bernardo Bertolucci's epic *1900,* after which he would, ironically, be tied up making *The Last Tycoon,* then *Taxi Driver*—that *Bogart Slept Here* could not start until the fall. De Niro took the part after a hasty meeting with Nichols at the Beverly Hills Hotel. Nichols thought he was worth waiting for.

Since *The Prisoner of Second Avenue,* the dynamic between Nichols and Simon had become uncomfortable; as Elizabeth Ashley put it, "I'm not sure Doc ever fully forgave Mike for everything he did for him." Nichols had won four Tonys for directing Simon's plays; Simon had won none, and was starting to feel that Nichols was getting credit for saving his plays as much as for staging them. "There was tension between Neil and Mike long before we went on location," says Mason. "We didn't discuss it much, but I know Neil was upset with Mike and felt that Mike's ego was really, really big at the time."

In fact, Nichols was still in bad shape emotionally, in the grip of self-doubt and a sense of purposelessness that had not really lifted in almost two years. After one meeting about *Bogart Slept Here,* he invited Mason and Simon to a test screening of *The Fortune.* The three of them stood in the back of a Century City theater, watching both the film and the indifferent audience. "It wasn't good," said Mason. "You could tell there was a problem. I remember Mike saying, 'I don't understand why it's not working. I just don't know what's wrong.'" This was not *The Day of the Dolphin,* which Nichols could tell himself was the wrong genre, the wrong story, the wrong script made for the wrong reasons. This was comedy—his wheelhouse. Just a few weeks earlier, he had watched the movie alone and told O'Steen it was his best film ever. "He had been so phenomenally successful," says Mason. "He had had carte blanche. And all of a sudden it didn't work. That's got to rock you to your core, especially men of that generation. I know Neil thought he had the pulse of the people, too, and when that started to unravel, he had a hard time."

When *The Fortune* opened a few weeks later, it got some good reviews—including from Vincent Canby, who had become a reliable champion of Nichols—but they were outnumbered by the bad ones. Of the whole creative team, Channing was the only one who walked away unscathed; she was discussed as the film's sole pleasant surprise. ("I thought it was going to be one of the great motion pictures of all time," she said. "It wasn't, but it changed my life.") Nichols wasn't caught off guard by the critics who noted "something hectic and ugly about watching a cad and a weasel trying to drown, however ineptly, an essentially defenseless innocent" or by the complaint that "watching this, one is hard pressed to remember where Nichols ever got the reputation for being clever." But he was taken aback by the film's swift box office collapse, and by the press's avid reporting of it. Newspapers and magazines were, for the first time, hungry for regular news about the financial performance of movies. *Jaws* was just a month from opening, and all through the summer of 1975, reports of its huge grosses would generate headlines, the mirror image of which was gleeful coverage of "flops of the year" and "summer's biggest turkeys." Hollywood movies as high-profile as the ones Nichols made would no longer fail quietly; *The Fortune* was a very public disaster, and Nichols was stunned by the enmity with which it—and he—was discussed. "Why won't they just let me make my insignificant comedies?" he asked a friend.

The film also cost him his partnership with Sylbert, who had left production design to become a senior executive at Paramount and trashed Nichols's choice to make *The Fortune* in *The New York Times*, calling it "a movie about two guys who want to kill a sweet, pretty young girl, for God's sake," and saying, "Who can identify with that?" Nichols viewed the comment as a public betrayal. "He was furious," says Davis. "And he had every right to be." Nichols and Sylbert did not work together again.

Amid the punishing headlines, Nichols kept his head down and tried to concentrate on *Bogart Slept Here*, but he was deeply worried. He had assembled an excellent cast that included Tony Lo Bianco, Linda Lavin, and Sam Elliott, and a team he trusted, including Surtees, his *Graduate* cinematographer; at Warner Bros., the film would be closely supervised by another ally, John Calley. "Two weeks before shooting, our sets were built, they were set-dressed, our locations were picked, our actors were cast, and I was so proud, as was Mike, that for the first time in his life he didn't have to think of anything but working with the actors," says the film's producer, Howard W. "Hawk" Koch. "Then we did the first table read, and it wasn't very funny." Even then, Nichols struck his colleagues as disturbingly detached; the movie was being prepared around him but not by him. "I hadn't really been paying enough attention," he said.

Nichols was so used to being in accord with Simon that he couldn't understand why, on this film, they seemed to move further apart with every draft. "Neil wrote it more as a romantic comedy," says Mason, "and Mike really wanted an overlay of satire about Hollywood. I was caught in the middle, as much as I tried to stay out of it."

And from the moment he arrived, everyone was alarmed by De Niro, who had just finished *Taxi Driver* days earlier and showed up not entirely ready to shift gears to light comedy. "Look, there was a hurry to start," De Niro says. "I had to get up to speed fast, and Neil's writing has to be done in a certain way . . . At the time, maybe I wasn't as agile with that kind of material. I just didn't feel connected. I had committed fast, and these days I would have said, 'Let's have a reading of this and make sure we all want to get into this together, and no hard feelings if we don't.'"

Every day, the problems got worse. De Niro's Method intensity was a wild mismatch for Simon's once-over-very-lightly comedy, and Nichols, ordinarily so skilled at burrowing into an actor's mind and helping him find his way to a character, was too checked out to dig into what could have been a rewarding collaboration. "Bobby called me one day and said that he wanted to live on the set!" Mason says. "I said, 'Well, I don't really work that way, and I think my husband might have thoughts about that, but if it works for you, you should do it.'" During rehearsals, De Niro asked Koch for a copy of a Bela Lugosi recording for a scene in which he was supposed to imitate Dracula for his young daughter. Koch obliged. When it came time to shoot the scene, De Niro spoke his line—"I vill not hurt you, I only vant to suck the chocolate syrup from your veins." The little girl playing his daughter was supposed to scream and run into her room. Instead she ran off the set, shrieking, "That man's not my daddy!"

"I felt like shit the whole time," says De Niro. "I was sitting in my camper and we were shooting on location in the Hollywood Hills, and I heard one crew guy say to another, 'He's just not funny.' The other guy said, 'He sure isn't.' I thought, *Oh my God.*"

"The set was not relaxed, and Bobby was very serious, and you couldn't really tell if he could be charming or not," says Mason. "So it was problematic for all of us. *The Fortune* was a real problem for Mike; it shook his confidence. I just felt, *This is not good.* I could feel the tension all the time. I think Mike was concerned for Bobby because he picked him. But from the get-go, nobody was in the right place at the right time."

One week into production, the problems came to a head. "There's a scene where De Niro and his wife and his two kids come out to California," says Koch. "A yellow cab pulls up to a yellow house. It's got a little yellow walkway, yellow flowers out front, and the door is yellow. When you open the door, we have yellow carpeting, yellow walls, yellow furniture . . . We even put yellow water in the pool." The dialogue that followed was prototypical Neil Simon:

Mason: Gee, it's very . . . yellow.
De Niro: Do you like yellow?
Mason: Yeah, I like yellow. I just never knew anyone would use it all up. Who found this place?
De Niro: Some woman from the studio . . . Well, she was sick . . .
Mason: Probably jaundice.

"By this time Mike was very insecure with De Niro," says Koch. "They were doing the scene and De Niro said, 'Mike, do I know this lady from the studio?'"

"I don't know, Bobby," Nichols sighed. "Why?"

"Well, how do I know she's sick?"

"Bobby, look at this place!" said Nichols. "Who would rent a place this ridiculous?"

"Well, did she send me pictures? Did I talk to her on the phone? I mean, could I say '*probably* sick'?"

"Mike turned around and looked at me with steam coming out of his ears and said, 'I will not work another minute with this,'" says Koch. "We called John Calley, we looked at the first six days, and Calley said, 'Okay, Mike, you can go ahead and fire him.' He fired him that afternoon."

Nichols spent two weeks trying to recast the role—they discussed moving Lo Bianco into De Niro's part or casting Raul Julia. Nothing felt right. "We looked at the dailies," Nichols said. "And I said, 'This is shit. This is no good.' Everyone said, 'No, don't be silly.' The editor said, 'I'll pull it together.' The composer said, 'We've got to do music.' I went to my office, and Anthea [Sylbert, the costume designer] came in and said, 'You're right. It *is* shit.' And I said, 'What should I do?' And she said, 'Stop.'"

He stopped. That day, Warner Bros. shut down the production of *Bogart Slept Here* for good. Firing an actor was one thing, but canceling a high-profile film after the cameras had already started to roll was a catastrophe so public that it would stain any director's reputation. The other actors were devastated. Lo Bianco hadn't even gotten to shoot a scene. "Oh, it was awful," says Lavin. "It would have been my first movie . . . I was getting ready to do my scene, and the wardrobe mistress called and said, 'The movie has wrapped.' 'Oh, no, no, no, movies don't fold,' I said. And she said, 'This one did.'"

Nichols packed his bags and went home to Connecticut, home to Annabel and his baby son and his forty horses, home to bed. "I get more narcoleptic than scared when things aren't going well," he said. "People said I was afraid of failure. I really just felt dead mentally." Four years earlier, *Carnal Knowledge* had given him a second chance. Now he left Los Angeles knowing he had squandered it. *The Day of the Dolphin* was strike one. *The Fortune* was strike two. This was strike three. He had essentially ended his working relationships with every writer he knew. He had no plans in movies or theater. He would not step behind a camera again to direct a feature film for seven years.

Back when his career as a director was just a few years old, when the instincts he now no longer believed he could trust were steady and sure and everything he touched routinely turned to gold, something happened to Nichols that he shrewdly shaped into a story that was crafted to disarm listeners, to let them know that fame isn't everything, that even he was at the mercy of fate. In the story he told, he was on a jet, leaving JFK, when it suddenly ran into mechanical trouble. The pilot announced that they were turning back—they had to make an emergency landing. A few passengers screamed or started to cry. Nichols had always known how to sell the anecdote, but now its punch line curled back at him like a scorpion's tail. As he strapped on his seat belt, he said, an angry woman a few rows in front of him wheeled around and glared at him.

"Well?" she snapped. "What are you going to do *now*, Mr. Success?!"

PART TWO

What Happened Next

Nineteen

EVERYTHING GOES
ON THE LINE
1975–1977

In the fall of 1975, Mike Nichols began to grasp the reality of his new status as a double exile—a filmmaker whose cold streak had grown ominously long and a stage director who hadn't had a big hit for four years. He tried to process his downgraded professional status as an earned punishment. At the start of his life as a director, he had embraced his new role as what he believed was a first step into fatherhood—a career as a surrogate parent to actors and playwrights and a way to outgrow the infantile, petulant side of his personality. Since then, having become an actual father, he had learned that directing was not parenting. It was, if anything, an even more dangerous job for what he called the "baby as king"; he presided over an empire in which there was no shortage of courtiers to say, "He wants his banana at 4" or "Oh-no-no-no, he *always* has his chair on the *left* side of the camera." Nichols had always taken to being pampered. Now, for the first time, he realized how completely he had come to feel entitled to it, especially in Hollywood. "I think he blamed L.A. and the ethos there, and he wasn't wrong," says Candice Bergen. "He and Annabel lived in such a beautiful, refined house, and I remember them talking about what a prince he had become. One morning they were having breakfast and he saw some stains on a coffee thermos and announced, 'I can't live like this.' It was that kind of thing." Now he was experiencing a trial that seemed designed to strip him of vanity. For the first time, a gossip column had even run an item about his hairlessness, a subject that until then had remained tactfully unmentioned in the press. It was one more small humiliation to endure.

If his movies had been succeeding, Nichols knew he would probably be in Los Angeles preparing the next one. But there was no next one, and it did not escape his notice that theaters were crowded with the work of directors who, like him, had risen in the past decade and were now making their masterpieces. Milos Forman, a friend whom Nichols had helped obtain sponsorship from the Directors Guild of America when he came to the United States, had just finished *One Flew Over the Cuckoo's Nest*. Sidney Lumet had worked with Pacino, an actor Nichols had been chasing since *Catch-22*, on *Dog Day Afternoon*. And *Nashville* was sparking the kind of conversation that Nichols's movies had not for years. Since *M*A*S*H*, he had seen Robert Altman's career path as the road not taken. "Altman," he told a colleague, "is doing what I would have expected me to be doing"—harnessing the techniques of improvisation in the service of a daring new kaleidoscopic naturalism. *Nashville* brought home to Nichols the fact that his own work had "gotten more and more formal and controlled," he said. But "every time I decide that I'm going to go in [Altman's] direction, something pulls me into a style that is much more spare and not so free."

Nichols was about to turn forty-four. The film-school generation—the kids inspired by *The Graduate*—were no longer kids at all but were, as the success of *Jaws* made clearer every week, reshaping the film industry. And in New York, he discovered that the culture he had left behind had, quite comfortably, moved on without him. The city's center of comedy was no longer the latest Neil Simon play; it was *Saturday*

Night Live, which had just debuted on NBC and was making the rest of the comedy-variety genre look timid and feeble. Twenty years earlier, the kind of young improv performers from Chicago and Canada whom Lorne Michaels had assembled for the show would have come to New York and made their names in nightclubs, as Nichols had done. That world was gone and, seemingly overnight, half the people he knew had been pulled into this new orbit—Candice Bergen, Paul Simon, Buck Henry, and even Tony Perkins were all among the show's first guest hosts.

Nichols didn't sulk or seethe. He recognized *SNL* not just as the hot new thing, but as a *good* new thing. He watched the show from the beginning, but, unlike many New York celebrities, he didn't attend the broadcasts or the A-list, cokey, long-night's-journey-into-day afterparties; instead he would shyly send word when he liked something. "At some point," said Michaels, "I was having dinner with Candy and she said, 'You know, you're Little Mike. You two should really meet each other.'" They became fast friends, and by the second season Michaels was turning to him as a casual consigliere when a cast member was acting up or an ego problem was brewing. In some ways, Nichols became to Michaels what Avedon had been to him—a guide to a new world. "I remember hearing Mike say to Elaine once, when they had to cancel a dinner with someone, 'He lives the same life we live—he'll understand,'" says Michaels. "It was the first time I put it all together—that this is a life, and that the small group of people who live it are different from Hollywood people. The New York version has stage and publishing and politics. When Mike said that, I started to see what it looked like to be nourished by being around people who are bright and funny—and how much he loved that."

Warner's new vice chairman, David Geffen, didn't know if Nichols had decided never to make another movie or just needed a break. He would send him scripts and try to interest him in going back to work, but in the aftermath of *Bogart Slept Here,* Nichols saw every opportunity as a potential mistake. "Everyone said I was afraid," he said, "and I thought, *Oh, bullshit*, but maybe in fact I *was* afraid"—whether of misstepping, blundering, or, worst of all, being made to look like a fool by repeating himself. When another possible reunion with Elaine May came up, he waved it off, saying they both felt that "there's something sort of sad about a crone and a geezer doddering out to give us their well-loved routines for the millionth time." That dismissiveness was a cover for apprehension. "I won't do anything as a performer," he said, "because I've lost that feeling of connection, and the ability to handle the audience as myself."

Nichols was looking for something that would make him love his work again. His salvation was a playscript that had arrived at his California office the day he shut down *Bogart Slept Here*. "I only know one thing about this valley," he said. "When you're in one of the troubled places, which happens to everybody . . . you must do something as small and serious and uncommercial as possible." The play was David Rabe's *Streamers*. Nichols would later call his production of it "the best work I ever did on the stage." Many who saw it agreed.

Rabe, then thirty-five, was something of a sensation when he approached Nichols; his play *Sticks and Bones* had won the Tony in 1972, and *In the Boom Boom Room* was nominated the following year. A toweringly tall Vietnam veteran who wrote long, edited grudgingly, argued strenuously, and often felt like an outsider in the clubby world of theater, Rabe was so passionate about his work that Joseph Papp, his mentor at the Public Theater, once said, "If [he] didn't write, he'd murder someone because his feelings are so strong."

"I'd been trying to catch Mike's attention for years," Rabe says, "but I was ready to get out of theater. Even when *Sticks and Bones* was on Broadway, I was making like a hundred dollars a week. I was in the throes of a divorce and went to L.A. looking for movie work. I would go talk to Mike about doing a movie, and he would start talking about theater because he was so sick of filmmaking." Rabe showed him

Streamers only reluctantly and was blunt about not wanting to subject an untested play to a New York opening. Fine, Nichols said, let's do it in New Haven and see how it goes.

Rabe had reason to be wary. He had written most of *Streamers* in a torrent of energy—"Mike said it read as though I'd done it at white heat in four days"—and the play's claustrophobic group portrait of young men in an Army barracks, where the combination of homosexuality, racial tension, and the dread of being sent to Vietnam prove combustible, included an unprecedented level of onstage carnage. Nichols was undeterred. Although *Streamers* was a world apart from anything he had put onstage, it was the sort of directing task he loved—a chance to use physical interplay to elucidate character. In addition, it would have to be cast with talented young actors rather than stars, a relief after years of massaging egos in the rehearsal room. He installed Rabe and his new girlfriend, Jill Clayburgh, in the guesthouse in Bridgewater and used their daily drive to the Long Wharf Theatre to stay on top of him. "He was on me about cuts all the time," says Rabe, "and I was trapped in the car. It was quite a struggle. We kind of wore each other to a frazzle, but I felt we were in it together."

That sense of forced camaraderie extended to the cast. The novice performers hired for the New Haven run were somewhat awed by Nichols; he disarmed them by opening up about his own life—his relationships, his fears, his children, even his wig—and by making a joke out of his own status. "After rehearsal, he would drive off in his Mercedes-Benz and wave like Queen Elizabeth from his car," says actor Ron Siebert.

But Nichols also knew how to bind his troupe together, and worked as teacher, guru, and drill sergeant to turn them into a unit. "We were a bunch of actors up in New Haven, separated from our families," says actor Herbert Jefferson Jr., "and we were thrown into this like a bunch of new guys in an actual Army barracks. We had no one but ourselves while we were doing the play." Nichols did all he could to sequester them. Rehearsals were long and punishing by design, and he had them all bunk in the same hotel. "After a couple of weeks, we had the opportunity to get away for a day or two and go down to New York to visit wives and girlfriends," says Jefferson. "Mike tried to talk us out of it."

The experience was doubly isolating for Peter Evans, the talented twenty-five-year-old whom Nichols cast in the crucial role of Richie, the gay recruit whose teasing boldness about his sexuality ignites the action. Evans himself was gay—the only member of the ensemble or creative team who was—but in 1976, even in theater, the subject was sensitive enough to be met with a decorous silence in rehearsals, and his feelings about a straight writer's depiction of a gay character were never discussed. "His take on Richie was that you never really knew what his orientation was," Jefferson says. "And we didn't know if Peter's sexuality was any of our business."

"Mike directed the first twenty minutes like a Noël Coward comedy," says Michael O'Keefe, who was hired as an understudy at nineteen and spent much of his time in the wings or the back of the theater watching Nichols. "He treated it as a door-slamming farce. He kept saying in rehearsal, 'Push the pace like it's a comedy. Don't slow down, don't indulge yourself.'" Nichols was especially forceful with John Heard, a rising stage actor whose skill was apparent to everyone but who tended to slow the action while he searched for his character's feelings and motives. "When you're young," says O'Keefe, "you try to parse every moment, but the effect of that in real time when we're watching is, we're just waiting for you to do something. Mike was like, 'Don't fall into that trap. Keep moving' . . . He would stand in the back of the theater and get really pissed when people were taking too much time. You could see him be like 'Say the line. Fucking *say* it!' He had incredibly honed instincts about what an audience would sit still for."

Nichols's focus on pacing was part of his overall design for the play. This was not a production on which he would just let it happen and pronounce everything wonderful; he wanted moment-to-moment precision and, when necessary, demanded it. He told his actors that the start of *Streamers* should feel "normal," a series of brisk entrances, exits, costume changes, trips to the shower, and routinized actions—making a bed, hanging up a uniform, closing a locker—that would make the audience believe it was seeing a service comedy, performed in a familiar and comfortable visual rhythm. Since *Barefoot in the Park*, he had been refining his ability to thread an offhand physicality through scenes until every piece of behavior seemed organic. He had always used the technique to elicit laughs. Now he deployed it as a weapon. When *Streamers* shifted to scenes of flirtation and seduction, he would unsettle the audience by slowing the tempo, turning the exchanges into something more intuitive and dreamlike, with a growing sense of menace. When that gave way to the bloody climax, he would have the violence erupt with terrifying suddenness and speed. "Mike directed it in such an intimate, naturalistic way," says Tony Walton, who designed the production, "that the switch to hair-raising viciousness would be almost physically disorienting."

It would also be exceptionally explicit. The actor playing one of the stabbing victims had one blood pack taped to his belly and another connected to a tube secured at his wrist; when the interloper Carlyle, who was played by an older Black actor named Joe Fields, knifed him, he would double over, surreptitiously uncork the wrist pack using his teeth, squirt a gout of fake blood into his mouth, and then stand up, stagger forward, and vomit it toward the audience.

The overall effect was something Nichols could not have anticipated. He had created a mood of such suffocating dread that, when the stabbings began, "we literally had people passing out, or getting out of their seats and running up the aisles to get out," says Jefferson. The Long Wharf's artistic director, Arvin Brown, had an office with a window that overlooked the stage, and he watched the walkouts and the fainting every night. "The reaction wasn't all about the blood," he says. "A lot of it was because of Mike's ability to create a sense of psychological terror." Brown says Fields's performance was so frightening that it seemed to "erase the kind of boundary line that always exists between the actor and the audience, that allows the audience to say, 'This is only a play—you're safe.'"

News quickly reached New York that something important was happening at the Long Wharf. "I am quite accustomed to seeing bloodshed on stage," wrote Walter Kerr in *The New York Times*. "I am not at all accustomed, however, to the sort of experience I had . . . in New Haven." As the violence broke out, he wrote, "the atmosphere in the auditorium changed radically, boiled over. A rather substantial portion of the audience got to its feet noisily, not hesitating to call out to companions to join them in leaving, stomping purposefully across the thin space that separates stage from spectators . . . Some hurled their programs into the acting space in a clear show of contempt . . . I have never seen a rebellion of these proportions before . . . Mr. Rabe is out to affect his audience . . . But he has not yet learned to affect it without alienating it." That tone of shocked umbrage was clearly going to sell as many tickets as a rave would—and there were plenty of those, with critics praising the "searing detail and overpowering realism of Nichols's direction."

The conversation about *Streamers* was itself incendiary. "Will the significance of the play outlast our current concern with homosexuality, a subject that has never been as politicized . . . as within the past ten years?" *Women's Wear Daily* wondered. Others asked if Rabe was suggesting that a gay soldier was, as a *New York Post* essay had it, a "neurotic and destructive force," or that the racial intermingling of soldiers could only lead to mayhem. Absolutely not, Nichols insisted. "You know what this play makes me think of?" he said at the time. "Ethel Rosenberg. That last grab for the matron before she was put into the electric chair. Which is certainly what any of us would do . . . There's a strong element of that in the play, of a quick grab and a hug—as you might do to the person sitting next to you on a plane if the plane were about to crash." Rabe added, "If you're in a dangerous situation, if you're lonely and frightened, you wish for somebody to grab hold of. Sex is probably the last thing on your mind. But say there's nobody around you but other men . . . What does it mean if you suddenly embrace one of them? Everything goes on the line, identities, everything."

Nichols, however, worried that "the later, violent portions of the play weren't . . . rooted in the earlier portions," and encouraged Rabe to keep revising. There wasn't much time; after those reviews, *Streamers* was headed for New York quickly. "Mike said he found out what the play was in New Haven, and now he needed to find out how to make it work," says actor Mark Metcalf. "And part of the way was to play all the comedy you could for the first three-quarters until it starts to turn violent. You make the audience comfortable, and then when you slap them with the bone-deep reality of the situation, they'll be so stunned they won't walk out."

That was close to Nichols's original plan, and in addition to sharpening the text and his own direction, he made several cast changes to get *Streamers* the rest of the way there. The increasingly recalcitrant John Heard was replaced by a gentler, more cooperative actor, Paul Ryan Rudd, at the insistence of Papp (who had retained the rights for the Public to co-produce the New York run). And as Carlyle, the GI whose rage finally boils over, Nichols replaced Fields with Dorian Harewood, a much younger, less physically imposing actor who would not tip the play's hand with his first entrance, as Nichols felt Fields had done. "Mike said that because I was more the size and age of the other actors, it would be more effective when I went off the rails," he says. Harewood wasn't sure he even wanted to be an actor, let alone one playing "such an ugly, self-hating character," but "Mike was the one who made it work," he says. "He made the audience understand my character and made me feel I could try anything without being afraid.

If something wasn't working, he would never be stern or harsh. He would just say, 'That was interesting,' and it made the point. His main focus was always on the truth of whatever a scene was."

When *Streamers* began previews in New York, there were still gasps and walkouts—at one performance, Liv Ullmann bolted from the theater, then sent the cast a note of apology, saying it was just too realistic—but not as many as there had been in New Haven. Word was out that Nichols was back in top form, and the theater community embraced his return. The opening of *Streamers* at Lincoln Center was an event, so much so that even though the small size of the Mitzi E. Newhouse Theater made it ineligible for the following year's Tonys, the American Theater Wing made a one-time-only exception, fearing a backlash if what was being hailed as a milestone of American stagecraft was locked out. Nichols's reascension was confirmed by the eagerness with which those in his circle raced to see the play. Lillian Hellman, who had chain-smoked through a day of rehearsals in New Haven, returned for another look. Warren Beatty came from Los Angeles; Dustin Hoffman got a ticket for opening night and congratulated the cast at the party afterward. Critics who had expressed reservations in New Haven were now fully on board; *Time* praised Nichols's work as "clean, powerful, and electric," and the *Daily News* called it "the most accomplished new American play in years." "Neither the author nor director has come close to this level of accomplishment in the past," Alan Rich wrote in *New York* magazine, "and I urge you to share with me the keen pleasure of having your faith restored in the power of American drama to make important and worthwhile sense."

By the time *Streamers* opened in April 1976, Nichols was back in the public eye as—to his own great surprise—the producer of a hit TV series. A couple of years earlier, he had gone to Michael Eisner, who had just taken over as ABC's head of prime-time programming, with a script by his Connecticut friend and neighbor Jay Presson Allen, who had written the screenplay for *Cabaret*. Allen and Nichols were both admirers of *An American Family*, the pioneering 1973 PBS documentary series that chronicled the lives of a contemporary Southern California household and allowed viewers to witness the breakup of a marriage and the coming out of a young gay man in seemingly real time. The series, which became a national obsession when it aired, inspired Allen to write an hourlong drama pilot that she called "The Best Years," about an upper-middle-class family—a husband, wife, and three children—who would deal with every issue the 1970s could throw at them, including premarital sex, drugs, divorce, health crises, financial woes, and generational rebellion. ABC thought Allen's script was too sophisticated and the characters insufficiently relatable; the network got on board only reluctantly, largely because of Nichols's involvement.

Nichols made several contributions to the pilot—he moved the family from a suburb of Philadelphia to Pasadena and oversaw the design of the house, which he insisted had to look like a real home, with laundry baskets, grocery bags, stacks of papers, and comfortable clutter. Most significantly, he oversaw the casting, bringing in the New York stage actors Sada Thompson and James Broderick to star. ("I think my father replaced somebody," says Matthew Broderick, "and I've always had the sense that that had something to do with Mike. When I was growing up, he was very well thought of in our house!") ABC liked the result enough to order six episodes, which it retitled *Family*, to avoid confusion with *The Best Years of Our Lives*. When the show aired that spring, reviews and ratings were so good that the network scrambled to sign the cast to long-term contracts. *Family* became a mainstay of ABC's schedule, and although he had virtually nothing to do with the series after the pilot, the words "A Mike Nichols Production" would begin every episode and literally make him a household name for the next four years.

Nichols himself was as close as he would ever come to settling into suburban tranquility. "I'm very happy the way my life is right now," he said. "I would like to lose 10 pounds, give up smoking, and have immortality." Max had just turned two, and Annabel was pregnant again—their daughter, Jenny, would be born that September. That spring, Nichols gave himself over to life in Connecticut and waved away one offer after another; the only thing he seemed interested in directing was a horse show. The two farms on which Nichols kept his Arabians—he had purchased a vast tract of land in California's Santa Ynez Valley—were now far more than a hobby; they had become an immense financial commitment to a kind of ever-fluctuating commodity market. Nichols would travel around the country and sometimes overseas to meet breeders and assess prospective purchases. He owned more than eighty horses, and when he decided to put half of them up for auction soon after *Streamers* opened, he brought a theatrical flair to the proceedings that drew hundreds of people to Connecticut—Jackie Onassis, Beatty, Hoffman, Bergen, and Henry among them, as well as reporters from *People* and *The New York Times*.

They were promised a spectacle, and they got one. Nichols hired Broadway designers to light the track on which his horses would be brought out in a carefully sequenced procession. He engaged a quartet of musicians to play as each horse appeared. He had workmen sprinkle glitter along the gravel paths and then conceal it beneath a layer of sawdust so that it would appear only when it was kicked up by hooves, and the pale blue filtered lights he had strategically placed to catch it worked their magic. The effect was designed to seduce, and it did; by the end of the auction, Nichols had sold thirty horses, for something close to a million dollars. "We all—Paul Simon, Lorne, and me—ended up buying horses," says Bergen. "And then we thought, *Now what do we do? Put them in our apartments?* But no one had ever done a horse auction the way he did."

Nichols was happy to assert his presence in every way except by taking a job. He even hosted a fundraiser for the legal defense of *Deep*

Throat star Harry Reems, who had been convicted of transporting obscene material across state lines. Nichols had been fascinated by the mainstreaming of porn over the previous few years, and he told guests at the benefit that "to help Harry Reems is to help ourselves. I don't want to go on a set someday and have an actor ask me what states the film would be shown in because he didn't want to go to jail." But he did not expect to find himself back on a set any time soon; he did everything he could to avoid it. As a gesture of friendship, he agreed to make a movie based on Lillian Hellman's *Scoundrel Time,* but he knew that her insistence on control was likely to make the deal fall apart and that, even if it didn't, Fred Zinnemann's pending Hellman adaptation *Julia*—which was announced the day before Nichols's deal—would likely consign his project to the back burner. And when Beatty approached him to direct *Heaven Can Wait,* a project that would have reunited him with both Buck Henry and Elaine May (who co-wrote it), he said no. He turned down an offer to direct *National Lampoon's Animal House* as well. "One of the lessons of *The Fortune,*" he said, "is that it's not enough to put together good people. You can't just wait for the idea. You have to *have* an idea."

He was less gun-shy about theater. He had already chosen his follow-up to *Streamers* and was planning to direct it on Broadway that fall. In some ways, *Comedians,* by the British playwright Trevor Griffiths, was almost *Streamers* redux—another ensemble piece featuring an entirely male cast in which dark comedy and naturalistic action give way to an eruption of ugliness from which there can be no recovery. The play, a success in London, concerned a group of working adults who want to become stand-up comics and take a class at a Manchester night school. Nichols loved its elegant structure—the first act was the class, the second was the stand-up performance in which some characters disintegrate and only the most ruthless or racist succeed, and the third was the bitter aftermath. And he relished the chance to grapple with material that explored the darkest aspects of trying to make people laugh, a

subject he knew well. "Griffiths is concerned with the difference between comedy that deals in prejudice and fear and comedy that con-
nects with something true," he said. "The first is easier, and tends to
corrode character."

It was a bold choice for a director who, though he publicly stated
that he had never been happier, privately "thought I had lost whatever
talent I had, not to mention my curiosity and my contentment," he later
said. Nichols was proud of *Streamers*, but his confidence and focus were
present only when he was in the rehearsal room; after a few months
away, it was harder for him to ward off depression. One day, he could
make himself believe that, all things considered, life was good; the
next, facing identical circumstances, he could feel only futility and despair. He was still in what he called "that fog" in July 1976, when, after
five years together, he and Davis-Goff got married in the garden of their
Bridgewater home. The wedding was small—she was seven months
pregnant and didn't want an elaborate ceremony. The minister and anti-
war activist William Sloane Coffin Jr. presided, and among the very
few guests were Hellman, Bergen, who took pictures, and Beatty, who
invited Trevor Griffiths to drive with him from New York. (The connection the two men sparked at the wedding led them to collaborate on
the screenplay that became *Reds*.)

Just before their daughter was born, Nichols and Davis-Goff had a
night out that ended up making him more money than any project in
his career up to that point. Jay Presson Allen and her husband, Lewis
Allen, had urged him to go see *Annie,* a new musical based on the
comic strip *Little Orphan Annie* that was struggling through a run at
the Goodspeed Opera House, in Connecticut; audiences enjoyed it,
but the reviews had been dismissive. Nichols saw that the show had
problems, but he was charmed and agreed to step in as something
between an adviser and a fixer. He recast the show's villain, Miss
Hannigan, bringing in an old friend, Dorothy Loudon; he helped
tweak plot points, tone, and pacing; and, perhaps most significantly, he

allowed the show to move forward with "Mike Nichols Presents" above the title on every poster, advertisement, and marquee. "If a musical appears to be a children's musical . . . it probably won't be a hit," said *Annie*'s composer, Charles Strouse. "But if it's an adult musical that parents can bring their children to, you've got the possibilities of a smash."

The show's untested director, Martin Charnin, resisted the idea, well aware that everyone would assume Nichols was now, in all but name, directing the show. But Strouse was adamant about how badly *Annie* needed help and threatened to pull his score unless his collaborators agreed to Nichols's billing. The show moved forward with Nichols as producer.

Annie's backers had their eye on a Broadway opening in the spring of 1977, but Nichols insisted that they first open the show, which needed considerable work, in Washington, D.C. With a run at the Kennedy Center booked and rewrites proceeding under his supervision, he turned his attention back to *Comedians*. The play was steeped in the culture and syntax of the north of England, where Trevor Griffiths had grown up. Nichols knew it was going to be a tough sell for a Broadway audience, but he was more worried about getting it right than making it accessible. Before rehearsals, he flew to Manchester, where Griffiths gave him a quick tour of the city's clubs and pubs. For Nichols, *Comedians* would be a labor of love; he would earn just $10,000 plus 5 percent of the weekly gross for a run that did not promise to be particularly long.

On *Streamers*, he had made a conscious effort to put actors who had never worked with him before at ease. His approach for *Comedians*, with Jonathan Pryce re-creating a performance that would win him a Tony, and a group of newcomers, including John Lithgow and Jeffrey De-Munn, working around him, was somewhat different. Perhaps because the play was in part about the terror of performing and of being judged, Nichols kept the atmosphere cool and slightly forbidding. "It was a pleasure to listen to him talk," says Jerry Adler, who served as production manager. "But that veneer was so thick—it was never personal, never revealing. He could be a psychiatrist or a mechanical genius with sets, but he never revealed himself. He was like a visiting monarch." And after *Streamers,* his word was law; on his first day in the theater, Nichols demanded that the Act I set for *Comedians* be torn down and rebuilt to make a hallway eight inches narrower. "He had looked at the model, but the reality struck him differently," says Adler. "If he said, 'Move it eight inches,' we were going to move it eight inches."

"At first it was hard and fun," DeMunn says. "But as we got closer to opening, and Mike started to get the sense that it wasn't quite working, it got a little rough." During one rehearsal, Nichols singled out a young actor for such withering treatment in front of the ensemble that he finally broke down and said, "Mr. Nichols, I don't know what you want me to do." The criticism continued until a more experienced performer, David Margulies, stepped in and cautioned Nichols, "There are other actors on the stage."

"Mike said, 'I was just doing that to show what I want to have happen in the scene,'" DeMunn recalls. "And we thought, *No, you weren't.* We were united by our reverence for his talent, but it also united us when we saw one of our number getting picked on."

By the time *Comedians* opened in November, Nichols had mended fences and fine-tuned the ensemble to such a degree that even Pryce, who found him "warm . . . and very understanding of actors," felt the production was better than the original. "The atmosphere that Mike creates is important," he said. "What he has brought to it is clarity." For the first time in his career, Nichols had a show that critics responded to better than audiences did. Reviews were enthusiastic; in *The New York Times,* Clive Barnes called the play "comedy with an aesthetic, moral, and above all political purpose" and praised its "un-self-consciously dazzling staging," and the *New York Post* wrote, "It is hard to imagine another director so completely understanding and sympathizing with the nature of solo comic performances." But all the good notices in the world couldn't sell tickets. To American audiences, says Adler, "the play was in a foreign language. We should have reset it in the Borscht Belt." Though it made a strong impression on many who saw it, *Comedians* would last less than five months on Broadway.

In January, Nichols went to Washington. Twelve years after they had performed at Lyndon Johnson's inauguration, he and May were invited to do the same for President Carter, and offered a reprise of their beloved "Mother and Son" sketch, this time as a call between Carter and his mother, Lillian. (The new president and first lady laughed heartily; the president's mother, Nichols said, "was not amused.") Many of Nichols's friends and colleagues—Simon, Beatty, Nicholson, the Bernsteins—were there to celebrate. One by one, they drifted out of the reception at the Kennedy Center until only Nichols and May, who had spent hours polishing the sketch while the Secret Service checked everyone's credentials, were left together at a corner table, old friends reminiscing and catching up. It had been a long time since they wrote anything new together; by the end of the happy night, they were even talking about a TV special.

First, however, there was *Annie* to attend to. While he was in Washington, Strouse says, Nichols put "many, many nights" into the show, and with every preview, the production took on more of his signature crispness and energy. "When Mike came in with his ideas, angels began to flap their wings," he says. "He was very modest about it. He would tell the actors a few things, and give notes quietly, but he made a big difference."

When the papers reported that Nichols was lending a helping hand, ticket sales started to surge. "I don't think Mike had any desire to be seen as the power behind the show," says Brooke Allen, Lewis and Jay Presson Allen's daughter. "It had a naked emotionalism that was not Mike's aesthetic at all. But he was very helpful and supportive."

Nichols described his role on *Annie* as "active producer"—"I jumped at the chance to invest," he said—but not surrogate director. "I didn't do much," he insisted. "I was friends with the guy who was directing it, and I would bug him and whisper in his ear in the back . . . I think once I said, 'They should probably bring in the Christmas tree earlier' . . . It took up a certain amount of time, and paid a certain amount of money." *Annie* opened on Broadway in the spring of 1977 for what became a six-year run that spawned national tours, overseas productions, and a movie sale, becoming what Nichols later called his "comic-book annuity." The "certain amount of money" it earned him ran into the millions.

When the Tony nominations were announced, Nichols was, for the first time in his career, a triple nominee. His work on *Streamers* and *Comedians* had won him two of the four slots for Best Director of a Play, and he was nominated as a producer of *Annie*, which won the award for Best Musical that June, giving him a fifth Tony. The *New York Post* declared him "this year's theater hero," capping a comeback that had *People* magazine proclaiming that "Nichols's decline was really little more than an awkward stumble. In any case, he is at the summit of his profession once again."

It sounded true. In many ways, it was true. But to Nichols, it never felt true. He still believed, he later said, that "it was the end of the line for me." Movie offers were rolling in again. He viewed them with nothing but fear. He felt as incapable of choosing wisely as he had when he left Hollywood. And on some level, perhaps he sensed what no one else did: He was about to plunge again.

Twenty

THE RAPTURE OF
MY DEPTH

1977-1980

When Nichols was in his sixties and finally believed that the most painful struggles of his life were in the past and unlikely to return, he looked back on the late 1970s and tried, without much success, to piece together what went wrong, what internal forces conspired to bring about years of false starts, missed chances, and bad decisions. "Dante says there is a dark forest in the middle of your life," he said. "You don't know it's coming, then you're in it, then you're out of it." He had always had a fondness for narrativizing his life that way—for presenting his own journey as a stumble toward enlightenment. But he could never find a way to turn his late forties, which were so characterized by fitfulness and indecision, into a tidy story. He claimed that his belief that he "waste[d] the middle" of his life impelled him to work more vigorously later, but he admitted that he never fully understood why, in the four years after *Annie,* he was so unable to find a path forward. Those years brought many failures, and also a few successes. But a part of Nichols felt that no matter what he was doing, he was sleepwalking through his own existence, a stranger to himself.

By the night of the 1977 Tony Awards, he was already turning his attention to a movie that he thought might get him back behind the camera. For months, he had been working with Bo Goldman, the co-screenwriter of *One Flew Over the Cuckoo's Nest*, on *Melvin and Howard*, a quirky, richly textured comedy-drama about Melvin Dummar, a small-time naïf who offered a lift to Howard Hughes and became a beneficiary in one of his many contested wills. Goldman had struggled with an early draft, and Ned Tanen, the head of Universal, thought Nichols would help steer him toward the wry, humane approach the story needed. Nichols liked Goldman, who had also grown up in New York and had briefly been one of his classmates at Dalton. The two worked together in long sessions at both the Beverly Hills Hotel and the Carlyle, in New York, where Nichols had taken a two-bedroom suite that served as office, pied-à-terre, and refuge on the many nights he didn't feel like going home to Connecticut. He pushed Goldman to bring Dummar's character into the foreground and turn the film from a portrait of a reclusive multimillionaire into a gentler, odder story about the American dream. His guidance brought *Melvin and Howard* close to the script that, four years later, would win Goldman the Oscar for Best Original Screenplay.

Goldman had every expectation that Nichols would direct the film, but he never quite committed to it, and once casting was under way, his intractability began to irritate Universal. For Melvin, Nichols wanted Jack Nicholson, who was interested but busy directing his own movie, *Goin' South*. When Nichols asked producer Don Phillips if he would postpone the shoot for a year to accommodate Nicholson's schedule, Phillips said, "I pulled off my shoe and pounded the coffee table . . . so hard that Mike's Valium went flying. And I said, 'There's no way in hell I'll wait a year.'" Nichols then turned to Elvis Presley, who was finishing a concert tour but said he liked the script and could start preparing for the role as soon as he was off the road. Two months later

Presley was dead, and Nichols was balking at the studio's insistence that the part (which was ultimately played by Paul Le Mat) didn't require a star.

Universal had had enough. "Mike came into my room at the Beverly Hills Hotel and said, 'I've been fired,'" says Goldman. "I said, 'Why?' And he said something like 'I wasn't addressing the project in the way that they thought I should be.' Art Linson, one of the producers, was a New Jersey guy who couldn't have been more different from Mike. He had a kind of impatient quality to him, like 'Nobody's going to impress *me*,' and I think he was having trouble getting Mike on the phone, which was the kind of thing that Mike, at that point in his career, was liable to subject somebody to." *Melvin and Howard* was given to Jonathan Demme, for whom the film became a major critical success. Reluctant to fire Nichols outright, Universal transferred his deal to another project, the Steve Martin comedy *The Jerk*. He worked on the film for less than a month, then gently pushed it away. "I remember walking down the street with Mike trying to convince him to direct the movie," says Martin. "This was at the point when he was saying no to everything, and the more he said no, the more people would ask him. I said, 'What a beautiful night,' and he looked up at the sky and said, 'Yes—isn't it ironic?'"

At the time, Nichols was more than happy to stick with theater. He was in a new marriage, and Davis-Goff did not relish the idea of his disappearing on location shoots for months while she stayed home with an infant and a preschooler. By the time *Melvin and Howard* fell apart, he had agreed to direct a play that would become a hit and further burnish his reputation. Early in 1977, Hume Cronyn had sent him *The Gin Game*, a seriocomic two-hander by an unproduced Texas playwright named D. L. Coburn. The play was a gentle story about a cantankerous old man and a widow in the same retirement home who turn their card games into both a means of connection and a fierce battle of wills. Cronyn and his wife, Jessica Tandy, were beloved lions of the stage who had spent the past three years touring in an evening Cronyn had devised for them called *The Many Faces of Love*. They were now nearing seventy and were heartily sick of what Cronyn called the "goddamn succession of Ramada Inns and airport coffee shops" that a life on the road meant. They were looking for a play that could run on Broadway, in London, or both for a good long stretch.

Nichols agreed to direct *The Gin Game* the day he read it; after his years with Elaine May, he knew exactly how a tug-of-war between a man and a woman could be mined for laughs and drama, and *The Odd Couple* had proved him to be one of the only directors who could stage a card game without making it static. He also knew that Cronyn and Tandy were self-sufficient professionals who would not turn the job into a heavy lift. The two actors agreed to a run at the Long Wharf for almost no money, then a quick tryout in Boston and a fall opening on Broadway.

Nichols later downplayed his contribution to *The Gin Game*'s great success. "I would not append the word 'happy' to that production," he said. "Perhaps I was content, or pleased, or startled. I have great respect for Hume and Jessie, and I was praying, I think, for some osmosis by being in their company . . . They approached that slight little play as if it were discovered in a Greek cave and answered all the world's questions. Having no faith in myself, I was wise enough to take on a play that had one set . . . and two incredible actors. Those two directed that play, and I just sat back and watched . . . I was in the rapture of my depth of depression."

Nichols may have felt distracted by the illness of a close friend. That summer, Leonard Bernstein's wife, Felicia Montealegre, was diagnosed with metastatic breast cancer. They were like family to him, and when Bernstein left for Europe, Nichols made a point of staying close to Montealegre and their three children. She lived for just one more year. "She was only fifty-six, and it was devastating," says their daughter Jamie Bernstein, "not just for her family but for all our close friends.

And the two who took it especially hard were Mike and Dick Avedon. Mike adored her."

As disconnected from his work as Nichols may have felt, his account of *The Gin Game* is at odds with the portrait of an engaged, sensitive, and focused director offered by both Cronyn and Tandy. Nichols was gentle with both stars, who took longer to feel comfortable with their lines than they might have a decade earlier. He rehearsed them at a library just two minutes from their home in Pound Ridge, New York. He hired an expert to teach them card tricks in order to get them more comfortable with handling a deck. And at one point when they were struggling to distinguish among the fourteen different hands of gin in the script, he urged them to "stop playing with clenched heads"—to deal less with the cards in their hands and more with each other.

"Mike has an honesty fetish," Cronyn said. "He stops me from 'acting.' I have a taste for the theatrical." Tandy agreed. "With Mike, everything has the quality of the first time, of not being manipulated," she said. "We don't know how much is enough. We need somebody to tell us." As Nichols had done on *The Prisoner of Second Avenue* and *Uncle Vanya*, he had Tandy and Cronyn lie down on couches he placed onstage the morning of the Broadway opening. When the playwright, Coburn, arrived at the theater, "I looked up," he recalls, "and they were there, reclining, running their lines quietly, and Mike was sitting there listening like a psychiatrist." When Coburn realized he had interrupted a rehearsal, he started to leave, but Nichols waved him in. He had come to ask Nichols whether he should wear a tuxedo that night. "No," Nichols said. "Just wear a suit. Don't let them know you care that much."

The Gin Game was an instant smash that made Nichols, Tandy, and Cronyn, all of whom were major investors, a good deal of money. The play, which was awarded the Pulitzer Prize, ran for well over a year, and won Nichols Tony nominations as both director and producer—his fourth and fifth in just two years.

He spent much of the following year consumed by two projects that came to nothing. His plans to produce a Black contemporization of *Alice in Wonderland*, written by Vinnette Carroll and Micki Grant, fell apart when the show closed just nine performances into what was intended to be a two-month trial run in Philadelphia; Nichols had invested $125,000 and lost it all. (A revised version of the musical, *But Never Jam Today*, came to Broadway in 1979, without his involvement, and also closed quickly.)

And when the director and choreographer Michael Bennett walked away from the film adaptation of *A Chorus Line* that he had been developing at Universal, Nichols agreed to step in as director and again work with Bo Goldman, who was writing the script. *A Chorus Line* presented a heightened version of the many problems that bedevil plays on their way to the screen: It had a major character, the director of the show within the show, who was offstage for long stretches, and almost all of the action, which took place in one day on one set, was contained in autobiographical vignettes. Nichols and Goldman tried to open it up, adding producers and songwriters as characters and varying the locations. They also developed the relationship between the director, Zach, and the dancer Cassie into a fuller romance that would resolve with her choosing to walk away from him, a modern and somewhat feminist ending that departed from the show but was very much in the mode of the just-released comedy-drama *An Unmarried Woman*. Universal balked at every change, but after Nichols had worked on the film for nine months, the studio agreed to go forward with the script and offered him a not unreasonable budget of $16 million. Nichols said no, complaining that it would have meant "shooting essentially the stage production, very carefully and very fast. It was impractical. You couldn't win. So I left."

Toward the end of 1978, he chose to direct a play that baffled almost everyone who read it, including many of the actors he cast. The novelist E. L. Doctorow had decided not only to try his hand at drama, but to write a play reflecting his conviction that "the theatrical mode has been . . . exhausted by television and film." He intended to cure America of its "defective understanding of what theatre is supposed to do" by ridding his play of elements like human psychology and "the idea of character as we normally celebrate it on the American stage." In its place would be "the arguing of ideas [as] a matter of life or death." The neo-Shavian vehicle that would house his precepts was *Drinks Before Dinner*, a play set in a luxurious Upper East Side apartment, at a party where one of the guests decides to hold another, a cabinet secretary, at gunpoint while he discusses, in a series of very long monologues, his belief that the world is coming to an end and that everyone watches too much television. Once he concludes that they are all, essentially, already dead, he puts down his gun, the hostage leaves in a huff, and they all go in to dinner.

Nichols knew his way around dinner parties like that (give or take the gun). More than many of his show business colleagues, he was at home with New York's moneyed elite and was used to attending dinners and benefits where he might be called upon to chat with anyone from Brooke Astor to Henry Kissinger. He was also avidly interested in and connected to the worlds of literature and publishing and well aware that the arrival of *Ragtime,* in 1975, had moved Doctorow to the forefront of American letters. Nichols's powerful new agent, ICM's Sam Cohn, had an unusual client roster that included directors, actors, playwrights, and novelists; he represented Doctorow, and talked Nichols into doing the play, knowing that he would not be able to resist the temptation to put his name next to one of the leading voices in contemporary fiction. After *Streamers,* Joseph Papp was eager to have him work under the umbrella of the Public Theater again and believed that his experience might compensate for the many aspects of stagecraft that eluded Doctorow. "I remember when Mike brought Doctorow around to meet Joe and see the theater," long before rehearsals started, says Papp's widow, Gail. When Nichols showed him the performance space and the stage, "Joe was struck by Doctorow's seeming unfamiliarity with theater because he asked him if there would be scenery."

"I adored Edgar Doctorow as a man and a writer, but not in that one," says Christopher Plummer, who played the monologist (also named Edgar). "He was around all the time, too, which was hard, because if you hated what you were doing, you had to watch your language. Mike was wonderful—he just stood back and let us do our work and fall on our asses, and then he came in and picked us up and put the cream on top."

It took Nichols weeks of patient and painstaking rehearsal before reality began to set in. "I think he thought it was something more than it turned out to be," says actor James Naughton. "We worked on it forever." Finally, Nichols realized he could do little but try to bring forward the few laughs the script offered. "Mike had a great brain that loved serious stuff, but he was also a comedian," says Naughton. "Those things were constantly in tension. Sometimes one side won and sometimes the other did."

After one session of notes, says Maria Tucci, who costarred in the play, "Mike waited for Edgar to leave the room and then he said, 'Well, I think we all know it's not a play.' I don't think we felt betrayed. It was pretty clear, and Mike made the whole rehearsal process a party."

The five-week run of *Drinks Before Dinner* had sold out quickly, and Papp, attempting to forestall the inevitable, postponed the critics' opening until a week before the final performance. Reviews were what Nichols feared; *The New Yorker* called the show "the first thoroughly boring play ever to be produced at the Public," and *The New York Times* expressed bewilderment at the "great blocks of talk . . . words that often seem to be assigned mainly as a matter of convenience to the nearest character available." Nichols, the review added, "has directed with great skill but a kind of glibness that unfortunately enhances the play's own." Papp, eager to keep Nichols in the fold, immediately hired him to step in as the director of *Sancocho*, a soon-to-open musical revue about the relationship between New York's Black and Latino communities, with a cast of twenty-six. After a couple of weeks, Nichols went to him and said he felt he had no business directing, on virtually no notice, a show about cultures that were completely unfamiliar to him, and quit.

In early 1979 he went home to Connecticut, in alternating states of misery and denial. David Hare, whose play *Plenty* Nichols had seen and admired in London, was working in New York for a year and remembers a weekend spent at Bridgewater with Nichols, who had invited him to the country. "I had never seen anybody who lived like that," Hare says. "It was what I called 'upper show business.' I think I slept in the screening room or something. Mike was talking about Hollywood, and what he was saying was 'I'm finally free. This is the best possible thing that ever could have happened to me. I've discovered after fifteen years that I don't have to do what they tell me to do, that I can just stop.' Those were his words—he talked as if something wonderful had happened to him—but his tone and his demeanor while he was saying them were suicidal depression, almost complete despair. And as I tried to talk him out of it, the weekend became profoundly uncomfortable—I left feeling that I had failed to cheer him up at a terrible low point in his life."

Nichols couldn't stay in the country for long. The winters, especially, made him feel confined and restless—there were movie premieres, plays, exhibitions, lunches, and dinners to attend, all the elements of a New York life that he hadn't anticipated he would miss as much as he did. His overnights at the Carlyle grew more frequent, and he started to bifurcate his life—alone in the city, with family at the house. One February night, he went down to the Public Theater to see his old friend Elizabeth Wilson in a new play called *Taken in Marriage*.

Wilson had gotten rave reviews for her performance, but it was another member of the cast who transfixed him. "He came backstage—to the shabby dressing room that the Public had then—and he just put the beams on me," says Meryl Streep. "He said, 'You do realize you were wonderful'—that kind of thing. And then he said, 'I think I might have something for you. Are you available?' Or something like that. I was in awe of him, but I thought it was a whopper." Streep, just a couple of years out of the Yale School of Drama, had started to make her name in New York theater and in television, where she had won an Emmy the previous fall for the miniseries *Holocaust*. The first movie in which she had a substantial role, *The Deer Hunter*, had just reached theaters.

She was surprised when, a short while later, Nichols called and asked her to come to the Carlyle and do a reading. "That was the first time I really met him, and I don't remember what we read," she says. "I just remember that there, curled at his feet like a cat, was little Carrie Fisher. He stroked her hair and she just sat there purring. He was besotted with her wit. Afterward, there arrived in my apartment a box from Tiffany's with a little silver pen, and I thought, *Oh my God, this is the most elegant person I've ever met*."

At the time Nichols first encountered Streep, his close friend William Styron was about to publish his long-awaited novel *Sophie's Choice*. The main character, a Polish Holocaust survivor with a tragic secret, was already being discussed as the role of the decade for whatever actress would star in the inevitable movie. Nichols topped the list of potential directors. For most of his life, he had not given much thought to his family history. He barely remembered Germany; what he described as the luck that had brought him to America was a fact of life that seemed to have nothing to do with him. But in his forties, his bitter good fortune and the pain his parents had carried with them to the United States— everything that had gone undiscussed during his childhood—started to push its way back into his consciousness. He came "very close," he said, to directing the film before recoiling from it. "I tried to picture myself on the crane saying, 'Okay, all you Jews: Camera left. SS guards on the right.' And I knew I couldn't do it. I don't think I can deal with the Holocaust . . . It's not that I read the script and burst into tears," he insisted. "It's that I'm physically incapable of dealing technically with those events."

A plan was briefly floated to have Nichols and Milos Forman direct the film together; Nichols would handle the scenes set in New York and Forman would take on the sequences set in Europe. "I never heard that," says Streep. "Is that right? Oh my God, what a terrible idea! But it could be, because there was that whole incestuous group out on Martha's Vineyard, and they all knew each other, and Styron was there. Sam Cohn"—who also represented Streep—"was at the very center of all of it. There was a little stable, and Sam was the one who put movie people and literary people together. That was how *Ragtime* happened, and he may have had something to do with *The French Lieutenant's Woman* as well." Streep herself was still a year or two from being cast in *Sophie's Choice*; she and Nichols never overlapped on the film, but they forged a personal and professional connection that would last for the next thirty-five years, during which there was almost never a moment when he was not either working with Streep or pursuing a film or play with her in mind.

Although *Annie* was still going strong, theater money isn't movie money, and Nichols, whose lifestyle was no less profligate than it had been when he was pulling down million-dollar Hollywood paychecks, was starting to worry about cash. In 1979 he decided to return to movies with a project that would, at least, carry the words "Directed by Mike Nichols" while allowing him to risk almost nothing. During the first years of *Saturday Night Live*'s run, he had become enchanted by Gilda Radner, whose ability to inhabit the characters she created reminded him of Elaine May. Radner had appeared in the series for four years; she was looking to branch out, and Lorne Michaels was searching for ways to keep his increasingly restive original ensemble happy.

"It was Gilda's dream to go to Broadway," says Michaels, "so we booked the Winter Garden for her, and it sold out quickly." The show, a collection of sketches directed by Michaels and featuring Radner's best-loved *SNL* characters, played for eight weeks during the summer, filled the 75,000 seats that were available for the run, and startled a theater community that was still steeped in snobbery about a television performer presuming to commandeer a Broadway stage. "John Calley and Mike were at the opening," Michaels says, "and Mike said, 'A triumph!' Which was one of his words." When Calley and Ted Ashley, who were then running Warner Bros., took Michaels out to dinner the next night, they told him they wanted to film the show and release it in theaters.

"I said, 'Well, it's not going to be a movie. I think this is what it was meant to be, and I don't really want my first movie to be a performance thing,'" Michaels says. "Anyway, I can't direct it," he added. "I've got to go back and rebuild the show.

"So John Calley says, 'What if Mike directed it?' And I think, *This is the safest bet for making sure it's not going to happen*, because Mike can't make a decision quickly and we only have five or six weeks to run. The next morning, Calley calls and says, 'Mike's in.' I go, 'Mike's in?' I mean, friendship's great, but I didn't think that was the movie he wanted to do next. I said to Mike, 'You said yes?' And he said, 'Well, they gave me my price . . . and fifty hours on the [corporate] plane.' I went, 'Jesus.'"

After the Winter Garden run ended, Nichols shot the performance—which was released as *Gilda Live*—in a couple of days in Boston. "He did a lovely job of committing to film what was already onstage without changing anything," says Paul Shaffer, the show's musical director.

"He never really spoke to me," Radner said later. "I think that once he told me to take one step to the left because I was out of the camera. I had to ask him, 'Do you ever talk to actors when you direct?' He said, 'You'd be surprised.'"

Nichols moved on. He spent a couple of weeks with screenwriter Patricia Resnick developing her script for *9 to 5*, helping her fine-tune some of the scenes in which the three women at the comedy's center deal with office politics—a stretch of work that may have served as a warm-up for *Working Girl*. "I did a draft," Resnick says. "I was really happy. He was really happy. We handed it in and literally everyone else hated it. [The studio didn't even say] 'let's try one more pass.' It was 'What director are we going to next?'" Nichols and Tommy Tune, a dancer and choreographer who had become a successful director of Broadway musicals like *The Best Little Whorehouse in Texas*, collaborated on the direction of a musical called *Double Feature*, a light, small-scale lark about two couples working out their relationship issues in a series of old-Hollywood pastiches. The show had all the earmarks of another Nichols success—an appealing design, a sleek movie theater set by Tony Walton, and a tryout in New Haven in late 1979 that paved the way for a Broadway run. "Mike Nichols seems to have another hit on his mitts," wrote *Variety*'s critic, who could find "no reason why it shouldn't follow *Streamers* and *The Gin Game* to New York and possibly be the biggest commercial hit of the three."

There was, it turned out, a reason: Jeffrey Moss, the show's author, adamantly refused to make the script changes that both Nichols and Tune thought were necessary. At another point in his career, Nichols might have summoned the years of experience he had dealing with the obstinacy and neuroses of writers to get them to act in what he thought was the best interest of the work. Not now. Rather than dig in for a fight, he simply shrugged and, as he had done so many times in the past few years, walked away. As the 1970s drew to a close, nothing felt worth the hassle to him. And no place felt like home.

Twenty-one

REUNIONS

1980–1981

arly in 1980, Nichols and Davis-Goff separated. Their relationship had frayed so gradually, with Nichols spending less
and less time in Bridgewater and more and more at the Carlyle,
that they found themselves living apart before either of them had made
a decision that they should split up. His frequent absences had been
hard on the marriage, and the time they did have together often turned
into an occasion for testy negotiation. She would complain about how
little he was around; he would sulk about how much was asked of him
when he was. (During one rough patch, he groused to a colleague that
their dynamic was "Look, as long as you're going upstairs, would you
mind carrying this anvil?") The Connecticut house now felt more isolating than tranquil; he preferred to spend his time in New York, and
she eventually took an apartment in the city and enrolled their children
in school there. It was a painful moment for her, for him, and for his
friends, some of whom had now watched three of his marriages fall
apart, and almost none of whom, at the time, would have described
him as an exemplary husband. "The secret of [your] later years is that
you finally give yourself a break, so you give other people a break," he

said long after their divorce. "Your body gives you a break. You're not following your dick everywhere."

Nichols could no longer tell himself that his string of abandoned, collapsed, and thwarted projects was merely a run of bad luck. He knew he needed some sort of reboot, and to that end, he decided to take one of the more unexpected risks of his career. He would revisit *Who's Afraid of Virginia Woolf?*, this time as an actor taking on one of the most challenging roles in the American canon, and he would do it with the woman he had known the longest.

Nichols and Elaine May had been discussing working together in the play for years. In 1976, their tentative plans for a production had been derailed by Albee, who announced that he was bringing *Virginia Woolf* back to Broadway and that he himself would direct Ben Gazzara and Colleen Dewhurst as George and Martha. Enough time had now passed for Nichols and May to dust off the idea—they were both forty-eight, an ideal age for the roles—and Nichols enticed her with a short-term commitment: a six-week run at the Long Wharf, where he had directed both *Streamers* and *The Gin Game*. He felt comfortable working there, and liked Arvin Brown, who ran the theater and would direct the production. "It will be good for me as a director to remember what it's like to be an actor," Nichols said, adding, "I don't want to sound like the grand old man coming out of retirement, [but] I'm very excited by the prospect of working with Elaine again. We haven't worked together [onstage] in 19 years, and now we both feel like it." Nichols asked James Naughton, whom he had directed in *Drinks Before Dinner*, to play Nick, and Swoosie Kurtz was cast as Honey.

If Nichols or May was worried that an intense collaboration on difficult material might mean revisiting the power struggles and injuries that had precipitated their breakup, their first days in New Haven put them both at ease. They were two old friends who knew everything about each other, including their eccentricities and weaknesses. May prowled through the play with an explorer's zeal—what if she whispered a line that had always been shouted? What if she brought out Martha's seductive side instead of the blowsiness and braying that other actresses emphasized? Nichols, by contrast, worked scene by scene and line by line, inching forward a beat at a time, always striving to understand exactly what he was doing and why. It had been his approach since his Strasberg days, and one he had always encouraged in the actors he directed. She was exploratory, he was methodical, but their styles didn't clash; they trusted each other utterly and fell back into their jokey, finishing-each-other's-sentences mind meld as if the previous two decades had been just a brief hiatus from their Broadway show.

His relationship with the show's director was rockier. "Arvin and I were both very constrained by the fact that I had done the movie and supposedly knew all about it," said Nichols. "Out of conviviality, I made myself as blank and open as I could." That didn't last long. For the first few days of rehearsal, Nichols kept himself from complaining or pushing back; after that, he didn't bother to try. Nichols the actor was up for anything; Nichols the director second-guessed every decision, complained that the scenic design was cheap and underfurnished, and made his disdain unmistakable. "It was fraught from the very beginning," Swoosie Kurtz says. "Mike was very clear, in his sardonic-bordering-on-sarcastic way, how much he loathed the set. When we were shown the model, he said, 'Hmmm, it's at a college, she's the daughter of the college president, four people . . . three places to sit. *Interesting*.' He would never let that go. In the first preview, Jimmy [Naughton] and I made our entrance, and Honey says something about how nice the house is, and Mike, in character, [improvised], 'Oh, do you like it? We've done the best we could since the fire.' Jimmy and I clutched each other—we didn't know whether to laugh or not."

"Arvin had a thankless task," says Naughton. "Mike and Elaine were challenging, at best. They were both used to doing things their way, and together they were like halves of one great personality. For Arvin, they were somewhat impenetrable."

Nichols couldn't conceal his fury when something went wrong. While May seemed to be settling into her role, sometimes paraphrasing her way through a not-quite-memorized portion of the script but always coming out the other side in a way that didn't throw her costars off balance, he was cranky, imperious, and easily rattled—exactly the kind of actor he had most feared becoming when he quit the profession. "There's a scene in which George smashes a bottle and yells 'Martha!' to shut her up," says Naughton. "We staged it so that he was going to bash the bottle against a door that was reinforced with metal, and the broken glass would go upstage into the doorway. It was a big, dramatic moment. In the first preview, he threw the bottle and it just bounced off the wall, *donk, donk, donk*. He said, 'Oh, shit!,' turned purple with embarrassment, and just walked off the stage."

As time ran out, Brown, Naughton, and Kurtz all became alarmed that neither Nichols nor May had fully memorized their lines for the third act, and seemed in no hurry to work on it. In the first read-through, Brown says, "it was clear that they were going to be able to bring something so unique to it. When I got to the last act, it was remarkable, strong, emotional work from both of them. I thought, *My God! They're going to stun everybody and make the transition from the spiky drawing room comedy in the first part to what happens as the play darkens.* But then came this tremendous reluctance to rehearse the last act. It was fear, to a certain extent. They both knew where they had gone in the read-through, and they were scared of going through that pain and finding a way to do it eight times a week without bleeding out."

"We were woefully underprepared because of Mike's process," Naughton says. "It was a truthful process, but he couldn't do something that most actors do. When you get to a difficult emotional moment, most actors say, 'I'm not quite sure what this is yet, but let's move on and I'll work on it some more.' Mike couldn't. Each block had to be right or he couldn't continue. As a result, we got to that first performance and we hadn't rehearsed the third act once."

"They were doing anything but," Kurtz says. "It was all 'Let's tell this anecdote, let's tell another story, let's eat up another ten minutes of rehearsal time.'"

Nichols and May had good reason for avoiding the last act of *Virginia Woolf.* They had the same take on the play—that George and Martha valued their enduring marriage and were spending the night toying with their guests rather than destroying each other—but the cruelty of the third act, in which George dismantles their shared fantasy and reduces Martha to tears, was resistant to that interpretation, and could not be avoided. It was, in a way, their nightmare—a revisitation, every evening, of the end of their "Pirandello" sketch, when the gloves would come off and they would lace into each other.

Even after so many years, May says, "we were still protective of each other," onstage and off. During one performance, Naughton decided to lunge at Nichols after George had baited Nick one time too many. "I went for Mike, just went for him," he says. "And Elaine was up off that couch like a shot—'Oh, no, no, honey.' I somehow knew she would never let me get to him." The final scenes would, they knew, be terribly punishing to play.

Starting with the second performance, they summoned their courage and did it. There were no more improvised lines or tantrums over mishaps. "I thought they were fucking brilliant," says Kurtz. "Elaine was the first sexy Martha I had ever seen—lithe and long and elegant. When she would writhe on the sofa, it wasn't embarrassing." And Brown thought "the banter between them was as powerful and incisive as I'd ever seen it in any production, including the original." Their working relationship became energized and playful again. As she had done when they were performing on Broadway, May would vary her performance each night just enough to keep Nichols on his toes, and he would gently steer the shape of their scenes in a manner that didn't infringe on her performance. "Arlene? Eileen? Irene?" he would teasingly call to May, sticking his head into the dressing room she shared with Kurtz. "Could you come in a little quicker with that line to me in Act II?"

When they decided to do *Virginia Woolf,* May says, her first reaction had been that "it was a play I had never liked that much. But he really wanted to do it." To make it more palatable for her, she says, Nichols promised that "there would be no reviewers, that nobody would even see it in Connecticut." The only unwelcome scrutiny they would have to endure would be from Albee—who came to the production and sourly remarked to Nichols on his way out, "When you were doing the film, you said you had insight into the play. I'm still waiting."

But there was no way that a sellout pairing of Nichols and May in the work that had made his reputation as a film director was going to escape the spotlight, especially once *The New York Times*'s drama critic, Frank Rich, got himself a ticket. "We arrive expecting to watch two rusty stand-up comics do a novelty act," he wrote in a Sunday column. "We leave having seen four thinking actors shed startling new light on one of the great dark plays of our time . . . The precise comic rhythms are not just the practiced style of two comedians; they testify to the long years that George and Martha have spent in unholy wedlock." Rich, understandably, thought the third act felt underdeveloped in the production, but he called the show "the happiest possible reunion . . . When Mr. Nichols goes in for the kill . . . well after the lights go down and plunge him into darkness, we retain the image of the fire rising in his steely eyes."

"Here's how intuitive Mike was," says May. "It was Sunday morning. I got up, and he called me and said, 'It's a good one! It's good!' He somehow knew I was picking the paper up. I had no idea Frank Rich had come. And it really was a good review—he said that we had made it comedic but hadn't hurt the play."

By then, however, Nichols and May had given their last performance. Just days after the show Rich had attended, Nichols was diagnosed with pneumonia and the rest of the run was canceled. Many speculated that he had gotten stage fright or that something had again ruptured between him and May, especially when there was no announcement of the Broadway transfer that Rich's review seemed to make a foregone conclusion. "No one believed he was sick," says May, "but it was the truth." Kurtz remembers him hunched over in his dressing room and coughing; she took his temperature, which was 103. Nichols, a heavy smoker, would be beset by recurring lung problems for the rest of his life. "You could see he was running on empty," says Kurtz. "The stage manager sent him home, and that was that."

Once he recovered, Nichols was firm about not wanting to continue with the play. He had loved working with his costars—he affectionately opened all of his subsequent correspondence with Kurtz, "Dear Angel Tits," and signed it "Big Fat Flop," both lines from the play—but he said he couldn't face playing George again: "I hear Uta [Hagen] and Arthur Hill," he said, "and I hear Richard and Elizabeth, and I hear Elaine and me. I can't get it all out of my head, and of course, the joy of doing a play is to discover what it is."

"I think he thought that bringing it to New York would be to say, 'I'll show *you*, Burton and Taylor,'" says May. "So we didn't think of doing it. But he put himself into it, with real access to his emotions. At the end of *Virginia Woolf* he would cry, just like he used to when we did 'Teenagers.' I was amazed that he wanted to do it at all."

Nichols had, for the first time in years, surprised himself. Despite the curtailed run, he came off *Virginia Woolf* more enthusiastic about returning to directing than he had been in some time, and he began strategizing a movie comeback with a vigor tempered only by the knowledge that, six years after *The Fortune*, "comeback" was exactly what everyone was going to label it. He had Sam Cohn place an item in a Hollywood column that said he was "planning his return to Hollywood with a vengeance" and was "anxious to shuck the image he's acquired around these parts . . . as that of a man who has a paranoia about the movie business." The item made sure to inform readers that "he's been asked to do many" films, and announced that he had settled on three: adaptations of Harold Pinter's play *Betrayal*, which had just ended its Broadway run, and of P. D. James's mystery *Innocent Blood*, and, most improbably, a remake of the 1932 Best Picture winner *Grand Hotel*, set not in Berlin but at the MGM Grand in Las Vegas. Nichols was not manic—at least, he was not diagnosed as manic—but his upswing into a period of unrelenting work startled those who knew him. At the same time as he was developing those projects, he was producing a play called *Billy Bishop Goes to War* in New York—first on Broadway and then, when it failed, off-Broadway—and preparing to direct Gilda Radner again in a new stage comedy called *Lunch Hour*. After years of dragging himself through his career in a torpor, he seemed frantic to make up for lost time.

The films came to nothing—in part because of circumstances, in part because Nichols's nerve seemed to desert him almost as quickly as he had rediscovered it. *Innocent Blood*, a thriller about a young woman who learns that the parents who gave her up for adoption were both convicted of murder, had been chosen by the longtime agent and dealmaker Irving "Swifty" Lazar as the picture that would mark his debut as a producer. Nichols clicked instantly with Tom Stoppard, whom Lazar hired to write the script; through several drafts, they became collaborators and friends. But Nichols's involvement lasted only until the moment Lazar sat both men down and said to the playwright, "All right, let me tell you what I see. Let me tell you the first fifteen minutes."

"Irving," said Nichols, "you're sitting with Tom *fucking* Stoppard. Are you nuts? Who gives a shit how *you* see it?"

Grand Hotel began as more of a whim, a chance for Nichols and novelist Diane Johnson, who was writing the screenplay, to fly to Las Vegas, where he spent too much money and, Johnson wrote, quickly had "any belief we might have had in the aristocracy of gamblers" destroyed by "the relentless democracy and low expectations of a . . . casino." MGM saw *Grand Hotel* as a feature-length advertisement for its hotel property, and Nichols and Johnson agreed that the only way to remake the movie would be with tongue in cheek. Perhaps Warren Beatty could play John Barrymore's role; maybe Dolly Parton was the new Garbo. Johnson, who found Nichols "delightful, smart, and funny," would fly to New York and stay at the Carlyle for a week at a time. Their work sessions were interrupted by field trips to art galleries, where, she said, his growing reputation as a collector would bring out "an especially unctuous solicitousness" from dealers trying to interest him in a Picasso or a Van Gogh. Their work continued fitfully until November 21, 1980, when a fire at the MGM Grand killed eighty-five people, and the studio quietly abandoned its plans.

It was Nichols's work on *Betrayal* that exposed him as a man still in crisis. He loved Pinter's semiautobiographical play, a dramatic love triangle about sexual jealousy and male competitiveness that unfolded in a dozen scenes in reverse chronological order; this was turf he had explored in *Virginia Woolf* and *Carnal Knowledge* and played with again in *The Fortune,* but the subject was by no means exhausted for him. He was warier about working with producer Sam Spiegel, whom he had found autocratic and overbearing during his brief stint on *The Last Tycoon.* But Spiegel had assembled a package Nichols couldn't resist: Pinter would adapt his own play, and Jeremy Irons and Meryl Streep, who had just finished filming his screenplay for *The French Lieutenant's Woman,* would star.

Nichols regretted his decision as soon as he had made it. "Sam said to me, 'I want you to make a lot of money on this,'" he recalled, "and I thought, 'Oh, God, am I in a lot of trouble.'" Right away, Spiegel issued his first edict: Nichols was to fly to London for an introductory meeting with Irons, the only member of the team he didn't know. The request was reasonable, but in it Nichols heard the engine of a major production, and of a producer who would never take no for an answer, starting to roar. "Mike told me that he said, 'I don't want to do that, Sam. I'm exhausted. I want to go home and see my little girl,'" said Pinter. But Spiegel insisted, so Nichols got on the plane for what turned out to be little more than a handshake with Irons. When, several weeks later, Pinter flew to New York to meet with Nichols, the man he encountered was "ashen-faced."

"He kept on saying, 'I can't do it, I can't do it,'" Pinter said. "I thought he was going to have a nervous breakdown." Nichols never gave a reason for his sudden emotional disintegration. He dropped out soon after that.

In the fall of 1980, no closer to making a film than he had been a year earlier, Nichols turned back to theater. Eager to work more closely with Radner, he had agreed to direct her in *Lunch Hour,* a slight, old-fashioned romantic comedy written by Jean Kerr, who had begun her career as a playwright in the late 1940s. Kerr was married to the drama critic Walter Kerr and was best known for fictionalizing their lives in the popular book *Please Don't Eat the Daisies,* a collection of vignettes that had been adapted as both a Doris Day movie and a TV sitcom. But she hadn't had a hit play since the early 1960s and was delighted when Nichols read *Lunch Hour* and signed on. "I have a good feeling about this," she said. "But then, every playwright who gets Mike Nichols feels good."

Her enthusiasm soon evaporated. Kerr got Nichols at his worst— what he described as a low point in his life as a director. The two were a mismatch from the start. Nichols didn't think much of her well-worn plot about two cuckolded spouses who discover that they belong with each other; he was interested only in Radner, and was chagrined to discover that Kerr had never heard of her. Kerr found him cold and condescending, and he found her intractable and resistant to the rewrites that he felt *Lunch Hour* desperately needed in order to become a show-case for its star. "Nobody talks like this!" he would snap at her. "Nobody thinks this way today!"

"He could manifest such intelligence and enthusiasm," said Max Wright, one of *Lunch Hour*'s costars, "but just below that layer was a man of ice. He made Jean Kerr cry and sweat from nerves. Nobody ever knew why he chose to do the play, but he kept telling her that the only way to make it up-to-date was to make it about Radner."

Publicly, Kerr and Nichols were pleasant about each other, but even in interviews, tension seeped through. Kerr told one reporter that he was "brilliant" but noted that "odd things bother him—his telephone service at the Carlyle, and waiters who refuse to notice him." What kept the production glued together, it turned out, was Radner, who was inexperienced onstage but game and generous; Kerr grew to like her immensely, and, as frustrated as the other actors may have been to see Nichols turn the play from an ensemble piece into a star vehicle, the laughs she got in the out-of-town tryouts showed the producers that Nichols knew what he was doing and why he was doing it. According to a reporter who observed the show's out-of-town tryout, Nichols shaped Radner's performance with attention to every detail: "'Gildaleh, I have one little suggestion,' he says. 'That line where you say, "Even the hygienist who cleaned her big white teeth fell in love with her"? If you say "big white teeth" this way'—he demonstrates, gritting his teeth, emphasizing each word—'you'll get your laugh.'"

Nobody in the rest of the cast suspected that Nichols's marriage was in crisis or that he was fighting depression every day. "He was never afraid to drop names—'I was having lunch with Jackie Onassis and Picasso'—but he was exceedingly bright and fun," says actor David Rasche. "And he was also the only one who really understood about Gilda. Under normal circumstances, Sam Waterston"—the play's male lead—"would have been the star, but she would take her bow and people would scream, 'We love you, Gilda!' It was the beginning of all of that—an adored television star showed up in a play on Broadway and not only brought the house down, but brought people in. The producers were dumbfounded. But Mike got it."

When *Lunch Hour* came into New York in November 1980, Nichols was disconsolate. He went to see Swoosie Kurtz in Lanford Wilson's play *Fifth of July*, which had just opened on Broadway to excellent reviews, and was playing just a couple of blocks from the Ethel Barrymore, where his production was beginning its run. "We went out afterwards," Kurtz says, "and he moaned, 'You're here doing art, and I'm across the street doing shit.' And he meant it." When *Lunch Hour* opened, critics treated it as a quaint relic. "In the '80s, people look for comedy with an edge," Edwin Wilson wrote in *The Wall Street Journal*. "Tame comedy, however amiable and charming, is almost a contradiction in terms." Nichols was treated more kindly; most said he had done what he could with the material, although Frank Rich, in a generally warm review that probably helped keep the play afloat for the eight months it ran, complained that the "klutzy sight gags . . . invite unwanted comparisons to Mr. Nichols's similar and fuller staging of Act I of *The Odd Couple*."

In the spring of 1981, his plate was so empty that when Neil Simon asked him to take over the direction of his new play on a day's notice, he packed a bag and left for Boston. Whatever tensions had arisen between the two during *Bogart Slept Here* had dissipated. Simon had reconceived the *Bogart* script and turned it into *The Goodbye Girl*, one of his biggest movie hits, and he had gone on to have a string of successes on Broadway—*California Suite, They're Playing Our Song, Chapter Two*—without Nichols at the helm. Now, though, he was having trouble. A new play he had written called *Fools* was dying onstage every night. Over the weekend, he had fired its director, Gordon Davidson. Would Nichols step in and save it?

He promised to try, although he knew from the start that there was no saving *Fools*. Set in old Russia, it offered a very thin fable about an idealistic schoolteacher hired as a tutor in a village whose residents had all been cursed by stupidity, and was stitched together by an unending succession of idiot jokes:

> **Yenchna:** Can you believe my daughter hasn't written to me in over a year?
> **Mishkin:** Doesn't your daughter live with you?
> **Yenchna:** It's a good thing. Otherwise I'd never hear from her.

"It was a reunion between Neil and Mike," says the play's star, John Rubinstein, "very emotional and celebratory . . . although delicately so, because they had been mad at each other for some years. Mike was avuncular and cynical and funny, and respectful of everyone who had just gone through a very bad time and was sort of traumatized by their director being fired. He laughed at all our jokes and told us, 'We're going to fix this thing, and you're all great,' and Neil was there, too, writing new jokes and talking about how great it was to work with him again."

All Nichols could do was infuse the cast with energy and work on individual moments. "Nothing could help the show," says Gerald Hiken, who was in the cast. "It was based on the wrong premise—that if a fool is happy, why educate him? There was nothing in that." After a couple of weeks, Hiken says, Nichols shrugged and said, "All we're going to do is trim the shrubbery." When the show moved to New York for its Broadway opening, Nichols did what he had never done as a director and walked away, leaving Simon to take the show to the finish line alone. "We were, for the second time, poleaxed as a cast," says Rubinstein. "That was bad. But I don't blame Mike. He said he had a commitment to his daughter [Daisy] to go to Europe, and he said, 'I cannot renege on that.' And we all understood—show business problems really pale in comparison to the heartbreak of a divorce where you don't see your children. It was very clear that it was a terrible trauma for him." The play, the fastest flop of Simon's career, closed in a month.

That spring, Sam Cohn pulled Nichols into a project that genuinely excited him: *The Queen of Basin Street,* a musical Americanization of the hit play *La Cage aux Folles,* the film adaptation of which had become a breakout success in the United States. The deal was complicated—Allan Carr, the producer, had obtained the rights to the French stage show but not the movie, and the package of talent involved was impressive but expensive. Nichols would direct, Tommy Tune would choreograph, Jay Presson Allen would write the script, and Maury Yeston—still a few years away from writing the Tony-winning hit *Nine* and at that time the sole untested member of the team—would write the music and lyrics.

It was a project with too many generals and an army of one—Yeston, who took a leave from his position on Yale's music faculty and got to work writing half a dozen songs while everyone else was still having Cohn hammer out their deals. Nichols was used to being the biggest personality on any project; so was Carr, an impulsive man with a fondness for caftans and chorus boys who was riding high after the success of the movie *Grease.* During their first meeting at the Carlyle, Nichols met his noisy showmanship with bored hauteur. "It was strange," says Carr's lawyer, John Breglio. "Allan was a crazy Broadway baby, and Mike was very cool and looking at him thinking, *This is going to be my producer?* The meeting had to be very late in the morning, because Mike liked to sleep, and when we got there nobody was offered anything. By about twelve thirty I started to think, *Allan is going to go nuts if he doesn't get something to eat.* Just then, Mike got up, walked to the kitchen, got a glass of water and a bowl with a bunch of grapes, came back to the table, and started eating them. No 'Would you like anything?' Nothing like that. Allan looked at me like 'What's happening here?' Mike was sending a message: *This is your show, but it's my baby, and I'm going to be in charge of how this goes.*"

Yeston tried to remain focused on the work as the weeks rolled by. Nichols did not. "When *The Queen of Basin Street* began," Yeston says,

"Mike was on some kind of mango diet, so someone would always call ahead to make sure there would be a mango waiting for him. We called him Mango Mike. But he also had other things he needed to do, and Jay would disappear altogether, and I would simply hear from the agent that they were having a devil of a time trying to make a deal." Everyone, Nichols most of all, knew there was a vast amount of potential profit at stake—and everyone wanted top dollar. "All I can tell you is that if you have Mike Nichols, Tommy Tune, and Jay Allen, and nobody wants to make less than anybody else," Yeston says, "then the kid on the team is going to be in trouble." At one point, Cohn called Yeston's agent and told her Yeston would be able to get only a 0.5 percent royalty instead of the 4 percent that was customary.

It soon became clear that Cohn had created a package of talent so formidable that it was unaffordable. A nasty rift opened up. Allen urged Carr to drop Nichols, a move that ultimately ended their friendship. Carr started to wonder if Tune, who had directed a couple of Broadway hits, could replace him. Nichols and Tune stuck together in solidarity. Jerry Herman, the composer of *Hello, Dolly!*, who badly wanted a crack at *La Cage* himself, started lobbying Carr to dump Yeston. John Breglio kept running the numbers. In July 1981, Carr flew to New York, where he and Breglio delivered a bombshell to Cohn: He was dumping the entire creative team.

"Sam always had his feet on his desk," says Breglio. "He brought his feet down, stood up, and said, 'You're kidding, right?' Allan said, 'No, I'm moving on. What you created was a monster. We can't finance this show based on what you're asking for.' Sam said, 'What am I supposed to tell my clients?' Allan said, 'Just tell them enough was enough.' And the meeting was over."

Nichols was stunned. Not only had a project he loved slipped away, but he had, for the first time, overestimated his clout and been informed of its limits in no uncertain terms. Beyond that, he was now approaching a financial moment of truth from which he had long been on the run. Money was no longer coming in the way he had assumed it always would, and he was still living at—and now beyond—the boundaries of his income. He felt both dejected and frightened.

At that moment, Annabel stepped back into his life. Their ten-year connection had been badly strained, but it was not severed, and those who knew them both say that when *The Queen of Basin Street* fell apart and Nichols started to worry that she and their children would be affected by the now perilous state of his career, she was caring, supportive, and solution-oriented. He didn't have to find the next thing right away; they could, and would, make do with less. "Mike Nichols and his wife Annabel, apart for a dog's age, have reconciled," the *Daily News* reported, "and that's why all the lights are burning in every socket on Broadway." Together, they returned to Connecticut for the rest of the summer to see if they could live as a family again. This time, no play or movie or commitment would pull him away. Slowly, Nichols began to put himself back together again. His depression started to lift. And as his fiftieth birthday approached, he read the script that would restart his career.

Twenty-two

AM I DOING THIS RIGHT?

1981-1982

By the time the script for *Silkwood* reached Mike Nichols, the project was already several years along a path to the screen so slow, vexed, and litigious that no one involved had any reason to believe it would ever get made. Almost seven years had passed since Karen Silkwood, an outspoken union organizer who became contaminated by radiation while working as a chemical technician at a Kerr-McGee processing plant in Oklahoma, died in a car crash on her way to meet a *New York Times* reporter. Silkwood's story—both her journey toward activism and the mysterious and, to many, suspicious circumstances of her death—had long interested Hollywood. Jane Fonda had tried to secure her life rights from Silkwood's father; when he turned her down, she decided to develop a thinly fictionalized version of the narrative before abandoning it altogether and approaching the dangers of radiation contamination from another angle, in the 1979 thriller *The China Syndrome*. Instead, Bill Silkwood placed his trust in Arthur "Buzz" Hirsch, an aspiring producer who had recently graduated from UCLA's film school. Hirsch had an avid interest in the case but no experience and few industry connections.

At the time, big-screen docudramas—especially those that named names and were blunt about corporate malfeasance—were quite rare, and when Kerr-McGee, which was already embroiled in a lawsuit with the Silkwood family, learned that a movie was in development, the company's attorneys pushed back hard, issuing a subpoena for Hirsch's interview transcripts and background materials. Hirsch refused. "Because I was having legal problems at the time," he says, "it was impossible to get the movie off the ground. No studio wanted to invest in a producer who might be going to jail." But Hollywood now had a rooting interest in the case, and the well-connected publicist Pat Kingsley reached out to clients like Marlon Brando, Gene Hackman, and Robert Wise to help form a legal defense fund for Hirsch. The result was a major federal court First Amendment decision in the spring of 1977 that extended journalistic protections to filmmakers who were doing factual research.

Silkwood began to pick up momentum when Sam Cohn saw an opportunity for a package deal for several of his clients, and reached out to one of them, Nora Ephron, to write a screenplay. It had been more than ten years since Ephron visited the *Catch-22* set and struck up a friendship with Nichols. Since then, she had become a nationally known journalist and essayist and had married Carl Bernstein, with whom she was now in the middle of a spectacularly acrimonious public split. Ephron had always been interested in Hollywood—she was the daughter of two screenwriters, and together she and Bernstein had tried their hand at a script treatment of *All the President's Men*. When Cohn approached her, she recalled, "I was perplexed, because I was extremely freshly divorced, with two infants, and I couldn't figure out how to get to Oklahoma to do the research that needed to be done." She turned to Alice Arlen, a fellow journalist and screenwriter who also had an interest in the case. They "disagree[d] on almost everything, sometimes violently," said Ephron. But they were a good team. Ephron said Arlen "almost never thinks like anyone else"; Arlen said Ephron, "thank God, has taught me . . . that you don't write a line you're not paid for. Not ever."

Once their first draft was completed, Cohn got in touch with Meryl Streep, who had heard about the project from Pat Kingsley and was keenly interested. By then, ABC Motion Pictures, a new production company, was on board to finance the film. "We were initially burdened by Sam's heavy-handed approach," says Bob Bookman, then ABC's head of production. Cohn represented the screenwriters and the prospective star; he was determined to have *Silkwood*'s director come from his client list as well. "At first," Bookman says, "he tried to impose Karel Reisz"—whom he had put together with Streep for *The French Lieutenant's Woman*. "His insistence was almost abusive." Not until ABC said no did Cohn mention Nichols.

"Remember, at this time, Mike really had one foot out of the business because of his serial failures," Bookman says. "We had the view that this is a talented guy who is very aware of how in jeopardy his career is, and this might be exactly the right time to get him." Nichols and Streep were eager to work together, but even so, *Silkwood* was never more than a step away from being scuttled. At a meeting in Cohn's New York office with Hirsch, Streep, Ephron, and Arlen, ABC Pictures president Brandon Stoddard said he wanted to see major changes in the screenplay before ABC would commit to the movie. "He wanted to turn it into a thriller," says Hirsch. "They wanted Kerr-McGee goons with mirrored sunglasses following Karen around, and a car chase or two. I could see Nora getting close to tears about how they wanted to pulverize what she had written." Hirsch told Ephron and Arlen to do whatever had to be done to get ABC's green light. He knew Nichols and Streep had enough clout to demand "pay or play" contracts that guaranteed them their full fees whether or not the movie was made. Once those deals were in place, Nichols could use a standard clause allowing for a "director's draft" of the script to restore *Silkwood* to the version they all wanted to make.

All the maneuvering was completed by August 1981. It had been a long time since Nichols last pulled a film production into shape, but Bookman soon discovered that his ability to protect the interests of his movie had not diminished in the slightest. "We had real arguments over the budget," Bookman says. "It was originally about $12 million. Mike said, 'You know, I've been thinking about it. I could shoot this thing in sequence, and that way I could have Meryl lose weight [as Karen Silkwood gets sicker]. It would aid her performance and the film so much, but because we would have to halt production for a few weeks, it's going to cost another $1.2 million.' We thought about it and said, 'Creatively, that's really smart.' So we signed off on it."

Nichols then called Streep and asked her if she thought she could be underweight at the very beginning of the shoot instead. By then, she had won the lead role in *Sophie's Choice* and was soon to begin shooting the movie; knowing that she would be coming directly from filming the Auschwitz scenes to the *Silkwood* shoot in Texas, she assured Nichols that showing up thin wouldn't be a problem. Nichols, having gotten ABC to guarantee the larger budget, then told Bookman, "On second thought, I don't think I *do* need to shoot it that way—I'll just do it the way I was going to before."

"He bought himself an extra $1.2 million for the film to play with," says Bookman. "I will never forget that."

Nichols didn't squander the money; there would be no excess or waste on *Silkwood*, but he wanted the locations to be varied and credible and the performances convincing, even if that meant flying New York stage actors to Texas and New Mexico for tiny roles as lawyers or factory employees. He had not invested so much attention in the details of a movie since *The Graduate*. "So often, the thing you've chosen turns out to be about your life at that moment," he said. "As we started to work, I discovered that *Silkwood* was, to me, about an awakening—Karen Silkwood, who went blindly through her life, beginning to awaken to what was being done to the workers in the factory. And I thought, *This is my awakening too. I've been asleep for seven years.*"

Nichols knew it was odd to feel such strong identification with a woman he had never met and whose circumstances were wildly different from his own, but he didn't shy away from the feeling. "That's the thing about movies—it always ends up to be about you," he said. "Afterwards, you think, *Look at this—there's my life!*" He was careful not to bend the script out of shape, but he did follow an instinct to turn his own sense of emerging from a slumber into an actual moment in the film. "Mike said, 'Let's have a scene where she wakes up. Not in the middle of the night, but early,'" says Hirsch. "It's in the film—she wakes up, she walks out on her porch, and then you see the sun coming up. There's a time-lapse, and she's sitting there reading [about plutonium poisoning] and [realizing], *This is bad news.*"

The months before production, while Streep was shooting *Sophie's Choice*, gave Nichols an unusually long time to develop the script, and through the winter and into the spring of 1982, he took full advantage of it in long sessions with Ephron and Arlen that would sometimes unlock a small plot point, sometimes a line of dialogue, sometimes just a visual image. "You free-associate all day long," said Ephron. "Then suddenly you get something that is good enough to find its way into the thing you're working on."

Nichols suggested that the apartment Silkwood shared with her boyfriend and her best friend be changed to a house, and he knew what he wanted it to look like: a ramshackle, dingy refuge with carefully simulated natural light—in contrast with the fluorescent look of the factory—that would stream in through the windows, slowly banishing the darkness. "He wanted the sense of family, and he wanted the house to look patched together with layers and seams and repairs," says Patrizia von Brandenstein, *Silkwood*'s production designer. "I think by then he knew that there was no easy way to make a family, and wanted to create the feeling that these people had tried to do it the hard way, and that the struggle was showing." Nichols also wanted Silkwood's life to unfold in seasons that would be reflected in the film's visual palette. "The spring was this exciting new technology that she was working with," says Hirsch. "Then she gets involved in the union, and that was almost like a blossoming or ripening—the summer. Then there's fall, when she realizes she's been contaminated, and then a slide into winter."

For the two main supporting parts—Karen's boyfriend, Drew, and her best friend, Dolly—ABC wanted names, and Nichols wanted actors who had something to prove, as he felt he did himself. He cast Kurt Russell, who was then making a transition from steady TV into action movies. And he found his Dolly at the Broadway play *Come Back to the Five and Dime, Jimmy Dean, Jimmy Dean,* in which Cher was making her stage debut as a waitress. Nichols had wanted to work with her ever since he turned her down for *The Fortune* and she had told him, "Someday you're gonna be sorry, 'cause I'm really talented!" After the show, he went backstage and greeted her by saying, "You're right!" When he said, "I want you to be in my new movie with Meryl Streep," said Cher, "I think at that moment I lost my hearing first, then my vision." Before Nichols sent her the script, he told her that Dolly was a lesbian ("a *wonderful* lesbian!" he threw in), something at which many actresses in 1982 would have balked. She hesitated for a moment, thinking about what it would be like to tell her mother. Then she said yes.

In preproduction, Nichols could still manifest the casual grandiosity with which he knew he had grown too comfortable. When he and von Brandenstein met to go over the film's design at his Manhattan office, he mentioned a look he wanted for a set. "He said, 'You know, when Picasso did such-and-such,'" she recalls, "and then he stopped and said, 'I can show you what I mean. Edward, bring in the small Picasso.' The *small* Picasso. Priceless. Someone brought it in and set it on the desk and we all just stared."

But once work on *Silkwood* moved to Texas, he was careful never to

come off as lofty. He put the "royal baby" side of his personality away
and it did not reemerge except for one weekend when, Streep joked, he
disappeared for twenty-four hours and the next day she saw a headline
announcing, "Arabian Horses Sold for Millions." There were no tantrums or fits of pique. He stayed in the same unluxurious hotels as
everyone else. The caterer and chef he had flown down to prepare
meals got sent home after a week or two. And when a severe flare-up
of back problems prevented him from traveling with von Brandenstein
to scout a location that could double for the Kerr-McGee plant, he was
mortified and fretful, telling her, "I know this makes such a bad impression on people."

"He was anxious," she said. "It was a very different, difficult subject.
None of us knew anything about plutonium processing or how fuel
rods were made. It was important to him to learn it and to get it right."

For the first time in years, he felt able to concentrate fully on the
work—and the work, for once, was unforced, relaxed, intuitive. After a
couple of weeks, Russell, impressed by the ease with which the shoot
was unfolding, asked Nichols, "Were you always this light on your feet
with the camera?"

"I said, 'Well, no,'" Nichols remembered. "I hadn't noticed that, instead of sending everyone away so I could think about it, I just did it.
It's like grammar—you don't have to think about grammar anymore
when you've spoken relatively grammatically most of your life. And
that happened in those seven years away . . . Everything was in the
back of my head, where I do my best thinking, instead of the front,
which is often wanting."

Over his first six features, Nichols had grown used to long huddles
with his cinematographer and editor over shot selection, planning out
every actor's movements in advance. He didn't do that on *Silkwood*. For
the first time, he was making a fact-based movie that depended for
verisimilitude on the ordinary, workaday rhythms of speech and interaction, and from the start, he decided to give his cast whatever room it

needed. In a factory scene in which several characters were introduced while doing their jobs, David Strathairn came up with the idea that he should chew gum and blow bubbles. Streep loved it and instantly figured out how to react. As Nichols, with clear delight, restaged the scene, "it broke open, for him, the whole idea of improv as a way to loosen up the blocking of a static scene in a movie," says Ann Roth, the film's costume designer. "All the actors started to contribute, and it got totally out of control—except it *wasn't* out of control, because Mike knew how to orchestrate it."

While he did, his cinematographer, Miroslav Ondricek, began to tap his cane on the floor. Nichols had hired him because of his work on five films for Milos Forman and loved the sweaty, sooty look he gave the movie, but Ondricek had little patience with actors: He thought rehearsals were a waste of time and believed performers were meant to be corralled, not indulged. On the set, he would pound the cane, jab the cane, even swing the cane to sweep everyone out of the way so he could see the monitor. Throughout production, Nichols kept his irritation in check: He was going to do *Silkwood* his way, harnessing everything he knew about film acting, stage acting, and improv. As he did, the tapping of Ondricek's cane became a metronome—a demand for order and regularity that he pointedly ignored.

Sam O'Steen, who was on the set consulting and editing, as he had always done, also noticed a change. On his previous few movies, Nichols had become enamored of long takes and had started to enforce, for no particular reason, a somewhat dogmatic principle that a movie should contain as few cuts as possible, an idea that had culminated in the lengthy unbroken shots in *The Fortune*. O'Steen disliked that aesthetic and told him, "The audience isn't going to give you a prize for holding off on making that cut." On *Silkwood*, Nichols realized he was right. "The long takes began to seem to me more self-regarding," he said. "For all the advantages [long] takes give you, [they] bring a certain theatrical quality that isn't always desirable . . . Cutting—cutting a lot—began to excite me and give me pleasures that most directors have right away. I came to it very late."

O f all the ways in which *Silkwood* would mark a fascinating and permanent transition in Nichols's career, perhaps the most significant was that, for the first time, he was surrounded by women. Men had been at the center of almost everything he had directed—whether *The Odd Couple* or *Streamers, Catch-22* or *Comedians*; the women in most of the new plays and movies he had worked on after *Virginia Woolf* were wives, girlfriends, goals, or objects, and his collaborators had been almost entirely male. *Silkwood* was his first major work about a woman—her actions, her consciousness, her goals, her fears—and the first movie on which his brain trust was mostly female. Nichols referred to the women around him on the set as "the coven," but he said it with affection. He was one of the few directors of his generation whose formative professional years had been spent with a woman who was his creative equal, and he felt at home around them. There were Ephron and Arlen, whom he wanted on the set as much as possible; there was Elaine May, whom he brought in to do a last-minute script polish; there were von Brandenstein and Roth, who was sharp-eyed and perceptive about on-set dynamics and the idiosyncrasies of actors, and unafraid to tell him when she thought he was making a mistake; there was Cher and, above all, there was Streep, whom Nichols viewed as a full partner from the moment he stepped onto the set.

"The pleasure of working with Meryl Streep!" he exulted. "Her joy at getting to do the role . . . is infectious. It reminded me of how much I loved *my* work. It was, I suppose, the confluence of the group of us, the subject, the way we all felt about one another, the excitement about what we were doing. I began to think, 'I'm pretty good at this, and it isn't as hard as I remembered.'"

She had arrived in Texas early, for two weeks of costume fittings, read-throughs, and rehearsals. "Mike told me that he had envisioned Snow White and Rose Red—blond Meryl and brunette Cher," says Roth. But as soon as she got to Texas, Streep, without telling him, chopped her hair short and dyed it dark brown, to match Silkwood's, in the sink at the Holiday Inn. "Mike almost died," Streep says. "He was so mad." But any reservations he had evaporated when she stepped out of the trailer after her first fitting. Nichols hadn't paid much attention to how she would look. "I thought, *Big deal.* I mean, it's contemporary, what's there to worry about?" he said. "And she came out in a very short denim skirt and cowboy boots and a tight T-shirt with her cigarettes rolled into one sleeve. And my heart started pounding. I had a kind of anxiety attack because she was so tough. She was already somebody else. She wasn't testing the costume. She was just there, in character. It was the most startling moment."

In Streep, Nichols realized he had found a kindred spirit, someone who liked to act the way he liked to direct, working out each moment, imagining what her character would do physically, how she would sound, move, think. And just as Nicholson had done on *Carnal Knowledge*, Streep forged a relationship with everyone she worked with, whether costar or crew member. By the fourth or fifth day of rehearsals, Nichols said, "Cher was her best friend." Throughout the shoot, Streep would take her on road trips to Dallas, where they would eat lunch and then take in double features. "Kurt was in love with her," Nichols said. "And the guys playing the factory bosses were terrified of her and stayed out of her way. She just somehow moved her soul around. All the relationships in the movie were people's relationships to her, so that when you were shooting a scene, they only had to show up and look at her."

Her effect on Nichols was transformative. They created a way of working—intense conversations about the character and the script, well before shooting started, but very little micro-direction once the cameras rolled—that would remain in place for decades. "One time, I saw Mike and Meryl standing in the same physical posture, their arms folded, thinking deeply about the same situation," says actor Bruce McGill. "I looked at them and thought, *My God, it's the same person, only one is male and one is female.* Even their faces, the shape of their noses, was alike. It was palpable how much they already admired and were nourished by each other."

They spent more than a day filming *Silkwood*'s harrowing shower sequence, in which a terrified Karen is frog-marched to decontamination, then scrubbed raw and bloody under a pulverizing spray. Streep had to be naked for the shoot, and the physical conditions were miserable. Her makeup artist, J. Roy Helland, "had really done a job on her," says Hirsch. "Her face and every exposed part of her body was scraped up." When Hirsch saw the dailies, he reluctantly went to Nichols with the Kerr-McGee manual, which specified that during a decontamination shower, extreme care had to be taken not to break skin. Nichols knew that they were risking a lawsuit. The entire sequence would have to be reshot. Streep didn't hesitate.

Nichols had spent much of his filmmaking career telling exhausted or shaky actors what he had told Dustin Hoffman on *The Graduate*: "I know you're tired, but you'll never get another chance to do this scene." On *Silkwood*, Streep's commitment seemed to issue the same challenge to him, and he rose to it, turning the cast and crew into a community with a shared mission. "What I remember about Mike on *Silkwood* is that he loved every single person," says Streep, "and every single moment of it. Nora, who would watch like a hawk, tickled him to death. He loved having her there. He had Sam O'Steen. He had Ann Roth, whom he adored. And he had a group of actors who thought he was the funniest thing in the world. I think it was probably exactly the opposite of something like *Catch-22* and a lot of unhappy men. He would cater dailies and expect everyone to come, which is something I had never experienced—I mean, I'd practically had to present my SAT scores to get into the dailies of *The Deer Hunter*."

Although it was still early in her career, Streep had worked with Reisz, Robert Benton, Fred Zinnemann, Michael Cimino, Alan Pakula, and Woody Allen, an array of experience that fascinated and slightly unnerved Nichols. Two weeks into the shoot, he asked her, "Am I doing this right? Does it feel right to you? It's like making love . . . You don't really know how other people do it, but you hope you're good." In fact, Streep told him, she hadn't worked with a director like him before. "He would take an idea from anybody," she says. "He wasn't threatened by other people, and many, many directors are—when you say something, you can just see them bracing themselves. Mike never did that, and it was glorious."

About some things, Nichols was unbending. He told Cher that he didn't want her character to wear makeup. She was so nervous she wept—"I am so convincingly ugly," she said. "I tried to get away with so many things . . . Mike would give me the white-glove test. He'd run his finger across my cheek. Once I tried to cheat and curled my eyelashes and Mike said, 'Don't do it again, my dear.' He said it sweetly, but I got the message." Even then, Nichols turned his strictness into an expression of faith—he knew that Cher was his biggest casting gamble, and made her believe he would take her through the production safely from the first moment on the set, when he dissuaded her from getting a butch haircut. "It'll be harder for you to bring across, but let's don't help you with something obvious," he told her. "Let's have you work to get everything out of her without externals."

"God, that was important!" said Cher. "It let me say, this is a girl, this is her way of life."

Nichols wanted no traces of glamour anywhere in the film. Early on, Streep told him, "I can't look like Karen Silkwood if everyone else is going to look like movie actors," and he listened. When the stage actress E. Katherine Kerr arrived in Texas and found out the factory worker she was playing had been reconceived and was now envisioned by Nichols as drab and dowdy, she spent the next day in her new costume, sulking. He spotted her on the set and called her over. "Kath-erine," he warned, "I can take anything but 'sullen.'" Kerr, thinking she was about to be fired, said, "Mike, it's just that when I look in the mirror, I look just like my mother. And I've been trying all my life not to be her!"

"And he said, 'Well . . . I guess it's time for you to reject your mother, then.' It was so shocking, so psychologically incorrect, that I bent over laughing," Kerr said. "And we never had another problem. He knew exactly what to say to get me out of my own head."

Ephron, who already knew she wanted to direct movies, said she was initially "in a state of shock . . . The first day Cher improvised a line, I practically had to take five aspirins." But she came to believe that Nichols would protect the best of her work, and what she learned about his style influenced her powerfully. "Mike . . . basically uses metaphors to direct actors," she said. "He'll say, 'It's like when you were in high school and nobody would choose you.' This gives an actor a way to connect to his character through some mutual experience." He had fa-vored that approach for almost twenty years; by the time he directed *Silkwood*, he had refined it to such a degree that every actor felt a per-sonal connection to him; both Cher and Russell were calling him "Dad" by the end of the shoot.

When all else failed, he would tell a story. For a critical scene in *Silkwood* in which Karen and Dolly make up on their porch after an argument, he sat down with Streep and Cher while Ondricek was light-ing them and started to deliver a long, thoughtful meditation about the real Karen Silkwood toward the end of her life—how terrified she must have been, how isolated she must have felt. "Mike is one of the great storytellers of all time," said Cher, "and he made this story so sad that tears started to well up in his eyes." As he kept talking, the two ac-tresses began to cry themselves. Nichols fell silent for a few moments, got up from the porch, called "Action," and shot the scene.

Silkwood wrapped production toward the end of 1982. Nichols would have more than a year to edit and shape it, and much of that year would be spent trying to fend off a legal challenge from Kerr-McGee, which announced in January that it would sue ABC if necessary, complaining indignantly that it had "never heard of existing, living companies being named in movies." Even that did nothing to dampen his spirits. With the completion of the film, a tremendous psychological burden had lifted. After almost a decade, he had fallen back in love with directing. "If the actors are good enough, something really begins to happen: Life occurs," he said. "Meryl woke me up. This time, I feel— knock on wood—I'll remain awake."

Twenty-three

OH, THIS IS TROUBLE

1983-1985

Nichols felt so revitalized by his experience on *Silkwood* that before it was even finished, he began contriving a way to reunite with Ephron and Streep. While in Texas, Ephron had been finishing *Heartburn*, her acidly funny, revenge-served-cold roman à clef about the breakup of her marriage to Bernstein. Nichols thought she should adapt the novel into a screenplay, and who better to play Ephron's fictionalized version of herself than Streep? But when he returned to New York in late 1982, *Heartburn* was still months from publication, and a prospective movie version was years down the road. So he returned to stage work, with a determination to prove that he was back in the game. Over the next two years, Nichols would put four consecutive hits on Broadway and, more than twenty years after *Barefoot in the Park*, reassert his centrality in New York theater.

The first of those shows was an unpromising rescue mission. After *The Queen of Basin Street* fell apart, Tommy Tune had decided to return to the stage as a performer, in a musical called *My One and Only*, a silly, old-fashioned pastiche that was an excuse to string together two dozen songs from the Gershwin catalog, a format that had started to stake a claim on Broadway a few seasons earlier with *Ain't Misbehavin'*. The show was prototypical early-Reagan-era stage entertainment—an expensive, defiantly retro throwback to a vague cultural notion of family-friendly "innocence." The director, Peter Sellars, was a twenty-five-year-old Harvard prodigy who was hailed as a boy wonder for his innovative stagings of classic plays and operas—Handel set in outer space, *Don Giovanni* reimagined as *Shaft*. But his sensibility could not have been a worse match for the crowd-pleasing exigencies of a Broadway-bound musical, and, in what he called a fight "between the forces of Brecht and the forces of *The Pajama Game*," Brecht lost in a first-round knockout. In January, a few days before the start of the show's Boston tryout, the producers fired Sellars, and Nichols's old friend Lewis Allen implored him to come take a look at the show and see what he could do.

When Nichols got to Boston, Tune was doing triple duty as co-director, choreographer, and star, and *My One and Only* was running close to four hours, not including the lengthy and apologetic "It's a work in progress" speeches that Tune was delivering after the curtain call to any audience members who had stuck around. Reviews were abysmal; Paramount, the musical's main financier, burned through much of the $2.8 million it had invested in Boston and contemplated tossing in the towel without opening in New York. Nichols and the show's new book writer, Peter Stone, persuaded the studio to postpone the Broadway launch until May, the very end of the season, and to put in another $1.3 million for two more months of rehearsals and pre-views. Then they started performing major surgery.

"The thing that struck me about Mike was his calmness," says the singer and music historian Michael Feinstein, who was tasked with representing the interests of the Gershwins. "He was very comforting, he exuded confidence and humor, and he just walked in and started doing the work. It was an interesting contrast. Tommy works entirely on instinct. And Mike certainly had extraordinary instincts, but he was also a great psychologist in the way he spoke to people."

"He was like a superfine machinist," says Bruce McGill, who joined the cast shortly after completing *Silkwood*. "The show was in deep trouble, and he came in and said, 'I'll try to fix it, but I don't want my name on it.' I remember him saying, 'All right, first we have to come up with a story that won't infuriate the audience.'"

Nichols told Stone to dial down a plotline that was predicated on amnesia—"in most cases," he said, "that drives people who are watching crazy." While Stone wrote a new story to fit the existing song list, Nichols went to work soothing the cast, which was rehearsing a new script every day and then performing the old show at night. "It was agonizing to go out and put on a happy face when you didn't have confidence in the material," says McGill.

"We had to use certain elements of the old show because the sets and costumes, which were gorgeous, had already been made," says Twiggy, who was about to make her Broadway debut as Tune's leading lady. "What Mike and Peter did was genius, really—creating a completely new show while working with what we had to keep. It was a bloody great jigsaw puzzle."

The show Nichols whipped into shape for New York was more than an hour shorter; the story was still tissue-thin, but at least coherent, and he made sure that all the performers, from the two leads to veteran supporting players like Roscoe Lee Browne and the dancer Charles "Honi" Coles, were appealingly showcased. Impatient to return to the *Silkwood* editing room, he stepped away once Tune brought Michael Bennett in to help and declined any official credit, but his role in turning *My One and Only* into a hit that ran for two years was publicly acknowledged by everyone involved. "When we were in our darkest hour," said Tune, shortly after he won two Tonys for the show, "Mike Nichols carried us through into the light."

Nichols then turned to a new play, one that he hoped would put him back together with Streep sooner than *Heartburn* would. On a trip to London, he had seen Tom Stoppard's comedy-drama *The Real Thing*, a contemporary, crisply intelligent exploration of love, infidelity, acting, and playwriting that had opened, in an imperfectly cast and designed production, to mixed reviews. Nichols was certain that he could make the play rocket along, get rid of the sluggish scene changes that one critic complained put him to sleep, and work with Stoppard to tighten and sharpen some of the play's interactions while leaving his intellectual arias intact. And he knew just who should star: Streep and Jeremy Irons, the two actors he had tried to put together for *Betrayal* a few years earlier. Irons would play Henry, a playwright who was a kind of mouthpiece for Stoppard's views on political theater; Streep would play Annie, the married actress with whom he has an affair.

The prospect of reuniting the two leads of *The French Lieutenant's Woman* on Broadway made its way into theater gossip columns almost immediately, but, although Irons was interested, Streep was not. She had just won her second Academy Award, for *Sophie's Choice*, and her second child, Mamie, was due in August; she did not relish the idea of out-of-town tryouts, rehearsals, and previews with a two-month-old. Beyond that, she was concerned that Annie was a character without much to say. *The Real Thing* provides several powerful moments in which the elegance of language and the sparkling expression of principle give way to simple, direct emotion—but almost all of that elegance and sparkle is given to Henry while Annie listens, something that was unlikely to change in Stoppard's rewrites. Nichols wasn't miffed when Streep passed on the role—she had already said she might be interested in *Heartburn*—nor was he any less excited about the play. He offered Annie to Glenn Close, who had started to make her mark in movies with high-profile supporting parts in *The World According to Garp* and *The Big Chill*. "It's a very tricky role," says Close, "thankless in some ways, because she's an inarticulate character in a highly articulate play." She took the part anyway.

Nichols's taste for living lavishly had not diminished with the years; he, Annabel, and their children had now settled into two connected brownstones on the Upper East Side, with a suite of offices for him and a giant, merged garden in the back—a home paid for largely by *Annie,* which had just ended its six-year run on Broadway. By the early 1980s, Nichols was a rich man who enjoyed living like an even richer man. He was a frequent bold-type name in lifestyle stories about conspicuous consumption: Which interior decorators were in favor? Who were the best florists? How do you cater a dinner for forty? More than ever, he was an acquirer—of horses, of art, of property—and he liked watching the people he knew spend money almost as much as he liked spending it himself; that spring he accompanied Jack Nicholson and Paul Simon to an auction at Sotheby's just to watch Nicholson drop almost half a million dollars on a Matisse.

Just before rehearsals for *The Real Thing* began in October 1983, he took a vacation to the south of France with Lorne Michaels and his wife, Susan Forristal, to see Simon & Garfunkel play a reunion concert in Nice. "We were having lunch," says Michaels, "and I remember him saying, 'Haut-Brion is for sale.' The château and the vineyard. It was one of those periods when the dollar was strong, and he said, 'It's only . . .' some sum, which I don't remember. 'It's eight hundred hectares,' and it's this and it's that. And I said, 'Well, when would we go there? You have your house in New York, and the Vineyard, and the farm . . .' But he loved checking stuff out. There's a certain risk thing which is inherent in the arts. But then there's this other kind of risk, one that you're less qualified for. Mike was perhaps prone to that."

Nichols did not buy the château or the vineyard. He had overextended himself before, and he would again, but at the moment he was confining his gambler's spirit to his work. When he embarked on *The Real Thing,* he gave Tony Walton a challenge. "The problem is that there are something like twelve full stage sets required—rehearsal rooms, railroad train carriages, living rooms, family rooms," Walton says. "Mike said, 'I can't afford to have a scene change last longer than four seconds in any instance.'" Walton started experimenting with the idea of three turntables onstage, each of which would house all or part of four different sets—a mathematical puzzle that kept him working until 3 a.m. on many nights, and a technological leap that almost no Broadway play had tried to take.

"It was so complex and intricate," says Close. "Mike's inspiration was that it should be filmic—it should change so fast that you shouldn't know it was changing." Nichols was obsessed with the physical production, starting with the very first scene, which ends with a door slamming and a house of cards collapsing on cue. Nichols had the house rebuilt every night; it was held together with wax and rigged to fall only when an actor stepped on a hidden pedal. And he couldn't figure out how to make one scene in Act II work until he got onstage and moved the furniture around himself. In Boston, where the turntables tended to break down mid-transition, he would stand in the back of the theater, clenching his fists. Stoppard, unflappable, amused, and thrilled with the way Nichols was transforming his play, would take a drag on his cigarette and calm him down.

"Even when he was pissed off, he was funny," says Kenneth Welsh, who was in the cast. "At one point I stumbled and the whole set had to stop for six seconds. I was so embarrassed. Mike came to my dressing room afterward and I said, 'I'm so sorry.' 'These things happen,' he said. 'I guess so,' I said, 'and after all, what's six seconds out of a lifetime?' He paused and said, 'Everything.'" Nichols's operatic level of distress at technical glitches became a running gag. "Once when he was working on a blackout, there was a tiny flicker of light, no more than a glowworm would cast," said Stoppard, "and Mike called, 'What in God's name is that *searchlight* doing onstage?'" And he once stopped a dress rehearsal in its tracks because he heard a noise no one else did.

"What *is* that?" he complained to the sound technician. "It's like *Apocalypse Now* in here!" The culprit turned out to be an electric fan two floors above them.

In the rehearsal room, *The Real Thing* came to life through the give-and-take of Nichols and Stoppard. They were an ideal pairing: Like Nichols, Stoppard was an émigré. His family had fled Czechoslovakia before the Nazi invasion, and he hadn't simply mastered English but had fallen in love with its eccentricities, double meanings, and rhythms. In Nichols he found, for the first time, a director with a natural ear for the European-tinged musicality of his dialogue. They were both formidable, effortlessly witty intellects who were secure enough to work in harmony, and Irons, lithe, handsome, and physically graceful, embodied their ideal selves. The cast also included Christine Baranski in her first high-profile role, Peter Gallagher, and Cynthia Nixon, a New York high school senior Nichols found to play Irons's daughter. Stoppard was not a co-director, but he was involved and present throughout rehearsals, offering notes at Nichols's invitation after every scene. "At one end of the table was Tom, smoking, and at the other was Mike, smoking," says Close. "Their brilliance informed what we were doing."

They were both strong-minded. Stoppard said he arrived with "prejudices about the noise [the] play should be making—how loud, how soft, how high, how deep, how fast, how slow the actors' voices should be." But he grew to love the "cunning and courtesy" with which Nichols expressed disagreement with him, and Nichols, in turn, adored Stoppard. "I take on the mood of the person I'm working with," he said. "David Rabe and I tend to get gloomy, Tom and I had nothing but laughs and joy."

While Nichols would use intimate stories about his marriages or his son, Max, to convey a point about love or insecurity or envy, Stoppard was more likely to be abstract or theoretical. "Once Tom was explaining part of the play really narrowly," says Gallagher. "And Mike said, 'No, Tom, this scene is about you! You and your wife.' And Tom said,

'Oh, no, no, no . . .' although of course it was. It was amazing to see Tom so immersed in storytelling and Mike so intent on making him aware that everything was personal."

Stoppard's erudition sometimes terrified the cast. At one point he said, "Cynthia, that passage wants to be a little more . . . plangent." The actors sat very still. "None of us had ever heard that word," says Gallagher. "Never even knew it existed. You could feel the collective quiet panic. I look out of the corner of my eye to Glenn, thinking, *I wonder if she has any*—no, she's got no idea. She's looking over at Jeremy. Jeremy's not even pretending to know. Cynthia's the only one honest and brave enough to say, 'I'm sorry. Tom, what's plangent?'

"'Oh, plangent . . .' Tom says. 'Mike?' Mike says, 'Fuck if I know.' Tom says, 'A guitar is more plangent than a trumpet.' Nothing. *Nothing*. Then he reaches down and he says, 'It's as if you were to take a pebble and drop it into a pool from a very small height. Plangent.' We're *Oh my God*. That was plangent."

The text of *The Real Thing* was largely set; Nichols didn't want Stoppard to touch the blistering diatribe at its center, a speech by Henry about how being a political playwright is worthless if you're not also a good writer. That stance would cause considerable controversy among some critics and playwrights who insisted it was a conservative writer's attack on the dominance of the left in British theater. Nichols's own politics at the time were socially liberal and globally indifferent. He did not see the play as a screed (and Stoppard himself saw *The Real Thing* more as a defense of his right to write nonpolitical plays than as an attack on leftist theater). In any case, he was not interested in amplifying the aspect of Stoppard's writing that had won him a reputation as a chilly playwright of ideas.

Nichols felt *The Real Thing*'s intellectual side would take care of itself. He was more interested in bringing forth the psychology and passion of its characters—people caught in a struggle between what they say and what they feel. Henry, a man living inside his own head and heedless of the effects of his remoteness on those around him, was a type all too familiar to him from his own life, and Nichols wanted every character's anguish around infidelity expressed as vividly as possible. "There's a scene where Annie comes home," says Nixon, "and her husband knows she's been sleeping with someone but hasn't yet revealed that he knows. Mike made a decision that Glenn should have taken a big bite of a candy bar, so that by the time it hits her—*Oh my God, he knows*—she has a mouthful of chocolate. What do you do? Do you chew? And also, your appetite, all of it, is suddenly on full display. It was a gift to the scene."

He was especially attentive to Close, who was sometimes frustrated at having to watch Irons make a meal of his part while she had little to do but react. "I remember thinking, *Oh, man, I just want to* act, *I want people to see what I can do*," she says. "Mike didn't want any of that, of course. He said, 'Just bring your day onto the stage with you,' I thought, *Oh my God, that's so boring*. But it has stuck with me my whole career: Bring your day, let it happen. When he felt that I was dying to get the audience to like me, he'd say, 'You have to be who that person is. If it's a great piece of writing, the moments you want will come. But you can't do it at the expense of the character.'"

Nichols also did everything he could to encourage the already apparent chemistry between his two leads. "We were trying to find a moment," Close says, "and he came up to Jeremy and me and said, 'If you ever get lost, just drown in each other's eyes.'" And early in the New York rehearsals, he gathered the actors around a table and, with seeming offhandedness, said, "The thing about having an affair is, you're totally casual around each other in public." As his eyes moved meaningfully from actor to actor, resting on each for a moment, starting with Irons and Close, he remarked, "If there were two people in this room who were having an affair right now, none of us would know."

"It was like, *gasp*," says Nixon. "It was so right. Mike knew that it was in everybody's interest, and in the play's interest, for us to wonder if something was going on, to make the world of the play completely permeate the rehearsal even more than it already was. But it was so delicious to just put it on the table like that."

Just as *The Real Thing* began previews in December, *Silkwood* opened. It was, in most respects, the film Nichols had set out to make, but Kerr-McGee's lawyers had scared ABC into changing the film's ending, which Nichols had shot to suggest that Silkwood's car was being followed and that she might have been run off the road. "Mike had final cut," says Buzz Hirsch, "but there was a clause that said ABC could make changes for legal reasons, and they did."

"Mike was upset," said O'Steen. "He did consult with a heavyweight lawyer to see what he could get away with, but there was nothing he could do." The final shot, of Silkwood driving at night and shielding her eyes from blinding headlights in her rearview mirror while the sound drops away and we hear her singing "Amazing Grace," came as close to raising the question of intent behind her death as was permissible. It was followed by a legally mandated end title that said drugs had been found in her system and that her death was ruled an accident.

That was not enough for any number of journalists, few of whom had grappled with the ethical complexities of films that dramatized current events or had seriously considered the difference between those movies and documentaries. Outside of the entertainment pages, newspaper coverage of *Silkwood* was harshly negative. One piece argued that fact-based movies simply should not be made until an event was old enough to be considered history. *The New York Times* wrote several critical stories, including one by David Burnham, the reporter Silkwood had been planning to meet, in which he said he insisted that his name be taken out of the movie and complained that "to be a character in a historical event which has been reinterpreted by Hollywood . . . is an irritating and frustrating experience." A *Times* editorial headlined "The

Chicanery of 'Silkwood'" argued that docudramas, "as a genre . . . deserve vigorous protest," and, after inaccurately claiming that the film "purports to be a documentary account," labeled it "a meretricious creation that breaks the rules of reporting." And in *The Washington Post*, a Heritage Foundation researcher who had written to Nichols in an unsuccessful quest to obtain a share of the movie's profits declared that Silkwood's life had been "exploited by a gang of causists—in this case, the anti-nuclear movement, the militant feminist cause and even anti-corporate ideology."

Given that outrage, *Silkwood*'s excellent reviews came as a pleasant shock. The *Times*'s Vincent Canby called it "a precisely visual, highly emotional melodrama that . . . may be the most serious work Mr. Nichols has yet done in films . . . For the first time in a popular movie America's petrochemical-nuclear landscape [has] been dramatized, and with such anger and compassion." Janet Maslin added, "Mike Nichols' direction and Meryl Streep's performance are the best screen work either one of them has done."

For those who had come to see Nichols as an elegant ironist whose studied camera compositions indicated cool detachment from his characters and their plights, *Silkwood* was an occasion for reassessment. "Nichols' directorial style gives the film a disquieting air of authenticity," Howard Kissel wrote in *Women's Wear Daily*. "One would not imagine a director as urbane and witty as Nichols having such a strong feeling for the semirural Southwest, but his understanding of this dispiriting milieu seems rich and thoughtfully nuanced." Some reviewers bristled at the film's portrayal of Kerr-McGee as an extension of what *Time* called "the radical-chic politics Nichols has always favored," and complained that "rarely has the desperation to square inspirational myth with provable, nonlibelous reporting been more apparent." But others, like *The Christian Science Monitor*'s David Sterritt, thought *Silkwood* was "a directorial triumph for a filmmaker who has artistically matured . . .

It's especially heartening to see Nichols direct a 'social-consciousness' movie so effectively after his past failures with *Catch-22* and *The Day of the Dolphin*."

Silkwood was widely seen as a pivot for Nichols, even if critics weren't quite sure what it was a pivot toward—politics, women, drama, sincerity, or an interest in the working class. But across the board, they were impressed by his handling of the actors, by the ease with which Cher played an unshowy dramatic role, and by the understated warmth and gentle social satire Nichols brought to the scene in which Karen and Drew contend with their feelings about Dolly's lesbianism. He had staged the exchange with the two characters alone in the kitchen after they had unexpectedly encountered Dolly and her lover, and he had directed Streep and Russell to avoid each other's eyes as they made breakfast and went about their morning routine.

> **Drew** (*muttering*): Well, personally, I really don't see anything wrong with it.
>
> **Karen**: No, neither do I.
>
> **Drew**: Guess it figures, doesn't it?
>
> **Karen**: I can handle it.
>
> **Drew**: Me, too.
>
> **Karen**: So why are we talkin' about it?

Silkwood turned out to be an unexpected and slow-building hit, grossing triple its budget and, in its seventh weekend of release, becoming the country's number-one movie. Many expected it to receive an Oscar nomination for Best Picture, and although the controversy may have derailed its chances, Nichols did get his first nomination for directing since *The Graduate*, and Streep, Cher, Ephron and Arlen, and O'Steen were nominees as well.

That recognition came on the heels of almost unanimous raves for

The Real Thing—*Variety* called it "a remedy for the ailing theater," and Clive Barnes noted that "the acting has exactly the one quality that Nichols always strives for . . . Irons, Close, and their companions seem to be making up Stoppard as they go along." The play would run for well over a year and sweep the Tonys, winning prizes for Stoppard, Irons, Close, Baranski, and Nichols—his fifth win for Best Director of a Play and his first in twelve years. In his effusive acceptance speech, he praised his colleagues but saved his final words for his family, saying, "I'd . . . like to thank my wife Annabel, who stuck with me through thin."

With his marriage on steadier ground, Nichols was hoping to avoid projects that took him away from New York and their children; he had not been much of a presence during Daisy's grade-school years and was determined to be around more for Max and Jenny, who were still preteens. *Heartburn,* if it happened, could be shot in the city, and if it didn't, he was happy to work as a full-time theater director. His mind was still on Streep, and in early 1984 he and his *Real Thing* co-producer Emanuel Azenberg approached her with a proposal that would have kept Nichols working on Broadway for the next two years. They wanted her to star in three plays: *A Streetcar Named Desire,* Noël Coward's *Private Lives,* and a Chekhov play, either *Three Sisters* or *The Seagull,* each of which would run ten weeks and all of which Nichols would direct. It was a dream Nichols had been nurturing since he staged *The Little Foxes* in 1967—a repertory company that would form the basis of an American national theater, with everyone working for reduced fees. The company he had in mind would also include Kevin Kline, Mandy Patinkin, and Amanda Plummer. The idea made the papers, excited huge interest, and immediately fell apart. "There was talk about it," says Streep. "But I don't think it was ever serious, because I had little children, and I don't know how people who work in the theater with little children can do it. You're gone when they come home from school, you're gone every night, and you're gone all weekend." (She adds, laughing, "I always told my children, 'I gave up the theater for you.' They couldn't care less. They said, 'You could have gone. We would have been fine.'")

By the time *The Real Thing* opened, Nichols had agreed to direct a new play that would take him out of New York, but only for a month or two. *Hurlyburly,* David Rabe's first major work since *Streamers,* was an exploration of the monstrous aspects of male competition, aggression, and jealousy, set in a milieu Nichols knew well—the movie business, specifically a Hollywood Hills home shared by a pair of cynical, decadent casting directors. When Emanuel Azenberg passed along Rabe's choices in an early meeting, Nichols turned them all down.

"Manny said, 'David wants Bill Hurt, Chris Walken, and Harvey Keitel,'" says Fred Zollo, who produced the play with Nichols. "Mike goes, 'Bill will never listen to me, so no. Harvey is crazy Actors Studio, so that's not going to happen. And Chris will do everything I want until opening night and then do what he wants.' They all got crossed off. And then they all got cast!" Nichols conceded to the irresistibility of star power: Hurt and Walken would play the housemates; Keitel would play an animalistic actor whose marriage is crumbling; Sigourney Weaver was cast as a photojournalist who sleeps with Walken's character, and Judith Ivey would play a good-hearted stripper who wanders in and out of the men's lives. Nichols rounded out the ensemble with Jerry Stiller and Cynthia Nixon, whom he plucked out of *The Real Thing* soon after its Broadway opening to play Donna, a blank-eyed teenage drifter whom the men use as a sexual plaything, "like a CARE package," says Ivey's character, "just to stay in practice. In case you run into a woman." They would take the play to Chicago's Goodman Theater, work out the kinks, and then bring it to New York.

By the spring of 1984, cocaine was so much a fact of life in Nichols's professional circles that its use barely raised an eyebrow. It was on movie sets and in rehearsal rooms, in galleries, nightclubs, and newsrooms, on trading floors, in restaurant bathrooms, and at weekend parties in the Hamptons, and the dividing line in his world was not between those who partook and those who abstained but between those who did it and those who overdid it. "In the case of *Hurlyburly,* the whole show is *about* cocaine," says Zollo, "and it was everywhere. I can't confirm it, but in Chicago there were moments when some of the cocaine onstage was . . . cocaine." Add the fact that, as the play's sound designer, Otts Munderloh, puts it, "every crazy person in the world was in the play at some point" and it is little surprise that the production of *Hurlyburly* was a study in chaos.

As work began in Chicago, the room was so full of male energy that the Goodman's artistic director, Gregory Mosher, suggested they all grow beards. ("How long are you willing to wait?" Nichols said dryly.) Misogynistic comments from the men—in character and out—were so frequent that Nichols had to tell them to knock it off. Once they read through the play a few times, their raunchy high spirits were dampened.

"Those terrific actors were confused as hell," says Peter Lawrence, the play's stage manager. "There was panic on their faces. Mike said, 'Don't worry about what the play is about. I'm going to build you a bridge of jokes from one end to the other. All you have to do every night is walk across that bridge.'"

"A lot of his direction was very technical," says Nixon, "but in a beautiful way. It was like listening to a musician talk about music. There was a lot of 'We have three jokes here, so we're going to push through the first two and get the big laugh on the third, rather than lose our momentum.'"

The actresses reacted to his approach better than the actors did. Ivey, who used a drawling Southern California accent, recalls that "in rehearsal, for a couple of days, he wouldn't let me use that dialect, because I was relying on it too much. It was horrifying to have him take it away and say, 'Just do Judy.' But it was a great lesson. I use that now whenever I have a dialect, because it's so easy to let the sound do the work for you that you can forget to tell the story."

Nichols was using cocaine regularly by then—he needed it to get through nights of marathon performances followed by long rehearsal days. He was generally blasé about his cast when it came to drugs—"he was avuncular," says Nixon, "but not paternal. It's not like anybody was there protecting me, and I didn't want to be protected!" But he was not prepared for the sybaritic commitment with which Hurt and Walken decided to embody the excesses of their characters offstage, or Keitel exposing himself to Ivey during a rehearsal and suggesting that he and Nixon act out an offstage sex scene, or the fact that he and Rabe would be at odds from day one.

On *Streamers,* their contentiousness over cuts to the text had ultimately been fruitful; this time it was not. In Chicago, the play ran over four hours, and although the audiences who filled the one-hundred-seat theater for what was an instant sellout run were not about to walk out, Nichols found the play unwieldy and indulgent. Rabe dug in, insisting that he and the actors be given time to see what worked. He was particularly incensed about Nichols's elimination of a long scene that he felt was necessary to make Keitel's character, Phil, something more than a "low-life thug." Nichols disliked it; he promised to rehearse it after they got the play up and running, but never did. "It got cut pretty quickly," says Ivey. "I think it was disturbing to David that it was never even tried."

"What Mike did with *Hurlyburly* was to allow the audience to tolerate the material," says Lawrence. "Rabe's point was that the length is part of the experience—that is, living with these guys for four hours *is* the story. And Mike felt that unless the audience could actually get through the experience, there is no play. They both had their points of view, but Mike had the muscle." In every run-through and performance, Nichols watched the show with pen in hand; Zollo sat behind him. "I could see the notes he was taking," he says. "At one point during a monologue, he kept writing, 'Who cares? Who cares? Who cares?' Three or four times. 'Nobody's going to care, I don't care.'"

Nichols started to feel at war with the play—and with his collaborators. "*Hurlyburly* was completely dysfunctional," says Nixon. "Seeing some of those actors in their full insanity . . . even though I knew things were bad, I didn't really understand how much William Hurt was in revolt, accompanied by the playwright. How impossible that must have been for Mike. He was used to productions on which everybody was in love with him and wanted to do his bidding, and many of us did, but it's hard when your lead and your writer think you're the devil. To them, anything that made it less palatable was a virtue. What was at stake, from their perspective, was the soul and integrity of the play and, by extension, the American theater, and here was this annoying showbiz guy, this Jewish *comedian*, trying to yuk it up and make it commercial."

"Our communication broke down completely," says Rabe. "I've come to terms with it, but I was deeply enraged. The play did need to be cut, but the way Mike did it was not the way to do it. Looking back, we got ourselves in a terrible box by having all those movie stars and not having some kind of developmental period. We were in such a high-profile situation that there wasn't any room to really work."

During the Chicago run, the writer Barbara Gelb arrived to interview Nichols for a long cover story for *The New York Times Magazine*. The piece appeared just as the play was beginning its run at the Promenade, an off-Broadway theater in New York, in May 1984. For the first time, some of the tension between Rabe and Nichols was public, and both men felt uncomfortably exposed. "I came into the theater, and Mike was down on the stage," says the show's press representative, Bill

Evans, "and he said, 'I can tell by your face! It's bad!' I said, 'It's not bad for you, but it's not good for David Rabe.' It was such a relief to me that it was okay for Mike that I hadn't noticed the picture of him and Annabel. Mike was way over here, and Annabel was way over there. It was icy, and I thought, *Oh, this is trouble*." ("Did you see the photograph of Mike Nichols, a fine director, on the [cover]?" Elia Kazan later wrote. "Did you notice how he smiles, how charming and friendly he seems— at first glance? Then look again and notice the glint in the corner of his eyes, recognize the cunning and determination there, the hardness? Why not? It's what saves us.")

If Nichols's marriage had suffered during his time in Chicago, nobody on *Hurlyburly* knew it. Despite its unhappy journey, the play was an almost impossible ticket when its New York run began, and the reviews, though not raves, made a transfer to Broadway inevitable. By then his relationship with Rabe had ruptured irretrievably. "In the end, Mike did not get the production he wanted, nor did I get the one I wanted," says Rabe. "My reputation took a big hit in the theater world with *Hurlyburly*. People knew I was unhappy. Few knew about the cut scene, and most probably wouldn't have cared. There I was with Mike Nichols directing half of Hollywood in my play . . . I'm sure I looked impossible, but I think any writer worth his salt would have felt as I did in those circumstances."

Hurlyburly ran for almost a year, turned a solid profit, and won a Tony for Ivey. Walken left the show before it moved to Broadway, and most of the rest of the cast departed as soon as their contracts were up; their replacements included Christine Baranski, Candice Bergen, Danny Aiello, and Frank Langella, who took Hurt's role for the end of the run. The night the play closed, "Mike came backstage and said, 'Come on, I'll drive you to the party,'" Langella says. "He had one of those big Bentleys. I was changing, and Mike was in the dressing room with me, and David Rabe walked in and gave me a hug. There they were, on opposite sides of my dressing room, standing in dead silence until David left. When Mike and I were driving toward the party, I said, 'I feel very bad, because I don't know David or you well enough to talk about the rift.'

"Mike said, 'What do you feel bad about?' I said, 'Well, because there you were, there he was . . . I sort of felt like going, "Come on, guys, it's the end of the show. Shake and make up."' And he said, 'Oh, I'm so glad you didn't.' I said, 'Why?' He said, 'Well, I have so few enemies, and there's something very exciting about being hated.'"

Twenty-four

A SHOT ACROSS THE BOW

1985–1986

At the beginning of 1985, Nichols had four hit shows running on Broadway. Although his name wasn't in the credits of *My One and Only*, it was on the checks that arrived each week, and as *The Real Thing* and *Hurlyburly* neared the ends of their runs, he would still show up to fine-tune the performances and take the actors out for a late meal at Orso or Joe Allen. Often, they were joined by the star of his fourth hit. Whoopi Goldberg had first met Nichols a year earlier, when he and Annabel, at the urging of Judith Ivey, had ventured downtown to see *The Spook Show*, a performance piece Goldberg had brought to a small space on West Nineteenth Street. Nichols knew nothing about her except that word of mouth had been attracting a stream of theater people to the show. He beamed throughout her act, a series of monologues in which she played an old man's Jamaican caregiver, a white teenage Valley Girl who learns she's pregnant, and a disabled person looking for love ("It was a good night—I was *on*," Goldberg said). And when her fourth signature character, a cosmopolitan junkie named Fontaine, talked about his visit to the Anne Frank museum,

Nichols wept. After the show, he went backstage, hugged her, and offered his help on the spot.

Nichols was always generous in praising new talent, but something about Goldberg touched him more deeply than he expected. He often compared her to Ruth Draper, whose recordings of her monologues influenced a generation of character-driven solo performers, but Goldberg's portraits-in-miniature and the deftness with which she could leap from social satire to poignancy owed just as much to Elaine May. She was starting to get acting offers but was determined to keep doing her own material: "If I have to shake my tits or play somebody's fuckin' maid for the rest of my life," she said, "it isn't worth it."

Nichols's first idea was to move Goldberg's show to the Promenade, the off-Broadway theater where *Hurlyburly* had played. When that proved unavailable, he told her they should take the show directly to Broadway. Goldberg was overwhelmed by his attention but slightly wary of going mainstream so quickly; she was used to working as a performer on the fringes, but also to being the master of her own fate. When she did a show, she said, "I like people to come without expectations, ready to have a good time . . . If they're rolling, the show can go on and on. If they're not, it's one, two, three." Nichols got it, and he got her. He had spent hundreds of hours onstage watching Elaine May stretch a sketch almost past the point of patience on one night, then move it along briskly the next. He knew that performers like Goldberg needed room to roam within their own storytelling structures, and accordingly, on a given evening, her show could run a crisp ninety minutes or a loose two hours.

Although Nichols didn't take a director's credit—"Production Supervised by Mike Nichols" was the billing—he acted as its director in every way, watching, listening, letting her know when she went too far or chased a laugh or needed to round out a vignette or deepen a moment. He had decades of experience being encouraging and intuitive with actresses, supportive and patient with writers, and tough and precise with comedians. Now he was working with all three at once, and he loved it. So did Goldberg; as they worked on shaping the show for Broadway, she felt he was speaking to her not just as a director but as a fellow performer with an uncanny sense of what an audience felt at any moment, and she trusted him completely. "Mike Nichols spoiled me," she said. "When it wasn't right, he told me. Not all actors like that, but for an actor like me who loves the process of creating a life—sort of like this God thing—it's wonderful to have a co-God." Beyond that, Nichols worked to bring Goldberg into his world, helping her make connections. His imprimatur helped to turn the show into an event that, just as *An Evening with Mike Nichols and Elaine May* had twenty years earlier, attracted the instant attention of Hollywood—including Steven Spielberg, who was looking for an actress to star in his adaptation of *The Color Purple.* But beyond that, Nichols wanted Goldberg to experience what he had loved—the dynamism and energy and late-night sociability of life as the star of a hit show. When he realized that, as a solo performer, she had nobody to go out with once the curtain fell—a Broadway rite that he had loved for twenty-five years—he essentially had the *Real Thing* company adopt her for post-performance dinners that would last late into the night.

As he started making plans to shoot *Heartburn* during the summer, other offers flooded in. John Lindsay, the former mayor of New York, was heading a search committee charged with finding someone to take over as the artistic manager of the two theater stages at Lincoln Center; Nichols declined, saying he was uninterested in a full-time administrative role. He had also said no several months earlier when Larry Kramer sent him his play *The Normal Heart.* Nichols's life was already touched by the AIDS epidemic; a few colleagues in the theater had gotten sick, and many more were terrified of what might lie ahead. In the spring, he and May would reunite again for a Comic Relief benefit for AIDS research, the start of a twenty-year commitment to AIDS fundraising on his part. He didn't think he was right for the impassioned cry of rage and condemnation that Kramer had written, but the play moved him. "I think along the way I sent him every play I wrote," said Kramer, "and he always wrote back in a way [that demonstrated] he had really read what I sent. Even though he said it wasn't for him, I thought, what a gentleman!"

After the miseries of *Hurlyburly*, Nichols wanted to return to lighter material; he was considering a new play called *Social Security*, by Andrew Bergman, the co-screenwriter of *Blazing Saddles*, that read as the kind of laugh-packed urban farce he had not directed since his run of Neil Simon hits. Bergman's main character, Barbara Kahn, is a nouveau riche Jewish socialite living with her husband, an art dealer, on the East Side. When her mother, an old-world kvetch from Long Island, unexpectedly moves in with them, Barbara has to confront everything about her origins that she has willed herself to forget. For Nichols, the play, a swift, funny literalization of Freud's theory of the return of the repressed, hit close to home. He was pulling together a reading at the Carlyle when real life intervened. He got a call from Philadelphia. His mother was dying.

In the decades since Brigitte Nichols had remarried, she and her son had found their way to a peaceable but not especially warm relationship. Nichols was fond of her husband, Franz, and financially generous to both of them. But the injuries of an anguished adolescence had never fully healed. For most of his adulthood, he had kept his distance, maintaining their connection, which his brother describes as "polite and indulgent," by telephone. "He bought them new houses, summer homes, extravagant gifts," says Robert Nichols. "His public relationship with her was as a very good son, but his true feelings were complicated. Mike suffered the most from our mother's phobias and neuroses, which were numerous." In recent years, their visits had been brief and had occurred mostly at the urging of Annabel, who had, during their marriage, won her mother-in-law's affection; she was the first of Nichols's wives to pass muster.

He could not afford to hesitate about a trip home. As he had gotten older and had his own children, the facts of his mother's terrible early life had stirred a kind of pity and empathy in him that he had not been able to find when he was a younger man. He could never entirely like her, but he could, at last, understand and forgive her. The unhappy manipulator whose flair for inducing guilt had inspired more than one Nichols and May routine was also the woman who took him to his first movies, calmly explained to him what anti-Semitism was, bought him his first wig, and kept the family from insolvency as a young widow. He reached Philadelphia in time to be at her bedside with Robert when she died, on January 10, 1985, at the age of seventy-eight. Nichols was deeply affected by her loss. "Mike broke down and wept—sobbed, actually—which surprised me," says Robert.

"My mother had always been sick with one thing or another, and we thought of her as a permanent invalid," said Nichols. "And then she had cancer, and was dying, and ended up being as courageous as anyone I've ever seen. It moved us very much, and it helped everything. We were able to really love her completely. Finally you say, *All right, well, let's declare a truce.*"

That spring, Nora Ephron was ideal company for Nichols. "They had their own language," wrote her friend Richard Cohen, "a matter of nods and frowns and common cultural references. They knew whose marriage was a sham and who could not act and who had a bad drug problem. They knew the business of movies and the business of theater and, because they were hyperventilating readers, the business of books and magazines. [And] they had words, a torrent of them." Over the years, their bond had deepened from what Cohen called "mentor/ mentee" into close friendship. Ephron possessed every quality Nichols loved in the people closest to him—wit, intellectual fluency, and such strong-mindedness that when she died, in 2012, he asked, unironically, "Who will tell all of us what we should do?" She was a Jewish mother whose own Jewish mother had been as formidable and complex as Nichols's. After Brigitte's death, the trust between them grew even deeper. For Ephron, giving Nichols *Heartburn*—her own story, less raw than it had been a few years earlier but still the expression and repository of a great deal of hurt—was an act of faith. She had once said on a talk show that the only way she could fantasize about infidelity was "to kill my husband for a couple of minutes—and then I get to marry Mike Nichols."

Reaction to the novel, which had come out in the spring of 1983, had been explosive. The first-person story of Rachel Samstat, a Jewish cookbook author whose second marriage ends when she discovers, while seven months pregnant, the infidelity of her husband, Mark, was manifestly Ephron's own, told in her intimate and cutting voice and even punctuated by her recipes, and she barely bothered to pretend otherwise. *Heartburn* mixed real names—including a warm reference to Elaine May—with barely disguised versions of Ephron's friends, colleagues, and nemeses. When it was published, *The New York Times* called it "a tough, funny, bitchy and sometimes touching report from the scene of the disaster in the form of a novel." Some critics, particularly men, excoriated it as the work of "an effective self-publicizer"; in *Vanity Fair*, Leon Wieseltier, hiding behind the pseudonym "Tristan Vox," went so far as to call the prospect of a movie "child abuse," claiming that Bernstein's misdeeds were nothing compared with "the infidelity of a mother toward her children" in writing about them. But the outrage of those who felt repelled—or perhaps menaced—by *Heartburn* only helped speed it to the bestseller list.

Carl Bernstein was livid about being transformed from the hero of Watergate into the bad guy—a man "so horny he was capable of having sex with a Venetian blind"—in what he called "a national soap opera."

At first, his public stance was calculated stoicism: "I've always known that Nora writes about everything that happens in her life," he said. "The book is just like her—it's very clever." But when he learned that *Heartburn* was to become a movie, he went to war, calling the novel "nasty . . . smarmy . . . prurient" and complaining that it "obliterates everybody's dignity . . . I should have had no reason to be surprised," he said, "but . . . your marriage, particularly your children, ought to be something you keep for yourself. When you give away what you sing to your infant child in the nursery . . . you give away your soul!" He took Ephron to court, and their battle resulted in one of the most unusual celebrity divorce agreements in history. Bernstein won the right to read all drafts of the screenplay and submit notes, extracted a pledge that Ephron would never turn *Heartburn* into a TV series, mandated that a trust for their two young sons be created with part of the film's profits, and won her guarantee that "the father in the movie 'Heartburn' will be portrayed at all times as a caring, loving and conscientious father in any screenplay prepared or executed with my name attached to it." Nichols himself was a signatory to the final settlement.

Nichols did not view *Heartburn* as an act of betrayal but as a response to one. He was moved by the way Ephron had turned a crushing emotional blow into a statement of survival, and he initially saw it as a movie about "a woman doomed to be right, and therefore alone."

"I can't believe you're going to do this," Bernstein said to him when they met at the Russian Tea Room to discuss the movie. "Particularly since, more than anybody I know, you're a person who cherishes his privacy and that of your children."

"Somebody is going to make this movie," Nichols told him, "and you're much better off if I make it, because I'm your friend." Streep insisted that the movie be treated as fiction; she wanted to star in an emotional comedy about a contemporary woman's life, not a tell-all drama, and on that point, her word was law. "Mike at that time was a romantic, and a total womanizer," says *Heartburn*'s producer, Robert

Greenhut. "But what he felt about Streep was love and respect. He listened to her."

In some ways, Nichols's choice for Rachel's husband was a natural for a director who often looked to theater when casting his movies. By 1985, Mandy Patinkin had won two Tonys and was beginning to get noticed by Hollywood, with major roles in Barbra Streisand's *Yentl* and in Sidney Lumet's adaptation of E. L. Doctorow's *The Book of Daniel*. Patinkin was a Sam Cohn client, and Cohn was constantly in Nichols's ear about how right he was for the part. He was earnest, he was emotional, he was Jewish; he was also, in the memories of those who worked on *Heartburn*, a lot to handle. "Mandy was at the top of his game," says Juliet Taylor, the film's casting director. "But when he came in to read with people, we got to a point where he sings"—Mark exuberantly breaks into "Soliloquy," from *Carousel*, when Rachel tells him she's pregnant—"and he sang it. The whole song. Every single verse. We were all just dying and thinking, 'Oh, he is going to be so high-maintenance.'"

During *Heartburn*'s two weeks of rehearsal, Nichols started to worry. Many of Patinkin's questions seemed to emanate from his skepticism about the bad behavior of his character. "Mandy would constantly say, 'I don't know, I don't understand, would a guy really do this? Would a man really cheat on his wife while she was pregnant?'" says Richard Masur, who played one of Rachel's friends. "Mike and I were the only two men in the room, and we found ourselves talking about our own lives and saying, 'Yes, men do terrible things!' He never got it. I think on some level he wanted his character to be the hero of the movie, or at least to be softer and more likable."

Streep wasn't worried. "Mandy's a questioner, right?" she says. "That's the way he was the very first time we worked together in *Trelawny of the 'Wells,'*" the play in which she made her off-Broadway debut in 1975. "He's a rabbinical actor. He wears everyone down with questions, and that's how he solves the mystery of the thing for himself."

But by July 19, the first day of production, Nichols had begun to convince himself that he had made a mistake that could put the entire movie at risk. In *Heartburn*, Rachel has to fall in love with Mark, marry him, go into a tailspin when she discovers his betrayal, leave, reconcile with him, realize she was right the first time, and leave again. For the movie to work, Mark would have to be alternately seductive and contrite, gentle and loutish, imploring and impatient, someone she could love, hate, and need.

They shot for five days. "Neither Meryl nor Mandy had any idea there was a problem," says Greenhut. "They thought everything was hunky-dory." Soon after filming a restaurant scene, Nichols went to Greenhut and said, "'This is not happening. I think we should try and replace Mandy.' He couldn't even articulate what it was, except that there was no real excitement in the relationship. He asked me to give Mandy the bad news, and I said, 'I really think you should be the one carrying the water on that,'" Greenhut says. "We sat in my car—I had one of the first car phones. I said, 'You call him, and I'll sit here and hold your hand or whatever.' It was a very emotional experience for both of them. I sat next to Mike and I could hear Mandy gasp on the other end. It was very, very rough."

Streep was stunned. Nichols had not told her of his decision, and, she says, "I never really understood it. He just took a dislike. Mandy was wonderful, and it was so early in the shoot. I did say to Mike, 'I think it's a bad idea.' And it was so sudden! Just like shaking an Etch a Sketch, and he was gone." Patinkin later faulted himself for listening "to all the relatives who said, 'Yes, you win Tony Awards, but how's the movie career going?'" and said that he was "ambivalent" about the role and believed that Nichols had always wanted another actor for the job. He was devastated, he said, when Nichols fired him.

"I've felt awful about it all my life," Nichols said. "But on film I couldn't see the chemistry I wanted. I had to move fast." Unless he could get a new costar for Streep on a moment's notice, the production would shut down, and it would be *Bogart Slept Here* all over again. He reached out to Kevin Kline, who was Streep's friend and had worked well with her in *Sophie's Choice*, but Kline wasn't interested; "I liked the book," he said, "but when I read the screenplay, the character just seemed like a jerk." Nichols then called Jack Nicholson, who agreed to step in immediately—for $5 million, which was about $5 million more than Paramount had been paying Patinkin. "When I called him," said Nichols, "the first thing he said to me was 'If you need me, Nick, I can be there in two days.' Then comes the bill, and it's very high, but that's also part of 'If you need me.' Because you can read it, 'If you need *me*.'" The studio did some quick calculus about whether Nicholson's drawing power was worth what would amount to a substantial increase in *Heartburn*'s sub–$20 million budget, and approved his hiring.

Both Streep and Ephron worried that Nicholson's arrival would throw *Heartburn* out of balance. Patinkin had been striving, needy, serious; Nicholson—who was nobody's idea of Jewish—was sly, confident, and indefatigably charming. "Now everyone will like him, that son of a bitch," Ephron fretted.

"Suddenly, there were a lot of ideas about how we were going to enhance the part," says Streep. "The *man's* part. This was a movie about a woman, which was even more unusual in those days than it is now, and I thought it was a unique opportunity to explore things from her perspective, from Nora's perspective. That was the first time in my life that I got mad at Mike. Jack Nicholson was a movie star, and it was intimidating to have him come in, and maybe a little piece of that made me go, 'Hey, don't lose me in this just because you bring your friend in.' I went to Mike and said, 'This movie is about the person who got hit by the bus. It's not about the bus.' He heard me—he really did hear me on that. And all the nonsense about new scenes stopped."

Nicholson himself turned out to be nervous—he and Streep had never met, and there was no prep time before their first scene. Nichols decided to use their awkwardness to the film's advantage by starting with a scene in which Mark and Rachel uneasily attempt a step toward reconciliation while remaining unsure of how to deal with each other. "If you look at the movie, Meryl's doing that thing that girls do," he said. "She's blotchy—parts of her face are blushing. The thrill of them with each other, and us with them together, is sort of what made the joy of that movie." For the first time, he started to take pleasure in the shoot. "It became clear to me that it was at least alive," he said. He no longer felt that *Heartburn* was about a woman doomed to be alone, but about the struggle, even if unsuccessful, to connect. "I think maybe my subject is the relationships between men and women, without much of anything else, centered [on] a bed," he said at the time. "I don't know how to narrow it down any more."

Streep and Nicholson's breakthrough came not in that uncomfortable first encounter but in a sequence in which Mark and Rachel eat a takeout meal and chat aimlessly while sitting on their bed in the house they've just moved into. Nichols suggested they should eat pizza; Streep proposed that they serve it with a trowel, because their kitchen utensils would probably still be packed. She and Nicholson started trying to remember lyrics to old songs, singing with their mouths full, recalling snatches of melodies, getting them wrong, moving on to something else. In just one take, Nichols captured the kind of private throwaway moment in a married couple's life that almost never makes it into movies.

He was glad to work with Nicholson again—they soon rediscovered the "Nick and Nick" dynamic they had had fifteen years earlier, although, Nichols said, "*Carnal Knowledge* is far blacker and bleaker than I feel now." But, like *Silkwood, Heartburn* was a set on which his most significant collaborators were women: Ann Roth, Carly Simon, whom he hired to write the score, Streep, and Ephron. "Nora was always there," says Streep. "He and she always had that confab. They were the Gang of Two. And often they didn't even have to say much—there was so much between them that was understood." Nicholson couldn't have been happier. "He didn't know how to talk to men unless you were talking about sports or something he was interested in," says Masur. "But with women, he was engaged, connected, funny. He would light up. In the wedding scene, he was wonderful with the little girls—he would listen to every word they said—charming to the old ladies, great to the women who were extras. I said to Mike, 'What do you think that comes from?' and Mike said, 'That's what happens when you grow up with two mothers. He didn't have a father to kill.'"

Streep trusted Nichols so completely that she allowed her daughter Mamie, then just two, to appear in several scenes as Rachel's toddler; their connection is unmistakable, and Nichols delightedly left much of their interaction in the movie, whether Mamie is pulling her mother's glasses off her face or climbing a flight of stairs to an airplane one deliberate step at a time as his camera watches patiently and insists that the audience do the same. Their scenes in *Heartburn* were the first he ever shot with a father's eye.

To fill in her own performance, Streep watched Ephron every day. "It wasn't like trying to play Margaret Thatcher or something," she says, "but there were parts of her essence that were important to me. Nora was a tough girl, but she was also girly, and she had certain fey mannerisms that I wanted to capture."

For Nichols, the making of *Heartburn* became a more personal experience than he had expected, sometimes uncomfortably so. The cast was full of people he knew—Maureen Stapleton, Stockard Channing, his old friends Cynthia O'Neal and Milos Forman. And for the first time, he was depicting his own milieu—a world of casual socializing among successful urbanites, of dinner parties and receptions and tense drives home, of prewar co-ops and expensive renovations, and of friends who gossip about one another's secrets. More painfully, he was trying to do justice to the plight of a woman with two young children who realizes that her husband will never become the man she needs him to be. At the time, Nichols's own marriage was once again in decline, and he brought a bitter force to the scenes in which Rachel attempts to continue with Mark but realizes she will never trust him.

With Streep, he was true to his word: The film's visual showpiece is the scene in which *Heartburn* announces that it is indeed about the woman who was hit by the bus—a two-minute slow push toward Rachel's face as she sits in a salon and overhears a conversation that makes her realize her husband has been cheating on her. The only major scenes he cut after shooting them were a couple of fantasies in which Rachel gets to step away from what she's actually facing. Although the film remained a comedy, Nichols wanted it to carry a sting that audiences wouldn't fully feel until the end. In most of his movies, he had embedded a thematic statement somewhere in the first five minutes. In *Heartburn*, he saved it for the end, when Rachel's friend says to her, "Don't give me that New York psychological bullshit about how people are capable of change. They are not." The lyrics Carly Simon wrote for the film's main theme, "Coming Around Again"—"I know nothing stays the same / But if you're willing to play the game . . ."—offer more hope than that, but only in the wake of loss and disillusionment. Simon consulted closely with Nichols and Ephron about the lyrics; he chose to thread the song through the film, his first extensive use of music to illuminate a story's theme since *The Graduate*.

Nichols finished the movie in October, not quite sure what he had shot, or what life he was going back to. He had been spending more nights and weekends at the Carlyle, often preparing for the coming week's work late into Sunday night. During one of those sessions, when Robert Greenhut was working with Nichols, *60 Minutes* came on the TV in the background. Nichols lifted his head from the shooting schedule, looked at Diane Sawyer, and said, "Wow. How can I get to meet her?"

"You're a famous guy," Greenhut told him. "I'm sure you can figure it out."

T he first edit of *Heartburn* got the most tepid possible endorsement from Carl Bernstein, who insisted that the movie was "a silly little story about two people who fucked up" but conceded that it "come[s] quite close to the truth of what really happened in the marriage." For the first time in his career, Nichols had no idea how critics or audiences would respond to a movie he had made. His own feelings about his movie, and his marriage, had shifted from optimism to discourage-ment and back so many times that he didn't quite know where, or if, he had finally landed.

With the film's release set for the summer of 1986, he turned back to *Social Security*, which was aiming for a spring opening on Broadway. Nichols cast the play entirely with friends and colleagues: He had known Marlo Thomas, who would play Barbara, since the 1960s, and in the past couple of years he had worked with Ron Silver (who played her husband), Joanna Gleason (her sad-sack sister), and Kenneth Welsh (her brother-in-law). When he did a reading of the play before shooting *Heartburn*, Elaine May had stepped in to play Barbara's mother as a favor; for the Broadway run, he cast Olympia Dukakis. Following that reading, which happened soon after his mother's death, Nichols en-couraged Bergman to take the second act in a new direction. Instead of a guest-who-wouldn't-leave comedy, *Social Security* would become "a play about a mother who seemed like a schlepper but who really showed up those wiseass, smarty-pants Upper East Siders," says Peter Law-rence, the stage manager. "He turned the play on its ear because of what happened to his mother. Everything Mike did was personal to him, and in this case he wanted to do a play about a difficult mother that did not end up being a mockery of the mother."

In January, he began rehearsals in anticipation of a March tryout in Washington, D.C. "He'd come in and start every day with a joke or something funny," says Welsh. "His point was 'If it's not fun, why are we doing this?'" He played games to loosen up the cast, making them answer questions like "If you could be anyone in this room besides yourself, who would you pick?" And he encouraged them to risk dignity and go as far as they dared; *Social Security*, with a slapstick scene that featured Dukakis standing helplessly in the living room in her underwear while a ninety-eight-year-old dinner guest is being hidden in a closet, was not a comedy that asked to be underplayed.

One afternoon, Nichols was rehearsing a scene in which Gleason and Welsh arrive at the apartment. The actors were mining the moment for all the self-pity, jealousy, passive-aggression, and resentment they could muster; Nichols, watching from his chair, was laughing hard but wanted more. "Make it worse!" he told them. They did.

"Mike started laughing again—he had this unbelievable laugh," says Bergman. "Then he turned red and suddenly said, 'I'm not feeling very well.'" He looked at Lawrence and said, "Pete, I want you to call this number. It's my cardiologist. I think I'm having a heart attack."

"Do you want me to call 911?" Lawrence asked. "No," Nichols said, "I'm just going to get in a cab and go to the doctor."

Nichols spent two days in the hospital for what the press called "observation and testing," after chest pains that revealed "no major problem." Publicly, what had happened was described as nothing more than a scare that would require him to rest for a couple of weeks before resuming rehearsals. "It wasn't called a heart attack," says Lorne Michaels. "It was called whatever it was called, because a heart attack could stop you from working. But it was a heart attack."

Nichols had not been taking care of himself; he was overweight, smoking, eating poorly, working long hours, and increasingly succumbing to his appetite for cocaine. By the mid-1980s, that included crack. Many of Nichols's peers, even those who regularly indulged in coke, would never have considered buying or using what they thought of as a cheap, dangerous street drug for the lower class. It is not clear when, or with whom, Nichols first tried crack, but his hunger for it was powerful, he quickly figured out where and how to obtain it, and he later admitted that his drug use was, in part, responsible for his health crisis. When he returned to *Social Security* a couple of weeks later, he was at least temporarily clean, several pounds lighter, and cranky about his new diet. "He was always bitching that he wanted a cheeseburger," says Bergman, "and Marlo would make these completely tasteless vegan cookies. He was not happy, but he was sassy and mentally on top of his game."

"When he came back, the atmosphere changed, because he was vulnerable," Gleason says. "I also remember that he had bought pearls for Annabel—that relationship was on the cusp, near the end. I'd be watching him: *Is he coughing? Is he short of breath?* But I must say, he seemed fine. I think the heart attack was less debilitating and more cautionary—a shot across the bow."

Nichols and the cast worked so efficiently that no substantial postponement was necessary. *Social Security* had a quick run in Washington, and by the time the play began previews in New York on March 26, the heart attack was more than two months behind him and he seemed like his old self. Not long before the play opened, he took a quick trip to Europe and came back with an anecdote for all the friends and colleagues who knew about his most recent crush. "He was talking all about Diane Sawyer," says Gleason. "They had flown back together, and he was full of stories."

The meeting was an accident. Nichols had run into her in Paris as he was waiting for his flight back to New York. Sawyer hadn't slept for three days. She had flown there to deal with a sudden emergency involving her mother, who had developed what appeared to be an erratic heartbeat while on vacation. She was now escorting her and her stepfather back to America and, she said, "had spent the night outside my mother's door . . . listening to her breathe, and was in a blind panic." In the morning, she had thrown on old jeans and a stained turtleneck and gotten her family to the airport; she was now waiting to board the same

Concorde flight as Nichols. She spotted him before he saw her, and tried to avoid him until he walked up and said, "You're my hero."

"And you're mine," she replied. She told Nichols what was going on; he talked about the loss of his mother and the stress of dealing with sick parents. They didn't banter; they opened up to each other quickly, finding unexpected common ground at a vulnerable moment. "Nothing fundamental had changed," she said. But "in the first 90 seconds, I knew he was at the center of the dance."

If lightning struck instantly, professionalism kicked in minutes later. Nichols was still married; Sawyer was involved with the diplomat Richard Holbrooke. She knew he had a movie coming out, and she spent some of the three-hour flight to JFK trying to wrangle him for an interview on *60 Minutes* timed to the release of *Heartburn*. "Do you ever have lunch?" she said as they reached New York. He said he did. They exchanged pleasantries and went their separate ways.

At the opening night of *Social Security*, Nichols was upbeat and cheerful; he and those around him all assumed he was out of the woods. He was not. The worst ordeal of his life was about to begin. "It was," he said, "the year I went crazy."

Twenty-five

BORROWED TIME

1986-1987

I t took months for the people who knew Nichols to realize that he
was having a nervous breakdown. The personality they knew—the
humor, the energy, the optimism, the sociability—fell away from
him layer by layer until what was left was a stranger: a gaunt, paranoid,
desperate man whose life appeared to be in grave and immediate peril.
As early as the spring of 1986, he seemed off balance, but there were
plenty of explanations: He had lost his mother and suffered a heart
attack, two reminders of mortality that everyone knew could shake a
man in his mid-fifties, especially one who had been as careless about
his health as Nichols. A degree of emotional unsteadiness was only
natural.

To his friends, Nichols did not seem shaken when *Social Security*
received mixed reviews, many of which dismissed the play as a sitcom
and questioned why, at this point in his career, he would want to work
so hard to "polish up this tinsel until it glitters like fool's gold." He
could take that—it wasn't the first time that John Simon had called
him "a genius of the second-rate" or that Frank Rich had said he "isn't

in top form," and in any case, the play looked like it was going to become a mild hit even without raves to spark ticket sales.

But the pending reception of *Heartburn* felt more ominous. Soon after *Social Security* opened, he started screening the movie for his friends and colleagues; Paul Simon agreed to host one of the showings. Nichols's list of invitees was, he later said, "a cruel, harsh audience that has never liked anything I've done nearly as much as the public or, dare I say, the critics. I call this audience 'The Dwarf' because the Roman conquerors, during the triumphal processions, kept a dwarf on their shoulders to whisper, 'Fame is fleeting and life is short.'" At that point, Nichols didn't need any reminders; the audience at Simon's screening had watched *Heartburn* indifferently and had not bothered to hide their coolness toward the film. To some, it even felt like an act of betrayal akin to Truman Capote's long-awaited novel *Answered Prayers*; Nichols had been invited into their world, had pried into their marriages and divorces, and had exploited what should have remained behind closed doors.

There were times when he could keep negative reactions to his work from getting under his skin. "The first screening of *any* picture is awful, because the film changes in your mind from the greatest picture ever made to a perfectly nice picture that needs a lot of work," he said. "Then you always have that depressed night, and you get . . . a lot of calls from friends who think the picture would be fine if only you cut a particular scene. It's hard to forget what everybody said and go back and cut the picture right." But that night, he was rattled. "There was a dinner afterward," says Tracey Jackson, a young woman with whom he had become friendly and occasionally flirtatious. "It was clear it hadn't gone well, and nobody wanted to talk about the movie. Afterward, we were crossing Central Park and he said, 'You know, people think that because I'm Mike Nichols, I don't need praise. I need a lot. Nobody gets that.' He seemed so bereft and alone, more than I had ever seen."

By the time *Heartburn* opened in July, a more widespread negative verdict was in. Today, the film stands as perhaps his most underappreciated comedy; it's both funny and unfailingly acute about the manners and mores of the privileged class of people it depicts, and also one of the few studio films of the period in which a male director subordinated himself to the perspective of a female screenwriter and a female protagonist. (*Silkwood* is another.) A year later, Vincent Canby caught up with *Heartburn*, predicted a healthy afterlife for the film in the newly popular medium of home video, and called it "an exceptionally good movie . . . an accumulation of tiny, wonderfully observed details [that] never for a second mistake[s] rueful, satiric comedy for something pathetic or sentimental . . . I can't understand what all the carping was about."

Decades later, the reason for the carping is clearer. "There must be a side to Carl Bernstein's behavior of which we have not been made aware either in the book or the movie," Andrew Sarris wrote, complaining in *The Village Voice* about the "one-sided sympathy" that the film extends to Rachel. In *Time*, Richard Corliss sighed over the "tunnel-vision point of view of the offended party." Roger Ebert shrugged, "There's not much in the marriage for him to betray," noting that Streep seemed "dowdy and querulous," and *Newsweek* was certain that Ephron had left out important information about Rachel that would explain why Mark slept with other women, asking, "Is he disgusted by Rachel's pregnant body? Tired of her cuddly, smart-homebody personality?" Almost every male critic who disliked the movie expressed bafflement that Nichols would take on a subject as minor as domestic unhappiness from a woman's point of view—"he's no dum-dum," wrote Stanley Kauffmann, wondering why he would "waste [his talent] on flimsy material." The good reviews for the film—and there were several—could not overcome a general perception that Nichols had blown it by making a trifle of a "woman's picture," and *Heartburn*'s box office performance (it opened in second place but grossed only about $25 million during its run) confirmed it as a failure.

By then Nichols was in far worse shape than he had been—too emotionally unsteady to do more than a bare minimum of press, and spiraling further into what had first seemed to be a severe depression but was starting to look more like psychosis. He had always worried about money, particularly when it stopped flowing. With *My One and Only, The Real Thing, Hurlyburly,* and Whoopi Goldberg's show all having reached the natural conclusions of their successful runs, he was now in a dry period, and he had overextended himself in the horse market again. But none of that explained why he was suddenly talking to everyone he knew about his certainty that he was headed for destitution, and his terror that Jenny and Max, then just nine and thirteen, would be left to starve. The fear grew into an obsession, and his friends became used to disoriented calls late at night, when Nichols, alone in his suite at the Carlyle—he and Annabel were now spending a lot of time apart—would become overwhelmed with terror and would reach out with mad questions or requests.

One night he called Tom Stoppard and said, "Could I come and live with you? Will you take care of me?" On another, he called Stephen Sondheim. "He went on and on about how he was going broke," says Sondheim, "and how there would be no money to educate his kids. I thought, *What am I hearing? Mike is having some kind of paranoid break.* I didn't tell anybody, because I didn't know who I would tell. I just said, 'Mike, I think, I really think . . . are you seeing a psychiatrist?' He said, 'Oh, yeah, yeah.' I thought it was just his usual strangeness about money. One evening . . . he had said to me in a sort of semi-drunken phone call that one of his biggest regrets in life was that he wasn't a millionaire. In those days, 'millionaire' meant billionaire. And I thought, *Wow.* I knew he liked money and luxury goods and living high. But that he was upset at 11:30 in the evening, when he'd had a lot of brandy,

that he wasn't a millionaire? I had nothing helpful to say, and I sure
didn't want to go to friends and say, 'What am I going to do about
Mike?'"

But it was a question people who knew Nichols were starting to ask.
Some took him at his word, as irrational as he sounded. "He called me
one night and said, 'A terrible thing has happened, I've lost all my
money, and I have nothing,'" Streep recalls. "I said, 'Well, Mike, you
have so many rich friends—everybody's going to lend you money.' I was
shocked, because it wasn't a kind of conversation that we would ever
have—it was so out of the blue and disconcerting. I thought, *Something's wrong with him,* but I didn't know what."

It didn't occur to Streep, or to most people, that Nichols might have
developed a drug problem. "I'm the kind of person who never knows
about that," she says. "When their nose is running all the time on the
set, I give them the name of an ear, nose, and throat specialist, and it's
always years later that I go, *Oh! Wow!* But Carrie [Fisher] knew. She
talked to him and said, 'He's out of his mind. He's on a drug.' When
she said it, I thought she was imagining it, because she always thought
everybody was using. But she was right."

Soon after Nichols was released from the hospital following his
heart attack, he had told his doctors that he was anxious and having
trouble sleeping. One of them prescribed him Halcion, a benzodiaze-
pine whose side effects can include paranoia and suicidal thoughts. The
pill worked for a while; then it didn't. The more anxious he became,
the more he took; the more he took, the deeper his paranoia got. Eventually he went from one pill at night to six just to fight off the palpita-
tions and shakes that going cold turkey would cause. "At first I was
enormously depressed," he said. "Then I was delusional. I thought I
was broke. And I made hideous mistakes."

He started selling everything, often at cut-rate prices to the first
available buyer. He fired his driver and got rid of his Mercedes. He sold
a Balthus that hung over his bed after Anjelica Huston and Susan

Forristal visited him and, trying to shake him out of his depression, joked that he'd start getting laid again if he got rid of it, and he regretted it so quickly that he started taking even more Halcion. He would talk openly to friends about what would become of his children, in such stark terms that some of them feared he was planning to commit suicide as soon as he felt certain that he could leave them enough money. He would sit with John Calley and compulsively go over a list of his assets. "I'd add the numbers up," Calley told the writer John Lahr. "I'd say, 'Thirteen point six. Can you accept that?' And he'd say, 'The only thing I could accept would be you telling me that when I go into debtor's prison you will take care of the children.'"

To some who knew him, Nichols seemed to be living two lives at once: He was deranged enough to ask one wealthy friend who offered to loan him money, "Can you make it $25 million?" but rational enough to observe himself in free fall as if from a great distance. "Why is it," Maury Yeston asked him, "that the richest people are the greediest?"

"Because that one extra dollar is just a little more insurance that they'll never have to return to the time in their lives when they didn't have it," Nichols replied.

"Even when he was selling all the Monets or Manets or whatever it was," Yeston says, "he was able to discuss it with great aplomb. 'I'm selling everything, and I don't know why,' he would say, as if he were talking about someone else's life crisis."

Some of Nichols's intimates, including Buck Henry and Candice Bergen, knew that his obsession with money, though disproportionate, was not entirely irrational. "He really did have debt," Bergen says. "He lived like a prince, and there was a point when he needed John Calley to help him get out of it." Annabel, trying to help, had agreed that they should sell the Eighty-first Street brownstones and move back to Connecticut with the children. Others, like Streep, felt that Nichols needed to hit bottom in order to justify ending his marriage. "He was so unhappy," she says, "and he didn't know how to get out of it without making it a crisis." Richard Avedon thought his old friend was simply in a deep funk; he went over to the Carlyle, pulled Nichols out of bed on a cold fall day, bundled him up in a sheepskin coat, and walked him around the block, at one point pounding him on the back and yelling, "Snap out of it!"

That October, Forristal came to visit him in Connecticut. "Everything was coming apart at the same time," she said, "the work, the life, the marriage. Annabel called and said that he was very, very down, and why didn't I come for the weekend to try to cheer him up? We were taking a walk and he started telling me how awful he felt, how he wasn't looking forward to anything. I said, 'What are you taking to sleep?' And he said, 'I'm taking Halcion.' The summer before, I had been in Amagansett with Lorne. We had Randy Newman and Penny Marshall staying with us, and Penny was saying, 'I just want to kill myself.' And Randy said, 'What are you taking to sleep?' And she said, 'Halcion.' And he went, 'Exactly the same thing happened to me and my brother.'

"So I told Mike this, and he goes, 'No, no, no, Jay told me'—we all had the same doctor—'Jay told me this was fine.' And I said, 'I'm telling you, it's *not* fine.' So then we had the weekend. They had people over for lunch, and the kids were causing trouble, and it was just normal."

A few weeks later, Nichols asked Forristal to come to the Carlyle. When she got there, he started asking what she described as "calm, practical" questions about the suicide of her sister. It became clear that he was trying to figure out the most painless way to take his own life. Forristal and Carly Simon, whom Nichols had also asked to come over, realized there was no time to waste. They got him dressed, hailed a taxi, and took him to Columbia-Presbyterian. The drive was slow—it was November 2, 1986, the day of the New York City Marathon—but Nichols was too exhausted to do anything but go willingly and check himself into the psych unit of the hospital. His Halcion addiction was quickly confirmed, and as he was weaned off the drug, his delusion and paranoia abated in less than two weeks.

The crisis was over, but the aftershocks were considerable. Nichols's marriage was in ruins; Annabel had stuck by him loyally until the worst had passed, without knowing if it ever would, but too much had been said and done and broken for them to continue as husband and wife. ("In craziness," he once observed after a long dinner with a mentally ill colleague, "a fair amount of truth comes out.") Their parting was amicable. He bought an apartment in the Hotel des Artistes, on West Sixty-seventh Street, four blocks from where he had grown up, where she and the children could live; he would stay across Central Park at the Carlyle. There was, at that moment, no other woman in his life. Although he and Sawyer had had a couple of friendly lunches, it had been almost a year since they were last in touch. And even if he had felt ready to go back to work, there was no work to go back to, no plays or movies on the horizon, nothing in which he wanted to immerse himself. "I changed my life," he said. "I got divorced . . . I moved. I changed everything. I wanted another life. And then I got it."

For the first time in his adult life, Nichols started being careful—not simply cautious or strategic about professional decisions, but respectful of his own fragility. "After that six months of hell, my life was very different," he said. "Simplified." He returned to therapy and, after decades of barely giving his heritage a thought, started to contend with some of the feelings about his Jewishness that his mother's death had reawakened—"the idea that all of this is borrowed time, that I should have been six million and one." And he started to try to understand why his life had felt like a cyclical series of ascents and crashes. "You work better and better and you feel okay about it and people seem to go for it," he said, "and then [depression] comes creeping in, and you don't know when it started. You know that you're getting up later. You spend more time watching crap on television and eating Haagen-Dazs . . . Slowly what you're doing is turning into stone. You don't notice it, and then something cataclysmic happens, like a marriage breaking up, or a picture being disastrous for everyone, or getting sick. And then you think you're through."

This last plunge had scared him—so much so that when he finally found a job he wanted to take, his first impulse was to explain that he couldn't. By the end of the year, Nichols had started thinking about returning to directing. Undeterred by the reception of *Heartburn*, Nicholson wanted to work with him again and approached him about the possibility of directing *The Two Jakes*, the long-in-development sequel to *Chinatown*. But although Nichols's paranoia about money had subsided, his worry about it had not; he set a fee too high for the film's budget to accommodate, and negotiations ended quickly. He also traveled to London to see Christopher Hampton's *Les Liaisons Dangereuses* in the West End, at the urging of Scott Rudin, whom Nichols had known since he was a teenage casting director on *Annie* and who was now, at twenty-eight, the new president of production at 20th Century Fox. Rudin thought the play was perfect for a Nichols movie and bid half a million dollars for the rights on the strength of his interest; the play's producers declined, deciding instead to move the show to Broadway and increase its value to Hollywood even more.

Rudin also had a script that a young playwright named Kevin Wade had written called *Working Girl*, a Cinderella story set on modern-day Wall Street that excited Nichols's interest enough for him to ask Rudin to come to New York and have lunch. "He said, 'I really like this, and I'd like to do it, but I have complications,'" says Rudin. "'I'm not in any shape to do it yet. I've been having a nervous breakdown, and I'm still crazy. I don't know when I'll be better, but I'll be better, and when I'm better I'll do it. Could you wait for me?'"

Nichols told Rudin that he had an easier project in mind—something that would return him to moviemaking with what felt almost like a set of training wheels. He was talking to Neil Simon about directing the film version of *Biloxi Blues*, the autobiographical play about his stint in the Army during World War II that had finally, after seven losses, gotten Simon a Best Play Tony. Nichols was in an atoning frame of mind, trying to make things right with friends and loved ones as if he were moving through a twelve-step program. He told Rudin that he felt he owed the film to Simon, especially after *Bogart Slept Here*. "It's a very easy movie," he said. "I don't have to invent anything—I can do it with Matthew Broderick, who did it onstage. It's just basically shooting."

Most people in the industry had no idea Nichols had gone through anything worse than a period of idleness. "I didn't know what 'I'm crazy' meant," Rudin says. "He kind of told me, and then I heard from other people, 'Oh, well, you know, Mike sold everything . . .'" Rudin passed along Nichols's request to his boss, Barry Diller, then in his second year as Fox's chairman and CEO. "He agreed to ice it for a year, which was menschy, because at the time we had very few movies that were good enough to make," Rudin says, "and *Working Girl*, which had three star parts, was one that was ready to go." Nichols was deeply appreciative; Rudin and Diller were among the only people in Hollywood to whom he had opened up about his struggles, and they remained friends for the rest of his life.

Twenty years earlier, Nichols had launched his career in Hollywood as a rookie directing two legends. When production of *Biloxi Blues* got under way in Fort Smith, Arkansas, in April 1987, he was, for the first time on a movie set, a legend directing rookies. Nichols had retained only Broderick and one other actor from the Broadway production; for many in the young cast, this was their first substantial experience on a set.

Some of the actors playing GIs had never heard of Nichols and May; they hadn't been born when Nichols had directed his first Broadway hit. "It was sort of like having a magical prince from a foreign land whose greatest dream was to be around actors," says Corey Parker, then a twenty-one-year-old whom Nichols cast as a bookish, high-minded Jewish recruit suspected of homosexuality by his barracks mates. "He was almost worshipful about acting and about what the atmosphere of a set was supposed to be. The only time I ever saw him get angry was when he thought the crew was making too much noise. 'There are actors on the set about to go in front of the camera!' he said. It was sacred to him."

Nichols had rarely treated an ensemble of actors more solicitously. "He was a leader, he was a host, and he was a coach," Broderick says. But the decade since *Streamers* had also given him a more fatherly touch. "He would take us all for beers and pizza, but what really impressed me was that he turned one of the barracks buildings in Fort Smith into a movie theater, and every weekend we would all watch a movie together that Mike would pick," says Broderick. The films were all from the late 1930s or early '40s—exactly what the soldiers on the base would have had access to. Nichols was especially fond of Preston Sturges comedies like *Hail the Conquering Hero* and *Sullivan's Travels*. "It helped us all feel like a group," says Broderick, "but in retrospect, he was also helping us live in that period and understand the comedy of that time in a completely painless way." The cast received a weekly education in film history, but also in the kind of man their director was. "He showed us *Camille,* with Greta Garbo," says Parker, "and you could watch the movie or you could watch him watch the movie. He cried at the end. There was nothing protecting his heart."

He could not, it turned out, rekindle the easy relationship he had once had with Simon. Too much time had passed, and Simon's sense of injury was too acute. Nichols had asked for rewrites that would put Broderick's character closer to the center of the action, and he had also insisted that Simon cut more than thirty minutes of text. Although they would remain friendly in later years, *Biloxi Blues* marked their last collaboration. "They just didn't seem to like each other," says Park

Overall, who played a local prostitute. "That was evident and palpable, but Mike never let it get in the way. He had a tone he wanted to set, and he set it."

Nichols was not above a few tricks. He hired Christopher Walken to play the drill sergeant, in part because he knew Walken's counterintuitively low-key line deliveries and complete unpredictability would be, as Parker put it, "sufficiently scary to make us ready to do whatever the hell he told us to do . . . I could hear him in his room screaming into his pillow, working on the voice . . . [and] he often carried an apple and sometimes an onion, which he ate like an apple, putting them down right before shooting." Nichols knew that Walken's performance would also affect Broderick's: "He was scary, but in a totally different way than Bill Sadler had been onstage," says Broderick. "So I had to give up the laughs that had become dependable and easy in a year on Broadway. I think that decision is what made the movie Mike's, in a way."

Nichols became a different director for each young actor. With Broderick, he developed an easy and specific shorthand based on his theater training. With Parker, he was soft-spoken and inquisitive, asking about his past, his family, and his spiritual beliefs, and at one point offering to get high with him. (His intoxicant of choice right after the Halcion episode was nothing stronger than a joint at the end of the day; Parker declined.) Markus Flanagan, who played another of the GIs, remembers that he "would find Mike's eyes in the room and he would give me a subtle nod or a little tip of the head, and it meant 'That's what I wanted' or 'You could do better' or 'There's a little more for you to explore.' And for Chris [Walken], he could just say, 'Less.' Every single person had a different way of communicating, and Mike intuited what the best way was very quickly." Nichols was understanding about youthful misbehavior; when one young actor got drunk and was arrested trying to break into an actual Army barracks, Nichols walked in, talked for several minutes with local law enforcement and military police, and left with everybody smiling and the actor in his custody.

Biloxi Blues was, for Nichols, largely an exercise in self-rehabilitation. The rhythms of Simon's dialogue were second nature to him, and he couldn't pretend that he felt deeply engaged by the small bromides and life lessons of the script. The goal was to remain even-keeled; there would be no explosions, no retakes to blow up the shooting schedule or the budget, no last-minute firings; most of all, he would try to remain balanced rather than suspend the rules of ordinary living just because he was making a movie. He stayed on course during the day, remaining unflappable in the scorching heat and laughing off the chiggers, ants, and water moccasins that plagued the shoot. At night, he went back to his hotel and slept. On Passover, he took a break and drove Simon and three of the actors to a makeshift seder at the local Holiday Inn.

Only occasionally did he betray a slight impatience to return to New York. "I met a woman," he told his first assistant director, Mike Haley, one day while they were driving to a location. "Diane Sawyer."

"Oh, good," Haley said.

"I'm going to marry her," he said.

Nichols had not yet shared that plan with Sawyer—he had not, in fact, spoken to her since the beginning of his crash. But in the summer of 1987, after *Biloxi Blues* had wrapped, he returned to New York City, called her, and said, "Meet me at the Russian Tea Room."

"She had wondered what had happened to me," he said, "and was sort of hurt." Nevertheless, she agreed to have lunch with him. "And then it went very very fast," he said.

In less than a month, they were engaged.

Twenty-six

PINOCCHIO AND CINDERELLA

1987–1988

Long after they got married, Nichols liked to say that his relationship with Diane Sawyer "turned Pinocchio into a real boy." But when they started to see each other that summer, he was, although deeply sentimental about her, much less so about himself. He did not view his own story as the narrative of a child come to life; if any fairy tale was on his mind, it was the one about a beast who desperately wants to become a man. While he and Sawyer were dating, he said to Douglas Wick, the producer of *Working Girl*, "If I don't find a woman who'll kick my ass when I'm rude to a cabdriver, I'm over as a human being."

"He said he had always liked the lazy romantic pathway," says Wick, "but he also needed someone to help him fight his worst instincts." In Sawyer, he had fallen for a woman who had her own career, ambitions, interests, and social world—and who was more "sidewalk-famous" than he was. At forty-two, she had lived almost as many lives as Nichols had. The daughter of a Republican politician and a schoolteacher, Sawyer, who was born and raised in Kentucky, was a former national beauty pageant winner; when Nichols was directing *Barefoot in the Park* in

1963, she was being crowned America's Junior Miss. She had gone on to Wellesley and a job as an aide to Richard Nixon. (Rumors that she was "Deep Throat" were so persistent that she finally asked Bob Woodward to bat them down, which he did.) In the 1970s, she moved into journalism and fought her way up in a field still dominated by men. In 1984, she became the first woman to coanchor *60 Minutes*; four years later, she was a prime-time star being avidly pursued by other networks that thought she could carry her own show. Her status helped Nichols keep his own in perspective, and he loved it.

To his friends and colleagues, the change in his demeanor was striking. "You see these survivors after a big earthquake, looking dazed as they come out into the light," says actress Kate Nelligan. "He was like that. I've never seen a man so grateful for anyone. He just felt like the luckiest man in the world, and he never made any secret of it. He was always very self-reportedly clear about not having been this person his whole life. Her love made him accept himself, and after that he wanted to make everybody's life better, because his had been made better."

"He fell in love with her instantly," says Candice Bergen, "and he wanted to be a better man for her. He had always talked about his 'black heart,' and I think he meant it. After Diane, his anger diminished. He paid more attention to others."

At the end of 1987, an item strategically placed in Liz Smith's gossip column made their relationship public. "I thought he was the most heart-stoppingly funny and limitless person I'd ever met," Sawyer said. "You know what Napoleon said: 'A woman laughing is a woman conquered.'"

Among those who gave Sawyer their stamp of approval, the most important was, without question, Nichols's soon-to-be ex-wife. Davis-Goff knew that anyone Nichols married would be spending a lot of time with her children; when Sawyer, more than a little nervous, arrived at her home for dinner, she answered the door wearing an apron that Max and Jenny had given her as a Mother's Day gift, with the word MOM emblazoned across it—"completely inadvertent," she insisted. Sawyer flinched, but only internally. Because she was used to interviewing people but dreaded being on the receiving end of questions, "I began to recite to [Annabel] all the people Mike could have married who were far worse than me," she said. "It was a gamble."

They found themselves in quick agreement about why the choices on that list would be disastrous; Davis-Goff, who described her split with Nichols as "the most civilized divorce possibly in the history of the world," soon assured her that she thought they were right for each other. What Sawyer called "one of those hazardous dances of modern culture—the dance of the wives" had gone well. "I still had my moments of petty jealousy, rivalry, fear of the unknown," Sawyer said. And there would be bumps, including a first Thanksgiving at which the teenage Max said to the haplessly unculinary Sawyer, "If my mother were here, everything would be finished on time and it would taste good." But the two women were able to move forward on a path of mutual respect. "Friends?" said Sawyer. "No, that doesn't seem quite right. Successors? That doesn't sound quite right either. We really became something else—which is family." Their mutual goodwill went a long way toward creating a settled domestic life for Nichols and his children that he once might have thought impossible.

For the second time in three years, Nichols was offered the stewardship of a major New York theater when Joseph Papp, who was ill with cancer, approached him about taking over the Public. Nichols said no; he was interested only in directing. After seeing *The Colored Museum* at the Public, he asked Papp to put him in touch with the play's author, George C. Wolfe (who would himself take over the Public several years later).

After his harrowing year, Nichols was eager to tackle a project about addiction. "He wanted me to write a version of *A Star Is Born* set in the world of stand-up comics," Wolfe says. "Whoopi Goldberg was going to be the rising comedian, and Richard Pryor was going to be the comedian on his way out. I went to comedy clubs all over the place. And I'd go to his office and he would tell me stories about his time in comedy and why he quit. He told me this joke about the comedian who finishes his set and a woman says, 'Here's my hotel key. Come to my room. You can do anything you want to me.' And the comedian says, 'Which set did you see, the first or the second?' He said that when he clicked into that brain, that's when he knew he had to do something else . . . He was totally opening up and using himself as a source for whatever I might write. He told me about his money issues, about smoking crack, all these incredibly intense personal things. It fell apart before I ever wrote a script, and it was totally my fault because I got tied up writing other things."

Nichols found a different door into the subject when he read a debut novel that Carrie Fisher had just written. *Postcards from the Edge* was a darkly comic, semi-autobiographical portrait of an actress making her way back into Hollywood after a stint in rehab. Nichols knew Fisher well enough to understand how much of it was her own story; on some level, he also felt it was his. Beyond that, he knew that Streep and Fisher had become friends and that Streep would find the lead role irresistible. By the time the book was published, he had signed on as director and had agreed to make the film after *Working Girl*, which was now scheduled to start production in early 1988.

At the same time, he was considering a return to theater. The tripartite challenge he had set for himself twenty years earlier—to direct Chekhov, Beckett, and Pinter—was still two-thirds unmet, and Nichols had viewed his one try at Chekhov, *Uncle Vanya*, as such a failure that he felt he was basically starting from scratch. Beckett had never left his thoughts ever since he played Lucky in Chicago thirty years earlier, and he had been actively pursuing the idea of a New York production of *Waiting for Godot* for some time. In 1984, when Dustin Hoffman was on Broadway in *Death of a Salesman*, Nichols asked him if he wanted to play Estragon. Hoffman was interested, and the following summer, shortly before he started shooting *Heartburn*, Nichols had a reading at the Carlyle with Hoffman, Brian Bedford as Vladimir, John Malkovich as Lucky, and Vincent Gardenia as Pozzo. (Malkovich's then wife, Glenne Headly, played the small role of the boy.) The actors worked on the text for weeks beforehand, and their interpretations were "inspired," according to the critic Mel Gussow, who was invited to attend. But Hoffman could never find time for a full production and eventually let it go.

Nichols did not. Soon after he finished *Biloxi Blues*, he flew to France to meet Beckett, then eighty-one, to try to secure the rights to stage the play at Lincoln Center. It had been a long time since Nichols had auditioned for anyone, and he went into their meeting well prepared, with respectful, specific questions about which variations in different editions of the text Beckett preferred. "I asked him at one point what one of the tunes was to one of the little songs in the play, and he sang it for me and cracked himself up," Nichols said. After six months of further discussions, he got the go-ahead. He would stage *Waiting for Godot* in a limited run off-Broadway in the fall of 1988, with Steve Martin, Robin Williams, Bill Irwin, and F. Murray Abraham. The casting of Martin and, particularly, of Williams generated instant speculation that Nichols intended to use Beckett's play as the pretext for an improvisatory clown show; among theater critics, there was still widespread skepticism that he could take something as serious as Beckett seriously. Nichols reminded everyone that Beckett himself called the play "a tragicomedy" and promised, "We'll do it all Sam's way," remarking that "when the play is over, you sit there utterly depressed because there seems to be no hope at all, and then you walk 15 blocks and you feel good, and finally you feel great, because somebody has told the truth . . . It can uplift you and make you feel actually joyous."

W hen *Biloxi Blues* opened in March, a few reviewers complained that Nichols couldn't possibly have found anything in Neil Simon's play to engage his intellect or his talent. "Isn't it time for Nichols to start acting more like a real filmmaker and less like a guy on retainer?" Roger Ebert wrote. Even those who enjoyed the movie, like *New York*'s David Denby, conceded that "a more lightweight film couldn't be imagined." "Here is one adaptation of a stage piece that has no identity crisis," wrote Vincent Canby. "Never for a minute does it aspire to be anything but a first-rate service comedy." There was condescension even in the praise—"now that Nichols has resigned the auteur claims of his early film career in favor of more self-effacing commercial assignments, he seems a much stronger director; he has learned to serve his material," said the *Daily News*. But the movie was what Nichols hoped it would be—a reasonable commercial rebound after *Heartburn* (its $43 million gross made it a modest hit) and proof to anyone who had heard rumors about his breakdown that he was back in form and capable of delivering, including as a director for hire.

Working Girl, however, would be a bigger swing—a movie for which he and 20th Century Fox had high hopes, and a production to which he would be expected to bring both fairy-tale romanticism and urban gleam. The story of a working-class secretary from Staten Island trying to make the leap to executive at the brokerage firm where she works was an unembarrassed product of the late Reagan years—an enthrallment with high finance and big business was baked into the script, so much so that its original director, James Bridges (*The China Syndrome*), who had planned to make the movie with Demi Moore, declined to move forward unless a new draft trained a more critical eye on Wall Street, as Oliver Stone had just done.

Nichols wasn't interested in celebrating conspicuous consumption. In fact, he had just produced *The Thorns,* a failed ABC sitcom that satirized the excesses of the moment; he said the show represented his take on "a greedy family living beyond its means—you could say it's about the Reagan years." His politics were far from Reagan's, but he was a first-generation American who needed no convincing about the irresistible allure of money and success. What he saw in Kevin Wade's screenplay was a portrait of a new generation of invisible and unrespected quasi immigrants—newcomers from an outer borough hungry for a piece of the American dream. He envisioned an opening scene that would illuminate their place in the pecking order: a swirling helicopter shot of the Statue of Liberty that would give way to an image of dozens of women spilling off the Staten Island Ferry—"I had all these private images of galleons, and worker bees," he said—to go toil in the new world of Wall Street, where they were treated as faceless, interchangeable drudges by a sleek new iteration of the financial ruling class. Among those hopefuls would be Tess, the movie's princess-in-waiting. Nichols planned to end the film with another helicopter shot: Once Tess has finally gotten both her prince and her dream—a job with upward mobility and a window office—he would have the camera hover outside the skyscraper, watching her, and then move back, revealing hundreds of windows just like hers. She would still be just a face in the crowd—but the crowd would be different.

"Some people feared this was a TV movie, and it could have been, but he made everything more specific," says Wick. "The first shot and the last shot—the pull-away that says, 'You want it so bad, and when you get it, it's overrated'—were all Mike."

"I thought, *This will be fine*," Nichols said, "because *Cinderella* will take care of us, and we can work on *detail* . . . The joy was . . . in getting to [give] all our time to what things were really like—what status is, how you achieve status, and what the tokens of status really are." He hired J. Roy Helland, Meryl Streep's hair designer, to go to Staten Island and photograph "the real working girls"—their clothes, hair, makeup. He looked through hundreds of pictures before he found the overprocessed dye job that would define Tess at the movie's start without a word of dialogue. For Nichols, a man to whom Staten Island was practically a foreign country, the pictures were a revelation. "I thought, *Surely this is not what they do with their hair and their faces! This is so extreme!*" he said. "And [Roy] said, 'Well, come on the ferry.'"

"I knew he would be analytical," says Wick. "Right away he started talking about the trader bars as watering holes for animals, and then about every moment in the story. But I didn't know he would be so romantic, or so raw about connecting to the dream and the longing."

Nichols was already thinking about the casting of Tess when Wick visited him on the *Biloxi Blues* set in early 1987. Both men faced a decision they knew would shape the entire movie: Was the role a star part, or a star-making part? Scarcely an actress in her twenties or thirties went unmentioned. After watching Madonna flirt and banter with Johnny Carson on a confident *Tonight Show* appearance, Nichols was intrigued by the idea of using her; after they met in New York, he encouraged her to test herself by acting onstage, as Cher had done. Cher herself was on his list for a while, as was Whoopi Goldberg, and Fox was, at various times, interested in Goldie Hawn and Shelley Long. Wick had met with Meg Ryan, who had yet to play the lead in a big movie, and thought she was a strong contender. "And Michelle Pfeiffer was interested," he says, "but we talked about how, if she was at the desk out front, people would be lining up around the block to marry her."

Nichols ultimately decided to push for Melanie Griffith, who had had leading roles in Brian De Palma's thriller *Body Double* and Jonathan Demme's *Something Wild* but had yet to carry a mainstream romantic comedy. Griffith wanted the part badly enough to read and screen-test for it; in her, Nichols believed he had found the right combination of sexuality, bravado, and guilelessness. He also thought she would pair well with the male lead he wanted, Alec Baldwin, a TV mainstay ready to make the jump to movie stardom. And Sigourney

Weaver, fresh off an Oscar nomination for *Aliens,* was everyone's first choice for Tess's boss and nemesis.

It was Fox that vetoed the pairing of Griffith and Baldwin as an insufficient draw for audiences. The studio had gone back and forth about how much star power the movie needed, initially encouraging the idea of Harrison Ford and Sigourney Weaver, then turning away from Ford after deciding that two star salaries would drive the $20 million budget too high. Now Fox reversed itself; it wanted Ford after all. "The studio said, 'Two unknowns as your leads? You can't do that,'" says Juliet Taylor, who cast the film. "Mike was really set on choosing Melanie. If he had to bend, he was going to bend about the male." Reluctantly, Nichols asked Baldwin how he would feel about taking the smaller role of Tess's working-class boyfriend. He said he'd be happy to.

At thirty, Griffith was not an entirely comfortable fit for a 1988 version of Cinderella. She had appeared nude in Arthur Penn's thriller *Night Moves* when she was still a teenager, and since then she had married, divorced, and remarried; her résumé included two dozen movie and television credits, plus a stay in rehab for alcohol and drug use, and she had already been the subject of a comeback story in *People* magazine four years earlier. Nichols knew how difficult it would be to make moviegoers feel they were meeting someone new.

He shot *Working Girl* almost entirely on location in New York, and it went into production at a time when cocaine use was still rampant on both movie sets and Wall Street itself. "You can't talk about the movie without talking about cocaine," says Ann Roth. "It was everywhere," says Wick. "But the idea was that you would do it on the weekends, and that way it wouldn't interfere with the job." After a couple of weeks of filming, it became clear that Griffith was once again having a serious problem with both cocaine and alcohol. She would show up late, often looking exhausted and puffy. Once the cameras rolled, according to Sam O'Steen, "she used to say, 'I gotta go down to my trailer for a minute.' They all knew what she was doing."

"The shoot was difficult—it was always verging on bad and verging on glorious at the same time," says Mary Bailey, who began a decades-long association with Nichols as the movie's script supervisor. "I think everyone felt that we might have something exciting and special and wonderful, but it could all come apart."

"Melanie was very charming and funny, but there were times Mike wanted to strangle her," says production designer Patrizia von Brandenstein. "He was very understanding, but, in a strange way, he was very moral about the idea that whatever was going on in your personal life, you had to be respectful of the work." The problem came to a head one night when Nichols was shooting on Staten Island; Wick had taken an evening off and was having dinner at Orso, in Midtown Manhattan. "Mike called me at the restaurant and said, 'She's really high—can you come back?'" Wick returned to the set and, on the advice of a colleague, told Griffith, "We're gonna shut down, and we're gonna charge you for the three hours that we're losing. We love you, but you have to deal with this." Wick was struck by how helpless Griffith seemed—she was not a diva, and genuinely wanted to do well—but, he says, "what really shocked me was how vulnerable Mike was. He was a serious artist, and she was his instrument, and if his instrument was impaired, he couldn't do his work. He couldn't play her. It was as if *he* were in danger. She was such a crazy, open spirit, and when you got her, you got her guts. He needed that, and he couldn't get it."

That talking-to didn't solve the problems, and a few nights later Nichols himself laid down the law, telling Griffith that she had to pull herself together—for him and for her colleagues. He reminded her of the opportunity that the role afforded her and told her she was in danger of blowing it. "He did it, and he did not do it privately," says von Brandenstein. "It was the middle of the night, but there were people around. With actresses, he could be stern, but somehow he also knew what they needed to hear. It penetrated, and she got it."

Griffith recommitted herself to her work, and as she did, Nichols started to have an easier time. Ford, who told him, "I don't have to have a lot of wonderful things to do—all I really want is to advance the action," was, he said, "the best collaborator on earth—a guy who knows his job," and he could see that Sigourney Weaver and the relatively unknown Joan Cusack were both walking away with their scenes. Soon after production ended, Griffith would enter an addiction treatment program. But for the rest of the shoot, she strove to give Nichols everything he wanted; her on-time record improved, and she threw herself into the role's comic and romantic possibilities. She even suggested that she go topless for a scene in which she vacuums a rug. "His face was like, 'Of *course* it would be fucking okay!'" she said.

While Nichols was making the movie, he and Sawyer were planning their wedding, and he realized that he was becoming something he had not been since his days squiring Jacqueline Kennedy around the city: an object of gossip column fascination. "The closer to the wedding they got, the more attention there was," says Sabrina Padwa, who worked in his office at the time. "The tabloids were calling every five seconds."

The unexpected pairing of a director heading into his fourth marriage with a glamorous broadcaster heading into her first was an irresistible story. At a moment when the media was starting to trade in power lists and items about power couples, Nichols and Sawyer's highly visible courtship became something of a fixation. (She even got a thumbs-up from Avedon, although, Nichols said, "I got pissed at [him] when he had the nerve to congratulate me on having finally married a woman who, when we walked into an A-list party together, I didn't have to worry that people would be speaking only to me.")

"Oh, God, Mike was in seventh heaven. I'd never seen him just floating on fucking air," says Mike Haley. "I'd go pick him up in the morning and she'd come tumbling out of the building first and he'd follow and they'd jump in the car—they were like a couple of teenagers." Sometimes a limousine would pull up to a floodlit location shoot late at night and, Haley says, "she would step out of the car in an evening gown, because she had just been at some event but what she really wanted to do was watch Mike work. It was like a separate romantic movie was happening right next to the one we were making."

The two seemed to enhance each other's celebrity merely by the pleasure they took in visiting each other's worlds. When Sawyer arrived, even the actors in *Working Girl* would find themselves angling for a glimpse of, or an introduction to, the star in their midst. And while she knew how to put people at ease and did so quickly, he was tickled by how abashed they were. "With Diane, he became a lot happier, but also a lot more regal and more intimidating," says Matthew Broderick. "They'd walk toward the table and you'd think, *Oh my God!* But both of them were very good at getting you over that."

Their engagement dinner was at the Rainbow Room. "I stood up to make the toast," says Lorne Michaels, "and there was Jacqueline Onassis and the Aga Khan and Oscar and Annette [de la Renta] . . . What struck me most was how easily Mike could go from rehearsals with actors who were living in, metaphorically, cold-water flats to *that*. And he didn't feel out of place in either world."

When the time came, Nichols and Sawyer were able to keep the press away. On April 29, 1988, soon after *Working Girl* wrapped, they married in a small ceremony on Martha's Vineyard, where they would soon buy Chip Chop, an estate once owned by the actress Katharine Cornell. They invited Carly Simon and her then husband, Jim Hart, and Rose and William Styron to renew their own vows at the same time. "Diane made wreaths of big white flowers for our hair," said Rose Styron. "We all looked gorgeous, and then we went back to Carly's house and had a beautiful reception."

"We had this thing where we each brought a poem, and my husband didn't cry, in fact he was laughing a lot of the time," Sawyer said.

"I was laughing because he was so funny, and the minister sobbed. Everybody [was] looking at him because the rest of us [were] perfectly merry the whole time."

For Nichols, their wedding was, he said, the moment when "my ultimate happiness began." For Sawyer, it was a realization of the Christina Rossetti line "The birthday of my life is come." If things had been different, she said, "I would have had children earlier . . . But Mike already had three children with two other women, and he was fifty-eight when we married. And I chose him."

Twenty-seven

STILL HERE

1988–1990

I'm genuinely happy, probably for the first time," Nichols told his therapist. "I love my wife. I love my life. I love my kids—they're turning out to be great people. I love my work. Why am I still so pissed off? Why hasn't that gone away?"

"It can't," his therapist replied. "That's who you are."

Nichols didn't argue. As he settled into a luxurious and largely happy late middle age, he was in some ways a changed man: On a set or in a rehearsal room, he had learned how to prevent his impatience from flaring into snappishness or disdain, and he had gotten better at controlling his temper—at least most of the time. But the motive that lay just beneath his poise—an almost punitive need to prove his detractors wrong—was nothing that falling in love was going to vanquish, and, despite his complaining, it was an element of his personality he thought might now protect him from complacency at a moment when the temptation to coast was stronger than it had ever been.

As much as he wanted to keep pushing himself, Nichols was also determined to find a new kind of balance in his life, something about which he hadn't cared much before his breakdown. Soon after his recovery, he surprised many who knew him when he reconnected with two colleagues he had barely seen since the mid-1950s—his Chicago mentor Paul Sills and his Strasberg classmate George Morrison—and announced the creation of the New Actors Workshop, a two-year instructional program in New York City. The curriculum would be half improvisation technique taught by Sills and half a version of the Method taught by Morrison; Nichols would lead a scene-study class once a week for four hours in the evening. During the school's first year, he conducted the sessions in the rented community room of a Greek Orthodox church.

"We would pick and rehearse scenes on our own," says director Diane Paulus, an acting student in the workshop's inaugural class. "It was about thirty people, and six or eight would present a scene every week—Shakespeare, Chekhov, Neil Simon. Mike didn't have the text in front of him. Sometimes he would make you do it again, but rarely. Mostly he would just sit and talk: 'What is the event of this scene? What's the story? What happens, and *then* what happens?' Sometimes he'd say, 'What's the secret cause?' 'The scene is a ball of yarn, and if you pull, eventually you'll get to the secret at the center.' And just as often, he would use analogy: 'What is this *like*?' Then he'd have you fill it in, or he would."

"It was unlike any scene-study class I've ever been in," says another early student, Laura Pierce. "It wasn't a teacher critiquing for twenty minutes, or saying, 'Work on this aspect and then bring it back.' It was so much about his storytelling, but always stories that would illustrate some aspect of the work."

The sessions could turn surprisingly personal. "In the process of going deeper into the scene, he would share everything about his life, his history, and the way he thought about directing in drama," Paulus recalls. "He would say, 'What's the dead whale?' Meaning, what's the thing under this scene that's stinking up the whole room that no one is talking about? Sometimes Diane Sawyer would come and watch the class. And when he couldn't be there because he was making a movie, he would bring in Meryl Streep or David Mamet. He was idealistic about it—he didn't think of the school as being about professional training, but about pure teaching and learning."

Many people assumed his involvement was a temporary fancy, but New Actors Workshop survived for twenty-two years, and he stayed connected to the school for most of its existence. For him, the program was a refuge from the spotlight: He made it clear to his ambitious, sometimes starstruck students that they shouldn't view their work with him as a de facto audition, and he discouraged publicity about his involvement until the school had been up and running for several years.

Nichols began teaching at a moment when the pleasurable, sequestered intimacy of directing actors in a rehearsal room had become a rarity for him. As he started work on *Waiting for Godot*, he felt almost menaced by the amount of scrutiny he was receiving. There is no question that Nichols enjoyed virtually everything his celebrity entailed, but his position in theater was now a kind of booby trap: For everyone who believed that a new Mike Nichols production was by definition an event, there were others who insisted it was *only* an event—a self-consciously glittery collection of A-list players who had been calculatedly assembled by a publicity-savvy director without any thought given to whether they were suited to the task at hand. Nichols's *Godot*, which would play for just eight weeks in the 291-seat Mitzi E. Newhouse Theater at Lincoln Center, was the fall's toughest ticket, but some asked if it would be anything more than an excuse to gawp at movie people lured by a master of the middlebrow, all of them looking to purchase legitimacy at the expense of a modern classic.

Both Steve Martin and Robin Williams were more than experienced enough to understand that their involvement was viewed with as much resentment as anticipation. Bernard Gersten, the executive producer of Lincoln Center Theater, explained to Nichols and his stars that more than half of the theater's thirty-six thousand subscribers would be locked out of *Godot* unless they moved the play to a larger house. Nichols was not averse to a Broadway run, but his leading men resisted, particularly Martin, who argued that Broadway would inflate the production into something other than the low-key enterprise he still imagined it could be. "He thought it would have made too big a deal of it," says his costar Bill Irwin, "but of course, the difficulty was that it was a big deal already and the impossibility of getting tickets made it a bigger one."

The backlash was intense. Lincoln Center was then viewed as the closest thing New York had to a national theater, and, especially given the stream of famous names that would doubtless be in attendance each night, the production started to be perceived as an anti-populist capitulation to celebrity culture. Gersten admitted that he "gritted [his] teeth" at the decision to keep the play in a small house and said that hundreds of subscribers had complained. "Is [this] any way to run a theater?" one newspaper demanded.

"Anxiety was very high," says Irwin. "It's a very difficult play. I don't know that you ever get it all in a production—you're lucky if you get part of it. And I'm not sure Mike knew quite what he was getting into." Nichols saw his work on *Godot* as exploratory, but he was also looking for a one-size-fits-all explanation about the need for human connection that could encapsulate Beckett's intention in a single aphorism. He often said that he couldn't direct anything until he found its central metaphor. He never found *Godot*'s, and, late in the process, he realized he never would: "You can do anything with this play," he said.

Rather than struggle endlessly over the text, he focused on the performances. The styles of his four actors—Williams's manic verbosity, Martin's absurdist drollery, Irwin's matchless physical skill, and F. Murray Abraham's ear for classical declamation—all needed to be brought into harmony with Beckett's austere, idiosyncratically colloquial universe. Nichols wanted to create a spirit of democracy in the room and to banish any sense that Irwin and Abraham were there only to serve the stars. At one point, when Martin and Williams had been dominating the table, he abruptly said, "Let's change parts," and had Irwin read Martin's role and Abraham read Williams's. He let the scene play for some time before saying, "Okay, that's enough." Martin nodded and said, "I learned a lot" from reading Lucky. Nichols replied, "It's not so easy, is it?"

Both leading men were at similar turning points; they had made the jump from stand-up to television, from television to movies, and from overt comedy to more offbeat projects. Williams had recently received his first Oscar nomination, for *Good Morning, Vietnam,* and Nichols had offered Martin notes on his screenplay for the *Cyrano* update *Roxanne.* But their styles could not have been more dissimilar. Williams had annotated his script line by line with questions about meaning and instructions to himself, but he was still the free-associative wild man who, with Nichols's permission, would use a two-word stage direction from Beckett—"General outcry"—to riff on whatever flew into his mind, including the Oscars. Martin was drier, quieter, more intellectual and subdued.

"Steve and Robin never quite found the same wavelength," says Irwin. "One moment I remember—and this was part of the joy of being in that room, even though the joy was fraught—was that Mike said, 'Does anybody know anything about . . .' and he named some breed of dog that his kids wanted. And Robin became a spaniel for a minute or two. Nothing delighted Mike more than watching Robin go. His eyes were just so alive watching him. And Steve waited until Robin had done everything he wanted to do, and then said, 'They're great dogs, but don't ever give one a loaded gun.' Those were the two wavelengths they were on."

"Mike had such a strong sense of himself," says David Hyde Pierce, who understudied Irwin. "In rehearsal, Robin would go off on some long rant, and then rein it back in. And Mike would allow it—he wouldn't wrangle Robin or say, 'Okay, let's get back to work,' because he knew that eventually the gravitas of the play, and his own incredible gravitational pull, would win out. And he had true respect for the material." When that meant pulling the actors back, he didn't hesitate. "When we were rehearsing," Martin says, "we did a scene, and Mike took a handkerchief and dabbed tears from his eyes, and said, 'It's so beautiful.' And then he paused and said, 'I wonder, though, if we want to be *this* beautiful at exactly *this* moment.'"

When *Godot* opened, many of the reviews were admiring. "The only real mistake that can be made in staging *Godot* is to make it too overtly or poetically pessimistic," wrote Clive Barnes in the *New York Post*. "It is a mistake that Nichols never makes." In the *Chicago Sun-Times*, Hedy Weiss noted that Williams's improvisatory effusions, which included a snatch of the *Twilight Zone* theme that riffed on Vladimir's nickname ("Didi . . . Didi . . . Dididi, didididi"), came only at points in the text at which Beckett had left room for nonspecific clowning, and argued that the cast was "entirely faithful to Beckett's spirit . . . What shines through most clearly in Nichols's production is the notion that we're all actors—continually trying out some little jig or song, some hat trick or comic routine, to help us slog through the muck of life." And in *Newsweek*, Jack Kroll quoted Beckett, who himself had Americanized one joke for the production, as saying, "All my plays should be played light and fast. I don't want to dwell upon their seriousness."

But others were outraged. John Simon bemoaned "the tragedy of a

[play] turned into shtick." And in *Time,* William Henry called the comic interjections "inexcusable" and labeled Williams "the chief sinner," complaining that he "enacts the audience's presumed boredom at having to think." Almost every review had something snide to say about the circumstances of the production—its hype, its stunt casting, its limited seating. And the only verdict that really counted—Frank Rich's in *The New York Times*—was sternly admonitory: The blasted desertscape set was too Sam Shepard–like, the jokes too referential, the pacing too fast to leave any room for existential despair. "The naked realism of *Godot* . . . does not suit a director whose gift is for comedy strongly rooted in contemporary social detail," he wrote. Rich had praise for Abraham and Irwin, saying that while they were onstage, "one feels privileged to be at this *Godot.* But those denied that privilege should not feel that the loss is a tragedy."

"Before the show opened, during previews, everybody ate us up," said Martin. "Cheers, bravos, the whole bit. Then as soon as the reviews came out, the audience started sitting there without reacting—no laughter, nothing. It was chilling. I thought I had had every kind of experience on stage, but this was sheer torture."

Nichols was not surprised by the audience's response. He had been directing long enough to know that theatergoers wanted their choice to purchase a ticket to be ratified by a rave in the paper of record; if they were told they had placed their bet on the wrong show, their collective mood could become sour and withholding. Overnight, Nichols's *Godot* became a production it was chic not to like and vulgar to be seen enjoying. Lewis Allen and Jay Presson Allen walked out at intermission. Stung, Nichols sent a messenger to their home the next day with a letter saying, "Dear Jay: Thanks so much for coming. It got even better in the second act."

"We were shell-shocked when we were finished," said Williams. "Very strange sensation . . . we put our ass out and got kicked for it."

Nichols shook off his disappointment quickly; he was, that year, in too positive a frame of mind for another downward spiral. *Godot* closed on November 27, just two weeks before *Working Girl* was to open, and Nichols was feeling sanguine about the movie. His first cut had run well over two hours, and, according to Douglas Wick, "it didn't work. There was just enough time at the beginning and especially at the end of every scene for you to pull back—to say, 'Does this really make sense? Would it happen like this? Would this person really burst through the door?' We couldn't have that extra reality intruding. *Working Girl* is a confection. Sam O'Steen called it a puck sliding over thin ice: As long as it was in motion, it was fine, but if it gave you time to think too much about any detail, that was trouble." Nichols and O'Steen went back into the editing room, cut more than twenty minutes, and added Carly Simon's anthemic "Let the River Run," with its churchlike chorus and hosanna to Wall Street as "the new Jerusalem."

In some ways, the film became something simpler and blunter than Nichols had intended when he agreed to direct it. The bemused detachment that he had wanted the final shot of Tess in her office to convey was legible only to him; for its largely delighted audience, *Working Girl* played as an unironic celebration of upward mobility. There were those who saw the movie's giddy embrace of the raise, the promotion, the jump up the ladder as a betrayal of the working class, of feminism, and of the counterculture ethos that they believed Nichols had once represented. It was as if he had taken the moment from *The Graduate* when a well-wisher says to Benjamin, "Plastics," and decided that it was good advice rather than a punch line about bankrupt values. In *The New York Times*, a Vassar professor deplored what she saw as the film's Reaganite ideology and argued that its sometimes cruel depiction of a female boss as wicked stepmother constituted "an attack on a woman holding power of her own."

"As Nichols & Co. see the world, it is working-class drone or corporate yuppie," Linda Winer wrote in *Newsday*. "What is impossible to ignore . . . is the wholesale acceptance—the simpleminded celebration—of yuppiehood as the Cinderella dream of today. Tess operates in a Wall Street that never heard about indictments for insider trading, or ethical questions about the desirability of gross materialism and an office with a view."

But Winer also wrote that "a lot of people say I should lighten up about *Working Girl*," and that attitude was reflected in the mostly excellent reviews it received, including from many of the men who had loathed *Heartburn*. Ebert gave the film four stars and called it Nichols's best work since *The Graduate*, and *Time*'s Richard Corliss argued that it was both "a fond anthology of old Hollywood's romantic comedies" and "as modern as the 21st century challenge that faces America—how will the working class be educated to survive and thrive in the computer age?" Women cast a sharper eye over the film—columnist Ellen Goodman called it "post-feminist . . . a story of the era when just enough women have moved up the ladder to shatter the dream of sexual solidarity." And Janet Maslin called it "enjoyable" but also "surprisingly primitive," conceding that the movie, "like its heroine, has a genius for getting by on pure charm."

Working Girl arrived at the last moment before the beginning of the American indie revolution; a month later, Steven Soderbergh's *sex, lies, and videotape* would debut at the U.S. Film Festival (the forerunner of Sundance) and launch the era in which Harvey and Bob Weinstein's company, Miramax, would reshape the Oscars. But for one last time, the studios had the playing field to themselves, and 20th Century Fox mounted a large-scale campaign for the film. Nichols intended *Working Girl* to be both an awards player and a blockbuster, and when he started to sense that the picture wasn't breaking through—it opened in fourth place and never ranked any higher—he worked himself into a rare volcanic fury. "The only time Mike ever really got angry with me, and it was scary anger, was over the marketing of *Working Girl*," says Barry Diller. "He was really tough, saying that I was not supporting the movie, and I was trying to mollify him and explain that we were. He was mad for about six months."

"It wasn't easy," says Wick. "We never got a great poster with all three people on it, Melanie wasn't particularly well known, and she looked weird to the audience in her makeup and costumes. We never found our *Pretty Woman* campaign." And any case that could be made to Academy voters that the movie was actually a critique of Wall Street values disintegrated when George Bush chose the film as the first to be screened at the White House after his inauguration. (He warned his guests that it had some "dirty parts.")

Working Girl was a solid success—it grossed $64 million in the United States, more than double its budget—"but it didn't catch a wave," says Wick. The Oscar campaign did, and resulted in nominations for Best Picture, Best Actress for Griffith, and Best Supporting Actress for both Weaver and Cusack; it also brought Nichols his fourth nomination for directing. But by then, he knew the film would be an also-ran. On Oscar night he lost to *Rain Man*'s Barry Levinson, and *Working Girl* took just one statuette, for Carly Simon's song.

During awards season, Sawyer was in the headlines more than Nichols; ABC had just poached her from *60 Minutes* by signing her to co-anchor its upcoming newsmagazine *Primetime Live,* which was intended as a younger, less staid alternative to CBS's ticking-clock approach. Among its innovations was the idea that Sawyer and Sam Donaldson would appear in front of a studio audience every week (a notion that was dropped a few months into the show's run). Nichols and Sawyer generally stayed out of each other's professional lives, but doing her job in front of a couple hundred people was new to her, and as the August 1989 premiere date neared, he stepped in to help, asking Swoosie Kurtz if she would volunteer to be interviewed by Sawyer in front of a rehearsal audience. "I spent a long evening at ABC," says Kurtz, "and I watched him sort of direct her—he gave her notes afterward, but in the most loving way."

Primetime Live was based in New York, and its first three months on air would mark Nichols and Sawyer's first extended separation; he would be shooting his next movie, *Postcards from the Edge*, almost entirely in Los Angeles. As he had done with *Heartburn*, Nichols was adapting the work of a woman who had chosen to process a recent and still raw trauma in a comic novel, and again he was playing with the work's well-publicized guessing-game elements. Most readers of Carrie Fisher's book assumed that the brief scenes exploring Suzanne Vale's tug-of-war with her mother, Doris, an old-Hollywood actress who isn't ready to cede the spotlight, were virtual transcripts of Fisher's interactions with her mother, Debbie Reynolds, and that the long section set in rehab was basically a diary entry from an actress who had been disarmingly candid about her struggles with addiction.

By Fisher's own admission, *Postcards* offered its readers "no plot . . . I'm not a big plotter." She had sent the novel to Nichols to see if it could be turned into a solo performance piece for her. He told her he saw it as a movie—but only if she could rework it. Fisher said she "[threw] the book into the backyard and [set] fire to it" in order to write the screenplay. As she sat in his office and talked through scenes, writing them out on legal pads on the spot, Nichols helped Fisher find the spine of a storyline. "Write more scenes with the mother," he would instruct her after every draft. Finally, she produced a version that downplayed Suzanne's stream-of-consciousness rehab wisecracks in favor of a mother-daughter seriocomedy. Dawn Steel, the president of Columbia Pictures, saw it as a chance to get Shirley MacLaine back in *Terms of Endearment* mode and green-lit the movie.

Publicly, Fisher dismissed talk that her work was autobiographical. "It's easier for them to think I have no imagination for language, just a tape recorder with endless batteries," she said. Nichols backed her up, claiming that "Carrie doesn't draw on her life any more than Flaubert did—it's just that his life wasn't so well known." But everyone involved in the movie knew that the latest chapter of a complex and painful dynamic was being played out both in the script and behind the scenes. When the artist Norman Sunshine, who had been commissioned to create a poster, arrived at the Four Seasons in Beverly Hills for a meeting, he recalls, "there was Mike, there was Meryl Streep, there was Ann Roth, and there was Carrie Fisher on the floor, quite stoned and telling us these terrible personal things about Debbie Reynolds, about her wigs and this and that. I was embarrassed."

Reynolds herself may have been slightly mortified by her fictional doppelgänger, but she was far more disappointed that she hadn't been asked to costar in the movie. "She was mad that Shirley was playing her!" says Streep. "She wanted to have that part, you know? That just tickled Carrie to death. They were close, and she didn't want to hurt her mother's feelings. But at the same time, she really had fun with the whole thing."

Nichols wasn't interested in casting Reynolds any more than he wanted Fisher to play Suzanne. The parental psychodrama was the hook for audiences, but initially he was just as interested in telling a story of addiction and the fragility of recovery. If his own experience with Halcion had been the impetus for his involvement, his struggles with Melanie Griffith during *Working Girl* had become just as central to his vision of what *Postcards* should be. The film's pre-credit sequence takes place on a set on which Suzanne bungles her lines, then goes to her trailer to wake herself up for a retake by doing some coke. Nichols essentially added himself as a character—a fatherly but tough director who chews her out in front of crew members, saying, "You fuck up my movie, I'm gonna kill you . . . I don't care what you do to your body on your time, but this is *my* time, my movie. I don't intend to have some spoiled, selfish, coked-up little actress ruin my movie. Pull yourself together . . . or I'll kill you before you kill yourself." To play the role, he cast Gene Hackman, with whom he hadn't worked since firing him from *The Graduate,* and made sure to shape his scenes with care and generosity. Once production started, Nichols found himself facing the same situation again: Dennis Quaid, whom he had cast as Suzanne's boyfriend, had a serious cocaine problem of his own and went into rehab almost as soon as *Postcards* was finished; another actor had to redub some of his lines in postproduction.

Like most of Nichols's movies over the previous decade, *Postcards* was driven by women: Streep and MacLaine; von Brandenstein and Roth, who oversaw the production and costume design; Carly Simon, who was again hired to compose a score; and Fisher, who was present for daily on-the-spot rewrites. Nichols shot the film largely on a soundstage; he had not worked so extensively on a backlot since *The Fortune.* And despite Dawn Steel's enthusiasm, he had only $22 million to work with, even less than *Heartburn* or *Working Girl* had cost; his shift to telling women's stories had brought an end to the high budgets he had enjoyed during the 1960s and '70s.

Postcards was his third collaboration with Streep, and by that point they had developed such a relaxed shorthand that almost no performance adjustments needed to be made on the set. His relationship with MacLaine was more difficult; her comedy style was different, and her on-set talk about extraterrestrials irritated some of her colleagues.

For both actresses, musical numbers promised to be the film's biggest challenge. Streep would have to sing the Ray Charles song "You Don't Know Me," a choice that represented her character's uncertain first step into her own identity, and MacLaine's big number—Stephen Sondheim's famous showstopper for an older woman, "I'm Still Here"—was meant to sweep her daughter's choice aside. Her performance would have to demonstrate both the character's old-school talent and her inability to resist upstaging her own child. Sondheim not only agreed to give Nichols the song but wrote new lyrics that played off MacLaine's own image ("I'm feeling transcendental—am I here?").

After the first work session in New York, Nichols drafted Scott Frankel, the young pianist and composer who would go on to write the songs for the musical *Grey Gardens,* to work with both actresses. "He was interested in young talent," says Frankel, "and I checked enough boxes to warrant a lunch. Mike knew that youth was a currency and a way to stay central to the marketplace. He had been this unbelievable flavor when he was young. He never forgot the entrée and access that that gave him, and he decided to pay it forward and look for that energy in other people."

When production began, Nichols flew Frankel to Los Angeles to continue rehearsals. "Shirley and Meryl were competitive—Shirley was out of the studio system, and Meryl was the post–*Deer Hunter* generation, and there was a kind of natural wariness between the two of them," says Frankel. "First I went to Meryl, who was in a rented house in Brentwood. We sang her song and she turned beet red. I said, 'What's wrong?' She said, 'I'm so nervous to sing. It fills me with agita.' Then I drove to Shirley, who was very curious about Meryl: 'What does she sound like? What was working with her like? Was she nice to you? Is she gonna be good?'"

The sing-off would take place during a welcome-home party for Suzanne at her mother's house. "Carrie was there, and she was shy—I think the pain of that scene cut very close to the bone for her," Frankel says. "Mike wasn't a yeller or a screamer—he was cerebral in his approach, and he knew what to say to Carrie and Meryl and Shirley."

When Nichols thought MacLaine wasn't digging deep enough, he let her see his frustration—especially that day. "He rehearsed that scene over and over," says Mike Haley. "He really kind of beat the shit out of Shirley—she had choreography and she had to move around the room, and he kept her doing it until I almost said, 'Come on, you're killing her.'" But Nichols knew how much she could take. "She's a dancer," he said. "And she had the discipline and approach of a dancer." By the time they shot the scene, Nichols had gotten her to the exact pitch of weariness, iron determination, and hunger for applause that the number required. "He knew just how to get what he needed from both of them," Haley says.

The shoot was not an entirely happy experience for Nichols. For the first time, he felt at the mercy of budget restrictions, particularly for a dream sequence in which Streep was supposed to glide along a highly reflective floor toward a cabinet of glowing pills. "The studio kept taking inadequate measures to give us what we wanted, until I was literally on my hands and knees trying to polish the floor," says von Brandenstein. "Mike wasn't used to not being given what he felt he needed to make the movie his way, and it left a bad taste."

In January 1990, two months after Nichols finished *Postcards*, the film lost its most important champion when Dawn Steel quit her job and left Columbia, saying, "I feel like I've been let out of a cage." Steel had been the only woman running a studio; her replacements were Peter Guber and Jon Peters, two brash Hollywood operators whose sensibilities had nothing in common with Nichols's. *Postcards* was not due to open until September, but Nichols knew how easily an unluckily timed regime change could orphan a movie; there was nothing to do but wait.

Nichols spent the spring directing a new Jules Feiffer play that he called "a direct outgrowth of what Elaine May and I worked on and of what *Carnal Knowledge* was for Jules and me." *Elliot Loves* was pure Feiffer—it begins with a monologue, by a divorced man nearing forty, about the history of his troubled relationships with women and then moves into a scene in which he takes his new girlfriend to meet his high school buddies; when they fight and she walks out, the evening devolves into a long, ugly look at how men talk about women when they're not around.

When he first read the play, in 1987, Nichols had loved its savagery: "It's about women trying to do the many contradictory things that are asked of them, and men's fears of women who can't handle things and their greater fears of women who can," he said. But three years later, his life had changed, and so had his relationship to the work. *Elliot Loves* would try out in Chicago and then move to New York's Promenade Theater, the same path that Nichols had taken with *Hurlyburly,* but without the movie stars or the misogyny that had defined that production. He assembled a cast of actors with whom he had recently worked, among them Christine Baranski, David Hyde Pierce, and Oliver Platt (who had a small role in *Working Girl*), and surprised himself by bringing a gentleness to the material that might not have reflected his first impulse to tackle it. "It's a play about misogyny," says Peter Lawrence, his stage manager. "But after he read it, he fell in love with Diane Sawyer, and he somehow made it into a play about a man who has very close male friends who finds a woman that he loves and crosses over into the world of women."

"I think Mike related to the play on a personal level," says Platt. "And the sway that he held over the cast—his ability to share that vision, which he often did by stopping and telling a story rather than by saying 'Go there' or 'Do that,' was remarkable, because invariably, the stories illuminated something in the play."

"What I noticed in that production was the way Mike would say, 'It's just us here. It's just us talking,'" says Pierce. "The idea that when you're acting, you don't have to put anything on, because the reality that you bring to your work is sufficient—I mean, I'd been in enough scene-study classes where people are just themselves, and you want to hang yourself because it's so boring. But Mike, if he was happy with who he picked, was able to say to an actor, 'You are enough.' That felt like a great gift."

If the tone of *Elliot Loves* changed from page to production, it happened with Feiffer's endorsement. "There was a lot of Nichols and May in what I was writing," he says. "It was on a darker level, but I could not have conceived it without their precedent. I found Mike's work deeply moving and pertinent and solid and wonderful, and preview audiences were rapturous. My friend John Guare was about to have a play called *Six Degrees of Separation* open at Lincoln Center, a few blocks away, and I thought, *Oh, poor John. Those fuckers aren't going to allow two successful plays to open at the same time. I'm gonna get the reviews and he's not.* And the rest is history." *Elliot Loves* was brutally dismissed by most critics, who called it twenty years out of date. "The problem is that Elliot's buddies have come in from . . . another generation altogether," said one review. "Their woman-hating sensibilities are stuck in an older, simpler, less sneaky style of misogyny than today's."

"You can imagine what a heavy opening night it was," says Platt. "I mean, everyone shows up for a Mike Nichols opening night. I was sandwiched between Elaine May and . . . name the legend, and suddenly there was Mike holding an advance copy of the [*Times*] review. He was very upset. The party was suddenly tangibly thinner. He tried to rally. He said all the right things. But he knew what it meant."

Feiffer was profoundly demoralized and told Nichols he had had his fill of theater and was through being a "pro bono playwright . . . Whatever I do that I think is good, they're gonna kill." ("It took me ten years to get over it," he would later write. "Actually, I got past it, not over it.") *Elliot Loves* closed a few weeks later, losing its entire $600,000 investment. Nichols had hoped he was directing a hit that would move to Broadway in the fall, just as *Postcards* was opening; instead he was responsible for what was then the costliest non-musical failure in off-Broadway history. And though he had endured worse reviews, the language of these felt like a warning: *Dated. Fusty. Out of touch.*

While he was working on the play, Nichols was, for the first time, honored with a retrospective of his film work, by New York's Museum of the Moving Image. That, too, was disorienting. He didn't feel ready.

At fifty-eight, he still had fewer than a dozen films on his résumé. As he watched audiences sigh over clips of *Who's Afraid of Virginia Woolf?* and *The Graduate*, he could only see them as "artifacts." He wasn't sure whether he was being enshrined in the pantheon, consigned to the dust heap, or both.

Twenty-eight

IT NEVER GOES AWAY

1990–1993

As the 1990s began, Nichols's place in the rapidly changing movie business felt shaky to him. Studio culture had become indistinguishable from money culture. Grosses were reported in newspapers and announced every Monday on *Entertainment Tonight*, and budgets, paychecks, and first-weekend numbers were tracked avidly by the mainstream press as indices of ever-shifting currency and clout, benchmarks that could move an actor or filmmaker up or down on an annual power list. Just two years earlier, the $5 million that Bruce Willis received for *Die Hard* had been labeled an outrageous example of salary inflation. Now, the announcement of a $5 million deal meant only that someone hadn't earned a spot in the ranks of stars who were getting $10 million or $15 million. And salaries for directors were soaring as well; filmmakers who had proven their drawing power now stood to reap windfalls as if they were lottery winners.

Nichols wasn't in that mix. *Working Girl* had gotten him close, but not close enough. Making money mattered to him not just as a practical need—although he had largely stepped back from the Arabian-horse world, he still spent profligately—but as a yardstick of respect and as proof of his centrality. For much of the next decade, he would chase success, sometimes with projects that were close to his heart, sometimes not.

In the spring of 1990, he faced a choice between two movies that represented as clear a fork in the road as he had yet confronted. One was *The Remains of the Day*. Harold Pinter had bought the rights to Kazuo Ishiguro's Booker Prize–winning novel about the relationship between a loyal butler and a strong-minded housekeeper in the mansion of a British fascist sympathizer in the years before World War II and was writing the screenplay. Nichols's first thought, just as it had been with *The Real Thing* and *Betrayal,* was that the film could serve to reunite Meryl Streep and Jeremy Irons—although a literary period piece about suppressed emotions was unlikely to command a budget that could accommodate star salaries. The other film was *Regarding Henry*, a comedy-drama by a twenty-three-year-old Sarah Lawrence grad named J. J. Abrams (then writing as Jeffrey Abrams) about a driven, callous lawyer who gets shot in the head and, to the surprise of his family and co-workers, has all of his negative traits wiped clean and is reborn as a kinder, gentler man.

Nichols said yes to both movies—but he said yes to *Regarding Henry* first, and fast. He was still worried about how *Postcards from the Edge* would be handled by Columbia, and wanted a new film in production before the verdict was in. *The Remains of the Day* would take time, craftsmanship, and the coordination of schedules; *Regarding Henry* would be so much easier.

In some ways, Abrams's screenplay dovetailed with Nichols's sense of himself as a man who had been granted a second (or fourth) chance by the cosmos; he frequently discussed his marriage to Sawyer as a bolt from the blue that allowed him to reform himself. To him, *Regarding Henry* read as the literalization of a guilty man's do-over fantasy, but it wasn't a passion project so much as an act of pragmatic calculation. The film had a male protagonist (to be played by Harrison Ford), which would help show the industry that Nichols had not become a niche director, it could shoot in New York, and he could start right away, although that would mean skipping the time he usually spent developing a script in order to make a film his own.

At the time, Nichols spoke of *Regarding Henry* as "a personal tale of redemption." "Certainly in my life," he said, "there's a crisis . . . and then a simplification in starting what appears to be your real life. Something similar happened to me, and I think happens to many people." But in fact, "there was no Mike in it at all," says Scott Rudin, who produced the film. "I mean, he loved Harrison and thought he could be a brilliant light comedian like Clark Gable. And I was thrilled, because I had just gone to Paramount, and five minutes later I was able to bring them a movie with Harrison and Mike."

Nichols had second thoughts almost as soon as he signed his deal. "We all loved J.J.," he said. "[But] at some point, Harrison said, 'Are we making a terrible mistake?' I said, 'I don't know! It's too late!'" Without time to dig into the screenplay—to ask the questions about meaning and intention that were central to his work and that he always pushed his acting students to consider—he latched on to what interested him most: the step-by-step anguish of recovery from a traumatic brain injury. "We met a guy to whom this had happened, and he was extraordinary, and we tried to stay with the reality of it," he said. "But what I think we didn't realize was, never mind that it's real, it seems like a soap opera concept, doesn't it? Too sentimental, even though it happens all the time."

"At that point in our relationship, I was afraid of Mike," Rudin recalls. "I didn't know him well enough to know how much I could say. The script had one wonderful, joyous scene in which Henry, after his injury, goes to his daughter's private school and gets all these kids playing tag. In the first minute of the first meeting, Mike says, 'Well, of course the tag scene has to go.' I thought, *What am I supposed to say? He's completely wrong!* It was the moment when he revealed he was not the right person to do the movie, and I just had no idea how to say it."

Nonetheless, Nichols started *Regarding Henry* in good spirits. The new Columbia regime had not, it turned out, mistreated *Postcards from the Edge,* but had shrewdly picked a quiet weekend in mid-September to launch the film. *Postcards* opened the day *Regarding Henry* began production; it received reasonably good reviews from a critical corps that was weary of summer action films dominated by men, and, despite playing in just a thousand theaters, it finished the weekend in first place.

The movie became no more than a modest success, but for Nichols, the pressure was off. He was on to a new film, and if he was uncertain about the script, he was happy with his actors. As Ford's wife, he cast Annette Bening, a rising star whom he had chased for the female lead in *Elliot Loves* and had given one quick scene in *Postcards.* Nichols told a self-deprecating story about how many great actors he had fired, from Gene Hackman to Robert De Niro. Ford listened and said, "Have you ever fired any really mediocre ones?"

"I remember being nervous, but I also remember Harrison and Mike saying how nervous *they* were," says Bening. "That made a big impression. I thought, *Oh, I get it. It never goes away. It doesn't stop just because you're an experienced person.*"

During production, Nichols concentrated almost entirely on the performances. With Kamian "Mikki" Allen, the eleven-year-old who played Henry's daughter, he was curious, playful, and solicitous—"he was very good about making sure the set felt homey," she says, "and the first time I saw myself onscreen, he was there with me and held my hand." And with Bill Nunn, who played Henry's rehab therapist, he was both encouraging and forceful. "He helped me tremendously," Nunn said. "I was being too sympathetic to Henry, and Mike told me, 'You gotta kick some butt.' That one sentence changed everything."

"I know he was invested in it emotionally," says the writer-director Rebecca Miller, who was cast in a small role. (Nichols knew her as the daughter of his friends Arthur Miller and Inge Morath.) "I saw him crying in front of the monitors a couple of times, which surprised me, because, really, it was sort of soggy. In some ways, it was a vulnerable moment for him. It was a time when all these masters of the 1960s and '70s—Alan Pakula was another—made sort of lost movies where they were trying to guess what the audience wanted and thinking, *Who am I and how do I still fit in?* With *Regarding Henry,* I don't know what he was after, and I'm not sure he did, but he was hardly the only giant to have an identity crisis around that period."

Nichols knew *Regarding Henry* was pulling its punches—gesturing toward the comic possibilities of a sudden personality transplant, toward the inspirational notion of rebirth, toward the emotionalism of a family melodrama, and toward the terror of a life-altering medical crisis without committing to any one tonal approach. Having forgone the immersion that was usually part of his process, he essentially treated the film as a day job—one more item on a calendar dotted with dinners and fundraisers and charity auctions not unlike those attended by the film's well-heeled characters. For the first time, he cut corners: The weeks of rehearsal he had long believed to be vital were, on *Regarding Henry,* compressed into a couple of days, and he paid little attention to the cinematography; the film has the flat, bland lighting and framing of a typical early-1990s television drama.

When he did put his foot down, it was, somewhat surprisingly, about food. The merging of the film with his own Upper East Side lifestyle reached an absurd apotheosis in a scene in which partygoers attend a formal soiree in a grand town house. "Oh my God, the caviar story," says Robert Greenhut. "It was so decadent it was embarrassing. Mike got a little crazy. There were extras standing around in formal clothes, and we had big bowls of cheap caviar that was supposed to look like beluga."

Nichols dipped a spoon into a dish, had a taste, and stopped the production cold. "We can't do this," he said. "This is disgusting. It's not fair to make the cast eat all this sub-caviar caviar . . . And we can't do this unless we have the right caviar, because if we don't, then . . . who are these people? How wealthy can they even be?"

"This is all an artifice," Nichols explained. "That's all movies are. This room is not really where these people live. They didn't choose these chairs or pick out these clothes. So if we start saying, 'These other things will do just fine'—if we undermine the production designer who says, 'It should be *these* dishes,' if we decide that no one will notice—the whole thing comes crashing down." Extras waited for hours while a producer was dispatched to buy several thousand dollars' worth of New York's best caviar before shooting could resume. At the end of the day, Nichols walked into the room where dailies were running, scooped up an untouched bowl, and took it home.

Partway through filming, the threat of a technicians' strike upended production, and *Regarding Henry* had to relocate to the Paramount lot in Los Angeles, where sets were re-created. Nichols was not happy to leave New York, or Sawyer. Her work took her out on the road frequently—"Do you hate that I travel so much, or would you like more time alone?" she once asked him, to which he replied, "Both." Before they married, he resolved that he would never try to put any fetters on her career, and that he, for once, would be the one willing to wait at home, eager to greet his spouse after her time away. More than that, he wanted them to *have* a home; two years into their marriage, they were still living in a gorgeous but small suite of rooms atop the Carlyle. She was happy there, but Nichols had been urging them to buy a real apartment, and she was coming around. "He's almost gotten me to yearn for a nest," she admitted. "Although I fall asleep in the swatches part." Having to leave for Hollywood was a disruption he resented.

What was supposed to be an easy shoot became a harder one, and Nichols's temper got the worst of him; it turned out there was no such thing as a magical banishment of old personality traits after all. During one morning of filming, he discovered that the set of a penthouse with a sweeping terrace included gaps that would limit the angles from which he could shoot the next day's scenes.

"We had saved a fortune by doing it that way, and I think I even got his approval," says Tony Walton. "But he'd forgotten, and he just had a meltdown. He said, 'There's no way we can do the scene. It's not possible to cheat it.' We tried to show him how it could work, and he wouldn't hear it. He was so pissed off. He said, 'What have you done? What have you done to *me*?'"

As it happened, that night Sawyer was flying out to visit Nichols. When she got there, he told her how angry he had gotten and what he had said to Walton, and, knowing how close the two men were, she said, "Why would you?" Nichols showed her the set to explain what he meant, and she gently said, "Come on. It looks fantastic. There must be a way." He knew she was right.

"Sometime after midnight, he phoned me," Walton says. "I was asleep and couldn't quite understand him, but it was clear he was sorry. By morning, things were all right again. I think she made him apologize."

One soundstage over from *Regarding Henry,* Kenneth Branagh was directing the romantic thriller *Dead Again,* in which he and his then wife, Emma Thompson, were costarring. Branagh and Thompson had arrived on the film scene a couple of years earlier, with his widely acclaimed version of *Henry V*; this would mark their first American movie. Nichols had met them a couple of times, but now he and Thompson struck up a deeper friendship, "a connection," she says, "that felt like one very long conversation that carried on for fifteen years. We connected completely. Sometimes that conversation was about the work we were doing together, but very often it was not. It was about our lives, and even when we weren't working together, we would see each other. I would go to the Vineyard, or he would come to England. He gave me away when I married Greg [Wise, in 2003]. That's what it was like—

a conversation neither of us ever had any interest in finishing." His bond with Thompson was the closest he had forged with an actress since he met Streep; within the year, it would end up reshaping the film that he intended to be his next project.

*R*egarding Henry opened in the summer of 1991, and its reviews amounted to a personal indictment. What had struck Nichols as a touching fable of self-reinvention played to others as mawkish and smug. "An unimaginably bad movie from none other than Mike Nichols, who appears to have lost his mind," wrote David Denby in *New York*. "Does the man who once directed *Who's Afraid of Virginia Woolf?* believe a word of this drivel?" said *Newsweek*. "If this is Hollywood's idea of a heartwarming, life-affirming spectacle, we should probably all go out and get ourselves shot in the head." *The New Yorker* proclaimed it "the worst-performed, limpest, least credible Nichols movie yet." And in *The Wall Street Journal*, Julie Salamon wrote, "I don't think Mr. Nichols believed in this story for an instant."

The collective reaction imparted jolting news to Nichols about exactly who they thought he was—a cynic and a pessimist who disdained warmth and sentiment. It was a notion of his personal and directorial aesthetic that had calcified sometime around *Carnal Knowledge* and had not been altered by the humanism of *Silkwood*, the gentle comedy of *Biloxi Blues*, or the savvy romanticism of *Working Girl*. There was a Nichols they liked and a Nichols they hated. The Nichols they liked was the acid anatomist of human behavior whose movies were extensions of his barbed, unsparing routines with Elaine May in which vanities and pretensions were laid bare almost prosecutorially. The Nichols they hated was a valorizer of the celebrated and well-to-do, a man who had become complacently attached to what *Rolling Stone* dismissed as "haute bourgeois marital dramedy" and unwilling to explore any personal sacrifice deeper than the one depicted in the movie—the trauma of downsizing from a sprawling suburban home to a large and well-appointed city apartment.

Nichols knew he had been too casual with the film, starting with his decision to make it. Next time, he would proceed with far more caution. *The Remains of the Day* was still in his sights, and, shortly before *Regarding Henry* opened, he set up a reading of Pinter's script in Los Angeles with Streep and Irons.

"The reading went really well," says Streep. "But at the time, I was very, very pregnant with my fourth child. I walked in, and Mike looked at me, and I could see that the light just went out of his eyes."

What happened next led to the only real rift between Nichols and Streep in thirty years. "Soon after," she says, "he started calling and saying, 'Are you sure you want to do this? Are *we* sure *we* want to do this?' I said, 'I think so! Did you not think the reading went well?' He said, 'Oh, yes, but do we really want to think about all these privileged people?' I was surprised, but I said, 'Okay, we don't have to do it if you don't want to.' It was very weird. I could tell he was trying to weasel his way out of it. And then I heard that he was going to go ahead and make it with Emma."

Nichols had always been reluctant to deliver bad news; in this case he told ICM's Sam Cohn, who represented both him and Streep, to handle it for him. But when the time came to tell Streep, Cohn was evasive. "He didn't tell me the truth," says Streep. "I guess he just didn't want to say, 'Mike doesn't want to do it with you because you're fat,' you know? Even though we would have started six months after I gave birth." Streep was hurt and angry. "I blamed Sam for something bad that Mike did," she says. "Mike [knew] what he did, but unfortunately Sam [bore] the scar." Nichols was deeply embarrassed, and livid at Cohn, who he believed had mishandled a delicate situation and damaged an important relationship.

Their falling-out over *The Remains of the Day* became public, and both Nichols and Streep would soon fire Cohn, leave ICM, and sign with CAA. Within a year or two, Streep had patched things up with Nichols (and with Cohn, although she did not return to him as a client). "Mike is someone I share an enormous amount of history with," she said at the time. "He has a big part of my heart. I was very upset to *be* upset."

Nichols never talked about the episode, but it left him less certain that he wanted to direct the movie. He stayed on for about six more months, toying with the idea of Emma Thompson and Irons, then bringing in Anthony Hopkins, with whom Thompson had just worked on the soon-to-open *Howards End,* instead. All of his public rationales for quitting the movie were contradictory: At one point, he said that Columbia wanted him to reduce the budget from $26 million to $12 million. At another, he claimed he was having trouble finding his way into the material, "because I'm not English . . . I have to learn more about it," an odd statement from someone who had worked enthusiastically with Pinter, Stoppard, and Trevor Griffiths. At still another, he said, "Harold wrote a very good script . . . but I couldn't work it out with my schedule because I had this other picture I was committed to." That much, at least, was true: Nichols had decided to direct, of all things, a werewolf movie.

At the beginning of 1992, he handed off *The Remains of the Day* to *Howards End*'s director, James Ivory. He stayed on as a co-producer with John Calley, and the film ended up receiving eight Oscar nominations, including one that he shared for Best Picture, though he was only minimally involved. "I didn't see much of Mike while we were making *Remains,*" Thompson says. "You couldn't have one eminent older American director in the room with another—that just would not have been a happy circumstance." Ivory shaped his delicate, subdued film at the same time that Nichols was developing his next attempt at a blockbuster. "We were turning Jack Nicholson into a wolf," he said, "while they were sorting the silverware."

Before he made *Wolf*, Nichols returned to the theater to direct his first Broadway play in six years. Right after the release of *Regarding Henry*, he flew to London to see *Death and the Maiden*, a melodrama set in an unnamed South American country a few years after the fall of a violent totalitarian regime and the restoration of democracy; the action begins when a man brings a stranger home to meet his wife, and she suspects that he is the sadistic physician who raped and abused her while the former government was in power. The playwright, Ariel Dorfman, had served as a cultural adviser to Salvador Allende and was forced to flee Chile at the start of the Pinochet years; he eventually settled in the United States, where he taught at Duke University. In London, his play was given a stark, bare-bones staging at the Royal Court Upstairs, a tiny, dark space that seated just sixty and maximized the sense of suffocating dread at the drama's core.

London critics treated *Death and the Maiden* as an urgent, conscience-pricking news bulletin from South America as well as a parable about guilt, revenge, and doubt. Nichols instantly made plans to bring the play to Broadway. "It didn't get off to a good start," Dorfman recalls. "I was suspicious of Mike—I guess I had just seen *Working Girl*, which felt like an homage to capitalism, and I was scared that he would try to tamp down such dark material. But I liked him, I thought he was brilliant, and he understood the play so well."

It did not occur to Nichols to look for Latino actors—the British production had not had any either. He cast Richard Dreyfuss as the husband and Gene Hackman as the accused guest, and petitioned Actors' Equity, the American theater union, to allow Juliet Stevenson, who had played the wife at the Royal Court, to reprise her role. When Equity ruled that she was insufficiently famous to merit an exception to its rule that American actors be cast in Broadway plays, he signed Glenn Close. By then the showdown over Stevenson had made the papers. "Glenny," said Nichols abjectly, "after I've been so insensitive in not coming to you first, will you consider taking the role?"

"Do you think I'm completely bananas?" she said. "It's a great part!"

"But will you ever forgive me?" he said.

"Well, Mike," she replied, laughing, "I don't know. You'll just have to wait and see!"

Before rehearsals began, "Richard and Gene and I were invited over to where Diane and Mike were living, and we had a beautiful meal and they served margaritas because it was supposed to be in South America, right?" says Close. "They were very strong margaritas, to the point where I had to concentrate on whether I could lift my fork to my mouth without making a total asshole of myself. Gene told me later that he was terrified through the whole meal—he thought Mike was going to fire him again! I mean, one of the greatest actors who will ever grace stage or screen . . . you know, we're fragile as actors, and you have to will yourself to stay fragile in order to do work that really resonates with people."

Hackman's trouble started with the first read-through—but it wasn't with Nichols. "Gene had a terrible time," says Tony Walton. "He was screwing up and seemed very troubled, and at the end he made a big apology and said, 'I know how distracting that can be. But not only am I dyslexic, I have no idea how to play this character. Am I guilty? Did I do all these things? Or am I innocent, as I protest I am?' He looked at Close. 'Is she wrong?' he asked. 'Or is she right?'

"Mike said, 'Well, since we have him here, I defer to our author.' And Dorfman said, 'That's the point of the play. We don't know.' And Gene said, 'Well, fuck that! I can't play *I don't know*. So as far as I'm concerned, he's guilty and that's the way I'm going to play it.'"

"It was so unfair to Gene," says Close. "You don't dick around—that's another word that Mike used a lot—with the question of torture. Even if you withhold the answer from the audience, not to help the actor was a cop-out. And in terms of my character, I never thought it was fair that you say this person has been tortured, and then keep the audience in the dark as to whether this person, who would have viscerally known his voice, was crazy or not."

The relationship between Nichols and Dorfman soon started to curdle. Dorfman was given to hyperbole when he was distressed. "Ariel used to say, 'Having car batteries attached to my genitalia wouldn't be as bad as working with Mike Nichols,'" says producer Fred Zollo. At one point, Nichols asked for an exchange to be shortened. "I just should have let him do it," Dorfman says. "But I had spent eighteen or twenty years fighting a dictatorship, fighting for every last word, fighting for the idea that the writer is central." Dorfman told him that every cut line of text was the equivalent of an assault on a character in the play. Nichols could not contain his contempt and started targeting him. During one rehearsal, Dorfman leaned on the back of Nichols's chair and said, "You know the writer who has inspired me the most?"

"No, who?" Nichols said.

"Shakespeare," Dorfman replied.

"Oh, Ariel," Nichols said, without looking up. "He's *awful*."

"The whole world wanted this play," says Dorfman, "and I didn't know how to handle it. Success on that scale, for someone as ambitious as I am, is very difficult. Mike would take me aside sometimes as if he were trying to teach me a lesson—'You should not believe any of this. Don't abuse the power that you now have.' He would say, 'Do you *really* need a chauffeur to take you to and from the airport?' I thought it was resentment, but now I think it may have been the good advice of a wise older brother." Eventually, both men had had their fill of each other. "Ariel," Nichols finally said, "why don't you just go back to North Carolina and let me make you very, very rich?" There are few combinations in the theater more toxic than a playwright convinced that a director is sabotaging his work and a director convinced that a playwright is sabotaging himself. Nichols finally issued an ultimatum. "He's in the theater or I'm in the theater, but we're not in the theater at the same time," he told Hal Luftig, another of the producers. "It fell on me to tell Ariel he was not welcome in rehearsals," says Luftig, "and it did not go well."

"Ariel was really making himself persona non grata," says Close. "But he had seen how it had been done in London—dark and fast—and it had worked. And the more we worked, the more problems started to become clear." Dorfman, it turned out, was right to be concerned. In a crucial miscalculation, Nichols had decided to replace the stripped-down London set with a large, semi-realistic representation of a Malibu-style beach house. For him, it was almost a foundational principle to start by asking, "Who are these people? Where do they live? What exactly would it look like?" Dorfman, Luftig says, warned him that the design choice was "wrong, wrong, wrong—you needed to feel the squalor and desperation of the time." Once the play was transposed from an abstract setting intended to convey life after a recent apocalypse to a large and recognizably lavish home, and played in front of a thousand people instead of sixty, the behavior of its characters seemed extreme and implausible. The play started getting too many laughs; on more than one occasion, Nichols had his actors lean into them.

"Mike made it his mission to make the play mean something real . . . but the play is more metaphorical than real, and he struggled with that," says Peter Lawrence. Advance sales were so strong that *Death and the Maiden* was in profit almost before it opened, but it arrived trailing controversy: A group of Latino actors protested the inappropriate casting and eventually founded the Labyrinth, which became a well-regarded off-Broadway theater company, in response.

Walton had come up with one design coup Nichols loved: a scrim that could be lit to be opaque or transparent and that would drop at the play's climax to reflect the audience and suggest that the past implicates everyone. The moment would, they hoped, unsettle the Broadway theatergoers, for whom Dorfman felt increasing distaste; "it has depressed him," said one news account, "to hear the set clapped, the stars applauded when they enter, and spectators spending the intermission talking about their dinner plans." By opening night, though, a gallows atmosphere had settled in on the creative team. "Mike started this tradition during previews," says Close, "where we would line up behind that curtain, when it was lit so nobody could see through it, and moon the audience." On opening night, forty people did it in front of the oblivious invited crowd. "Mike's ass must have been about four feet from Whoopi Goldberg, who was in the front row," says Lawrence. "I'll never forget it."

Death and the Maiden opened on March 17, 1992. ("Only six more to go!" said Hackman with grim jolliness after their curtain call. "Months, that is.") Most of the important critics were not pleased with what they saw. By then news of the differences between Dorfman and Nichols had made the papers, and some reviewers took sides—Benedict Nightingale called it "a pitiful travesty of a fine play," and Frank Rich wrote, "It is no small feat that the director Mike Nichols has managed to transform *Death and the Maiden* into a fey domestic comedy. But what kind of feat, exactly? History should record that Mr. Nichols has given Broadway its first escapist entertainment about political torture."

"I don't think Mike got, finally, to the savage core of the play," says Dorfman, "but I thought a lot of the criticism was incredibly unfair to him. The laughs that they complained about are there in the play itself—a lot of what happens is intentionally absurd." Nichols took in the criticism and kept revising the staging well after reviewers had come and gone. After revisiting the London production to remind himself of why he had found the play powerful, he returned to New York and, while he did not undertake a drastic overhaul, changed several lighting cues and redirected a number of moments to clarify the stakes and reduce the laughter. "I genuinely made some mistakes," he said at the time. "Nobody likes to get criticized in reviews, but in this case I didn't disagree." And Dorfman, while still publicly ruing the fact that he himself had "done violence to the play" and "tortured" it in a devil's bargain to have it run on Broadway, said that "whatever he is

Nichols and May as George and Martha (with James Naughton and Swoosie Kurtz as Nick and Honey) in the Long Wharf Theatre's foreshortened run of *Who's Afraid of Virginia Woolf?*

"Meryl woke me up," said Nichols of his *Silkwood* star. "This time, I feel—knock on wood—I'll remain awake." They would work together for the next thirty years.

"His main focus was always on the truth of whatever a scene was": Dorian Harewood, standing over Peter Evans as Paul Rudd watches, in Nichols's incendiary production of *Streamers*.

Nichols with his third wife, the novelist Annabel Davis-Goff, at the 1985 Tony Awards, where he won Best Director for his work on Tom Stoppard's *The Real Thing*.

Nichols before
an auction of the
Arabian horses he
collected and bred,
at his Bridgewater,
Connecticut, farm.

Meryl Streep and
Cher in *Silkwood*.

"I can't afford to have a scene change last longer than four seconds in any instance": Jeremy Irons and Glenn Close in Nichols's Swiss-watch production of *The Real Thing*.

Sigourney Weaver, Cynthia Nixon, and Judith Ivey taking a break during Nichols's fraught and contentious production of *Hurlyburly* just before its move to Broadway.

"You have to understand you're unique, and if I don't help you realize this, you will always be ordinary because that's how you think of yourself," Nichols told Whoopi Goldberg.

Jack Nicholson, stepping in after Nichols fired Mandy Patinkin from *Heartburn*, the director's second film with Streep.

Christopher Walken and Matthew Broderick in *Biloxi Blues*, the only Neil Simon script Nichols ever filmed.

"I thought, *This will be fine*," Nichols (with Melanie Griffith and Harrison Ford) said of *Working Girl*. "Cinderella will take care of us, and we can work on *detail*."

"He fell in love with her instantly," said Candice Bergen of Diane Sawyer, "and he wanted to be a better man for her." They married in 1988.

Nichols and Davis-Goff with their son, Max, and daughter, Jenny, in New York City, 1987.

Nichols with Jenny; Daisy, his daughter with his second wife, Margot Callas; and Sawyer at the Museum of Television and Radio Honors, 1992.

Streep in Nichols's adaptation of Carrie Fisher's *Postcards from the Edge*, the second time he directed her to an Oscar nomination.

"Werewolves are a lousy metaphor," Nichols said of *Wolf* (with Jack Nicholson), "because they're not a metaphor for anything that *happens* to people."

After his contentious production of Ariel Dorfman's play *Death and the Maiden* (with Richard Dreyfuss and Glenn Close), Nichols did not direct on Broadway again for thirteen years.

"I remember Harrison and Mike saying how nervous they were," said Annette Bening of *Regarding Henry.* "I thought, *Oh, I get it. It never goes away.*"

Nichols with, from left, Robin Williams, Hank Azaria, Nathan Lane (in wig cap), and cinematographer Emmanuel Lubezki (foreground) on the set of *The Birdcage,* on which he once again collaborated with Elaine May.

"So much of filmmaking is winging it, because you don't have the time to dig in the way Mike did," said John Travolta (with Nichols on the set of *Primary Colors*).

Nichols with Greg Kinnear and Garry Shandling on the set of *What Planet Are You From?*, his unhappiest film production and biggest box office failure.

Nichols with the man he said taught him how to be famous, his lifelong friend and mentor Richard Avedon, in 1990.

The artist Eric Fischl with his portrait of Nichols at the Mary Boone Gallery in New York City, 1999.

Nichols on the New York set of *Angels in America* with Emma Thompson. Their friendship, she said, was like "a conversation neither of us ever had any interest in finishing."

"Everything he did was always interesting," said Streep of Al Pacino in *Angels in America*. "Even in a late take, he'll throw you a curve."

A birthday visit from the Rockettes on the *Angels* set.

"The kiss in this scene is the hippo's toe in *Fantasia*," Nichols told Julia Roberts and Jude Law on the *Closer* set. "Everything balances on just the toe."

Nichols's Christmas card from the Morocco shoot of *Charlie Wilson's War*.

Nichols (with Julia Roberts) shot parts of *Charlie Wilson's War*, his last film, on the same soundstage as *The Graduate*.

Hank Azaria, David Hyde Pierce, and Tim Curry are joined by
Nichols for the opening-night curtain call of *Spamalot*.

Nichols backstage at his poorly received revival of *The Country Girl*.

Nichols, joined by Daisy and Sawyer, at the presentation of his American Film Institute Life Achievement Award in 2010. "I promise, no more achievements," he said.

In 2012, forty-eight years after winning his first Tony for directing, Nichols won his last, for his revival of *Death of a Salesman* (with, from left, Linda Emond, Philip Seymour Hoffman, and Andrew Garfield).

A commemorative paperweight created by Nichols's longtime theater press representative and friend Bill Evans for his memorial service in New York City.

"The thing about directing a movie is that every day you think, *Oh no.... I cannot get out of this corner.... She's awful, he's awful, I'm awful....* And you talk your way out of the end of the world. You shoot one more scene, and you're saved again." —Mike Nichols

doing, he certainly has my approval. It's admirable for a man of Mike Nichols's stature to keep working on a play." Despite the reviews, *Death and the Maiden* was a hit, and Nichols briefly considered extending the run after the original actors' contracts were up by replacing them with an all-Black cast that would have been led by Whoopi Goldberg. But he ultimately decided against it; he was tired of working on the play, tired of theater and its discontents, and, for reasons he was just beginning to understand, tired of everything.

He began, for the first time, to feel the weight of his own mortality. He had turned sixty the previous December. The AIDS epidemic was ravaging the gay community in numbers that had seemed unimaginable five years earlier and was tearing through the worlds of theater and movies. In April, soon after the opening of *Death and the Maiden,* Nichols had attended a sixtieth-birthday party for his old friend Anthony Perkins, who had kept his diagnosis a secret for two years, fearing that he would never be hired again. By August, Perkins was so sick that Nichols flew to Los Angeles to sit at his bedside and say goodbye. He died two weeks later. Nichols also lost his young assistant Jerry Caron, who had worked on *Heartburn, Working Girl,* and *Regarding Henry.* Barely a month went by when he wasn't asked to speak at a memorial service or host a fundraiser. He said yes to everything he could, including a pair of performances with May to benefit the AIDS charity Friends In Deed, which he had founded in 1991 with his friend Cynthia O'Neal.

He began to believe, he said, that everything that had happened to him since "having escaped, for no particular reason, the Holocaust" was an accident. At a dinner given by E. L. Doctorow, he found himself seated next to Cornelia Foss, the wife of the composer Lukas Foss. They had not met, but when they started chatting, Nichols discovered that they had been born in Berlin within months of each other, and had escaped from Germany at around the same time. Foss told Nichols that when she described her own overwhelming guilt to her husband, he had told her, "We've been looking for you for a long time."

"What are you talking about?" she said.

"We've found the person responsible for the death of six million Jews," he replied.

When Foss recounted the story to Nichols, he said, "I burst into tears . . . It was extremely embarrassing. It had never occurred to me [in] 50-odd years that I [had] felt this guilt. In the days and weeks and months following this experience, I began to realize to what extent I [had] never looked at my own feelings about this."

Nichols started reconsidering his life not as an ongoing search for meaning in art but as a decades-long flight from himself. Whether he was reacting to recent professional disappointment or to a sense that time was slipping away is unguessable, but he started to feel that expressing himself through movies and plays was a fool's errand. "Metaphor has left art and gone into current events," he complained. "Who in the fuck is going to compete? Where is there a hero who can fall from greater heights than Michael Jackson? Where is there more naked rivalry than between Tonya Harding and Nancy Kerrigan? What couple can you write about that is a stronger metaphor about relations between the sexes than the Bobbitts? These are incidents . . . that would be thrown out by even a second-rate writer. Who's going to cut someone's dick off in a novel?"

By early 1993 Nichols had made a decision and announced it with a flourish. He was going to walk away from his career. "With the end in sight, I'm dreaming of stopping," he said. "Suddenly I want to make my own choices, to follow my own dreams and fantasies." In an alternately bitter and philosophical interview with *The New York Times,* he said that after *Death and the Maiden,* he had sworn off directing Broadway theater, and he railed against the way the press had treated him.

"When somebody talented starts, it startles everybody, and expectations get higher and higher," he said. "It gets harder to find material, it gets harder to surprise people, it gets harder to fulfill expectations and keep going and renew yourself. And finally, it gets hard because you don't get credit for doing it . . . Sure, you're hoping for some astonishing piece of movie material that knocks you out. That doesn't happen . . . Why should I have to defend myself? Who's still doing it so well after so long? Can you name me six guys? Why do I get punished for making two or three or however many great movies that I'm granted? Where are the things I *should* be doing?"

It was over, said Nichols. He was done. This was his goodbye. There was, he explained, just one catch: First, there were six final movies he wanted to make.

Twenty-nine

THE BEST ROUTE
TO REVENGE

1993–1996

Nichols had spent the better part of a year hoarding projects that could serve as the final fireworks display of his abilities when he revealed them en masse in early 1993. In some ways, his estimation of what he could accomplish was correct; he would, in fact, direct six more movies over the next twenty years (as well as a TV movie, a miniseries, and despite his insistence that he was through with theater, four Broadway shows). But the work that would fill the long and prolific last act of his career would bear almost no resemblance to the sextet of movies he announced. One of them, a film version of a romantic thriller called *The Impersonator,* by Diana Hammond, was never mentioned by him again. Most of the others were also literary adaptations—Scott Smith's *A Simple Plan,* Cormac McCarthy's *All the Pretty Horses,* and Robert Harris's what-if-the-Nazis-had-won-World-War-II suspense novel *Fatherland*; he would develop and then walk away from all three. And he had already produced the fifth project, *The Remains of the Day,* which would be released at the end of the year.

The sixth film on Nichols's list was the only one he would actually direct, and he had already been working on it for two years. *Wolf* had begun as a brainstorm during a bender, a half-formed idea concocted by Jack Nicholson and Jim Harrison, a rugged novelist whose work explored myth and masculinity and whose appetite for hunting, fishing, food, and alcohol was bottomless. The idea that had come to them over one long, hard-drinking weekend was an updated werewolf story that producer Douglas Wick described as "Willy Loman Eats Spinach," about a sad sack, tamed and beaten down by the modern world, whose transformation gives him access to the primal male energy he has long suppressed.

Harrison worked on the concept for years. By the early 1990s, the success of finding-your-inner-wild-man books like Robert Bly's *Iron John* had given it some momentum, and Nicholson's involvement sparked the curiosity of a number of directors, Milos Forman and Peter Weir among them. But Harrison was not a natural screenwriter, and could never crack the plot. "I told Mike the ambitions of the story—a civilized guy connecting with his id," says Wick. "He was fascinated. But he also said, 'We have to put the main character in a world that I can bring the details to.'"

For *Wolf* to work, Nichols knew it would have to combine the high stakes and high concept of a genre film with something more idiosyncratic. But he and Harrison were oil and water; he was not about to put on waders, go fly-fishing in a Montana stream, and then sit around a campfire and talk about the beast within. "Mike was torn," says Wick, "because he loved Jack, and he thought it might be a gigantic commercial enterprise." But he felt no connection to the heart of the film. "A movie's artistic success depends on the metaphor that is the central engine," he said. "If the audience knows why they're there, you can soar. If [they] don't . . . no amount of cleverness with the camera or talent on the part of the actors can lift it." And he had one worry he couldn't ever set aside: "Werewolves are a lousy metaphor," he said, "because they're not a metaphor for anything that *happens* to people."

Wick disagreed. "The movie was about the celebration of oblivion—losing yourself, getting fucked up," he says. "I realized in retrospect that Mike could not see it as celebratory—he could only see it as loss. When he talked about it, he talked about AIDS and the friends he had lost. I was trying to sell him more on how great it is to leave the burden of your brain behind." To keep Nichols on board, Wick brought in Wesley Strick, an experienced, adaptable screenwriter who had written Martin Scorsese's remake of *Cape Fear*. Strick found Harrison's draft "exceedingly dense" and "impenetrable"; Harrison himself later said it would have resulted in "a three-hour horror movie with blood coming off the fucking walls." "Please give me some scenes that I can direct," Nichols said.

Strick worked on the film for months, changing the profession of Nicholson's character, Will Randall, from white-shoe lawyer to mild-mannered literary editor; Nichols had just depicted a high-powered law firm in *Regarding Henry* and felt that he could bring fresher observation to the world of publishing. But he still couldn't find *Wolf*'s deeper meaning, if any existed. "Is it really about AIDS?" he would ask Strick. "Or the death of God?" Was being a werewolf a stand-in for politically incorrect thought, for rape fantasies, for unacceptable impulses? "Free-associating with Nichols always felt like a privilege, a hoot," Strick wrote, adding, "and a grand waste of time."

Several drafts later, the script had progressed—Will's journey from man to werewolf and the idea of his professional interactions becoming increasingly feral had been more playfully developed. But neither Nichols nor Strick had given much thought to the female lead—"sometimes she was Nicholson's love interest, sometimes she was his sister," Strick wrote. Columbia wanted to put Michelle Pfeiffer opposite Nicholson, but she passed, saying the part was thin and underconceived. "It was 'the girl,'" she said. "I hadn't done that in a long time."

With production nearing, a script that he didn't feel was yet shootable, and no lead actress, Nichols took a deep breath, picked up the phone, and called the collaborator he still trusted more than any other.

At sixty-one, Elaine May had not been afforded the opportunities or second chances that Nichols had. She had received an Oscar nomination for co-writing *Heaven Can Wait*, and she had directed four movies. The noisy failure of the most recent, *Ishtar*, had ended her career behind the camera. But it had not tarnished her status as Hollywood's most valuable invisible woman—a stealth rewriter whose reputation in the industry was unrivaled. Handed a broken screenplay, May knew how to diagnose the problem and find a fix; she would work fast, pocket a substantial paycheck, and always decline credit. Nobody knew how many scripts she had improved, solved, or saved. "It's like some Taoist thing with her," said a clearly impressed Jim Harrison. "Very mysterious. Come in, do the work, take the money, leave no tracks." After thinking about *Wolf* for a weekend, she told Nichols, "Mike, you have a story about a guy who wants to become a wolf, so he becomes a wolf. I think this is going to be a very short movie."

"I read it and thought, *I can't lick this*," she says. "To want to be a wolf—to give up thought and human nature—what kind of a cluck would do this? 'Oh, good, I'm becoming a wolf' is not a story, and a movie almost always has to have a story. A play doesn't, but a movie does. But it was going to be made, so he was stuck with it."

Nichols begged her to try some rewrites anyway. She agreed to step in. Strick and Harrison would share screenplay credit; her name would appear nowhere on *Wolf*, although Nichols could not resist including a callback to one of their best-loved sketches by using her in one scene as the voice of a telephone operator.

Their renewed bond would end up reshaping the next several years of his working life. "There were old friendships that informed a lot of the things we did [on *Wolf*]," he said. "And at the heart of it was Elaine and me. Because we rekindled something we hadn't done—except for inaugurations and stuff—for 35 years. That was very emotional for us. And very exciting."

May first concentrated on the female lead. She made Laura—who was now the daughter of Will's boss—a sharp-tongued, self-sufficient, unflappable sparring partner; Pfeiffer read her redraft and signed on. And she dug deeper into the acerbic comedy of the publishing-house scenes, giving a cast that included Christopher Plummer, David Hyde Pierce, and James Spader a bit more to do. These were Band-Aids, not solutions—the material that she and Nichols enjoyed still alternated uncomfortably with scenes in which their star would have to howl at the moon. But there was no time to do more: Nicholson had a limited window of availability, and *Wolf*, with a $70 million budget that included shoots in Vermont, New York, and Los Angeles, needed to start by March in order to make a Christmas 1993 release date.

Over the next twenty years, a rush to production with rewrites done on the fly would become typical for large-scale studio movies. But it was alien to the way Nichols had always worked, and Sam O'Steen, who would not edit another of his movies after *Wolf*, was annoyed. He felt Nichols had been negligent by declining to storyboard the shots and by forgoing any meaningful rehearsals with his cast: "Mike was just not well prepared when he started shooting. He said, 'I like coming on the [sound]stage and [having] it all sort of come to me.' I think he was just being lazy."

Nichols may have believed that he and Nicholson would generate ideas on the spot, as they had done since *Carnal Knowledge*. Instead, he faced a leading man who seemed surly, distracted, and unhappy to be there. Nicholson's role was arduous; he spent long mornings in the makeup chair, and shooting days could stretch to seventeen hours. He was in the middle of a split with his girlfriend, Rebecca Broussard— they had two children under three at the time—and would often arrive in a foul temper and stay that way. "Everyone was scared to death of him," O'Steen said. "He was in such a horrible mood, even with Nichols. Poor Michelle—she'd be waiting on the set for Jack to show up . . . She was ignored because Jack consumed so much of Mike's time, and Mike was intimidated by Jack's moods."

"It was a great disappointment to Mike," says script supervisor Mary Bailey. "Jack wasn't the Jack that he remembered, the pal that he had been on their previous projects. Mike would talk about how great that had been a lot."

The shoot took longer than Nichols had anticipated. The December release date gave way to March, and then to June, and an awareness that the film was in trouble pervaded the set. "We all kind of knew that this movie wasn't up to Mike's A-1 scratch," Plummer says, "or indeed any of ours. But he never showed his displeasure or impatience. It was as if he had put the movie in a kind of slot, and told himself, 'All right, I'll work from that and shut up about the problems.' He never looked for a second like he was struggling. We adored him for that."

"In *Wolf*, I had to eat breakfast with Jack Nicholson," says Kate Nelligan. "I was the wife he was going to cheat on, so I couldn't be too glamorous. So I ate, normally, and Mike came over and said, 'Kate . . . She's a beautiful woman, eating ravenously.' He wanted me to look ugly while I ate. A lot of directors don't know what to do in that moment—they don't know how to ask for that. Mike knew exactly how to ask. *Ravenously*."

Nichols let the mask drop just once. "I remember going to the snack table, which drew him like a moth to a flame," says Nelligan. "I knew he wasn't happy, and I said, 'How are you doing, Mike?' He said, 'It's like Vietnam. I got in, and now I can't get out.' He said it like Eeyore, quietly. With a normal director, you'd be alarmed. With Mike, it was just hilarious."

Soon after *Wolf* wrapped, the news broke that Nichols was leaving Cohn for CAA. *The New York Times* cited the *Remains of the Day* flap but also said he was "intent on earning far more money by making potential blockbusters" and "seeking to expand his reach into producing." The story seemed to frame the still-unreleased *Wolf* as a final misstep rather than a stride in a new direction. Postproduction did not go smoothly; Nichols had made a picture poised uneasily between sophisticated satire and horror—one that needed a lot of work. "There was a good deal of rancor between the studio and Mike," says Bo Welch, *Wolf*'s production designer. "It was the first time I worked with him, and on that one, there was hardship."

"We did a preview in Dallas, where we got some bad laughs," says Wick. "So we trimmed some of the wolfman stuff that was playing funny. And the score seemed to tell people that Jack's character was having a dream, where we wanted it to be scary. We did two days of reshoots—a bunch of little things to re-steer it—and for the first time, Mike was in his element. He knew exactly what he wanted to do. But until then, everything had been makeshift. Given its ambitions, we were all disappointed."

"We were more worried about the ending than anything," said O'Steen. After trying several alternatives, Nichols settled on one in which Will reveals himself as a werewolf and Laura consents to join him in his new life. "I'm thinking, 'Jesus, she's going to go off and fuck this wolf? Come on,'" said O'Steen. "The ending was terrible. Mike never even previewed it. I bet that cost them $40 million [at the box office]."

Wolf received mixed reviews, many of which praised the performances and the workplace comedy while noting that it all fell apart by the end. Nichols was by no stretch an action director, and many of the shots in the werewolf scenes and the climactic fight sequence are presented in ultra-slow motion, an indicator of how little usable footage O'Steen had to work with. For its first half, *Wolf* plays as the movie Nichols wanted to make—an acid look at the savagery that lurks within even a profession as outwardly genteel as publishing, and about the need to become a predator in a predatory era. But it gives way to the movie he had to make: an effects-driven thriller shot with little flair and a tired and unfocused star.

Nichols insisted that *Wolf*'s June 1994 premiere, at New York's Ziegfeld Theater, also serve as an AIDS fundraiser. The film reached screens not long after movies like *The Flintstones* and *City Slickers II*, and most critics gave him the benefit of the doubt for at least trying to do something adult in an increasingly infantilized movie season. "Audiences may well have forgotten the joys to be had from this brand of sophisticated confection, rich and dark, laced with bitter little jokes," wrote Anthony Lane in *The New Yorker*. "From *The Graduate* on, he has relished the spectacle of Americans at one another's throats, but this is the first time he has introduced sharp teeth and long claws into the process, and it's not really his field." The film grossed $65 million, enough to place it among the year's top twenty. It neither threatened nor improved Nichols's place in an ever more competitive industry.

"A lot of very good work went into *Wolf*," he said. "[But] it didn't matter. The metaphor didn't sail. We had to start pushing and pulling. And once you start doing that, it is usually too late." Nonetheless, he was elated that the film had brought him back together with May. Soon after *Wolf* was completed, they performed at a New York Public Library benefit where they had planned to read passages from Nabokov. According to Bob Morris, who covered the event for *The New York Times*, "It had seemed like such a worthy literary idea when they had planned it. But then, during dinner, they started noticing how glum everyone looked . . . 'Can I see you?' Ms. May asked, taking Mr. Nichols's arm with a charming smile about to shatter into a million pieces . . . Not long after that, Marshall Rose, the library's chairman, was announcing, 'There are two people whose talents have placed them in the upper stratosphere of show business.' Then they were front and center, taking a backward plunge into the comfort of the familiar. 'Hello?' Mr. Nichols said, shedding 35 years as he picked up an imaginary telephone. 'Hello, Arthur,' Ms. May said. 'This is your mother. Do you remember me?'"

"We're really excited," Nichols said. "We're two people who increase each other when we work. So we're nuts not to work together."

He was being wooed for several projects, including a remake of Billy Wilder's *Sabrina* that would have reunited him with Harrison Ford. He wasn't interested. He only wanted to collaborate with May again.

Nichols had been living through a moment that felt valedictory. His peers were entering their lifetime-achievement-award years—he had just presented one to Nicholson, at the American Film Institute—and he had lost two old friends within a month of each other: Saint-Subber, his first Broadway producer, and Jacqueline Kennedy Onassis, who was just a year older than Nichols and had died at sixty-four. He and she had remained so close that he was asked to do a reading of scripture at her private funeral mass.

It felt too soon for so many goodbyes. The idea of planning a well-choreographed last act suddenly lost any appeal it had for him. With May's reentry into his life, talk of retirement was off the table. He wanted to work, and a new film was foremost in his mind. In the almost fifteen years since Allan Carr had fired him from *The Queen of Basin Street*, Nichols had not lost his enthusiasm for *La Cage aux Folles*. The musical had been a big hit on Broadway, and Carr wanted to turn it into a film, but he had a problem: Because he didn't own the rights to the original movie, he would be unable to use any of the plot elements the filmmakers had invented—including the comic centerpiece in which the two gay protagonists, Albin and Georges, strip their home of its outré decor and transform it into a virtual monastery to impress their priggish in-laws-to-be.

John Calley had just taken over United Artists and was trying to revitalize the label—and UA had, it turned out, bought the American remake rights fifteen years earlier as part of its deal to distribute *La Cage* in the United States. Nichols had Calley quietly renew the option, and then announced it as his next film: He would direct and, for the first time, serve as sole producer, and May would write the script. In one stroke, he had thwarted Carr's plans. "The best route to revenge," he said, only half joking, "is to sit around and wait."

May knew exactly how she wanted to adapt the plot: Georges—now Armand—would still run a nightclub with a locally famous drag show. Albin—now Albert—would be his partner of twenty-five years and the club's star attraction. Mindful that almost no studio had put gay characters front and center in a mainstream comedy, she and Nichols repeatedly insisted that the movie would not be political—"It's about family" was the agreed-upon talking point, a not uncommon approach at the time. But May made some changes to reflect the bigotry and hatred that was then making headlines. Albert and Armand's prospective in-laws would now be an outspoken Moral Majority politician and his wife. This version of *La Cage*—Americanized as *The Birdcage*—would be the unmistakable product of a moment in which gay people were in peril, and it would clearly identify those who demonized them. The script included a brief acknowledgment of the AIDS crisis and a reference to right-wing anti-choice politics; it retained the broad farce of the original while being blunt about the stakes—and the Pat Buchanan–like villains.

"We had a twinge about this," said Calley. "But Mike . . . said, 'By the time the movie comes out, you won't be able to parody these guys anymore—they'll be parodying themselves' . . . And he was right."

Nichols's first impulse was to cast his two *Waiting for Godot* stars—he saw Robin Williams as the hysterical, self-dramatizing Albert and Steve Martin as the restrained, forbearing Armand. But Martin felt he was wrong for the material ("He didn't think he could do the camping that goes with [the role]," Nichols said), and Williams didn't want to play Albert. "Robin decided, because of *Mrs. Doubtfire,* that he had already been in a dress, and perhaps the other part would open up a different kind of challenge for him. And that," says Nathan Lane, "is where I came in." Lane was, at the time, a much-loved stage actor who was appearing on Broadway in Neil Simon's *Laughter on the 23rd Floor*; he was stunned when Nichols went backstage and asked him to play Albert.

"It seems crazy, but I had to turn the movie down," Lane says. He was committed to return to Broadway in the lead in a revival of *A Funny Thing Happened on the Way to the Forum* that Scott Rudin was producing. "After that, I'd get a call from Mike and he'd say things like 'Well, I talked to Kevin Kline, but I just keep thinking you're the person who should do this.' That's how Mike was with actors. He fell in love with you, and like all great men in love, he made you feel like you were the most important person in the world." Finally, Nichols called Rudin, who postponed *Forum* for a year so that Lane could make the movie.

Despite his demurrals, every choice Nichols made on *The Birdcage* was, to some degree, political, and he was alert to danger zones regarding sexuality and race in a way he had not been before. He had struggled with how to portray Black servants as far back as *The Little Foxes*, and had used actors of color in comical housekeeper roles in *Postcards from the Edge*. For *The Birdcage*, a film that would be largely about stereotypes, he knew he would have to think differently. Originally, he planned to cast a Black actor, as the French film had done, in the role of Albert and Armand's drag-queen maid; he was especially interested in Adrian Lester, a young British actor he had spotted in an all-male production of *As You Like It*.

"I came in, I did the lines, and then we started talking about what it would mean to have a Black actor play that role," Lester says. "'I have to be honest,' I said. 'It feels like the lines don't give him enough depth for us to see past the slapstick elements, and it starts to be a bit negative.' And Mike said, 'Yes, I think we're past that. It doesn't feel right. It feels like we're pointing at something that is not an eye-opener and not informative—it's the opposite.' Never in my life had someone opened up that kind of honest conversation about why I shouldn't play a part, and still left me feeling positive and confident. I was bowled over."

Nichols asked May to reconceive the role; she merged it with another character, Albert's dresser, and Nichols cast Hank Azaria. "I worked up different versions," Azaria says. "One was more understated, barely obviously gay, almost a street tough. And one was the character that ended up in the movie. Both felt real to me—I had grown up with Puerto Rican street queens who were very effeminate and flamboyant and others who weren't. I tried both versions out for a friend who was a drag queen, asked which one he liked better, and got his seal of approval."

Lane was the only gay actor cast in a major role in *The Birdcage*. He had never addressed his sexual orientation publicly; when the film was released, he would come out by telling an interviewer, "I'm forty, I'm single, and I work in musical theater. *You* do the math." But in preproduction, it was a subject Nichols declined to broach, whether out of awkwardness, uncertainty, or tact. "There was a point when Robin Williams was not certain he was doing it," Lane said. "And Mike would say, 'What do you think of Billy Crystal as your husband?' or 'What do you think of Robert Redford?' I joked, 'Well, if you can make *that* happen, all my dreams will come true!' So *he* knew. And then Robin came in, and he was just a sensitive, beautiful soul, generous and kind from the get-go. I think that Mike cast me in part because he knew it would probably be good to have an actual gay person in the midst of this old-fashioned French farce. But we didn't talk about it—and I didn't talk about it with Robin, either."

On *The Birdcage*, Nichols reverted to the habits that had served him best: He threw himself into research, flying with May and Bo Welch to drag shows in Chicago, Savannah, and, at Welch's behest,

South Beach, a trip that inspired him to change the movie's setting from New Orleans to Miami. He cast only actors he loved, including Gene Hackman, Dianne Wiest, and Christine Baranski. He treated May as a full creative partner, keeping her by his side throughout the process. And he built three weeks of rehearsal into the schedule. "He would say, 'Don't worry about laughs. Just tell the story,'" says Lane. "And he was very protective of Elaine—she would be at the catering table eating something and if there were crumbs on her blouse, he would gently brush them away. You could tell it was a real reunion."

Nichols was protective of May's script as well; improvising was fine, but the final decision on what to use would be his and May's—and would be locked down by the end of rehearsals. "Mike said, 'I want you guys to know exactly what you're doing by the time we shoot,'" says Azaria. "'Elaine's going to take down all of your ad-libs, and we'll decide what to use together, but once we're shooting, we're not going to try nineteen different versions.'"

In rehearsals, Williams let his instincts carry him anywhere; Lane eventually felt comfortable enough to join him. That process yielded one of Williams's most inspired moments, a scene in which Armand is choreographing a number and shows Albert what he wants by doing a furiously compressed history of modern dance, from Michael Kidd to Twyla Tharp to Bob Fosse to Madonna. "Stop!" Nichols yelled, choking with laughter. "I don't want to see this again until we're doing it! How does it end? How do we get out of it?" It was Lane who provided Williams with the punch line that ends the scene: "But you keep it all *inside.*"

Nichols and his cinematographer, Emmanuel Lubezki, had mapped out an opening shot about the joy of giving yourself over to a well-executed visual illusion that could be seen as a thesis statement about both moviemaking and drag. The camera would glide, *Miami Vice* style, over water toward the Florida coast, then, as if the cameraman had simply hopped off the prow of a boat and kept going, push across a busy street full of revelers and up to, then through, the doors of the club, where a group of performers are onstage lip-syncing to the song that's been playing (also a thesis): "We Are Family."

The playful but elaborate shot was characteristic of the precision with which Nichols undertook *The Birdcage*. He planned every detail—with one glaring exception. "Bo [Welch] was really good," says May. "But he had designed a home for Albert and Armand that was more a gay set than a family house. It was supposed to be where they had raised a kid, cooked meals, their private space. And it wasn't. Mike said, 'I have to change it, don't I?' And I said, 'You really do, because if you don't, then the visual story is that they had orgies here while the kid was growing up.' Everything in a movie has to tell the story—the clothes, the performances, the sets. With this one set, we had forgotten that. Maybe because he and I knew so well what we wanted to do that we just assumed everyone did."

The occasional tentativeness Nichols and May brought to depicting homosexuality in *The Birdcage* was characteristic of a moment when gay culture was about to go mainstream with remarkable speed but had not done so yet. There was a vast chasm between the independent film realm, where New Queer Cinema was thriving, and the world of studio movies and network TV, where Ellen DeGeneres was still looking for a boyfriend on her sitcom and gay characters were either marginal or nonexistent. Nichols was not uncomfortable with the material or with gay men. For forty years, they had been his friends, mentors, confidants, and colleagues, and his own possible bisexuality had long been a subject of speculation. In an era when other directors of his generation simply avoided the subject, Nichols had not—homosexuality was central to *Streamers* and *Biloxi Blues*, he had included a lesbian character in *Silkwood*, and at the time he made *The Birdcage* he was developing a biographical drama about Oscar Wilde. For him, gay characters had long been part of the canvas, whether they were a pair of bored cater-waiters in *Heartburn* or the man in *Postcards from the Edge* who adoringly tells Shirley MacLaine's character that he does her in his act. But *The Birdcage* was different: Gay men *were* the canvas.

Nichols drew on what he knew, even if some of it was from an earlier era. At one point, Azaria was struggling with a scene in which Agador has to contend with Albert's pre-performance meltdown. "I said, 'Mike, I don't know how to play this—this must happen every time, so why is Agador treating it as a disaster?' And Mike said, 'No, no, dear boy'—only Mike could get away with calling me that—'your character is partly based on Judy Garland's dresser. Judy would panic before every performance and her dresser would panic with her, and then panic *more* than her, so that she'd have to be the one to tell him to calm down. That was their ritual.' I was like, 'Brilliant!' No other directors say things like that to you, at least in my experience."

Nichols later called *The Birdcage* "one of the happiest times of my life"; he would laugh so hard while filming that his monitor had to be moved to a separate room, where a blanket was thrown over him to keep his irrepressible giggles away from the microphones. But there were a few moments when a generation gap between Nichols and May and the younger actors became apparent. "The script used the word 'fag' a lot. 'Well, Alexander the Great was a fag,' like that," says Lane. "The day we had to shoot it, I said, 'I'm a little uncomfortable saying *fag*.' We had this long discussion about why he wanted to use the word, and ultimately I said, 'Yeah, but as the only fag in the room, let me tell you. It's making me uncomfortable. Can we *try* other things?' He said, 'Absolutely.' He still used it in the movie, though. It was interesting. The word was not as offensive to them because it had been a punch line for years. They were two of the smartest, most sophisticated people in the world, but they couldn't quite let go of it."

Ultimately, Nichols and May assigned the most notable use of the word not to Lane but to Williams. "Yes, I wear foundation," May has Armand say. "Yes, I live with a man. Yes, I'm a middle-aged fag. But I know who I am. It took me twenty years to get here. And I'm not gonna let some idiot senator destroy that. Fuck the senator. I don't give a damn what he thinks."

Throughout production, Nichols would sit before his monitor and repeat to himself quietly, "Never underestimate the audience. Never underestimate the audience." He kept his eye out for what he called "the expensive laugh"—the joke that came at the cost of believability, consistency, or emotional honesty—and would often rethink a scene if he saw it going in that direction. "There were no rules," Azaria says, "but when he changed something, he would always err on the side of making it small and real and human."

N ichols did not view *The Birdcage* as his last chance to make a hit comedy, but he did view it as his best chance, and he went into the first preview concerned. "He'd gone through a rough period," says Lorne Michaels, who accompanied him. "He said, 'You go in for meetings with the studio people. They're all much younger, and they talk to you about your famous work, which they grew up on. They all assume you're in the Hall of Fame. They think, *Why would you still want to be doing this when you've already achieved the thing we're all aiming for?* They don't understand that you're not desperate. It's just that this is what you *do*—and suddenly, decades have gone by without you realizing it, and people think you've had your moment and you should stop.' After the preview, which just *destroyed*, Mike said, 'I'm so happy. It's going to be a hit.'"

The Birdcage opened on March 5, 1996, with a strong endorsement from the Gay and Lesbian Alliance Against Defamation (GLAAD), which praised the movie for going "beyond the stereotypes to see the characters' depth and humanity" and urged people not only to buy tickets but to write letters of support to United Artists. Critics mostly saw

the film as an effective, expertly handled update of dated material—
Variety tallied twenty-two positive, eight mixed, and one negative review. Among gay artists and activists, *The Birdcage* was more divisive;
in a long and angry essay titled "Why Can't Hollywood Get Gay Life
Right?" the essayist Bruce Bawer decried it as "strained, awkward, synthetic." "I saw the movie with a gay friend," he complained to *Entertainment Weekly*, "and we sat there in horror and disbelief, while the
straight audience around us was just laughing it up . . . They don't get
anything outside of a narrow Hollywood idea of gay life."

"That poor schmuck," Nichols said. "He says this isn't how gay people act? Let him hang out with RuPaul for a couple of days. They're not
the nice couple that works in the agency and goes shopping together in
their horn-rimmed glasses and khaki suits. We're not just talking about
gays—we're talking about drag divas, theatrical stars!"

But many gay writers rose to the film's defense, including Larry
Kramer, who called it "proof-positive evidence that if you have two male
stars shown having an honest gay love affair, it would be dynamite box
office." Kramer was right; *The Birdcage* opened in first place, stayed
there for four weeks, and grossed $125 million, more than any of Nich-
ols's films since *The Graduate*. "Who would have guessed that we live
in a country where Robin Williams and Nathan Lane are a sexier box
office pair than Robert Redford and Michelle Pfeiffer [in *Up Close &
Personal*]?" wrote Frank Rich in an essay called "Beyond the Birdcage"
in which he speculated that "same-sex marriage could be the next
bloody battleground of the culture wars." In a way, the picture was
Nichols's *Guess Who's Coming to Dinner*—a breakthrough that was revolutionary not in its content but in the degree to which its instant
mainstream acceptance signaled a shift at America's center.

As his sixty-fifth birthday approached, Nichols could write his own
ticket once again. He had known it was coming ever since he showed
the film's creative team his final cut on Martha's Vineyard. As they

celebrated at lunch, he sat quietly, surprised at his own emotions. "I couldn't speak," he said. "I realized I'd had no inkling of my anger at the people who had written me off. My reaction, instantaneously, was 'Fuck you bastards! You thought I couldn't do this anymore? Well, look at this.'"

Thirty

SOMETHING SCARY

1996-1999

A couple of months before *The Birdcage* opened, Nichols was given thirty minutes on the phone to sell himself to a stranger. The auction for the movie rights to Joe Klein's novel *Primary Colors* was one of the oddest in the history of publishing. Klein, a political journalist for CBS and *Newsweek*, had written a barely disguised fictional account of Bill Clinton's 1992 presidential campaign that hit stores in the middle of Clinton's reelection bid, and, because he was still covering the presidency as a journalist, he had decided to conceal his identity. The instant bestseller dug into everything readers could want to know about candidate "Jack Stanton," from his insatiable appetite to his troubled partnership with his intelligent, frustrated wife to his compulsive and clumsy infidelities—and the words "By Anonymous" on the cover created an additional wave of publicity. *Primary Colors* was a tell-all that was also a whodunit, and thus a very hot property.

Amateur sleuths were already using computer programs to compare the book's phraseology and sentence structure to the work of journalists who had covered the Clintons, but at the time of the auction, Klein's identity was still a secret. Nichols chased the book hard, pitching himself to direct and produce and May to write. He had met the Clintons four years earlier and liked them, but he had not let personal relationships get in the way of *Heartburn* or *Postcards from the Edge*. He decided to take a gamble. He would go up against movie studios and major producers, attempt to buy the rights with his own money, and, if he obtained them, make back his investment and then some by selling the property, with himself attached, to a studio. The bidders each had half an hour to convince a listener whose identity they still didn't know. "I had an advantage," Nichols said. "I knew what I wanted to do with the [book]. I said, 'It's about honor.' In my view . . . it's deep in the heart of almost any serious movie, because it's always the issue at stake."

Klein said Nichols won him over during the call by expressing his belief that the novel had no villains. "I'd never met him, but I felt safe," he said. "He wouldn't turn the satire into burlesque. He would treat the characters with respect." He sold Nichols the rights for $1.5 million.

Guessing games about casting began right away. Stanton's wife, Susan, was seen as a natural fit for Meryl Streep, Glenn Close, or Emma Thompson. Tom Hanks led most lists, including Nichols's, to play Jack. Klein's third main character was Henry Burton, the idealistic young operative who joins the campaign and whose journey toward disillusionment as he observes Stanton forms the story's main arc. The character was Black; several news outlets, including *The New York Times*, suggested that the easiest course for Nichols would be to make Henry white so that someone like Michael J. Fox could play him.

Nichols had no intention of changing Henry's race, but casting him would have to wait. While May worked on the screenplay, he would be busy with a commitment so unlikely that he surprised himself by making it. Wallace Shawn, whose writing he had long championed, had recently gathered a group of friends at Richard Avedon's apartment for a read-through of his new play, *The Designated Mourner*, a knotty,

challenging three-character drama, told in monologues, about coward-
ice and culpability under a fascist regime. Shawn and his companion,
Deborah Eisenberg, gathered around a dining room table with Avedon, David Hare (who had agreed to direct the play in London), and
designer Bob Crowley. Shawn had enlisted the poet Mark Strand to
read the part of Howard, a dissident writer who becomes a target of the
murderous government, Julianne Moore played his daughter, and
Nichols read Jack, an envious academic who is the play's central (and
most compromised) character.

"When Mike read the script, it was so extraordinary," Shawn says.
"It had a kind of naturalness, spontaneity, and intimacy that you would
not really expect. It seemed uncannily as if it was written to fit his vocal
patterns. On top of that, he wept at the end of it."

"The part has to be done by somebody comfortable with convoluted, long sentences, with the convoluted thought behind them and
the convoluted emotional quality they contain," says Eisenberg. "Watching Mike throw around those languid, self-justifying skeins of self-
deception . . . it was like he turned himself inside out to become his
own evil twin."

"Debbie and Hare and I conferred for about two seconds before we
asked Mike if he wanted to do it," Shawn says. To our great surprise,
he said, 'How long do I have before you need a decision?' We said, 'Two
weeks.' He took the full two weeks and then said yes."

Nichols agreed to star in a twenty-five-performance run of the play
at the Cottesloe, a small stage at London's National Theatre. He said
up front that he would be too busy with *Primary Colors* to repeat the
performance if the play moved to New York, and that he would probably need either an earpiece or a hidden prompter to get through the
massive, text-heavy role, which required him to do most of the talking
for two hours. "There was no reason under the sun for him to take this
incredibly arduous job as an actor, which was something he had not
done for years," says Eisenberg, "in a play that is demanding of the

audience, accusatory, assaultive, intellectual, rarefied, unbelievably painful. I thought of Mike as anything but a risk-taker. I mean, he was a risk
as a human being—he was so alive to possibilities that every second of
his life, in a way, was an experiment. But in his work, not."

"I wanted to do something scary. Something that can't do me any
possible good," said Nichols, who made his decision after Sawyer and
May both urged him to take the role. "I can't go skydiving or climb
Annapurna, but I can do this."

In April 1996, he began rehearsals in London. "Mike said that as a
director, when he listened to actors, he would always think, *Why can't
you make it sound more like life?* and that's what he did," says Hare. "Because of his background in improvisation, he was trained to make everything sound spontaneous. Once I wanted him to do a line differently,
and he said, 'Well, why don't you do it the way you want it done?' I
walked over, in what Wally describes as the longest ten seconds of his
life, and did it. Mike said, 'Oh, that's what you want,' and did the line
exactly as I had done it. It didn't bother him at all. He had no vanity as
an actor."

"He could have been such a diva," says Eisenberg, "but he was unbelievably well behaved." Shawn adds that "his theater discipline was a
thousand percent. He never came late, never said, 'I'm going to have to
step out to take this call.' And once performances began, all of London
was at his feet, really." Critics were dazzled; the *Evening Standard* wrote
that his "meticulous performance of this vast role is a triumph of creation." Streep flew over to see him work; so did May. "He gave one of
the greatest performances I've ever seen," May says. "He just went right
to the audience with it, and it went to him."

The reception delighted Nichols, who agreed to spend three days
repeating the performance at Pinewood Studios, without an audience,
for what he understood to be a record of the play that would be shown
only on British television; when it was released theatrically in the United
States, he was as furious as if his private letters had been published, and

refused to participate in publicity. "The film didn't make me happy," he said. "The play was a very specific event between the three of us actors and the living audience . . . I played a monster who was able to charm the audience, and just as they began to realize he was a monster, he could get them to laugh one more time . . . During that process, they began to wonder if they were in any way like this monster, which was both the purpose of the play and the fun of the performance . . . If you take that away, the film isn't a complete [record of the play]. But the play was an experience."

When Nichols returned to New York, *Primary Colors* was still on the bestseller list, and in the news: Klein, after several denials, admitted he was its author, and his journalistic colleagues, with not a little schadenfreude, rebuked him for playing both sides of the fence. Nichols didn't see what the fuss was about. "My wife had to explain it to me," he said. "I said, 'What's so terrible? If you say you're anonymous and you're hiding, of course you would say, "No, it's not me." Isn't that the point of being anonymous?' And she said, 'You don't understand. It's like if there's a vice cop, he has to answer the question, "Are you a cop?"'"

Nichols shrugged it off. May was close to finishing a draft—"I didn't fully know what to do with it," she says, "but I think it had a story by the time I was done"—and his roll of the dice was about to pay off spectacularly. *Primary Colors* was once again the subject of a bidding war, this time with Nichols as the object; the winning buyer, Universal, agreed to pay him $8.5 million, against 12.5 percent of the gross, to direct and produce.

By June, he had a cast—or thought he did; *Variety* reported that the film would star Hanks, Thompson, Jack Nicholson, and John Malkovich. Of those four, only Thompson would make it to the first day of shooting. "Maybe I erased it, but I don't think he ever talked to me about it," says Streep. "It was always Emma—he had just seen the movie she wrote [*Sense and Sensibility*] and was so in love with her for the role."

Thompson's commitment was firm. "We had been talking about doing a very funny Elaine May script about a woman who kidnaps a politician and strands him in the middle of a field," she says. "Then Mike said, 'Look, can we ditch this and do *Primary Colors*?' I said, 'Sure.' I loved the book. I thought it was so perspicacious about politics and power structures in general, never mind about the Clintons and our deep naivete about sexuality in politics and all of that."

Hanks was cagier. In August, just days after it was reported that he was all but signed to play Stanton, he told Nichols he was out. Nichols was shocked. "He didn't say anything like 'Oh, okay, I understand,'" says Hanks. "He literally said, '*Why?* Why is it suddenly no longer for you?'" Nichols later said he believed that Hanks, who was coming off back-to-back Oscars for playing intensely sympathetic characters in *Philadelphia* and *Forrest Gump*, had not wanted to play a philanderer or to alienate the Clintons. Hanks says it was more complicated. He wanted to star in Steven Spielberg's *Saving Private Ryan*, which would shoot at the same time, and he also felt uncomfortable about the phenomenon the novel had become. "*Primary Colors*, at first, felt almost like this counterculture thing, a little subversive," he says. "And it transmogrified into something mainstream. It was 'Oh, this is the movie about Bill Clinton.' And I've always felt, if you're going to do *that* story, do the real thing, find out what really happened. I didn't want to do all this work and have an asterisk on it, like 'This is Tom Hanks's version of this book's version of Bill Clinton.'"

In addition, Hanks, at forty, wasn't sure he had the gravitas to play Stanton, and didn't necessarily want to acquire it. "I didn't think I could pull off a viable president, or even a candidate," he said. "I viewed myself as a kind of out-of-shape young man—but a young man. I said, 'I'm just not hungry to do this,' and he said, 'Well, that's a thing. Don't do it if you don't want to throw yourself into it.' I wasn't on some kind of shit list with him for dropping out, but he thought I was wrong."

Hanks's participation in the movie had been crucial to Universal; when he walked away, the studio told Nichols the deal was off. Nicholson and Malkovich moved on to other projects. For much of the rest of the year, *Primary Colors* was in serious peril.

Then Nichols met John Travolta. "We had lunch in his trailer," Nichols said. "We had all his favorite things, turkey and stuffing—it was his favorite meal." It was also Nichols's. They were two of Hollywood's most famous on-set gourmands—Travolta had a chef prepare special meals for him on his movies, and Nichols felt a catering table should be a groaning board of treats. They bonded quickly. "I said, 'Have you read *Primary Colors*?' And he said, 'No, no one sent it to me,' which I thought was the perfect movie-star answer," Nichols said. "I did, he read it, he liked it." With Travolta in place, Universal was back on board, but cautiously. The studio, worried about the film's lack of overseas appeal, forced Nichols to reduce the budget from $80 million to $65 million.

By early 1997, Nichols had cast Billy Bob Thornton in the James Carville part, Kathy Bates, and Adrian Lester (who ended up beating out Cuba Gooding Jr., then hot off the success of *Jerry Maguire*, for the role of Henry). The movie was under a microscope before a foot of film was shot; a *New York Observer* story pointed to Nichols and Sawyer's place in "the Martha's Vineyard power crowd," of which the Clintons had become a part, and noted that Carville, former Clinton press secretary Dee Dee Myers, and George Stephanopoulos, the reported inspiration for Lester's character, had all turned down offers to serve as consultants. "If somebody told you that Mike Nichols was gonna be directing a film about you and an Oscar nominee was gonna play you, you'd watch," said Carville. "It's another thing to be pulling for it." And Nichols had to fend off whispering campaigns from both flanks—

some insisted he would use the movie to trash the Clintons, others said he would use it to placate them.

Nichols again insisted on extensive rehearsals. For Travolta, it was a new experience. "So much of filmmaking is winging it, because you don't have the time to dig in the way Mike did," he says. "He treated his actors like royalty. The days weren't too long. We were rested, we knew our staging, we talked through everything we were going to do, and we were certain about every move we made." Lester recalls rehearsing one scene in which he had to come out of a shower and change into clothes that were on a bed. "We rehearsed, and Mike said, 'Okay, let's do it again.' These two prop guys stepped forward to reset my clothes. I stopped them and did it myself. Then Mike asked to do it a third time. He was just watching quietly, and when the guys stepped forward again, his hand moved and indicated, 'Don't. Leave Adrian alone.' He knew I needed to do it myself, and that by doing it, I was trying to make it my own. That was his theater instinct."

When the film started shooting in April, May was once again at his side. "Every morning, they would tell each other the story of the movie," says Mary Bailey. "'This is a movie about a man who wants to do this. Then he meets these people. Then there's this setback.' If they couldn't remember something, that was a red flag for them—a scene that needed to be fixed or a story point that wasn't in the right place. For them it was an exercise about seeing both the details and the big picture."

"They were wonderful to watch," says Thompson. "Between the two of them, there'd been so much blood under the bridge by then. Elaine is not the world's most social creature, but I was never so happy as when we were all together."

Nichols's two stars took sharply different approaches. Thompson didn't want to try an impression of the first lady. "Hillary was much less imitable at the time," she says, "and in any case I wasn't interested in that—to me it was not a story about the Clintons, but politics and the press. John *was* interested." Travolta wore a frosted wig, adjusted his vocal pitch and body language, and eased into a gently Clintonian accent. "I was doing a literal interpretation," he says—one that landed him and the film on the cover of *Time* with the words "Yep, he's Bill." "It felt right for the movie and for me, and Mike was very supportive."

Travolta was, in some ways, a challenge for Nichols—a star used to having his way, who didn't hesitate to push for it. Ann Roth wanted to put him in cheap, Men's Wearhouse–style suits to emphasize that Stanton was running as an outsider. "There was a particular pale blue-gray suit that Clinton wore, from a guy in Fayetteville. Travolta was darling, but he didn't want that, and I kept bitching about it. He wanted Donna Karan, and Mike gave it to him," says Roth. "I hated, hated, hated it." And while "May was adamant that we not ad-lib," says Kathy Bates, "which was fine, because there was really no need to screw up her writing," Travolta didn't always stick to the script. When a line didn't sit easily, he says, "I would play Mom and Dad against each other—I'd go to Elaine and say, 'I don't want to say this and Mike is making me,' and she'd say, 'Mike, don't make him say it,' and he'd say, 'Oh, all right, fine.' It worked!"

"I always feel that a really good director is a scout," Bates says. "They know every inch of the landscape, and if you don't know how to get there, it's okay, because they know how to get you there." Her role—a brash, foulmouthed, mentally unstable lesbian who becomes the movie's tragic conscience—was a potential tour de force, and Bates credits Nichols for the strength of her performance. She had two big scenes—one in which she realizes that the Stantons are willing to resort to blackmail, and another in which, sitting in a truck, she reveals that the knowledge has shattered her.

"I knew the character was gay," says Bates, "but I thought she was let down because the Stantons revealed themselves as greedy and vicious. I didn't go deeper until Mike said, 'This is personal for her. She's gay. Their behavior is a betrayal of who she is.' Suddenly it clicked.

Usually a director will say, 'You know, it needs to be more emotional—maybe you cry.' He didn't direct like that. With Mike, it was about discovering who the character was and what was important to her, and helping you to make that discovery. After I got to that place, he mimed tears coming out of his eyes. He didn't say anything. He just looked over with his fingers on his face, and I knew I had accomplished that for him."

In January 1998, two months before it was to open, *Primary Colors* was hit with two unpleasant surprises. The first was the arrival of Barry Levinson's topical satire *Wag the Dog*, which had jumped into Oscar season at the end of the year and was entering wide release. The film—about an administration and a Hollywood producer who manufacture a war to divert attention from a presidential infidelity—was getting a warm response from critics and audiences; at a moment when the packaging of politics as a TV show was becoming a subject of discussion, it felt savvy and topical.

A week later, the world was introduced to Monica Lewinsky, and the *Primary Colors* team knew they were in the kind of trouble from which a movie might not recover. A film that suggested Americans were both hypocritical and hysterical about White House sex scandals was not going to play well while every night's newscast led with the biggest such scandal in history. Overnight, the film went from current to dated. "This girl went down on him in the Oval Office, and just like that, it became a tame movie!" says May. "That was really all we thought—you couldn't wait another two months?"

"We were all in L.A.," Thompson says. "I remember Mike calling a meeting and all of us sitting down. Mike and Elaine and I were eating rice and beans out of polystyrene containers, and John had, you know, a sixty-five-course meal laid out for him, and the conversation was 'What are we going to do? Life would appear to be imitating art at this moment, and it's going to make selling this movie incredibly hard.' And we were right. It did."

Primary Colors became grist for endless rumors about recuts, frantic changes, last-minute appeasements—in Nichols's words, "a shit magnet." Universal stuck with its plan for a March release—"We're staying the course, with our heads high," insisted the studio's chairman, Casey Silver—but *The New York Times* quoted a rival studio head as saying, "I would hang myself." Nichols put on a brave face. "It's not about Clinton, but about the 'Clinton thing,'" he claimed. He talked about his fantasy that the Clintons would see the movie ("I would hope that they would be able to see past some of the specifics and know how much the movie . . . feels for them," he said, while insisting, "I don't think we've prettified anything"), and he pointed to positive reactions at test screenings. But shortly before the film opened, he admitted, "It's the only time in my life I cannot imagine what will happen."

What happened came close to the worst-case scenario. Critics were respectful, and sometimes more; *Variety*'s Todd McCarthy called *Primary Colors* "frequently funny, wonderfully performed, eerily evocative of recent history and gratifyingly blunt in its assessment of what it takes to get to the top." But even the kinder reviews felt almost like condolence notes; the intimate look inside the life of the president that the film had teased was now available for free, and ad nauseam, on TV around the clock. The bad reviews pulled no punches. "*Primary Colors* is old news," Rex Reed wrote. "Who cares what happened in 1992? We're too busy trying to get through 1998 . . . . The movie is two and a half hours long, and you can't wait to get out of there to see what happened while you were sitting in the dark." The film won Oscar nominations for Bates's moving performance and May's screenplay, but it faded fast, grossing $39 million in the United States and just $13 million in other countries.

"I liked the book, I made the movie. Them's the breaks—I have to take my lumps," Nichols said. "When the movie came out, I was [at] the big *Time* magazine party where everyone who had ever been on the cover was gathered. I remember getting my picture taken with Gorbachev and Sophia Loren—that's the kind of party it was. At the beginning, the president and first lady were coming in and I thought, *I can't do this to them. I have to stay out of their way.* I thought we had treated them with great sympathy, but of course, it's not true—they're accused of monstrous things. As they were passing, I turned to pretend to be talking to the person on the other side of me. And when I thought it was safe to turn back, I was face-to-face with Hillary. Her manners were perfect. She asked how I was. And I said, 'Nervous—I have a picture opening.' And she said, 'Yes, well, there's nervous and then there's nervous.'"

There was no reason for Nichols to rush into his next movie, and he didn't. He and May were considering an Americanized update of the 1949 dark comedy *Kind Hearts and Coronets,* but without any particular urgency. After years of indecision, he finally dropped *All the Pretty Horses*; during the *Primary Colors* shoot, he had talked up the project to Billy Bob Thornton and convinced him to take over as director. At one point, he read *American Beauty* and put himself forward to Steven Spielberg and David Geffen as a possible director, but Spielberg was already well down the road with a newcomer to movies, Sam Mendes, and although he regretted having to tell Nichols no, he was also mindful of what hiring him would do to the projected $15 million budget. Nichols immediately backed away and wished Mendes well. ("From the beginning," producer Dan Jinks says, "we all said, 'We want the next Mike Nichols. Who is that?'")

For a while, Nichols was content to dabble, scheduling promising meetings with interesting people that kept him in the game but committed him to nothing. Barbra Streisand wanted to know if he would direct her farewell tour. Tom Cruise and Nicole Kidman had seen a play by Patrick Marber called *Closer* and were thinking of buying the film rights; Nichols also liked the play, so perhaps he would bid against—or partner with—them. Anthony Minghella wanted to write and direct an adaptation of the German novel *The Reader*; did he want to produce?

Nichols could pass months that way, but at sixty-seven, he could not afford another long stretch of indolence and hesitation. It was too late in his career to pull another disappearing act and expect the industry to welcome his return whenever he decided he was ready, and too early to drift into a twilight of discarded projects and retrospective honors. (He had just been selected as the Film Society of Lincoln Center's career achievement award recipient.) It was fun having his portrait painted by Eric Fischl, or driving around Martha's Vineyard with Candice Bergen in search of the island's best oysters, or arriving home at the Fifth Avenue apartment he and Sawyer had finally bought to find a box of desserts from Nora Ephron, who was always discovering New York's best brownies or the perfect chocolate chip cookie. There were new restaurants to try, new plays to drag Sawyer to, new people to have dinner with afterward, whether from her world or his.

But their lifestyle was about to change. At the end of 1998, Sawyer, at ABC's urging, agreed to step in as co-anchor of *Good Morning America*, a decision that would necessitate a drastically altered schedule. Time together would be harder to find. Her alarm would go off at 4 a.m. five days a week. Their late evenings out and about—in fact, evenings, period—would now be a treat reserved for weekends. (The move resulted in such a dramatic upswing in the struggling show's fortunes that Sawyer became ABC News' most valuable player, and what was intended to be a temporary run lasted ten years.)

Nichols knew it was time to get back to work. He dreaded a return to shooting in Los Angeles. "There's a virus I have no protection against if I'm there," he said at the time. "How am I perceived? You can do whatever you like—put towels at the bottom of the door, not read the trades . . . [but] if you're vulnerable to the virus, you've got to stay away from its matrix." When he finally made a decision, it was an unfortunate one; he picked the movie that would make him the most money. Calley, who had taken over Sony in 1996, brought him the script for a Garry Shandling sex comedy, an extended sketch called *What Planet Are You From?*, in which Shandling would play an alien sent to find an Earth woman to impregnate. Calley offered his old friend $8 million to direct. He said yes.

It was not an entirely cynical decision. Nichols was an avid fan of Shandling's cable comedy *The Larry Sanders Show,* which had just ended an acclaimed six-year run. "Mike got crushes," says Douglas Wick. "He was going through a bit of a downturn, and suddenly this script came along from someone he thought was good, and Calley said, 'We'll pay your full price.'" His entire career had been predicated on going with his gut; if he couldn't trust his first instinct, he couldn't trust anything.

His involvement instantly changed the movie's nature for the worse. Shandling was friends with Warren Beatty and Annette Bening; he had been developing the screenplay with them in a series of readings. "Unlike many comedians, in a day-to-day setting, Garry was this lovely guy—not a tortured, unhappy person," Bening said. "But the screenplay, we all felt, was this quirky, eccentric thing that perhaps didn't need to be big." With Nichols's involvement, it went from being the kind of off-kilter indie that might have attracted someone like Spike Jonze or David O. Russell to a scaled-up studio movie. His paycheck alone would make the film costly enough to require stars; those stars would all demand that they be paid their asking prices, because their director was. What had been conceived as a $12 million movie would, by the time Nichols stepped onto the set, be budgeted at $53 million. "I said, 'Garry, do you remember saying that if you ever were to do movies, they would be small and personal, like Albert Brooks's? What's happening to this movie? It's changing!'" says Ed Solomon, one of the screenwriters. "But I don't think he wanted it to go back to what it was supposed to be."

Nichols's Lincoln Center gala took place on May 3, 1999. Three thousand people attended the evening at Avery Fisher Hall, in which clips of his movies alternated with tributes from Bergen, May, Streep, Ephron, Buck Henry, Harrison Ford, Nathan Lane, Matthew Broderick, Paul Simon, and Art Garfunkel. The tone was occasionally roast-like—Bergen insisted that he was more than "the man who washes out Diane Sawyer's underthings"—but mostly adoring. Nichols, who joked that they must have "run out of geezers" in order to pick him, wiped tears from his eyes as he got up to speak. "Where the hell was Dustin Hoffman?" he joked. "It's like the monster not showing up at a tribute to Dr. Frankenstein . . . I have half a mind to cut him out of *The Graduate* and use Harrison Ford." He told the story of his Atlantic crossing, with the two-sentences-of-English anecdote that he had, by then, polished until it gleamed; he spoke in unusually personal terms of his upbringing and his parents' stormy marriage, and he lavished individual praise on every speaker. "All this would be hollow," he finished, "without the person who is my life and without whom I would be—as Dustin would be without *The Graduate*—merely an aging Jew, my wife, and without those three people who give my existence meaning, Daisy, Max, and Jenny Nichols."

Then he reeled off a short list of jokes about what directing films had taught him, ending with "There is absolutely no substitute for genuine lack of preparation." As the audience rocked with laughter, he said, "Tomorrow I go to L.A. to start a new picture. I'm making it for the same reason I made the others: Movies give us a chance to live other lives, and we walk on the set every morning thinking, *Anything can happen*."

The shoot was a disaster. Nichols wasn't kidding; he had indeed underprepared. Physically, he had never been in worse shape; he had gained a great deal of weight after the failure of *Primary Colors* and may have been on steroids to treat what had become chronic lung inflammation. He had scheduled a week of rehearsal, which wasn't enough; worst of all, he had no real connection to Shandling, who, it turned out, could not have been a poorer match for him. "Garry was very limited in terms of his acting," says Solomon. "He tried so hard, he took classes, he worked to be real, but he didn't have the technical skill. He never forgot the moment after the first shot when Mike looked at the playback and saw Garry and rolled his eyes. He saw that, and he was devastated."

"I got to the set," Nichols later told Cary Brokaw, who would produce his next three movies, "and I thought, *Oh my God. What do I do? Who do I have to fuck to get off this movie?*"

Nichols's aversion to Shandling was so visceral that, to many of the actors and crew members, it felt personal. From his perspective, it was a doomsday scenario—a TV series had tricked him into believing that a non-actor was an actor. Years earlier, Elaine May had told him, "If an actor isn't good by the end of the fifth day, fire him—they never get better." But this was Shandling's movie; there was no replacing him.

A month into the shoot, Nichols stepped onto a piece of canvas that was covering a hole in the floor of a raised soundstage. "I saw him fall right through," says Mary Bailey. "He had to spend the rest of the shoot on crutches. After that, it never got even a little better. It only got worse." Nichols had always been a physically active director; if he saw that a moment wasn't working, he would jump out of his chair and walk over to the actors, sometimes demonstrating what he wanted in broad gestures, sometimes telling a story, sometimes just putting an arm around a performer's shoulders and whispering a word of guidance. Now he was virtually immobile and had to use a "God mic"—a personal microphone connected to speakers on the set through which everyone could hear him. He didn't even bother to temper his harsh moods. "He couldn't walk around, so he was booming into it like the director in *A Chorus Line*," says Wick, who visited him on the set. "He was shooting something with Annette Bening, and hair and makeup came in for final touch-ups, and suddenly Mike yelled, 'Scat, dwarves!' He was more miserable than I'd ever seen him."

By then, he and Shandling were at each other's throats. Shandling wasn't shy about saying something when he thought Nichols was ruining the tone of a scene; and Nichols, who referred to him as "Shambling" to a visiting reporter, "went totally nuts" when he made a suggestion about how Bening should play her character. "Her clothes are kooky, the sets are kooky, her lines are kooky—you want her to *act* kooky, too?" he shouted at Shandling. "Why don't you come in prepared and do your own work?"

"I find it hard to talk about," says Bening, who intervened and told Nichols privately that she couldn't stand to see him behave that way toward a colleague. "I'm sad to say that Mike just treated Garry terribly, in a way that I had never seen. He was humiliated. And it was more upsetting because Mike was a hero to us—we all knew how much he loved actors."

"It was hysterical on the page," says Bo Welch. "But honestly, Mike was not the right guy for that job, and Garry was not the right lead, and they were a terrible combination. It was brutal, but especially for Garry."

"Garry was a very honest person," says Nora Dunn, who appeared in the movie. "He was extremely insecure, and he did talk about those insecurities a lot, which is something I don't think Mike Nichols had any time for on a set. We knew the relationship wasn't working because at six o'clock Mike would say, 'All right, that's it for the day,' and Garry's face would go white. I just thought, *Boy, he's kind of written this off.* I think we all did."

On December 31, 1999, two months before *What Planet Are You From?* opened, Nichols made a list of all of his wishes for the new century. He and his wife were at the home of Rose and Bill Styron on Martha's Vineyard. They spent Y2K eve together, ready to hunker down if all the computers broke and the lights went out. All four contributed to the list, filling it with their hopes for a better world. "We put it in some kind of container," says Rose Styron, "and we buried it at the roots of a tree, but I can't remember where. I called Diane and she didn't remember, either. The trees have all blown down now. We've had such terrible storms, I don't know where to look. It's a shame."

The fights between Nichols and Shandling were widely reported; they were too numerous and public for stories of discord not to leak. It was not until well after Nichols had completed the movie that he realized the reason for his disproportionate rage and his cruelty. In Shandling, a congenitally nervous comedian, insecure about his attractiveness to women, terrified that people were smirking at his hair, he had seen a nightmare version of his own reflection. For his entire life, he had worked to compose a surface self, an impeccably polished "Mike Nichols" capable of concealing any insecurity with an epigram, a decisive piece of direction, or a brilliantly inscrutable, wide-eyed grin whose infinite variations could mean anything from "How true" to "What a terrible idea" to "Only you and I know that we're on the *Titanic*."

Shandling had no such veneer; on the set, he had been all worry, anxiety, naked need. "Garry gave away the secret of everything Mike was afraid people might be thinking," says Hannah Roth Sorkin, who assisted Nichols. By the time Nichols recognized how his own insecurities had contributed to their friction, it was too late. *What Planet Are You From?* opened in March 2000. Reviews were merely indifferent, but the public's verdict was devastating. The film grossed just over $6 million before vanishing from theaters; it lost Sony almost $90 million. And with no immediate prospects for a project that might rehabilitate him in an increasingly unforgiving industry, Nichols suddenly found himself at what looked like the end of his run as a feature film director.

Thirty-one

THE ULTIMATE TEST

2000-2001

The weekend after *What Planet Are You From?* opened, Nichols and Sawyer hosted a dinner party for eight people, including her ABC colleagues Charles Gibson and Jeffrey Toobin and their spouses. The timing couldn't have been worse. Canceling would have been even more embarrassing than going through with it; in either case, there was no way for anyone to pretend they hadn't heard the verdict on the movie. "He was furious," Toobin says, "and sort of baffled in the face of complete failure. I think people knew not to discuss it too much, but he did. He hated Shandling at that point, and he was not taking the high road or brushing it off."

At sixty-eight, Nichols would have to remake his career once again. There was no longer anything surprising to him about the anger, the self-pity, the obsessive recapitulation of what went wrong that could engulf him in the wake of a flop—or about what followed: the listless days spent at home, with no desire for anything but solitude and cocaine, a habit with which he had long struggled. The desire for the drug had not left him; he once told a young colleague that if he knew the world was about to end, he would just lie back on his couch and freebase. "We would talk about it, as addicts do," says Aaron Sorkin, who met him at a party in the early 2000s, soon after being arrested himself for cocaine possession, and was disarmed by how frank Nichols was about his own history. "He had read about what happened to me, and he made a point of taking me aside. It's very hard to talk about those things with non-addicts, because to them it sounds unfathomable that you'd be out looking for drugs at four in the morning. He told me about his own problem because he wanted to reach out and lend a hand to me. I couldn't believe that he would do that."

What Nichols would not do, even when mired in what he ruefully called "darkness, my old friend," was lie to himself. More than anything, he wanted to understand his own behavior, and his distress about the way he had acted during production of *What Planet Are You From?* sent him back into therapy. Soon after the movie's release, he saw Bening at a party. John Lahr had written a long the profile of him for *The New Yorker* that included considerable detail about the problems on the set, and she had been forthright about a few of the issues. "John was completely ethical," Bening says, "but I felt so guilty, because I had never before said anything publicly that was remotely negative. So I went up to Mike and said, 'I've got to tell you, I'm really sorry,' and he said, 'No, no, no. You were right. I feel terrible about what I did. There was something in Garry that brought up my own fear that all I was was a hack Jewish comic.' He was working so hard to process it, and he felt bad. It was very touching."

Nichols had long believed that the only way to rebound from a professional disaster was with a small-scale labor of love. Twenty-five years earlier, he had rediscovered his passion for directing after a string of failures by throwing himself into *Streamers*. This time, he would turn to Chekhov. He went to Meryl Streep, who had not appeared onstage in decades, to see if she would be interested in playing the vain, destructive actress Irina Arkadina in a revival of *The Seagull*. To his surprise, she said yes. She wanted the production to run at the Delacorte, the 1,800-seat open-air theater in Central Park where the vast majority of tickets every summer were free to anyone who stood in line long enough. She and Kevin Kline were eager to work together on the play, but she wouldn't be available until the summer of 2001, fifteen months later.

Streep had recently turned down another high-profile part. Producer Cary Brokaw had offered her the lead in the film version of Margaret Edson's Pulitzer Prize–winning play *Wit*, an intimate, devastatingly sad drama about a terminally ill poetry professor, an expert in the work of John Donne, who gradually comes to terms with her mortality. Vivian Bearing was a showcase role for any actress, but Streep had received an Oscar nomination just a year earlier for playing a mother with cancer in *One True Thing*. "I've died in too many movies lately," she said. "I just don't want to do this."

Wit was not planned as a theatrical release; it would be made for HBO, at the time the sole home for the kind of prestigious dramatic film that network television had largely stopped making. HBO's reputation had risen sharply with the premiere of *The Sopranos* a year earlier, and its movies dominated the Emmys every fall, but HBO Films president Colin Callender was still fighting a perception among top-tier actors and directors that cable was a step down. He and Brokaw were elated when Emma Thompson agreed to star in the film and Rob Reiner agreed to direct. But Thompson, who had just had a baby daughter, wanted *Wit* shot in London; Reiner, whose wife was pregnant, didn't want to leave Los Angeles.

"Emma said she'd had a great experience with Mike on *Primary Colors*," Brokaw says. "And Colin and I were like, 'Yeah, Mike Nichols—in our dreams.' It was our good luck that he had just had a significant failure. He was not in director jail, but he was close to it, reevaluating things and licking his wounds."

"What drew me to *Wit* was the question we're all gonna face one way or the other," Nichols said. "[Dying] is the ultimate test: Can you bring honor to it? Can you find something to be proud of yourself for? Is it possible to have some kind of courage about what's coming?"

Edson was an elementary school teacher when she wrote the play. Before the movie rights were sold, *Wit*'s first producer told her, "You can either be completely involved or not at all. But you can't be a little bit involved." She wasn't sure, she said, how a play that "is so much direct address, with the main character speaking to the audience, could be translated to film—and if you take that away, it's just a sad story. So I decided to be not at all involved. I didn't want to spend three years learning how to write a screenplay. So I said, 'I'm just going to hand this to you.'"

Nichols was unfazed. "Emma's a writer," he told Brokaw, "and I can do it with her." The screenplay that resulted, which eliminated many of Vivian's disquisitions on Donne but otherwise preserved Edson's structure and language, was credited to Nichols and Thompson, although "we didn't write it in any way," says Thompson, "and I'm sure Mike would agree with me. It was written by Margaret. What the two of us did had more to do with editing, actually. We sat down to look at what we needed to take out. We had this shared credit, but it was because of something incredibly prosaic that had to do with people's contracts, and Margaret was too untroubled by egotism to care about it."

Wit was the first of three consecutive adaptations of plays that Nichols would film, and he approached it curatorially, handcrafting every moment to enhance rather than conceal its inherent theatricality. He did not alter Vivian's monologues; they would be delivered conversationally to the camera instead of to an audience. But he gave more thought to how cinematography could shape the story than he had in many years. As Vivian drifts through her memories, alternating between lucidity and reverie, he worked out a way to render her stream of consciousness in cinematic terms, with the camera panning seamlessly from her sickbed to her office, classroom, or childhood home. Sometimes she would appear in a flashback as her healthy self. Then, with one cut, she would be back in a hospital gown, her hair gone, IV tubes in her arm, but still in the same scene, interacting with someone from her past. It was a concept that required his creative team to be in sync from the start, and he worked closely with his new production designer, Stuart Wurtzel, and editor, John Bloom, to achieve it.

Wit became a kind of laboratory in which Nichols could put into practice everything he had learned about what he needed to make a production congenial and obtain a worthy result. Thompson fulfilled his first requirement—a creative partner he trusted who would be there every day. Her presence freed him to fill out the small cast idiosyncratically. He asked Harold Pinter to play Vivian's father, and Eileen Atkins, herself a cancer survivor (years earlier, he had offered her his home as a place to recover when he learned she was ill), to play Vivian's mentor. His other choices were all counterintuitive: Audra McDonald as a nurse, in one of her first dramatic screen roles; Christopher Lloyd as the presiding physician; and Jonathan M. Woodward, a twenty-six-year-old newcomer, as a callow resident.

The brief shoot at Pinewood Studios began in September 2000. It was the first time Nichols had directed a movie outside the United States in thirty years, and he was working with a much smaller budget than he was used to. He made only two demands—that HBO hire his longtime script supervisor Mary Bailey and assistant director Mike Haley, and that rehearsals be built into the schedule. "We had plenty of time," says Woodward. "Mike was mapping out the shots, which were very specific, at the same time that he was mapping out the human interaction to make sure that all those dynamics were in place before we started shooting."

Anyone on *Wit* who expected a grim slog through a painful play during a chilly London autumn was soon disarmed by the esprit de corps Nichols and Thompson worked to create. He would take Woodward or

McDonald out to the theater at night; she would cook Saturday lunches at her home for the cast and any other American strays. "I mean, Harold was not a *cheerful* person," says Woodward. "He came to the table read the first morning and announced, 'I've written a poem. It's called "Death."'" But everyone else was. Mike and Emma took the approach that we should treat everything with joy and spirit, that you don't play tragedy as tragedy but as comedy with fewer jokes."

"I turned up at Pinewood," says Atkins, "and coming towards me in one of those [golf carts] were Mike and Emma, who already had her head shaved, and they were screaming with laughter. That was the mood—that it was all going to be lovely—and that was Mike."

"It was glorious," says McDonald. "He became a dad to all of us, and even though it was such dark material, we had a ball. What was so unique was that you didn't feel the direction. He did it so subtly that it felt like he was just lightly touching a ball that was already rolling down a hill. When it was great, he just said, 'Oh, man.' And when it wasn't, he would say, 'I'll tell you what . . .' and then he'd go into a story or he'd have a discussion with you, as if he wanted to figure out the moment *with* you."

"What I remember him saying is 'This moment is like *this*,'" says Woodward. "Everything was a story or a metaphor or an analogy. If I was pushing too hard, he would say, 'Why are you trying to give a prostitute an orgasm?' And the other thing was, he wanted everything to be surprising." In one scene, Woodward and McDonald are catheterizing Vivian, who lies between them, unconscious. "In rehearsal, it had been very moving," says Brokaw. "But when Mike blocked it and filmed it, he said, 'This is completely flat. It's not working; it's dead on its feet. Everybody take a break, we're going to regroup.' A few minutes later he said, 'I know what I want to try.' He called in Audra and Jonathan and said, 'All the lines are the same, the staging is the same, but play it as if you're looking at each other—really looking—for the first time ever.'"

Nichols then took Woodward aside and told him, "Hospitals are the sexiest places in the world. People are desperate to do it, because otherwise it's horrible all the time. Sex is how they console themselves." He sent a runner to his hotel to fetch a bottle of his cologne, then pulled Woodward into a corner and told him to dab it on without letting McDonald know. "Suddenly there was an extra element for us to have fun with," says Woodward. "That was his style."

One morning, as they were driving to the studio, Nichols asked Brokaw what else he was working on. Brokaw said he had been trying to get a film version of Tony Kushner's *Angels in America* off the ground for the past seven years. Nichols had seen the first part of the play, *Millennium Approaches,* on Broadway in 1993 but had missed part two, *Perestroika.* "I'd really like to read it," he said.

"I got my office to send me an autographed bound copy of the play," Brokaw says, "and I gave it to Mike as we went to the set on a Friday. Diane was supposed to fly to London for a long weekend with Mike— Monday was a bank holiday—so I wasn't expecting a fast reaction. His attitude was more 'I'll read it when I can.' The next time I saw him was Tuesday—it had been a typical rainy London weekend, and he had a grin on his face. 'Diane got sick and didn't come,' he said. 'I had nothing to do all weekend but read. I love it!'"

Nichols was not ready to commit himself. He had never met Kushner, and he was no longer interested in working on any film without a writer he liked at hand. He was also trying to keep his head completely in the work he was doing. Throughout production, he and Thompson checked in with each other constantly, almost subliminally. "We'd do a take, then one of us would lift an eyebrow or make a little move with their mouth, and we'd do it again, or we'd nod and move on," says Thompson. "It was very instinctive. We talked a lot, but this other thing was ineffable. His love of exploration is what I remember. He never got tired of the text or of the actors. The myriad ways in which a human being can respond at any moment fascinated him endlessly."

When production ended, "Mike made a big emotional speech, as he always did, about how this was the best crew he had ever worked with," says Thompson, "and then he thanked everyone—absolutely everyone— except me. When I pointed that out, which of course I did, he grabbed me and said, 'Oh my God, you know why? Because you are blood of my blood, and bone of my bone.' I understood that completely. We had worked so closely that we didn't separate at all."

For once, there had been no mitigating circumstances; Nichols had made exactly the movie he wanted to make—a poem about death. To him, *Wit* had felt not like a demotion, but a reclamation of what he cared most about. "In the end, this awful, tragic story made us all very happy to work on [it]," he said. "I loved having something small that you can concentrate on and get as right as you can. It's not a giant, sprawling thing."

*A*ngels *in America* was a giant, sprawling thing, one that Kushner had all but decided could never become a movie by the time he walked into Trattoria Dell'Arte, a restaurant in Midtown Manhattan that was one of Nichols's favorites, for an introductory lunch in late October. There had been interest in a two-part movie version of the seven-hour, eight-actor play ever since its Broadway run. Kushner had written a pair of *Nashville*-like scripts for Robert Altman that departed from the stage version radically; at one point, Altman started to think about a cast that might include Jodie Foster, Robert Downey Jr., and Al Pacino as Roy Cohn. But the challenges of mounting two very long movies about AIDS, gay men, Mormons, Roy Cohn, the ghost of Ethel Rosenberg, and an angel in 1980s Manhattan were more than any studio was interested in. New Line, where Altman had hoped to make the film, said no to a $25 million budget, and no again when Brokaw reduced it to $20 million; in 1995, HBO Films said even

$12 million was too rich. After Altman drifted away, other directors, from P. J. Hogan (*My Best Friend's Wedding*) to Neil LaBute, expressed interest, but nothing came of it. "Once in a while, Cary and I would have lunch," says Kushner, "and he'd have index cards in the breast pocket of his jacket with names of directors on them. But I had pretty much given up."

Going into the lunch, "my main question," says Kushner, "was would we be politically compatible? Was he going to find me this irritating doctrinaire lefty, and was I going to think he was this entertainer who really didn't want to do something political?" They talked for three hours—about Kushner's childhood and Nichols's ancestry, food and Brecht, movies and theater. "There were a couple of things that made me feel I was absolutely going to let him do this, which I knew I was by the end of the meal," says Kushner. "One was, I talked to him about how Altman and I had tried to reinvent the play. Bob had said, 'The play is written like a screenplay, so it's extraordinary onstage because it has cinematic form, but if you make a movie of it, then it's just a screenplay.' I had thought that was a great insight, but Mike was skeptical. He said, 'I don't know that that's true. I want to do the play, and what I love about it is the relationships, who those people are and what they want and need from each other.'"

Nichols eventually combed out some of the more hallucinatory scenes that had been written for Altman—one in which the stricken Prior Walter, on his way to heaven, passes through an African AIDS ward, and another in which Cohn, delirious and on his way to the hospital, briefly imagines himself in a police van with the handcuffed Ethel Rosenberg. But at that first meeting, Kushner was most struck by his willingness to depart from strict naturalism; Nichols told him he wanted to keep the play's doubling. (*Angels* is staged with actors playing multiple roles: The same actress plays Ethel, the acerbic Utah Mormon Hannah Pitt, and an ancient rabbi.) "He said, sort of as a joke, 'I want to see Meryl play all those parts,'" says Kushner. "But he was the first person to suggest that the theatricality of it—even the artificiality—could be part of the fun rather than something to overcome."

Angels was not going to happen quickly. Even if HBO Films, which was now under new leadership, could be reapproached, a fresh budget would have to be drawn up and a new script would need to be written from scratch, with both plays divided into three hourlong installments that would allow the network to air the resulting miniseries any way it wanted—in two intermissionless blasts, hourlong episodes over six consecutive nights, or an hour a week every Sunday.

But HBO wanted to keep Nichols in the family; late in 2000, David Chase even gave him a role in what turned out to be a pivotal episode of *The Sopranos,* as the psychiatrist who warns Carmela Soprano that she has morally compromised herself, perhaps irretrievably, in staying married to her husband and tells her to "take only the children—what's left of them—and go." "Yes, I was Mrs. Soprano's shrink for half a week when I fired myself," he said. "I said, 'You need another Jew—I'm the wrong Jew for this particular shrink.'" (He was right; Chase replaced him with an actor named Sully Boyar whose Old Testament severity gave the series one of its most memorable scenes.) "David Chase and I became friends through that self-firing," Nichols said. "That should be the title of my biography—'The Wrong Jew.'"

The relationship between Nichols and HBO was cemented by the network's handling of *Wit,* which it treated like a theatrical feature, sending it to the Berlin International Film Festival in February and throwing a premiere at an East Side movie theater before it aired in March. Edson—who didn't sit down for lunch with Nichols and Thompson until that day and saw the film for the first time with its premiere-night audience—said she thought Nichols's work was "beautiful" and was impressed by how much it "challenged the idea I had always had that the direct address was a problem rather than something that could work in a movie." Critics were unanimously complimentary;

in *New York*, John Leonard wrote that the movie "deserves not only an Emmy but our baffled gratitude," and *Variety* praised its "subtle yet crucial shifts from theatrical to film conventions" and "Nichols's measured, top-of-his-game direction . . . [His] legendary way with actors is in evidence again." To many critics, *Wit* represented not just a return to form, but a return to his roots, in particular the shrewdly intuitive handling of stage material with which he had begun his film career.

A recent success almost always erases the stain of a less recent failure, and it would not have been difficult for Nichols to leverage the acclaim for *Wit* into a return to features. He wasn't interested; he was too happy about the fact that "there was no opening weekend to worry about, nothing else except the piece itself." *Wit* could have served as an elegant curtain call, but retirement held no interest for him. He wanted to work, and that meant rooting himself in New York and, for the first time in a decade, going back to theater.

Streep's participation alone would have made *The Seagull* one of the year's defining New York theater evenings, but she and Nichols had also gotten commitments from, among others, Kline, Christopher Walken, John Goodman, and Natalie Portman, whose role in the then-ongoing second *Star Wars* trilogy turned the play's five-week Central Park run into an event that saw teenagers camping out for tickets and required the hiring of additional security staff. (Nichols was distantly amused by the hubbub around *Star Wars*, which to him was truly a galaxy far, far away; he had cast Portman based on her work on Broadway in *The Diary of Anne Frank*.) Months earlier, he had done a reading with Cynthia Nixon as Masha and Wes Bentley as Arkadina's son, Konstantin (Kostya). "But Cynthia was doing *Sex and the City*, so she wasn't available, and Wes Bentley was not a good fit," says the show's casting director, Rosemarie Tichler. The part of Masha went to Allison Janney and then, when she had to drop out, to Marcia Gay Harden.

For Kostya, Nichols took his most daring leap, casting Philip Seymour Hoffman, who had impressed him in a Broadway revival of Sam Shepard's *True West*. The character was generally played as a darkly romantic, dramatically self-tormenting artist, but Nichols had seen the British actor Simon Russell Beale play Kostya as a depressed shlub and found it revelatory. "Mike had the best casting sense of any director I ever worked with," says Tichler. "He wanted a neurotic, frightened guy, someone uncomfortable in his own skin, to play that part, and he thought Philip had the soul of the role."

Nichols had not been in a rehearsal room for a long time when he assembled his cast to begin work. The production of *The Seagull* was both down-to-earth—all the actors would rehearse at the Public Theater, be paid $646 a week, and share dressing rooms in the cramped underground tunnels of the Delacorte—and impossibly elite, with every night's audience composed of those free enough to spend a summer day waiting for a seat and those connected enough to obtain one by other means. His return to theater marked the beginning of what Matthew Broderick called "the grand-old-gentleman phase of his career," a mode of warm benignity and discursiveness that delighted some actors and frustrated others. Those who had not worked with him before—and even some who had—were surprised by his initial reticence. "The first week he barely said anything," Kline says. "He loved actors—he was thespiphilic, even though there's no such word. But I said to Meryl, 'Is he always like this when he directs? He says so little.' And she said, 'No, it's odd.'"

"In fact, I was one of those people backstage who was kind of whining, 'Well, when is he going to start directing it?'" says Streep. "He was *really* willing to trust his actors and to let them find their way." Nichols didn't walk into the production with an argument he wanted to make about what *The Seagull* meant or how it should be played; as days passed, it became clear that his plan was to have the production be the sum of its performances rather than the realization of a vision. "He would say that casting is destiny, casting is everything," Kline says. "So in the room, he would let the actors follow their impulses, and then, rather than direct in any dictatorial sense, he would sort of edit."

Nichols wanted the scenes to be both naturalistic and theatrical, sad and funny—"he would always say that the problem with New York theater was that everybody forgot it needed to be fun, and the audience was filled with couples who would rather be anywhere except with each other at home," says Portman. Most of all, he expected his actors to "tell the story"—an instruction that became a mantra. He wanted a relaxed ensemble atmosphere that would allow everyone to ease into the casual lassitude that opens the play. His troupe, he felt, should be a family—he even gave Streep's son, Henry, a small role. ("He was wildly in love with Natalie," Streep says. "Who wasn't?")

"I remember all of us sitting around the table," says director Trip Cullman, who was then assisting him, "and Mike anecdotalizing for hours on end. I was thinking, *When are we going to* work? It took me a while to realize that he was creating trust. It was such an enormous lesson—that you don't have to start controlling everything right away." (When Nichols felt lost, he would turn to Cullman, who had had Konstantin Stanislavski's directorial notes for the play's original Moscow Art Theatre production translated, and whisper, "What did *he* do?")

To his actors, Nichols presented himself as a man who had, after a lifetime of trying, vanquished his demons. His drug use was in the past; the cigarette habit that even Sawyer could not get him to break was his darkest remaining vice. He told them of the "no assholes" rule he had insisted on since working with Walter Matthau and George C. Scott, but, says Portman, "he added that there were many times when he didn't figure out *he* was the asshole until it was too late." One night, during a round of secret-sharing over Russian vodka, he startled his cast by saying, "Someone at this table had a cocaine problem that almost killed him."

"I was like, 'Chris Walken,'" says Portman. "And he said, 'No.' I kept guessing, because there was no shortage of suspects, until I think I had guessed literally everyone, and I said, 'Meryl?' And Mike said, 'No. Me.'"

"He became, at that point, so supportive and appreciative," says his friend Jack O'Brien. "He told me, 'I was a terrible person for a long time.' I don't think he was, but it was clear that the drug period was bad and that he felt he had been mean to people. I mean, there was a lot of broken crockery behind him."

Not every actor on *The Seagull* received the same degree of affection or attention. Performers like Stephen Spinella, Marcia Gay Harden, and Debra Monk, who had signed on hoping to experience his vaunted specificity about performance, were left to fend for themselves, without the performance notes and adjustments that many actors crave; some of them grew frustrated. ("It's not you," Harden was told. "Mike just doesn't like characters who are losers.") He focused almost exclusively on four actors. He was always available for Streep and Kline, although he knew they would find their own way. ("I like the reins off, just being allowed to roam," says Streep, "and Kevin does as well, so that was heaven.") He worked closely with Hoffman, whose psychological and emotional commitment was exceptionally intense; he arrived armed with grave, thoughtful questions for Nichols every day. And he took great care with Portman, the least experienced principal cast member, who was playing Nina before returning to Harvard in the fall. The role of a beautiful young actress who must be shallow and vapidly insensitive in *The Seagull*'s first half and moving and mature in its second can present an insurmountable challenge. "It's the Juliet problem," says Tichler. "If you're young enough to be cast as Nina, you're probably too young to play her."

"I was nineteen," says Portman, "and I hadn't done anything I had needed to research except for *Anne Frank*. I'd watch Phil write down question after question in his notebook, and Meryl would make up songs to sing and put them in her pocket just in case her character suddenly wanted to burst into song." She feared she was out of her depth and turned to Nichols, whom she found to be not only a sensitive director but also "the only older man who mentored me without there ever being a creepy element in it." It was a need that Nichols would fill for many actresses—not just Portman, but Emma Thompson, Julia Roberts, Mary-Louise Parker, and Whoopi Goldberg. With men, "there would be a period of light shining on you," says Matthew Broderick, "and then it would shine on someone else, not because it was fake but because there were always new, talented people to meet." But once Nichols loved an actress, his devotion was constant; he would see them through breakups and health crises, legal problems and career mishaps, pivotal decisions and disappointments, serving as everything from kindly uncle to levelheaded adviser to sympathetic shoulder to reliable source for the best lawyer, doctor, or psychiatrist. "I think he was a genuine feminist," says Portman. "There was nothing, nothing, nothing there except him seeing you as a creative, interesting, talented human. It is the rarest, finest quality, and not many directors of his generation had it."

Nichols's jovial, energetic production of *The Seagull* opened on August 12, 2001, after a few weeks of previews. Many critics were moved by the work he had done. "For three brief, captivating, unforgettable hours," Linda Winer wrote in *Newsday*, "it is possible to see what an American national theater might have been if Hollywood and New York were in the same place." But what Winer called "an exquisitely integrated ensemble of star turns" struck other critics as spotty and uneven, although there was a great deal of praise for the anguished intensity of Streep's and Hoffman's scenes. "It was a real mishmash of acting styles," says Kline. "You had Philip Seymour Hoffman, who was doing something that I thought at the time was very middle-American, but fine and unexpected. And Meryl and I were doing the mid-Atlantic, Juilliard-Yale-training version of Chekhov, where you can't sound like you have any accent. And Chris was doing Chris, which was inimitable and riveting. But I remember reviews saying it was all over the place."

Ticket demand was so overwhelming that discussions began about an eight-week transfer to Broadway, but the schedules of various actors would make it impossible. When it became clear that the show would not have a life after its scheduled close at the end of August, Kline suggested that they wrap up with a free come-one, come-all screening on Central Park's Great Lawn. "I would leave the theater and see people waiting with sleeping bags and tents for the next day's tickets. It was insane," Kline says. "I said, 'Why don't we get ten cameras, film a performance, and put up a big screen and show it?' And Mike said, 'No, the whole point of Chekhov is that you have to be able to see everything, every character, in one picture. You can't do a close-up of this thing or that thing. His plays are one big master shot.'"

Nichols did consent to have the production filmed for the theater archive at the Library for the Performing Arts at Lincoln Center, where he had started to pay regular visits, watching a tape of George C. Wolfe's Broadway production of *Angels in America* over and over to see how it had worked. He would spend the next two years working on the miniseries. "You have to prepare like a maniac," he told Cullman. "Research and research and research. Know everything there is to know. And then, on that first day, be willing to throw it all away."

Thirty-two

MORE LIFE

2001–2003

Nichols had not attended the Emmy Awards since 1959, when he and Elaine May had performed a sketch in which he took the stage, beaming, to accept a prize for never having done any work of value whatsoever. Forty-two years later, he was a triple nominee, for producing, directing, and cowriting *Wit*. He had planned to fly to Los Angeles for the September 16 ceremony, but after the 9/11 attacks, the show was postponed until October, then postponed again because of the start of the war in Afghanistan. When the ceremony finally took place, on November 4, Nichols stayed home. It was two days before his seventieth birthday, and he was in New York City holding auditions for *Angels in America*. The stars were on board; Streep had said yes during *The Seagull*, and Thompson earlier than that, and Pacino had agreed to portray Roy Cohn, the play's vicious, droll, and profane embodiment of ruthlessness and self-deception. "I wanted Mike to cast Dustin Hoffman," says Kushner. "I love Al Pacino, and of course I ended up thrilled with his Roy. My only initial worry was that when he was young, he was gorgeous. He was Michael Corleone—someone born into power. What I wanted for Roy was someone who'd had to struggle all his life for every bit of power he had. The day after Pacino was announced, I was at a party and I felt someone kind of hit me from behind. I turned around and it was Dustin Hoffman, and he said, 'Al Pacino's Jewish?! Fuck you, and fuck Mike, too!'"

Although Pacino, Streep, and Thompson were still finalizing their deals, their participation looked secure enough to get Nichols a green light from HBO, at a budget that would top $60 million. But when the network said it wanted big names for the remaining roles, he told them no. "People like Matt Damon and Reese Witherspoon were on the list," says *Angels* producer Celia Costas, "and Mike said, 'Movie stars are not going to be able to handle the language, let alone memorize as much as they're going to have to in order to shoot what will be a normal day for us. I need people from theater.'" He also needed actors who were available to give a full year to the job. The *Angels* schedule was a marathon—preproduction in January and February, rehearsals in March, and shooting from April to December; Nichols's insistence on a long summer break was the only concession he made to his age.

Jeffrey Wright had won a Tony for playing the fierce, morally exacting nurse Belize, and at thirty-five, he was still young enough for the role. "My thought was that no one was going to play Belize other than me," he said, "and if they tried to bring that into being, some sets might mysteriously burn to the ground." After rewatching the Broadway production and seeing him onstage in Suzan-Lori Parks's play *Topdog/ Underdog*, Nichols believed he was the only choice; no other actors were considered. Nor were any actresses called in for the Valium-addicted Mormon wife, Harper Pitt; Nichols offered the part to Mary-Louise Parker, who had won a Best Actress Tony for *Proof* a few months earlier. But to cast the remaining three roles—the reluctant visionary Prior Walter, his unfaithful, relentlessly self-questioning boyfriend, Louis, and the closeted Mormon lawyer Joe Pitt—Nichols, Kushner, and casting director Juliet Taylor spent several days in his production office on West Fifty-seventh Street, seeing dozens of actors.

"Mike would sometimes fall in love with whoever the latest hot person was," says Taylor. "Hollywood actors did come up in conversation—'What about so-and-so?' But some of those monologues were two pages, and his first instinct was right. Most of them couldn't handle it, and it was a revelation when somebody could."

Not all the surprises were pleasant. After Adrien Brody read for Louis, his agent called to say he was uneasy about the role, which included intimate scenes with other men. Another actor was perhaps too comfortable with his body. "He auditioned with a scene that takes place at a urinal," says Taylor, "and . . . I'll just say he did it in very specific detail. We were all sitting there going, 'What? You don't need to . . .'" Then there was the television star who decided to make up his lines. "Mike stopped him and said, 'I'd like you to do the script as written,'" says Kushner. "He said, 'Can I see the script? I don't really know it.' That was the first time I saw that Mike could be scary. He had this smile where he opened his eyes very wide and his eyebrows went straight up. He was technically smiling, but also baring his teeth. You had the feeling that if he had been less charming and polite, he might have said something devastatingly nasty. But he just looked at him with beautifully performed shock and said, 'Why not?' And the actor said, 'Come on . . . it's *film*. Don't you want to see what I can bring to it?' And Mike said, still smiling, 'I don't know that I do.'"

Ben Shenkman had played Roy Cohn in a student production and later played Louis in San Francisco. "I'd just been in *Proof* with Mary-Louise and I knew Mike liked it, so I was terrified," he says. "I thought, *I want to have this great experience of auditioning, but I don't want to get it, because I'm not up to it.* But I wasn't going to deliberately tank the audition!"

"When he read Louis," Taylor says, "we wanted to weep." Nichols liked Shenkman so much that he asked him to stick around and read with potential Priors and Joes. "I knew I was connecting with Mike," he says. "I said, 'Of course!' and then I had an hourlong break and I stood

on the sidewalk thinking, *The world has changed.* And I immediately
played out all that anxiety." He said to Nichols, "To be totally honest,
I'm not sure I can do what I did in the audition again, and I think you
should know that I might not be able to duplicate it in front of a camera." Without meaning to, Shenkman had, in his confession, perfectly
embodied a character about whom Prior says, "Watching him stick his
head up his asshole and eat his guts out over some relatively minor moral
conundrum . . . was the best show in town." Nichols laughed and told
Shenkman, "The thing I've finally realized after all this time is: You
have to not care. Sometimes it'll be there and sometimes it won't. The
potential is all."

"For him to say, 'The thing I've finally realized . . .' was so generous," says Shenkman. "As if he was saying, 'Yes, my boy, we're all artists. This is what we all think about. Everyone is like you.'" He got the
part and ended up reading with the two other actors Nichols went on
to cast, Justin Kirk and Patrick Wilson. Kirk had come close to working with Nichols before—he was almost hired to play Robin Williams
and Nathan Lane's son in *The Birdcage,* and he's fleetingly seen in a
photograph in *Wolf* as Michelle Pfeiffer's late brother. "Nice face," Jack
Nicholson says in the movie. Nichols agreed. "He looks like religious
art," he said, "like a quattrocento painting. That's what I want Prior to
look like." And Wilson, cast as Joe Pitt after Billy Crudup passed on
the role, was "very, very new," says Taylor. Like Kirk, he was rising fast
in New York theater and getting regular work on Broadway. "But I
don't think I had ever been in a film or even in front of a camera before," he says. "I didn't know about lights, angles, lenses, where to look,
anything."

"They were all young, all very raw," says Costas. "Mike embraced
that innocence. He wanted actors whose core he believed in. If that was
there, he felt the rest would follow."

By January, the screenplay was almost finished. "I had gone to his apartment with the script for the first hour of *Millennium*," says Kushner. "I'd put in language about point of view, this angle, that angle. We had lunch, and he said, 'Have you ever worked on a movie?' I said, 'No, I've never even been on a set.' He said, 'I can sort of tell that. The good news is, you don't need to know about making movies. I know how to make movies. You just have to tell me what you want the actors to say and what you want people to see, and you don't have to tell it in any kind of fancy way.' Later I learned how to write with the camera in mind and do other things that screenwriters do, but that was the moment when Mike made it possible for me to become a screenwriter."

Nichols had not asked for the play's sexuality or politics to be toned down; the cuts he wanted—most of which were in *Perestroika*—had more to do with anything that pulled attention from the core characters (a speech by an elderly Russian revolutionary that opens the second play was jettisoned) or that violated his sense of the supernatural acts in *Angels* as hallucinations. He told Kushner to eliminate a scene in which pioneers in a diorama at the Mormon Visitors' Center come to life, because its objective leap outside of reality broke the rules the play itself had set up. "I can't do . . . Mormons coming across the desert without snapping [the thread of the narrative]," Nichols said.

"Other than Mike, no director has ever called me on that," says Kushner. "But also, he wasn't interested in the ooky-spooky stuff at all. He was not going to make the play New Agey. I never wanted the play to be that, but it didn't bother me that some people did. It bothered Mike. He was not interested in creating fantasy. Mike's version of the play strips away a lot of the bells and whistles—he was interested in telling a story of people who love each other and betray each other and themselves and construct lives based on lies, and sometimes they find their way back to each other and sometimes they pay a terrible price. That was an important lesson for me: that that is fundamentally what the main event of *Angels* is."

In March, Nichols gathered the cast in New York, where almost all of the shoot would take place, for a month of read-throughs and rehearsals, wardrobe and makeup tests, and immersion in the world of *Angels*. Most of them needed no education about the toll AIDS had taken; nonetheless, he arranged for them to visit his friend Cynthia O'Neal's charity Friends In Deed to learn more. "The rehearsals were hugely digressive and seminar-y. We rarely stood up," says Shenkman. "We'd be in a room with some incredible table of snacks and we'd read the scenes and talk about them." Some actors felt their way into their roles gradually; others were ready to go. "I was amazed at how prepared Pacino was," says Kushner. "He had two old paperback copies of the play, filled with notes, all splayed open—they had obviously fallen into the bathtub at some point." By the first day of rehearsal, Pacino had done weeks of preparation with his own team of colleagues and coaches. "Al works very hard before we ever see him," said Nichols. "He needs a long time to familiarize himself with the words and make them his own."

Nichols carved out extra rehearsal time with Shenkman and Kirk. "He wanted to give Justin and me a shot to flesh out what the relationship between Prior and Louis had been," says Shenkman, "because the structure of the play is, you meet them and immediately the relationship explodes. So it was a backstory kind of thing." It was also the moment at which both young actors realized how hard Nichols was going to push them. "At the first rehearsal, I said the last line of the play, and Mike turned to me in front of this table and said, 'Well . . . you're the prophet,'" says Kirk. "I suddenly had Al Pacino looking at me! I felt like: I'm *cooking*! A couple of weeks of rehearsal go by and I get a message saying, 'Mike wants to see you at lunch. Come to his office.' I went in, and the gist of what he said was 'It's not working. It's not landing. And I talked to someone who said that during rehearsals you need a kick in the ass.'"

Kirk's head started to spin. "My first thought was: *Who can it possi-*

bly be?" he says. "I found out later that it was Joe Mantello," who had played Louis in the Broadway *Angels* and recently directed Kirk on-stage. "I couldn't decide whether to be angry or not, but that was the kick in the ass. From that day forward, I was terrified. On the first day we shot, Mike came over to me and said, 'We got it. It's great. What you're doing is perfect.' But for the whole shoot, I never lost the fear. I went home every night thinking, *You didn't hit it.*"

On March 20, Nichols went to Washington, D.C., to receive a National Medal of Arts alongside Johnny Cash, Kirk Douglas, Helen Frankenthaler, and Yo-Yo Ma. Three weeks later, he was shivering in Central Park on a chilly April night, about to film two men starting to have anonymous unprotected sex. *What the fuck am I doing here?* he thought.

The first week of production had not gone smoothly. Nichols had begun with two days of shooting in a cramped Queens diner—a difficult scene described on the call sheet as "Louis' diatribe on race in America," a long monologue that he later said was exactly the wrong place to begin nine months of filming. He would end up unable to use most of the footage. Now, standing under banks of floodlights placed along Central Park South, watching extras in black leather cruise one another as production assistants used smudge pots to fill the park's lamplit walkways with fog, he felt lost. Streep would not arrive to begin work until the following week, and Thompson and Pacino would not start until a few weeks after that.

He and his cinematographer, Stephen Goldblatt, were also off to a rough start. "He was so obnoxious and difficult at the beginning that I finally told him, 'I quit,'" says Goldblatt, "and as soon as I did that, he apologized profusely and we were fine for the rest of the shoot." At the moment, Nichols was working with the cast's least experienced actors; he had not contended with so many novices in major roles since directing Hoffman and Katharine Ross in *The Graduate*. He had envisioned a shot in which the camera would push from the bar at the Plaza Hotel, where Roy was trying to seduce Joe professionally, across Central Park South and into a different jungle with its own rites of male negotiation and persuasion. But nothing was coming together. At 10 p.m., he called Kushner and said, "You've got to come! I don't know what I'm doing! I don't know how to get a performance out of these actors—they're baby narcissists!"

Kushner was also worried. Early in the production, he wrote in his diary, "Everything still feels glum and depressed and second-week-of-rehearsal-ish." When he got to the park, he told Nichols, who had calmed down, "You know they're extraordinary actors, so if they're stuck on something, there's a reason." But Nichols was also stuck. "When Tony wasn't there," says Trip Cullman, who served as Nichols's on-set assistant, "I was, shockingly, the only gay guy on the production most of the time. So Mike asked me to teach him and the actors what cruising looked like. Which I have to say was a lot of fun."

After that night, Nichols started to unclench, and so did his actors. "Patrick Wilson was astonishing," he said. "He never looked down for a mark, never did anything phony, always looked in the right direction . . . He walked right in, like a little kid sometimes does in a movie, and knew how to do it. But as the play asked more and more of them, they all grew."

A month later, when Pacino showed up, the production kicked into a higher gear. Pacino, all of whose scenes were to be shot in a five-week sprint in May and June, did not like to act in front of writers and had Nichols boot Kushner from the Kaufman Astoria Studios set the first morning he got into costume and makeup. ("When can I come back?" Kushner asked Nichols. "When he's done," came the reply.) His arrival changed the rhythm of the filming. Nichols and most of his actors preferred to move on after a few takes of each scene, and sometimes not even that. "Mike always fell in love with the master"—the start-to-finish shot in which all the actors are visible, which is usually filmed before close-ups—"and I would have to beg him to do more takes," says Goldblatt. But Pacino never wanted to quit, even after the twelfth, sixteenth, or eighteenth try at a scene. "Yeah, he likes that," says Streep. "Everything he did was always interesting, though—even in a late take, he'll throw you a curve. He's like De Niro. Some actors just don't want to go home!"

"He kept cursing Ron Leibman [who had played Cohn on Broadway]," says Brian Markinson, who shared a scene with Pacino. "He would say, 'That fucking guy had all those performances and so much time with the text. It takes time to get it in your belly!'"

"I'd say to him, 'I can't imagine anything better, I'm very happy,'" said Nichols. "And he'd say, 'I'll give you one more for free.' And it would be better. He was working toward a facility with the whole thing. The words he had, my God, the long speeches. They were completely digested, and came out in music and fire."

Pacino and Shenkman had no dialogue scenes together, but Shenkman came to the set anyway. "It was the day they were shooting the scene when Roy's doctor tells him he has AIDS," he says. "Pacino was a hero of mine. It was the only time I said to Mike, 'Would it be okay if I watched?' I sat there and watched him act, and I watched Mike direct. They did the scene a bunch of times. Mike turned to me and said, 'So what have you learned?' I said, 'Keep it simple?' And he said, 'No. That's not the right answer. The right answer is: See how hard it is? Even for the master, even for your idol? See how many times he has to try it? You've just watched ten takes, and I know you can see it was great here but not there, and then great again but not great right at that important moment. That's what film acting is. We're not trying to draw the perfect line. You do whatever you need to do—be real, be fake, be quiet, be loud—and then leave the rest to me. I'll know it when I have it, and I'll put it all together.'"

Nichols summoned every bit of technique he had learned over the decades for *Angels in America*. He took a two-minute scene with no dialogue that is only referenced in the play—the ornate funeral of a beloved local drag queen who has died of AIDS—and turned it into a wordless essay on grief and celebration, filling the pews with real drag queens, and capturing Prior's despair and alienation, Belize's concern for and impatience with him, the quiet heartbreak of a family out of its element, the affinity between a gospel choir and a drag performer, and the way the stricken gay community used excess, spectacle, and song as a bulwark against endless loss. For a late-night scene in which Belize talks a dying Roy through his hallucination as Ethel Rosenberg watches, he had Goldblatt use a swaying, almost hypnotic camera to suggest that Roy was drifting inexorably out to sea, or perhaps being rocked to sleep by Belize's evocation of the afterlife. He filmed a slow dance between Prior and a spectral version of Louis with a romantically spinning camera that moved in from the two men holding each other in a close embrace to Prior's face, then pulled back to show him alone, a piercingly sad moment that could not have been achieved onstage. And when Shenkman and Kirk struggled with their first scene together, in which Prior tells Louis he has AIDS—"Like Justin, I always went home feeling I screwed up," says Shenkman—Nichols took both actors to his trailer and choreographed their interaction beat by beat, working through every line and telling them how to time each physical gesture. At one point Shenkman said, "I feel like I'm pushing." Nichols said gently, "It's only bad to push in comedy. In emotional scenes, sometimes it's okay."

"*Angels* can get really tough for actors," says Kushner. "If they go deep inside the characters to find the terrible things they're feeling before they've internalized the language, it can get very teary and become an exercise in bathos." Nichols fought against that. "The idea that acting is *feeling* . . . is such nonsense and so useless and leads us into a corner of unintelligible people muttering," he said. "It's the ultimate perversion of Lee Strasberg and the Method."

Throughout the shoot, he worked to keep the playing field level. He did not want a set on which newcomers felt intimidated by movie stars. "He didn't differentiate that way," says Cullman. "He put Ben and Justin and Patrick right on the level of anyone else. He made everyone feel like they were his best friend, receiving the juiciest tidbit of gossip or theater history or lore or keen observation. It was absolutely strategic. In order for them not to go mad with anxiety that they were working with Emma and Meryl, he made everyone part of the gang. And he knew exactly what each actor needed, whether it was a lot of takes for Pacino or for Mary-Louise to be left alone so she could be focused and internal in her prep work."

The sheer duration of the filming was more punishing than anyone involved could have imagined. Production had to shut down briefly when Thompson got sinusitis after days of "playing an angel having an orgasm while hanging eighty feet up on a wire. The wind machines were blowing all the studio dust up my nose," she says. "It was one of the highlights of my life, but it stretched us all as far as we could go. At one point, I came in and Mike said, 'It'd be great if the angel were a lot taller than Prior, but it'll take us two hours to raise the floor she's standing on,' and I just burst into tears."

But a deep sense of comradeship usually prevailed. Streep knew just when one of the actors needed a few murmured words of encouragement about how much Mike liked them, and often the actors would hang around on set even during their downtime; one morning, Thompson, who was off duty, snuck into the back of a funeral-chapel set to watch Streep, almost unrecognizable as a rabbi, deliver a eulogy. "Emma and I talked about this," says Streep. "*Angels* was like making three movies one right after another. Usually when you worked with Mike, you said goodbye to him after a couple of months and that was it. With this, we kept coming back."

Nichols's health began to suffer, and the respiratory problems that had afflicted him for years began to flare up into a terrifyingly protracted racking cough. "When I first worked with him," says Mary

Bailey, "I read Cocteau's diary in which he talks about being in the hospital and says, 'The person next to me had this horrible cough, and sounded like'—it's translated as 'a lacerated orchid.' That's what Mike's cough sounded like."

"He would sneak cigarettes with Mike Haley behind the scenery," says Costas, "which was terrible, because he was very susceptible to lung infections, anything pulmonary, and then he would get sick and take steroids, which are not good for the personality. You just wanted him to take a few days and slow down, but it was very difficult for him."

After several months, production fell slightly behind schedule, and for the first time since the beginning, his spirits started to flag. "I walked over to his office on the set in Queens," says Brokaw, "and he was at his desk looking despondent, with his chin in his hands. I said, 'What is it?' He said, 'I'm tired. I'm just tired. I don't want to do this today.' And I took a breath and said, 'Mike, there are 165 people outside on that stage, so pull it together. What would cheer you up?'"

Sometimes it was a visitor—Maurice Sendak spent a day on location in a cemetery, playing a rabbi, alongside Kushner, and Natalie Portman would drop by just to hang out and watch Nichols work. But most often, the answer was food. "I would get in his chauffeur-driven car and go to Peter Luger's every day to get him and the cast burgers for lunch," Cullman says. "Part of my job was to de-stress him with snacks or cigarettes or candy, or a joke, or a conversation, which is what he really wanted. Sometimes his anger would flare up, but it wasn't often, and it was never about something stupid or petty. It was always about incompetence, someone not doing their job as well as he knew they could or as well as he was."

The shooting of *Angels* went on for so long that at one point or another, almost everyone involved was given a birthday party; thanks to HBO's very free spending, each one was more elaborate than the last. Nichols's, thrown on an Astoria soundstage, featured a performance by the singer Diana Krall, ten Rockettes, and a guest appearance by

Whoopi Goldberg in full angel raiment. "It was all accomplished in an hour and twenty minutes," says Costas, "because we had to get back to work."

In November, production moved to Hadrian's Villa, outside Rome, where Nichols had decided to film the scenes set in heaven, in which Prior tells a council of angels how much he wants to live and excoriates God for abandoning the world in the face of human suffering. The scene was particularly arduous for Kirk, not just textually but physically; he would spend much of one day wading through a pool of hip-deep dirty water in a hospital gown that concealed a wetsuit.

"I feared for Justin when we were in Italy," Streep says. "That was really hard. In the theater, you can make the scene work with lighting, production design, and the momentum of everything that has carried you to that point. But it's different when you're trying to speak those words in the middle of a daylit tourist area with people milling around."

"Justin had got really thin, and he worried a lot," says Thompson, who mentored Kirk throughout the shoot and worked closely with him in Italy to help him through the scene. "He may have worried even more than Ben. I adored those boys—they threw every ounce of themselves into it. I'd tell them, 'Don't worry so much,' and they'd say, 'Oh, yeah, easy to say,' and then we'd go and drink in an Irish pub."

"Believe me, it was overwhelming," says Kirk. "It was a baptism by fire. It's possible that all the insecurities I had served the character, who was always off balance, and the story. And I always felt that Mike was in my corner. But after that, I was a changed actor. I was never intimidated by material or co-workers again."

The cast and crew returned to New York, and on a cold late-autumn morning, Streep, Wright, Kirk, and Shenkman gathered at Bethesda Fountain to shoot the scene that ends the film, an epilogue set five years after Prior's return from the celestial world. Although there was still a month of production to go, it felt like a goodbye of sorts. Parker had already filmed her last scene as Harper Pitt and had burst into tears as soon as she finished; the actors and Nichols felt they had been through something epic together. Sawyer came to Central Park to see her husband film the send-off, as did a number of Nichols's friends. "Justin had gotten better and better and better," said Nichols, "and then he had had these difficulties with the stuff in heaven. And then, at the end, he suddenly relaxed. And we were all extremely moved. You could see that something important had happened to him. He trusted me, and he trusted Tony, and he trusted the place we were in. And he was amazing."

That day, as Kirk spoke Prior's last lines—"I bless you. More life. The great work begins"—to the camera, Nichols found himself weeping. "He was always living the scene with you, whatever it was," says Streep. "It was so wonderful to feel there was someone in the same groove. And yes, he liked to cry. He was an easy crier. And no eyelashes, so there was no place for the tears to hide and nothing ever to stop them."

Thirty-three

BIG ISN'T TRUE

2003-2005

Nichols spent much of the winter and spring of 2003 in the editing room. "He was exhausted," says Kushner. "The stuff in Hadrian's Villa had been complicated, and he was not entirely sure he'd gotten it right. Finally he finished, and he showed me his cut. I loved it. I went over to the editing room, where he was still working, and I told him it was magnificent and I hugged him. He looked enormously pleased, and he just said, 'Well. It's what I meant.'" "In the end, if I have to pick something I'm proudest of, it's that," Nichols said. "For a year of going to work every day and shooting, all of us forgot that it would ever be seen by anyone. That was very fulfilling."

If *Wit* had been a small victory, *Angels* was a large one; the reviews were among the most laudatory of Nichols's filmmaking career, with Frank Rich, who had often been tough on his work, invoking his directing hero Elia Kazan in calling the miniseries "the most powerful screen adaptation of a major American play since *A Streetcar Named Desire*," and *Variety*'s Todd McCarthy praising him for "once again proving, after 40 years at or near the forefront of the American performing arts scene, that he knows how to put a work of theater on the screen to maximum effect . . . Ever the great director of actors, Nichols allows everyone—stars and newcomers alike—to shine." The praise began a yearlong march through awards ceremonies that included both a competitive win and a lifetime achievement honor from the Directors Guild of America, a Producers Guild of America Award, and, finally, an Emmy sweep: All eight of *Angels'* main cast members were nominated; Streep, Pacino, Parker, and Wright won; and Nichols picked up trophies as both producer and director. He accepted the latter in a brief and modest speech in which he reminded the audience that AIDS remained a worldwide crisis and said, "We must all do what we can."

On December 7, 2003, the night HBO aired the first part of *Angels,* Nichols and Sawyer were in Washington, D.C. He had been named a Kennedy Center honoree and was being feted by, among others, Streep, Candice Bergen, Christine Baranski, Patrick Wilson, and Philip Seymour Hoffman. Many of his friends, including Nora Ephron and her husband, Nicholas Pileggi, made the trip from New York just to be in the audience. Tom Stoppard joked that Nichols had been "awarded . . . eighty-seven medals, including hygiene." To keep him humble, he said, "we follow him around and remind him that he made that Garry Shandling movie." Then Elaine May addressed the crowd. "Mike has chosen to do things that are really meaningful, and that have real impact and real relevance," she said, "but he makes them so entertaining and exciting that they're as much fun as if they were trash."

Earlier in the year, the producer Bill Haber had approached Nichols with a rough script and a handful of songs for a stage musical based on the 1975 film *Monty Python and the Holy Grail.* Nichols and Eric Idle were old friends whose families had vacationed together in Barbados. Nevertheless, his first reaction, he said, was "Please go away."

He was all too familiar with the misery and sweat required to bring a musical to Broadway. "I directed *The Apple Tree*, I produced *Annie*, and I saved *My One and Only* together with Peter Stone," he said. "It's enough. I hate doing musicals. I hate being out of town with musicals. I hate watching the thing that you've already cut but it has to stay in for five days until the [new] orchestrations arrive."

Nichols was a Python fan, and, having seen Richard Burton through the run of *Camelot* on Broadway forty years earlier, he had affection for the troupe's hilarious, violent, anarchic take on the Arthurian legend. He wondered if a Broadway version of *Holy Grail* might somehow avoid turning into the "special kind of hell" that directing musicals always became. But he told Haber he couldn't even think about doing the show for a year. He was already preparing his first feature film since *What Planet Are You From?*—an adaptation of Patrick Marber's *Closer* that was everything *Spamalot* was not: small-scale, adult, and completely within his control.

On paper, *Closer* looked like an elegantly symmetrical conclusion to Nichols's filmmaking career. Like *Virginia Woolf*, the play was a four-character adult drama that focused on gamesmanship and jealousy; like *Carnal Knowledge*, it trained its most merciless gaze on misogynistic male competitiveness; and like *Betrayal*, it explored infidelity as a shatteringly destructive force. It was also a shrewdly judged way to return to movies without risking another costly catastrophe. The film, which consisted of a dozen or so long scenes, would cost only about $27 million, and casting—still Nichols's forte—would be half the work.

Marber had once hoped to direct the adaptation himself; when it became clear that that wasn't going to happen, he gave his screenplay to Nichols and Brokaw, who made a deal with Sony. Several years earlier, when the play debuted in London, Clive Owen had starred as Dan, a young, smug author who suffers a brutal comeuppance; he now wanted to play that character's rival, Larry, a betrayed doctor who coolly awaits his moment of vengeance. Nichols hired Jude Law to play

Dan and cast Natalie Portman as Alice, a younger woman who becomes involved with both men and eventually takes work as a stripper. "I know she can do it," he told Brokaw. "And I think it's a great opportunity for her to show herself as an adult woman."

To play Anna, a photographer who becomes the fourth corner of *Closer*'s sexual quadrangle, Nichols signed Cate Blanchett. "They all knew the play," says Brokaw. "We did a back-of-the-napkin budget and figured we needed nine weeks of shooting. They green-lit the movie . . . and then we were told that Cate Blanchett is pregnant and that she's going to be in her sixth or seventh month when we're shooting. As it was written, there was nudity in the role, and replacing her was going to be highly problematic in terms of sex discrimination. So we settled Cate out. I won't disclose the terms, and it wasn't contentious, but it was a bit of a difficult negotiation."

Nicole Kidman and Tom Cruise, who had considered going after the movie rights when the play was on Broadway, had since divorced, but Kidman was still interested in playing Anna. So was Julia Roberts. "It was painful," says Brokaw. "We talked about it for a week, and Mike said the contrast between Julia and Natalie felt better to him."

"I was so smitten with her," Nichols said. "She was like a goddess." He arranged to meet Roberts at a Los Angeles restaurant. "I was beside myself," she says. "I didn't know what to wear. I left ridiculously early and sat in my parked car on the side of the road thinking, *What's a good time to go in?* I walked in ten minutes early, just as Mike was coming out of the washroom. We looked at each other and he gave me that smile and said, 'You're early. That's cheating!' I went in knowing I was his second choice, but I was surprised how immediately I was at ease with him."

In his years on *Wit* and *Angels*, Nichols had become committed to a working style that combined film and theater. On *Closer*, he tried something that was rare for plays but almost unheard of for movies: a workshop several months ahead of time. His plan was born out of necessity—a week in mid-2003 was the only slot all four stars had before filming began in London the following January—but Nichols also believed in the value of immersion followed by a long stretch away from the material. "In making movies," he said, "time is so short—because it is so expensive—that we tend to neglect the place from which the best ideas come, namely that part of ourselves that dreams. The unconscious is our best collaborator."

Nichols told his actors that he had chosen them in part because they all reminded him of one another. "He said he saw all the characters in the play as different facets of one person, which I found fascinating," says Portman. Owen says the workshop "was basically the four of us sitting around drinking up Mike Nichols every day. It's not like we rehearsed the scenes; instead we would read them and then discuss the themes they brought up. It would spin off into very personal areas. It felt like a safe place for airing experiences. Mike was nothing short of dazzling in that period, so knowledgeable, so smart, so funny, so good at talking about life. After that, I really started to hold on to the idea of thinking about something challenging early in the process."

During that week, Nichols tried something he had first attempted with May during *Primary Colors*. "He said, 'We're all going to keep ourselves on the same page of what's happening in every scene by naming every moment,'" Portman says. "'This is the scene where he realizes that she's cheating. This is the scene where she falls out of love.' He wanted us to go through it in that explicit a manner, to make sure we were all telling the same story."

The process was more familiar to Owen, Portman, and Law, who had all acted onstage, than it was to Roberts, who shyly confessed that in fifteen years of starring in movies, she had never participated in a workshop. "She was very nervous in the beginning," says Mary Bailey. "And by the end, she brought books for us all that she had loved—Jeanette Winterson novels. She said she felt like something about them related to the themes of the script, and she wanted to share that with everybody."

Private, cloistered, and emotionally charged, the shooting of *Closer* at London's Elstree Studios represented the kind of moviemaking Nichols loved, and he drew on strategies he had developed over decades to bind his actors to one another and to him. After work, he took them out for meals; on weekends he showed them old movies that connected to the one they were making. And when a moment wasn't landing, he always had an analogy ready. "At the start of shooting," says Roberts, "we spent the day doing a scene where Jude comes in and I take his picture and we end up kissing. It was complex and intimate and intense, and we didn't know each other that well, so it was also a little uncomfortable. A couple of days later, Mike called for a conversation. I think we went into Jude's dressing room. I was sitting on the floor, and Mike said, 'I've seen the dailies, and it just didn't work.' My heart was pounding so hard. He said, 'It's entirely my fault. I put the camera in the wrong place. But I've figured out what the scene is now. Have you ever seen *Fantasia*?' Jude and I kind of looked at each other. And Mike said, 'The kiss in this scene is the hippo's toe in *Fantasia*. Everything balances on just the toe.'

"Well, first of all, I've never felt more pressure kissing someone in my life!" she says, laughing. "But I remember the complete clarity that it brought—the movie is the hippo, this kiss is the toe, we must accomplish it perfectly. We did it one more time. He was so clear. There was no confusion about what he wanted from me, ever."

Nichols prodded his actors to explore the story's darkest ramifications. "To me, it's about how mysterious sex is," he said. "Sometimes it's great. Sometimes it's not so great, but it's still great . . . It can ruin you, it can make people lose everything they have . . . but if anyone understands it, I don't know them." When he shot the roughest exchange, in which a livid Owen confronts Roberts about her unfaithfulness, "it was the physicality that he was focused on," says Owen. "He spent a lot of time making sure the way I followed her around the apartment was right, and that turned out to be the unlocking of the scene. I remember someone telling me about another filmmaker, 'Oh, you're gonna love this guy, he's an actor's director.' And usually what that means is they talk a lot, which isn't always the best thing. Mike didn't do that kind of line-by-line directing. He put you in a place where he made you feel you could do it, and then he let you go and made you want to deliver for him." On *Closer*, Nichols let his actors play out the scenes in long takes, which Owen says was "demanding but hugely satisfying. It's not just that the takes are long, it's that there aren't many, so you have to come ready to work."

With Portman, Nichols was careful and protective, particularly in the strip club sequence, for which, at her request, he was happy to eliminate some of the nudity. "He wants to see my bare ass [even] less than my father would," said Portman at the time. He made sure she was comfortable with the angles, the costumes, and the movement, and walked her through the scene until she felt ready. "What he did for me . . ." she says. "Lord, may I have that ability to offer that kind of mentorship and guidance to one other person."

He couldn't imagine slowing down. He and most of his oldest friends were still thinking about the next show, the next movie, the next job. Back in New York, soon after the opening of a revival of the musical *Assassins*, he had dinner at the theater haunt Orso with Sondheim, Calley, and Avedon. Their conversation soon turned to a can-you-top-this *alter kocker* exchange of stories about their various heart problems and medical close calls. Old age was starting to chase them all; there was nothing to do but try to outrun it. Just six months later, Avedon would be gone, dead of a cerebral hemorrhage at eighty-one. The loss tore at Nichols. Avedon's reported contention that they had once been lovers remains uncorroborated, but they had indisputably been the closest of friends for forty years. Avedon's assistant Norma Stevens said that Nichols was the third person she called the day Avedon died; he was almost too stricken to speak, and crushed that they had quarreled—as was often the case, it was over something insulting that Avedon had said—during what turned out to be the last meal they shared.

For Nichols, the question "What happens next?" remained not just a pleasure but a necessity, even an addiction. He talked about slowing down and making a place in his life to do nothing, but he couldn't really imagine it. In the summer, he flew to Los Angeles at Streep's request to present her American Film Institute Life Achievement Award, and he remained on the hunt for projects that could reunite them. He and Julia Roberts were thinking about doing another film together. And he had started to work with May on an adaptation of Carl Hiaasen's comic mystery *Skinny Dip*; Nichols paid for the movie rights himself, as he had done on *Primary Colors*. "Watching the two of them go back and forth in his office was one of the greatest days," says Hiaasen. "He was already talking about casting, and of course he had everyone's phone number. I've done enough meetings so that I take it all with an amused grain of salt. But he wasn't a bullshitter, which many of them are. He threw himself into it."

Eric Idle was still waiting. He had continued to work on *Spamalot*, and when Nichols read his newest draft, he said, "Oh, shit! I have to do this." He agreed to a New York workshop in October, a tryout in Chicago over Christmas and New Year's, and a Broadway opening in February. The cast would include Tim Curry as King Arthur as well as two Nichols favorites, David Hyde Pierce and Hank Azaria. Nichols started supervising Idle's redrafts, meeting with him and the show's songwriter, John Du Prez, and giving them marching orders to come up with a workable narrative.

The show needed one. Idle and Du Prez had conceived a strange, scattershot hybrid—a semi-faithful transposition of the movie crossed with a random parody of every musical-theater cliché they could think of, with Andrew Lloyd Webber a particular target. Nichols was determined not to let *Spamalot* turn into a series of blackout sketches. "We [have] to have at least the pretense of a plot," he said. "Not an elaborate plot, just a plot." He added, "There is no story at all in [*Holy Grail*]. It's a revue, secretly or not so secretly. And they give up in the end and have everyone arrested. [But] if you have people come to a theater, there's a kind of understanding between you that you will tell them a story."

Nichols assumed that *Closer* was proceeding smoothly toward its release, so it was an unhappy surprise when test screenings revealed that audiences hated the film's ending, which came directly from the play and revealed the death of one of the principal characters. "It really did not work," says Brokaw. Before he undertook *Spamalot*, Nichols would have to reconceive the movie's last ten minutes, reassemble his cast, and spend a week doing reshoots.

The screening reaction was bad enough to alarm Sony chief Amy Pascal, who called Scott Rudin and said, "Oh, my God, it's a total disaster. The audience hates it." Rudin, who owned the rights to the play, asked to see the film. "She showed it to me," he says, "and I said, 'It's a great movie, and I know how to solve this. Let me take it over'" as executive producer. Nichols, who had had a falling-out with Brokaw over what was required of him in the reshoot, was grateful for the intervention. "*Closer* was where our relationship really got cemented," Rudin says. For the next ten years, he would be Nichols's most powerful champion, and a loyal friend and ally.

With the reshoot finished and a slightly less bleak version of the film in the can, Nichols gathered his *Spamalot* cast in New York. By his side was choreographer Casey Nicholaw, who had never worked on Broadway before. Nichols hired him to stage the dance numbers, but as their partnership evolved, Nicholaw, who had a strong sense of comedy, would end up serving as an uncredited co-director; Nichols concentrated on the text, tone, pacing, and performances but entrusted Nicholaw with almost all of *Spamalot*'s physical staging.

Early on, Nichols announced, "There's only one rule in a show like this: If it's not funny, it has to go. If it's funny, it stays." But through weeks of rehearsals—during which Idle was bringing in new material every morning, Nicholaw was turning it into dance and action on the spot, and the cast was performing the latest draft from beginning to end almost every afternoon—that rule changed: Funny wasn't enough.

"What Mike wouldn't let go of," Azaria says, "is that *Spamalot* couldn't be just a send-up of musicals. He'd say, 'You can't just make fun of the form—you also have to deliver a lovely, heartfelt musical in the end. Even if it's juvenile, even if it's simplistic.' At one point, I thought the whole thing should end in classic Python fashion with us all bombing the play and vomiting onstage. Just as it's starting to feel sentimental, you undercut it with violence. Mike was like, 'Oh, dear boy . . . that's awful.'"

The room was, at times, an uneasy mishmash of comedy styles. Azaria was the Pythonhead, the true believer who had internalized the source material almost fanatically. When Nichols expressed astonishment that he knew his dialogue inside and out by the third day, Azaria replied, "Mike, I've been off book on this since I was twelve!" Curry, who was struggling with some health issues, had trouble with his lines and complained that he never should have taken the role. And Hyde Pierce, a master of understatement who had just finished eleven seasons on *Frasier,* at first felt daunted by the demands of a big musical. At one point, he says, "Casey did a demonstration of the 'Knights of the Round Table' number, probably sixteen bars, with forty-seven steps in each bar. He said, 'Okay, let's try it!' Of course, the entire ensemble did it perfectly, and when it was over, I was still there with one foot in the air. Casey stopped and looked at me and said, 'All right, let's go back.' And I said, 'To California?'"

Rehearsal-room laughs often seemed to dictate who was in or out of favor with Nichols. Some actors found him warm and responsive; to others, he was distant. Most were surprised by how completely he was leaving the hands-on directing to Nicholaw, "not just the numbers but the whole thing, really," says Azaria. "But Mike trusted the people he hired to get it right, and he was very focused on working with Eric to make sure the book was as funny and tight as it could be." At times, he would warn the actors to keep it real, telling them, "If you don't take it seriously, why should the audience?" On other days, he would wave off questions about character or motive with uncharacteristic dismissiveness, saying, "It's just sketch comedy." Late in the process, he admitted that he would have no sense of whether the show was working until he saw it in front of a live audience in Chicago.

Nichols was not in good shape during *Spamalot*. He was overweight, suffering from acute back pain, and taking medication that sometimes dulled his responses; as soon as the workshop was over, he underwent successful surgery for a herniated disk. He was also worried about *Closer*, which was scheduled to open at the beginning of December. Rudin had pushed back against the idea of a standard "It's a story about relationships" ad campaign. "Nobody should try to make the movie into something it isn't," he said. "The only chance this has to work is to lead with the fact that it's bracing and very ugly. Julia Roberts in a movie this nasty? We can make that into an event." Sony listened.

The week before the film opened, *The New York Times* published a long career appreciation by A. O. Scott that called Nichols "a wonderfully self-confident technician" whose movies are distinguished by an "unobtrusive but nonetheless palpable intelligence . . . [He stakes] out a territory bounded on one end by cynicism, on the other by sentimentality . . . most of the time he calculates the distances pretty well. His mockery is nearly always leavened by tolerance, and his moments of uplift tempered by an acute sense of imperfection . . . Mr. Nichols may be the last of a venerable line that stretches from Ernst Lubitsch through Billy Wilder."

Since his return to filmmaking with *Silkwood*, Nichols had so often been treated as a director who complacently subsumed his interests to those of writers and actors or, worse, Scott wrote, as "just another feel-good hack," that an essay examining his movies as a thematically consistent body of work was a rare and welcome surprise. He began to relax, knowing the piece would help position *Closer* for the respectful treatment it turned out to receive. While some reviewers, like the *Los Angeles Times*'s Kenneth Turan, dismissed the film as "all slick surfaces, a bauble polished to such a high gloss that finding an emotional handhold is impossible," most critics praised Nichols's treatment of the material and the performances. He received a Golden Globe nomination, and Owen and Portman were both Oscar nominees. *Closer* was also a modest hit, with a worldwide gross of $115 million that confirmed Nichols as, once again, a viable hire for studios. At a moment when contemporaries like Arthur Penn and Norman Jewison were winding down, that validation mattered. At seventy-three, despite the fact that every studio meeting still began with someone saying, "I'll never forget the first time I saw *The Graduate*," he knew that Hollywood had no interest in his résumé, only in his ability to deliver.

That would be put to the test in Chicago, where *Spamalot* was extensively reshaped. Nichols was still recovering from surgery. "There were some days with real low energy," says Azaria, "and some mornings when he couldn't come in at all and Casey had to do the heavy lifting" so that Nichols could be sharp in the afternoon, then be able to sit through each night's performance and give notes afterward. The first performances were, as critics pointed out, long, ungainly, and sometimes tentative. "It was not fated that it was all going to be great," says Azaria. "It took a lot of work. It was very problematic." For one thing, there was simply too much material. Nichols had insisted that Idle interpolate the popular Python song "Always Look on the Bright Side of Life," originally sung by men on crucifixes in *Life of Brian*, and the creators had fallen in love with the huge voice and comic skills of the show's female lead, Sara Ramirez, giving her something like half a dozen songs. There was also a good deal of mugging, moment-taking, embellishing, and laugh-milking; none of the actors seemed sure how much was too much for a show so dedicated to, and self-aware about, its own silliness.

As Nichols regained his strength, his toughest instincts kicked in. When he directed a drama, his attitude toward actors was generous, exploratory, even indulgent. But to him, getting an honestly earned laugh was a science: Comedy had rules, it had boundaries, and it required absolute discipline. It was hard work, and he would not tolerate carelessness. "There was an incident during the Chicago previews that stuck with me," says Hyde Pierce, "because it speaks to Mike's power and how he would wield it. We were doing a scene in a tower, and Mike couldn't hear us. He said, 'What's going on?' One of the actors, Steve Rosen, said, 'My microphone's in my helmet for this scene and the helmet isn't up here.' They did it again, and for a second time, the helmet wasn't where it was supposed to be. Mike asked that Steve's dresser come out onstage. He was a bit of a lackadaisical guy. Mike said, 'What happened? You didn't set the hat.' The guy's response was kind of 'Yeah, I guess not.' There was a pause, and Mike said, 'What's your name?' Nothing more. And we knew that not only would he never be seen again in that theater, he might never be *seen* again."

If Nicholaw was, much of the time, serving as *Spamalot*'s director, Nichols became its strict and exacting editor. "He made that show a bullet," says associate director Peter Lawrence. "Day by day, he streamlined it, he whittled it, he made it into an arrow that just flew through the air." After agonizing, Nichols cut his own favorite first-act number, "The Cow Song," a riff on a scene from the movie in which a cow is launched into the air by a catapult. ("It broke the most important rule— she wasn't a cow," he said. "If you're going to catapult a cow toward the audience, then a hot lady dressed in a black-and-white thing is not the same as an actual cow that lands on a guy.") Another song, performed by witches being burned at the stake, was also eliminated. "They were two of everyone's favorite numbers," says Christian Borle, who gave a breakthrough comic performance in the show. "We were shocked, but he believed in that idea of killing your babies, of losing things even if you loved them. And instantly, it worked a million times better."

But most of what Nichols did was delicate scalpel work on moments, lines, gestures. He was especially tough about what he called "the presentational pause." "It's a two-second delay," he said. "It says, 'Something funny is coming.' It's that telegram that says, 'Wait 'til you hear this!'" "He would just skewer actors for doing that," says Lawrence. "He could be absolutely brutal in some of those note sessions."

"He let people play to their strengths," says Nicholaw. "We had such amazing comedians in the show, and he did build in one moment where Hank could improvise a little. But the note he gave the most often was 'Terrific. Now cut the bullshit and do it as *you*.'"

"It was surprising," says Borle. "I thought it was going to be all of us coming out and doing shtick and making it big. But he was constantly scaling us back." In his scenes with Azaria and Hyde Pierce, Borle remembers being bewildered that "they would say a line, get a laugh, and then hold forever. I thought that as a comic actor, you had to push forward, drive the scene. They were doing something else—waiting for people to laugh themselves out so they could hear the next joke, because if they jumped in too fast, it'd be lost. For them it was about relaxation, calm, and confidence—about not ruining a moment out of your anxiety. That was all born of Mike and his ethos."

"What he fundamentally did," says Hyde Pierce, "even when we were doing outrageous things, is help us find out how we could tap the range of that script, its comedy and its bleakness, but still be us. That's what he wanted, and once we were able to find that, it gave us great freedom."

By New Year's Eve, *Spamalot* was taking shape, getting bigger laughs, and moving more fleetly. The advance sales for Broadway were huge, and Sawyer flew to Chicago to celebrate with her husband as 2005 arrived. "By then everyone was feeling very happy and good," says Borle. "We all had little crowns and hats on, and just looking over and seeing him gently rest his hand on Diane's butt was the sweetest moment. After *Spamalot*, I was a convert. Working with him switched on something in my brain about the process of comedy."

The show opened in New York six weeks later. "Go out there and make them wish they were dead!" he told his cast. *Spamalot* was an instant smash, the biggest of Nichols's career as a theater director; that June, it won him his sixth Tony for directing, his first in twenty years. ("I guess you're thinking age before beauty," he quipped in his acceptance speech. "Me, too.") But by the end of its first month, he was already checking back in, warning his actors, "As soon as you have figured out how to get your laugh, don't do that."

"Nine out of ten directors would never say that. They'd say, 'We decided how that moment is supposed to go. Why did you change it?'" says Hyde Pierce. "He called it the 'squeak and turn'—the cute thing you do that you know guarantees the audience will howl. He'd say, 'Drop it. You can always do it again the next night, but just let it go.' The effect of that is huge on a company: *A*, it keeps the show from calcifying, and *B*, it means there's never the conversation where someone says, 'Oh, but if he does that, I'll lose my laugh there,' because there's no such thing as 'your' laugh."

Spamalot ran on Broadway for four years. Nichols could not always be present for what turned out to be innumerable cast changes, but his words were—a kind of last will and testament of comedy labeled "Guiding Principles for SPAMALOT (and Comedy in General) from Mike Nichols" was always close at hand backstage. He filled it with specific instructions about how to play the show from its first scene ("Be careful that the top of the show not be too musical-theater . . . It can get relentless if overplayed") and general precepts. "It's easy to get a laugh," he wrote. "It's NOT easy to get a laugh when it's connected to an idea or the other people on stage. Stay connected to each other . . . The laughs cannot—and should not—be uppermost on your mind."

Nichols warned his troupe that "we're nothing without our tiny, fragile, but perfectly good story," and added:

> It's the details that move us and remind us of life. Therefore, what you do can't be big—big isn't true . . . When the response is low, instead of going higher you should concentrate more on each other and the truth . . . This is the first rule of comedy and you had better learn it.

REMEMBER:
> Portray human beings in the course of their lives
> Stop playing for the laughs
> Say the lines
> Don't get in the way of your own jokes
> Stop mugging at the audience
> Strip back to the basics—what you do must remind us of real people
> Pursue your task.

Thirty-four

GOOD NIGHT, STARS

2005-2009

When you're in your mid-seventies, even if your two most recent accomplishments are a successful movie and a Broadway hit, nobody puts you at the top of their must-hire list; nobody makes you their first call of the day. In the year after *Closer* and *Spamalot* opened, Nichols's phone did not ring off the hook with offers. Producers and executives and writers and actors assumed he was doing his own thing, or easing into a less active life, or enjoying a period of post-victory leisure. The last, at least, was true; he didn't find it difficult to fill his time. There were long lunches with younger filmmakers whom he would call just because he loved their work; they would accept his invitation shyly and then find themselves in the company of a new friend who was also the repository of half a century of show business wisdom. There were weeks on Martha's Vineyard, DVD commentary tracks to record with the help of his close pal Steven Soderbergh, tributes to receive, vacations to take, theater people to bless by producing short runs of their plays or godfathering their careers. And there was time with old colleagues who, for the rest of his life, would turn to him for advice or consolation or just an evening of good stories.

But work itself—the thing that had always impelled him—was subsiding. *Spamalot* had, for the first time, brought Nichols face-to-face with the reality that his stamina and energy were waning; he could no longer jump out of his chair to direct a scene or work from dawn until long after the theater curtain fell. The prospect of putting himself back in that position held no appeal. And the adaptation of Carl Hiaasen's novel *Skinny Dip,* which he had hoped would be his next movie, was slowly foundering. CAA had tried to broker a marriage between Nichols and the star he hoped to cast, George Clooney. "They had the same agent," says producer Celia Costas, "but Mike wanted George to do it and George didn't want to, and agents always seem to take a very long time to figure out an acceptable way for one important client to say no to another. It dragged on and on."

During those discussions, Elaine May became seriously ill, and it was unclear when she would be able to continue to work on the script. By the time she recovered, Nichols had given up on the film. In an appearance with her at Lincoln Center, he was uncharacteristically sour. He bemoaned the state of theater, saying, "People are forever sending me to plays, and I say, 'Son of a bitch, they've done it again. Somebody I thought I could trust has sent me to this piece of shit.' I get really angry. It's harder and harder to find someone who sees theater the way you do." And he was no happier about movies. "Hollywood doesn't *want* to be a better place," he complained, railing against the type of studio executive who thinks "that expressing an opinion in a meeting is a creative act, because that's all he ever gets to do." He griped about films being overtaken by technology, about studios being swallowed by conglomerates, even about the influence of the Golden Globe Awards, before concluding, "I'm a pain in the ass." "Yes, you're a pain in the ass," said May, "but amusing."

His spirits started to sink. He missed making movies. "It's something I never want to stop doing," he said. "When you're doing it with a group of people who you love and who love you . . . something begins to happen."

When Tom Hanks asked Nichols to direct *Charlie Wilson's War*, it was the summer of 2006, he was months from turning seventy-five, and he hadn't been behind a camera in more than two years. Hanks, who would both star in and produce the movie, had commissioned a script from Aaron Sorkin, who sent it to Nichols before Hanks even thought of pursuing him.

"The bottom line is I don't believe that Mike had his heart in it," says his editor, John Bloom. "It's a film that he agreed to do out of a sense of obligation to a cast and crew who had been hanging around for over a year waiting for him to go ahead with [*Skinny Dip*]." Hanks wanted Nichols enough to allow him to bring on most of the team he had kept on hold—Bloom, Costas, Mike Haley, Mary Bailey, and cinematographer Stephen Goldblatt. Nevertheless, the reality was that *Charlie Wilson's War* was a director-for-hire job; Nichols would, for the first time in his career, be working for his leading actor. "In retrospect, I wish I had been more objective about whether he should do it," says Costas. "There was so much that needed to be worked on with the material, forget about his health. But he was itching to make a movie."

Charlie Wilson's War was a politically complicated project; George Crile's book recounted the history of a hard-partying, staunchly anti-Communist Democratic congressman from Texas who spearheaded a CIA push to funnel weapons to the Afghan mujahideen in their fight against the Soviet Union in the 1980s. (According to Nichols, Wilson had, much earlier, gone on a couple of dates with Diane Sawyer. Her verdict: "He was crazy.") Sorkin's script had streamlined the story into a parable about the unintended consequences of blundering idealism; the movie he envisioned would end with 9/11, and with the same lines the book did: "These things happened. They were glorious and they changed the world . . . And then we fucked up the endgame."

"There isn't a person who read Sorkin's script who didn't want to do it," says Hanks. "It had that crackling-ass patter that everybody loves to wrap their heads around—it was a hypnotically great screenplay. But it wasn't dead-solid accurate as far as what really went on, because Charlie Wilson was very vociferous." Many of Wilson's rougher edges were sanded down; his appetite for cocaine was left out after Hanks and Sorkin both said audiences would not be able to forgive the character for drug use. "As we got into it," Hanks says, "Mike at one point said, 'I'm never going to do a movie about someone who is alive again.'"

To Universal's delight, Nichols was able to attract Julia Roberts to play a right-wing Texas socialite with a special interest in Afghanistan, and Philip Seymour Hoffman as a gruff CIA operative. *Charlie Wilson's War* was starting to look like a Mike Nichols movie. But from the beginning, he lacked the time he knew he needed to make the film his own. In part, that was because his working method had become digressive to the point of avoidance; "rehearsals" would end up being a long, loose series of tales about Hollywood and theater, with little attention to the scenes at hand until the end; work sessions with Sorkin, who was preoccupied with launching his new drama series *Studio 60 on the Sunset Strip* for NBC, would similarly take too long to get to the point, and then Sorkin would have to leave after fifteen or twenty minutes of actual discussion about the screenplay. Nichols went into the film underprepared, and he couldn't afford to be. Unlike *Closer, Charlie Wilson's War* had a large cast, a $75 million budget, and a complicated schedule of location shooting; it would begin production less than three months after he signed on, with months of filming under punishing conditions in Morocco.

By October he was in Marrakesh, and in trouble. Much of the shoot took place at high altitudes and amid intense pollution, both of which exacerbated his respiratory problems. "He had been a smoker, and a recreational pot smoker, for a long time," says Hanks. "And he had a deep, guttural cough that got really bad—to a degree that worried everyone and affected his ability to plan the shoot."

"I never should have let him shoot in Morocco," says Costas. "We should have done it in Southern California, the way a lot of people do. We all thought Mike was invulnerable, but when we were scouting locations, we took him up in the mountains, and suddenly I thought, *This is insane. He's a seventy-five-year-old guy who isn't in good health. What are we doing?*" Every day, Nichols and the cast and crew were trucked up to the location. At one point, a windstorm destroyed the entire set. "We lost the whole thing in less than twenty-five minutes, and much of the crew was stranded on the mountain," says Goldblatt. "We were actually very lucky that nobody got killed."

Many of the Morocco scenes involved large numbers of non-English-speaking extras doing things like firing rocket launchers; Universal thought all the action was necessary to justify the budget, but Nichols felt utterly lost. "Our hotel rooms in Marrakesh were on top of each other," says Costas, "so I knew when he was up, because I'd hear him walking around. I'd text with him, and it was 'Are you up? Are you up? Are you up? I'm scared. I'm scared.' He was having anxiety attacks. He understood the script's politics and its comedy, but Mike was not an action director, and he felt he was half stuck making an action movie."

"We ended up reshooting a number of big things," says Hanks, "because they were just not mounted in the way that was needed, and, to Mike's credit, when we came back to the United States, he knew it."

Once production moved to Los Angeles for the second half of the shoot, Nichols was in better health and more in his element. "We restaged a number of things that had been shot in Morocco with all these Afghan refugees who now lived in Fresno, believe it or not," says Hanks. "But there were peaks and valleys to his acumen and his abilities during that shoot." Nichols's bleak mood lifted more and more as he got to work with Roberts, whose scenes involved the kind of minutely detailed social comedy that he loved. "I had to do so much visually to accomplish her," she says. "I would have my wig cap put on particularly tight to create the strained look of having had a lot of face-lifts. Mike was super into that. It was so much fun having little things to play with that I could show him." For an exchange that takes place after her character sleeps with Wilson, Nichols said, "I can't do one more scene where the guy gets out of bed in his boxer shorts and the sheet is right up to here on the woman . . . Why not have them in the bathroom afterwards, and he's in the bathtub . . . Julia [had] a long speech about armaments and gun bores and the detailed characteristics of weapons, and I said, 'Couldn't you be doing your makeup?'" The result was a classic Nichols moment of revealing character through action, as she made a steely speech—"the words came out like a machine gun," Nichols said—while looking in the mirror with cool self-assessment and separating her lashes with a pin she held millimeters from her eyeball.

Freed from the misery of waiting for a translator to move masses of extras around or standing on a mountain hoping the light wouldn't change, Nichols was able to concentrate on executing Sorkin's screenplay to the letter. "He was so nice," says Denis O'Hare, who had a small role, "except for one moment when I messed up a line. I was inverting something or leaving something out, and he said, in the most hard-ass way I'd seen from him, 'The line is *seventeen thousand* in the script.' It put the fear of God in me, which I appreciated. I thought, *Right, this guy is not just a congenial uncle—he's a high-level professional who expects high-level execution from everyone.* It was the only time I'd ever seen the teeth behind the grin. I never felt any sense that he was just letting us do what we wanted—he was keenly aware of what *he* wanted. He had practically memorized the script and was listening for the words closely."

"That's really when it sailed," Hanks says. "We had one extended scene, a scene between me and Philip Seymour Hoffman talking about the best way to shoot down helicopters, that is still the best three days I've ever had shooting. It was vintage Mike." At one point, a crew member asked Nichols if he remembered the Los Angeles soundstage where he had shot most of *The Graduate*. He paused for a moment and looked around. "This one," he said, and then asked for another take.

Nichols didn't know that the day *Charlie Wilson's War* wrapped would be the last he ever spent shooting a movie. Over the next seven years, until the week he died, he would continue to develop new projects, never doubting that he had one more film in him. But after forty-two years, his career as a movie director was over.

A major creative battle, one that would pit Hanks and Universal against Nichols and Sorkin, remained. Sorkin's script establishes early on that Wilson can see the Pentagon from his office; it's the setup for a final scene in which he watches the building burn on September 11, 2001. Sorkin intended that image to be the last thing people saw before they read "We fucked up the endgame" on a black screen.

"Sorkin saw everything that happened to Charlie Wilson as a precursor to 9/11," says Hanks. "And we did shoot that scene, because I thought there was about a 50 percent chance it'd work. But it wasn't the point of the book, or the movie, or the performance I was giving. I can understand a guy as good as Sorkin saying, 'I love that there.' But when I saw it put together, I don't think we connected the dots. I said, 'We took a shot, but this ain't it.'"

"Charlie Wilson himself didn't want the scene in the movie, because he was afraid that people were going to blame the people of Afghanistan for 9/11," says Sorkin. "And Tom didn't like playing 'the guy who caused 9/11.' I thought those were silly reasons, but what happened was, by the time we got into the editing room, Mike did not like the job he had done during production, when he had been so sick. And he felt that he had lost the creative authority to tell the studio or producer

or star no. We call the first cut of the movie 'the suicide cut,' because it
can really take it out of you. And Mike was not able to recover from the
suicide cut. So Gary [Goetzman, the head of Hanks's company Play-
tone] and Tom won that fight. I want to emphasize that they were not
taking advantage of a sick Mike Nichols. They simply had a creative
vision as strong as the one that Mike and I had, and theirs won."

"I wasn't terribly thrilled with some of Tom and Gary's ideas," says
Bloom. "And I told Mike that. But he said, 'Well, you know, they got
the film off the ground. It is theirs.' And I thought, *My God, the Mike
I know would have told them to fuck off.*"

Nichols labored through an extra two months in the editing room,
addressing, without much enthusiasm, a long series of notes from Universal after a test screening. *Charlie Wilson's War* opened in December
2007 to decent reviews and mild business; it received a single Oscar
nomination, for Hoffman's performance. Nichols was more philosophical than disheartened. "People who expect wonderful things have serious
problems," he said. "I don't know anyone of significant talent who goes
into something thinking, *This is gonna be great!* Artists fear the worst,
and for good reason. Every time the worst doesn't happen, it's a miracle." His friendship with Hanks would survive their disagreement—
Hanks had stood by Nichols in Morocco when other producers might
have replaced him. And he was already thinking about what he wanted
to work on next—a play, in New York, so he could be home every night
with Sawyer and near his doctors should he need them. In the summer,
he announced plans to direct two shows in 2008—a revival of Clifford
Odets's 1950 drama *The Country Girl,* and *Farragut North,* a political
play by Beau Willimon, a rising thirty-year-old writer who had worked
on Howard Dean's presidential campaign a few years earlier and turned
his experience into a *Primary Colors*–like inside peek at how idealism
gets ground up by realpolitik.

By the time it reached Nichols, *Farragut North* was the industry's
shiny object of the moment; Warner Bros. was considering it as an op-

portunity to team George Clooney and Leonardo DiCaprio in a movie, and Jake Gyllenhaal was interested in starring onstage. Willimon already had a handshake deal for a production with an off-Broadway theater company, but Nichols wanted more—the chance to direct the play on Broadway, make the movie, or both. He invited Willimon over to talk.

Few directors were as skilled in the art of professional courtship. Nichols knew exactly how agog a young writer would be walking into the Fifth Avenue penthouse with the wraparound terrace—and just how the warm welcome, the quick glimpse of Sawyer in the background, and the carefully chosen pastries would set the stage for a long, intimate, deeply engaged talk. It was all calibrated to produce an effect—and it was also all sincere. "At that point in my life, he was perhaps the most brilliant person I'd conversed with," says Willimon. "Everything he said seemed like it should be embroidered on a pillow."

They talked for three hours, with Willimon discussing his hopes for the play and Nichols offering insights that were both sharp and personal. "Because my play has to do with power dynamics and the ways in which people become cruel," he says, "Mike started telling me about seeing a production of *The Heiress* and sitting in the audience watching the scene in which the heiress's lover of many years comes back and says to her, 'My God, how cruel you've become,' to which she replies, 'I learned from masters.' And then Mike started to weep. He said, 'I'm just thinking about the beauty of that line and how we're all taught to be cruel,' and how that feeling drew him to this play of mine. He's full-on crying in front of me, and I'm thinking, 'How the fuck did I get here? How is this even possible?'"

Nichols dried his tears and told Willimon his play needed a new ending. "You think you've written a Greek tragedy," he said, "but this is the twenty-first century. There are no gods. There is no fate. The tragedy for this character is winning, with nothing to curb him. He must turn into the monster. We must see him victorious."

"I'll always be grateful to him for that," says Willimon, who went on to create the American version of *House of Cards*. "The direction he pointed me in for that play informed a lot of stuff that I wrote later." Willimon was reeling when he left, but their partnership would go no further. By the time they met, other producers were already involved, and Nichols insisted on complete control as a condition of his participation. "I don't know how to function any other way," he said several weeks later, "and at this point, I don't see a need to change my way of doing things." Willimon thanked him, and they parted ways.

"Several months later, I was at a party in Los Angeles and saw Jake Gyllenhaal," Willimon says. "And Jake said, 'What happened with all that? It just seemed to fall apart with Mike.' I told him the story of our meeting, and when I got to the part where Mike brought up *The Heiress*, Jake said, 'Hold on. Did he tell you about the line *I learned from masters* and start to cry? Same thing with me.' What I realized in that moment was that Mike was an actor, a Jedi master of intellectual seduction, someone who could bring you into his orbit in ways that verged on sorcery. At the time, I remember feeling like that had completely devalued our amazing meeting. Could he really call up those tears at will? Had I fallen prey to an act? But as I've gotten older, I've realized that we all have our stories that work. We burnish them as we retell them, and it's pretty natural. It's just part of living in the world. But I never met anyone better at it than he was."

Nichols moved on to *The Country Girl,* and once again he found himself on shaky ground from the moment he started work. "It was a struggle," says Peter Gallagher, who played one of the three principal roles. "It's a very difficult play. And while we were doing it, I think Mike was genuinely scared for his life."

Odets's downbeat look at the working lives of a fragile, alcoholic stage actor, his drab, loyal wife, and the producer and director who are determined to get him working again had debuted on Broadway when Nichols was a teenager, but the 1954 movie with Bing Crosby and Grace Kelly had left a stronger impression on him, and his own professional experiences had seemed to confirm for him the idea that the play contained some real wisdom about the relationship between addiction and life as a performing artist. He had watched Richard Burton struggle to get through a monologue without tremors, George C. Scott practically destroy entire productions and himself with his uncontrolled drinking, and Art Carney drive himself to a breakdown. He viewed their alcoholism as the way they had coped with the constantly heightened sensitivity they needed to draw on to do their work. "There's no question that a great actor hears what people are thinking," he said. "That's the only way he can do it. And he survives by doing anything to stem those bad opinions." Nichols told some friends that he viewed *The Country Girl* as his chance to come to terms with his memories of Scott. He also wanted to do something he had never done—a backstage story. "There is a kind of neurosis," he told one of his actors, Remy Auberjonois, "that only finds satisfaction or solace in self-dramatization. Jewish mothers and theater people compete for the prize of being most put-upon."

"There is great life under the surface [of the play]," says Jon Robin Baitz, whom Nichols brought in to help make trims and adjustments. "Two wounded veterans leaning against each other like old athletes with a lot of scars—a picture of a marriage. I'm not sure we ever saw that version of the play, but it was the one Mike talked about."

To secure financing, Nichols miscast both leads with stars he hadn't worked with and didn't know, Morgan Freeman and Frances McDormand. Race-blind casting in a naturalistic American play set in the 1940s raised all kinds of questions about what had caused years of strain in the marriage of the two main characters; Nichols was not interested in asking or answering them. "Morgan's casting . . . What was in Mike's head, I have no idea," says Albert Wolsky, the play's costume designer. "The play didn't support it, and we needed a little more context than Mike gave it. And Frances McDormand is a wonderful actress, and can be very sexy, but he kept saying, 'I want her to look like Grace Kelly,' and that's not who she is."

Rehearsals did not go well. "Mike was not fully himself," says Baitz. "His coughing was kind of cataclysmic, and his approach to rehearsing was mostly to use anecdotes and inference—tell stories about himself and his life that might direct an actor towards an impulse. But you had to be a Mikeologist, and some actors [could] not find a path through the maze of stories that [would] enable them to make choices." After four weeks, with previews looming, the central relationship between Freeman's and McDormand's characters had gone undiscussed, and several actors still didn't know their lines. "Usually, by the time you leave the rehearsal room, you have the lines locked down. They were still paraphrasing," says B. T. McNicholl, the production's assistant director. "As we were walking down the alley towards the theater for a preview, Mike said, 'If this were Philadelphia or New Haven, we'd be about halfway there.' And I realized, *Oh my God, he's completely miscalculated the trajectory.* He had worked in an era when you had three stops before New York, and now there were none."

"Well," Nichols said, "I guess there's nothing left to do but go down with the ship."

"I will never forget Mike in the alley, smoking a bummed cigarette, coughing and smiling, rheumy-eyed, saying, 'Don't tell Diane, she'll kill me,'" says Baitz. "Anybody who has a spouse who is in their corner could identify with that play. That moment in the alley . . . Why couldn't *that* show up onstage?"

When Clifford Odets's son, Walt, came to see a preview, Freeman was still "dropping lines right and left. I remember sitting with Mike in the back and saying, 'Listen, this is your production and I don't want to interfere, but if it were me, I would tell Morgan to go back to his hotel room and think about the scene and learn his lines,'" says Odets.

"Mike looked at me and his eyebrows went up, and he said, 'He's Morgan Freeman.' And I thought, *And you're Mike Nichols.*" As a younger man, Nichols would have known how to deploy an arsenal of strategies to deal with a veteran movie star who was having line trouble. But now he was struggling himself, and he didn't have the kind of relationship with Freeman that would have made a frank discussion between two men in their seventies possible. McDormand, meanwhile, was growing impatient with the fact that Nichols had given her almost no direction. Audiences were reacting with indifference. And Michael Riedel, the *New York Post*'s theater gossip columnist, began to savage the production as a catastrophe in the making. Nichols found himself living in a new, less forgiving world, one in which each night's performance was instantly reviewed by anonymous internet commentators. As his cough deepened into a serious chest infection, he checked the sites compulsively. Early on, he called Jack O'Brien and said, "You've got to come down—it's a disaster, it's terrible, it's unfixable." O'Brien watched the play and pointed out that the set design Nichols had approved gave his actors so little room to move that they were practically shouting their lines into the wings. "It hadn't occurred to him to put a table and chairs on the stage," says O'Brien. "Mike, who had always been so careful about blocking. I thought, *Uh-oh.* I said to him, 'You've been away, and you're forgetting you can't get the results you want unless you stage them.'"

Nichols was braced for the reviews, which were largely negative. ("How could this be?" *The New York Times* asked of the "inert" revival. "Mike Nichols picks up Tonys the way cashmere picks up lint.") "He sent a note backstage to the cast," says McNicholl, "that said something to the effect of 'You're all wonderful, and anything that went wrong was my fault.'"

He had always made a point of carefully maintaining his shows during their runs; years into *Spamalot*, he would still routinely drop by the Shubert to watch a performance, give notes, and sometimes even guide a new actor through a rehearsal or two. But as *The Country Girl* played out its limited run, he barely had the strength to go in and check on the performances. When Paul Sills died, in June, he was almost too unwell to attend the funeral, but it was important to him to pay his respects to his first mentor, to see May, and to have a moment to mend fences with his onetime nemesis, the Compass Theater's cofounder David Shepherd. After the service, says Shepherd's wife, Nancy Fletcher, "Elaine came rushing up and said, 'Isn't this wonderful? To be all together again?' Whatever bad feelings there were had passed."

A month later, Nichols was diagnosed with a heart blockage and underwent a coronary bypass. The surgery took place a few days before *The Country Girl* closed. The operation was a success, but his recovery at home would be slow—months, not weeks. His breathing problems made everything harder, as did a lifetime of bad habits. "Mike was, you know, not a guy to get on the treadmill or anything like that," says Hanks.

Nichols's daytime social life revolved around regular restaurant lunches with friends and colleagues at one of his three or four favorite spots. But during his convalescence, his world had to come to him. Lunches and meetings were at his apartment and lasted only as long as his energy held out. "There was never a moment when he wasn't interested in something," says Tony Kushner. "I remember going to have lunch with him soon after the surgery. His appetite wasn't good. He was trying to eat the things that he liked, but he couldn't do it, and he wasn't able to focus very well. But he was already talking about an idea he had to remake *A Little Night Music* with Meryl Streep on some island off the coast of Sweden."

He still felt the weight of *The Country Girl*'s failure. As soon as he was well enough, he sat on his sofa and, on a legal pad, started to write a list of everything he believed he had done wrong in the production.

"They're all great actors," he told Scott Rudin. "But I just didn't know them. They weren't my company in a way that would have allowed me to make a show in four weeks. I didn't know how to do it." "*The Country Girl* really left him feeling like 'Maybe I don't want to do this again,'" Rudin says.

Unable to go out very often, he watched more television. After devouring the first season of *Mad Men*, he emailed a fan letter to Matthew Weiner and asked him over for breakfast. "He had just had the bypass—there was still a bruise on his arm from the intravenous line," says Weiner. "But Mike was like a heat-seeking missile for anything he found artistically interesting—just on top of it and affected by it and emotional about it." Nichols became a trusted friend and adviser. "Outside of the immediate world of *Mad Men*," says Weiner, "Mike and David Chase are the two people I would run my ideas by." (It was Nichols who counseled Weiner to get Don Draper into a quick second marriage, telling him, "A divorced guy in the 1960s is going to want someone to put that steak on the table.")

By the end of 2008, Nichols was feeling healthier than he had in a long time. Rudin, in particular, had taken him in hand, seeing him through his recovery by bringing him project after project until he got interested in working again; they were now starting to plan an update of the 1962 Akira Kurosawa kidnapping thriller *High and Low*, with a David Mamet script that was being rewritten by Chris Rock. And there were other films on the horizon—Nichols pulled together a reading of an adaptation of Nick Hornby's novel *How to Be Good* with Jon Hamm, Julia Roberts, and Buck Henry, and he briefly became attached to direct an adaptation of Patricia Highsmith's suspense thriller *Deep Water* for 20th Century Fox.

But over the next couple of years, it became clear that he was happy to keep projects at arm's length—to live the professional life of someone who was perpetually considering another movie or play but would probably not actually direct one. Readings, story meetings, and lunches were a way to keep a foot in working life, but nothing ever went further than that. Nora Ephron had written a play called *Lucky Guy* in which Hanks had agreed to make his Broadway debut. Nichols did a reading and told her he thought it wasn't ready; she moved on. He gathered a group of actors to read John Patrick Shanley's play *Storefront Church*; he decided not to direct it but stayed in touch with one of the actors, Lin-Manuel Miranda, and offered encouraging words when Miranda later told him he was working on a musical about Alexander Hamilton. Streep brought him *Hope Springs*, a comedy-drama about a long-married couple dealing with their dwindling passion in late middle age. Nichols arranged a reading, and those who participated watched his enthusiasm dwindle in real time. "Oh, no, no, no, he would never have said yes to making that movie," says Streep (who eventually starred in the film opposite Tommy Lee Jones for director David Frankel). "It was about a man experiencing failure, insufficiency. There are very few men who want to touch that." During the reading, according to Patrizia von Brandenstein, "Mike had a kind of hooded look throughout. They had laid on this enormous fancy lunch buffet for all of us, and he was nice to everyone, but he called me the next morning and said, 'I can't do it. The story is too sad. If it doesn't make me laugh, I can't make other people laugh.'"

When old friends had new work, he was a loyal cheering section. He flew to Minneapolis for two days to see a festival of three plays by Kushner, and made a point of going backstage and congratulating each of the casts. "Every time I saw him," Kushner says, "he had always just seen a movie or read a book or gone to a play that he was excited about. Once in a while, it would be something he thought was garbage, but he didn't really like to talk about the things he hated. He loved talking about things that excited him, that he found extraordinary."

Nichols knew that his film legacy was either complete or close to it, and he felt it was shaky enough to need defending. In 2009, the Museum of Modern Art honored him with a retrospective. Rajendra Roy, who oversaw the festival, wanted it to be almost comprehensive. Nichols did not. "We debated over *The Day of the Dolphin*, *Wolf*, and *The Fortune*," Roy says. "I won on *The Fortune*. I didn't win on the other two. My read was, if he felt that he had let anybody down, he didn't want to revisit that heartbreak and personal pain. But when he watched *The Fortune* again, what he saw was that it was a good movie, and that the hurt was that it wasn't embraced, not that he had failed anyone."

In October 2009, just before his seventy-eighth birthday, Nichols was named the recipient of the American Film Institute Life Achievement Award. "We sent save-the-date cards to the twenty-five most imperative people," says AFI head Bob Gazzale. "Tom Hanks, Julia Roberts, Elaine May, Robin Williams, Meryl Streep . . . In one day, twenty-four of them said, 'I'll be there.' It was one of the first times people called to say, 'Can I come?' Steven Spielberg said, 'I want to be there for Mike.' Oprah Winfrey said, 'How do I buy a table?' It had never happened before, and I don't know that it will happen again."

The gala was scheduled for the following June, and Nichols was an active, if sometimes cranky, participant in the creation of the film-clip packages that would be spread throughout the evening. ("You're not telling my story" was a frequent refrain as the clips were assembled.) As the night approached, he found himself nervous. "I told him, 'Go watch *Wild Strawberries*,'" says Weiner. "He started to laugh. I said, 'You're going to pass your own hearse on the way, it's going to break, and you're going to sit there and remember everything good that happened and be embarrassed you're so old.' He liked that."

Shortly before the tribute, Nichols, Sawyer, and many in their social circle were rocked by the arrest of Kenneth I. Starr, who had been their business manager and was eventually convicted of cheating his clients out of between $30 million and $60 million in a Ponzi scheme and sent to prison. Starr had also handled the financial affairs of, among others,

Nora Ephron and Nicholas Pileggi, Richard Avedon, Neil Simon, Candice Bergen, and Carly Simon. Nichols and Sawyer had fired him after his negligence damaged a trust fund that had been set up for one of his children; they were spared his greater misdeeds, but the news generated a certain amount of gallows humor at the ceremony in Los Angeles.

Nevertheless, it was a happy and emotional night for both of them. After ten years, Sawyer had left *Good Morning America* to become the anchor of ABC's *World News Tonight*. For the first time since the 1990s, their nights were their own again, and he loved the extra time they had together. She beamed and laughed throughout the dinner, which was warm, joshing, deeply affectionate. Roberts opened up the speeches by announcing, "Anybody who knows Mike personally knows that most of the really great stories about him contain the words *ratfuck* or *bullshit*, so that's tricky for TV." Nora Ephron joked that "we could all be in a Buñuel movie—a pack of people who owe Mike everything and are doomed to spend all of eternity giving him awards." Elaine May brought down the house with a perfectly polished routine about "little Igor" and his cousin Albert Einstein. Dustin Hoffman came out and said, "You said in New York, 'If it wasn't for me, you'd be just another aging Jew.' You are an ageless Jew. Keep doing it." Tributes poured forth from Candice Bergen, Jack Nicholson, Warren Beatty, Robert Redford, Cher, Nora Ephron, and Natalie Portman. Eric Idle emerged from backstage, dressed as the Angel from *Angels in America,* to serenade him with "Always Look on the Bright Side of Life."

At the end of the evening, Streep presented him with the award, as he had done for her six years earlier. He received a two-minute standing ovation.

"Wow," he said. "I got to see my own memorial and I'm still alive, sort of. I make a solemn promise here and now, especially to Elaine and Nora and Meryl, who have given new meaning to the phrase 'I gave at the office'—I promise, no more achievements."

Nichols almost always effused over his actors. That night, he chose instead to thank his writers, his designers, his composers, and the longest-standing and most loyal members of his crew. Summing up, he said, "I thank my film family and my own family, first and foremost my kids, a constant source of wonder and pride, not to mention gratitude for their patience with me."

At the top of his speech, Nichols joked, "This is no time for sincerity." But he ended his remarks with what felt like a fond and sorrowful goodbye to a world he could not quite bring himself to say was now part of his past. "I love the process of making a movie, and doing it with all of you was—despite the fear, the pressure, the budget—happiness," he said. "As a little kid in a sometimes hard place, I went to the movies as often as I could. Movies—making them, seeing them—is not something that could ever lose its pleasure for me. That puts them on a short list of things that eternally give me joy . . . I could go on all night, but you have the idea. You get it. Good night, moon. Good night, stars. I'll see you on the set, and on the beach, and in the kitchen, and at the movies."

Thirty-five

WAY OUT THERE
IN THE BLUE

2010–2014

He had one last mountain to climb.

In the summer of 2010, Nichols started talking to Scott Rudin about directing a revival of *Death of a Salesman* on Broadway. Nobody, including Nichols himself, was sure he would be able to do it.

He had never escaped the shadow of Arthur Miller's play, and he had never wanted to. The look, the sound, and the impact of Elia Kazan's original staging remained as vivid to him as if the sixty-two years since he saw it as a teenager had been no more than a week. *Salesman* was etched in his consciousness, a touchstone to which he returned so frequently that no cobwebs had ever grown over his memories of a production that he called "sainted." "I'm aware that that production was part of the greatest year Kazan ever had, with *Streetcar* and *Salesman* one after the other. Unbelievable. Those two plays and the way they were presented are certainly the reason I'm in the theater," he wrote to Linda Emond, the actress he asked to play Linda Loman. "On my last reading of *Salesman*, I was keenly aware that the collapsing of time, the idea that causes the play to lift off . . . is the result of what to me is the whole point of the theater, even though the phrase belongs to a great novelist: Only connect. Miller and Kazan found that time-reality *together*. Just as, in a mini way, Buck Henry and I found the [*Graduate*] montage of being on top of Mrs. Robinson and at home at the same time together. You need a buddy to find the nonrealistic true things."

Nichols told Emond he intended to schedule a workshop that would allow his cast to become partners with him—"a process in which we dream together, and bring to the rehearsal the things that are ours, is the sacred part of what we do," he said. "Little thing by little thing, pebble by pebble, till we are basically saying to the audience, 'This is our life. You recognize it, don't you? It's yours, too.'" He had strived for that finger-snap moment of discovering common ground ever since his first improv sketch in a Chicago bar. But as much as he yearned for collaboration, his deepest reason for directing *Death of a Salesman* was personal. For him, approaching the play was akin to making a private offering—to Kazan, to the theater, to memory, and to his own sixteen-year-old self, the bright, alienated, lonely boy whom he could finally and fully remember with compassion.

Rudin was willing to tailor the production to Nichols's needs and to his advanced age. Since he was no longer up to the rigors of the road, there would be no out-of-town tryout, but he would have as much time as he needed—upward of a year—to cast, plan, and rehearse a production that would not begin previews until the fall of 2011, just in time for his eightieth birthday. He already had his Willy Loman. At forty-three, Philip Seymour Hoffman was too young for the part (just as the original Willy, Lee J. Cobb, had been at thirty-seven), but ever since *The Seagull*, Nichols had known that Hoffman had the anger, the fear, the desperation, and the lumbering sadness to play Willy, and the commitment and technique to dig as deep as the role demanded.

From the start, Nichols was adamant about a design concept: He wanted to stage *Salesman* on an exact replica of Jo Mielziner's original set, and to use Alex North's 1949 underscore as well. In photographs, the skeletal frames that Mielziner, who had started designing in the 1920s, had used to create the humble kitchen and bedrooms of the Loman house looked quaint and small, a relic of a pre-technological theater era when brilliant designers used efficient but modest visual gestures to connote seriousness and modernism. "When he said, 'The Mielziner set can't be bettered,'" says Rudin, "I said, 'Okay, if that's what you want, we'll do it.' But what I was thinking was: *We've just made the most catastrophic mistake.*"

Nichols secured Andrew Garfield, his choice for Biff Loman, during a phone call. "I was in L.A., staying with a director of Mike's generation and trying to decide between a movie he was going to do and *Salesman*," Garfield says. "I remember asking Mike why he decided to be a New Yorker rather than get seduced, and he said, 'Why would I want to live in a city where I can tell what my stock is on a daily basis by how the valet parking attendant looks at me?' He somehow managed to key in to everything I was wrestling with, and I knew in that moment I was going to go to New York."

But Garfield had just signed on to play Spider-Man and would have to shoot throughout much of 2011. The negotiation with Sony to secure his participation was complicated, and Rudin pushed *Salesman* to the spring of 2012. It was a dangerously long time to try to hold on to everyone, especially, given his fragility and tendency to waver, Nichols himself. Every year now was a year of loss. In the spring, he wept when he heard that Elizabeth Taylor had died, and fall brought the death of his closest and oldest friend in Hollywood, John Calley, a man who had championed his work since *Catch-22* and whom he viewed as "a life saver." More homebound than he had been before his health started to falter, he had gotten interested in television, and, in the wake of the success of *Downton Abbey* (which he loathed), he had started talking to the writer-producer Tom Fontana about collaborating on an *Upstairs, Downstairs*–style drama based on the Bouvier family in the early twentieth century. He was doubtful about his ability to be insured for a film, but in TV he could produce or consult without subjecting himself to the strain of a daily shooting schedule. He had also started to worry about losing his memory. "Forgetting names was frustrating for him," says Fontana. "He'd be on a roll with a story, and then he'd stumble over a name and be so upset he wouldn't finish."

It would have been easy for him to retire. His son Max's wife, Rachel, had just had twin daughters, and, like many men of his generation who felt guilty about their absence from their children's early lives, he became a delighted and doting grandfather, drinking in every minute he could. "We don't go anywhere," he told a reporter who asked about his marriage. "We have weekends, we have most nights, we have our own secret life in our own little place. And we just go play with our grandkids."

"When his son and daughter had children, he went crazy, he was so happy," says Celia Costas. "I think he never knew that there was anything new that could delight him in that really basic way." His take on little girls was indulgent and cheerfully retro. "Let them do anything they want," he told a friend who asked for advice about how to entertain his nieces. "Give them ice cream and toys and keep telling them it's because today is a special occasion. And make sure that every so often a woman comes in and gives them orders." And later, when his daughter Jenny's baby son was born, he proudly announced that he "may be the Messiah, although it's early to be certain." Walking away from work was, for the first time, truly tempting; he started talking to Sawyer about a day when they might both slow down and devote themselves to a few years of family, rest, and pleasure.

But he showed up for the fall 2011 workshop ready to engage with *Salesman* as best he could. "I remember the process as being in very hushed tones," says Finn Wittrock, who played Happy Loman. "We sat around the table for a lot of the time, and Mike went about it by telling stories of his own life, not talking too directly about the practicalities of the play." ("I do [tell stories], to an almost embarrassing extent,"

Nichols had said several years earlier. "I hope they're not getting longer as the years go by. What I'm trying to encourage is that we all do that.")

"I could sense that as time went on, people were getting a little unsure," says Wittrock. "Like, 'The deadline is looming—do we have to have another story about you and Richard Burton getting drunk together?'" At times, Nichols almost seemed to mirror Willy's flights into memory and his inability to contend with the present. "There was seemingly no thread," says Garfield, "but it was like he was seeping stuff into our unconscious about what the play was about for him and what it should be about for us."

"Because Mike opened up, everyone started sharing their stories as they related to the play," says Wittrock. "His goal was getting the four of us, as a family, as close and in love with each other as possible, so that by the time we were in previews, we would feel like he had guided us onto the ship and he could wave goodbye as we sailed off. And that's what happened."

"He created an environment that was really helpful, and he did it in a different way from other directors," Emond says. "When something would happen onstage that moved him, he would share things from his past on a very personal level—about his mental health, for instance—because he felt it would be useful. It was a generous thing to do. And he would also tell stories that were funny when he felt he needed it or we needed it, because the play was so brutal. He did it for the room—it was necessary relief."

"We really listened to those stories," says Bill Camp, who played Charley. "When he talked about his childhood or his professional life, my imagination would be fired in a way that aided me in feeling liberated, even before we got up in the rehearsal room and started moving around."

"Safety is such a huge thing when you're making a play, and he was basically saying, 'It's safe here,'" says Rudin. "'If you have a bad idea, you can make a fool of yourself if that's what you need.'"

Early on, it was apparent that Philip Seymour Hoffman was going to take charge as much as Nichols was. He kept pulling the room back toward the play, asking dozens of pointed questions about the characters and their interactions, and he was the first to walk onto the set that Rudin had had constructed for the workshop to see how it felt. "There were times when Mike kind of let Phil lead the room," Wittrock says. "It was purposeful, because he was Willy and we were all in his brain. He would take his cues from whatever Phil's instincts were and go down any road he was curious about."

"You can't really say Phil was directed by Mike," says Rudin. "Mike and Phil made the production together."

Whatever misgivings the actors may have had about the way in which *Salesman* was coalescing, when they disbanded, they were electrified at the prospect of reuniting in January to begin full rehearsals. The break was not, however, useful for Nichols, who tried to back out of the production, as Rudin, who had watched him toy with and then turn away from projects for years, had feared he might. "Why am I doing this?" Nichols said. "I don't want to do this. This is a terrible idea. I'm only gonna be compared to Kazan. There's nothing in this for me."

"I have a contract, and I'm going to enforce it," Rudin told him. "I'm not indulging this nonsense anymore. It's the great American play, and you have invented yourself as the great quasi-American director. You're just scared. And you're not scared of the Kazan part, you're scared of the Arthur Miller part, because it confronts a lot of things in your life, like your father and your brother, that you've never looked at closely. It starts in a week, and you're going to show up."

"And he did," Rudin says. "And in the most gentle, kind, low-key way of guiding the company toward the play, he was unbelievable every day."

The relationship between Hoffman and Nichols was not easy. Nichols was physically debilitated—"I remember walking with him and asking, 'What's the hardest part of your health issues?'" says Emond. "He said, 'The breathing. It's so frustrating.'" The medications he had to take made him drowsy, and he frequently nodded off during re-hearsals. When that happened, Hoffman would glance over at the assistant director and sometimes pick up and just continue the work. "I noticed a couple of times that Mike didn't have the energy to sustain a long rehearsal morning or afternoon," says Garfield, "but also, I think he wanted us to be a little on edge and not to have all our questions answered. He wanted the play to live in crisis and in a state of discovery every night. Yes, he was definitely an old man, but he was still so full of longing—to realize his vision and to provide something of worth."

Partly because Hoffman was himself on shaky ground—terrified of the darkness of the role, he was taking an unusually long time to get off book—his realization that Nichols would not be able to take him in hand and re-create the detailed, beat-by-beat engagement they had had ten years earlier on *The Seagull* was painful. "There were times when he'd come home panicked and freaked out," says his widow, Mimi O'Donnell. "Some of it was the difficulty of the role, some of it was that he had seen Dustin Hoffman do it. He knew that even if Mike couldn't give him everything he wanted, he wasn't going to let him fuck up. But I do remember his feeling of *I'm a little alone in this.* He felt afraid. One night, he was venting, and I said something like 'Someday you're going to be that old.' He suddenly realized he'd been talking about Mike Nichols. Mike! Someone he loved! His anger dissipated, and we just started laughing about age and aging."

When Nichols was alert, "his style was conversational and analytical," says Rebecca Miller, who had entrusted her father's play to him. "That can be the opposite of the most efficient way to direct. But to Mike, they were a group of people trying to answer the questions of the play. He was saying, 'You guys are smart. Let's figure this out together.'"

By the end of rehearsals, Hoffman and Nichols had found a way to work in harmony. Hoffman would steer the cast toward specific decisions while Nichols kept his focus on the play's themes, the Loman family dynamic, and the production's overall tone. "Phil seemed like the stronger hand," says Matthew Stern, the stage manager, "and Mike was more the guiding force." He didn't do much physical direction or positioning of the actors, but he understood what Hoffman needed and found a way to give it to him. "Mike had this phobia of giving a bad note to an actor," says Wittrock. "Phil said that in a final rehearsal of *The Seagull*, Mike gave him a note and I guess that night's show didn't go too well. Mike hardly talked to him after that, and Phil thought, *Oh, well, I just fucked up that relationship.* And then he got a note from Mike months later that said, 'I'm so sorry I gave you that terrible note.' He had been carrying around that guilt! So, during *Salesman* previews, at one point Phil said, 'Am I yelling too much? Is it too angry?' Mike said, 'Yes.' Phil said, 'When?' Mike said, 'I don't want to tell you, but it's a little too angry.' That was it. In the next show, Phil toned it down. Mike knew he'd figure out when and how to do it."

Once previews started, it was clear that Nichols's most daring bet—his use of the original set—would pay off. The design was so cramped and the rooms so oddly configured that Hoffman, Emond, Garfield, and Wittrock had no choice but to embrace their unnerving, sometimes awkward proximity. The design, as Nichols knew it would, forced a kind of intimacy among their characters; the Lomans became a family bound together in suffocating and misshapen ways, with the house serving as both a cause and a representation of their dysfunction. The version of the play that the actors began to embody once they got on their feet was the one Nichols had held in his head and heart for more than six decades.

Death of a Salesman opened on March 15, 2012. Nichols was upset by a disappointed review from *The New York Times*'s Ben Brantley, who called it "an immaculate monument to a great American play" but felt that, while "you admire every detail of construction and leave . . . feeling that you have learned something of worth," the production "never quite achieves greatness." But almost all of the other reviews were raves.

The Wall Street Journal's Terry Teachout wrote that "the genius of Mr. Nichols's unostentatiously right staging of *Death of a Salesman* is that each part of it is in harmony with Mr. Hoffman's plain, blunt acting . . . the result is a production that will be remembered by all who see it as the capstone of a career."

"Nichols's unequivocal admiration for Elia Kazan's legendary directorial contributions to the play's original production hasn't inhibited him from advancing his own views," Marilyn Stasio wrote in *Variety*. "Willy is his hero—a weak, foolish, deeply flawed man, but still his hero—and Nichols understands and indeed loves him enough to forgive him his many sins."

The show's limited run was a major success—"an astonishingly good time," says Rudin, "with no real bumps except for Phil and Andrew's complete inability to mark it," that is, to lock their performances the way many actors do during the run of a play. "They never stopped. They were both so ruthlessly hard on themselves when they did not feel the things they were meant to express, and they would not rely on just technique to power through the show, ever."

"The part was brutal," says O'Donnell. "Every night, Phil would come home and go beat by beat over what worked and what didn't and why it didn't and what felt off. Theater stops your life to a certain extent, but this was different. I had never seen that before with him." Often, he couldn't wait to get out of the theater. Before his last scene, he would put on his street clothes under his costume; the minute the curtain call ended, he would strip off Willy's suit and walk straight off the stage, through the Barrymore Theater's side door, and across the street to the Glass House Tavern, where he would wait for the other actors to join him. The work took a terrible toll. "He would drink with the cast," says O'Donnell. "He'd never done that before. He knew he couldn't go onstage if he had used drugs. So in some ways I think doing the play kept it at bay. But I knew the minute the show was done, drugs would come into the picture."

Night after night, *Salesman* numbered among its attendees people who had worked with Nichols ten, thirty, and fifty years earlier. "I saw him backstage," says Tony Roberts, who had been a replacement in Nichols's first Broadway show, *Barefoot in the Park*, "and he turned to me and said, 'Oh, Tony, you were always my favorite,' with that great smile of his where you never knew if he was kidding or not." For Nichols, it was a moment to embrace old colleagues and, if possible, heal old wounds, or at least avoid reopening them. When he heard that Mandy Patinkin was backstage congratulating the cast, he quietly left the theater, texting Emond, "I stayed out of the way not to make Mandy unhappy." And when the producers threw a celebratory luncheon after the show received seven Tony nominations, he requested that David Rabe be seated at his table. The two had barely spoken in the thirty-five years since their falling-out over *Hurlyburly*. "I was surprised he put me there," says Rabe, "and I was grateful and glad. I didn't want to stay mad at him. It doesn't change anything that happened, but you get older and you want to hold on to the things about him that were gracious and winning."

Death of a Salesman ended its run the week before the Tonys. Nichols was the heavy favorite to win his seventh award for directing, forty-eight years after his first. The ceremony was held at the Beacon Theatre, the former movie house where he had so often escaped his warring parents as a little boy. Toward the end of the play's run, he had grown weaker; he looked gaunt, and his breathing was more labored than ever. "That was the only moment during *Salesman* when he was really infirm, when I worried about his stamina," says Rudin. Hours before the ceremony, Rudin took him to the theater. "I think you're going to win," he said, "and there are some steps you'll have to walk up. You should make sure you can do it, because you're going to be on camera when your name is called."

They practiced the walk to the stage together. Hours later, Nichols won the Tony. The standing ovation he received seemed to throw him off balance; he was winded and coughing by the time he reached the podium. "You see before you a happy man," he said. As he started to thank the actors—"a cast straight from heaven," he said—his voice broke. He was near tears. "God damn it," he said. "I can't talk about them. I love them too much . . . There's not a person in this theater that doesn't know what it is to be a salesman, to be way out there in the blue, riding on a smile and a shoeshine," he said, reading from a sheet of paper. "And as we know, a salesman has got to dream. It goes with the territory. Thank you." He raised his hand to his forehead, gave the audience a farewell salute, and left the stage.

Two weeks after the Tonys, Nora Ephron died. She was seventy-one and had fought leukemia for years but had kept her illness a secret from even her closest friends, including Nichols, until very near the end of her life. He was terribly shaken and told more than one friend it seemed wrong that he had outlived her. "As always, she quietly taught us a lesson," he wrote in an email. "If the worst happens, control it. Do what you want . . . Make the decisions, choose who will speak at your funeral . . . Die as you live: in control. Sort of helps a little."

Mortality was, inescapably, on his mind. His schedule grew cluttered with doctors' appointments—cardiologists, pulmonologists, eye doctors to deal with his weakening vision—and when he was asked to do something in public, it was usually because someone had died. In the fall, he was drafted to coordinate a memorial for the composer Marvin Hamlisch at the Juilliard School, at which Aretha Franklin, Liza Minnelli, and Barbra Streisand would all perform. He spent the day in minuets of diplomacy; Streisand would have to sing last, Franklin would have to be told that Streisand was going to sing last, Minnelli would have to be reminded not to take a bow and wait for applause. ("Why don't you just turn and bow to the picture of Marvin on the stage?" he gently suggested.) "It was so much fun watching him take each of these people and turn them into putty in his hands," says Ebs Burnough, who coordinated the event with him. "At the end, he said to me, 'Let's not overdo it. We don't want to get a reputation as funeral planners.'"

In 2013, he decided to direct another Broadway play, one he had wanted to stage for thirty-five years, Harold Pinter's *Betrayal*, with Daniel Craig and Rachel Weisz. Rudin thought more work was the best way for him to keep depression and anxiety at bay. Sawyer worried that he was too weak for another production and that a full rehearsal schedule would overtax him. But Nichols wanted to do it, and in twenty-five years of marriage, neither had ever stood in the way of the other's professional passion. Rudin scheduled the production for late that year. Serving as co–lead producer would be Nichols's close friend Barry Diller, on whose boat he had vacationed more than once. ("It's the ninth-largest yacht in the world," Nichols wryly remarked to a friend. "I feel anything larger would be vulgar, don't you?") Nichols's longtime assistant Colleen O'Donnell would be by his side as assistant director. He would be taken care of in every way possible.

In a sense, Nichols had outlived his passion for the play without realizing it. When he first saw *Betrayal*, he was a troubled and some-what angry man in his late forties, determined to make his brand-new third marriage work. Back then, Pinter's depiction of the deceit and cruelty of infidelity had struck him as an exposé of the dark heart of the war between men and women. "It's a play about marriage, but it's also about a question of middle age," says Ian MacNeil, who designed the show. "Are you going to do it right, or are you going to fuck it up again?"

Nichols was past all that now; at eighty-one, he had come to see *Betrayal* as a human comedy about how sexual desire drives everyone mad. The stakes no longer felt as high to him; the play's insistence on futility was something his own life had disproved. "At one point he was talking to a young woman, about twenty-five, about her marriage, and he said, 'Is this your first husband?' MacNeil remembers. "She said yes, and he said, 'The first and the fourth marriage are always the best.' That had been the journey of his life: learning to love more and more. But that wasn't the play."

"It's a nasty piece of work about jealousy and power and men who are pigs," says Brian MacDevitt, who designed the lighting for both *Salesman* and *Betrayal*. "And he made it a big lovefest about 'What are we going to do? We all love each other so much!'"

A workshop in the spring went promisingly. "It was Mike doing the kind of comedy he completely owned," says Rudin, "that granular behavior, every second explicated, subtext in everything, people deploying language in a way that made it clear they were lying—all the major skeins of his work. But when they returned and started rehearsals in the fall, that just never came back." By September, there was no hiding how enfeebled Nichols was. Many days had to be cut short for doctors' visits, and on others, he was too sick to come in at all. "It was bumpy in part because he was so upset," says MacDevitt. "He was really ill, and he'd get into coughing fits that would shut everything down. He was so pissed off about it. He would curse the health issues and say, 'If only I hadn't abused my body so much back in the day.'"

The production that resulted felt jagged and unsteady, including to those who were working on it. Daniel Craig was patient and deferential, but everyone involved was worried. Nichols and MacNeil spent endless hours at odds about the way the set design slowed the transitions between scenes. "*Betrayal* is like an exhale," says Rudin, "and the production felt more like a series of short breaths. Everybody knew it was in trouble, so there was an undertow of panic during previews. I think Mike thought from the beginning that he wasn't going to get away with it."

Friends and colleagues from across the decades—Aaron Sorkin, Julia Roberts, Candice Bergen, Julie Andrews, and Tony Walton among them—showed up to support Nichols on opening night. But reviews were mixed. In the *Chicago Tribune*, Chris Jones wrote that the play "has been infused with an aching ennui by the redoubtable Mike Nichols, a director who has lived long enough to see that even adultery grows old, and the aging adulterers sad and pathetic." But Ben Brantley called the production "crude and clunky . . . This *Betrayal* shrivels Pinter's play to the dimensions of the minor tale of infidelity that London critics called it when the show first opened . . . Time may have proved those critics wrong, but this production seems determined to show that they were right."

The review devastated Nichols. "He was really wounded," says Bergen. "It just seemed to blunt him, in a way." In the past, he had said that he found that bad reviews injured him less if he didn't tell Sawyer about them, but this time there was no hiding his feelings. "He was home, and I went to see him, and he didn't say anything about it," says Bergen, "but he lost his spark. I was so angry. I thought, *Aren't you supposed to be kinder to people when they're older?* What would it have cost?"

What appeared to be an emotional crash turned out to be the onset of a severe physical illness. Nichols lost twenty-five pounds in just a few weeks. "Nobody ever enjoyed food more than he did," says Rudin. "And suddenly I would go eat with him and there would be the same parade of food, but he wouldn't take more than two bites of bread." Some friends thought he was dying; a rumor that he had cancer had to be kept out of the papers. He turned out to have a systemic infection; once it was treated, he rapidly regained weight and a measure of strength, but each successive illness left him weaker than he had been before.

Philip Seymour Hoffman died in February 2014. "I can't stop talking to him," Nichols wrote. "[He] could have been OK and far more. Onward is the only direction." He had to keep going. Rudin encouraged him, telling him that David Lean had still been directing in his early eighties. (He was fudging by a few years, but it cheered

Nichols up.) They started talking about a revival of *Our Town*, and Nichols got excited at the idea of directing Tom Hanks as the Stage Manager. "Think of the marquee," he told Hanks. "Our names . . . Our Town!" This time, Sawyer put her foot down. "Diane called me," says Rudin, "and said, 'Don't do this. He's not well enough.' I said, 'Well, here's the thing. I have to hear it from him. I can't be the guy who says to him, "You're done."'" When Hanks said he wasn't interested, they started to think about Lily Tomlin. Rudin knew they were fighting against time and reality, but it gave Nichols a project to care about.

He saw friends, went out for meals, and watched as artists many generations younger developed their new work. He exulted over a workshop presentation of *Hamilton* to which Miranda invited him. And on nights when he was up to it, he headed out to the theater, always sure to stay and congratulate the casts of whatever he saw, although there were times when he couldn't climb the stairs to their dressing rooms. His car and driver were always close by, and when Sawyer couldn't be with him, she made sure a safety net was in place. In the spring, Eric Fischl, who had painted a striking portrait of Nichols several years earlier, called him and made a date for them to go see an exhibit of "Degenerate Art"—paintings from the years Nichols had been a child in Germany. Soon after they had arranged to meet at the Neue Galerie, which was just a few blocks from Nichols's apartment, Sawyer called Fischl and said, "Don't tell Mike I'm asking you to do this, but I'd feel better if you came and picked him up and took him there."

"Of course I said I would," Fischl says. "He insisted on walking, so we walked very slowly and took our time. At one point in the gallery, he broke away, and when I went into another room to find him, he said he had had to sit down. He said the exhibit was too emotionally difficult for him—there was more documentation of the Nazi horror than he was able to handle. It was not the way I wanted our last time together to be."

Nichols started spending time with Jack O'Brien to do interview sessions for a documentary about his life, and after years of vowing he would never write an autobiography, he became intrigued by the idea of collaborating with John Lahr on a professional memoir, though nothing came of it. "The funny thing is that toward the end of his life," says Matthew Weiner, "which of course I was not aware it was going to be, he told me with great joy that he had retired." Sawyer had decided to step down as the anchor of ABC's evening newscast; they both hoped they would be lucky enough to have a couple of years together. "Mike encouraged me, when *Mad Men* was almost over, to do nothing and start over emotionally and just take time to appreciate my family," says Weiner. "Two weeks after that conversation, I called him and said, 'What are you doing?' and he said, 'I'm in preproduction.' 'What are you talking about?!' I said. 'What about just living life?' 'I know,' he said, 'but it's now or never.'"

In July, HBO announced that Nichols would direct Meryl Streep in a film adaptation of *Master Class,* Terrence McNally's play about Maria Callas. It sounded impossible; Rudin, who says, "It never occurred to me that Mike was not going to live forever," was concerned enough to call Celia Costas and ask, "Are you sure he's strong enough to do this?" But Nichols insisted he was, and started formulating a plan to make the movie by staging seventeen or eighteen performances of the play in a studio in Queens and filming them all. He opened a production office and began sketching out ideas. "I wanted it to be true," Streep says. "We worked on it with Terrence, and I thought about the role, but I never, deep in my heart, thought it was going to happen."

That summer, Nichols started seeing a psychiatrist to help him accept the fact that his time was limited and to talk about his fear of dying. His friends had already noticed a change in his demeanor—an emotionalism that rose to the surface on even minor occasions. "His quips and asides could be . . . smart and mean and sharply observed when he was in his prime," says Streep. "But, chastened, I guess, by all his brushes with the reaper, he willfully, heartfully changed. Every phone call, email, and in-person exchange was charged with an embarrassing, coursing current of love. Goodbye always had tears. It upset me. But it readied me for what came, I guess."

In October, he attended a Broadway revival of *The Real Thing*. Cynthia Nixon, who had played the main character's daughter for Nichols at seventeen, was now playing the girl's mother. Two of her original costars, Christine Baranski and Peter Gallagher, went to the opening night, as did Tom Stoppard. Nichols tried to sit through the play, but his cough got the better of him and he quietly walked up the orchestra aisle to a lounge where he wouldn't disturb anyone. A few days later, the impromptu reunion turned into a real one when Baranski organized a lunch at his favorite restaurant, Marea, for the women of Nichols's 1984 productions: She was joined by Glenn Close, Whoopi Goldberg, and Nixon. They knew his birthday was coming up in a few days and wanted to do something special for him. "It was fantastic," Nixon says. "He told stories and talked a lot about his grandchildren. Sometimes he'd talk about a show and he wouldn't remember a name, and he would get upset, and Christine would calmly remind him. And we also told stories, especially Whoopi and Glenn. They gave themselves to him as gifts—you know, 'This is what my experience was, this is what you did for me, this is what you meant to me . . .'"

On November 6, Nichols turned eighty-three. He woke up to an email from his first wife, Patricia Scot. Like Nichols, she was now on her fourth and happiest marriage and was living in Florida; they had been back in touch over the previous decade, initially at the urging of Sawyer, who had done a great deal to unite the different threads of Nichols's family and past. "I wrote to him and said, 'Happy birthday, dear old friend. I hope you have a wonderful day and all your wishes come true.' He emailed back," Scot says. "It was very nice, because after all those years, that's what he finally was—a dear, old friend."

The last week of his life was a busy one. He and Sawyer went to dinner at Lorne Michaels's house, where they saw Paul Simon and Edie Brickell and Tina Fey. He touched base with John Patrick Shanley about Shanley's desire to have him direct a new play called *Prodigal Son*. "Just promise me you won't die," said Shanley. "I'll try," said Nichols. He went to a conference room at CAA to listen to the actors Josh Charles, Nina Arianda, and Jon Hamm read a play whose director he had mentored, and he participated as an actor in a reading of a new play called *Evening at the Talk House*, by his old friend Wallace Shawn. "He was very ill," says Shawn, "and it was even more moving to me that he would do it, that he would expose himself to being watched by people. His cough was terrifying—at one point I thought, *Maybe this will be the end of his life, right here*. He walked out for a good twenty minutes, and then he came back in and said, 'I'm fine. This happens.'" The actor Larry Pine, whom Nichols had cast in *The Seagull*, sat next to him and helped him keep his place in the script. He had rehearsed his part, and when the time came for him to read his lines, he did it effortlessly.

On November 18, he had lunch with Candice Bergen. He had just gotten an eye examination and was having trouble reading street signs and addresses; he got to the lunch late and was slightly disoriented and frightened. He told her that he was having a minor medical procedure the next day—an adjustment to his pacemaker, and possibly the insertion of a stent. After lunch, he went to play with his granddaughters, and then to the hospital to sit by the bedside of his friend Buck Henry, who had just suffered a severe stroke. He firmed up lunch plans with Bob Balaban. And he and Sawyer saw Terrence McNally. "It's dumb nuts and bolts," Nichols told him, "but I have to have this thing done, and I can either get it over with or wait until next week." "Get it over with," McNally advised him. "Thank you for that," Sawyer said.

The next evening, after the procedure, Mike and Diane went out to dinner with Daisy, Max, and Jenny. As they got back to the apartment, he complained of feeling dizzy and collapsed. He died a short time later, at home, surrounded by the people he loved the most. He left behind an appointment book for the coming week that was completely full.

EPILOGUE

A few hours after Mike died, his three children divided up the long list of people who needed to be told he was gone and started making calls. The outpouring of love and grief was immense. In the morning, Whoopi Goldberg broke down when she tried to announce his death on *The View*. That night, Glenn Close and John Lithgow, who were costarring onstage in Edward Albee's *A Delicate Balance*, sang one of Mike's favorite songs, "Happy Trails," to the audience after their curtain call. The night after that, Broadway's theaters dimmed their lights in his honor.

Movie people reacted to his death with heartfelt paragraphs delivered by their publicists to trade publications for use in memorial round-ups. Theater people reacted to his death by getting together in the back room of a Midtown restaurant for an impromptu wake after the curtains on that Thursday night's shows fell, to hug and cry and laugh and swap stories and drink. And several dozen people who were close to Mike gathered that Sunday at the home he and Diane shared, chatting quietly and observing the rites of condolence as grandchildren too young and tiny to be sad scampered obliviously between the legs of the people in his many circles, some of whom were meeting for the first time and discovering that his world was wider than even they had imagined.

One year later, not much more than a mile from where the SS *Bremen* had deposited a seven-year-old boy ashore in his new country in 1939, about 250 of Mike's friends gathered in the IAC Building, where Barry Diller had turned the high-ceilinged, Frank Gehry–designed lobby into an event space that could accommodate what he described—invoking Mike's favorite word, to the delight of the crowd—as "the last ratfuck." It was November 8, 2015, a long-awaited send-off that Diller, CAA head Bryan Lourd, and Lorne Michaels had planned, and a night so packed with celebrities that even the famous dropped their guard and gazed at one another in fascination. It was a convocation of different realms: Anna Wintour and David Remnick and Frank Rich, Meryl Streep and Julia Roberts and Emma Thompson, Stephen Sondheim and Tom Stoppard and John Patrick Shanley and Terrence McNally, Steven Spielberg and Stanley Donen and James L. Brooks and Bennett Miller. Oprah Winfrey and David Geffen, publishers and designers and artists and agents and news anchors and billionaires. Diane had decided on the food—it would be Thanksgiving dinner, Mike's favorite meal. A dais of transparent cubes filled with autumn leaves collected from the park along the Hudson River had been erected in front of the dining tables at the center of the long, narrow space.

The night had the feeling of a large and unusual family reunion—a gathering of people who had never, until now, realized that they were members of the same tribe, united only by their deep connection to the man who wasn't there. The angry girl who first met Mike in Chicago stood up to talk and said, "Can everybody hear me?" "Yes," roared the room. "Can everybody *see* me?" said Elaine May. Shouts of "No!" came from distant tables. "No?" she said. "I look *fabulous*." Tom Stoppard got up to say that he had always felt "overestimated by Mike . . . People ask, 'Do you write for yourself or for the audience?' For the last thirty-five years, I've wanted to say, 'No, I write for Mike Nichols.'"

"I never understood why Mike was my friend," said Whoopi Goldberg. "He told me, 'You have to understand you're unique, and if I don't help you realize this, you will always be ordinary because that's how you think of yourself.'" She paused, as expertly as he would have wanted her to, then added, "And so it is his fault that I am the egotistical bitch that I am." Tony Kushner spoke about Mike's mind and heart and life as an immigrant. Meryl Streep read his emails and talked about a relationship that was based on "the love of working," adding that they had learned only late in his life that they were distant cousins. "We shared a nose," she said. Julia Roberts spoke of her love for Mike and fought back tears. Christopher Walken, who had seen the film of *The Designated Mourner* dozens of times, said, "Mike was a great actor—that doesn't get talked about much." Paul Simon sang "Homeward Bound" as many people in the room wept. He said, "When I sang this at Anne Bancroft's memorial service, I thought, *I don't ever want to sing 'Mrs. Robinson' for Mike*." Then he sang "Mrs. Robinson." People craned their necks at the lean, gray-haired, diffident-looking older man who had been given a place of honor. Many of them did not realize until he got up to speak that Mike had a brother. People leaned forward, as if a secret code were about to be cracked.

Many in the room commented that Mike was the last of a certain kind of cultural celebrity—someone who could travel between film and theater, who understood art and politics and fashion and history and money, a man of the world and of his century. "I don't think anyone here will have this many people at their memorial service," said Mia Farrow, her son Ronan on her arm.

There were funny stories and personal stories, there was gossip and the sharing of his favorite aphorisms; people compared notes and exchanged memories and talked about an era ending. "How did he make us all feel like we were the special one?" one actress asked. There were posters of Mike's work to examine, and the images on them filled the room with ghosts—Taylor and Burton, Tandy and Cronyn, Walter

Matthau and Art Carney, George C. Scott and Maureen Stapleton, Robin Williams and Philip Seymour Hoffman. People spoke with special fondness of those who couldn't be there—John Calley and Richard Avedon and Nora Ephron. They would have known what to make of a moment like this, they said, and then: *He* would have known what to make of it, better than anyone. Finally, there was Mike himself, filling the room with both his presence and his absence. The night ended with an audio clip of an old Nichols and May routine, an improvisation about a male nurse that he couldn't get through without disintegrating into hysterics. That sound—the sound of Mike breaking into hilariously helpless laughter—sent the guests out into the pleasantly cool night, the breeze from the Hudson River on their faces, feeling that they had heard him happy one last time.

Fifty years earlier, in a state of agitated anxiety, he had told an interviewer, "I don't care about being forgotten. I fear getting to the end of my life and feeling I've wasted it. I don't want to get to the end and think I haven't tasted enough and touched other people enough and had a good enough time."

In old age, that fear had vanished. All of his desperate urgency had given way to a serenity he had taken a lifetime to find. At one of his favorite restaurants, he had lunch with a friend whose son was about to go out on his own; he was looking for some advice he could share. Did he have any wisdom to offer?

He thought for a moment.

"Well," he said, "just so long as he knows that things that start out poorly don't always end poorly."

He thought some more.

"That," he said, "and study improv."

Acknowledgments

I began research for this biography in early 2015, after seeking the consent of Diane Sawyer, Daisy Nichols, Jenny Nichols, and Max Nichols. They gave it with no conditions attached; they did not ask that any subject or area of inquiry be placed off limits, nor did they ask to see any part of the manuscript before publication. I am more grateful to them than I know how to express for allowing me to take this journey into the life of a man they all loved, and I hope this book repays their trust.

My sincere thanks to the people who agreed to talk to or correspond with me about Mike Nichols—many of whom also invited me into their homes; shared letters, photographs, and diaries; opened up private collections; and made introductions to others. They are, in alphabetical order, Jerry Adler, Alan Alda, Brooke Allen, Kamian Allen, Dan Allentuck, Amy Aquino, Elizabeth Ashley, Ed Asner, Eileen Atkins, Remy Auberjonois, Hank Azaria, Mary Bailey, Jon Robin Baitz, Bob Balaban, Barbara Barrie, Kathy Bates, Annette Bening, Richard Benjamin, Candice Bergen, Andrew Bergman, Jamie Bernstein, John Bloom, Peter Bonerz, Bob Bookman, Christian Borle, John Breglio, Matthew Broderick, Cary Brokaw, Arvin Brown, Ebs Burnough, Bill Camp, Joy Carlin, Josh Charles, Glenn Close, D. L. Coburn, Jill Cordle, Celia Costas, Trip Cullman, Peter Davis, Jeffrey DeMunn, Robert De Niro, Barry Diller, Paul Dooley, Ariel Dorfman, Olympia

Dukakis, Nora Dunn, Margaret Edson, Deborah Eisenberg, Linda Emond, Bill Evans, Ron Fassler, Jules Feiffer, Michael Feinstein, Eric Fischl, Robert Fitch, Markus Flanagan, Nancy Fletcher, Calista Flockhart, Tom Fontana, Susan Forristal, Gary Frank, Scott Frankel, Will Frears, Morgan Freeman, Penny Fuller, Peter Gallagher, Herbert J. Gans, Andrew Garfield, Bob Gazzale, David Geffen, Joanna Gleason, Stephen Goldblatt, Bo Goldman, Lee Grant, Robert Greenhut, Mike Haley, Jon Hamm, Tom Hanks, Marcia Gay Harden, David Hare, Dorian Harewood, Sheldon Harnick, Kathy Hendrickson, Cal Herrmann, Carl Hiaasen, Barbara Hiken, Gerald Hiken, Arthur Hirsch, Jane Stanton Hitchcock, Anna Maria Horsford, Bill Irwin, Judith Ivey, Tracey Jackson, Andrew Jarecki, Herbert Jefferson Jr., Richard Jenkins, Dan Jinks, Susan Kellermann, E. Katherine Kerr, Justin Kirk, Kevin Kline, Michael E. Knight, Howard W. Koch Jr., Jon Korkes, Larry Kramer, Swoosie Kurtz, Tony Kushner, Nathan Lane, Frank Langella, Linda Lavin, Peter Lawrence, Lesley "Twiggy" Lawson, James Lecesne, Adrian Lester, Norman Lloyd, Tony Lo Bianco, Hal Luftig, Brian MacDevitt, Ian MacNeil, Brian Markinson, Steve Martin, Marsha Mason, Richard Masur, Audra McDonald, Bruce McGill, Terrence McNally, B. T. McNicholl, Joanna Merlin, Mark Metcalf, Lorne Michaels, Rebecca Miller, Lin-Manuel Miranda, Kirby Mitchell, Susanna Moore, Marianne Mosbach, Gregory Mosher, Otts Munderloh, James Naughton, Kate Nelligan, Craig T. Nelson, Casey Nicholaw, Cynthia Nixon, Jack O'Brien, Walt Odets, Mimi O'Donnell, Denis O'Hare, Michael O'Keefe, Park Overall, Clive Owen, Sabrina Padwa, Gail Papp, Corey Parker, Diane Paulus, Austin Pendleton, David Hyde Pierce, Laura Pierce, Larry Pine, Oliver Platt, Christopher Plummer, David Pogue, Natalie Portman, David Rabe, David Rasche, Robert Redford, Pamela Reed, Patricia Resnick, Howard Rittner, Julia Roberts, Tony Roberts, Gordon Rogoff, Temi Brodkey Rose, Ann Roth, John Rothman, Rajendra Roy, John Rubinstein, Scott Rudin, Harvey Sabinson, Julian Schlossberg, Arthur

Schmidt, George Segal, Paul Shaffer, John Patrick Shanley, Wallace Shawn, Alan Shayne, Ben Shenkman, David Shepherd, David Shire, Ron Siebert, Douglas Sills, Anna Deavere Smith, Ed Solomon, Josef Sommer, Stephen Sondheim, Aaron Sorkin, Hannah Roth Sorkin, Steven Spielberg, Gloria Steinem, Matthew Stern, Ben Stiller, Barbara Siman Strouse, Charles Strouse, Rose Styron, Susanna Styron, Thomas Styron, Norman Sunshine, Juliet Taylor, Emma Thompson, Rosemarie Tichler, Jeffrey Toobin, John Travolta, Leo Treitler, Jonathan Tropper, Maria Tucci, Patrizia von Brandenstein, Tony Walton, Matthew Weiner, Bo Welch, Ken Welch, Kenneth Welsh, Douglas Wick, Beau Willimon, Patrick Wilson, Finn Wittrock, George C. Wolfe, Albert Wolsky, Jonathan M. Woodward, Max Wright, Maury Yeston, and Fred Zollo. Every one of them added pieces to a fascinating puzzle, and I hope none of them will feel slighted if I express an extra measure of gratitude to Elaine May, Dr. Robert Nichols, Meryl Streep, and Patricia Scot Yorton for their exceptional generosity in sharing their memories and insights. In addition, the perspectives and recollections shared with me by Susan Anspach, Warren Beatty, Alexandra Berlin, Eileen Brennan, William Daniels, Wynn Handman, William Hanley, Buck Henry, Dustin Hoffman, Norman Jewison, Peter Nelson, Arthur Penn, Ronald Ribman, Joel Schiller, Michael Tolan, Lawrence Turman, and Elizabeth Wilson for my earlier book *Pictures at a Revolution* were of great value in preparing this one.

For answering questions, sharing information, facilitating introductions, offering support, volunteering transcripts, clearing up misconceptions, or generally making a biographer's life easier, I thank Ryan Bernstein, Chris Bonanos, Isaac Butler, Chris Connelly, Leslee Dart, Thom Geier, Michael Golding, Bill Goldstein, Jay Handelman, Claire Kenny, Glenn Kenny, Dan Kois, Bryan Lourd, Kristie Macosko Krieger, Peggy McRae, Barry Mendel, Richard Nelson, James Nicola, Rick Pappas, Ben Schwartz, Brian Siberell, Alisa Solomon, George

Stevens Jr., Kyle Stevens (the author of *Mike Nichols: Sex, Language, and the Reinvention of Psychological Realism*, an insightful study of Nichols's films), Moises Velasquez-Manoff, Julie Welch, and John Sacret Young. I am especially grateful to Chris Nashawaty and the American Film Institute's Bob Gazzale for providing full transcripts of their interviews with Mike, to Steven Soderbergh for sharing transcripts of his fascinating discussions with Mike for the DVD editions of *Who's Afraid of Virginia Woolf?*, *The Graduate*, and *Catch-22*, and to Annabel Davis-Goff for graciously allowing me to fact-check parts of this biography with her.

In researching this book, I benefited from the work of many writers who, over the decades, interviewed and/or wrote about Nichols. I want to express particular appreciation for the histories of improv comedy written by Janet Coleman and Jeffrey Sweet, and for John Lahr's extraordinary 2000 *New Yorker* profile "Making It Real," an essential starting point for anyone who wants to understand its subject. Over the years that I spent plundering the resources of the New York Public Library for the Performing Arts, the apparently inexhaustible patience of John Calhoun, Suzanne Lipkin, and the entire staff of the third-floor research room and the Theatre on Film and Tape Archive was a gift I won't forget. My thanks as well to the staff of the Scholars Room at the Paley Center for Media in New York, to the Museum of Modern Art, and to the team at Film at Lincoln Center, in particular Eugene Hernandez, Michael Koresky, and Jordan Raup.

My great thanks to my agent, Andrew Wylie, for his enthusiasm, support, perspective, and clear-sightedness. I have been lucky to have a home at Penguin Press for more than fifteen years, and even luckier to be in the hands of the inestimably smart, kind, perceptive, and patient Scott Moyers and Ann Godoff, who brought me into their world. They and the team that worked on this book, especially Mia Council, Will Palmer, Bruce Giffords, Amanda Dewey, Darren Haggar, Claire Vaccaro, and the spectacular photo editor Michele Romero, are all any biographer could wish for.

Heartfelt thanks as well to my other editors—the ones who kept me employed during the years it took to write this book—particularly Lane Brown, Jeff Giles, David Haskell, Radhika Jones, Adam Moss, Nic Rapold, and Carl Swanson. My friends and family are champions at bearing with me through mood crashes, fogs of distraction, and last-minute absences—I'm in serious debt to Scott Brown, Kate Clinton, Elly Eisenberg, Linda Emond, Oskar and Laurie Eustis, Dan Fierman, David Harris, Gabriella Maurer, Michael Mayer, Lisa Schwarzbaum, Urvashi Vaid, and Roger Waltzman, all of whom, to quote Mike, stuck with me through thin.

This book would not exist without the love and steadfastness of my husband, Tony Kushner, my best friend, kindest and sharpest reader, and most preposterous piece of good fortune. Nor would it exist without the time I was lucky enough to spend with its subject. My own journey with Mike began in 2001, when he decided to take on the job of directing the HBO adaptation of Tony's play *Angels in America*. Soon after that, I interviewed him for my first book, which is in part about the making of *The Graduate*. To know Mike in the later phases of his life and career was a privilege, to be in his company was never less than a special occasion, and to listen to him and learn from him was always a joy. I hope he will forgive me for not taking his suggestion and calling this book *The Wrong Jew*. Mike's warmth and generosity to me were great gifts, and there was not a day I worked on this book that I didn't think of one more question I wish I had asked him. I hope I found my way to some of the answers.

Notes

Abbreviations Used

ACC Alexander Cohen Collection, New York Public Library for the Performing Arts

AI Author interview

CNP Claire Nichtern papers, New York Public Library for the Performing Arts

NYPLPA New York Public Library for the Performing Arts

Unless otherwise indicated, all descriptions of Mike Nichols and Elaine May's television appearances are based on my viewing of the archived broadcasts, most of which are located at New York's Museum of Television and Radio.

EPIGRAPH

ix **"You don't know":** Deirdre Carmody, "Mike Nichols Reflects on Movies—and Life," *New York Times*, April 20, 1985.

CHAPTER ONE: STARTING FROM ZERO

3 **"Maybe," he said:** AI with Robert Nichols. Unless otherwise noted, the details of Mike Nichols's ancestry, family, and early life in New York in this chapter come from this interview and from Robert Nichols, "German Tragedies: Robert Nichols Remembers," February 15, 2012, Holocaust Living History Workshop, University of California, San Diego, https://library.ucsd.edu/dc/object/bb94562426.

4 **The story he told:** Nichols told the story to countless interviewers; the first may have been John Keating. See Keating, "From Bistros to Broadway," *New York Times*, December 18,1960.

4 **"We all had to learn":** Joseph Berger, "No Ordinary Reunion," *New York Times*, November 10, 1992.

5 **"I suppose I've spent":** Patrick Goldstein, "Primary Concerns," *Los Angeles Times*, March 15, 1998.

5 **"A Jew in Nazi Germany"**: Joan Juliet Buck, "Live Mike," *Vanity Fair*, June 1994.

5 **the "family legend"**: Nichols, interview by Bob Gazzale, for Nichols's American Film Institute Life Achievement Award, 2010, unpublished transcript.

5 **a cousin of Albert Einstein**: *Faces of America with Henry Louis Gates Jr.*, aired on PBS, February 23, 2010.

5 **mine on Sakhalin Island**: Jesse Green, "When in Doubt, Seduce," *New York*, March 2, 2012.

6 **"I always had"**: *Faces of America*, PBS.

6 **"There wasn't the"**: Brigitte Landauer, interview, in Paul Avrich, *Anarchist Voices: An Oral History of Anarchism in America* (Chico, CA: AK Press, 2005).

7 **"My beloved children"**: Gustav Landauer, *Revolution and Other Writings: A Political Reader*, ed. Gabriel Kuhn (Oakland, CA: PM Press, 2010).

8 **"By the time I spelled Peschkowsky"**: C. Robert Jennings, "The *Playboy* Interview: Mike Nichols," *Playboy*, June 1966.

8 **April 28, 1939**: *Faces of America*, PBS.

8 **"unbelievable, undeserved"**: Nichols, interview by Chris Nashawaty for *Entertainment Weekly*, March 1, 2012, unpublished transcript.

9 **"I remember everything"**: Nichols gave similarly worded accounts in two documentaries: "Mike Nichols," *American Masters*, dir. Elaine May, aired on PBS, January 29, 2016, and *Becoming Mike Nichols*, dir. Jack O'Brien, aired on HBO, February 26, 2016.

9 **"years, decades"**: Nichols, interview by James Lipton, *Inside the Actors Studio*, season 3, episode 8, aired on Bravo, 1996, viewed at the Theater Film and Tape Archive, NYPLPA.

9 **"I remember when we got to the end"**: Nichols, Gazzale interview.

9 **"was ill"**: *Becoming Mike Nichols*, HBO.

9 **"if you were alone"**: Nichols, Nashawaty interview.

10 **"I remember looking for the prow"**: Paul Rosenfield, "Did Mike Nichols Squander His Luck on 'Heartburn'?," *Los Angeles Times*, August 3, 1986.

10 **"test pee-lote"**: Nichols, Gazzale interview.

10 **"The first thing I saw"**: Nichols, Nashawaty interview.

11 **"They were awful"**: John Lahr, "Making It Real," *New Yorker*, February 21 and 28, 2000.

11 **for the next year and a half**: Letter written by Brigitte Landauer, October 23, 1941, in "German Tragedies: Robert Nichols Remembers."

11 **"we had somehow miraculously"**: Nichols, Nashawaty interview.

11 **At the time the Nichols family settled**: Information on the geography and demography of Jews in pre–World War II New York comes from Jeffrey S. Gurock, *Jews in Gotham—New York Jews in a Changing City, 1920–2010*, vol. 3 of *City of Promises: A History of the Jews of New York*, ed. Deborah Dash Moore (New York: New York University Press, 2012), 4–24, 55.

13 **"not as funny"**: Mel Gussow, "'Vanya' Stars Tie Success to Nichols," *New York Times*, June 17, 1973.

13 **"I remember being on the schoolbus"**: Keating, "From Bistros to Broadway."

13 **"To this day," he said at thirty-five**: "Mike Nichols: Lighting Up Broadway," *Newsweek*, November 14, 1966.

13 **"He printed everything"**: AI with Jack O'Brien.

13 **"a series of very chic"**: Gordon Cotler, "For the Love of Mike—and Elaine," *New York Times Magazine*, May 24, 1959.

14 **"the most popular of the unpopular"**: Lahr, "Making It Real."

14 **"What I loved him for"**: Lahr, "Making It Real."

14 **"What I understood"**: Gordon Rogoff, email to author, February 19, 2016.

14 **And when Mike's parents**: AI with Marianne Mosbach.

15 **"I was motivated then"**: Sam Wasson, *Improv Nation: How We Made a Great American Art* (New York: Houghton Mifflin Harcourt, 2017), 10–11.

15 **"I came home a little concerned"**: *Faces of America*, PBS.

16 **"It was sort of my playground"**: *Becoming Mike Nichols*, HBO.

16 **where he felt "landlocked"**: Lahr, "Making It Real."

16 **her older sister's emigration**: Letter from Brigitte Landauer, "German Tragedies: Robert Nichols Remembers."

16 **"It was hard for them to have a fresh"**: Barbara Gelb, "Mike Nichols: The Special Risks and Rewards of the Director's Art," *New York Times Magazine*, May 27, 1984.

16 **The new school**: "Lighting Up Broadway," *Newsweek*.

16 **"I think there is an immigrant's"**: Peter Applebome, "Always Asking, What Is This Really About?," *New York Times*, April 25, 1999.

17 **"said I was intelligent"**: "Lighting Up Broadway," *Newsweek*.

17 **"You must learn to hear people"**: Sam Kashner, "Who's Afraid of Nichols and May?," *Vanity Fair*, January 2013.

17 **The opening was coincident:** AI with Tony Kushner.

17 **Sometimes they'd attend a Broadway:** Nichols, Gazzale interview.

17 **"you can be a very great writer":** "Mike Nichols," *American Masters.*

17 **"I liked the theater":** Nichols, Gazzale interview.

18 **"As my mother later explained":** Peter Biskind, "Who's Afraid of the Big Bad Wolf?," *Premiere,* March 1994.

18 **"There were a lot of problems":** AI with Mosbach.

18 **"All his doctor friends":** Alice Arlen, "Mr. Success," *Interview,* December 1988.

19 **"I wish I'd known him":** *Becoming Mike Nichols,* HBO.

19 **"He died before he could see":** Lahr, "Making It Real."

CHAPTER TWO: AGENT X-9

20 **"He would always refer to the wig":** AI with Robert Nichols.

21 **Anything they needed was purchased:** AI with Robert Nichols.

21 **But in 1946:** Robert Nichols, "German Tragedies: Robert Nichols Remembers," February 15, 2012, Holocaust Living History Workshop, Digital Library Collection, University of California, San Diego, https://library.ucsd.edu/dc/object/bb94562426.

21 **from migraines to:** Robert Nichols, "German Tragedies."

22 **"We weren't clean":** John Lahr, "Making It Real," *New Yorker,* February 21 and 28, 2000.

22 **"Everything wounded her":** Lahr, "Making It Real."

22 **"I don't think Mike":** Robert Nichols, email to author, June 15, 2018.

22 **he liked the horses:** Mike Nichols, interview by Barbara Walters, *Today,* NBC, July 29, 1966.

22 **"never had a friend":** Lahr, "Making It Real."

22 **At least one Walden faculty:** AI with Peter Davis.

23 **"I was stranger than them":** Lahr, "Making It Real."

23 **"Mike often used":** Robert Nichols, email to author, November 7, 2017.

23 **"being too snappish":** Edmund Wilson, *The Sixties: The Last Journal, 1960–1972,* ed. Lewis M. Dabney (New York: Farrar, Straus, and Giroux, 1993), 721.

23 **"met this nice girl":** C. Robert Jennings, "The *Playboy* Interview: Mike Nichols," *Playboy,* June 1966.

24 **"He looked golden":** AI with Tony Kushner.

24 **Mike was interested in plays:** Mike Nichols, interview by James Lipton, *Inside the Actors Studio,* season 3, episode 8, aired on Bravo, 1996, viewed at the Theater Film and Tape Archive, NYPLPA.

24 **"It sounds very dramatic":** Mike Nichols, interview by Bob Gazzale, for Nichols's American Film Institute Life Achievement Award, 2010, unpublished transcript.

25 **"and the curtain comes up":** "Mike Nichols," *American Masters,* dir. Elaine May, aired on PBS, January 29, 2016.

25 **Wendy Hiller:** Gavin Smith, "Of Metaphors and Purpose," *Film Comment,* May–June 1999.

25 **"totally devastated":** Jesse Green, "When in Doubt, Seduce," *New York,* March 2, 2012.

25 **"Lazy and disorganized":** "Mike Nichols," *American Masters.*

25 **Instead, he began a year of drudgery:** Robert Rice, "Profiles: A Tilted Insight," *New Yorker,* April 15, 1961.

26 **"The hard times dissolved":** AI with Robert Nichols.

26 **"Show up at Mandel Hall":** "Mike Nichols," *American Masters.*

26 **"Yes, I had a tough childhood":** Barbara Gelb, "Mike Nichols: The Special Risks and Rewards of the Director's Art," *New York Times Magazine,* May 27, 1984.

26 **"In high school you figure":** "Some Are More Yossarian Than Others," *Time,* June 15, 1970.

27 **"the great discovery":** Nichols, *Playboy* interview.

27 **"We talked about books":** Lahr, "Making It Real."

27 **"I don't usually have alliances":** AI with Peter Davis.

27 **"I wouldn't say [we were] misfits":** Lahr, "Making It Real."

27 **"was paradise":** Gelb, "Mike Nichols."

27 **"something out of":** Lahr, "Making It Real."

28 **staying in bed:** "Some Are More Yossarian Than Others," *Time.*

28 **"A persona takes energy":** Lahr, "Making It Real."

28 **"He was very outspoken":** Lahr, "Making It Real."

28 **He was particularly taken with a humanities:** Gordon Cotler, "For the Love of Mike—and Elaine," *New York Times Magazine,* May 24, 1959.

29 **"It threw me":** "Mike Nichols," *American Masters.*

29 **"why my rich friends":** Gerald Nachman, *Seriously Funny: The Rebel Comedians of the 1950s and 1960s* (New York: Back Stage Books, 2004), 328.

30 **"bullshit about theater":** *Becoming Mike Nichols,* dir. Jack O'Brien, aired on HBO, February 26, 2016.

30 **Sills, in turn:** Nichols, Gazzale interview.
30 **Rather, he believed that the games:** Viola Spolin, *Improvisation for the Theater*, 3rd ed. (Evanston, IL: Northwestern University Press, 1999).
30 **In one of his first exercises:** Janet Coleman, *The Compass: The Improvisational Theatre That Revolutionized American Comedy* (Chicago: University of Chicago Press, 1991), 21–22.
30 **"a 'revolutionary' group":** Jeffrey Sweet, *Something Wonderful Right Away: An Oral History of the Second City & the Compass Players* (Montclair, NJ: Limelight Editions, 1978), 73.
30 **"I was extremely good":** *Becoming Mike Nichols*, HBO.
30 **"I liked him":** Coleman, *The Compass*, 18.
31 **"At the University of Chicago":** AI with Joy Carlin.
31 **"I was still always oversleeping":** AI with Mike Nichols.
31 **"There were times when I resented him":** AI with Edward Asner.
32 **Throughout his life, *A Place*:** *Becoming Mike Nichols*, HBO.
32 **the length of each shot:** AI with Mike Nichols.
32 **"Watch it twenty-five times":** AIs with Gregory Mosher and Matt Weiner.
32 **"It just really got to me":** Nichols, Gazzale interview.
33 **"the highest possible level":** Sam Wasson, *Improv Nation: How We Made a Great American Art* (New York: Houghton Mifflin Harcourt, 2017), 19–20.
33 **"I can't tell you how bad":** Nichols, Gazzale interview.
33 **"about four feet away":** Nichols, *Inside the Actors Studio*.
33 **"I knew she knew":** Sweet, *Something Wonderful*, 73.
34 **"That was probably true":** AI with Elaine May.
34 **"Ha!" she barked:** Sweet, *Something Wonderful*, 73. Versions of this story also appear in many other interviews.
34 **Nichols approached her:** "Mike Nichols: Lighting Up Broadway," *Newsweek*, November 14, 1966.
35 **"I met Elaine several ways":** Mike Nichols, interview by Chris Nashawaty for *Entertainment Weekly*, March 1, 2012, unpublished transcript.
35 **"I knew then that she was the best":** Wasson, *Improv Nation*, 23.

CHAPTER THREE: A SENSE OF YOUR POSSIBILITIES

36 **Eventually they moved:** Janet Coleman, *The Compass: The Improvisational Theatre That Revolutionized American Comedy* (Chicago: University of Chicago Press, 1991), 38–39.
36 **worked as a private investigator:** Thomas Thompson, "Whatever Happened to Elaine May?," *Life*, July 28, 1967.
37 **"loathed [him] on sight":** Gordon Cotler, "For the Love of Mike—and Elaine," *New York Times Magazine*, May 24, 1959.
37 **"Hi, Elaine":** John Lahr, "Making It Real," *New Yorker*, February 21 and 28, 2000.
37 **"We were both seductive":** Gavin Smith, "Of Metaphors and Purpose," *Film Comment*, May–June 1999.
37 **"reputations on campus":** Jeffrey Sweet, *Something Wonderful Right Away: An Oral History of the Second City & the Compass Players* (Montclair, NJ: Limelight Editions, 1978), 131.
37 **"the three days":** Coleman, *The Compass*.
37 **"We live very quietly":** "The Road: Two Characters in Search . . . ," *Time*, September 26, 1960.
38 **"No," he told *Playboy*:** C. Robert Jennings, "The *Playboy* Interview: Mike Nichols," *Playboy*, June 1966.
38 **"only sort of for a minute":** Michael Wilmington, "How Mike Nichols and Friends Created a 'Wolf,'" *Chicago Tribune*, July 4, 1994.
38 **Soon after they met:** Sweet, *Something Wonderful*, 131.
38 **"She could, God knows":** Thompson, "Whatever Happened to Elaine May?"
38 **"I'm a much more negative person":** Elaine May, in discussion with Nichols, Walter Reade Theater, Film Society of Lincoln Center, February 26, 2006.
38 **were "safe from each other":** Sweet, *Something Wonderful*, 131.
38 **"she wouldn't lose interest":** Lahr, "Making It Real."
38 **"I thought I would become extremely":** Cotler, "For the Love of Mike—and Elaine."
38 **He took whatever nearby jobs:** Nichols, interview by James Lipton, *Inside the Actors Studio*, aired on Bravo, 1996.
39 **"Once every [so often]":** Coleman, *The Compass*, 28.
39 **The two envisioned:** AI with David Shepherd.

39 **"She just wandered in":** Nichols, interview by Bob Gazzale, for Nichols's American Film Institute Life Achievement Award, 2010, unpublished transcript.

40 **"There is no news tonight!":** AI with Cal Herrmann.

40 **"There was a lot of folk":** AI with Deborah Eisenberg.

40 **"He was funny":** Lahr, "Making It Real."

41 **Sills was performer driven:** Sweet, *Something Wonderful,* 1–17.

41 **But both men imagined:** Paul Sills and Bernie Sahlins, in *Compass Cabaret 55,* dir. Mike Siska (Chicago: Siska Films, 2014).

41 **"I have built a miserable":** David Shepherd, journal entry, May 25, 1954, in Sweet, *Something Wonderful,* xxi.

42 **Neal agreed to do it:** Steven Michael Shearer, *Patricia Neal: An Unquiet Life* (Lexington: University Press of Kentucky, 2006), 165.

42 **"At some point at Playwrights":** AI with Joy Carlin.

42 **Howard Johnson's:** Nichols, *Playboy* interview, and many subsequent interviews.

43 **Joy Carlin moved:** AI with Joy Carlin.

43 **"nervous young man":** Lahr, "Making It Real."

44 **"I couldn't find any part":** Nichols, "A Show Soliloquy: Mike Nichols and the Midas Touch," *Show,* March 1965.

44 **"he was exceptionally gifted":** Carroll Baker, *Baby Doll: An Autobiography* (New York: Arbor House, 1983), 83.

44 **"he'd end up directing you":** Carroll Baker to Guy Flatley, 1976, quoted on Moviecrazed.com.

44 **"What I didn't really understand":** Nichols, Gazzale interview.

44 **"I keep thinking, we can do":** Nichols to Joy Carlin, letter, December 11, 1954.

44 **"Strasberg . . . said the best thing":** Nichols, Gazzale interview.

44 **"It's the most useful":** Barbara Gelb, "Mike Nichols: The Special Risks and Rewards of the Director's Art," *New York Times Magazine,* May 27, 1984.

45 **"how to be in the course":** Nichols, *Inside the Actors Studio.*

45 **if he couldn't get cast in great roles:** Lahr, "Making It Real."

45 **"hit the jackpot":** Nichols to Carlin, letter, December 11, 1954.

45 **For a while, he worked:** "Mike Nichols: Lighting Up Broadway," *Newsweek,* November 14, 1966. In this interview, Nichols mistakenly recalls his job at Caedmon as being in 1952.

46 **Joy Carlin's husband:** AI with Joy Carlin.

46 **during his time at Howard Johnson's:** Sam Wasson, *Improv Nation: How We Made a Great American Art* (New York: Houghton Mifflin Harcourt, 2017).

46 **"the smell of acetone":** AI with Joy Carlin.

46 **"I was in class":** Nichols to Carlin, letter, December 11, 1954.

47 **"The idea," he told Carlin:** Nichols to Carlin, letter, December 11, 1954.

47 **For several months, Nichols enjoyed:** Robert Wool, "Mike & Elaine: Mirrors to Our Madness," *Look,* June 21, 1960.

47 **"Like all little stations":** Jerome Toobin, *Agitato: A Trek Through the Musical Jungle* (New York: Viking, 1975), 13–17.

47 **"couldn't stand Philadelphia":** Wool, "Mike & Elaine: Mirrors to Our Madness."

47 **Playwrights Theatre Club:** Coleman, *The Compass,* 83–84.

48 **Sills himself had:** Coleman, *The Compass,* 119.

48 **As an incentive:** Nichols, *Inside the Actors Studio.*

48 **he went over to dinner:** Herbert R. Gans, email to author, October 22, 2017.

49 **"If I'd stayed in New York":** Nichols, "A Show Soliloquy."

49 **"her and that train station":** Wasson, *Improv Nation,* 34–36.

CHAPTER FOUR: THE FIRST THING WE EVER DID TOGETHER

50 **"got all the parts":** Gordon Cotler, "For the Love of Mike—and Elaine," *New York Times Magazine,* May 24, 1959.

50 **"If I kiss":** Gerald Nachman, *Seriously Funny: The Rebel Comedians of the 1950s and 1960s* (New York: Back Stage Books, 2004), 329.

50 **"Elaine was very much":** Janet Coleman, *The Compass: The Improvisational Theatre That Revolutionized American Comedy* (Chicago: University of Chicago Press, 1991), 68.

50 **"Physical reality"**: Sam Wasson, *Improv Nation: How We Made a Great American Art* (New York: Houghton Mifflin Harcourt, 2017), 24.

51 **"She knew everything"**: Coleman, *The Compass*, 66, and Nachman, *Seriously Funny*, 329.

51 **"Every time she came in"**: Jeffrey Sweet, *Something Wonderful Right Away: An Oral History of the Second City & the Compass Players* (Montclair, NJ: Limelight Editions, 1978), 105–6.

51 **"a kind of generosity"**: Coleman, *The Compass*, 113.

51 **At first, "we were guided"**: Sweet, *Something Wonderful*, 69.

51 **"David was the sociopolitical"**: Sweet, *Something Wonderful*, 69.

52 **"They all seemed"**: Sweet, *Something Wonderful*, 27–28.

52 **"he latched on to Elaine"**: AI with David Shepherd.

52 **"It was like a summit"**: Coleman, *The Compass*, 128.

52 **"not a man with a natural sense"**: Jeffrey Sweet, in *Compass Cabaret 55*, dir. Mike Siska (Chicago: Siska Films, 2014).

52 **"He didn't seem well"**: AI with David Shepherd.

53 **At one point during a sketch**: Wasson, *Improv Nation*, 35–36.

53 **"I was horrible."**: "Mike Nichols," *American Masters*, dir. Elaine May, aired on PBS, January 29, 2016.

53 **"One night we were"**: Sweet, *Something Wonderful*, 50–51.

53 **the know-it-all**: AI with Elaine May.

53 **"He would root himself"**: Sweet, *Something Wonderful*, 50–51.

54 **Then they would eat**: AI with Elaine May.

55 **May reeled him in**: AI with Elaine May.

56 **May couldn't help him**: AI with Elaine May.

57 **"For a month I was a disaster"**: Sweet, *Something Wonderful*, 76.

57 **"I was desperate"**: Nichols, "A Show Soliloquy: Mike Nichols and the Midas Touch," *Show*, March 1965.

57 **"But if you keep at it"**: Nichols, "Show Soliloquy."

57 **May says that it wasn't**: AI with Elaine May.

57 **"Come quick"**: Coleman, *The Compass*, 129.

57 **"What is implied"**: John Lahr, "Making It Real," *New Yorker*, February 21 and 28, 2000.

58 **"Our work was"**: Peter Applebome, "Always Asking, What Is This Really About?," *New York Times*, April 25, 1999.

58 **And "the referential joke"**: Lahr, "Making It Real."

58 **"if you screwed up"**: Nachman, *Seriously Funny*, 233–34.

58 **"With Elaine, I got"**: Nichols, "Show Soliloquy."

58 **Together they came to realize**: Gavin Smith, "Of Metaphors and Purpose," *Film Comment*, May–June 1999.

58 **"When you're making"**: Nichols, interview by James Lipton, *Inside the Actors Studio*, aired on Bravo, 1996.

59 **"The audience says"**: Coleman, *The Compass*, 129.

59 **she told Nichols that everything**: AI with Mike Nichols.

60 **"Shelley Berman was great"**: Nichols, interview by Chris Nashawaty for *Entertainment Weekly*, March 1, 2012, unpublished transcript.

60 **Their first triumph**: Coleman, *The Compass*, 110–11.

60 **"Elaine and I had a rule"**: Sam Wasson, *Improv Nation: How We Made a Great American Art* (New York: Houghton Mifflin Harcourt, 2017), 339.

61 **one moment during the Jack Ego**: Nichols, "Life, with a Little Tenderizer," *New York Times*, May 26, 1991.

61 **"People would drive"**: Coleman, *The Compass*, 153.

62 **"I was flabbergasted"**: AI with Patricia Scot Yorton.

62 **"with wall-to-wall carpeting"**: Coleman, *The Compass*, 148.

62 **"They had made something"**: Sweet, *Something Wonderful*, 68–69.

63 **"Mike hated the whole idea"**: Coleman, *The Compass*, 191.

63 **Not everything they did**: Coleman, *The Compass*, 170–71.

63 **Late in 1956**: AI with Elaine May.

64 **"The audience didn't give a shit"**: AI with Elaine May.

65 **"Shelley is the first person"**: Nachman, *Seriously Funny*, 338.

65 **"as happy an experience"**: *New Theater Review* 1, no. 4, ca. fall 1988.

65 **"I [had] never seen Mike so physical"**: Coleman, *The Compass*, 219.

65 **"I was not in his league"**: AI with Patricia Scot Yorton.

66 **"I remember going to a furrier"**: AI with Joy Carlin.

66 **"Isn't it a beautiful"**: Lahr, "Making It Real."

66 **"our so-called honeymoon"**: AI with Patricia Scot Yorton.

66 **Just weeks after he and Scot:** AI with Patricia Scot Yorton.

66 **"We just weren't mature enough":** Sweet, *Something Wonderful*, 141.

67 **"I'm flying down":** AI with Patricia Scot Yorton.

67 **There were rumblings:** Coleman, *The Compass*, 234.

67 **Example: If two actors:** Sweet, *Something Wonderful*, 141.

67 **"I persecuted the shit out of Del":** Lahr, "Making It Real."

68 **"Mike and Elaine crisis":** Coleman, *The Compass*, 236.

68 **"I was basically fired":** Alice Arlen, "Mr. Success," *Interview*, December 1988.

68 **"You can't copyright":** AI with David Shepherd.

68 **"was a lot of fun":** "Mike Nichols," *American Masters*, January 29, 2016.

CHAPTER FIVE: THIS BOY AND GIRL

69 **"Elaine would go on":** Gerald Nachman, *Seriously Funny: The Rebel Comedians of the 1950s and 1960s* (New York: Back Stage Books, 2004), 340–42.

70 **They were relieved:** Whitney Bolton, unheadlined column, *New York Morning Telegraph*, June 9, 1961.

70 **The Blue Angel was dark, plush:** John Gavin, *Intimate Nights: The Golden Age of New York Cabaret*, rev. ed. (New York: Back Stage Books, 2006), 48.

71 **"The trick was":** AI with Elaine May.

72 **he stepped in a couple of times:** AI with Mike Nichols.

72 **"Jack bought Mike a new shirt":** Nachman, *Seriously Funny*, 341.

72 **"I said, 'Mom, can I call you'":** Nichols, interview by Bob Gazzale, for Nichols's American Film Institute Life Achievement Award, 2010, unpublished transcript.

73 **"they were the hottest thing":** Gavin, *Intimate Nights*, 162.

73 **"A large crowd gathered":** Gene Knight, "The Knight Watch: Comedy Team Scores at Blue Angel," *New York Journal-American*, October 24, 1957.

74 **"hipsters' hipsters":** *Variety*, November 13, 1957.

74 **"Taking shelter from the damp":** Douglas Watt, "Tables for Two," *New Yorker*, December 21, 1957.

74 **"New York is not only fashion-driven":** Nachman, *Seriously Funny*, 332–33.

74 **He "looked pale":** Nachman, *Seriously Funny*, 332–33.

75 **"Do an improvisation, kids":** Lester Sweyd, "Lemons for Breakfast," *TV Guide*, date not available (circa 1960).

76 **"I made a deal":** Nachman, *Seriously Funny*, 341–42.

77 **"The only two interludes":** Jack Gould, "'Suburban Revue': 'Hilarious Look' at Country Life on NBC Fails to Get Beyond City Limits," *New York Times*, January 15, 1958. Gould's follow-up column ran on January 19, 1958.

77 **"should go skyrocketing":** *Time*, cited in Gavin, *Intimate Nights*, 164.

77 **"Everyone had said to Rollins":** AI with Elaine May.

77 **"We did twenty minutes":** Nichols, interview by Chris Nashawaty for *Entertainment Weekly*, March 1, 2012, unpublished transcript.

78 **Rollins started planning:** Gavin, *Intimate Nights*, 164.

78 **"It takes me three hours":** AI with George Segal.

78 **"I had sharkskin suits":** Nachman, *Seriously Funny*, 341–42.

78 **"nothing operationally different":** Robert Rice, "Profiles: A Tilted Insight," *New Yorker*, April 15, 1961.

78 **"Oh my God":** AI with Jules Feiffer.

79 **"Mike and I just":** AI with Stephen Sondheim.

79 **And Paar had changed his mind:** Sweyd, "Lemons for Breakfast."

80 **everything about "Teenagers":** *The Perry Como Show*, aired on NBC, February 1, 1958.

80 **"The bigger the nightclub":** Barbara Gelb, "Mike Nichols: The Special Risks and Rewards of the Director's Art," *New York Times Magazine*, May 27, 1984.

80 **"early on . . . we discovered":** Alice Arlen, "Mr. Success," *Interview*, December 1988.

81 **"I felt very left out":** AI with Patricia Scot Yorton.

81 **"I remember one performance":** Thomas Thompson, "Whatever Happened to Elaine May?," *Life*, July 28, 1967.

82 **"go there to drink":** *Becoming Mike Nichols*, dir. Jack O'Brien, aired on HBO, February 26, 2016.

82 **"There's no such thing as a brilliant production":** "Theater: View from the Penthouse," *Newsweek*, April 5, 1965. "The Red Mill" aired on CBS, April 19, 1958.

82 **"doesn't bear thinking about":** Gavin Smith, "Of Metaphors and Purpose," *Film Comment*, May–June 1999.

82 **The two went over to CBS:** AI with Elaine May; also "Mike Nichols: Lighting Up Broadway," *Newsweek*, November 14, 1966.

83 **"I had this big revelation":** "Mike Wallace Asks . . . ," *New York Post*, April 1, 1958.

83 **During one segment:** Joseph Roddy, "Elizabeth Taylor and Richard Burton: The Night of the Brawl," *Look*, February 8, 1966. The reference is to the December 28, 1958, episode of *The Dinah Shore Chevy Show*.

84 **"I had never actually heard":** "Nichols & May: Take Two," *American Masters*, dir. Phillip Schopper, aired on PBS, May 22, 1996.

85 **"Most of the time":** John Lahr, "Making It Real," *New Yorker*, February 21 and 28, 2000.

85 **Were they comics:** "Fresh Eggheads," *Time*, June 3, 1958.

85 **"actors who don't rely":** Nichols and May, interview on *Sunday Evening with Mitch Miller*, September 14, 1958.

85 **"No Fooling, They're Actors":** Florence Wessels, "No Fooling, They're Actors," *New York Journal*, November 3, 1958.

86 **"because I didn't have a big shiny car":** Sweyd, "Lemons for Breakfast."

86 **"This was a neighborhood":** AI with Patricia Scot Yorton.

CHAPTER SIX: A NEW AND VERY STRANGE EXPERIENCE

88 **"In the short period":** *The Dinah Shore Chevy Show*, NBC, May 31, 1959.

88 **"The more we became the talk of the town":** Jeffrey Sweet, *Something Wonderful Right Away: An Oral History of the Second City & the Compass Players* (Montclair, NJ: Limelight Editions, 1978).

89 **May heard the pitch:** AI with Barbara Siman Strouse and Charles Strouse; also Charles Strouse, *Put On a Happy Face: A Broadway Memoir* (New York: Union Square Press, 2008), 72.

89 **"What do you want":** Bob Salmaggi, "Asleep at the Switch," *New York Herald Tribune*, May 24, 1959.

89 **May approached the podium:** "The 11th Emmy Awards," aired on NBC, May 6, 1959.

90 **"broke new ground":** John S. Wilson, "Satirists Heard in Program Here," *New York Times*, May 2, 1959.

90 **"From the throng of pilgrims":** Gordon Cotler, "For the Love of Mike—and Elaine," *New York Times Magazine*, May 24, 1959.

90 **as "a scene that not only":** Wilson, "Satirists Heard."

90 **Nichols's annual income:** Michael Braun, "Mike and Elaine: Veracity-Cum-Boffs," *Esquire*, October 1960.

90 **May began writing a play:** Sam Zolotow, "Miss Colbert Ill, Misses Two Shows," *New York Times*, April 2, 1959.

91 **"He took me and [Pat]":** Norma Stevens and Steven M. L. Aronson, *Avedon: Something Personal* (New York: Spiegel & Grau, 2017), 99–102.

91 **"This is really hard to explain":** AI with Patricia Scot Yorton.

92 **"Being famous was":** Stevens and Aronson, *Avedon*, 100.

92 **"Do celebrities only know":** Braun, "Mike and Elaine."

93 **Avedon "said to me":** Stevens and Aronson, *Avedon*, 100.

93 **"Thank heaven for the investigation":** *The Fabulous Fifties*, aired on CBS, January 31, 1960.

93 **"the day after the show":** *Life*, headline and date not available, in Elaine May file, NYPLPA.

95 **"It was a childhood disease":** *Monitor*, NBC Radio. The blog *Isn't Life Terrible* hosted seventy-three tracks from the program, from which these transcripts were drawn. They have since been removed and, as of this writing, are not publicly available.

96 **would cost $50,000:** Alexander Cohen to investors, undated letter, ACC.

96 **"Elaine quit when":** Guy Flatley, "Blood and Funny Are the Range of Mike Nichols' Remarkable Back-to-Back Hits on Broadway," *People*, January 10, 1977.

96 **"I just would have liked":** Gavin Smith, "Of Metaphors and Purpose," *Film Comment*, May–June 1999.

97 **"the impression was":** Review, *Variety*, April 19, 1960.

97 **scheduled a lunch:** Alexander Cohen to Elaine May, telegram, April 22, 1960, ACC.

97 **they had attended a rehearsal:** Steven Michael Shearer, *Patricia Neal: An Unquiet Life* (Lexington: University Press of Kentucky, 2006), 165.

97 **"We had to have someone":** AI with Elaine May.

98 **For the more established:** AI with Arthur Penn.

98 **"Because he's a very good director":** Smith, "Of Metaphors and Purpose."

98 **"I was still very much the Avedons'":** Stevens and Aronson, *Avedon*, 185–87.

98 **"We are trying to get Elaine examined":** Cohen to Nichols, letter, July 25, 1960, ACC.

99 **Nichols and May settled on:** AI with Howard Rittner.

99 **As they improvised:** William Goldenberg, interview by Whitney Bolton, presumably from *New York Morning Telegraph*, undated, Mike Nichols file, NYPLPA.

99   **"With his hands":** Elliot Norton, "Comic Pair at Falmouth Refreshing Entertainers," *Boston Daily Record*, August 23, 1960.

99   **Cohen, watching their first:** Cohen to May, Nichols, and Penn, letter, August 16, 1960, ACC.

100   **"They brought the curtain down":** Gerald Nachman, *Seriously Funny: The Rebel Comedians of the 1950s and 1960s* (New York: Back Stage Books, 2004), 344.

100   **They set box office records:** Box office statements for week ending September 16, 1960, Westport Country Playhouse, 1960, ACC.

100   **Harry Belafonte, Lucille Ball:** Harvey Sabinson to Cohen, letter, September 30, 1960, ACC, and AI with Sabinson.

100   **"they have been known":** Walter Kerr, "First Night Report," *New York Herald Tribune*, October 10, 1960.

101   **"The preponderance of":** Howard Taubman, "Theatre: Pair of Jokers," *New York Times*, October 10, 1960.

101   **"laureates of the fatuous":** "Fun with Human Foibles," *Life*, November 21, 1960.

101   **"the voice of outraged intelligence":** Robert Brustein, "Comedians from the Underground," *New Republic*, October 31, 1960.

102   **"accept mannerisms for originality":** Howard Taubman, "Cry for Comedy," *New York Times*, December 25, 1960.

102   **Each of its stars was taking home:** Cohen to Robert Goodfellow, letter, October 19, 1960, ACC.

102   **the $75,000 they had made:** Braun, "Mike and Elaine."

102   **the $30,000 they now commanded:** Robert Wool, "Mike and Elaine: Mirrors to Our Madness," *Look*, June 21, 1960.

102   **the $160,000 apiece:** Braun, "Mike and Elaine."

102   **"I told Mike":** Thomas Thompson, "Whatever Happened to Elaine May?," *Life*, July 28, 1967.

CHAPTER SEVEN: THE MOST IMPORTANT PEOPLE

103   **"If somebody came":** AI with Elaine May.

103   **"Even after I had ceased":** Edmund Wilson, *The Sixties: The Last Journal, 1960–1972*, ed. Lewis M. Dabney (New York: Farrar, Straus, and Giroux, 1993).

104   **Another ardent admirer:** Peter Feibleman, *Lilly: Reminiscences of Lillian Hellman* (New York: William Morrow, 1988), 164–65.

104   **"pretend[ed] to be hopeless":** Lillian Hellman, "And Now—an Evening with Nichols and Hellman," *New York Times*, August 9, 1970.

104   **"Mike said he didn't mind":** Peter Davis, email to author, January 4, 2019.

104   **"Nothing that Peter said":** Kenneth Tynan, *The Diaries of Kenneth Tynan*, ed. John Lahr (New York: Bloomsbury, 2001), 202.

104   **When Avedon threw him:** Kathleen Tynan, *The Life of Kenneth Tynan* (New York: William Morrow, 1987), 182.

105   **"Sometimes Elaine would come":** AI with Tony Walton.

105   **whom he found "too formidable":** "Some Are More Yossarian Than Others," *Time*, June 15, 1970.

105   **the stage manager's log:** Time sheet logs, *An Evening with Mike Nichols and Elaine May*, ACC.

106   **"For him the slightest detail":** Barney Lefferts, "Now the Mike Nichols Touch," *New York Times*, November 22, 1964.

106   **"I was narcissistic":** John Lahr, "Making It Real," *New Yorker*, February 21 and 28, 2000.

106   **"Their health is at stake":** Cohen to Rollins, letter, December 7, 1960, ACC.

107   **"One night in 'Teenagers'":** AI with Elaine May.

108   **Although some writers came up:** Joseph Brownstone, stage manager for *An Evening with Mike Nichols and Elaine May*, and Harvey Medlinsky, the show's assistant stage manager, kept a record of every first line, last line, and literary style used for the out-of-town tryouts and Broadway run of the show; they are preserved in the Alexander Cohen Collection.

108   **"WE ARE THE ONLY SHOW":** Cohen to Brownstone, memo, February 3, 1961, ACC.

108   **"there is little carefulness":** Robert Rice, "Profiles: A Tilted Insight," *New Yorker*, April 15, 1961.

109   **In an interview she and Nichols:** Nichols and May, interviewed on *The Mitch Miller Radio Show*, January 14, 1961.

109   **Cohen once estimated:** Rice, "A Tilted Insight."

109   **"She got so bored":** Alice Arlen, "Mr. Success," *Interview*, December 1988.

109   **"I would start playing games":** Jeffrey Sweet, *Something Wonderful Right Away: An Oral History of the Second City & the Compass Players* (Montclair, NJ: Limelight Editions, 1978), 83.

109 "I had to push the sketch": Barbara Gelb, "Mike Nichols: The Special Risks and Rewards of the Director's Art," *New York Times Magazine,* May 27, 1984.

109 "She was a real actress": *Becoming Mike Nichols,* dir. Jack O'Brien, aired on HBO, February 26, 2016.

110 "I have enjoyed my association": May to Cohen, letter, June 1, 1961, ACC.

110 "We're not going to do": Stuart W. Little, "Theater News," *New York Herald Tribune,* June 14, 1961.

110 "He felt guilty": AI with Elaine May.

110 "Elaine pulled back": Joan Juliet Buck, "Live Mike," *Vanity Fair,* June 1994.

111 "do a show for a year": Sam Wasson, *Improv Nation: How We Made a Great American Art* (New York: Houghton Mifflin Harcourt, 2017), 73.

111 "She is very good-looking": Wilson, *The Sixties.*

111 He packed a box of books: AIs with Jamie Bernstein, Peter Bonerz, Temi Rose, and Stephen Sondheim.

111 "not for dinner or anything": AI with Stephen Sondheim.

111 By the fall, Nichols and Brown: AI with Temi Rose.

111 "I love this girl": Herbert Whittaker, "Mike Nichols to Be Married, but Not to Partner May," *New York Mirror,* date not available.

112 But other friends: Norma Stevens and Steven M. L. Aronson, *Avedon: Something Personal* (New York: Spiegel & Grau, 2017), 384.

112 "She told a story to me": AI with Temi Rose.

112 "It was unwise": Nichols, interview by Bob Gazzale, for Nichols's American Film Institute Life Achievement Award, 2010, unpublished transcript.

113 Nichols agreed to star: "O'Connell Named to Replace Tone," *New York Times,* January 11, 1962.

113 He signed on: AI with Ken Welch.

113 "really threw me for a loop": "Mike Nichols," *American Masters,* dir. Elaine May, aired on PBS, January 29, 2016.

113 In Rome, he met Taylor: Nichols, DVD commentary, *Who's Afraid of Virginia Woolf?* (Burbank, CA: Warner Home Video 2016), special ed. DVD.

114 "She never had": William J. Mann, *How to Be a Movie Star: Elizabeth Taylor in Hollywood* (New York: Mariner Books, 2009), 317–18.

114 In just a few days: Walter Wanger and Joe Hyams, *My Life with Cleopatra: The Making of a Hollywood Classic* (1963; repr., New York: Vintage, 2013), 177.

114 "Do you do personal wigs?": Michael Schulman, "The Hairdo's and Don'ts of Wig Design," *New Yorker,* April 8, 2019.

114 "gag on Richard Burton": Kimberly Cutter, "Mike Nichols Collaborates with Richard Avedon," *Harper's Bazaar,* November 2007.

114 "Well, they were certainly": Stevens and Aronson, *Avedon,* 100–101.

115 "Elaine and I were never": AI with Sheldon Harnick.

115 "If things had been different": Their routine was reprinted in *Show,* August 1962.

115 "We were on the dance floor": James Kaplan, "True Colors?," *New York,* March 2, 1998.

116 "It was Mickey and Judy": AI with Stephen Sondheim.

116 "as soon as he returns home": AI with Jules Feiffer.

116 "At one point while we were rehearsing": AI with Jules Feiffer.

117 "As the work advanced": Jules Feiffer, *Backing into Forward: A Memoir* (New York: Nan A. Talese/Doubleday, 2010), 340–41.

117 "didn't work for me": Sweet, *Something Wonderful,* 84.

118 "to make him ridiculous": Wilson, *The Sixties,* 174–75.

118 "It was pretty much an unmitigated": Gavin Smith, "Of Metaphors and Purpose," *Film Comment,* May–June 1999.

118 "I was, God knows": Nichols, Gazzale interview.

118 she felt unsupported: Gelb, "Mike Nichols."

118 "there was something about": AI with Elaine May.

118 "as soon as we weren't": Gelb, "Mike Nichols."

119 "something to do with the realities": Sam Zolotow, "'Position' Closes on Road," *New York Times,* October 10, 1962.

119 "those members of the audience": *Philadelphia Daily Bulletin,* cited in Lahr, "Making It Real."

119 "We stayed in each other's lives": AI with Elaine May.

119 "It took years": Gelb, "Mike Nichols."

CHAPTER EIGHT: PLAYING THE ROLE OF A FATHER

120 **In November, a few weeks:** AI with Elaine May.
120 **"state of deep depression":** John Lahr, "Making It Real," *New Yorker,* February 21 and 28, 2000.
120 **"In a way, it was the worst":** Gerald Nachman, *Seriously Funny: The Rebel Comedians of the 1950s and 1960s* (New York: Back Stage Books, 2004), 332.
121 **"I felt for a long time":** "Mike Nichols: Lighting Up Broadway," *Newsweek,* November 14, 1966.
121 **"Oh, Mikey":** Janet Coleman, *The Compass: The Improvisational Theatre That Revolutionized American Comedy* (Chicago: University of Chicago Press, 1991).
121 **"enormously jealous":** Nichols, interview by Bob Gazzale, for Nichols's American Film Institute Life Achievement Award, 2010, unpublished transcript.
121 **"the two main characters compete":** Mel Gussow, *Edward Albee: A Singular Journey* (New York: Applause Books, 2001), 235.
121 **"they enjoy each other's prowess":** *"A Daring Work of Raw Excellence,"* DVD featurette, *Who's Afraid of Virginia Woolf?* (Burbank, CA: Warner Home Video, 2016), special ed. DVD.
121 **"austere and restrained":** Gussow, *Edward Albee,* 235.
122 **"As Richard and I read":** "Lighting Up Broadway," *Newsweek.*
122 **"Get me out of this!":** Lahr, "Making It Real."
123 **"Stark Hesseltine, my agent":** AI with Elizabeth Ashley.
123 **"wanted to meet with us":** Neil Simon, *Rewrites: A Memoir* (New York: Touchstone, 1998), 132.
124 **"At the time, my attitude":** AI with Elizabeth Ashley.
124 **"I experienced that frisson":** Michael Feeney Callan, *Robert Redford: The Biography* (New York: Alfred A. Knopf, 2011), 96–97.
124 **"There was always this thing":** AI with Elizabeth Ashley.
125 **"When I got word":** AI with Robert Redford.
125 **"It felt slightly perverse":** AI with Robert Redford.
125 **He was reluctant:** Callan, *Robert Redford,* 96–97.
125 **Nichols walked into:** Simon, *Rewrites,* 132–33.
126 **"Mike looked at me":** Simon, *Rewrites,* 132–33.
126 **"this was the job":** Nichols, interview by James Lipton, *Inside the Actors Studio,* aired on Bravo, 1996.
126 **"All the Strasberg":** "Mike Nichols," *American Masters,* dir. Elaine May, aired on PBS, January 29, 2016.
126 **"If you're missing your father":** Nichols, *Inside the Actors Studio.*
126 **"I had a sense of enormous relief":** Lahr, "Making It Real."
126 **"made me unhappy":** Barbara Gelb, "Mike Nichols: The Special Risks and Rewards of the Director's Art," *New York Times Magazine,* May 27, 1984.
126 **"Look at this!":** "Mike Nichols," *American Masters.*
126 **"Once they're relaxed":** Simon, *Rewrites,* 133.
127 **"Let's do it as though we don't know":** Lahr, "Making It Real."
127 **"As if the people were alive":** Sam Wasson, *Improv Nation: How We Made a Great American Art* (New York: Houghton Mifflin Harcourt, 2017), 90.
127 **Standing next to Nichols:** Simon, *Rewrites,* 234–35.
127 **"Mike would bring people":** AI with Elizabeth Ashley.
128 **"George would always":** AI with Elizabeth Ashley.
128 **"I knew they were all solid":** Callan, *Robert Redford,* 97–98.
128 **"I don't want you being cute":** *Becoming Mike Nichols,* dir. Jack O'Brien, aired on HBO, February 26, 2016.
128 **"He was pissed a lot":** Callan, *Robert Redford,* 98.
128 **"I said the first grown-up thing":** Nichols, Gazzale interview.
129 **The Biltmore's owner:** John Keating, "Come-on-a My House," *New York Times,* November 17, 1963.
129 **"KEEP YOUR HAIR UP":** AI with Tony Walton.
129 **"My memory is of her":** AI with Rose Styron.
130 **"I learned that things":** "New Director," *New York Times,* September 8, 1963.
130 **"Do you think you could have a cold?":** "Mike Nichols," *American Masters.*
130 **"I could wake [Mike]":** Lahr, "Making It Real."
132 **"He said, 'Look'":** AI with Elizabeth Ashley.
132 **"I behaved badly":** Callan, *Robert Redford,* 99.
132 **"I had agreed to do the play":** AI with Robert Redford.
132 **"Look, I know how":** Nichols, interview by Chris Nashawaty for *Entertainment Weekly,* March 1, 2012, unpublished transcript.

132 **"I know what you're doing"**: AI with Robert Redford.

133 **"He said, 'I think'"**: AI with Robert Redford.

133 **"When we did the show"**: Callan, *Robert Redford*, 99.

133 **With every performance**: AI with Elizabeth Ashley.

133 **"I said, 'Can you excuse me'"**: *Becoming Mike Nichols*, HBO.

134 **"in five seconds"**: Joan Juliet Buck, "Live Mike," *Vanity Fair*, June 1994.

134 **"Everybody relax," Redford says**: AI with Robert Redford.

134 **the 1960s was "revolutionary"**: AI with Lorne Michaels.

134 **"Doc Simon owed more"**: AI with Elizabeth Ashley.

135 **"Mike Nichols—you can call him"**: Walter Kerr, "The Making of a Nice Big Fat Hit," *New York Herald Tribune*, November 10, 1963.

135 **"Ah, what the actors"**: Unbylined review, *Cue*, November 2, 1963.

135 **"These entrances could become"**: Howard Taubman, "Theater: Bubbling Comedy," *New York Times*, October 24, 1963.

135 **"Every reviewer in town"**: Richard Watts, "Two in the Aisle," *New York Post*, November 10, 1963.

136 **he had been paid just $4,000**: Sam Zolotow, "'Barefoot' Goes Off and Running," *New York Times*, October 25, 1963.

CHAPTER NINE: OKAY, THAT'S GREAT, NOW LET'S TRY THIS

137 **His mother called during the party**: AI with Stephen Sondheim.

137 **"I think people try to become"**: Barney Lefferts, "Now the Mike Nichols Touch," *New York Times*, November 22, 1964.

138 **"only made it worse"**: Elizabeth Ashley with Ross Firestone, *Actress: Postcards from the Road* (New York: M. Evans, 1978), 68–69.

138 **In shock, Ashley left**: AI with Elizabeth Ashley.

138 **The production put out**: *New York Daily News*, December 6, 1963.

138 **"But I had cracked up"**: AI with Elizabeth Ashley.

139 **They went into the bedroom**: AI with Stephen Sondheim.

139 **"Mike, I've got to tell you"**: Ashley, *Actress*, 25.

139 **"Mike was the opposite"**: AI with Elizabeth Ashley.

139 **"Mike was one of the first"**: Joan Barthel, "A 'Cat' in Search of Total Approval," *New York Times*, September 21, 1974.

140 **"Would you be interested in some extras"**: *That Was the Week That Was*, aired on NBC, November 10, 1963.

140 **they would make half a dozen**: Nichols and May's deal to appear on NBC's *The Jack Paar Program* was announced on May 1, 1964; the sketches aired from September 1964 to June 1965.

140 **"Miss May and I"**: William Glover, "Ad-Lib Dividends," Associated Press, September 20, 1964.

140 **"Once we got over"**: Gerald Nachman, *Seriously Funny: The Rebel Comedians of the 1950s and 1960s* (New York: Back Stage Books, 2004), 351.

141 **"things have reached"**: Lefferts, "Mike Nichols Touch."

141 **"He's calling the notion"**: Lewis Funke, "Along the Rialto: Actors Studio Theater Sets Its Season," *New York Times*, October 20, 1963.

141 **"The audience can appreciate"**: Nick Lapole, "Mike Proves Right Again," *New York Journal American*, August 16, 1964.

142 **"I was Mister Theater"**: AI with Mike Nichols.

142 **Nichols committed to *The Public Eye***: A. H. Weiler, headline not available, *New York Times*, January 12, 1964.

142 **"I'm laid out"**: Lewis Funke, "News of the Rialto," *New York Times*, March 8, 1964.

143 **"the funny nervousness"**: AI with Lawrence Turman.

143 **"questions about the psychological motivation"**: Orville Prescott, "Books of the Times: Talent Busting Out All Over," *New York Times*, October 30, 1963.

143 **"It seemed to me totally unoriginal"**: AI with Mike Nichols.

143 **he left Turman a phone message**: Lawrence Turman, *So You Want to Be a Producer* (New York: Three Rivers Press, 2005), 99.

143 **"I remember crawling around"**: AI with George Segal.

144 **"You think you're pretty clever!"**: Ann Jellicoe, *The Knack* (New York: Samuel French, 1958).

144 **"I remember saying"**: AI with George Segal.

144 **"Mike was in deep distress"**: AI with Tony Walton.

145 **"Give Mike Nichols":** Howard Taubman, "Theater: Original 'Knack,'" *New York Times*, May 28, 1964.

145 **"a restless, ceaseless quest":** Whitney Bolton, "'Knack' Often Funny at New Theater," *New York Morning Telegraph*, May 29, 1964.

145 **Nichols himself called the marriage:** Nichols, interview by Chris Nashawaty for *Entertainment Weekly*, March 1, 2012, unpublished transcript.

145 **"Where, in an eleven-month":** AI with Aaron Sorkin.

145 **That may have been:** AI with Tony Walton.

146 **"a small fortune":** John McCarten, "Mike and Max," *New Yorker*, April 11, 1964.

146 **"I was still in my first mode":** AI with Mike Nichols.

147 **"nice . . . it was all right":** AI with Mike Nichols.

147 **two of its three characters:** May played Jackson's role in the 1967 film version of *Luv*, opposite Peter Falk and Jack Lemmon.

147 **"always grab the hot director":** Eli Wallach to Claire Nichtern, letter, October 31, 1963, CNP.

147 **"Should I write to Mike":** Wallach to Nichtern, letter, February 6, 1964, CNP.

147 **"Mike will be diagnostician":** Wallach to Nichtern, letter, June 18, 1964, CNP.

148 **"Walter is a wonderful actor":** Nichtern to Wallach, letter, February 19, 1964, CNP.

148 **"Doing what you've hoped":** Joanne Stang, "Alan Arkin: Brooding About How Happy He Is," *New York Times*, February 28, 1965.

148 **"has a way of speaking":** Lefferts, "Mike Nichols Touch."

148 **"I only knew I'd done something wrong":** AI with Richard Benjamin.

149 **"It's only when rehearsals start":** Nichols, "A Show Soliloquy: Mike Nichols and the Midas Touch," *Show*, March 1965.

149 **"In *Luv* there's a scene":** Nichols, "Show Soliloquy."

150 **"He wasn't dictatorial":** AI with Gloria Steinem.

150 **"at a party or an opening":** AI with Gloria Steinem.

150 **"not a play that everyone":** Nichols, "Show Soliloquy."

151 **"I was friends with John Kenneth Galbraith":** AI with Gloria Steinem.

151 **"Then [critics] said it":** Nichols, interview by Charlie Rose, *Charlie Rose*, aired on PBS, April 26, 2005.

151 **"a delicious spoof":** Howard Taubman, "Theater: Schisgal's 'Luv' Is Directed by Nichols," *New York Times*, November 12, 1964.

151 **"one of the best comedy directors":** Richard Watts Jr., "Two on the Aisle," *New York Post*, November 29, 1964.

151 **"He not only knows what is funny":** Henry Hewes, "Adieu from the Bridge," *Saturday Review*, November 16, 1964.

151 **"It is almost a new play":** Harold Clurman, headline unavailable, *Nation*, November 30, 1964.

151 **3 percent of the box office:** "'Luv' Can Earn 8G Profit per Week," *Variety*, November 18, 1964.

151 **"I would rather do *Luv*":** Nichols, "Show Soliloquy."

152 **"Joe would like a piece":** "Milt" to Samuel Zolotow, assignment memo with Zolotow's handwritten notes, *Luv* file, NYPLPA.

152 **"I never quite knew that Larry":** AI with Mike Nichols.

153 **"People know how Uta Hagen":** Mel Gussow, *Edward Albee: A Singular Journey* (New York: Applause Books, 2001), 233.

153 **"twenty years too young":** Gussow, *Edward Albee*, 232.

153 **"they'll eat our director alive":** Gussow, *Edward Albee*, 234.

153 **"The people in the play":** *Becoming Mike Nichols*, dir. Jack O'Brien, aired on HBO, February 26, 2016.

153 **"our popular hero":** Peter Bart, "Nichols to Direct 'Virginia Woolf,'" *New York Times*, December 12, 1964.

153 **He would be paid $250,000:** C. Robert Jennings, "The *Playboy* Interview: Mike Nichols," *Playboy*, June 1966.

154 **"I'm almost certain":** Bart, "Nichols to Direct."

CHAPTER TEN: THE FUNNIEST DISTANCE BETWEEN TWO POINTS

155 **He often said that the first spoken line:** AI with Mike Nichols.

155 **"I'm more anxious to do films":** Faye Hammel, "Director at Work," *Cue*, November 7, 1964.

155 **"There are movie directors":** C. Robert Jennings, "The *Playboy* Interview: Mike Nichols," *Playboy*, June 1966.

156 **"if I foul up on the first":** Stuart W. Little, "Success Wafts Mike Nichols to Hollywood," *New York Herald Tribune*, December 28, 1964.

156 **"He told Mike how to get through"**: AI with Norman Lloyd.

156 **"He was my mentor"**: "Mike Nichols," *American Masters*, dir. Elaine May, aired on PBS, January 29, 2016.

156 **"It was the most useful"**: Nichols, interview by Chris Nashawaty for *Entertainment Weekly*, March 1, 2012, unpublished transcript.

157 **Jewison was several months**: AI with Norman Jewison.

157 **"the writer-producer who"**: AI with Mike Nichols.

157 **"It's my play"**: Mel Gussow, *Edward Albee: A Singular Journey* (New York: Applause Books, 2001), 243.

157 **In a memo to the studio**: Ernest Lehman or Geoffrey Shurlock to Abe Lastfogel, undated letter, in "Too Shocking for Its Time," DVD featurette, *Who's Afraid of Virginia Woolf?* (Burbank, CA: Warner Home Video, 2016), special ed. DVD.

158 **"I thought, *This is a gag*"**: AI with Mike Nichols.

158 **He calmly returned to his hotel**: The film was eventually made in 1972 as *Follow Me!*, with Sir Carol Reed directing Mia Farrow and Topol.

158 **"There was something unpleasant"**: AI with Mike Nichols.

158 *The Odd Couple*, **which had**: Stuart W. Little, "Theme for Neil Simon: Divorce as Men See It," *New York Herald Tribune*, December 18, 1964.

159 **"They start to treat"**: Nichols, interview by Bob Gazzale, for Nichols's American Film Institute Life Achievement Award, 2010, unpublished transcript.

159 **"Walter, do me a favor"**: Neil Simon, *Rewrites: A Memoir* (New York: Touchstone, 1998), 154–55.

160 **"Art Carney was a saint"**: Nichols, Nashawaty interview.

160 **"What do we do?"**: Simon, *Rewrites*, 156–57.

160 **"One of the things he said"**: AI with Paul Dooley.

161 **he had put his own money**: Certificate of Limited Partnership for Odd Couple Company, filed at New York County Clerk's Office, February 4, 1965.

161 **"Go home and try *anything*"**: Simon, *Rewrites*, 158–59.

161 **"I somehow began to go out"**: AI with Gloria Steinem.

162 **"Why do a bad third act well"**: Simon, *Rewrites*, 164.

162 **"there were so many changes"**: Rob Edelman and Audrey Kupferberg, *Matthau: A Life* (Lanham, MD: Taylor, 2002), 60.

162 **"All right, you bastard"**: Simon, *Rewrites*, 165.

162 **"Mike was in some ways a very conventional"**: AI with Ann Roth.

163 **"The play had a different"**: Nichols, Nashawaty interview.

163 **"For twenty-five years I've been"**: Edelman and Kupferberg, *Matthau*, 142.

163 **"He never stopped"**: AI with Paul Dooley.

164 **"cunning manipulator who makes"**: Elliot Norton, "Elliot Norton Writes," *Boston Record American*, February 2, 1965.

164 **"A lightbulb did not go on"**: Simon, *Rewrites*, 168.

164 **"Let's play poker!"**: Neil Simon, *The Odd Couple: A Samuel French Acting Edition* (New York: Samuel French, 1966).

165 **"Props!" Nichols yelled**: Versions of this story are told in Edelman and Kupferberg, *Matthau*; Gerald Nachman, *Seriously Funny: The Rebel Comedians of the 1950s and 1960s* (New York: Back Stage Books, 2004), 331; and "Some Are More Yossarian Than Others," *Time*, June 15, 1970.

165 **"I was restaging something"**: *Becoming Mike Nichols*, dir. Jack O'Brien, aired on HBO, February 26, 2016.

165 **"And I [thought], *Thanks*"**: Nichols, Nashawaty interview.

165 **Walter Kerr wrote**: Kerr, cited by Richard Watts Jr. in "Two on the Aisle," *New York Post*, March 21, 1965.

165 **"All of Nichols's trademarks"**: "Divorce Broadway Style," *Newsweek*, March 20, 1965.

166 **"It is a bad idea"**: Maurice Zolotow, ". . . And the Even Couple," *New York Times*, May 21, 1965.

166 **"I'm bored in the theater"**: "Theater: View from the Penthouse," *Newsweek*, April 5, 1965.

166 **"Why is my pleasure gone?"**: "Mike Nichols—Right on Top of Broadway's World," *Times* (London), June 28, 1965.

166 **"Here I am with plays"**: Nichols, *Playboy* interview.

167 **"I said to Elaine"**: "Mike Nichols," *American Masters*.

167 **"Mike was aware of the violence"**: AI with Gloria Steinem.

167 **Sammy Davis Jr., Harry Belafonte**: *King: A Filmed Record . . . Montgomery to Memphis*, prod. Ely Landau (Commonwealth United, 1970).

167 **"were met by a guy"**: "Mike Nichols," *American Masters*.

168 **"I was never a fan":** AI with Robert Redford.

168 **seemed "close enough to":** Nichols and Soderbergh, DVD commentary, *Who's Afraid of Virginia Woolf?*

168 **"Elizabeth and [her ex-husband]":** AI with George Segal.

168 **The show's star, Sandy Dennis:** Gussow, *Edward Albee*, 236.

168 **"her stomach protrudes":** Ernest Lehman, diary entry, July 15, 1965, in Lehman, "He Was Very Afraid," *Talk,* April 2000.

169 **While Nichols was on the road:** "View from the Penthouse," *Newsweek.*

169 **As soon as casting was finished:** AI with Candice Bergen.

169 **"By the way," the announcer said:** Tony Awards, June 13, 1965, audio archives, Museum of Television and Radio, New York.

169 **"I was so sure I knew":** Nichols and Soderbergh, DVD commentary, *Who's Afraid of Virginia Woolf?*

CHAPTER ELEVEN: I WANT TO KNOW THIS PLACE

171 **"I, first gently and then not very":** Nichols and Steven Soderbergh, DVD commentary, *Who's Afraid of Virginia Woolf?* (Burbank, CA: Warner Home Video, 2016), special ed. DVD.

171 **"was sick and tired of having":** Ernest Lehman, interview, *American Film*, October 1976.

171 **"I didn't have the patience":** Nichols and Soderbergh, DVD commentary, *Who's Afraid of Virginia Woolf?*

171 **"This must be beautifully":** AI with Mike Nichols.

171 **"Ernie was whining, 'I don't'":** Sam O'Steen, as told to Bobbie O'Steen, *Cut to the Chase: Forty-five Years of Editing America's Favorite Movies* (Studio City, CA: Michael Wiese Productions, 2001), 39–40.

171 **who was so worried:** Ernest Lehman, diary entry, May 21, 1965, in Lehman, "He Was Very Afraid," *Talk,* April 2000.

172 **"He told me when he got":** Lehman, diary entry, June 15, 1965, in Lehman, "Very Afraid."

172 **he believed it was the best:** C. Robert Jennings, "The Playboy Interview: Mike Nichols," *Playboy,* June 1966.

173 **"Here's the thing about":** *Becoming Mike Nichols,* dir. Jack O'Brien, aired on HBO, February 26, 2016.

173 **"in his usual candid way":** Haskell Wexler, DVD commentary, *Who's Afraid of Virginia Woolf?*

173 **"absolutely overwhelmed":** Lehman, diary entry, May 19, 1965, in Lehman, "Very Afraid."

173 **"Oh, Harry," he said:** AI with Mike Nichols.

174 **"I was a real snot":** Nichols, interview by Bob Gazzale, for Nichols's American Film Institute Life Achievement Award, 2010, unpublished transcript.

174 **"a pile of crap":** Lehman, diary entry, July 9, 1965, in Lehman, "Very Afraid."

174 **"stay, not run out of the theater":** Howard Thompson, "Unafraid of 'Virginia Woolf,'" *New York Times,* September 5, 1965.

174 **"I have actually seen":** Melvyn Bragg, *Rich: The Life of Richard Burton* (London: Hodder & Stoughton, 1988), 309.

174 **"wasn't pleased with himself":** William J. Mann, *How to Be a Movie Star: Elizabeth Taylor in Hollywood* (Boston: Mariner Books, 2009), 392.

175 **"I could have written one-half":** Lehman, diary entry, July 1, 1965, in Lehman, "Very Afraid."

175 **"the world's most beautiful eyes":** Nichols, *Playboy* interview.

175 **"I did my investigating":** Nichols and Soderbergh, DVD commentary, *Who's Afraid of Virginia Woolf?*

175 **In just three days:** *Becoming Mike Nichols,* HBO.

175 **"as searching, or vicious":** Nichols and Soderbergh, DVD commentary, *Who's Afraid of Virginia Woolf?*

175 **"I said . . . 'You gotta have'":** Nichols, Gazzale interview.

176 **"The titles were all":** AI with Susanna Moore.

176 **a Fourth of July party:** A full account of Fonda's party appears in my book *Pictures at a Revolution* (New York: Penguin Press, 2008), 102–8.

176 **"It's like asking a chocolate milkshake":** Lehman, diary entry, July 6, 1965, in Lehman, "Very Afraid."

177 **$1.1 million for her, $750,000 for him:** Bragg, *Rich.*

177 **"moderate and in good taste":** Mann, *Movie Star,* 345–46.

177 **"I've never seen people":** AI with George Segal.

177 **That morning, Nichols:** Lehman, diary entry, July 7, 1965, in Lehman, "Very Afraid."

177 **"They had a real student-teacher":** AI with George Segal.

178 **"Elizabeth and I were quite":** Roy Newquist, "Behind the Scenes of a Shocking Movie," *McCall's,* June 1966.

178 **"You must be sure to":** Mann, *Movie Star,* 356.

178 **She refused Nichols's request:** Lehman, diary entry, July 15, 1965, in Lehman, "Very Afraid."

178 **When Lehman dismissed:** Mann, *Movie Star,* 352.

178 **"politically, she ran the production":** AI with George Segal.

178 **"He would yell at her"**: Nichols, interview by Chris Nashawaty for *Entertainment Weekly*, March 1, 2012, unpublished transcript.

179 **"In *Virginia Woolf,* there's"**: Nichols and Soderbergh, DVD commentary, *Who's Afraid of Virginia Woolf?*

179 **"I can't act until you say"**: Mann, *Movie Star*, 357.

179 **"You prepare your ass off"**: Nichols, Gazzale interview.

179 **"can keep in her mind"**: Mann, *Movie Star*, 357.

180 **"I had my light meter"**: Wexler, DVD commentary, *Who's Afraid of Virginia Woolf?*

180 **"She was brilliant at extreme states"**: Nichols and Soderbergh, DVD commentary, *Who's Afraid of Virginia Woolf?*

180 **"His behavior, his manner"**: Mel Gussow, *Edward Albee: A Singular Journey* (New York: Applause Books, 2001), 239.

180 **"He'd walk around saying"**: O'Steen, *Cut to the Chase.*

181 **"they [didn't] . . . get into"**: Nichols, *Playboy* interview.

181 **"Mike just wet his pants"**: O'Steen, *Cut to the Chase*, 42–44.

181 **"I wanted to cry"**: Elaine Dundy, "The Theater of Logical Exaggeration," *New York World Journal Tribune,* October 16, 1966.

181 **"he left because I didn't"**: *Becoming Mike Nichols*, HBO.

181 **"Wake up!" he would bark**: Nichols, interview by Barbara Walters, *Today*, July 29, 1966.

182 **"A week later I say"**: Nichols, *Playboy* interview.

182 **Nichols often told a story**: AI with Mike Nichols; contradicted by Ernest Lehman's August 5, 1965, diary entry in Lehman, "Very Afraid."

182 **"I had done films before"**: Wexler, DVD commentary, *Who's Afraid of Virginia Woolf?*

182 **When Lehman asked him**: AI with Mike Nichols.

182 **a location Steinem had suggested**: AI with Gloria Steinem.

183 **"There was a first-class"**: Gussow, *Edward Albee*, 240.

183 **"Elizabeth's gone to see"**: Thompson, "Unafraid of 'Virginia Woolf.'"

183 **"They tried to tell me"**: Nichols, Gazzale interview.

183 **"When Richard was drinking"**: Nichols, Nashawaty interview.

183 **During a fight scene**: AI with Mike Nichols.

184 **"He became my nemesis"**: AI with Mike Nichols.

184 **"You will notice that all"**: Joseph Roddy, "Elizabeth Taylor and Richard Burton: The Night of the Brawl," *Look*, February 8, 1966.

185 **"We did it over and over"**: AI with George Segal.

185 **"Richard was not so great"**: Nichols and Soderbergh, DVD commentary, *Who's Afraid of Virginia Woolf?*

185 **"We watched the first five minutes"**: AI with Stephen Sondheim.

186 **"an ill omen"**: Lehman, diary entry, September 27, 1965, in Lehman, "Very Afraid."

186 **"I told her I didn't think"**: Lehman, diary entry, November 19, 1965, in Lehman, "Very Afraid."

186 **"I think you can actually see"**: Gavin Smith, "Of Metaphors and Purpose," *Film Comment*, May–June 1999.

186 **"Here were four stage people"**: Nichols and Soderbergh, DVD commentary, *Who's Afraid of Virginia Woolf?*

187 **"She finally did it"**: AI with Mike Nichols.

187 **"I did know"**: Smith, "Of Metaphors and Purpose."

CHAPTER TWELVE: ONE CONSIDERABLE INTELLIGENCE

188 **a *New York Times* profile**: Vincent Canby, "The Cold Loneliness of It All," *New York Times*, January 23, 1966.

188 **a widely read article**: Sherman L. Morrow, "The In Crowd and the Out Crowd," *New York Times Magazine*, July 16, 1965.

188 **he chose ANOMIE**: AI with Robert Bookman.

189 **traded his Lincoln Continental**: C. Robert Jennings, "The *Playboy* Interview: Mike Nichols," *Playboy*, June 1966.

189 **then told NBC he had sold the car**: Nichols, interview by Barbara Walters, *Today*, NBC, July 29, 1966.

189 **"could live on a loaf"**: "Mike Nichols: Lighting Up Broadway," *Newsweek*, November 14, 1966.

189 **"his large, imposingly baronial home"**: Nichols, *Playboy* interview.

189 **"he was never bothered"**: Canby, "Cold Loneliness."

189 **"My God, we've got"**: Thomas Thompson, "A Surprising Liz in a Film Shocker," *Life*, June 10, 1966.

190 **"he was thrown off the lot"**: Sam O'Steen, as told to Bobbie O'Steen, *Cut to the Chase: Forty-five Years of Editing America's Favorite Movies* (Studio City, CA: Michael Wiese Productions, 2001), 46–58.

190 **"That's where O'Steen proved"**: Nichols and Steven Soderbergh, DVD commentary, *Who's Afraid of Virginia Woolf?* (Burbank, CA: Warner Home Video, 2016), special ed. DVD.

190 **"You're a good actor"**: Rob Edelman and Audrey Kupferberg, *Matthau: A Life* (Lanham, MD: Taylor, 2002), 145.

190 **"The problem is that Walter"**: AI with Paul Dooley.

191 **Nichols promised that he would arrange**: AI with Mike Nichols.

191 **"They did the Watusi and the Frug"**: Earl Wilson, "It Happened Last Night," *New York Post*, January 14, 1966.

192 **"My play is not a farce"**: Roy Newquist, "Behind the Scenes of a Shocking Movie," *McCall's*, June 1966.

192 **"It's my play"**: Mel Gussow, *Edward Albee: A Singular Journey* (New York: Applause Books, 2001), 241–43.

192 **"I almost killed myself"**: AI with Alan Shayne.

192 **"That M. Nichols really gets"**: Richard Burton, *The Richard Burton Diaries*, ed. Chris Williams (New Haven, CT: Yale University Press, 2012), entries dated April 5, 1966, and April 11, 1966.

193 **A modern apartment building**: "Lighting Up Broadway," *Newsweek*.

193 **"Children survive extraordinary things"**: Nichols, *Playboy* interview.

194 **"It's the only time in my life"**: Nichols, interview by Bob Gazzale, for Nichols's American Film Institute Life Achievement Award, 2010, unpublished transcript.

194 **"We put *Virginia Woolf* in what"**: Thomas Thompson, "A Surprising Liz in a Film Shocker," *Life*, June 10, 1966.

194 **"hit the American public"**: "Too Shocking for Its Time," DVD featurette, *Who's Afraid of Virginia Woolf?*

194 **"Mike was a basket case"**: O'Steen, *Cut to the Chase*, 48.

194 **"I thought I was going"**: Nichols and Soderbergh, DVD commentary, *Who's Afraid of Virginia Woolf?*

194 **"It took me years"**: "Mike Nichols and Jason Reitman Talk 'Carnal Knowledge' in 2011," Walter Reade Theater, posted by Film at Lincoln Center, November 25, 2014, https://www.youtube.com/watch?v=ETR0 -lcfsgQ.

195 **"committed all the classic errors"**: Andrew Sarris, review of *Who's Afraid of Virginia Woolf?*, *Village Voice*, July 28, 1966.

195 **"the screen has never held"**: James Powers, "'Who's Afraid of Virginia Woolf?' Is a Motion Picture Masterpiece," *Hollywood Reporter*, June 22, 1966.

195 **"he has . . . made the most"**: Stanley Kauffmann, "Screen: Funless Games at George and Martha's," *New York Times*, June 24, 1966.

195 **"an example of daring"**: Bosley Crowther, "Who's Afraid of Audacity?," *New York Times*, July 10, 1966.

195 **the year's third-highest grosser**: Cobbett Steinberg, *Reel Facts: The Movie Book of Records* (New York: Vintage, 1978), 350.

196 **"You are without a doubt"**: Nichols, interview by Barbara Walters, *Today*, NBC, July 29, 1966.

196 **"Yes," he replied**: AI with Mike Nichols.

197 **"in every way unacceptable"**: AI with Mike Nichols.

197 **"It didn't take more than ten pages"**: AI with Buck Henry.

197 **"The book is filled"**: AI with Buck Henry.

197 **"was more fun than anything"**: Nichols, Gazzale interview.

197 **"Are we too old-fashioned"**: Buck Henry, interview by Terry Gross, *Fresh Air*, NPR, 1997.

197 **"I knew it was a perfect"**: AI with Mike Nichols.

198 **Nichols offered to work around**: Steven Michael Shearer, *Patricia Neal: An Unquiet Life* (Lexington: University Press of Kentucky, 2006), 272–73.

198 **He also went to Jeanne Moreau**: AI with Mike Nichols.

198 **"It's the hardest thing"**: Peter Bart, "Mike Nichols, Moviemaniac," *New York Times*, January 1, 1967.

198 **He also cast Barbara Harris**: Stuart Ostrow, *Present at the Creation, Leaping in the Dark, and Going Against the Grain* (New York: Applause Books, 2006), 34–40.

199 **"Then why are you here?"**: Ostrow, *Present at the Creation*, 34–40.

199 **"I improvised a little moment"**: AI with Alan Alda.

199 **"threw up all over"**: Ostrow, *Present at the Creation*, 34–40.

199 **"Mike," Sondheim says**: AI with Stephen Sondheim.

200 **"He was an actor's director"**: AI with Alan Alda.

200 **"Like all good directors"**: AI with Sheldon Harnick.

200 **"hired a terrific comedy director"**: Ostrow, *Present at the Creation*, 34–40.

200 **"I admired very much"**: AI with Alan Alda.

201 **"They were light boxes"**: AI with Tony Walton.

201 **"Alan *is* in the tree"**: AI with Jerry Adler.

201   **"He was very worried":** AI with Sheldon Harnick.

202   **"mildly pleasant" was typical:** William Glover, Associated Press, date and headline unavailable.

202   **"flaccid and maladroit":** "Triple Play," *Newsweek*, October 31, 1966.

202   **"The myth of Director Mike Nichols":** "Plop Art," *Time*, October 28, 1966.

202   **"had emasculated the satirical thrust":** AI with Jules Feiffer.

202   **"I can't do this anymore":** AI with Alan Alda.

202   **"Broadway scared the hell":** AI with Jerry Adler.

203   **"and never see [them] again":** "Lighting Up Broadway," *Newsweek*.

203   **He was enraged by a quote:** The disputed quote originally appeared in *Newsweek*'s November 1966 cover story, "Mike Nichols: Lighting Up Broadway." When it was reprinted in *The New York Times* ("Man in the News: Sought-After Director," January 25, 1967), Nichols asked for a correction; his letter ran in the newspaper the next day.

203   **"The question is, how ambitious":** "Lighting Up Broadway," *Newsweek*.

204   **As 1967 began:** Bart, "Moviemaniac."

204   **"I really am":** AI with Jerry Adler.

CHAPTER THIRTEEN: PROVE YOU BELONG HERE

205   **Originally, "Mike and I never":** This account of the making of *The Graduate* is based on the author's interviews with Alan Alda, Candice Bergen, Joy Carlin, William Daniels, Buck Henry, Dustin Hoffman, Mike Nichols, Robert Nichols, Robert Redford, Joel Schiller, Lawrence Turman, and Elizabeth Wilson. The interviews with Daniels, Hoffman, Mike Nichols, Schiller, Turman, and Wilson were for my book *Pictures at a Revolution* (New York: Penguin Press, 2008). The interviews with Alda, Bergen, Carlin, Robert Nichols, and Redford were for this book. Unless otherwise noted, all quotations and information in this chapter come from those interviews.

207   **his girlfriend, Anne Byrne:** Hoffman and Byrne married two years later; they divorced in 1980.

211   **"The picture is entirely":** Barry Day, "It Depends on How You Look at It," *Films and Filming*, November 1968.

215   **"Oh, I'm sick of that shirt off":** Betty Rollin, "Mike Nichols: Wizard of Wit," *Look*, April 2, 1968.

216   **"She's driving me fucking crazy":** Sam O'Steen, as told to Bobbie O'Steen, *Cut to the Chase: Forty-five Years of Editing America's Favorite Movies* (Studio City, CA: Michael Wiese Productions, 2001).

217   **"Sometimes Katharine and I":** Dustin Hoffman, DVD interview, *The Graduate* (Irvington, NY: Criterion Collection, 2016), DVD.

217   **"Part of me must have known":** Nichols and Steven Soderbergh, DVD commentary, *The Graduate*.

217   **"Remind me when this is over":** Nichols and Soderbergh, DVD commentary, *The Graduate*.

218   **"He doesn't say it":** Rollin, "Mike Nichols: Wizard of Wit."

CHAPTER FOURTEEN: IT'S BEGINNING TO MAKE SENSE

220   **"You can't do this":** Sam O'Steen, as told to Bobbie O'Steen, *Cut to the Chase: Forty-five Years of Editing America's Favorite Movies* (Studio City, CA: Michael Wiese Productions, 2001).

220   **"in the grip of something":** AI with Mike Nichols.

220   **"the whole experience had been many":** AI with Elizabeth Wilson.

220   **"looked like something out of":** AI with William Daniels.

221   **"Ha, ha, ha":** AI with Elizabeth Wilson.

221   **"They were, as they were about":** AI with Mike Nichols.

221   **"It was the only thing to do":** AI with Mike Nichols.

222   **"He was thinking":** AI with Dustin Hoffman.

223   **"They were dead for me":** AI with Mike Nichols.

224   **"I wanted him to do it":** Lillian Hellman, "The Time of the 'Foxes,'" *New York Times*, October 22, 1967.

224   **During an early read-through:** Richard F. Shepard, "'Little Foxes' Gets a Start in Low Key," *New York Times*, September 20, 1967.

224   **When she took to striding through:** AI with Austin Pendleton.

225   **"screwed up":** Joyce Wadler, "Mike Nichols: The Trouble Is . . . ," *New York Post*, May 24, 1975.

225   **"I think it was a sexual thing":** AI with Austin Pendleton.

225   **"How dare you," she said:** AI with Maria Tucci.

226   **"It's the way you walk":** AI with Austin Pendleton.

226   **"This is the best company":** AI with Maria Tucci.

227   **"He told me on the set":** AI with Austin Pendleton.

227   **"The first people who saw":** AI with Buck Henry.

227   **"I remember," said Nichols:** AI with Mike Nichols.

227   **"I heard him say":** Mike Nichols, interview by Michael Fleming, *Deadline*, May 30, 2012.

227   **"[Kazan] was my hero":** AI with Mike Nichols.

227   **"it didn't hit me the way":** AI with Elizabeth Wilson.

227   **"I didn't make any judgment":** AI with William Daniels.

227   **"hoping it would be a great flop":** AI with Jules Feiffer.

228   **Hoffman sat in the back row:** AI with Dustin Hoffman.

228   **"We were speechless":** Nichols, interview by Chris Nashawaty for *Entertainment Weekly*, March 1, 2012, unpublished transcript.

228   **"a television commercial":** Pauline Kael, "Trash, Art, and the Movies," *Harper's*, February 1969.

228   **"rock-bottom" music:** John Simon, "Nulla Cum Laude," *New Leader*, February 26, 1968.

228   **"one of the best seriocomic":** Bosley Crowther, "Film: Tales Out of School," *New York Times*, December 22, 1967.

228   **"The film demonstrates":** Archer Winsten, "'The Graduate' at Lincoln, Coronet," *New York Post*, December 23, 1967.

229   **David Brinkley called it:** David Brinkley, "What's Wrong with *The Graduate*," *Ladies' Home Journal*, April 1968.

229   **"the latest symbol":** Richard Schickel, "Fine Debut for a Square Anti-Hero," *Life*, January 19, 1968.

229   **"almost felt personally attacked":** Hollis Alpert, "*The Graduate* Makes Out," *Saturday Review*, July 6, 1968.

229   **Soon after *The Graduate* opened:** "Over-50s Vote for Oscars's 'Bests' but Film Audience 48% Under 24," *Variety*, January 24, 1968.

229   **"a nearly mandatory":** Jacob Brackman, "Why Do We Love '*The Graduate*,'" *New Yorker*, July 27, 1968.

230   **"speak with a special fervor":** Robert Windeler, "Study of Film Soaring on College Campuses," *New York Times*, April 18, 1968.

230   **"a victim of the sophomore":** "The Graduate," *Time*, December 29, 1967.

230   **four unrelated short plays:** Simon would reuse the device in *California Suite* (1976) and *London Suite* (1994).

230   **"a drama, a satire":** Neil Simon, *Rewrites: A Memoir* (New York: Touchstone, 1998), 254–56.

230   **"to show what Mike Nichols's":** Edmund Wilson, *The Sixties: The Last Journal, 1960–1972*, ed. Lewis M. Dabney (New York: Farrar, Straus, and Giroux, 1993), 811–12.

230   **"Jacqueline Kennedy's brace":** Doris Lilly, "Mike Nichols Is in Love," *New York Post*, April 4, 1968.

231   **"she was like a ghost":** AI with Jane Stanton Hitchcock.

231   **"You sometimes meet couples":** AI with Wallace Shawn.

231   **"Inside he may be going through":** Rex Reed, "George Is on His Best Behavior Now," *New York Times*, March 29, 1970.

232   **"Mike was a behaviorist":** AI with Bob Balaban.

232   **"his style, his tricks":** Simon, *Rewrites*, 265–67.

232   **Everyone seemed happy:** Simon, *Rewrites*, 265–67.

233   **"The next day," Stapleton said:** Maureen Stapleton and Jane Scovell, *A Hell of a Life: An Autobiography* (New York: Simon & Schuster, 1995), 194–96.

233   **In New Haven, Scott complained:** David Sheward, *Rage and Glory: The Volatile Life and Career of George C. Scott* (New York: Applause Books, 2008), 170.

233   **"George had a vicious, terrible":** AI with Bob Balaban.

234   **"I'm finally in a goddamn hit":** Simon, *Rewrites*, 268–72.

234   **"You mean if I don't eat ice cream":** Simon, *Rewrites*, 268–72.

234   **"There was no obviously":** AI with Bob Balaban.

234   **One-sixth of the show's:** Sam Zolotow, "Albert Finney to Appear Here in 'Joe Egg,' a London Success," *New York Times*, December 12, 1967.

235   **"reminiscent of the shrewd":** Harold Clurman, *Nation*, March 4, 1968.

235   **"His direction on its own":** Whitney Bolton, "'Plaza Suite' Wild Simon Comedy," *New York Morning Telegraph*, February 16, 1968.

235   **"It used to be straightforward":** AI with Mike Nichols.

235   **A few days later he returned:** Earl Wilson, "It Happened Last Night," *New York Post*, April 4, 1968.

236   **"I said, 'I won't go'":** AI with Mike Nichols.

236   **"I was Mister Anhedonia":** AI with Mike Nichols.

236   **"If you're ever the golden":** Nichols, "A Show Soliloquy: Mike Nichols and the Midas Touch," *Show*, March 1965.

237   **"Wait!" he said:** "Mike Nichols: Lighting Up Broadway," *Newsweek*, November 14, 1966.

CHAPTER FIFTEEN: THE ONLY WAY TO LIVE YOUR LIFE

238 **"He is living in more or less luxury":** Edmund Wilson, *The Sixties: The Last Journal, 1960–1972*, ed. Lewis M. Dabney (New York: Farrar, Straus, and Giroux, 1993), 682–83.

239 **Playwrights, including Neil Simon:** Lewis Funke, "News of the Rialto," *New York Times,* January 19, 1969.

240 **"One could take a hundred":** Norman Mailer, "Some Children of the Goddess—Norman Mailer vs. Nine Writers," *Esquire,* July 1963.

240 **He mapped the novel:** Marcia Seligson, "Hollywood's Hottest Writer—Buck Henry," *New York Times,* July 19, 1970.

241 **His first attempt:** Tracy Daugherty, *Just One Catch: A Biography of Joseph Heller* (New York: St. Martin's, 2011), 307.

241 ***Catch-22* is about dying":** Barry Day, "It Depends on How You Look at It," *Films and Filming,* November 1968.

241 **"the picture [would]":** Nora Ephron, "Yossarian Is Alive and Well in the Mexican Desert," *New York Times Magazine,* March 16, 1969.

241 **"We asked in our":** "Some Are More Yossarian Than Others," *Time,* June 15, 1970.

242 **"10,000 desolate acres":** Buck Henry, "A Diary of Planes, Pilots, and Pratfalls," *Life,* June 12, 1970.

242 **By the time production started:** Ephron, "Yossarian Is Alive and Well . . ."

242 **Paramount also spent:** Leonard Lyons, "The Lyons Den," *New York Post,* January 8, 1968.

242 **Over the years, Heller had been approached:** Daugherty, *Just One Catch,* 283–84.

243 **"he'd start to say":** AI with Peter Bonerz.

243 **"We saw loads of actors":** AI with Alan Shayne.

243 **"No way . . . It's just awful!":** Rex Reed, "George Is on His Best Behavior Now," *New York Times,* March 29, 1970.

243 **"Arkin was in my mind":** Nichols and Steven Soderbergh, DVD commentary, *Catch-22* (Hollywood: Paramount Home Video, 2006), DVD.

243 **"the only part I've ever":** "Some Are More Yossarian," *Time.*

243 **"I lost a solid":** Maureen Stapleton and Jane Scovell, *A Hell of a Life: An Autobiography* (New York: Simon & Schuster, 1995), 197.

243 **"Mike was the conductor":** AI with Lee Grant.

244 **"Who's going to fly the plane":** Buck Henry, diary entry, November 23, 1968, in Henry, "Planes, Pilots."

244 **On January 2, 1969:** Ephron, "Yossarian Is Alive and Well . . ."

244 **Not a single foot:** Charles Grodin, *We're Ready for You, Mr. Grodin: Behind the Scenes at Talk Shows, Movies, and Elsewhere* (New York: Charles Scribner's Sons, 1994), 243.

244 **"lying on his back":** Henry, diary entry, January 11, 1969, in Henry, "Planes, Pilots."

245 **"I loved him":** Nichols, in onstage conversation with Steven Soderbergh at the Directors Guild of America, 1999.

245 **"Here's a little secret":** AI with Richard Benjamin.

245 **"lapsing into a coma-like":** Henry, diary entry, January 18, 1969, in Henry, "Planes, Pilots."

245 **"the idea was to fill up":** AI with Peter Bonerz.

246 **"I was really scared":** AFI transcript.

246 **Mike said, 'It's not'":** AI with Peter Bonerz.

246 **"As soon as they were":** Nichols, interview by Bob Gazzale, for Nichols's American Film Institute Life Achievement Award, 2010, unpublished transcript.

246 **"would sit around":** Patricia Bosworth, "I Want to Be America's Best Classical Actor," *New York Times,* October 19, 1969.

246 **"Sitting around in Mexico":** AI with Peter Bonerz.

246 **"The nearest airport":** AI with Bob Balaban.

247 **"All that waiting":** Rex Reed, "Tony Perkins: All Steamed Up About Directing," *New York Times,* July 26, 1970.

247 **"We make bets":** Ephron, "Yossarian Is Alive and Well . . ."

247 **"Martin Balsam walking":** Mark Shivas, "'Midnight Cowboy' Turns Revolutionary," *New York Times,* September 28, 1969.

247 **"It's such a powerful memory":** Nichols, interview by Chris Nashawaty for *Entertainment Weekly,* March 1, 2012, unpublished transcript.

247 **Gilliatt came and went:** Wilson, *The Sixties,* 760–61.

248 **"She stayed," he said:** Nichols, Nashawaty interview.

248 **"It was good to be":** Lillian Hellman, "And Now—an Evening with Nichols and Hellman," *New York Times,* August 9, 1970.

248 **Some of the actors:** Barbara Gelb, "Mike Nichols: The Special Risks and Rewards of the Director's Art," *New York Times Magazine,* May 27, 1984.

248 **"When Nichols is unhappy":** Henry, diary entry, April 5, 1969, in Henry, "Planes, Pilots."

248 **"I'm certain he felt":** AI with Peter Bonerz.

248 **"I couldn't get ahold":** Nichols and Soderbergh, DVD commentary, *Catch-22.*

249 **"He did his best":** AI with Austin Pendleton.

249 **"Whenever Mike did a master":** AI with Peter Bonerz.

249 **"Day after day, he told fascinating":** Ephron, "Yossarian Is Alive and Well . . ."

249 **He insisted on multiple:** Sam O'Steen, as told to Bobbie O'Steen, *Cut to the Chase: Forty-five Years of Editing America's Favorite Movies* (Studio City, CA: Michael Wiese Productions, 2001).

250 **When Welles turned to Pendleton:** Nichols and Soderbergh, DVD commentary, *Catch-22.*

250 **"The Welles situation":** Ephron, "Yossarian Is Alive and Well . . ."

250 **"Not only was he forced":** Nichols, Gazzale interview.

250 **"He said beautiful":** Ephron, "Yossarian Is Alive and Well . . ."

250 **"Better late than early":** O'Steen, *Cut to the Chase.*

251 **The mood on the set:** Charles Winecoff, *Split Image: The Life of Anthony Perkins* (New York: E. P. Dutton, 1996), 280.

251 **"It was this wonderful":** AI with Bob Balaban.

251 **"That was good terror":** Henry, diary entry, March 18, 1969, in Henry, "Planes, Pilots."

251 **"You carry on":** "Some Are More Yossarian," *Time.*

251 **"It just sits there":** AI with Austin Pendleton.

251 **"We are trying to make up for it":** Ephron, "Yossarian Is Alive and Well . . ."

252 **"We were such prigs":** Nichols and Soderbergh, DVD commentary, *Catch-22.*

252 **A month after Nichols:** Daugherty, *Just One Catch,* and AI with Bob Balaban.

252 **"the presence of Mike Nichols":** Don Heckman, "View from Simon's Bridge," *New York Times,* February 27, 1972.

252 **"The Only Living Boy in New York":** Alexandra Pollard, "Simon and Garfunkel: 10 of the Best," *Guardian,* February 8, 2017.

252 **It took them two months:** Nichols, Nashawaty interview.

253 **"He finishes when he finishes":** O'Steen, *Cut to the Chase.*

253 **"Mike would not let me see it":** AI with Jon Korkes.

253 **"We worked on the front-projection":** Nichols and Soderbergh, DVD commentary, *Catch-22.*

253 **"Simplicity," he announced:** Vernon Scott, "Mike Nichols Believes in Simplicity," UPI, July 27, 1969.

253 **"how I want to live":** Daugherty, *Just One Catch,* 314.

253 **"I feel like I'm pregnant":** "Some Are More Yossarian," *Time.*

253 **"The thing about directing":** "Mike Nichols," *American Masters,* dir. Elaine May, aired on PBS, January 29, 2016.

CHAPTER SIXTEEN: COLD TO THE TOUCH AND BRILLIANT TO THE EYE

255 **"completely unethical and a danger":** AI with Stephen Sondheim.

255 **Perkins and his longtime boyfriend:** The story of Perkins and Dale was confirmed by two interviewees who asked not to be identified.

256 **Newman and Berkowitz had:** AI with Stephen Sondheim.

256 **who had recently telephoned:** Edmund Wilson, *The Sixties: The Last Journal, 1960–1972,* ed. Lewis M. Dabney (New York: Farrar, Straus, and Giroux, 1993), 807–8.

256 **"constant interruption of the drama":** Guy Flatley, "So Truffaut Decided to Work His Own Miracle," *New York Times,* September 27, 1970.

256 **"I resent Mike Nichols":** "D-e-n-n-i-s. H-o-p-p-e-r!," *New York Times,* October 18, 1970.

256 **In his 1969 book:** William Goldman, *The Season: A Candid Look at Broadway* (New York: Harcourt, Brace & World, 1969), 243–47.

257 **"may require another book":** Walter Kerr, headline unavailable, *New York Times,* August 31, 1969.

257 **When a test screening:** Sam O'Steen, as told to Bobbie O'Steen, *Cut to the Chase: Forty-five Years of Editing America's Favorite Movies* (Studio City, CA: Michael Wiese Productions, 2001), 85–96.

257 **"I want you to come":** "Some Are More Yossarian Than Others," *Time,* June 15, 1970.

257 **"almost everybody in the movie":** Joseph Heller, December 1970 onstage talk, quoted in *A Catch-22 Casebook,* ed. Frederick Kiley and Walter McDonald (New York: Thomas Y. Crowell, 1973), 353.

258 **"When the lights came up":** Peter Biskind, "Who's Afraid of the Big Bad Wolf?," *Premiere,* March 1994.

258 **"I almost passed out"**: Sam Wasson, *Improv Nation: How We Made a Great American Art* (New York: Houghton Mifflin Harcourt, 2017), 147–48, and Nichols and Steven Soderbergh, DVD commentary, *Catch-22* (Hollywood: Paramount Home Video, 2006), DVD.

258 **"the legendary unfinished"**: Roger Greenspun, "'M*A*S*H' Film Blends Atheism, Gore, Humor," *New York Times*, January 26,1970.

258 **"I saw it at an invited screening"**: AI with Austin Pendleton.

258 **"People begged me"**: Nichols and Soderbergh, DVD commentary, *Catch-22*.

258 **"And of course, we did"**: Nichols, interview by Bob Gazzale, for Nichols's American Film Institute Life Achievement Award, 2010, unpublished transcript.

259 **"It was the first preview"**: Nichols and Soderbergh, DVD commentary, *Catch-22*.

259 **"We saw the audience"**: Buck Henry, interview by Steven LaFreniere, Vice.com, September 30, 2010.

259 **"not about human behavior"**: Wasson, *Improv Nation*.

259 **"the best American film"**: Vincent Canby, "Nichols Captures Panic of 'Catch-22,'" *New York Times*, June 25, 1970.

259 **"possibly the biggest"**: John Mahoney, "'Catch-22' Brilliant but Cynical and Bitterly Cold," *Hollywood Reporter*, June 5, 1970.

259 **Andrew Sarris pronounced it**: Andrew Sarris, "Films in Focus," *Village Voice*, June 25, 1970.

259 **"cold to the touch"**: "Some Are More Yossarian," *Time*.

259 **in *New York*, Judith Crist wrote**: Judith Crist, "All That Glitters Is Not Nichols," *New York*, June 29, 1970.

260 **"Help him! Help the Bombardier!"**: "Catch-All-22," *Mad*, March 1971, reprinted in *A Catch-22 Casebook*.

260 **"I never intended"**: Lillian Hellman, "And Now—an Evening with Nichols and Hellman," *New York Times*, August 9, 1970.

260 **"I never found the heart"**: Joan Juliet Buck, "Live Mike," *Vanity Fair*, June 1994.

260 **"I could have scored it"**: Nichols and Soderbergh, DVD commentary, *Catch-22*.

261 **taken care of "the despairing"**: Nichols, Gazzale interview.

261 **"I'd had all these hits"**: Nichols, interview by Chris Nashawaty for *Entertainment Weekly*, March 1, 2012, unpublished transcript.

261 **The culinary indulgences**: R. Smith, "Eye Too," *Women's Wear Daily*, July 18, 1971.

261 **"a kind of adolescent"**: Jules Feiffer, interview by Sam Adams, *A.V. Club*, July 28, 2008.

262 **"It had to do with the expression"**: Barbara Gelb, "Mike Nichols: The Special Risks and Rewards of the Director's Art," *New York Times Magazine*, May 27, 1984.

262 **"I said, 'What about'"**: AI with Jules Feiffer.

262 **"Arkin didn't like it"**: AI with Jules Feiffer.

263 **"going to be our most"**: Patrick McGilligan, *Jack's Life: A Biography of Jack Nicholson* (New York: W. W. Norton, 1994), 220.

263 **"We never talked about it this way"**: Nichols, in onstage discussion with Steven Soderbergh at Directors Guild of America, 1999.

263 **"there was this thing"**: "Mike Nichols and Jason Reitman Talk 'Carnal Knowledge' in 2011," Walter Reade Theater, posted by Film at Lincoln Center, November 25, 2014, https://www.youtube.com/watch?v=ETR0-lcfsgQ.

263 **"She'll act for me"**: Gerald Nachman, *Seriously Funny: The Rebel Comedians of the 1950s and 1960s* (New York: Back Stage Books, 2004), 357.

263 **"Mike Nichols just offered"**: Rex Reed, "Jane: Everybody Expected Me to Fall on My Face," *New York Times*, January 25, 1970.

264 **"It was like, they knew that she"**: Nichols and Steven Soderbergh, Directors Guild of America, 1999.

264 **he had signed Nichols**: "Lantz Agented Nichols' Coin Take; May Settle Suit," *Variety*, March 21, 1971.

264 **"Nichols will be the boss"**: A. H. Weiler, "Nichols Meets Jules Feiffer," *New York Times*, October 26, 1969.

264 **"I wanted to see those who were not"**: "Mike Nichols and Jason Reitman Talk 'Carnal Knowledge,'" Walter Reade Theater.

264 **He told Nicholson**: Jules Feiffer, *Backing into Forward: A Memoir* (New York: Nan A. Talese/Doubleday, 2010), 399.

265 **"Mike felt, properly"**: Richard Warren Lewis, "The *Playboy* Interview: Jack Nicholson," *Playboy*, April 1972.

265 **"He worked very hard"**: AI with Candice Bergen.

265 **He took Garfunkel**: Art Garfunkel, *What Is It All but Luminous: Notes from an Underground Man* (New York: Alfred A. Knopf, 2017), 71.

265 **"First of all"**: "Mike Nichols and Jason Reitman Talk 'Carnal Knowledge,'" Walter Reade Theater.

265 **"It was a picture"**: O'Steen, *Cut to the Chase*, 99.

266 **"When you take a film"**: AI with Candice Bergen.

266 **"not a crew guy"**: AI with Mike Haley.

266 **"was the first actor"**: Nichols and Soderbergh, Directors Guild of America, 1999.

266 **"They're all his friends"**: Nichols, Gazzale interview.

266 **"He said, 'All right'"**: Nichols, Nashawaty interview.

266 **"Well, everybody has to do it"**: Nichols, interview by James Lipton, *Inside the Actors Studio*, aired on Bravo, 1997.

267 **"He brought you up to your best"**: Garfunkel, *What Is It All*, 228.

267 **"Finally, she was completely hysterical"**: Nichols, Gazzale interview.

268 **"the psychological line"**: Ann-Margret with Todd Gold, *Ann-Margret: My Story* (New York: G. P. Putnam's Sons, 1994), 208–9.

268 **"I had the instinct"**: AI with Jules Feiffer.

268 **"but that just pulled the timing"**: Gelb, "Mike Nichols."

268 **"He started screaming"**: Ann-Margret and Gold, *Ann-Margret*, 210.

268 **"Jack had no voice"**: Nichols and Soderbergh, Directors Guild of America, 1999.

269 **"I sat on the edge"**: Ann-Margret and Gold, *Ann-Margret*, 210.

269 **The diversion that:** "Arabian Horses, Bred in Poland, Are Finding New Homes in America," *New York Times*, April 2, 1972.

269 **"all of the literary"**: AI with Jules Feiffer.

270 **whispered to Nichols, "We're dead"**: Feiffer, *Backing into Forward*, 403.

270 **"It's a picture"**: Peter Feibleman, *Lilly: Reminiscences of Lillian Hellman* (New York: William Morrow, 1988), 27.

270 **"a nearly ideal"**: Vincent Canby, "Film," *New York Times*, July 1, 1971.

270 **"There is not one moment"**: Stephen Farber, "A Film That Forgets That Sex Can Be Fun," *New York Times*, August 1, 1971.

270 **"I'm not sure"**: Rosalyn Drexler, "Do Men Really Hate Women?," *New York Times*, September 5, 1971.

270 **"unconscious vindictiveness"**: John Simon, "An Appalling Plague Has Been Loosed on Our Films," *New York Times*, September 19, 1971.

271 **"I was profoundly hurt"**: Kristin Linklater, letter to the editor, *New York Times*, November 14, 1971.

271 **"show business fundamentalism"**: Pauline Kael, "The Current Cinema," *New Yorker*, July 3, 1971.

271 ***Carnal Knowledge* was:** *Variety*, December 22, 1971.

271 **"I thought it was a religious"**: *All in the Family*, season 2, episode 2, aired on CBS, September 25, 1971.

271 **"What we have here"**: Roger Ebert, "Why Do They Say They Don't Like 'Carnal Knowledge'?," *Chicago Sun-Times*, December 5, 1971.

272 **"nothing in the movie"**: *Jenkins v. Georgia*, 418 U.S. 153 (1974).

CHAPTER SEVENTEEN: DOLPHINS ARE SMARTER THAN HUMAN BEINGS

273 **"I've gotta tell you"**: Chris Chase, "Mike Nichols: Man on the Dolphin," *New York*, September 17, 1973.

274 ***God's Favorite*, a modern-day:** *God's Favorite* opened on Broadway in 1974, in a production directed by Michael Bennett. It received tepid reviews and ran only a few months.

275 **"Mike did not write"**: Mel Gussow, "Recipe for a Happy Crowd: Mix 1 Simon and 1 Nichols," *New York Times*, November 15, 1971.

275 **Setbacks that others:** Peter Falk, *Just One More Thing* (New York: Carroll & Graf, 2006), 204.

275 **"to knock it out"**: AI with Lee Grant.

275 **"Mike turned to me"**: AI with Lee Grant.

276 **"He explained," the actor:** Falk, *Just One More Thing*, 205.

276 **"I was running around"**: Chris Chase, "Peter Picked a Pip," *New York Times*, November 26, 1971.

276 **"He made Peter and me"**: AI with Lee Grant.

276 **"I was wrong"**: AI with Jules Feiffer.

276 **"only takes a risk"**: "Some Are More Yossarian Than Others," *Time*, June 15, 1970.

277 **"immaculately restrained"**: Walter Kerr, "'The Prisoner' Merely Complains," *New York Times*, November 21, 1971.

277 **"perfect for the play"**: Clive Barnes, "Stage: Creeping Paranoia and Crawling Malaise," *New York Times*, November 12, 1971.

277 **"everything was purple"**: AI with Rose Styron.

277 **"girls who have never"**: Gerri Hirshey, *Not Pretty Enough: The Unlikely Triumph of Helen Gurley Brown* (New York: Sarah Crichton Books, 2016), 276.

278 **"Living with one woman"**: Peter Feibleman, *Lilly: Reminiscences of Lillian Hellman* (New York: William Morrow, 1988), 28–29.

278 **"We're waiting for a script"**: A. H. Weiler, "Movies," *New York Times*, July 4, 1971.

278 **"I didn't like it"**: Guy Flatley, "Blood and Funny Are the Range of Mike Nichols' Remarkable Back-to-Back Hits on Broadway," *People*, January 10, 1977.

278 **"couldn't imagine going to work"**: Barbara Gelb, "Mike Nichols: The Special Risks and Rewards of the Director's Art," *New York Times Magazine*, May 27, 1984.

278 **"pretty horrible experience"**: Rod Lurie, "Still Avant-Garde After All These Years," *West Side Spirit*, October 9, 1990.

278 **it was Franklin J. Schaffner**: A. H. Weiler, "Mike Nichols' 'Dolphin,'" *New York Times*, March 12, 1972.

279 **"At one point Mike said"**: Buck Henry, DVD interview, *The Day of the Dolphin* (Home Vision Entertainment and Janus Films, 2003), DVD.

279 **"Dolphins are smarter"**: *Monitor*, NBC Radio, undated, early 1960s.

280 **"I thought it was a stupid book"**: Buck Henry, interview by Steven LaFreniere, Vice.com, September 30, 2010.

280 **The screenplay, a science-oriented**: Nora E. Taylor, "Mike Nichols's Latest: Filming with Dolphins," *Christian Science Monitor*, December 27, 1973.

280 **"the worst actress"**: AI with Tony Walton.

280 **book ten nights**: Val Adams, "Best of Nichols and May," *New York Daily News*, May 26, 1972.

281 **just a week after agreeing**: Bob Wiedrich, "Tower Ticker," *Chicago Tribune*, June 5, 1972.

281 **"the rhythm and tone"**: Mel Gussow, "Nichols, Fortune Made, Looks to the Future," *New York Times*, June 3, 1975.

281 **They talked about McGovern's**: McCandlish Phillips, "Rock 'n' Rhetoric Rally in the Garden Aids McGovern," *New York Times*, June 14, 1972.

281 **"We were just stunned"**: Glenn Collins, "A Double Reunion, 2 Decades Later," *New York Times*, May 2, 1992.

281 **"Is this the whole thing?"**: Chris Chase, "Mike Nichols: Man on the Dolphin," *New York*, September 17, 1973.

281 **he never thought that Mike should**: AI with Susanna Moore.

281 **"Mike never really"**: Sam O'Steen, as told to Bobbie O'Steen, *Cut to the Chase: Forty-five Years of Editing America's Favorite Movies* (Studio City, CA: Michael Wiese Productions, 2001), 113–17.

282 **But he had only recently**: "Lantz Agented Nichols' Coin Take; May Settle Suit," *Variety*, May 31, 1971.

282 **"If only it could talk"**: Joan Juliet Buck, "Live Mike," *Vanity Fair*, June 1994.

282 **"He was very unhappy"**: AI with Alan Shayne.

282 **"Mike instantly answered"**: AI with Jon Korkes.

283 **"His narrative ideas"**: Buck Henry, DVD interview, *Day of the Dolphin*.

283 **"George dragged Trish"**: O'Steen, *Cut to the Chase*, 113–17.

283 **Scott and Van Devere**: David Sheward, *Rage and Glory: The Volatile Life and Career of George C. Scott* (New York: Applause Books, 2008), 236–37.

283 **"two terrifying German shepherds"**: Nichols, interview by Bob Gazzale, for Nichols's American Film Institute Life Achievement Award, 2010, unpublished transcript.

283 **"Those dogs were dead"**: AI with Jon Korkes.

283 **"Bodyguards?" Weaver asked**: Sheward, *Rage and Glory*, 236–37.

283 **"What can I tell you"**: Buck Henry, DVD interview, *Day of the Dolphin*.

283 **"They'd do everything that was called for"**: Chase, "Mike Nichols."

284 **"We were on location"**: Edward Herrmann, DVD interview, *Day of the Dolphin*.

284 **"One morning George called up"**: AI with Tony Walton.

284 **a young assistant director**: AI with Michael Haley.

285 **As his captive guests**: AI with Jon Korkes; Leslie Charleson, DVD interview, *Day of the Dolphin*.

285 **"It was very hard"**: Buck Henry, DVD interview, *Day of the Dolphin*.

285 **"You can't imagine"**: AI with James Naughton.

285 **"It made me realize"**: John Lahr, "Making It Real," *New Yorker*, February 21 and 28, 2000.

285 **"I'd send notes"**: O'Steen, *Cut to the Chase*, 113–17.

286 **"The last day of the shoot"**: Buck Henry, DVD interview, *Day of the Dolphin*.

287 **"worth its weight"**: Mel Gussow, "'Vanya' Stars Tie Success to Nichols," *New York Times*, June 17, 1973.

287 **They all let him lead**: AI with Joanna Merlin.

287 **"there was an ugly"**: Gussow, "'Vanya' Stars."

287 **"He is an entertainer"**: Gussow, "'Vanya' Stars."

287 **By opening night**: "Briefs on the Arts," *New York Times*, August 11, 1973.

288 **"The play is full"**: George Oppenheimer, "'Vanya' Comes Bearing Gifts," *Newsday* [June 1973?].

288 **"more than its usual"**: Brendan Gill, "Scenes from Country Life," *New Yorker*, June 9, 1973.

288 **"Chekhov without tears"**: John Beaufort, "George C. Scott in 'Vanya,'" *Christian Science Monitor*, June 7, 1973.

288 **"mano a mano"**: T. E. Kalem, "Unrequited Lives," *Time*, June 18, 1973.

289 **"You'd better," said Scott**: AI with Tony Walton.

289 **"Where's Daddy's face?"**: AI with Mark Metcalf.

289 **"You'll never really be the fullest artist"**: AI with Peter Davis.

289 **"I never forgave"**: AI with Nathan Lane.

CHAPTER EIGHTEEN: MR. SUCCESS

291 **"no different than the negative"**: Nichols, interview with James Grissom, 1992, "Mike Nichols: The Metabolism of Success, Part One," http://jamesgrissom.blogspot.com/2018/08/mike-nichols-metabolism-of-success-part.html.

291 **Davis-Goff was away**: Chris Chase, "Mike Nichols: Man on the Dolphin," *New York*, September 17, 1973.

291 **The Bridgewater house**: *New York Times*, November 10, 1973.

292 **"a Flipper film"**: Vincent Canby, "Film: Underwater Talkie," *New York Times*, December 20, 1973.

292 ***Lassie Come Home* for fish"**: Rex Reed, *New York Daily News*, December 21, 1973.

292 **"the most expensive"**: Pauline Kael, "The Current Cinema," *New Yorker*, December 31, 1973.

292 **"it's hard to relate"**: Archer Winsten, *New York Post*, December 20, 1973.

292 **"If Mike Nichols and Buck"**: Kael, "The Current Cinema."

292 **After the *Dolphin* reviews**: Natasha Fraser-Cavassoni, *Sam Spiegel* (New York: Simon & Schuster, 2003), 316–18.

292 **"It was nothing ever but a pleasure"**: Buck Henry, DVD interview, *The Day of the Dolphin* (Home Vision Entertainment and Janus Films, 2003), DVD.

293 **"You personally lost"**: Nichols, in discussion with Elaine May, Walter Reade Theater, Film Society of Lincoln Center, February 26, 2006, video recording courtesy of Film at Lincoln Center.

293 **"Don't regret anything"**: AI with Mike Nichols.

293 **"Sam was paying me"**: Fraser-Cavassoni, *Sam Spiegel*, 316–18.

293 **he was "bogged down"**: Stephen Farber, "Hollywood Takes On 'The Last Tycoon,'" *New York Times*, March 21, 1976.

293 **"At the time I informed"**: Nichols, letter to the editor, *New York Times*, April 4, 1976.

294 **"a time in America"**: Mel Gussow, "Nichols, Fortune Made, Looks to the Future," *New York Times*, June 3, 1975.

294 ***The Fortune* was**: Gussow, "Nichols, Fortune Made."

294 **"which of course God always punishes"**: Suzanne Finstad, *Warren Beatty: A Private Man* (New York: Harmony, 2005), 420–25.

294 **Nichols had taken the script**: Finstad, *Warren Beatty*.

295 **according to Henry, "severely strange"**: Peter Biskind, *Star: How Warren Beatty Seduced America* (New York: Simon & Schuster, 2010), 199.

295 **"I like being an amateur"**: Peter Biskind, *Easy Riders, Raging Bulls: How the Sex-Drugs-and-Rock 'n' Roll Generation Saved Hollywood* (New York: Simon & Schuster, 1998), 194.

295 **Nicholson and Beatty**: Ellis Amburn, *The Sexiest Man Alive: A Biography of Warren Beatty* (New York: HarperEntertainment, 2002).

295 **"There are two kinds"**: Amburn, *Sexiest Man Alive*, 200.

295 **"a bit on my high horse"**: James Kaplan, "Anjelica Rising," *New York Times Magazine*, February 12, 1989.

295 **Nichols gave her**: Lacey Fosburgh, "Funny, Serious, Bright, Pretty Stockard Channing," *New York Times*, June 11, 1975.

296 **"The script was 345 pages"**: Biskind, *Star*, 205–8.

296 **"he kept cutting"**: Biskind, *Easy Riders*, 195.

296 **"surrounded by yes-men"**: From Polly Platt's unpublished memoirs, quoted in the podcast *You Must Remember This: Polly Platt—The Invisible Woman*, episode 5, 6/22/20.

296 **"I had to do what I could"**: Nichols, interview by Bob Gazzale, for Nichols's American Film Institute Life Achievement Award, 2010, unpublished transcript.

296 **"didn't read *The Fortune*"**: Biskind, *Star*, 199–202.

296 **"silly story"**: Frank Rich, "The Misfortune of Mike Nichols: Notes on the Making of a Bad Film," *New Times*, July 11, 1975.

296 **"misbehaving as if"**: AI with Warren Beatty (2006).

296   that "little tickle": Finstad, *Warren Beatty*, 424.

297   "I heard the word": Rich, "The Misfortune of Mike Nichols."

297   "[He] works almost": Rich, "The Misfortune of Mike Nichols."

298   "He was weeping": *Drama-Logue*, June 16–22, 1994.

298   Nicholson was so devastated: Patrick McGilligan, *Jack's Life: A Biography of Jack Nicholson* (New York: W. W. Norton, 1994).

298   Nichols had lent: AI with Peter Davis.

299   "somewhat sleep-disheveled": AI with David Shire.

299   When Nichols told: Norma Stevens and Steven M. L. Aronson, *Avedon: Something Personal* (New York: Spiegel & Grau, 2017), 187.

299   "Mike asked me if": AI with Rose Styron.

300   "It's about 'If we don't get'": AI with David Shire.

301   "I meant *The Fortune*": Gussow, "Nichols, Fortune Made."

301   turned it down: Aljean Harmetz, "Will 'Mr. Goodbar' Make Voyeurs of Us All?," *New York Times*, July 24, 1977.

301   "they seemed to me": Gussow, "Nichols, Fortune Made."

301   But their reconnection: Joyce Wadler, "Mike Nichols: The Trouble Is . . . ," *New York Post*, May 24, 1975.

302   De Niro took: AI with Robert De Niro.

302   "I'm not sure Doc ever": AI with Elizabeth Ashley.

302   Just a few weeks earlier: Sam O'Steen, as told to Bobbie O'Steen, *Cut to the Chase: Forty-five Years of Editing America's Favorite Movies* (Studio City, CA: Michael Wiese Productions, 2001), 180.

302   "He had been so phenomenally": AI with Marsha Mason.

303   "I thought it was going to be": Martin Kasindorf, "A Film Actress Aims at TV 'Oomph,'" *New York Times*, March 4, 1979.

303   "something hectic and ugly": Paul D. Zimmerman, "Madcap Murder," *Newsweek*, May 26, 1975.

303   "watching this, one is": Jay Cocks, "Small Change," *Time*, May 26, 1975.

303   "Why won't they just let me": AI with Peter Davis.

303   "He was furious": AI with Peter Davis.

304   "Two weeks before shooting": AI with Howard W. Koch Jr.

304   "I hadn't really been paying": Nichols in discussion with May, Walter Reade Theater, February 26, 2006.

304   "Neil wrote it more": AI with Marsha Mason.

304   "Look, there was a hurry": AI with Robert De Niro.

304   "Bobby called me": AI with Marsha Mason.

305   "I vill not hurt you": AI with Howard W. Koch Jr.

305   "I felt like shit": AI with Robert De Niro.

305   "The set was not relaxed": AI with Marsha Mason.

306   "Mike turned around": AI with Howard W. Koch Jr.

306   "We looked at the dailies": Nichols in discussion with May, Walter Reade Theater, February 26, 2006.

306   "Oh, it was awful": AI with Linda Lavin.

307   "I get more narcoleptic": Barbara Gelb, "Mike Nichols: The Special Risks and Rewards of the Director's Art," *New York Times Magazine*, May 27, 1984.

307   "What are you going to do *now*": John Lahr, "Making It Real," *New Yorker*, February 21 and 28, 2000.

CHAPTER NINETEEN: EVERYTHING GOES ON THE LINE

311   It was, if anything: Barbara Gelb, "Mike Nichols: The Special Risks and Rewards of the Director's Art," *New York Times Magazine*, May 27, 1984.

311   "I think he blamed": AI with Candice Bergen.

312   For the first time, a gossip column: Robin Adams Sloan (pseudonym for a team of writers), unheadlined column, *New York Daily News*, July 13, 1975.

312   "gotten more and more": Jeffrey Sweet, *Something Wonderful Right Away: An Oral History of the Second City & the Compass Players* (Montclair, NJ: Limelight Editions, 1978), 86.

313   "I remember hearing": AI with Lorne Michaels.

313   He would send him scripts: AI with David Geffen.

314   "Everyone said I was afraid": "Mike Nichols," *American Masters*, dir. Elaine May, aired on PBS, January 29, 2016.

314   "there's something sort of sad": Guy Flatley, "Blood and Funny Are the Range of Mike Nichols' Remarkable Back-to-Back Hits on Broadway," *People*, January 10, 1977.

314 **"I won't do anything as a performer"**: Sweet, *Something Wonderful,* 86.

314 **Many who saw it**: Joan Juliet Buck, "Live Mike," *Vanity Fair,* June 1994.

314 **"If [he] didn't write"**: Helen Epstein, "The N.Y. Shakespeare Festival—Does Biggest Mean Best?," *New York Times,* February 27, 1977.

314 **"I'd been trying"**: AI with David Rabe.

315 **"Mike said it read"**: Robert Wahls, "Onstream with Rabe," *New York Daily News,* April 25, 1976.

315 **"He was on me"**: AI with David Rabe.

315 **"After rehearsal, he would"**: Ron Siebert, email to author, December 17, 2018.

315 **"We were a bunch"**: AI with Herbert Jefferson Jr.

316 **Evans himself was gay**: Evans died of complications from AIDS in 1989, at thirty-eight.

316 **"His take on Richie"**: AI with Herbert Jefferson Jr.

316 **"When you're young"**: AI with Michael O'Keefe.

317 **"Mike directed it"**: AI with Tony Walton.

317 **The actor playing**: AI with Mark Metcalf.

317 **"we literally had people"**: AI with Herbert Jefferson Jr.

318 **"erase the kind of boundary"**: AI with Arvin Brown.

318 **"I am quite accustomed"**: Walter Kerr, "When Does Gore Get Gratuitous?," *New York Times,* February 22, 1976.

318 **"searing detail and overpowering"**: William Glover, review of *Streamers,* Associated Press, February 9, 1976.

318 **"Will the significance"**: Christopher Sharp, "The Theater," *Women's Wear Daily,* April 22, 1976.

318 **"neurotic and destructive"**: Martin Gottfried, *New York Post,* February 14, 1976.

318 **"You know what this play"**: Robert Berkvist, "How Nichols and Rabe Adapted 'Streamers,'" *New York Times,* April 25, 1976.

319 **"the later, violent"**: Berkvist, "Nichols and Rabe."

319 **"Mike said he found"**: AI with Mark Metcalf.

319 **"Mike said that because I was"**: AI with Dorian Harewood.

320 **When *Streamers* began**: AI with Dorian Harewood.

320 **"clean, powerful, and electric"**: T. E. Kalem, "War Without End," *Time,* May 3, 1976.

320 **"the most accomplished"**: Rex Reed, "'Streamers' Shatters Broadway's Doldrums," *New York Daily News,* April 23, 1976.

320 **"Neither the author"**: Alan Rich, review of *Streamers, New York,* May 10, 1976.

321 **ABC thought Allen's script**: Rowland V. Barber, "Three Strikes and They're On," *TV Guide,* January 21, 1978.

321 **"I think my father"**: AI with Matthew Broderick.

322 **"I'm very happy"**: Ann Guarino, "Mike Nichols and His Immortality Deal," *New York Daily News,* June 15, 1975.

322 **The effect was designed**: Marsha Cochran, "They Sell Horses, Don't They? Not the Spectacular Way Mike Nichols Does It," *People,* June 7, 1976.

322 **"We all—Paul Simon"**: AI with Candice Bergen.

323 **who had been convicted**: Tom Goldstein, "Notables Aid Convicted 'Deep Throat' Star," *New York Times,* June 29, 1976.

323 **"to help Harry"**: "Harry Reems' $250,000 Fund Goal," *Variety,* July 7, 1976.

323 **Fred Zinnemann's**: Unbylined item, *Women's Wear Daily,* July 1, 1976, and Lacey Fosburgh, "Why More Top Novelists Don't Go Hollywood," *New York Times,* November 21, 1976.

323 **And when Beatty**: "Mr. Hollywood," *Time,* July 3, 1978.

323 **He turned down an offer**: Larry Getlen, "House of Cads," *New York Post,* April 8, 2012.

323 **"One of the lessons"**: Paul Rosenfield, "Did Mike Nichols Squander His Luck on 'Heartburn'?," *Los Angeles Times,* August 3, 1986.

324 **"Griffiths is concerned"**: Mel Gussow, "Mike Nichols for the Fun of It," *New York Times,* November 26, 1976.

324 **what he called "that fog"**: Gussow, "Nichols for the Fun of It."

324 **The connection the two men**: Peter Biskind, *Star: How Warren Beatty Seduced America* (New York: Simon & Schuster, 2010), 227.

325 **"If a musical"**: Charles Strouse, *Put on a Happy Face: A Broadway Memoir* (New York: Union Square, 2008), 229–30.

325 **Before rehearsals, he flew**: Daniel Rosenthal, "Comedians: Racist and Sexist Standups Who Messed with Audiences," *Guardian,* February 20, 2015.

325 **he would earn**: *Variety,* September 15, 1976.

325 **"It was a pleasure"**: AI with Jerry Adler.

326 **"At first it was"**: AI with Jeffrey DeMunn.

326 **"The atmosphere that Mike"**: Warren Hoge, "He Makes Them Laugh Until They Squirm," *New York Times*, December 5, 1976.

326 **"comedy with an aesthetic"**: Clive Barnes, "The Weighty Matter of Comedy," *New York Times*, November 29, 1976.

326 **"It is hard to imagine"**: Martin Gottfried, "'Comedians'—an Affirming Attitude," *New York Post*, November 29, 1976.

327 **"the play was"**: AI with Jerry Adler.

327 **"was not amused"**: Nichols, interview by James Lipton, *Inside the Actors Studio*, aired on Bravo, 1996.

327 **One by one, they drifted**: Sally Quinn, "Citywide Celebrations on the Day Before the Big Day," *Washington Post*, January 21, 1977.

327 **It had been a long**: Richard Coe, "Mike Nichols, Producer," *Washington Post*, March 2, 1977.

327 **"many, many nights"**: AI with Charles Strouse and Barbara Siman Strouse.

327 **"I don't think Mike had any desire"**: AI with Brooke Allen.

327 **"I jumped at"**: Nichols, interview with James Grissom, 1992, "Mike Nichols: The Metabolism of Success, Part One," http://jamesgrissom.blogspot.com/2018/08/mike-nichols-metabolism-of-success-part.html.

328 **"I was friends with the guy"**: Nichols, interview by Bob Gazzale, for Nichols's American Film Institute Life Achievement Award, 2010, unpublished transcript.

328 **"comic-book annuity"**: Grissom, "Metabolism of Success."

328 **"this year's theater hero"**: Martin Gottfried, "Mike Nichols: This Year's Theater Hero," *New York Post*, May 28, 1976.

328 **"Nichols's decline was really"**: Flatley, "Blood and Funny . . ."

328 **"it was the end"**: Grissom, "Metabolism of Success."

CHAPTER TWENTY: THE RAPTURE OF MY DEPTH

329 **"Dante says there is"**: "Why Mike Nichols Is Working Without a Net," *Newsweek*, May 5, 1996.

329 **"waste[d] the middle"**: "Working Without a Net," *Newsweek*.

329 **But a part of Nichols**: "Mike Nichols," *American Masters*, dir. Elaine May, aired on PBS, January 29, 2016.

330 **Goldman had struggled**: Luke Ford, *The Producers: Profiles in Frustration* (Lincoln, NE: iUniverse, 2004), 268–69.

330 **"I pulled off"**: Ford, *Producers*.

331 **"Mike came into my room"**: AI with Bo Goldman.

331 **He worked on the film**: *Daily Variety* reported that Nichols would direct *The Jerk* on October 6, 1978; *The Hollywood Reporter* noted that he had "bowed out" of the film on November 1, 1978.

331 **"I remember walking"**: AI with Steve Martin.

332 **the "goddamn succession"**: *Women's Wear Daily*, October 31, 1977, and Marilyn Stasio, "The Couple Game," *Cue*, November 12–25, 1977.

332 **"I would not append"**: Nichols, interview with James Grissom, 1992, "Mike Nichols: The Metabolism of Success, Part One," http://jamesgrissom.blogspot.com/2018/08/mike-nichols-metabolism-of-success-part.html.

332 **They were like family**: AI with Jamie Bernstein.

332 **"She was only fifty-six"**: AI with Jamie Bernstein.

333 **He rehearsed them**: Mel Gussow, "Tandy and Cronyn Play Gin for Money," *New York Times*, September 1, 1977.

333 **"stop playing with clenched"**: "The Cards," *New Yorker*, October 24, 1977.

333 **"Mike has an honesty"**: Gussow, "Tandy and Cronyn."

333 **"I looked up"**: AI with D. L. Coburn.

334 **His plans to produce**: Ken Mandelbaum, "Looking Back: Alice," Broadway.com, June 3, 2004.

334 **They also developed**: Samuel G. Freedman, "'Chorus Line' vs. Hollywood: A Saga," *New York Times*, November 11, 1984.

334 **"shooting essentially the stage production"**: Freedman, "'Chorus Line' vs. Hollywood."

335 **"the theatrical mode"**: E. L. Doctorow, *Drinks Before Dinner* (New York: Theatre Communications, 1996).

335 **"I remember when"**: Gail Papp, email to author, February 14, 2019.

336 **"I adored Edgar"**: AI with Christopher Plummer.

336 **"I think he thought"**: AI with James Naughton.

336 **"Mike waited for Edgar"**: AI with Maria Tucci.

336 **"the first thoroughly"**: Edith Oliver, "Off Broadway," *New Yorker*, December 5, 1978.

336 **"great blocks of talk":** Richard Eder, "Stage: Doctorow's 'Drinks Before Dinner,'" *New York Times*, November 24, 1978.

336 **Papp, eager to keep:** Carol Lawson, "New Jobs for Tune and Nichols," *New York Times*, December 13, 1978.

337 **After a couple:** Carol Lawson, "Nichols Withdraws as Director of New Musical," *New York Times*, January 23, 1979.

337 **"I had never seen anybody who lived":** AI with David Hare.

338 **"He came backstage":** AI with Meryl Streep.

339 **He came "very close":** Peter Biskind, "Who's Afraid of the Big Bad Wolf?," *Premiere*, March 1994.

339 **"It's not that I read":** Barbara Gelb, "Mike Nichols: The Special Risks and Rewards of the Director's Art," *New York Times Magazine*, May 27, 1984.

339 **"I never heard":** AI with Meryl Streep.

340 **"It was Gilda's dream":** AI with Lorne Michaels.

340 **"He did a lovely":** AI with Paul Shaffer.

340 **"He never really spoke to me":** John Corry, "Gilda Radner to Make Dramatic Debut on Broadway," *New York Times*, August 19, 1980.

341 **"I did a draft":** AI with Patricia Resnick.

341 **"Mike Nichols seems":** Mart. (pseudonym for Markland Taylor), *Variety*, November 30, 1979.

CHAPTER TWENTY-ONE: REUNIONS

342 **"Look, as long as":** AI with Maury Yeston.

342 **"The secret of [your] later years":** "Why Mike Nichols Is Working Without a Net," *Newsweek*, May 5, 1996.

343 **"It will be good":** Carol Lawson, "Mike Nichols, Elaine May Bringing 'Virginia Woolf' to Long Wharf," *New York Times*, June 21, 1979.

344 **"Arvin and I":** Mel Gussow, *Edward Albee: A Singular Journey* (New York: Applause Books, 2001), 245–46.

344 **"It was fraught":** AI with Swoosie Kurtz.

344 **"Arvin had a thankless":** AI with James Naughton.

345 **"There's a scene":** AI with James Naughton.

345 **"it was clear":** AI with Arvin Brown.

345 **"We were woefully":** AI with James Naughton.

346 **"They were doing anything":** AI with Swoosie Kurtz.

346 **"we were still protective":** AI with Elaine May.

346 **"I went for Mike":** AI with James Naughton.

346 **"I thought they were":** AI with Swoosie Kurtz.

346 **"the banter between them":** AI with Arvin Brown.

347 **"Arlene? Eileen? Irene?":** AI with Swoosie Kurtz.

347 **"it was a play":** AI with Elaine May.

347 **"When you were":** Karen Isaacs, "Long Wharf's Artistic Directors Look Back on 50 Years," *Two on the Aisle*, January 8, 2016, https://2ontheaisle.wordpress.com/tag/arvin-brown/.

347 **"We arrive expecting":** Frank Rich, "Who's Afraid of Nichols and May?," *New York Times*, May 4, 1980.

347 **"Here's how intuitive":** AI with Elaine May.

348 **"No one believed":** AI with Elaine May.

348 **"You could see he was running":** AI with Swoosie Kurtz.

348 **"I hear Uta":** Gussow, *Edward Albee*, 245–46.

348 **"I think he thought":** AI with Elaine May.

349 **The item made sure:** Marilyn Beck, column, *New York Daily News*, July 24, 1980.

349 **"Irving," said Nichols:** Joan Juliet Buck, "Live Mike," *Vanity Fair*, June 1994.

350 **"an especially unctuous":** Diane Johnson, *Flyover Lives* (New York: Viking, 2014), 197–201.

351 **"He kept on saying":** Natasha Fraser-Cavassoni, *Sam Spiegel* (New York: Simon & Schuster, 2003), 331–32.

351 **He dropped out:** Streep walked away from *Betrayal* soon after Nichols did. A film version of *Betrayal* with Irons, Patricia Hodge, and Ben Kingsley was directed by David Jones and released in 1983.

351 **"I have a good":** Carol Lawson, "'Sunday Runners' Starts Its Paces," *New York Times*, March 19, 1980.

351 **Kerr got Nichols:** Barbara Gelb, "Mike Nichols: The Special Risks and Rewards of the Director's Art," *New York Times Magazine*, May 27, 1984.

351 **Nichols didn't think:** Susan Watters, "Eyeview," *Women's Wear Daily*, October 27, 1980.

352 **"He could manifest":** AI with Max Wright.

352 **Kerr told one reporter:** Watters, "Eyeview."

352 **"'Gildaleh, I have one'":** Elizabeth Stone, "Gilda Radner: Goodbye, Roseanne, Hello, Broadway," *New York Times Magazine*, November 9, 1980.

352 **"He was never afraid":** AI with David Rasche.

353   "We went out afterwards": AI with Swoosie Kurtz.

353   "In the '80s": Edwin Wilson, "Jean Kerr's New Comedy; Chekhov," *Wall Street Journal*, November 14, 1980.

353   "klutzy sight gags": Frank Rich, "Stage: Jean Kerr's 'Lunch Hour' Opens at Barrymore Theater," *New York Times*, November 13, 1980.

354   "It was a reunion": AI with John Rubinstein.

354   "Nothing could help": AI with Gerald Hiken.

354   "We were, for the second": AI with John Rubinstein.

355   "It was strange": AI with John Breglio.

355   "When *The Queen of Basin Street*": AI with Maury Yeston.

356   "Sam always had": AI with John Breglio.

357   "Mike Nichols and": *New York Daily News*, September 21, 1981.

CHAPTER TWENTY-TWO: AM I DOING THIS RIGHT?

358   Jane Fonda had: Aljean Harmetz, "Fallout from 'China Syndrome' Has Already Begun," *New York Times*, March 11, 1979.

359   "Because I was": AI with Arthur Hirsch.

359   But Hollywood now: Larry Cano (Hirsch's producing partner), letter to the editor, *Los Angeles Times*, September 4, 1988.

359   The result was a major: Deirdre Carmody, "Court Extends Right of Press to Filming," *New York Times*, October 2, 1977.

359   "I was perplexed": John Blades, "When Nora Met Alice . . . ," *Chicago Tribune*, February 13, 1990.

360   "Remember, at this time": AI with Bob Bookman.

360   "He wanted to turn it into": AI with Arthur Hirsch.

361   "We had real arguments": AI with Bob Bookman.

361   "So often, the thing": Nichols, interview by James Lipton, *Inside the Actors Studio*, aired on Bravo, 1996.

362   "That's the thing about": "Mike Nichols," *American Masters*, dir. Elaine May, aired on PBS, January 29, 2016.

362   "Mike said, 'Let's have'": AI with Arthur Hirsch.

362   "You free-associate": John Lahr, "Making It Real," *New Yorker*, February 21 and 28, 2000.

362   "He wanted the sense": AI with Patrizia von Brandenstein.

363   "The spring was": AI with Arthur Hirsch.

363   "Someday you're gonna": Mark Bego, *Cher: If You Believe* (New York: Taylor, 2004), 153.

363   "a *wonderful* lesbian": Janet Maslin, "Cher Hoping 'Silkwood' Is Her Turning Point," *New York Times*, January 7, 1984.

363   "He said, 'You know'": AI with Patrizia von Brandenstein.

364   He put the "royal baby": AI with David Hare.

364   The caterer and chef: Michael Hausman, DVD interview track, *Silkwood* (New York: Kino Lorber, 2017), Blu-ray Disc.

364   "He was anxious": AI with Patrizia von Brandenstein.

364   "I said, 'Well, no'": Nichols, interview by Bob Gazzale, for Nichols's American Film Institute Life Achievement Award, 2010, unpublished transcript.

365   As he did, the tapping: AI with Ann Roth.

365   "The audience isn't going to give you": Sam O'Steen, as told to Bobbie O'Steen, *Cut to the Chase: Forty-five Years of Editing America's Favorite Movies* (Studio City, CA: Michael Wiese Productions, 2001), 182–85.

365   "The long takes began": Nichols and Soderbergh, DVD commentary, *Catch-22* (Hollywood: Paramount Home Video, 2006), DVD.

366   as "the coven": Richard Cohen, *She Made Me Laugh: My Friend Nora Ephron* (New York: Simon & Schuster, 2016), 164–67.

366   a last-minute script polish: Sam Wasson, *Improv Nation: How We Made a Great American Art* (New York: Houghton Mifflin Harcourt, 2017), 335.

366   "The pleasure of working": Barbara Gelb, "Mike Nichols: The Special Risks and Rewards of the Director's Art," *New York Times Magazine*, May 27, 1984.

367   "Mike told me that": AI with Ann Roth.

367   "Mike almost died": AI with Meryl Streep.

367   "I thought, *Big deal*": Nichols, Gazzale interview.

367   Streep would take her: Cher, *The First Time* (New York: Simon & Schuster, 1998).

367   "Kurt was in love": Nichols, Gazzale interview.

367 **"One time, I"**: AI with Bruce McGill.

368 **"had really done"**: AI with Arthur Hirsch.

368 **"What I remember about Mike"**: AI with Meryl Streep.

369 **Two weeks into**: AI with Meryl Streep.

369 **"God, that was"**: Bego, *If You Believe*, 153–54.

369 **"I can't look like"**: AI with Mike Nichols.

370 **"Katherine," he warned**: AI with E. Katherine Kerr.

370 **"Mike . . . basically uses metaphors"**: Lawrence Frascella, "On the Front Lines with Nora Ephron," *Rolling Stone*, July 8, 1993.

370 **both Cher and Russell**: Gelb, "Mike Nichols."

370 **"Mike is one of"**: Bego, *If You Believe*.

371 **"never heard of existing"**: Diana Maychick, "Battle Breaks Out over Meryl Streep's New Film," *New York Post*, January 12, 1983.

371 **"If the actors are"**: David Richards, "Mike Nichols, Directly," *Washington Post*, March 21, 1986.

CHAPTER TWENTY-THREE: OH, THIS IS TROUBLE

373 **"between the forces of Brecht"**: Carol Lawson, "Broadway," *New York Times*, January 28, 1983.

373 **When Nichols got to Boston**: Kevin Kelly, "Falling on Its Funny Face," *New York*, February 28, 1983.

373 **Nichols and the show's new book writer**: Don Shewey, "How 'My One and Only' Came to Broadway," *New York Times*, May 1, 1983.

373 **"The thing that struck me about Mike"**: AI with Michael Feinstein.

374 **"He was like a superfine machinist"**: AI with Bruce McGill.

374 **"It was agonizing"**: AI with Bruce McGill.

374 **"We had to use certain elements"**: AI with Twiggy Lawson.

374 **"When we were in our darkest hour"**: Carol Lawson, "Broadway," *New York Times*, July 22, 1983.

375 **She had just won her second Academy Award**: AI with Meryl Streep.

375 **"It's a very tricky role"**: AI with Glenn Close.

376 **accompanied Jack Nicholson**: Rita Reif, "Sotheby Auction Sets Record of $37 Million," *New York Times*, May 19, 1983.

376 **"We were having lunch"**: AI with Lorne Michaels.

376 **"The problem is"**: AI with Tony Walton.

377 **"It was so complex"**: AI with Glenn Close.

377 **Nichols had the house rebuilt**: Martin Burden, "The (Card) House That Jan Built," *New York Post*, January 12, 1984.

377 **And he couldn't figure out**: AI with Glenn Close.

377 **"Even when he was pissed off"**: AI with Kenneth Welsh.

377 **"Once when he was working on a blackout"**: Barbara Gelb, "Mike Nichols: The Special Risks and Rewards of the Director's Art," *New York Times Magazine*, May 27, 1984.

377 **And he once stopped a dress rehearsal**: AI with Otts Munderloh.

378 **"At one end of the table"**: AI with Glenn Close.

378 **"I take on the mood"**: Gelb, "Mike Nichols."

379 **"Cynthia, that passage"**: AI with Peter Gallagher.

380 **"There's a scene where Annie"**: AI with Cynthia Nixon.

380 **"We were trying to find a moment"**: AI with Glenn Close.

380 **"It was like, *gasp*"**: AI with Cynthia Nixon.

381 **"Mike had final cut"**: AI with Arthur Hirsch.

381 **"Mike was upset"**: Sam O'Steen, as told to Bobbie O'Steen, *Cut to the Chase: Forty-five Years of Editing America's Favorite Movies* (Studio City, CA: Michael Wiese Productions, 2001).

381 **"to be a character"**: David Burnham, "Screen Credit: A Reporter Who Said No," *New York Times*, February 12, 1984.

382 **"as a genre"**: "The Chicanery of 'Silkwood,'" editorial, *New York Times*, December 24, 1983.

382 **"exploited by a gang of causists"**: Op-ed cited by Sol Stern in "The Smearing of *Silkwood*," *Village Voice*, date unavailable, found in NYPLPA clipping file on *Silkwood*.

382 **"a precisely visual"**: Vincent Canby, "Film: Karen Silkwood's Story," *New York Times*, December 14, 1983.

382 **"Mike Nichols' direction"**: Janet Maslin, "In the Arts: Critics' Choices," *New York Times*, January 8, 1984.

382 **"Nichols' directorial style"**: Howard Kissel, *Women's Wear Daily*, December 13, 1983.

382 **"the radical-chic politics"**: Richard Schickel, "A Tissue of Implications," *Time*, December 19, 1983.

382 **"a directorial triumph":** David Sterritt, "And from Russia a Demanding, but Very Rewarding, 'Nostalghia,'" *Christian Science Monitor,* January 5, 1984.

384 **"a remedy for the ailing theater":** Review of *The Real Thing, Variety,* January 11, 1984.

384 **"the acting has exactly":** Clive Barnes, "'Real Thing': A Really Fine Theatrical Event," *New York Post,* January 6, 1984.

384 **"There was talk":** AI with Meryl Streep.

385 **"Manny said, 'David wants Bill Hurt'":** AI with Fred Zollo.

386 **"In the case of *Hurlyburly*":** AI with Fred Zollo.

386 **"every crazy person":** AI with Otts Munderloh.

386 **"How long are you willing to wait?":** AI with Bill Evans.

386 **"Those terrific actors":** AI with Peter Lawrence.

386 **"A lot of his direction":** AI with Cynthia Nixon.

387 **"rehearsal, for a couple of days":** AI with Judith Ivey.

387 **"he was avuncular":** AI with Cynthia Nixon.

387 **"low-life thug":** AI with David Rabe.

387 **"It got cut pretty quickly":** AI with Judith Ivey.

387 **"What Mike did with *Hurlyburly*":** AI with Peter Lawrence.

388 **"I could see the notes":** AI with Fred Zollo.

388 ***Hurlyburly* was completely dysfunctional":** AI with Cynthia Nixon.

388 **"Our communication broke down":** AI with David Rabe.

388 **"I came into the theater":** AI with Bill Evans.

389 **"Did you see the photograph":** Elia Kazan, *A Life* (New York: Alfred A. Knopf, 1988), 299.

389 **"In the end, Mike":** Rabe restored the scene Nichols had omitted for later productions of the play.

389 **"My reputation took a big hit":** AI with David Rabe.

389 **"Mike came backstage":** AI with Frank Langella.

CHAPTER TWENTY-FOUR: A SHOT ACROSS THE BOW

391 **"It was a good night":** Guy Trebay, "The Whoopi Goldberg Variations," *Village Voice,* October 30, 1984.

392 **"If I have to shake":** Janet Coleman, "Making Whoopi," *Vanity Fair,* July 1984.

392 **He knew that performers:** Enid Nemy, "Whoopi's Ready, but Is Broadway?," *New York Times,* October 21, 1984.

393 **"Mike Nichols spoiled me":** "Whoopi Goldberg," *Screen Actor,* Fall 1988.

393 **John Lindsay, the former mayor:** Harold C. Schonberg, "Search for Artistic Chief Extended at Beaumont," *New York Times,* January 8, 1985.

394 **"I think along the way":** Larry Kramer, email to author, October 12, 2018.

394 **"polite and indulgent":** AI with Robert Nichols.

395 **"Mike broke down":** AI with Robert Nichols.

395 **"My mother had always been":** Mike Nichols, interview by Bob Gazzale, for Nichols's American Film Institute Life Achievement Award, 2010, unpublished transcript.

395 **"They had their own language":** Richard Cohen, "On the Celibate Love Affair of Nora Ephron and Mike Nichols," Literary Hub (website), September 12, 2016.

396 **"Who will tell all of us":** Mike Nichols, email to author, 2012.

396 **"to kill my husband":** Nora Ephron, on *The Dick Cavett Show,* February 22, 1971, in *Everything Is Copy,* dir. Jacob Bernstein and Nick Hooker (San Francisco: HBO Documentary Films, 2015).

396 **"a tough, funny":** Grace Glueck, "A Dishy Roman a Clef With Recipes," *New York Times,* April 23, 1983.

396 **But the outrage:** Christopher Lehmann-Haupt, "Books of the Times," *New York Times,* April 8, 1983.

397 **"nasty . . . smarmy":** Tony Schwartz, "The Playboy Interview: Carl Bernstein," *Playboy,* September 1986.

397 **"the father in the movie":** Chuck Conconi, "Divorce with a Heartburn Clause," *Washington Post,* June 28, 1985.

397 **"Somebody is going to make this movie":** Schwartz, *Playboy* interview.

397 **"Mike at that time was a romantic":** AI with Robert Greenhut.

398 **"Mandy was at the top of his game":** AI with Juliet Taylor.

398 **"Mandy would constantly":** AI with Richard Masur.

398 **"Mandy's a questioner":** AI with Meryl Streep.

399 **"Neither Meryl nor Mandy":** AI with Robert Greenhut.

399 **"I never really understood it":** AI with Meryl Streep.

399 **"to all the relatives who said":** Alex Witchel, "Mandy Patinkin: 'I Behaved Abominably,'" *New York Times Magazine,* August 25, 2013.

399 **"I've felt awful about it"**: Witchel, "Mandy Patinkin."

400 **"I liked the book"**: AI with Kevin Kline.

400 **"When I called him"**: Peter Biskind, "Who's Afraid of the Big Bad Wolf," *Premiere*, March 1994.

400 **"Now everyone will like him"**: Sam O'Steen, as told to Bobbie O'Steen, *Cut to the Chase: Forty-five Years of Editing America's Favorite Movies* (Studio City, CA: Michael Wiese Productions, 2001).

400 **"Suddenly, there were a lot of ideas"**: AI with Meryl Streep.

401 **"If you look at the movie"**: Nichols, Gazzale interview.

401 **"It became clear to me"**: David Richards, "Mike Nichols, Directly," *Washington Post*, March 21, 1986.

401 ***Carnal Knowledge* is far blacker"**: Michael Healy, "Nichols' 'Heartburn' Sweetens the Bitterness," *New York Post*, August 2, 1986.

401 **"Nora was always there"**: AI with Meryl Streep.

401 **"He didn't know how to talk to men"**: AI with Richard Masur.

402 **"It wasn't like trying to play"**: AI with Meryl Streep.

403 Nichols lifted his head: AI with Robert Greenhut.

404 **"a silly little story"**: Schwartz, *Playboy* interview.

404 **"a play about a mother"**: AI with Peter Lawrence.

404 **"He'd come in and start every day"**: AI with Kenneth Welsh.

405 **"Mike started laughing again"**: AI with Andrew Bergman.

405 **"Pete, I want you to call this number"**: AI with Peter Lawrence.

405 **Publicly, what had happened**: "Director's Chest Pains Delay 'Social Security,'" *New York Times*, January 10, 1986.

405 **"It wasn't called a heart attack"**: AI with Lorne Michaels.

406 **"He was always bitching"**: AI with Andrew Bergman.

406 **"When he came back"**: AI with Joanna Gleason.

406 **"He was talking all about Diane Sawyer"**: AI with Joanna Gleason.

407 **"And you're mine"**: Joan Juliet Buck, "Live Mike," *Vanity Fair*, June 1994.

407 **"the year I went crazy"**: Mike Nichols, conversation with author, ca. 2012.

CHAPTER TWENTY-FIVE: BORROWED TIME

408 **"a genius of"**: John Simon, "Sisters and Brothers," *New York*, April 28, 1986.

408 **Rich had said he "isn't"**: Frank Rich, "Stage: 'Social Security,' with Ron Silver and Marlo Thomas," *New York Times*, April 18, 1986.

409 **"a cruel, harsh audience"**: Alice Arlen, "Mr. Success," *Interview*, December 1988.

409 **"The first screening"**: Alice Arlen, "Mr. Success," *Interview*, December 1988.

409 **"There was a dinner"**: AI with Tracey Jackson.

410 **"an exceptionally good movie"**: Vincent Canby, "Film View: VCR's Give Movies a Fresh Start," *New York Times*, August 30, 1987.

410 **"There must be a side"**: Andrew Sarris, *Village Voice*, date unavailable, ca. August 1986.

410 **"tunnel-vision point of view"**: Richard Corliss, "Cinema: Love's Something You Fall in Heartburn," *Time*, August 4, 1986.

410 **"There's not much in the marriage"**: Roger Ebert, review, *Chicago Sun-Times*, July 25, 1986.

410 **"Is he disgusted"**: David Ansen, headline unavailable, *Newsweek*, July 25, 1986.

410 **"he's no dum-dum"**: Stanley Kauffmann, headline unavailable, *New Republic*, date unavailable, ca. July–August 1986.

411 **"Could I come and live with you"**: AI with Jack O'Brien.

411 **"He went on and on"**: AI with Stephen Sondheim.

412 **"I'm the kind of person who never knows"**: AI with Meryl Streep.

412 **"At first I was enormously depressed"**: Joan Juliet Buck, "Live Mike," *Vanity Fair*, June 1994.

412 He sold a Balthus: Susanna Moore, email to author, April 18, 2019.

413 **"I'd add the numbers up"**: John Lahr, "Making It Real," *New Yorker*, February 21 and 28, 2000.

413 **"Why is it," Maury Yeston asked him**: AI with Maury Yeston.

413 **"He really did have debt"**: AI with Candice Bergen.

413 **"He was so unhappy"**: AI with Meryl Streep.

414 **"Snap out of it!"**: Norma Stevens and Steven M. L. Aronson, *Avedon: Something Personal* (New York: Spiegel & Grau, 2017), 629.

414 Forristal and Carly Simon: AI with Susan Forristal.

415 **"I changed my life"**: Sean Mitchell, "Nichols on Nichols," *Newsday*, July 9, 1991.

415   **"After that six months"**: Matthew Gilbert, "Mike Nichols: Still Hollywood's Czar of Zeitgeist," *Boston Globe*, July 7, 1991.

415   **"the idea that all of this is borrowed"**: Nichols on *Faces of America with Henry Louis Gates Jr.*, aired on PBS, February 23, 2010.

415   **"You work better and better"**: Arlen, "Mr. Success."

416   **Undeterred by the reception**: Samuel G. Freedman, "'Two Jakes' Picks Up the 'Chinatown' Trail," *New York Times*, August 5, 1990.

416   **Rudin thought the play was perfect**: Aljean Harmetz, "Film Makers in a Race over 'Les Liaisons,'" *New York Times*, February 10, 1988.

417   **"I didn't know what 'I'm crazy' meant"**: AI with Scott Rudin.

417   **"It was sort of like having a magical prince"**: AI with Corey Parker.

418   **"He was a leader"**: AI with Matthew Broderick.

418   **"He showed us *Camille*"**: AI with Corey Parker.

418   **"They just didn't seem to like each other"**: AI with Park Overall.

419   **"sufficiently scary to make us ready"**: Corey Parker, "On Making *Biloxi Blues* with Mike Nichols," *The Actors Work* (blog), December 2, 2016.

419   **"He was scary, but"**: AI with Matthew Broderick.

419   **With Parker, he was**: AI with Corey Parker.

419   **"would find Mike's eyes"**: AI with Markus Flanagan.

419   **Nichols was understanding**: AI with Park Overall.

420   **"I met a woman"**: AI with Mike Haley.

420   **"She had wondered"**: Buck, "Live Mike."

CHAPTER TWENTY-SIX: PINOCCHIO AND CINDERELLA

421   **"turned Pinocchio into"**: Mike Nichols, conversation with author.

421   **"He said he had always"**: AI with Douglas Wick.

422   **"You see these survivors"**: AI with Kate Nelligan.

422   **"He fell in love"**: AI with Candice Bergen.

422   **At the end of 1987**: Liz Smith, *New York Daily News*, December 16, 1987.

422   **"I thought he was the most"**: Sheila Weller, *The News Sorority: Diane Sawyer, Katie Couric, Christiane Amanpour—and the (Ongoing, Imperfect, Complicated) Triumph of Women in TV News* (New York: Penguin Press, 2014), 149–53.

423   **"Friends?" said Sawyer**: "Diane Sawyer Interviews Annabel Davis-Goff," transcript of June 11, 2002, interview on *Good Morning America*, ABC News, https://abcnews.go.com/amp/GMA/story?id=126042&page=1.

423   **when Joseph Papp**: Helen Epstein, "How a King Did and Did Not Seek a Successor," *New York Times*, August 21, 1994.

423   **"He wanted me to"**: AI with George C. Wolfe.

425   **interpretations were "inspired"**: Mel Gussow, "The Tramps Who Remade the Theater," *New York Times*, November 6, 1988.

425   **It had been a long time since Nichols**: Mel Gussow, "Beckett, as a Beckettian, Isn't Always the Purist," *New York Times*, November 16, 1988.

425   **called the play "a tragicomedy"**: Mervyn Rothstein, "Nichols Tries to Put the Fun Back in 'Godot,'" *New York Times*, September 13, 1988.

426   **"Isn't it time"**: Roger Ebert, *Chicago Sun-Times*, March 25, 1988.

426   **"a more lightweight film"**: David Denby, review of *Biloxi Blues*, *New York*, March 28, 1988.

426   **"Here is one adaptation"**: Vincent Canby, "Film: Simon's 'Biloxi Blues,' Coming of Age in the Army," *New York Times*, March 25, 1988.

426   **"now that Nichols has resigned"**: Dave Kehr, "'Biloxi' Steps Lively to the Screen," *New York Daily News*, March 25, 1988.

426   **The story of a working-class**: AI with Douglas Wick.

427   **"a greedy family"**: "1988: Previews from 36 Artists," *New York Times*, January 3, 1988.

427   **"Some people feared"**: AI with Douglas Wick.

428   **"I thought, *Surely*"**: Nichols, interview by Bob Gazzale, for Nichols's American Film Institute Life Achievement Award, 2010, unpublished transcript.

428   **"I knew he would be analytical"**: AI with Douglas Wick.

428   **"And Michelle Pfeiffer"**: AI with Douglas Wick.

429   **"The studio said"**: AI with Juliet Taylor.

429 **the subject of a comeback:** Todd Gold, "A Former Sex Kitten, Tippi Hedren's Daughter Melanie Griffith Decides Her Racy Past Was for the Birds," *People*, June 4, 1984.

429 **"You can't talk about the movie":** AI with Ann Roth.

429 **"It was everywhere":** AI with Douglas Wick.

429 **"she used to say, 'I gotta'":** Sam O'Steen, as told to Bobbie O'Steen, *Cut to the Chase: Forty-five Years of Editing America's Favorite Movies* (Studio City, CA: Michael Wiese Productions, 2001).

430 **"The shoot was difficult":** AI with Mary Bailey.

430 **"Melanie was very charming":** AI with Patrizia von Brandenstein.

430 **"what really shocked":** AI with Douglas Wick.

430 **"He did it, and he did not":** AI with Patrizia von Brandenstein.

431 **"the best collaborator":** Nichols, Gazzale interview.

431 **"His face was like":** Chris Gardner, "'Working Girl' Turns 30: On-Set Romances and Secrets of the Staten Island Ferry Revealed in Juicy Oral History," *Hollywood Reporter*, December 3, 2018.

431 **"The closer to the wedding":** AI with Sabrina Padwa.

431 **"I got pissed at":** Norma Stevens and Steven M. L. Aronson, *Avedon: Something Personal* (New York: Spiegel & Grau, 2017), 629.

431 **"Oh, God, Mike was":** AI with Mike Haley.

432 **"With Diane, he":** AI with Matthew Broderick.

432 **"I stood up to":** AI with Lorne Michaels.

432 **"Diane made wreaths":** Julia Wells, "Film Director Mike Nichols Is Remembered by Island Friends," *Vineyard Gazette*, November 20, 2014.

432 **"We had this thing":** *"Good Morning America* Reveals Its Own True Love Stories," ABC News, June 20, 2019, https://abcnews.go.com/amp/GMA/story?id=126110&page=1.

433 **"I would have had children":** Weller, *News Sorority*, 156.

CHAPTER TWENTY-SEVEN: STILL HERE

434 **"It can't," his therapist replied:** Joan Juliet Buck, "Live Mike," *Vanity Fair*, June 1994.

435 **"We would pick":** AI with Diane Paulus.

435 **"It was unlike any scene-study class":** AI with Laura Pierce.

435 **"In the process of":** AI with Diane Paulus.

437 **"He thought it would have made":** AI with Bill Irwin.

437 **"Is [this] any way":** Barbara Isenberg, "'Godot' Leaves Them Waiting for Tickets," *Los Angeles Times*, November 22, 1988.

437 **"Anxiety was very high":** AI with Bill Irwin.

438 **"It's not so easy":** AI with Bill Irwin.

438 **"Steve and Robin":** AI with Bill Irwin.

439 **"Mike had such":** AI with David Hyde Pierce.

439 **"When we were rehearsing":** AI with Steve Martin.

439 **"The only real mistake":** Clive Barnes, "Mortuary Glee," *New York Post*, November 7, 1988.

439 **"entirely faithful to Beckett's":** Hedy Weiss, headline unavailable, *Chicago Sun-Times*, November 8, 1988.

439 **himself had Americanized:** Beckett wrote *Waiting for Godot* in French and then translated it himself. For Nichols's production, he changed a scatological pun, in which "Macon country" became "cackon country," to "Napa country" and "crappa country." See *New Theater Review* 1, no. 4.

439 **"All my plays":** Jack Kroll, "Sam's Heartbreak Vaudeville," *Newsweek*, November 21, 1988.

439 **bemoaned "the tragedy of":** John Simon, "Yuppie Godot," *New York*, November 21, 1988.

440 **called the comic interjections "inexcusable":** William A Henry, "Clowning Around with a Classic." *Time*, November 21, 1988.

440 **"The naked realism":** Frank Rich, "'Godot': The Timeless Relationship of 2 Interdependent Souls," *New York Times*, November 7, 1988.

440 **"Before the show opened":** Dave Itzkoff, *Robin* (New York: Henry Holt, 2018), 236.

440 **"Dear Jay: Thanks":** AI with Bill Evans.

440 **"We were shell-shocked":** Itzkoff, *Robin*, 236.

441 **"it didn't work":** AI with Douglas Wick.

441 **"an attack on a woman":** Mona Harrington, "'Working Girl' in Reagan Country," *New York Times*, January 15, 1989.

442 **"a lot of people":** Linda Winer, "The Trouble with 'Working Girl,'" *Newsday*, January 6, 1989.

442 **"a fond anthology":** Richard Corliss, *Time*, December 19, 1988.

442   **called it "post-feminist":** Ellen Goodman, "Taps for Feminism?," *Chicago Tribune*, January 8, 1989.

442   **Maslin called it "enjoyable":** Janet Maslin, "The Dress-for-Success Story of a Secretary from Staten Island," *New York Times*, December 21, 1988.

442   **"The only time Mike ever really":** AI with Barry Diller.

443   **"It wasn't easy":** AI with Douglas Wick.

443   **had some "dirty parts":** Maureen Dowd, "Review of Bush's First Week," *New York Times*, January 29, 1989.

443   **"but it didn't catch a wave":** AI with Douglas Wick.

443   **"I spent a long evening":** AI with Swoosie Kurtz.

444   **offered its readers "no plot":** Rod Lurie, "Author on the Edge," *West Side Spirit*, October 2, 1990.

444   **"[threw] the book":** Margot Dougherty, "Hi, Mom!," *Entertainment Weekly*, September 22, 1990.

444   **"Write more scenes":** Carrie Fisher, DVD commentary, *Postcards from the Edge* (Paramount Home Video, 2006), DVD.

444   **"Carrie doesn't draw on":** Dougherty, "Hi, Mom!"

445   **"there was Mike, there was":** AI with Norman Sunshine.

445   **"She was mad":** AI with Meryl Streep.

446   **Once production started:** Judith Newman, ". . . And Some Call for a Voice," *New York Times*, January 19, 1992.

447   **"Carrie was there":** AI with Scott Frankel.

447   **"He rehearsed that":** AI with Mike Haley.

447   **"She's a dancer":** Nichols, interview by Bob Gazzale, for Nichols's American Film Institute Life Achievement Award, 2010, unpublished transcript.

448   **"He knew just how":** AI with Mike Haley.

448   **"The studio kept taking":** AI with Patrizia von Brandenstein.

448   **"I feel like I've been let out":** Aljean Harmetz, "Dawn Steel Quits Columbia Pictures Post," *New York Times*, January 9, 1990.

449   **"It's about women":** "1988: Previews from 36 Artists," *New York Times*, January 3, 1988.

449   **"It's a play about misogyny":** AI with Peter Lawrence.

449   **"I think Mike related":** AI with Oliver Platt.

449   **"What I noticed in that production":** AI with David Hyde Pierce.

449   **"There was a lot":** AI with Jules Feiffer.

450   **"The problem is":** Linda Winer, "All Right, Now—Who Does Elliot Love?," *Newsday*, June 8, 1990.

450   **"You can imagine":** AI with Oliver Platt.

450   **"pro bono playwright":** Sam Adams, "Jules Feiffer," *A.V. Club*, July 28, 2008.

450   **"It took me ten years":** Jules Feiffer, *Backing into Forward: A Memoir* (New York: Nan A. Talese/Doubleday, 2010), 422–23.

450   ***Elliot Loves* closed:** *Variety*, July 18, 1990.

451   **see them as "artifacts":** Mike Nichols, interview by David Schwartz, Museum of the Moving Image, March 19, 1990, http://www.movingimagesource.us/files/dialogues/2/18025_programs_transcript_pdf_203.pdf.

CHAPTER TWENTY-EIGHT: IT NEVER GOES AWAY

452   **the $5 million:** Aljean Harmetz, "Bruce Willis Will 'Die Hard' for $5 Million," *Chicago Tribune*, February 18, 1988.

454   **"Certainly in my life":** Nichols, interview by Christopher Connelly, unpublished transcript.

454   **"there was no Mike":** AI with Scott Rudin.

454   **"We met a guy to whom":** Nichols, interview by Bob Gazzale, for Nichols's American Film Institute Life Achievement Award, 2010, unpublished transcript.

454   **"At that point":** AI with Scott Rudin.

455   **"Have you ever":** AI with Scott Rudin.

455   **"I remember being":** AI with Annette Bening.

455   **"he was very good about":** AI with Kamian Allen.

455   **"He helped me tremendously":** Glenn Plaskin, "And Then There Was Nunn," *New York Daily News*, July 7, 1991.

456   **"I know he was invested":** AI with Rebecca Miller.

456   **"Oh my God":** AI with Robert Greenhut.

457   **"We can't do this":** AI with Tony Walton.

457   **"This is all an artifice":** AI with Mary Bailey.

457   **"Do you hate":** Joan Juliet Buck, "Live Mike," *Vanity Fair*, June 1994.

457   **"He's almost gotten":** Buck, "Live Mike."

458 "Sometime after midnight": AI with Tony Walton.

458 "a connection," she says: AI with Emma Thompson.

459 "An unimaginably bad": David Denby, "The Trouble with Henry," *New York*, July 22, 1991.

459 "Does the man": David Ansen, "You Need This Movie Like . . ." *Newsweek*, July 15, 1991.

459 "the worst-performed": Michael Sragow, capsule review, *New Yorker*, August 26, 1991.

459 "I don't think": Julie Salamon, headline unavailable, *Wall Street Journal*, July 18, 1991.

459 "haute bourgeois marital": Sragow, *New Yorker*.

460 "I blamed Sam": AI with Meryl Streep.

460 "Mike [knew] what": Bernard Weinraub, "Her Peculiar Career: Meryl Streep," *New York Times*, September 18, 1994.

461 "Mike is someone": Weinraub, "Her Peculiar Career."

461 At one point, he said that Columbia: Benedict Nightingale, "Merchant-Ivory and Friends: On the Job Again," *New York Times*, January 24, 1993.

461 "because I'm not English": Matthew Gilbert, "Mike Nichols: Still Hollywood's Czar of Zeitgeist," *Boston Globe*, July 7, 1991.

461 "Harold wrote a very": Nichols, in "Love and Loyalty: The Making of *The Remains of the Day*," Blu-ray featurette, available on *The Remains of the Day* anniversary edition (Sony Pictures Home Entertainment, 2013).

461 "I didn't see much": AI with Emma Thompson.

461 "We were turning": Nichols, "Love and Loyalty . . . ," DVD featurette.

462 "It didn't get off": AI with Ariel Dorfman.

463 "Glenny," said Nichols: AI with Tony Walton.

463 "Richard and Gene": AI with Glenn Close.

463 "Gene had a terrible": AI with Tony Walton.

463 "It was so unfair": AI with Glenn Close.

464 "Ariel used to say": AI with Fred Zollo.

464 "I just should have let him": AI with Ariel Dorfman.

464 "You know the writer": AI with Glenn Close.

464 "The whole world": AI with Ariel Dorfman.

464 "Ariel," Nichols finally said: Mike Nichols, conversation with author.

464 "He's in the theater": AI with Hal Luftig.

465 "Ariel was really": AI with Glenn Close.

465 "wrong, wrong, wrong": AI with Hal Luftig.

465 "Mike made it his": AI with Peter Lawrence.

465 A group of Latino actors: Anthony Scaduto, Doug Vaughn, and Linda Stasi, "Doctor Watch at Death & Maiden," *Newsday*, March 18, 1992.

465 eventually founded the Labyrinth: John Ortiz, quoted in David Kaufman, "Theater: A 'Gym' for Acting, It's a Company, Too," *New York Times*, December 10, 2000.

465 "it has depressed him": Benedict Nightingale, "'Death and the Maiden' Becomes a Tale of Two Cities," *New York Times*, May 10, 1992.

466 "Mike started this tradition": AI with Glenn Close.

466 "Mike's ass must": AI with Peter Lawrence.

466 "Only six more": AI with Glenn Close.

466 "a pitiful travesty": Benedict Nightingale, headline unavailable, *Times* (London), March 18, 1992.

466 "It is no small feat": Frank Rich, "Close, Hackman, and Dreyfuss in 'Death and the Maiden,'" *New York Times*, March 18, 1992.

466 After revisiting the London: AI with Hal Luftig.

466 "I genuinely made some mistakes": Bernard Weinraub, "Mike Nichols Plans a Career Finale," *New York Times*, March 15, 1993.

466 said that "whatever he is": Alex Witchel, "On Stage, and Off," *New York Times*, April 17, 1992.

467 Despite the reviews: AI with Ariel Dorfman.

467 By August, Perkins: Charles Winecoff, *Split Image: The Life of Anthony Perkins* (New York: E. P. Dutton, 1996), 456, 460.

467 Nichols also lost: AI with Bill Evans.

467 including a pair: Glenn Collins, "A Double Reunion, 2 Decades Later," *New York Times*, May 2, 1992.

467 At a dinner: James Kaplan, "True Colors," *New York*, March 2, 1998.

468 "I burst into tears": Peter Biskind, "Who's Afraid of the Big Bad Wolf?," *Premiere*, March 1994.

468 "Metaphor has left art": Joan Juliet Buck, "Live Mike," *Vanity Fair*, June 1994.

468 "When somebody talented": Weinraub, "Career Finale."

CHAPTER TWENTY-NINE: THE BEST ROUTE TO REVENGE

471   **Jim Harrison, a rugged novelist:** Harrison's 1971 novel *Wolf* was unrelated to the movie.
471   **"Willy Loman Eats Spinach":** AI with Douglas Wick.
471   **"I told Mike the ambitions":** AI with Douglas Wick.
471   **"Mike was torn":** AI with Douglas Wick.
471   **"A movie's artistic success":** Gavin Smith, "Of Metaphors and Purpose," *Film Comment*, May–June 1999.
471   **"Werewolves are a lousy metaphor":** Nichols, interview by Bob Gazzale, for Nichols's American Film Institute Life Achievement Award, 2010, unpublished transcript.
472   **"The movie was about":** AI with Douglas Wick.
472   **"exceedingly dense" and "impenetrable":** Wesley Strick, "Of Mike and Me," Hollywoodjournal.com, November 23, 2014.
472   **"a three-hour horror":** "Jack Cries Wolf," *Newsweek*, June 19, 1994.
472   **"Free-associating with Nichols":** Strick, "Of Mike and Me."
472   **"sometimes she was":** Strick, "Of Mike and Me."
472   **"It was 'the girl'":** Peter Biskind, "Who's Afraid of the Big Bad Wolf," *Premiere*, March 1994.
473   **"It's like some Taoist thing":** "Jack Cries Wolf," *Newsweek.*
473   **"I read it and thought":** AI with Elaine May.
473   **"There were old friendships":** Michael Wilmington, "How Mike Nichols and Friends Created a 'Wolf,'" *Chicago Tribune*, July 4, 1994.
474   **"Mike was just not":** Sam O'Steen, as told to Bobbie O'Steen, *Cut to the Chase: Forty-five Years of Editing America's Favorite Movies* (Studio City, CA: Michael Wiese Productions, 2001), 217–21.
475   **"Everyone was scared":** O'Steen, *Cut to the Chase.*
475   **"It was a great disappointment":** AI with Mary Bailey.
475   **"We all kind of":** AI with Christopher Plummer.
475   **"In *Wolf*, I had":** AI with Kate Nelligan.
476   **"intent on earning":** Bernard Weinraub, "The Talk of Hollywood: Movers and Shakers Shaken Up by a Move," *New York Times*, August 23, 1993.
476   **"There was a good deal":** AI with Bo Welch.
476   **"We did a preview":** AI with Douglas Wick.
476   **"We were more worried":** O'Steen, *Cut to the Chase.*
477   **"Audiences may well":** Anthony Lane, "The Current Cinema," *New Yorker*, July 11, 1994.
477   **"A lot of very good work":** Smith, "Of Metaphors and Purpose."
477   **"It had seemed like such":** Bob Morris, "Great Expectations," *New York Times*, November 14, 1993.
478   **"We're really excited":** Wilmington, "Created a 'Wolf.'"
478   **He was being wooed:** Philip Weiss, "Hollywood at a Fever Pitch," *New York Times Magazine*, December 26, 1993.
479   **"The best route":** AI with Maury Yeston.
479   **"We had a twinge":** Bernard Weinraub, "'Birdcage' Shows Growth in Older Audience's Power," *New York Times*, March 11, 1996.
479   **"He didn't think":** Benjamin Svetkey, "Tickled Pink," *Entertainment Weekly*, March 29, 1996.
479   **"Robin decided, because of":** AI with Nathan Lane.
480   **"It seems crazy":** AI with Nathan Lane.
480   **"I came in, I did the lines":** AI with Adrian Lester.
481   **"I worked up different versions":** AI with Hank Azaria.
481   **"I'm forty, I'm single":** Nathan Lane, interviewed in *Us Weekly*, 1996.
481   **"There was a point":** AI with Nathan Lane.
481   **On *The Birdcage*, Nichols:** AI with Bo Welch.
482   **"He would say, 'Don't worry'":** AI with Nathan Lane.
482   **"Mike said, 'I want you guys'":** AI with Hank Azaria.
482   **"But you keep it all *inside*":** Sam Wasson, *Improv Nation: How We Made a Great American Art* (New York: Houghton Mifflin Harcourt, 2017), 335–37.
483   **"Bo [Welch] was really":** AI with Elaine May.
484   **"I said, 'Mike, I don't'":** AI with Hank Azaria.
484   **"one of the happiest":** Wasson, *Improv Nation*, 335–37.
484   **"The script used":** AI with Nathan Lane.
485   **"Never underestimate":** AI with Calista Flockhart.
485   **"There were no rules":** AI with Hank Azaria.

485 **"He'd gone through"**: AI with Lorne Michaels.

485 **"beyond the stereotypes"**: GLAAD, "GLAAD Applauds 'The Birdcage,'" press release, March 5, 1996.

486 **"strained, awkward"**: Bruce Bawer, "Why Can't Hollywood Get Gay Life Right?," *New York Times*, March 10, 1996.

486 **"That poor schmuck"**: Svetkey, "Tickled Pink."

486 **"proof-positive evidence"**: Larry Kramer, *Variety*, April 8, 1996.

486 **"Who would have guessed"**: Frank Rich, "Beyond the Birdcage," *New York Times*, March 13, 1996.

487 **"I couldn't speak"**: John Lahr, "Making It Real," *New Yorker*, February 21 and 28, 2000.

CHAPTER THIRTY: SOMETHING SCARY

489 **"I had an advantage"**: John Lahr, "Making It Real," *New Yorker*, February 21 and 28, 2000.

489 **"I'd never met him"**: Joe Klein, *Time*, November 20, 2014.

489 **suggested that the easiest**: Bernard Weinraub, "Let Emma Thompson Play Everyone," *New York Times*, February 25, 1996.

490 **"When Mike read"**: AI with Wallace Shawn.

490 **"The part has to be"**: AI with Deborah Eisenberg.

490 **"Debbie and Hare and I"**: AI with Wallace Shawn.

490 **"There was no reason"**: AI with Deborah Eisenberg.

491 **"I wanted to do something scary"**: Jack Kroll, "Why Mike Nichols Is Working Without a Net," *Newsweek*, May 5, 1996.

491 **"Mike said that as a director"**: AI with David Hare.

491 **"He could have been such a diva"**: AI with Deborah Eisenberg.

491 **"his theater discipline"**: AI with Wallace Shawn.

491 **"He gave one of the greatest"**: AI with Elaine May.

492 **"The film didn't"**: Gavin Smith, "Of Metaphors and Purpose," *Film Comment*, May–June 1999.

492 **"My wife had to"**: Peter Biskind, "The White House Unzipped," *Premiere*, April 1998.

492 **"I didn't fully know"**: AI with Elaine May.

492 *Primary Colors* **was once**: *Variety*, August 16, 1996.

492 **"Maybe I erased"**: AI with Meryl Streep.

493 **"We had been talking"**: AI with Emma Thompson.

493 **"He didn't say anything"**: AI with Tom Hanks.

494 **"I said, 'Have you'"**: Nichols, interview by Bob Gazzale, for Nichols's American Film Institute Life Achievement Award, 2010, unpublished transcript.

494 **The studio, worried**: Biskind, "The White House Unzipped."

494 **"If somebody told you"**: Warren St. John, "Mike Nichols' All-Star Clinton Gamble," *New York Observer*, March 3, 1997.

495 **"So much of filmmaking"**: AI with John Travolta.

495 **"We rehearsed, and Mike said"**: AI with Adrian Lester.

495 **"Every morning, they would"**: AI with Mary Bailey.

495 **"Hillary was much less"**: AI with Emma Thompson.

496 **"I was doing a literal"**: AI with John Travolta.

496 **"There was a particular"**: AI with Ann Roth.

496 **"May was adamant"**: AI with Kathy Bates.

496 **"I would play Mom and Dad"**: AI with John Travolta.

496 **"I always feel that a really good"**: AI with Kathy Bates.

496 **"I knew the character"**: AI with Kathy Bates.

497 **"This girl went down"**: AI with Elaine May.

497 **"We were all in L.A."**: AI with Emma Thompson.

498 **a shit magnet**: Ruth Stein, "'Primary' Campaign Director," *New York Daily News*, March 16, 1998.

498 **"We're staying the course"**: Biskind, "White House Unzipped."

498 **"I would hang myself"**: Bernard Weinraub, "Real Life Intrudes on Political Movie," *New York Times*, January 26, 1998.

498 **"It's not about Clinton"**: Todd S. Purdum, "The Way We Are in the Era of Clinton," *New York Times*, March 15, 1998.

498 **"I would hope that"**: Stein, "'Primary' Campaign Director."

498 **"I don't think"**: Biskind, "White House Unzipped."

498 **"It's the only time":** James Kaplan, "True Colors," *New York,* March 2, 1998.

498 **"frequently funny":** Todd McCarthy, *Variety,* March 16, 1998.

498 ***"Primary Colors* is old news":** Rex Reed, *New York Observer,* March 23, 1998.

498 **"I liked the book":** Nichols, interview by Chris Nashawaty for *Entertainment Weekly,* March 1, 2012, unpublished transcript.

499 **"From the beginning":** AI with Dan Jinks.

500 **Barbra Streisand wanted to know:** *New York Post,* September 7, 1998.

500 **Tom Cruise and Nicole Kidman:** Michael Riedel, "Theater Talk," *New York Post,* April 23, 1999.

500 **Anthony Minghella wanted:** *Variety,* May 24, 1999.

500 **driving around Martha's Vineyard:** AI with Candice Bergen.

501 **"There's a virus":** Peter Applebome, "Always Asking, What Is This Really About?," *New York Times,* April 25, 1999.

501 **He said yes:** John Lippman, "What 'Planet' Were They On?," *Wall Street Journal,* March 3, 2000.

501 **"Mike got crushes":** AI with Douglas Wick.

501 **"Unlike many comedians":** AI with Annette Bening.

502 **What had been conceived:** Lippman, "What 'Planet'?"

502 **"I said, 'Garry, do you'":** AI with Ed Solomon.

502 **Nichols's Lincoln Center gala:** Film Society of Lincoln Center Gala, tribute to Mike Nichols, Avery Fisher Hall, May 3, 1999, videotape provided by Film at Lincoln Center.

503 **"Garry was very limited":** AI with Ed Solomon.

503 **"I got to the set":** AI with Cary Brokaw.

503 **"If an actor isn't good":** AI with Joanna Gleason.

503 **"I saw him fall":** AI with Mary Bailey.

504 **"He couldn't walk":** AI with Douglas Wick.

504 **"I find it hard":** AI with Annette Bening.

504 **"It was hysterical":** AI with Bo Welch.

504 **"Garry was a very honest person":** AI with Nora Dunn.

505 **"We put it in":** AI with Rose Styron.

505 **In Shandling, a congenitally:** AI with Annette Bening.

505 **"Garry gave away":** AI with Hannah Roth Sorkin.

506 **it lost Sony almost:** *New York Post,* January 11, 2001.

CHAPTER THIRTY-ONE: THE ULTIMATE TEST

507 **"He was furious":** AI with Jeffrey Toobin.

507 **he once told a young:** AI with Will Frears.

508 **"We would talk about it":** AI with Aaron Sorkin.

508 **"John was completely":** AI with Annette Bening.

509 **"I've died in too many":** AI with Cary Brokaw.

509 **"Emma said she'd had":** AI with Cary Brokaw.

510 **"What drew me to":** Nichols, interview by Bob Gazzale, for Nichols's American Film Institute Life Achievement Award, 2010, unpublished transcript.

510 **Edson was an elementary:** AI with Margaret Edson.

510 **"Emma's a writer":** AI with Cary Brokaw.

510 **"we didn't write it":** AI with Emma Thompson.

511 **his creative team:** Sam O'Steen, who had retired, died at seventy-six on October 11, 2000, while *Wit* was in production.

511 **"We had plenty of":** AI with Jonathan M. Woodward.

512 **"I mean, Harold":** AI with Jonathan M. Woodward.

512 **"I turned up at Pinewood":** AI with Eileen Atkins.

512 **"It was glorious":** AI with Audra McDonald.

512 **"What I remember":** AI with Jonathan M. Woodward.

512 **"In rehearsal, it had been":** AI with Cary Brokaw.

513 **Nichols then took:** AI with Jonathan M. Woodward.

513 **"I got my office":** AI with Cary Brokaw.

513 **"We'd do a take":** AI with Emma Thompson.

514 **"Mike made a big":** AI with Emma Thompson.

514 **"In the end, this awful":** Nichols, Gazzale interview.

514 **New Line, where Altman:** Isaac Butler and Dan Kois, *The World Only Spins Forward: The Ascent of Angels in America* (New York: Bloomsbury, 2018), 310.

515 **"Once in a while":** AI with Tony Kushner.

516 **"David Chase and I":** *The Leonard Lopate Show,* WNYC, September 25, 2013.

516 **thought Nichols's work was "beautiful":** AI with Margaret Edson.

517 **"deserves not only an Emmy":** John Leonard, "The I.V. League," *New York,* March 26, 2001.

517 **"subtle yet crucial":** Eddie Cockrell, *Variety,* February 15, 2001.

517 **"there was no opening":** Bernard Weinraub, "Little Screen, Big Ambition: Serious Films by Cable Networks Fill a Void Left by Hollywood," *New York Times,* January 3, 2001.

518 **"Mike had the best":** AI with Rosemarie Tichler.

518 **all the actors would:** Jesse McKinley, "On Stage, and Off," *New York Times,* February 2, 2001.

518 **"the grand-old-gentleman":** AI with Matthew Broderick.

518 **"The first week":** AI with Kevin Kline.

518 **"In fact, I was one of those people":** AI with Meryl Streep.

519 **"would say that casting is destiny":** AI with Kevin Kline.

519 **"he would always say that the problem":** AI with Natalie Portman.

519 **"He was wildly in love":** AI with Meryl Streep.

519 **"I remember all of us":** AI with Trip Cullman.

519 **"he added that there were":** AI with Natalie Portman.

520 **"He became, at that point":** AI with Jack O'Brien.

520 **"It's not you":** AI with Rosemarie Tichler.

520 **"I like the reins off":** AI with Meryl Streep.

520 **"It's the Juliet problem":** AI with Rosemarie Tichler.

520 **"I was nineteen":** AI with Natalie Portman.

521 **"there would be a period":** AI with Matthew Broderick.

521 **"I think he was a genuine feminist":** AI with Natalie Portman.

521 **"For three brief, captivating":** Linda Winer, *Newsday,* August 13, 2001.

521 **"It was a real mishmash":** AI with Kevin Kline.

522 **"I would leave the theater":** AI with Kevin Kline.

522 **"You have to prepare":** AI with Trip Cullman.

CHAPTER THIRTY-TWO: MORE LIFE

523 **"I wanted Mike to cast":** AI with Tony Kushner.

524 **"People like Matt Damon":** AI with Celia Costas.

524 **"My thought was that no one":** Isaac Butler and Dan Kois, *The World Only Spins Forward: The Ascent of Angels in America* (New York: Bloomsbury, 2018), 320.

525 **"He auditioned with":** AI with Juliet Taylor.

525 **"Mike stopped him":** AI with Tony Kushner.

525 **"I'd just been in *Proof*":** AI with Ben Shenkman.

525 **"When he read Louis":** AI with Juliet Taylor.

525 **"I knew I was connecting":** AI with Ben Shenkman.

526 **"He looks like religious":** AI with Tony Kushner.

526 **"very, very new":** AI with Juliet Taylor.

526 **"But I don't think I had ever been":** AI with Patrick Wilson.

526 **"They were all young":** AI with Celia Costas.

526 **"I had gone to his":** AI with Tony Kushner.

527 **"I can't do . . . Mormons":** Nichols, interview by Bob Gazzale, for Nichols's American Film Institute Life Achievement Award, 2010, unpublished transcript.

527 **"Other than Mike":** AI with Tony Kushner.

528 **"The rehearsals were":** AI with Ben Shenkman.

528 **"I was amazed":** AI with Tony Kushner.

528 **"Al works very hard":** Nichols, Gazzale interview.

528 **"He wanted to give Justin":** AI with Ben Shenkman.

528 **"At the first rehearsal":** AI with Justin Kirk.

529 **"You didn't hit it":** Butler and Kois, *The World Only Spins Forward,* 322.

529 **What the fuck am I:** Nichols, conversation with author.

529 **"He was so obnoxious":** AI with Stephen Goldblatt.

530 **"You know they're extraordinary"**: AI with Tony Kushner.
530 **"When Tony wasn't there"**: AI with Trip Cullman.
530 **"Patrick Wilson was astonishing"**: Nichols, Gazzale interview.
530 **"When can I come back?"**: AI with Tony Kushner.
530 **"Mike always fell"**: AI with Stephen Goldblatt.
531 **"Yeah, he likes that"**: AI with Meryl Streep.
531 **"He kept cursing"**: AI with Brian Markinson.
531 **"I'd say to him"**: Nichols, Gazzale interview.
531 **"It was the day"**: AI with Ben Shenkman.
532 **"Like Justin, I always"**: AI with Ben Shenkman.
532 ***"Angels* can get really"**: AI with Tony Kushner.
532 **"The idea that acting"**: David Ansen, "City of Angels," *Newsweek,* November 16, 2003.
533 **"He didn't differentiate"**: AI with Trip Cullman.
533 **"playing an angel"**: AI with Emma Thompson.
533 **"Emma and I talked"**: AI with Meryl Streep.
533 **"When I first worked"**: AI with Mary Bailey.
534 **"He would sneak"**: AI with Celia Costas.
534 **"I walked over to his office"**: AI with Cary Brokaw.
534 **"I would get in his chauffeur-driven"**: AI with Trip Cullman.
535 **"It was all accomplished"**: AI with Celia Costas.
535 **"I feared for Justin"**: AI with Meryl Streep.
535 **"Justin had got really"**: AI with Emma Thompson.
535 **"Believe me, it was"**: AI with Justin Kirk.
536 **"Justin had gotten"**: Nichols, Gazzale interview.
536 **"He was always living"**: AI with Meryl Streep.

CHAPTER THIRTY-THREE: BIG ISN'T TRUE

537 **"He was exhausted"**: AI with Tony Kushner.
537 **"In the end, if I have to pick"**: Nichols, interview by Bob Gazzale, for Nichols's American Film Institute Life Achievement Award, 2010, unpublished transcript.
537 **"the most powerful"**: Frank Rich, "Angels, Reagan, and AIDS in America," *New York Times,* November 16, 2003.
537 **"once again proving"**: Todd McCarthy, "Angels in America," *Variety,* December 1, 2003.
539 **"I directed *The Apple Tree*"**: Nichols, *Charlie Rose,* PBS, April 26, 2005.
540 **"They all knew the play"**: AI with Cary Brokaw.
540 **"It was painful"**: AI with Cary Brokaw.
540 **"I was so smitten"**: Nichols, interview by Chris Nashawaty for *Entertainment Weekly,* March 1, 2012, unpublished transcript.
540 **"I was beside myself"**: AI with Julia Roberts.
541 **"In making movies"**: Nichols, interview with *AARP, The Magazine,* January/February 2004.
541 **"He said he saw"**: AI with Natalie Portman.
541 **"was basically the four"**: AI with Clive Owen.
541 **"He said, 'We're all going'"**: AI with Natalie Portman.
541 **"She was very nervous"**: AI with Mary Bailey.
542 **"At the start of shooting"**: AI with Julia Roberts.
542 **"To me, it's about"**: Nichols, Nashwaty interview.
543 **"the physicality that he was"**: AI with Clive Owen.
543 **"He wants to see"**: "Page Six," *New York Post,* November 5, 2004.
543 **"What he did"**: AI with Natalie Portman.
543 **Their conversation soon**: Norma Stevens and Steven M. L. Aronson, *Avedon: Something Personal* (New York: Spiegel & Grau, 2017), 630.
544 **Avedon's assistant Norma**: Stevens and Aronson, *Avedon,* 629.
544 **He and Julia Roberts**: *Variety,* August 4, 2004.
544 **"Watching the two"**: AI with Carl Hiaasen.
544 **"Oh, shit! I have to do this"**: Bill Zehme, "King Mike and the Quest for the Broadway Grail," *New York,* March 14, 2005.

545   **"We [have] to have":** Zehme, "King Mike."
545   **"There is no story":** Nichols, *Charlie Rose*, PBS, April 26, 2005.
545   **Before he undertook:** AI with Cary Brokaw.
545   **"*Closer* was where":** AI with Scott Rudin.
546   **"There's only one rule":** Nichols, interview by Charlie Rose, *Charlie Rose*, aired on PBS, April 26, 2005.
546   **"Mike, I've been":** AI with Hank Azaria.
546   **"Casey did a demonstration":** AI with David Hyde Pierce.
547   **"not just the numbers":** AI with Hank Azaria.
547   **"If you don't take":** Eric Idle, *Always Look on the Bright Side of Life* (New York: Crown Archetype, 2018), 208.
547   **"Nobody should try":** AI with Scott Rudin.
548   **"just another feel-good":** A. O. Scott, "Who's Returning to Virginia Woolf?," *New York Times*, November 28, 2004.
548   **"all slick surfaces":** Kenneth Turan, "Love, Sadistically," *Los Angeles Times*, December 3, 2004.
548   **"It was not fated":** AI with Hank Azaria.
549   **"Always Look":** Idle, *Bright Side*, 206–8.
549   **"There was an incident":** AI with David Hyde Pierce.
549   **"He made that show":** AI with Peter Lawrence.
549   **"It broke the most":** Bill Zehme, "King Mike and the Quest for the Broadway Grail," *New York*, March 14, 2005.
550   **"They were two":** AI with Christian Borle.
550   **"It's a two-second delay":** "Guiding Principles for SPAMALOT (and Comedy in General) from Mike Nichols," unpublished memo, provided to author by B. T. McNicholl.
550   **"He would just skewer":** AI with Peter Lawrence.
550   **"He let people":** AI with Casey Nicholaw.
550   **"It was surprising":** AI with Christian Borle.
550   **"What he fundamentally did":** AI with David Hyde Pierce.
551   **"By then everyone":** AI with Christian Borle.
551   **"Go out there":** AI with David Hyde Pierce.
551   **"Nine out of ten":** AI with David Hyde Pierce.
552   **Portray human beings:** Nichols, "Guiding Principles for SPAMALOT."

CHAPTER THIRTY-FOUR: GOOD NIGHT, STARS

554   **"They had the same":** AI with Celia Costas.
554   **"People are forever":** Nichols, in discussion with Elaine May, Walter Reade Theater, Film Society of Lincoln Center, February 26, 2006.
555   **"The bottom line is":** AI with John Bloom.
555   **"In retrospect":** AI with Celia Costas.
555   **"He was crazy":** Richard L. Berke, "Sex! Drugs! (and Maybe a Little War)," *New York Times*, December 16, 2007.
556   **"As we got into it":** AI with Tom Hanks.
556   **In part, that was because:** Nichols, interview by Bob Gazzale, for Nichols's American Film Institute Life Achievement Award, 2010, unpublished transcript.
556   **"He had been a smoker":** AI with Tom Hanks.
557   **"I never should":** AI with Celia Costas.
557   **"We lost the whole thing":** AI with Stephen Goldblatt.
557   **"Our hotel rooms":** AI with Celia Costas.
557   **"We restaged a number":** AI with Tom Hanks.
558   **"I had to do":** AI with Julia Roberts.
558   **"the words came out":** Nichols, Gazzale interview.
558   **"He was so nice":** AI with Denis O'Hare.
558   **"That's really when":** AI with Tom Hanks.
559   **"Sorkin saw everything":** AI with Tom Hanks.
559   **"Charlie Wilson himself":** AI with Aaron Sorkin.
560   **Nichols labored through:** AI with John Bloom.
560   **"People who expect":** Nichols and Steven Soderbergh, DVD commentary, *The Graduate* (Irvington, NY: Criterion Collection, 2016), DVD.

562 **"I'll always be":** In 2011, Clooney produced, directed, co-wrote, and acted in a film version of *Farragut North* called *The Ides of March*, with Ryan Gosling in the role that had been considered by DiCaprio and Gyllenhaal.

562 **"Several months later":** AI with Beau Willimon.

562 **"It was a struggle":** AI with Peter Gallagher.

563 **"There is a kind":** AI with Remy Auberjonois.

563 **"There is great life":** Jon Robin Baitz, email to author, October 17, 2018.

563 **"Morgan's casting":** AI with Albert Wolsky.

564 **"Mike was not fully":** Jon Robin Baitz, email to author.

564 **"Well," Nichols said:** AI with B. T. McNicholl.

564 **"I will never forget":** Jon Robin Baitz, email to author.

564 **"dropping lines right and left":** AI with Walt Odets.

565 **"It hadn't occurred to him":** AI with Jack O'Brien.

565 **"How could this be?":** Ben Brantley, "Hungry for a Comeback, but Pretty Thirsty, Too," *New York Times*, April 28, 2008.

565 **"He sent a note":** AI with B. T. McNicholl.

566 **"Elaine came rushing":** AI with Nancy Fletcher.

566 **"Mike was, you know":** AI with Tom Hanks.

566 **"There was never a moment":** AI with Tony Kushner.

567 **"*The Country Girl* really":** AI with Scott Rudin.

567 **"He had just had the bypass":** AI with Matthew Weiner.

568 **He gathered a group:** AI with Lin-Manuel Miranda.

568 **"Oh, no, no, no":** AI with Meryl Streep.

568 **"Mike had a kind of":** AI with Patrizia von Brandenstein.

568 **"Every time I saw him":** AI with Tony Kushner.

569 **"We debated over":** AI with Rajendra Roy.

569 **"We sent save-the-date cards":** AI with Bob Gazzale.

569 **"You're not telling my story":** AI with Bob Gazzale.

569 **"I told him, 'Go watch'":** AI with Matthew Weiner.

570 **Nichols and Sawyer had fired:** AI with Jane Stanton Hitchcock.

570 **Roberts opened up the speeches:** American Film Institute Life Achievement Award gala, Tribute to Mike Nichols, June 10, 2020, unedited videotape provided by AFI.

CHAPTER THIRTY-FIVE: WAY OUT THERE IN THE BLUE

572 **"I'm aware that":** Nichols's texting and email style was often free of punctuation. In this case, I have added it for clarity.

573 **He had strived:** Mike Nichols to Linda Emond, email, September 23, 2010.

574 **"When he said":** AI with Scott Rudin.

574 **"I was in L.A.":** AI with Andrew Garfield.

574 **In the spring:** AI with Bob Gazzale.

574 **a life saver":** Nichols, quoted in Sophia Savage and Anne Thompson, "The Late Great John Calley: Businessman with Soul of Artist, Life Saver," Indiewire.com, September 13, 2011, https://www.indiewire.com/2011/09/the-late-great-john-calley-businessman-with-soul-of-artist-life-saver-184851/.

575 **"Forgetting names was frustrating":** AI with Tom Fontana.

575 **"We don't go anywhere":** Nichols, interview by Chris Nashawaty for *Entertainment Weekly*, March 1, 2012, unpublished transcript.

575 **"When his son":** AI with Celia Costas.

575 **"may be the Messiah":** Mike Nichols to Linda Emond, email, September 21, 2012.

575 **"I remember the process":** AI with Finn Wittrock.

575 **"I do [tell stories], to an":** Nichols, interview by James Lipton, *Inside the Actors Studio*, 1997.

576 **"I could sense that":** AI with Finn Wittrock.

576 **"There was seemingly":** AI with Andrew Garfield.

576 **"He created an environment":** AI with Linda Emond.

576 **"We really listened":** AI with Bill Camp.

576 **"Safety is such a huge":** AI with Scott Rudin.

577 **"There were times":** AI with Finn Wittrock.

577 "You can't really say": AI with Scott Rudin.

577 "And he did": AI with Scott Rudin.

578 When that happened: AI with Kathy Hendrickson.

578 "I noticed a couple of times": AI with Andrew Garfield.

578 "There were times when": AI with Mimi O'Donnell.

578 "his style was conversational": AI with Rebecca Miller.

579 "Phil seemed like": AI with Matthew Stern.

579 "Mike had this phobia": AI with Finn Wittrock.

579 "an immaculate monument": Ben Brantley, "American Dreamer: Ambushed by the Territory," *New York Times*, March 16, 2012.

580 "the genius of Mr. Nichols's": Terry Teachout, "A Smile, a Shoeshine," *Wall Street Journal*, March 16, 2012.

580 "Nichols's unequivocal admiration for": Marilyn Stasio, "Death of a Salesman," *Variety*, March 16, 2012.

580 "an astonishingly good time": AI with Scott Rudin.

580 "The part was brutal": AI with Mimi O'Donnell.

580 Before his last scene: AI with Finn Wittrock.

580 "He would drink": AI with Mimi O'Donnell.

581 "I saw him backstage": AI with Tony Roberts.

581 "I stayed out": Mike Nichols to Linda Emond, text, March 14, 2012.

581 "I was surprised": AI with David Rabe.

581 "That was the only": AI with Scott Rudin.

582 "As always, she": Mike Nichols to Linda Emond, email, June 26. 2012.

582 "It was so much fun": AI with Ebs Burnough.

583 "At one point": AI with Ian MacNeil.

584 "It's a nasty piece": AI with Brian MacDevitt.

584 "It was Mike doing": AI with Scott Rudin.

584 "It was bumpy": AI with Brian MacDevitt.

584 *Betrayal* is like": AI with Scott Rudin.

585 "has been infused": Chris Jones, "Pinter's 'Betrayal' Ages Well," *Chicago Tribune*, October 27, 2013.

585 "crude and clunky": Ben Brantley, "Threesome to Tantalize and Behold," *New York Times*, October 27, 2013.

585 "He was home": AI with Candice Bergen.

585 "Nobody ever enjoyed food": AI with Scott Rudin.

585 "I can't stop": Mike Nichols to Linda Emond, email, March 26, 2014.

586 "Think of the marquee": AI with Tom Hanks.

586 "Diane called me": AI with Scott Rudin.

586 "Of course I said": AI with Eric Fischl.

587 Nichols started spending time: Mike Nichols, conversation with author.

587 "Mike encouraged me": AI with Matthew Weiner.

587 "It never occurred to me": AI with Scott Rudin.

587 "His quips and asides": Meryl Streep, email to author, April 4, 2019.

588 "It was fantastic": AI with Cynthia Nixon.

588 "I wrote to him": AI with Patricia Scot Yorton.

589 He and Sawyer: AI with Lorne Michaels.

589 "Just promise me": AI with John Patrick Shanley.

589 He had rehearsed: AI with Wallace Shawn and Larry Pine.

589 He told her that: AI with Candice Bergen.

589 After lunch, he went: AI with Tracey Jackson.

589 And he and Sawyer: AI with Terrence McNally.

EPILOGUE

594 "I don't care about": C. Robert Jennings, "The *Playboy* Interview: Mike Nichols," *Playboy*, June 1966.

Bibliography

NONFICTION

Amburn, Ellis. *The Sexiest Man Alive: A Biography of Warren Beatty*. New York: HarperEntertainment, 2002.

Ann-Margret with Todd Gold. *Ann-Margret: My Story*. New York: G. P. Putnam's Sons, 1994.

Arkin, Alan. *An Improvised Life: A Memoir*. New York: Da Capo Press, 2011.

Ashley, Elizabeth, with Ross Firestone. *Actress: Postcards from the Road*. New York: M. Evans, 1978.

Avrich, Paul. *Anarchist Voices: An Oral History of Anarchism in America*. Chico, CA: AK Press, 2005.

Baker, Carroll. *Baby Doll: An Autobiography*. New York: Arbor House, 1983.

Barnett, David. *A History of the Berliner Ensemble*. Cambridge: Cambridge University Press, 2015.

Barthel, Joan. *A Death in Canaan*. New York: Thomas Congdon/E. P. Dutton, 1976.

Bego, Mark. *Cher: If You Believe*. New York: Taylor, 2004.

Bergen, Candice. *Knock Wood*. New York: Linden Press/Simon & Schuster, 1984.

Bernstein, Jamie. *Famous Father Girl: A Memoir of Growing Up Bernstein*. New York: Harper, 2018.

Biskind, Peter. *Easy Riders, Raging Bulls: How the Sex-Drugs-and-Rock 'n' Roll Generation Saved Hollywood*. New York: Simon & Schuster, 1998.

———. *Star: How Warren Beatty Seduced America*. New York: Simon & Schuster, 2010.

Bosworth, Patricia. *Jane Fonda: The Private Life of a Public Woman*. New York: Houghton Mifflin Harcourt, 2011.

Bragg, Melvyn. *Rich: The Life of Richard Burton*. London: Hodder & Stoughton, 1988.

Breglio, John. *I Wanna Be a Producer: How to Make a Killing on Broadway . . . or Get Killed*. Milwaukee: Applause, 2016.

Brooks, Tim, and Earle Marsh. *The Complete Directory to Prime Time Network and Cable TV Shows 1946–Present*. 9th ed. New York: Ballantine, 2007.

Burton, Richard. *The Richard Burton Diaries*. Edited by Chris Williams. New Haven: Yale University Press, 2012.

Butler, Isaac, and Dan Kois. *The World Only Spins Forward: The Ascent of "Angels in America."* New York: Bloomsbury, 2018.

Callan, Michael Feeney. *Robert Redford: The Biography*. New York: Alfred A. Knopf, 2011.

Charnin, Martin. *"Annie": A Theatre Memoir*. New York: E. P. Dutton, 1977.

Cher. *The First Time*. New York: Simon & Schuster, 1998.

Cohen, Richard. *She Made Me Laugh: My Friend Nora Ephron*. New York: Simon & Schuster, 2016.

Coleman, Janet. *The Compass: The Improvisational Theatre That Revolutionized American Comedy*. Chicago: University of Chicago Press, 1991.

Crile, George. *Charlie Wilson's War: The Extraordinary Story of the Largest Covert Operation in History*. New York: Atlantic Monthly Press, 2003.

Daugherty, Tracy. *Just One Catch: A Biography of Joseph Heller*. New York: St. Martin's, 2011.

Davis, Michael. *Street Gang: The Complete History of Sesame Street*. New York: Viking, 2008.

Davis, Stephen. *More Room in a Broken Heart: The True Adventures of Carly Simon*. New York: Gotham, 2012.

Edelman, Rob, and Audrey Kupferberg. *Matthau: A Life*. Lanham, MD: Taylor, 2002.

Falk, Peter. *Just One More Thing*. New York: Carroll & Graf, 2006.

Feibleman, Peter. *Lilly: Reminiscences of Lillian Hellman*. New York: William Morrow, 1988.

Feiffer, Jules. *Backing into Forward: A Memoir*. New York: Nan A. Talese/Doubleday, 2010.

Feinstein, Michael. *Nice Work If You Can Get It: My Life in Rhythm and Rhyme.* New York: Hyperion, 1995.

Filichia, Peter. *The Great Parade: Broadway's Astonishing, Never-to-Be-Forgotten 1963–64 Season.* New York: St. Martin's, 2015.

Finstad, Suzanne. *Warren Beatty: A Private Man.* New York: Harmony, 2005.

Ford, Luke. *The Producers: Profiles in Frustration.* Lincoln, NE: iUniverse, 2004.

Fraser-Cavassoni, Natasha. *Sam Spiegel.* New York: Simon & Schuster, 2003.

Garfunkel, Art. *What Is It All but Luminous: Notes from an Underground Man.* New York: Alfred A. Knopf, 2017.

Gavin, John. *Intimate Nights: The Golden Age of New York Cabaret.* Rev. ed. New York: Back Stage Books, 2006.

Goldman, William. *Adventures in the Screen Trade.* New York: Warner Books, 1983.

———. *The Season: A Candid Look at Broadway.* New York: Harcourt, Brace & World, 1969.

Grant, Lee. *I Said Yes to Everything: A Memoir.* New York: Blue Rider Press, 2014.

Grodin, Charles. *We're Ready for You, Mr. Grodin: Behind the Scenes at Talk Shows, Movies, and Elsewhere.* New York: Charles Scribner's Sons, 1994.

Gurock, Jeffrey S. *City of Promises: A History of the Jews of New York,* vol. 3: *Jews in Gotham—New York Jews in a Changing City, 1920–2010.* New York: New York University Press, 2012.

Gussow, Mel. *Edward Albee: A Singular Journey.* New York: Applause Books, 2001.

Harris, Mark. *Pictures at a Revolution: Five Movies and the Birth of the New Hollywood.* New York: Penguin Press, 2008.

Hart, Dennis. *Monitor (Take 2): The Revised, Expanded Inside Story of Network Radio's Greatest Program.* Lincoln, NE: iUniverse: 2003.

Heilbrun, Carolyn G. *The Education of a Woman: The Life of Gloria Steinem.* New York: Dial Press, 1995.

Hirshey, Gerri. *Not Pretty Enough: The Unlikely Triumph of Helen Gurley Brown.* New York: Sarah Crichton Books, 2016.

Hischak, Thomas S. *American Theatre: A Chronicle of Comedy and Drama, 1969–2000.* Oxford: Oxford University Press, 2001.

Hofler, Robert. *Party Animals: A Hollywood Tale of Sex, Drugs, and Rock 'n' Roll Starring the Fabulous Allan Carr.* New York: Da Capo Press, 2010.

Hunter, Allan. *Walter Matthau.* New York: St. Martin's, 1984.

Hyman, Ruth Link-Salinger. *Gustav Landauer: Philosopher of Utopia.* Indianapolis: Hackett, 1977.

Idle, Eric. *Always Look on the Bright Side of Life.* New York: Crown Archetype, 2018.

Itzkoff, Dave. *Robin.* New York: Henry Holt, 2018.

Johnson, Diane. *Flyover Lives.* New York: Viking, 2014.

Kael, Pauline. *Deeper into Movies.* New York: Warner Books, 1973.

Kazan, Elia. *A Life.* New York: Alfred A. Knopf, 1988.

Kessler-Harris, Alice. *A Difficult Woman: The Challenging Life and Times of Lillian Hellman.* New York: Bloomsbury, 2012.

Kiley, Frederick, and Walter McDonald, eds. *A "Catch-22" Casebook.* New York: Thomas Y. Crowell, 1973.

Kuhn, Gabriel, ed. Gustav Landauer: *Revolution and Other Writings: A Political Reader.* Oakland, CA: PM Press, 2010.

Kurtz, Swoosie. *Part Swan, Part Goose: An Uncommon Memoir of Womanhood, Work, and Family.* New York: Tarcher-Perigee, 2014.

Leaming, Barbara. *Orson Welles.* New York: Viking, 1985.

———. *Polanski: A Biography—The Filmmaker as Voyeur.* New York: Simon & Schuster, 1981.

Levy, Shawn. *De Niro: A Life.* New York: Crown Archetype, 2014.

Linson, Art. *A Pound of Flesh: Perilous Tales of How to Produce Movies in Hollywood.* New York: Grove, 1993.

Mann, William J. *How to Be a Movie Star: Elizabeth Taylor in Hollywood.* New York: Mariner Books, 2009.

Martinson, Deborah. *Lillian Hellman: A Life with Scoundrels and Foxes.* New York: Counterpoint, 2005.

McGilligan, Patrick. *Jack's Life: A Biography of Jack Nicholson.* New York: W. W. Norton, 1994.

Moreno, Rita. *Rita Moreno: A Memoir.* New York: Celebra, 2013.

Nachman, Gerald. *Seriously Funny: The Rebel Comedians of the 1950s and 1960s.* New York: Back Stage Books, 2004.

Nadel, Ira. *Tom Stoppard: A Life.* New York: Palgrave Macmillan, 2002.

O'Steen, Sam, as told to Bobbie O'Steen. *Cut to the Chase: Forty-five Years of Editing America's Favorite Movies.* Studio City, CA: Michael Wiese Productions, 2001.

Ostrow, Stuart. *Present at the Creation, Leaping in the Dark, and Going Against the Grain: "1776," "Pippin," "M. Butterfly," "La Bête" and Other Broadway Adventures.* New York: Applause Books, 2006.

Radner, Gilda. *It's Always Something.* New York: Simon & Schuster, 1989.

Rollyson, Carl. *Lillian Hellman: Her Legend and Her Legacy.* New York: St. Martin's, 1988.

Schickel, Richard. *Elia Kazan: A Biography*. New York: HarperCollins, 2005.

Shales, Tom, and James Andrew Miller. *Live from New York: An Uncensored History of "Saturday Night Live."* New York: Little, Brown, 2002.

Shearer, Steven Michael. *Patricia Neal: An Unquiet Life*. Lexington: University Press of Kentucky, 2006.

Sheward, David. *Rage and Glory: The Volatile Life and Career of George C. Scott*. New York: Applause Books, 2008.

Simmons, Matty. *Fat, Drunk, and Stupid: The Inside Story Behind the Making of "Animal House."* New York: St. Martin's, 2012.

Simon, John. *Reverse Angle: A Decade of American Films*. New York: Clarkson N. Potter, 1982.

Simon, Neil. *The Play Goes On: A Memoir*. New York: Touchstone, 2002.

———. *Rewrites: A Memoir*. New York: Touchstone, 1998.

Spolin, Viola. *Improvisation for the Theater: A Handbook of Teaching and Directing Techniques*. 3rd ed. Evanston: Northwestern University Press, 1999.

Stapleton, Maureen, and Jane Scovell. *A Hell of a Life: An Autobiography*. New York: Simon & Schuster, 1995.

Starr, Michael Seth. *Art Carney: A Biography*. New York: Fromm International, 1997.

Steinberg, Cobbett. *Reel Facts: The Movie Book of Records*. New York: Vintage, 1978.

Stevens, Kyle. *Mike Nichols: Sex, Language, and the Reinvention of Psychological Realism*. New York: Oxford University Press, 2015.

Stevens, Norma, and Steven M. L. Aronson. *Avedon: Something Personal*. New York: Spiegel & Grau, 2017.

Strouse, Charles. *Put on a Happy Face: A Broadway Memoir*. New York: Union Square, 2008.

Sweet, Jeffrey. *Something Wonderful Right Away: An Oral History of the Second City & the Compass Players*. Montclair, NJ: Limelight Editions, 1978.

Toobin, Jerome. *Agitato: A Trek Through the Musical Jungle*. New York: Viking, 1975.

Turan, Kenneth, and Joseph Papp. *Free for All: Joe Papp, the Public, and the Greatest Theater Story Ever Told*. New York: Doubleday, 2009.

Tynan, Kathleen. *The Life of Kenneth Tynan*. New York: William Morrow, 1987.

Tynan, Kenneth. *The Diaries of Kenneth Tynan*. Edited by John Lahr. New York: Bloomsbury, 2001.

Valenti, Jack. *This Time, This Place: My Life in War, the White House, and Hollywood*. New York: Harmony Books, 2007.

Wanger, Walter, and Joe Hyams. *My Life with Cleopatra: The Making of a Hollywood Classic*. 1963. New York: Vintage, 2013.

Wasson, Sam. *Improv Nation: How We Made a Great American Art*. New York: Houghton Mifflin Harcourt, 2017.

Weisberg, Jessica. *Asking for a Friend: Three Centuries of Advice on Life, Love, Money, and Other Burning Questions from a Nation Obsessed*. New York: Nation Books, 2018.

Weller, Sheila. *The News Sorority: Diane Sawyer, Katie Couric, Christiane Amanpour—and the (Ongoing, Imperfect, Complicated) Triumph of Women in TV News*. New York: Penguin Press, 2014.

Welles, Orson, and Peter Bogdanovich. *This Is Orson Welles*. New York: HarperCollins, 1992.

Whitehead, J. W. *Mike Nichols and the Cinema of Transformation*. Jefferson, NC: McFarland, 2014.

Wilson, Edmund. *The Sixties: The Last Journal, 1960–1972*. Edited by Lewis M. Dabney. New York: Farrar, Straus and Giroux, 1993.

Winecoff, Charles. *Split Image: The Life of Anthony Perkins*. New York: E. P. Dutton, 1996.

Wright, William. *Lillian Hellman: The Image, the Woman*. New York: Simon & Schuster, 1986.

FICTION

Anonymous [Joe Klein]. *Primary Colors*. New York: Random House, 1996.

Ephron, Nora. *Heartburn*. New York: Alfred A. Knopf, 1983.

Fisher, Carrie. *Postcards from the Edge*. New York: Simon & Schuster, 1987.

Friedman, Bruce Jay. *The Collected Short Fiction of Bruce Jay Friedman*. New York: Grove, 1997.

Gough, Simon. *The White Goddess: An Encounter*. Norwich, UK: Galley Beggar Press, 2012.

Heller, Joseph. *Catch-22*. 1961. 50th anniversary ed. New York: Simon & Schuster Paperbacks, 2011.

Ishiguro, Kazuo. *The Remains of the Day*. New York: Alfred A. Knopf, 1989.

Merle, Robert. *The Day of the Dolphin*. Translated by Helen Weaver. New York: Simon & Schuster, 1969.

PLAYS

Beckett, Samuel. *Waiting for Godot: A Tragicomedy in Two Acts*. Translated by the author. New York: Grove, 1954.

Bock, Jerry. *The Apple Tree: A New Musical*. Random House: New York, 1967.

Chekhov, Anton. *The Seagull*. Translated by Richard Nelson, Richard Pevear, and Larissa Volokhonsky. New York: Theatre Communications, 2017.

Chekhov, Anton. *The Seagull*. Adapted by Tom Stoppard. New York: Farrar, Straus and Giroux, 1997.

Coburn, D. L. *The Gin Game.* New York: Samuel French, 1977.

Doctorow, E. L. *Drinks Before Dinner.* New York: Theatre Communications, 1996.

Dorfman, Ariel. *Death and the Maiden.* New York: Penguin, 1994.

Edson, Margaret. *Wit.* New York: Farrar, Straus and Giroux, 1999.

Feiffer, Jules. *Elliot Loves.* New York: Grove, 1990.

Jellicoe, Ann. *The Knack.* New York: Samuel French, 1958.

Kushner, Tony. *Angels in America.* New York: Theatre Communications, 1995.

Marber, Patrick. *Closer.* New York: Grove, 1999.

May, Elaine. *Taller Than a Dwarf: A Samuel French Acting Edition.* New York: Samuel French, 1999.

Miller, Arthur. *Collected Plays 1944–1961.* New York: Library of America, 2006.

Pinter, Harold. *Betrayal.* New York: Dramatists Play Service, 1978.

Rabe, David. *Hurlyburly.* New York: Samuel French, 1985.

———. *The Vietnam Plays: Streamers and the Orphan.* New York: Grove, 1994.

Schisgal, Murray. *Luv.* New York: Dramatists Play Service, 1963.

Shawn, Wallace. *The Designated Mourner.* New York: Farrar, Straus and Giroux, 1996.

Simon, Neil. *Barefoot in the Park.* Samuel French Acting Edition. New York: Samuel French, 1964.

———. *The Collected Plays of Neil Simon.* 2 vols. New York: Plume, 1986.

———. *Fools: A Comic Fable.* Samuel French Acting Edition. New York: Samuel French, 1981.

———. *The Odd Couple.* Samuel French Acting Edition. New York: Samuel French, 1966.

All video and web material used in the book is cited in the endnotes.

Works by Mike Nichols

FILM AND TELEVISION (AS DIRECTOR)

Who's Afraid of Virginia Woolf? (1966)
The Graduate (1967)
Catch-22 (1970)
Carnal Knowledge (1971) **(P)**
The Day of the Dolphin (1973)
The Fortune (1975) **(P)**
Gilda Live (1980)
Silkwood (1983) **(P)**
Heartburn (1986) **(P)**
Biloxi Blues (1988)
Working Girl (1988)
Postcards from the Edge (1990) **(P)**
Regarding Henry (1991) **(P)**
Wolf (1994)
The Birdcage (1996) **(P)**
Primary Colors (1998) **(P)**
What Planet Are You From? (2000) **(P)**
Wit (2001) **(P)**
Angels in America (2003) **(P)**
Closer (2004) **(P)**
Charlie Wilson's War (2007)

THEATER (AS DIRECTOR, EXCEPT WHERE NOTED)

An Evening with Mike Nichols and Elaine May (Broadway, 1960) **(A)**
The World of Jules Feiffer (summer stock, 1962)
Barefoot in the Park (Broadway, 1963)

Key to Abbreviations
(A) = actor • **(P)** = also producer

The Knack (Off-Broadway, 1964)

Luv (Broadway, 1964)

The Odd Couple (Broadway, 1965)

The Apple Tree (Broadway, 1966)

The Little Foxes (Broadway, 1967)

Plaza Suite (Broadway, 1968)

The Prisoner of Second Avenue (Broadway, 1971)

Uncle Vanya (Broadway, 1973)

Streamers (Broadway, 1976)

Comedians (Broadway, 1976)

The Gin Game (Broadway, 1977)

Annie (Broadway, 1977) **(PP)**

Drinks Before Dinner (Off-Broadway, 1978)

Billy Bishop Goes to War (Broadway, 1980) **(PP)**

Who's Afraid of Virginia Woolf? (Long Wharf, 1980) **(A)**

Lunch Hour (Broadway, 1980)

Fools (Broadway, 1981)

Grown-Ups (Broadway, 1981) **(PP)**

My One and Only (Broadway, 1983) **(DU)**

The Real Thing (Broadway, 1984)

Hurlyburly (Broadway, 1984)

Whoopi Goldberg (Broadway, 1984) **(DU***)***

Social Security (Broadway, 1986)

Standup Shakespeare (Off-Broadway, 1987)

Waiting for Godot (Off-Broadway, 1988)

Elliot Loves (Off-Broadway, 1990)

Death and the Maiden (Broadway, 1992)

Word of Mouth (Off-Broadway, 1995) **(PP***)***

The Designated Mourner (London, 1996) **(A)**

James Naughton: Street of Dreams (Off-Broadway, 1999) **(PP)**

The Seagull (Central Park, 2001)

The Play What I Wrote (Broadway, 2003) **(PP)**

Whoopi (Broadway, 2004) **(PP)**

Spamalot (Broadway, 2005)

On the Line (Off-Broadway, 2006) **(PP)**

The Country Girl (Broadway, 2008)

Death of a Salesman (Broadway, 2012)

Betrayal (Broadway, 2013)

RECORDINGS

Improvisations to Music (1959)

An Evening with Mike Nichols and Elaine May (1961)

Mike Nichols & Elaine May Examine Doctors (1962)

Key to Abbreviations

(A) = actor • **(DU)** = direction uncredited • **(PP)** = producer or presenter

Image Credits

Index

Abbott, George, 123
ABC Motion Pictures, 360–61, 363, 371, 381
ABC News, 5–7, 500, 570, 587
ABC-TV, 320–21, 443
Abraham, F. Murray, 425, 438, 440
Abrams, J. J. (Jeffrey), 453–54
Actors Studio, 42
Adler, Jerry, 201, 202, 204, 325–27
AIDS:
  and *Angels in America*, 514, 515, 528, 531, 532, 538
  and *The Birdcage*, 479
  and *Friends in Deed*, 467, 528
  and *The Normal Heart*, 393–94
  and *Wolf*, 472, 477
Aiello, Danny, 389
Ain't Misbehavin' (musical), 373
Albee, Edward:
  and *A Delicate Balance*, 591
  use of language by, 157, 265
  and *Who's Afraid of Virginia Woolf?*, 121, 153, 157, 171, 181, 192, 343, 347
Alda, Alan, 199–200, 202, 206
Algren, Nelson, 239
Alice in Wonderland (theater), 334
Allen, Brooke, 327
Allen, Jay Presson, 321, 324, 355, 356, 440
Allen, Kamian "Mikki," 455
Allen, Lewis, 291, 324, 373, 440
Allen, Steve, 75–76, 77, 79
Allen, Woody, 369
Allende, Salvador, 462
All in the Family (TV), 271
All the President's Men (film), 359
All the Pretty Horses (film), 470, 499
Alonzo, John, 296
Altman, Robert, 258, 312, 514–15
"Always Look on the Bright Side of Life" (song), 548, 570
"Amazing Grace" (song), 381
American Beauty (film), 499

American Family, An (PBS-TV), 321
American Film Institute, Life Achievement Awards, 544, 569
American Tragedy, An (film), 32
Anderson, Dame Judith, 285
Andrews, Julie, 105, 113, 150, 584
Angels in America (film), 522, 523–36, 540, 570
  actors playing multiple roles in, 515–16
  and AIDS, 514, 515, 528, 531, 532, 538
  awards for, 538
  casting of, 514, 523–26
  and Kushner, 513, 514–16, 523–24, 525, 527, 528, 530, 534, 536, 537
  Millennium Approaches (part 1), 513, 527
  Perestroika (part 2), 513, 527
  rehearsals for, 528–29
  reviews of, 537–38
  screenplay for, 513, 514, 526–27
  shooting of, 529–36
  and Streep, 516, 523, 524, 529, 531, 533, 535, 536, 538
  themes of, 515, 527
Annie (musical), 324–25, 327–28, 339, 416, 539
Ann-Margret, 263–64, 267–69, 272
Apple Tree, The (musical), 198–202, 209, 223, 231, 539
Arianda, Nina, 589
Arkin, Alan, 204
  and *Catch-22*, 243, 245, 246, 248–49, 251, 253, 262
  and *Enter Laughing*, 148
  and *Luv*, 149, 157
Arlen, Alice, 359–60, 362, 366, 383
Arrick, Larry, 63
Asher, Aaron, 28, 40
Ashley, Elizabeth, 122–24, 127–34, 138, 139, 145, 302
Ashley, Ted, 340
Asner, Ed, 31, 39, 51
Assassins (musical), 543

Astor, Brooke, 335
Atkins, Eileen, 511, 512
Auberjonois, Remy, 563
Avedon, Richard, 111, 112, 284, 333, 431, 489–90,
    570, 594
    death of, 543–44
    and *The Fabulous Fifties*, 91
    and lifestyle, 91, 92–93, 98, 146, 169, 299, 313
    Nichols's friendship with, 91, 115n, 414, 543–44
    and photography, 97, 104, 114–15, 176
Azaria, Hank, 481, 484, 544, 546–47, 548, 550
Azenberg, Emanuel, 384, 385

Bacall, Lauren, 104
Bailey, Mary, 430, 475, 495, 503, 511, 533–34,
    541, 555
Baitz, Jon Robin, 563, 564
Baker, Carroll, 44, 45
Balaban, Bob, 232, 589
    and *Catch-22*, 242, 246–47, 251
    and Scott, 233, 234
Baldwin, Alec, 428–29
Baldwin, Billy, 169
Baldwin, James, 167, 224
Ball, Lucille, 100
Balsam, Martin, 246, 247, 249
Bancroft, Anne, 204, 593
    and *The Graduate*, 206, 208, 209–10, 213–14, 216,
        222, 229
    and *The Little Foxes*, 223, 225, 226
Baranski, Christine, 378, 384, 389, 449, 482, 538
Barefoot in the Park (theater), 137–38, 372,
    421, 581
    and awards, 145
    Broadway opening of, 134
    in Bucks County, 122, 125–26, 127, 128
    casting of, 122–25
    comparisons with, 159, 208, 223
    effects of, 143, 147, 274
    film rights to, 142
    Nichols's life transformed by, 126, 136, 141, 151
    Nichols's work with actors on, 126, 127, 128, 130,
        131–33, 161
    "Nichols touch" in, 135, 317
    as *Nobody Loves Me*, 122–26
    and Redford, 124–25, 127, 128, 130–35
    rehearsals for, 125–28
    reviews of, 132, 135, 141, 145, 147
    as success, 152, 165
    on tour, 142, 148–49
Barnes, Clive, 277, 384, 439
Barrymore, John, 350
Bates, Kathy, 494, 496–97, 498
Bawer, Bruce, 486
Beale, Simon Russell, 518
Beatty, Warren, 176, 202, 320, 322, 323, 501, 570
    and *The Fortune*, 294, 295, 296, 301
    and *Grand Hotel*, 350

and Nichols and May performance, 281, 327
    and *Reds*, 324
Beckett, Samuel, 204, 424, 425, 437–38, 439
Bedford, Brian, 425
Behan, Brendan, 108
Belafonte, Harry, 100, 167
Bening, Annette, 455, 501, 504, 508
Benjamin, Richard, 148, 242, 245, 246, 255
Bennett, Michael, 334, 374
Bentley, Wes, 517
Benton, Richard, 150
Benton, Robert, 369
Bergen, Candice, 570, 584, 585
    and *Carnal Knowledge*, 263, 265–66, 267
    and *The Graduate*, 205, 263
    and *Hurlyburly*, 389
    on Nichols's lifestyle, 311–12, 313, 322, 324, 413,
        500, 589
    and Nichols's marriages, 324, 422
    and *Saturday Night Live*, 313
    tributes to Nichols from, 502, 538
Bergman, Andrew, 394, 404, 405, 406
Berkowitz, Bernard, 255, 256
Berle, Milton, 85
Berlin, Jack and Ida, 36
Berlin International Film Festival, 516
Berman, Shelley, 53, 60, 63, 64–65
Bernstein, Carl, 359, 372, 396–97, 404, 410
Bernstein, Felicia Montealegre, 91, 111, 129, 188,
    235, 327, 332–33
Bernstein, Jamie, 332
Bernstein, Leonard, 332
    and Nichols's work, 91, 121
    and politics, 167, 235
    socializing with, 104, 111, 129, 188, 327
    at Tanglewood, 24
    and *West Side Story*, 79
Bertolucci, Bernardo, 302
Best Years of our Lives, The (film), 321
Betrayal (film), 349, 350–51, 375, 453
Betrayal (theater), 539, 583–85
Better Part of Valor, The (May), 90
Bill, Tony, 206
Billy Bishop Goes to War (theater), 349
Biloxi Blues (film), 425, 428, 483
    casting of, 417, 419
    Nichols's directorial style for, 419, 459
    reviews of, 426
    and Simon, 416, 417–20, 426
Birdcage, The (film), 479–87, 488, 526
Black, Karen, 263
Blanchett, Cate, 540
"Blob, The" (song), 104–5
Bloom, John, 511, 555, 560
Blue Angel, New York, 70, 72–74, 78, 79, 82, 83,
    85, 98
Bly, Robert, 471
Bobbitts, 468

Bock, Jerry, 198–99
Bogart Slept Here (film), 303–6
    casting of, 304
    film shut down by Warner Bros., 306, 313,
        314, 400
    as *The Goodbye Girl*, 353
    and Simon, 301–2, 304, 305, 417
Bogdanovich, Peter, 249
Bonaparte, Napoleon, 422
Bonerz, Peter, 244, 245–46, 248, 249, 250
Bookman, Bob, 360, 361
Borle, Christian, 550, 551
Bowen, Roger, 52
Boyar, Sully, 516
Bracken, Eddie, 191
Branagh, Kenneth, 458
Brandenstein, Patrizia von:
    and *Hope Springs*, 568
    and *Postcards from the Edge*, 446, 448
    and *Silkwood*, 362, 363, 364, 366
    and *Working Girl*, 430
Brando, Marlon, 24–25, 42, 263, 359
Brantley, Ben, 579, 585
Brecht, Bertolt, 203
Breglio, John, 355, 356
Brickell, Edie, 589
Bridges, James, 426
Brinkley, David, 229
Broderick, James, 321
Broderick, Matthew, 321, 417–19, 432, 502, 518, 521
Brodkey, Harold, 111
Brody, Adrien, 525
Brokaw, Cary:
    and *Angels in America*, 513, 514–15, 534
    and *Closer*, 539–40, 545
    and *What Planet Are You From?*, 503
    and *Wit*, 509, 510, 512
Brooks, Albert, 502
Brooks, James L., 592
Brooks, Mel, 197, 209, 216
Broussard, Rebecca, 474
Brown, Arvin, 317–18, 343–45, 346
Brown, David, 277
Brown, Helen Gurley, 277
Brown, Joanna, 111–12, 113
Browne, Roscoe Lee, 374
Bruce, Lenny, 81, 101
Brustein, Robert, 101, 203
Buchanan, Pat, 479
Burnett, Carol, 113
Burnham, David, 381
Burnough, Ebs, 583
Burstyn, Ellen, 263
Burton, Richard, 122, 288, 593
    alcohol consumption of, 183, 185, 231, 563
    and *Camelot*, 105, 539
    Nichols working with, 179, 180, 183, 184–85
    socializing, 113, 241
    and Taylor, 113, 114, 153, 174–75, 177–78, 241
    and *Who's Afraid of Virginia Woolf?*, 153, 170, 171,
        174, 175, 177–78, 180–81, 182–87, 189, 192,
        195, 348
Burton, Sybil, 113, 141
Bush, George H. W., 443
But Never Jam Today (theater), 334
Bye Bye Birdie (musical), 89
Byrne, Anne, 228

Cabaret (musical), 321
Callas, Margot, 127, 133, 137, 138
    and daughter Daisy, 145, 193, 261, 291, 300
    end of marriage, 145–46, 161, 299–300
    marriage of Nichols and, 129, 193, 261
    and Nichols's work, 144–45
Callender, Colin, 509
Calley, John, 270, 461, 594
    and *Bogart Slept Here*, 304, 306
    and *Catch-22*, 239, 241, 242–43, 245, 248, 257–58
    death of, 574
    and *Exorcist*, 278, 292–93
    and *La Cage/Birdcage*, 478–79
    Nichols's friendship with, 239, 413, 543
    and Sony, 501
    and United Artists, 478–79
    and Warner Bros., 278, 304, 306, 340
    and *What Planet Are You From?*, 501
Camp, Bill, 576
Canby, Vincent, 188–89, 259, 270–72, 303, 382,
    410, 426
Capote, Truman, 92, 188, 409
Carlin, Joy, 31, 42, 43, 45, 46, 47, 216
Carnal Knowledge (film), 262–72, 274, 294, 474
    casting of, 262–64
    and changing culture, 262, 271–72
    comparisons with, 300, 350, 367, 401, 539
    and Feiffer, 261–63, 264, 265, 268, 269–70,
        272, 448
    and Nicholson, 264–67, 268, 278, 294, 367, 401
    Nichols's direction of, 264–69, 298, 459
    reviews of, 269–72
    success of, 271–72, 278, 307
    as *True Confessions*, 261–62
Carney, Art, 594
    alcohol consumption of, 159, 231, 563
    and *The Odd Couple*, 159–60, 161, 163, 164,
        190–91
    and *Take Her, She's Mine*, 123
Caron, Jerry, 467
Caron, Leslie, 236
Carpetbaggers, The (film), 130–31
Carr, Allan, 355, 356, 478–79
Carroll, Vinnette, 334
Carson, Johnny, 428
Carter, Jimmy, 327
Carter, Lillian, 327
Carville, James, 494

Cash, Johnny, 529
Catch-22 (film), 227, 239–53, 255–61, 270, 272, 359,
    366, 368, 574
    and Arkin, 243, 245, 246, 248–49, 251, 253, 262
    and the book, 189, 195, 239–40
    casting of, 242–52, 260, 312
    and drug use, 248
    *M*A*S*H* as competition with, 257–58, 260
    negative effects of, 278, 383
    and Nichols's detractors, 256–57, 260, 262
    Nichols's hindsight about, 260–61, 264
    postproduction on, 257, 259
    reviews of, 259–60
    screenplay for, 239, 240–41, 243, 259
    shooting of, 241–42, 244–54, 255
    wrap of, 252–53
Catch-22 (Heller), 189, 195, 239–40
Channing, Stockard, 295, 296, 303, 402
Charles, Josh, 589
Charles, Ray, 446
Charlie Wilson's War (film), 556–60
Charnin, Martin, 325
Chase, David, 516, 567
Chekhov, Anton:
    and improvisation, 108
    Nichols's ambition to direct, 204, 290, 384, 424
    and *The Seagull*, 508, 521, 522
    and *Uncle Vanya*, 287, 288, 290
Cher, 295, 363, 366, 367, 369, 370, 383, 428, 570
Children's Hour, The (theater), 42
China Syndrome, The (film), 358, 426
Chinatown (film), 278, 294, 296, 298, 416
Chorus Line, A (musical), 334
Christie, Julie, 286, 287
Cimino, Michael, 369
Citizen Kane (film), 249
Clayburgh, Jill, 315
Cleopatra (film), 113, 174
Clift, Montgomery, 32
Clinton, Bill, 488–89, 493, 494–96, 498, 499
Clinton, Hillary, 489, 493, 494–95, 498, 499
Clooney, George, 554, 561
Close, Del, 66–67
Close, Glenn, 489, 591
    and *Death and the Maiden*, 462–63, 465, 466
    and *The Real Thing*, 375, 377, 378, 379, 380, 384
Closer (film), 500, 539–43, 545, 547, 548, 553, 556
Clurman, Harold, 151, 235
Cobb, Lee J., 573
Coburn, D. L., 331, 333
Cocteau, Jean, 534
Coe, Fred, 112–13, 118
Coffin, William Sloane, Jr., 324
Cohen, Alexander, 95–99, 101, 105–6, 108–10
Cohen, Richard, 395
Cohn, Roy, 514, 515, 523–24, 525, 530, 531, 532
Cohn, Sam, 335, 339, 349, 355–56, 359–60, 398,
    460–61, 475

Coleman, Cy, 122
Coles, Charles "Honi," 374
Color Purple, The (film), 393
Columbia Pictures, 444, 448, 453, 455, 461, 472
Comden, Betty, 91, 104, 150, 235
Comedians (theater), 323, 325–27, 328, 366
Comic Relief, 393–94
Como, Perry, 79
Compass Players, 50–65, 78, 142
    end of, 64, 66–68
    formation of, 48–49
    improvisation at, 52–53, 56–58, 67
    and May, 50–53, 55–59, 566
    and Shepherd, 37, 48, 51–53, 61, 63, 66, 68, 566
    and Sills, 48–49, 51, 52, 62–63
    and Sills's death, 566
Corliss, Richard, 410, 442
Cornell, Katharine, 432
Costas, Celia, 524, 526, 534, 535, 554, 555, 557, 575
Country Girl, The (theater), 560, 562–67
Coward, Noël, 108, 316, 384
Cox, Wally, 40
Craig, Daniel, 583, 584
Crile, George, 555
Crist, Judith, 259–60
Cronyn, Hume, 331–33, 593
Crosby, Bing, 563
Crowley, Bob, 490
Crowther, Bosley, 195, 228
Crudup, Billy, 526
Cruise, Tom, 500, 540
Crystal, Billy, 481
Cullman, Trip, 519, 522, 530, 533, 534
Curry, Tim, 544, 546
Cusack, Joan, 431, 443

Dale, Grover, 255
Damon, Matt, 524
Daniels, William, 208, 220, 227
Dante Alighieri, 329
Darden, Severn, 53
Davidson, Gordon, 353–54
Davis, Bette, 152–53, 176
Davis, Josie, 298
Davis, Peter, 104, 289, 298, 303
Davis, Sammy, Jr., 167
Davis-Goff, Annabel, 291, 297
    end of marriage, 415
    lifestyle of, 311–12, 376
    marriage in decline, 384, 389, 402, 406, 411
    marriage of Nichols and, 324, 331, 352
    and Nichols's mother, 394–95
    Nichols's relationship with, 270, 278, 342, 402,
        404, 406, 413–14
    pregnancy/children of, 285, 307, 322, 324
    reconciliation with, 357, 384
    and Sawyer, 422–23
    separation from, 342, 415

Day, Doris, 142, 158, 198, 351
Day of the Dolphin, The (film), 278–86, 290–92, 302, 307, 383, 569
Death and the Maiden (theater), 462–67, 468
Death of a Salesman (theater), 25, 32, 425, 572–82, 584
Deep Water (Highsmith), 567
Deer Hunter, The (film), 338, 368, 447
"Degenerate Art" (exhibit), 586
DeGeneres, Ellen, 483
de la Renta, Oscar and Annette, 432
Delerue, Georges, 291
Delicate Balance, A (theater), 591
Demme, Jonathan, 331, 428
DeMunn, Jeffrey, 325, 326
Denby, David, 426, 459
De Niro, Robert, 301–2, 304–6, 455, 531
Dennis, Sandy, 168, 177, 180, 183, 184, 186, 204, 213
De Palma, Brian, 428
Designated Mourner, The (theater), 489–92, 593
Desilu Productions, 82
Dewhurst, Colleen, 234, 280, 343
DiCaprio, Leonardo, 561
Diller, Barry, 417, 442–43, 583, 592
Dillon, Melinda, 168
Dinesen, Isak, 176
Directors Guild of America, 227, 235, 312, 538
Distler, Anna (grandmother), 8
Distler, Grigory (grandfather), 5
Doctorow, E. L., 334–36, 398, 467
Dog Day Afternoon (film), 312
Donaldson, Sam, 443
Donen, Stanley, 592
Donne, John, 509, 510
Dooley, Paul, 160, 163, 190
Dorfman, Ariel, 462–66
Double Feature (musical), 341
Douglas, Kirk, 529
Downey, Robert, Jr., 514
Draper, Ruth, 392
Dreiser, Theodore, 32
Drexler, Rosalyn, 270
Dreyfuss, Richard, 462, 463
Drinks Before Dinner (theater), 335–36, 343
Dukakis, Olympia, 404, 405
Dummar, Melvin, 330
Duncan, Andrew, 52, 65
Dunn, Nora, 504
Du Prez, John, 544

Eastman, Carole, 294–96
Ebert, Roger, 271, 410, 426, 442
Edson, Margaret, 509–10, 516
Ehrlich, Heyward, 28, 31
Eigen, Jack, 60–61
8½ (film), 172, 173, 194
Einstein, Albert, 5, 570

Eisenberg, Deborah, 40, 490, 491
Eisner, Michael, 320–21
Elliot, Cass, 298
Elliot Loves (theater), 448–50, 455
Elliott, Sam, 304
Embassy Pictures, 152, 207
Emond, Linda, 572–73, 576, 579, 581
Enter Laughing (theater), 148
Ephron, Nora, 256, 538, 568, 594
    and *Catch-22*, 247, 249, 250, 359
    death of, 396, 582
    and *Heartburn*, 372, 396–97, 400–403, 410
    Nichols's friendship with, 395–96, 500
    and *Silkwood*, 359–60, 362, 366, 368, 370, 372, 383
    tributes to Nichols from, 502, 570
Evans, Bill, 388–89
Evans, Peter, 316
Evening at the Talk House (theater), 589
Evening with Mike Nichols and Elaine May, An (Broadway), 96–102, 103, 105–10, 393
Exorcist, The (film), 278, 292–93

Fabulous Fifties, The (CBS-TV), 91, 93, 156–57
Falk, Peter, 275–76
Family (TV), 321
Fantasia (film), 542
Farber, Stephen, 270
Farragut North (theater), 560–61
Farrow, Mia, 192–93, 291, 593
Fatherland (film), 470
Feiffer, Jules, 101
    and *Carnal Knowledge*, 261–63, 264, 265, 268, 269–70, 272, 448
    and *Elliot Loves*, 448–50
    and *The Graduate*, 227–28
    and *Little Murders*, 227, 276
    and Nichols and May, 78–79, 262, 272
    and "Passionella," 116, 198, 199, 202
    and *The World of Jules Feiffer*, 113, 116–17
Feinstein, Michael, 373
Fellini, Federico, 155, 172, 264
Ferrer, José, 234
Fey, Tina, 589
Fields, Joe, 317–18, 319
Fifth of July (theater), 353
Film Society of Lincoln Center, 500, 502–3
First Amendment, 359
Fischl, Eric, 500, 586
Fisher, Carrie, 338, 412, 424, 444–45, 446, 447
Fitzgerald, F. Scott, 127, 292
Flanagan, Markus, 419
Flanders & Swann, 40
Flaubert, Gustave, 444
Fletcher, Nancy, 566
Fonda, Henry, 176
Fonda, Jane, 176, 196, 204, 263, 358
Fontana, Tom, 574–75

Fools (theater), 353–54

Ford, Harrison, 429, 431, 453–55, 478, 502

Forman, Milos, 312, 339, 365, 402, 471

Forristal, Susan, 376, 412–13, 414

Fortune, The (film), 293–301, 446, 569
   casting of, 294, 295, 363
   editing of, 298–99, 301, 365
   opening of, 302, 303
   previews of, 300, 302
   reviews of, 303
   screenplay for, 294–95, 296
   shooting of, 296–97
   themes of, 294, 297, 300, 301, 350
   as unsuccessful, 293, 301, 302, 305, 307,
     323, 348

Foss, Cornelia, 467–68

Foss, Lukas, 467

Fosse, Bob, 482

Foster, Jodi, 514

400 Blows, The (film), 172

Fox, Michael J., 489

Fraker, William, 285

Frankel, David, 568

Frankel, Scott, 447

Frankenheimer, John, 269

Frankenthaler, Helen, 529

Franklin, Aretha, 582

Freeman, Morgan, 563–65

French Lieutenant's Woman, The (film), 339, 350,
   360, 375

Freud, Sigmund, 255, 394

Friedkin, William, 292

Friends In Deed, 467, 528

Funny Thing Happened on the Way to the Forum, A
   (film), 480

Galbraith, John Kenneth, 151

Gallagher, Peter, 378, 379, 562

Gans, Herbert, 48

Garbo, Greta, 350, 418

Gardenia, Vincent, 425

Garfield, Andrew, 574, 576, 578, 579, 580

Garfunkel, Art, 242, 244, 252, 263, 264, 265,
   267, 502

Garland, Judy, 484

Gay and Lesbian Alliance Against Defamation
   (GLAAD), 485

Gazzale, Bob, 569

Gazzara, Ben, 343

Geffen, David, 313, 499, 592

Gehry, Frank, 592

Gelb, Barbara, 388

Gershwin, George and Ira, 373

Gersten, Bernard, 437

Gibson, Charles, 507

Gielgud, John, 122

Gilda Live (stage), 340

Gill, Brendan, 288

Gilliatt, Penelope, 217, 230–31, 235, 238, 242,
   247, 256

Gin Game, The (theater), 331–33, 343

Gish, Lillian, 286–87

Gleason, Jackie, 100

Gleason, Joanna, 404, 405, 406

Godard, Jean-Luc, 222

Goetzman, Gary, 560

Goldberg, Joe, 62

Goldberg, Whoopi, 428, 466, 467
   and comedy, 424
   and Nichols's death, 591
   Nichols working with, 392–93, 521, 593
   and *The Spook Show*, 391–93, 411
   and tributes to Nichols, 535, 593

Goldblatt, Stephen, 529, 531, 532, 555, 557

Goldenberg, William, 99

Golden Globe Awards, 235, 548, 554

Goldman, Bo, 330–31, 334

Goldman, William, 256–57

Gone With the Wind (film), 229

Goodbye Girl, The (film), 353
   see also Bogart Slept Here

Gooding, Cuba, Jr., 494

Goodman, Ellen, 442

Goodman, John, 517

Good Morning America (TV), 500, 570

Gorbachev, Mikhail, 499

Gordon, Bobbi, 55

Gordon, Mark, 51

Gordon, Max, 70, 74, 79

Gould, Jack, 77

Graduate, The (film), 205–19, 227–30
   and awards, 229, 236, 257, 383
   and Bancroft, 206, 208, 209–10, 213–14, 216,
     222, 229
   book of, 142–43, 196, 197
   casting of, 198, 204, 205–7, 218, 246, 301, 502
   comparisons with, 246, 361, 442, 446, 486, 530
   as cultural milestone, 228, 229–30, 262, 441, 548
   editing of, 222
   and film technique, 32, 211–13, 229, 573
   first line of, 155
   and Hoffman, 205–7, 209–10, 213–19, 222, 227,
     228–29, 267, 301, 368, 502, 530
   and later developments, 223, 236–37, 264, 477
   marketing of, 222
   music for, 208, 221–22, 256, 403
   and Nichols's moods, 217–18, 220–21, 285
   opening of, 224, 228, 231
   planning for, 152, 153, 189, 198
   production team of, 207–8, 304
   public reactions to, 227–28, 256, 451
   rehearsals for, 209–11
   reviews of, 228–30
   screenplay for, 196–98
   shooting of, 213–16, 218–19, 220, 263, 368
   success of, 229–30, 248, 262

Grand Hotel (film), 349–50
Grant, Lee, 243–44, 275–76
Grant, Micki, 334
Graves, Robert, 127
Green, Adolph, 91, 104, 150, 156, 235
Greenhut, Robert, 397–98, 399, 403, 456
Greenspun, Roger, 258
Griffith, Melanie, 428–31, 443, 445
Griffiths, Trevor, 323–24, 325, 461
Grodin, Charles, 206, 242
Guare, John, 450
Guber, Peter, 448
Guess Who's Coming to Dinner (film), 486
Guinness, Alec, 294
Gyllenhaal, Jake, 561, 562

Haber, Bill, 538, 539
Hackman, Gene, 359
    and *The Birdcage*, 482
    and *Death and the Maiden*, 462, 463, 466
    and *The Graduate*, 210, 246, 446, 455
    and *Postcards from the Edge*, 445–46
    and Strasberg classes, 44, 210
Hagen, Uta, 121, 153, 186, 348
Halcion, 412–13, 414–15, 419, 445
Haley, Mike, 266, 284, 420, 431–32, 447–48, 511, 534, 555
Halpern, Lucy, 24, 25
Hamilton (musical), 586
Hamilton, Alexander, 568
Hamilton, Murray, 210
Hamlisch, Marvin, 582
Hamm, Jon, 567, 589
Hammond, Diana, 470
Hampton, Christopher, 416
Hanks, Tom, 566, 569
    and *Charlie Wilson's War*, 555–60
    and *Lucky Guy*, 568
    and *Our Town*, 586
    and *Primary Colors*, 489, 492, 493–94
Hansberry, Lorraine, 224
Harden, Marcia Gay, 517, 520
Harding, Tonya, 468
Hare, David, 337, 490, 491
Harewood, Dorian, 319–20
Harnick, Sheldon, 104, 111, 113, 115, 198–200
Harris, Barbara, 39, 47, 48, 50, 53, 62, 198–202
Harris, Robert, 470
Harris, Sydney J., 33
Harrison, Doane, 181
Harrison, Jim, 471–73
Hart, Jim, 432
Hassilev, Alex, 27, 55–56
Hausberger, Franz, 25–26, 394
Hawn, Goldie, 428
HBO Films, 509, 511, 514, 516, 524, 534, 538
Headly, Glenne, 425
Heard, John, 316, 319

Heartburn (film), 375, 396–404, 425, 467
    book of, 372, 396–97
    casting of, 372, 398, 400, 483
    collaboration with women on, 400, 401, 402, 403
    comparisons with, 444, 446
    and court battle, 397
    as modest hit, 426
    Nichols's personal connection with, 402–3, 404, 489
    reactions to, 404, 409–11, 416, 442
    rehearsals for, 398–99
    screenplay for, 359–60, 362, 370, 383
    shooting of, 384, 393, 399, 400–402, 403
    themes of, 397, 403
Heaven Can Wait (film), 323, 473
Heiress, The (theater), 561, 562
Helland, J. Roy, 368, 427–28
Heller, Joseph, 189, 239–40, 241, 257
Hellman, Lillian, 104, 133, 190, 270, 278, 284, 299, 320, 324
    and *The Children's Hour*, 42
    and *The Little Foxes*, 189, 223–27
    and *Scoundrel Time*, 323
Henry, Buck, 265, 322, 413, 502, 589
    and *Catch-22*, 239–45, 246, 248, 251–52, 257
    and Dalton School, 14, 196
    and *The Day of the Dolphin*, 279–80, 283, 285–86, 292
    and *Get Smart*, 197
    and *The Graduate*, 205, 208, 209, 210, 214, 215, 219, 227, 229, 573
    and *Heaven Can Wait*, 323
    and *How to Be Good*, 567
    and *The Last Tycoon*, 292, 293
    and *Prisoner of Second Avenue*, 276
    and *Saturday Night Live*, 313
    and *Who's Afraid of Virginia Woolf?*, 197
Henry, William, 440
Herman, Jerry, 356
Herrmann, Cal, 40
Herrmann, Edward, 284
Hesseltine, Stark, 123
Hiaasen, Carl, 544, 554
High and Low (film), 567
Highsmith, Patricia, 567
Hiken, Gerald, 354
Hill, Arthur, 121, 186, 348
Hiller, Wendy, 25
Hirsch, Arthur "Buzz," 358–60, 363, 368, 381
Hoffman, Dustin, 198, 199, 204, 223, 320, 322, 570
    and *Angels in America*, 523, 524
    and *Catch-22*, 242, 260
    and *Death of a Salesman*, 425
    and *The Graduate*, 205–7, 209–10, 213–19, 222, 227, 228–29, 267, 301, 368, 502, 530
    and *Midnight Cowboy*, 242
    and *Waiting for Godot*, 424–25

Hoffman, Philip Seymour, 538, 594
  and *Charlie Wilson's War*, 556, 558, 560
  death of, 585
  and *Death of a Salesman*, 573, 577–80
  and *The Seagull*, 518, 520, 521, 573, 578, 579
Hogan, P. J., 515
Holbrook, Hal, 234
Holbrooke, Richard, 407
Hollywood:
  changing industry in, 195, 235, 262, 271–72,
    312–13, 452, 485, 501–2
  competition in, 257–58, 468, 477, 497
  "director's draft" used in, 360
  docudrama, 382–83
  First Amendment protections for filmmakers, 359
  and homosexuality, 272, 418, 479–87
  and indie revolution, 442
  large-scale studio movies, 474
  porn films, 323
Holocaust, 9, 338–39, 467
"Homeward Bound" (song), 593
Hope, Bob, 236
Hope Springs (film), 568
Hopkins, Anthony, 461
Hopper, Dennis, 256
Hornby, Nick, 567
Horowitz, Vladimir, 13
House of Cards (TV), 562
Howards End (film), 461
How to Be Good (Hornby), 567
Hudson, Rock, 158
Hughes, Barnard, 286
Hughes, Howard, 131, 330
Humphrey, Hubert H., 281
Hunter, Ross, 142, 146–47, 158
Huntley, Paul, 114
Hurlyburly (theater), 385–90, 391, 392, 394, 411,
    449, 581
Hurok, Sol, 13
Hurt, William, 385, 387, 388
Huston, Anjelica, 295, 412
Hyde Pierce, David, *see* Pierce, David Hyde

Icarus production company, 203
Idle, Eric, 538, 544, 546, 548, 570
Impersonator, The (film), 470
Importance of Being Earnest, The (theater), 122
Improvisations to Music (recording), 83–85, 88
"I'm Still Here" (song), 446
Innocent Blood (James), 349
Iron John (Bly), 471
Irons, Jeremy:
  and *Betrayal*, 350–51, 375, 453
  and *The French Lieutenant's Woman*, 350, 375
  and *The Real Thing*, 375, 378, 379, 380, 384
  and *Remains of the Day*, 453, 460, 461
Irwin, Bill, 425, 437, 438, 439, 440
Ishiguro, Kazuo, 453

Ishtar (film), 473
Ivey, Judith, 385, 386–87, 389
Ivory, James, 461

Jackson, Anne, 147, 149
Jackson, Michael, 468
Jackson, Tracey, 409
James, P. D., 349
Janney, Allison, 517
Jaws (film), 303, 312
Jax Beer, 90
Jefferson, Herbert, Jr., 315, 316, 317–18
Jellicoe, Ann, 141
Jewison, Norman, 93, 156–57, 158, 224, 548
Jinks, Dan, 499
Joffe, Charles, 72
Johnson, Diane, 350
Johnson, Lyndon B., 161, 327
Jones, Chris, 585
Jones, Tommy Lee, 568
Jonze, Spike, 501
Jordan, John, 252
Julia, Raul, 306

Kael, Pauline, 228, 271, 292
Kaliski, Lotte, 4
Kanin, Garson, 123
Kauffmann, Stanley, 195, 410
Kazan, Elia, 45, 227, 389
  and *America America*, 157
  and *Death of a Salesman*, 25, 572–73, 577, 580
  and *The Last Tycoon*, 293
  and *A Streetcar Named Desire*, 24–25, 537, 572
Keach, Stacy, 242, 246
Keitel, Harvey, 385, 387
Keith, Slim, 299
Kelly, Gene, 176
Kelly, Grace, 563, 564
Kennedy, Jacqueline, 188, 191, 194, 230, 431; as
    Onassis, 322, 352, 432, 478
Kennedy, John F., 102, 106, 108, 138–39
Kennedy, Robert F., 15–16
Kennedy Center Honors, 538
Kerensky, Alexander, 5
Kerouac, Jack, 90
Kerr, E. Katherine, 369–70
Kerr, Jean, 351, 352
Kerr, Walter, 100, 135, 165, 257, 277, 318, 351
Kerrigan, Nancy, 468
Kerr-McGee, 358–59, 360, 364, 368, 371, 381, 382
Khan, Aga, 432
Kidd, Michael, 482
Kidman, Nicole, 500, 540
Kind Hearts and Coronets (film), 499
King, Rev. Martin Luther, Jr., 236, 238
Kingsley, Pat, 359, 360
Kirk, Justin, 526, 528–29, 532, 533, 535, 536
Kissel, Howard, 382

Kissinger, Henry, 335
Klein, Joe, 488–89, 492
Kline, Kevin, 384
    and *The Birdcage*, 480
    and *The Seagull*, 509, 517, 518–19, 520, 521–22
    and *Sophie's Choice*, 400
Klugman, Jack, 191
Knack, The (theater), 141–42, 143–45, 152, 165, 168, 190
Knight, Gene, 73–74
Koch, Howard W. "Hawk," 304, 305, 306
Korkes, Jon, 253, 282, 283
Korman, Harvey, 65
Krall, Diana, 534
Kramer, Larry, 393–94, 486
Kramer, Stanley, 172, 224
Krim, Arthur and Mathilde, 115
Kroll, Jack, 439
Kubrick, Stanley, 238–39, 258
Kurosawa, Akira, 567
Kurtz, Swoosie, 343, 344, 346–47, 348, 353, 443
Kushner, Tony, 566, 568
    and *Angels in America*, 513, 514–16, 523–24, 525, 527, 528, 530, 532, 534, 536, 537
    tribute to Nichols by, 593

LaBute, Neil, 515
Labyrinth, 465
La Cage aux Folles (film), 355, 478–79
    see also Birdcage, The
Lachmann, Hedwig, 6, 27
La Dolce Vita (film), 194
Lahr, John, 413, 508, 587
Lampert, Zohra, 45
Landauer, Brigitte (mother), 4, 6–7, 8
    see also Nichols, Brigitte
Landauer, Gudula (aunt), 7, 8, 16, 21
Landauer, Gustav (grandfather), 6–7
Lane, Anthony, 477
Lane, Nathan, 480, 481–82, 484, 486, 502, 526
Langella, Frank, 389–90
Lantz, Robert, 120, 122, 158, 282
Last Tycoon, The (film), 292, 293, 302, 350
Laughter on the 23rd Floor (film), 480
Laurel and Hardy, 294
Laurents, Arthur, 79
Lavin, Linda, 304, 306
Law, Jude, 539, 541, 542
Lawrence, Peter, 49, 386, 387, 404, 405, 465–66, 549–50
Lazar, Irving "Swifty," 349
Lean, David, 195, 585
Lee, Gypsy Rose, 100
Legion of Decency (National Catholic Office for Motion Pictures), 157–58, 191, 194
Lehman, Ernest, and *Who's Afraid of Virginia Woolf?*, 152–53, 157–58, 166, 168, 170–78, 182–84, 186
Leibman, Ron, 531

Leigh, Carolyn, 122
Leighton, Margaret, 223, 225
Le Mat, Paul, 331
Lemmon, Jack, 242
Leonard, John, 517
Les Liaisons Dangereuses (theater), 416
Lester, Adrian, 480–81, 494, 495
"Let the River Run" (song), 441, 443
Levine, Joseph E.:
    and *Carnal Knowledge*, 264, 271
    and *The Day of the Dolphin*, 279, 280, 282, 284
    and *The Graduate*, 152, 207–8, 222, 264
Levinson, Barry, 443, 497
Lewinsky, Monica, 497
Library for the Performing Arts at Lincoln Center, 522
Life of Brian (film), 548
Lincoln Center gala, 500, 502–3
Lindsay, John V., 393
Linklater, Kristin, 271
Linson, Art, 331
Lithgow, John, 325, 591
Little Foxes, The (theater), 189, 223–27, 257, 384, 480
Little Murders (theater), 227, 276
Little Night Music, A (musical), 566
Lloyd, Christopher, 511
Lloyd, Norman, 156
Lloyd Webber, Andrew, 545
Lo Bianco, Tony, 304, 306
Long, Shelley, 428
Looking for Mr. Goodbar (Rossner), 301
Loren, Sophia, 499
Loudon, Dorothy, 116, 324
Lourd, Bryan, 592
Lubezki, Emmanuel, 482
Lubitsch, Ernst, 547
Lucky Guy (theater), 568
Luftig, Hal, 465
Lugosi, Bela, 305
Lumet, Sidney, 100, 172–73, 263, 312, 398
Lunch Hour (theater), 349, 351–53
Lunts (Alfred Lunt; Lynn Fontanne), 74
Luv (theater), 147–52, 157, 165, 169, 223, 243

Ma, Yo-Yo, 529
MacDevitt, Brian, 584
MacLaine, Shirley, 444–47, 484
MacNeil, Ian, 583–84
Mad Men (TV), 567
Madonna, 428, 482
Mailer, Norman, 81, 104, 188, 240
Malkovich, John, 425, 492, 494
Mamet, David, 436, 567
Mankiewicz, Joseph L., 156
Mantello, Joe, 529
Marber, Patrick, 500, 539
Margulies, David, 326

Mark, Mary Ellen, 284
Markinson, Brian, 531
Marshall, E. G., 223
Marshall, Penny, 414
Martin, Steve:
    and *The Birdcage*, 479
    and *The Jerk*, 331
    on Nichols and May, 84
    and *Waiting for Godot*, 425, 436–37, 438–39, 440
M*A*S*H (film), 257–58, 260, 312
Maslin, Janet, 382, 442
Mason, James, 152
Mason, Marsha, 301, 302, 304–5
Masur, Richard, 398, 402
Matter of Position, A (May), 112–13, 117–19, 120, 274
Matthau, Walter, 594
    and *Luv*, 147–48
    and "no assholes" rule, 231, 519
    and *The Odd Couple*, 159–60, 162–65, 166, 190–91
    personal traits of, 148, 160, 190
May, Elaine, 404, 450, 491, 503
    as collaborator, 473–74, 479, 481–83, 489, 495–97, 499, 541, 544
    comparisons with, 62, 340
    and Compass Players, 50–53, 55–59, 566
    early years of, 36
    and Harnick, 104, 111, 113, 115
    health issues of, 554
    influence of, 392, 396
    and Nichols, 34–35, 37–38, 293, 554
    one-liners of, 4–5, 37, 66, 73, 84
    personal traits of, 105, 121
    and Playwrights Theatre Club, 40
    and politics, 106, 166–67, 281
    and socializing, 103
    tributes to Nichols by, 502, 538, 569, 570, 592
    at University of Chicago, 36–37, 38
    as writer, 52, 65, 79, 90, 95, 110, 111, 117–18, 189, 274, 366, 473, 492, 493, 498
    see also Nichols and May
May, Ida, 81
May, Jeannie, 36, 81, 110
McCarthy, Cormac, 470
McCarthy, Eugene, 235
McCarthy, Mary, 263
McCarthy, Todd, 498, 537–38
McDonald, Audra, 511–13
McDormand, Frances, 563–64, 565
McGill, Bruce, 368, 374
McGovern, George, 281
McNally, Terrence, 587, 589, 592
McNicholl, B. T., 564, 565
Melcher, Martin, 198
Melvin and Howard (film), 330–31
Mendes, Sam, 499
Mengers, Sue, 263–64

Merle, Robert, 279
Merman, Ethel, 100
Metcalf, Mark, 319
MGM, 349, 350
Michaels, Lorne, 134, 313, 340, 376, 405, 414, 432, 485, 589, 592
Midler, Bette, 295
Midnight Special, The (radio), 40
Mielziner, Jo, 573–74
"Mike Nichols Presents," 325
"Mike Nichols Production, A," 321
Millennium Approaches (part 1 of *Angels in America*), 513, 527
Miller, Arthur, 91, 456, 572, 573, 577
Miller, Bennett, 592
Miller, Mitch, 83, 85
Miller, Rebecca, 456
Minghella, Anthony, 500
Minnelli, Liza, 582
Minnerles (neighbors), 54–55
Miracle Worker, The (theater), 97
Miramax, 442
Miranda, Lin-Manuel, 568, 586
Mitford, Jessica, 140
Mitford, Nancy, 98
Mocambo, Los Angeles, 81–82
Monitor (NBC radio), 90, 93–95, 110, 120, 130, 146, 279
Monk, Debra, 520
Monroe, Marilyn, 91, 115–16
Montealegre, Felicia (Bernstein), 91, 111, 129, 188, 235, 327, 332–33
Monty Python and the Holy Grail (film), 538–39, 545
Moore, Demi, 426
Moore, Julianne, 490
Moore, Marianne, 176
Moore, Susanna, 176, 281
Morath, Inge, 456
Moreau, Jeanne, 198
Morley, Robert, 45
Morris, Bob, 477
Morrison, George, 435
Mosbach, Marianne, 15
Moscow Art Theatre, 519
Mosher, Gregory, 386
Moss, Jeffrey, 341
Mostel, Zero, 242
Motion Picture Association of America, 194
Mrs. Doubtfire (film), 479
"Mrs. Robinson" (song), 222, 593
Munderloh, Otts, 386
Museum of Modern Art, New York, 568–69
Museum of the Moving Image, New York, 450–51
Myers, Dee Dee, 494
My One and Only (musical), 372–74, 391, 411, 539

Nashville (film), 312
National Catholic Office for Motion Pictures
    (Legion of Decency), 157–58, 191, 194
National Medal of Arts, 529
Natwick, Mildred, 126, 135, 138
Naughton, James, 336, 343, 344, 345, 346
Neal, Patricia, 42, 198
Nelligan, Kate, 422, 475
Nesbitt, Cathleen, 286–87
New Actors Workshop, 435–36
Newhart, Bob, 247
Newman, Mildred, 255–56
Newman, Paul, 43, 235, 243
Newman, Randy, 414
New Queer Cinema, 483
New York City, Jews in, 11–12, 15
New York Public Library, 477
Nicholaw, Casey, 545–47, 548, 549, 550
Nichols, Brigitte (mother):
    family background of, 4, 6–7
    health issues of, 8, 16, 21–22
    and her sister, 16, 21
    illness and death of, 394–95, 396, 407, 408, 415
    immigration to U.S., 9, 11
    marriage to Pavel/Paul, 7, 10
    and Mike's childhood, 4, 7, 8, 10, 11, 15, 17, 18
    and Mike's honeymoon, 66
    and Mike's teen years, 22, 23, 24
    and Pavel/Paul's death, 18–19
    in Philadelphia, 42
    second marriage of, 25–26
    work obtained by, 14, 18, 20–21, 23
Nichols, Daisy (daughter), 434, 502, 575, 590
    birth and childhood of, 145, 193, 203, 261, 278,
        291, 354, 384
    living in Europe, 145, 193, 300
    and parents' divorce, 261, 300
Nichols, Jenny (daughter), 422, 434, 502, 575, 590
    birth of, 322
    childhood of, 384, 411
Nichols, Max (son), 307, 422, 434, 502, 575, 590
    birth of, 291
    childhood of, 289, 322, 384
    and his father's work, 378
    teen years of, 411, 423
Nichols, Mike:
    as actor, 32–33, 41, 42–49, 52–53, 55–57, 65, 96,
        118, 343, 344–45, 490–91, 562, 589, 593;
        reviews of, 33, 347, 589
    as adviser/fixer, 324–25, 330, 354, 373–74,
        392–93
    and aging, 342–43, 408, 415, 450–51, 467–69,
        485, 506, 510, 524, 543, 544, 553–55, 556,
        559–60, 564–69, 571, 573, 574–76, 578, 582–89
    ambition of, 41–42, 96, 126, 203, 278
    art collection of, 350, 363, 412–13
    awards and honors of, 145, 169, 203, 208, 229,
        235, 236, 238, 239, 290, 328, 330, 333, 383,
        384, 443, 461, 500, 502–3, 523, 529, 538, 548,
        551, 569–71, 581–82, 592–94
    baldness and wigs of, 7, 20, 21, 27, 42, 46, 53, 78,
        95, 114, 289, 312, 315, 395
    birth of, 7
    and celebrity, 24, 103, 137, 141, 195–96, 236–37,
        248, 277, 431, 436, 593
    childhood of, 3–5, 8–17, 26
    children of, *see* Nichols, Daisy; Nichols, Jenny;
        Nichols, Max
    comebacks of, 328, 348–49, 371, 372, 383, 386,
        391, 420, 453, 508, 514
    and comedy, 44, 59, 60, 151, 235, 313, 319,
        323–24, 353, 393, 424, 549–50, 551–52
    and cultural change, 134, 195, 235, 312–13, 447,
        450, 484
    death of, 590, 591–94
    depressions of, 120–21, 122, 129, 146, 166,
        290–91, 293, 307, 324, 332, 337, 357, 411, 413,
        414, 415
    detractors of, 104, 256–57, 260, 262, 303, 312,
        434, 459, 466, 468, 476, 487
    as director, *see* Nichols, Mike, as director; *specific
        titles*
    and drug use, 197, 248, 265, 385–86, 387, 405–6,
        412, 414–15, 424, 445, 507–8, 519–20
    early jobs of, 22, 23, 25, 30, 38–39, 42–43, 45,
        46–47, 49
    and emotion, 106–7, 348, 418, 456, 536, 561, 562,
        574, 594
    family background of, 5–8, 338–39, 415, 468, 502
    as grandfather, 575, 589, 591
    health issues of, 348, 405–6, 408, 412–13, 503,
        533–34, 547, 556–57, 559, 564, 565, 566, 567,
        577–78, 581, 582, 584, 585, 589
    and his mother, *see* Nichols, Brigitte
    and homosexuality, 115n
    and horses, 146, 269, 277, 278, 299, 307, 322, 364,
        411, 452
    immigration to U.S., 8–10, 11
    and indecision, 329
    interviews with, 129–30, 141, 142, 152, 154, 166,
        188–89, 196, 388, 468–69, 508, 587, 594
    legacy of, 134, 568–69, 594
    and luxury, 24, 92–93, 98, 146, 169, 188–89,
        216–17, 238, 269, 277, 299, 311–12, 337, 339,
        350, 363–64, 376, 413, 456–57, 500
    and May, 34–35, 37–38, 293, 554; *see also* Nichols
        and May
    and money, 42, 90, 102, 146, 151, 153, 234–35,
        322, 324, 328, 333, 339, 350, 356–57, 376,
        411–13, 416, 424, 452, 476, 492, 501
    name of, 3, 10
    nervous breakdown of, 351, 352, 407, 408, 411–15,
        416, 426
    personal traits of, 64, 67, 86, 105–6, 120, 139, 148,
        174, 203, 215, 217–18, 261, 266, 285, 329, 344,
        389, 434–35, 458, 459, 505–6, 508, 536, 561–62

Nichols, Mike *(cont.)*
  as producer, 320–21, 325, 327–28, 426–27
  reputation of, 202, 274, 278, 303, 306, 459,
    547–48
  teen years of, 17–19, 20–28, 394
  at University of Chicago, 26–34, 137
  wives of, *see* Callas, Margot; Davis-Goff,
    Annabel; Sawyer, Diane; Scot, Patricia
  and women, 111–12, 127, 150, 192, 230, 256,
    342–43, 366
  as writer, 113
Nichols, Mike, as director:
  and apprehension, 314, 324, 328, 345
  and audience reactions, 317–19, 440, 492
  and believability, 127, 135, 351–52, 361, 364–65
  changes in technique of, 317, 365
  collaborations with women, 366, 400, 401, 402,
    403, 446; *see also specific individuals*
  comparisons with, 312, 313
  delving into the plot, 149, 160–61, 253–54, 262,
    274, 287, 316–17, 319, 344, 379–80, 428, 454,
    549–50
  detachment of, 304, 329, 341, 354, 355–56,
    560, 565
  double exile of, 307, 311, 360
  early stage productions, 116–17, 126
  first films, 141–42, 147, 169, 175, 179, 181, 195
  and improvisation, 365, 594
  as legend, 417
  low point of, 329, 351–52
  and "the Nichols touch," 135, 149, 307, 317, 361–63
  responsibility of, 285, 297, 311, 323
  style of, 149, 165, 180, 213, 232, 312, 317, 326,
    365, 378, 382, 419, 513, 522, 540–41, 542, 556
  success of, 135–36, 137, 229–30, 250, 262, 272,
    273, 302, 307, 332, 391, 453
  working with actors, 127, 130–33, 134, 139, 151,
    161, 179, 180–81, 200, 207, 214–15, 231–32,
    243, 266–67, 269, 275–76, 315–18, 319–20,
    326, 333, 341, 368–70, 380, 384, 386, 392–93,
    417–20, 430, 438, 439, 447–48, 449, 497,
    512–13, 518–21, 528–29, 531–33, 542–43,
    551–52, 576, 579
  working with other directors, 313, 341
  working with writers, 134, 159, 161, 179, 265,
    275, 330, 341, 370, 378–79, 387, 392, 404, 410,
    444, 464, 472, 527
Nichols, Mike, works by, 651–52
  retrospectives of, 450–51, 568–69
  reviews of, 132, 135, 141, 145, 147, 151, 164, 165,
    194–95, 202, 203, 226, 228–30, 235, 259–60,
    270–72, 276–77, 288, 291–92, 303, 318–19,
    320, 326, 336, 347, 353, 381–83, 408, 426, 439,
    441–42, 450, 459, 466, 486, 517, 521, 537–38,
    547–48, 565, 579–80, 585
Nichols, Paul (father), 287
  death of, 19
  early years of, 4–8

name change of, 8
  in U.S., 8, 10–12, 14, 16–19
Nichols, Robert (brother), 22, 23, 26, 42, 208,
    394–95, 593
  birth of, 7
  early years of, 3, 5, 7–8, 10–15, 18
Nichols and May, 417
  "Bach to Bach," 84
  breakup of, 118–19, 120, 129–30, 343
  Broadway show, 96–102, 103, 105–10, 393
  and civil rights, 167–68
  "Cocktail Piano," 84
  as comedy team, 34–35, 58, 59–65, 68
  comparisons with, 147, 180, 197, 214, 235, 262,
    272, 332
  and Compass Players, 37, 49, 50–65, 68, 78
  critical reviews of, 73–74, 75, 77, 99, 100, 101,
    102, 103
  "Dentist," 84
  "Disk Jockey," 73, 75, 88, 95, 99, 101
  at Emmy Awards, 89–90, 523
  and *The Fabulous Fifties*, 93, 156–57
  first encounter of, 34, 83
  and generational shift, 101–2
  "Grief Lady," 139–40
  improvisation, 69–70, 71, 73, 74, 90, 94, 99, 101,
    107–8, 594
  influence of, 143, 448, 449–50
  lessons learned by, 127, 135
  Monitor sketches, 93–95, 110, 120, 130,
    146, 279
  "Mother and Son," 72–73, 79, 99, 116, 327, 395
  mutual trust of, 94–95
  "Mysterioso," 34, 83–84, 196
  "Pirandello," 63–64, 73, 90, 98, 99–100, 107, 110,
    121, 346
  "PTA Fun Night," 107
  radio spots, 190, 301
  reconnections of, 115, 137, 139–41, 280–81, 301,
    314, 323, 327, 393–94, 473–74, 477–78, 479,
    481–82
  recordings of, 83–85, 88, 106, 120, 130, 652
  relationship of, 35, 37–38, 49, 54–57, 111, 112,
    118–19
  rifts between, 66–68, 108–9
  sketches becoming stale, 108
  success of, 77–80, 82–85, 89, 90, 459
  "Teenagers," 60, 69, 71, 73, 76, 78, 79, 80, 89, 106,
    107, 108, 214, 348
  "Telephone," 71, 76, 77, 79, 473, 477–78
  and *Who's Afraid of Virginia Woolf?*, 343–48
Nichols and May Examine Doctors (recording), 120
Nicholson, Jack, 478, 570
  art collection of, 376
  and *Carnal Knowledge*, 264–67, 268, 278, 294,
    367, 401
  and *Chinatown*, 278, 294, 296, 416
  and *Easy Rider*, 263

family background of, 298
and *The Fortune,* 294, 295, 296–98, 301
and *Heartburn,* 400–402, 416
and *Melvin and Howard,* 330
Nichols's friendship with, 266, 327, 376, 401
and *Primary Colors,* 492
and *Wolf,* 461, 471–72, 474–76, 526
Nichtern, Claire, 147, 148
Nightingale, Benedict, 466
9 to 5 (film), 341
Nixon, Cynthia, 378, 379, 380–81, 385, 386, 387, 388, 517
Nixon, Richard M., 115, 422
Nizer, Louis, 272
Nobody Loves Me (theater), 122–26
  see also Barefoot in the Park
Normal Heart, The (theater), 393–94
North, Alex, 189, 574
Norton, Elliot, 99, 164
Nunn, Bill, 455

O'Brien, Jack, 13, 520, 565, 587
Odd Couple, The (theater), 152, 154, 158–66, 243, 366
  and awards, 165, 169
  card game scene in, 159, 165, 332, 353
  and Carney, 159–60, 161, 163, 164, 190–91
  ending its run, 191, 223
  and Matthau, 159–60, 162–65, 166, 190–91
  rehearsals for, 158
  reviews of, 164, 165
  and Simon, 141, 158–61, 163–64, 190
  theme of, 159, 164
Odets, Clifford, 560, 562
Odets, Walt, 564
O'Donnell, Colleen, 583
O'Donnell, Mimi, 578, 580
O'Hare, Denis, 558
O'Horgan, Tom, 39
O'Keefe, Michael, 316
Omnibus (TV), 76–77, 78
Onassis, Jacqueline Kennedy, *see* Kennedy, Jacqueline
Ondricek, Miroslav, 365, 370
O'Neal, Cynthia, 81, 402, 467, 528
O'Neal, Patrick, 81
One Flew Over the Cuckoo's Nest (film), 312
O'Neill, Eugene, 17
On the Waterfront (film), 42
Osborne, John, 217, 230
O'Steen, Sam:
  and *Carnal Knowledge,* 264, 265, 269
  and *Catch-22,* 248, 249–50, 253
  and *The Day of the Dolphin,* 283, 285
  and *The Fortune,* 265, 296, 302
  and *The Graduate,* 208, 212, 216, 220, 221, 222, 257
  and *Silkwood,* 365, 368, 381, 383

and *Who's Afraid of Virginia Woolf?,* 171, 180–81, 184, 186, 190, 191–92, 194, 208
and *Wolf,* 474, 475, 476
and *Working Girl,* 429, 441
Ostrow, Stuart, 199–201
Oswald, Lee Harvey, 139
Our Town (theater), 586
Ouspenskaya, Maria, 36
Overall, Park, 418–19
Owen, Clive, 539, 541, 542–43, 548

Paar, Jack, 75, 79, 87, 140
Pacino, Al:
  and *Angels in America,* 514, 523–24, 528, 529, 530–31, 533, 538
  and *Catch-22,* 243, 312
  and *Dog Day Afternoon,* 312
Padwa, Sabrina, 431
Pakula, Alan, 369, 456
Paley, William and Babe, 92
Papp, Joseph, 314, 319, 335–36, 423
Paramount Pictures:
  and *Barefoot in the Park,* 142
  and *Catch-22,* 240, 242, 245, 253, 256, 261
  and *Heartburn,* 400
  and *My One and Only,* 373
  and *Regarding Henry,* 454, 457
  and Rudin, 454
  and Sylbert, 303
Parker, Corey, 417–19
Parker, Mary-Louise, 521, 524, 525, 533, 535–36, 538
Parker, Suzy, 114–15
Parks, Suzan-Lori, 524
Parton, Dolly, 350
Pascal, Amy, 545
"Passionella" (revue), 116, 198, 199, 202
Patinkin, Mandy, 384, 398–400, 581
Patton (film), 243, 280
Paulus, Diane, 435
Pendleton, Austin, 223, 224–26, 227, 242, 249–50, 258
Penn, Arthur, 97–98, 113, 117, 236, 429, 548
Peppard, George, 124, 128, 131, 138
Perestroika (part 2 of *Angels in America*), 513, 527
Perkins, Anthony:
  and *Catch-22,* 242, 246, 247
  and civil rights, 167
  death of, 467
  Nichols's friendship with, 175, 184, 242, 246, 467
  and psychologist, 255, 256
  and *Saturday Night Live,* 313
Perry Como Show, The (TV), 80
Peschkowsky, Igor Michael, *see* Nichols, Mike
Peschkowsky, Pavel Nikolayevich (father), 4, 5–6, 7–8
  name change of, *see* Nichols, Paul
Peter, Paul, and Mary, 167, 281

Peters, Jon, 448
Pfeiffer, Michelle, 428, 472, 474–75, 486, 526
Phillips, Don, 330
Pierce, David Hyde, 439, 449, 474, 544, 546, 549, 550
Pierce, Laura, 435
Pileggi, Nicholas, 538, 570
Pine, Larry, 589
Pinter, Harold:
  and *Betrayal*, 349, 350–51, 583, 585
  and *The Last Tycoon*, 293
  Nichols's ambition to direct, 204, 424, 583
  and *Old Times*, 276
  and *Remains of the Day*, 453, 460, 461
  and *Wit*, 511
Place in the Sun, A (film), 32, 172
Platt, Oliver, 449, 450
Platt, Polly, 296
Playhouse 90 (TV), 96, 112
Playwrights Theatre Club, 39–42, 46, 47, 51
Plaza Suite (theater), 230, 231–35, 239, 243, 280, 286
Plummer, Amanda, 384
Plummer, Christopher, 336, 474, 475
Poitier, Sidney, 224
Polanski, Roman, 278, 282
Portman, Natalie, 517, 519–21, 534, 540, 541, 543, 548, 570
Postcards from the Edge (film), 424, 444–48, 450, 453, 455, 480, 483, 489
Preminger, Otto, 156
Prentiss, Paula, 255
Presley, Elvis, 330–31
Pretty Woman (film), 443
Previn, Andre, 189
Primary Colors (film), 492–99, 503, 509, 541, 544, 560
Primary Colors (Klein), 488–89, 490, 492
Primetime Live (TV), 443–44
Prisoner of Second Avenue (theater), 274–77, 302, 333
Private Lives (film), 384
Producers Guild of America, 538
Production Code Administration, 157–58, 182, 194
Pryce, Jonathan, 325, 326
Pryor, Richard, 424
Public Eye, The (film), 141–42, 146–47, 152, 153, 158
Public Theater, 314, 319, 335, 337, 338, 423, 518

Quaid, Dennis, 446
Queen of Basin Street, The (theater), 355–57, 372, 478

Rabe, David, 378
  and *Hurlyburly*, 385, 387–90, 581
  and *Sticks and Bones*, 276
  and *Streamers*, 314–15, 318–19
Radner, Gilda, 339–41, 349, 351–53
Radziwill, Lee and Stanislaw, 188

Rae, Charlotte, 40
Ragtime (Doctorow), 335, 339
Ragtime (film), 339
Ramirez, Sara, 549
Rasche, David, 352
Rattigan, Terence, 223
Reader, The (film), 500
Reagan, Ronald, 198, 427
Real Thing, The (theater), 376–81, 385, 393
  casting of, 375, 453
  end of run, 391, 411
  ideas in, 379–80
  reviews of, 383, 384
  and set design, 376–77
  and Stoppard, 375, 377–79, 383–84
Redford, Robert, 138, 168, 204, 205, 481, 486, 570
  and *Great Gatsby*, 291
  and *Nobody Loves Me/Barefoot in the Park*, 124–25, 127–28, 130–35
Reds (film), 324
Reed, Clive, 246
Reed, Rex, 498
Reems, Harry, 323
Regarding Henry (film), 453–60, 462, 467, 472
Reiner, Carl, 148
Reiner, Rob, 509
Reisz, Karel, 360, 369
Remains of the Day, The (film), 453, 460–61, 470, 475
Remnick, David, 592
Renoir, Jean, 156
Resnick, Patricia, 341
Reynolds, Debbie, 444, 445
Rich, Alan, 320
Rich, Frank, 297, 347–48, 353, 408, 440, 466, 486, 537, 592
Richards, Beah, 224–25
Richardson, Tony, 244
Riedel, Michael, 565
Ritt, Martin, 172
Robards, Jason, 282, 286
Robbins, Harold, 71
Robbins, Jerome, 79, 198, 201
Roberts, Julia, 521, 544
  and *Betrayal*, 584
  and *Charlie Wilson's War*, 556, 558
  and *Closer*, 540, 541–52, 547
  and *How to Be Good*, 567
  and tributes to Nichols, 569, 570, 592, 593
Roberts, Tony, 581
Rock, Chris, 567
Rockettes, 534
Rogoff, Gordon, 14
Rollin, Betty, 75, 215–16
Rollins, Jack, 69–73, 75–79, 81, 106
Rose, Marshall, 477
Rosen, Steve, 549
Rosenberg, Ethel, 318, 514, 515, 532

Rosenheim, Edward, 28–29
Ross, Herbert, 200
Ross, Katharine, 206, 216, 217, 219, 222, 229, 530
Rossetti, Christina, 433
Rossner, Judith, 301
Roth, Ann:
   and costume design, 162, 446, 496
   and *Heartburn*, 401
   and *The Odd Couple*, 162
   and *Postcards from the Edge*, 445, 446
   and *Primary Colors*, 496
   and *Silkwood*, 365, 366, 368, 401
   and *Working Girl*, 429
Roth, Philip, 291
Rotunno, Giuseppe, 264, 267
Roy, Rajendra, 568–69
Rubinstein, John, 354
Ruby, Jack, 139
Rudd, Paul Ryan, 319
Rudin, Scott:
   and *Annie*, 416
   and *Betrayal*, 583, 584
   and *Closer*, 545, 547
   and *A Country Girl*, 567
   and *Death of a Salesman*, 572, 573–74, 576–77, 580, 581
   and *A Funny Thing Happened on the Way to the Forum*, 480
   and Nichols's health, 567, 581, 583, 585–86
   and *Regarding Henry*, 454–55
   and *Working Girl*, 416, 417
RuPaul, 486
Russell, David O., 501
Russell, Kurt, 363, 364, 367, 370, 383
Ryan, Meg, 428

Sabrina (film), 478
Sacks, James, 51
Sadler, Bill, 419
Sahl, Mort, 70–72
Sahlins, Bernie, 41
Saint-Subber [Arnold], 122, 123–24, 129, 136, 159, 478
Salamon, Julie, 459
Sancocho (revue), 337
San Francisco, performance in, 96–97
Sarris, Andrew, 195, 259, 410
Saturday Night Live (TV), 312–13, 339, 340
Saving Private Ryan (film), 493
Sawyer, Diane, 403, 415, 420, 555, 569–70
   background of, 421–22
   career of, 422, 443–44, 457, 500, 587
   influence of, on Nichols, 421, 449, 453, 458, 491, 502
   marriage of Nichols and, 432–33, 453, 575
   and Nichols's death and memorial, 590, 591, 592
   and Nichols's ex-wives, 422–23, 433, 588
   and Nichols's health, 519, 583, 586

   and Nichols's work, 436, 458, 536, 538, 560, 583, 585, 586, 589
   relationship of Nichols and, 406–7, 421–23, 431–33, 434, 453, 457, 560
   socializing, 494, 505, 507, 551, 589
Schaffner, Franklin J., 278
Schisgal, Murray, 147, 151, 265
Schlesinger, Arthur, Jr., 238
Schneider, Bert, 289
Schulberg, Budd, 227
Scorsese, Martin, 472
Scot, Patricia, 61–62
   later friendship with Nichols, 588–89
   marriage of Nichols and, 80–81, 86–87, 127
   relationship of Nichols and, 65–67
   separation and divorce, 91–92, 146, 267
Scott, A. O., 547–48
Scott, George C., 519, 563, 594
   and *The Day of the Dolphin*, 282–85
   and *The Little Foxes*, 223, 225
   and *Patton*, 243, 280
   and *Plaza Suite*, 231–34, 280, 286
   and *Uncle Vanya*, 280, 286, 287, 288–89
Seagull, The (theater), 384, 517–22, 523, 589
   archival film of, 522
   casting of, 508–9, 517–18
   and Kline, 509, 517, 518–19, 520, 521–22
   Nichols working with actors on, 518–21
   opening of, 521
   and P. S. Hoffman, 518, 520, 521, 573, 578, 579
   rehearsals for, 518–19
   reviews of, 521
   and Streep, 508–9, 517–21
Second City, Chicago, 30
Segal, George, 78
   and *The Knack*, 143, 144, 168
   and *Who's Afraid of Virginia Woolf?*, 177, 178, 180, 183, 184, 185, 186
Sellars, Peter, 373
Sellers, Peter, 104
Selznick, David O., 169
Sendak, Maurice, 534
September 11 attacks, 523, 559
sex, lies, and videotape (film), 442
Shaffer, Paul, 340
Shaffer, Peter, 141–42, 146–47
Shakespeare, William, 464
Shandling, Garry, 501–2, 503–5, 508, 538
Shanley, John Patrick, 568, 589, 592
Shawn, Wallace, 231, 489–90, 491, 589
Shayne, Alan, 243, 282
Sheen, Martin, 242
Shenkman, Ben, 525–26, 528, 531, 532–33, 535
Shepard, Sam, 440, 518
Shepherd, David, 39, 40, 41, 47–48
   and Compass Players, 37, 48, 51–53, 61, 63, 66, 68, 563
Shire, David, 299, 300

Shore, Dinah, 79, 86, 88, 90
Shurlock, Geoffrey, 194
Siebert, Ron, 315
Silkwood (film), 358–71, 372, 374, 410, 483
  casting of, 360, 363
  and Cher, 363, 366, 367, 369, 370, 383
  collaboration with women on, 366, 401
  humanism of, 358, 361–63, 459
  and Nichols's directorial style, 365–66, 367–68, 369–70, 459
  and Nichols's return to filmmaking, 360, 362, 371, 548
  reviews of, 381–83, 548
  screenplay for, 359–60, 362, 370, 383
  shooting of, 361, 364–65, 368
  and Streep, 360–69, 371, 382, 383
Silkwood, Karen, 358, 361–63, 368, 369, 370, 381–82, 383
Silkwood family, 358–59
Sills, Paul:
  acting classes given by, 39, 44
  and Compass Players, 48–49, 51, 52, 62–63
  death of, 566
  and Harris, 47, 48, 53
  and New Actors Workshop, 435–36
  and "Passionella," 116
  and Playwrights Theatre Club, 39–42, 46
  and Tonight at 8:30, 30–31
  at University of Chicago, 29–34, 37
Silver, Casey, 498
Silver, Ron, 404
Simon, Carly, 401, 403, 414, 432, 441, 443, 446, 570
Simon, John, 228, 270–71, 408, 439–40
Simon, Neil, 179, 239, 256, 265, 312, 394, 570
  and *Biloxi Blues*, 416, 417–20, 426
  and *Bogart Slept Here/The Goodbye Girl*, 301–2, 304, 305, 353–54, 417
  and *Fools*, 353–54
  and *Laughter on the 23rd Floor*, 480
  and *Nobody Loves Me/Barefoot in the Park*, 122, 123, 125–30, 133–35, 138, 145, 159
  and *The Odd Couple*, 141, 158–61, 163–64, 190
  and *Plaza Suite*, 230, 232, 234–35, 244
  and *Prisoner of Second Avenue*, 274–77, 302
Simon, Paul, 322, 327, 376, 409, 589
  and *Saturday Night Live*, 313
  as songwriter, 221–22, 252, 593
  and tributes to Nichols, 502, 593
Simon & Garfunkel, 208, 221–22, 281, 376
Simple Plan, A (film), 470
Sirk, Douglas, 142
Six Degrees of Separation (theater), 450
60 Minutes (TV), 403, 422, 443
Skinny Dip (Hiaasen), 544, 554, 555
Smith, Liz, 422
Smith, Maggie, 142
Smith, Scott, 470
Social Security (theater), 394, 404–7, 408

Soderbergh, Steven, 442, 553
Solomon, Ed, 502, 503
Sondheim, Stephen, 255, 411, 592
  and "I'm Still Here," 446
  Nichols's friendship with, 79, 104, 111, 127, 139, 543
  and "Passionella," 116, 199
  and *West Side Story*, 79
  and *Who's Afraid of Virginia Woolf?*, 184, 185–86
Sontag, Susan, 27, 127, 203
Sony Pictures, 501, 506, 539, 545, 547, 574
Sophie's Choice (film), 339, 361, 362, 375, 400
Sophie's Choice (Styron), 338
Sopranos, The (TV), 516
Sorkin, Aaron, 145, 508, 555–56, 558, 559, 584
Sorkin, Hannah Roth, 505
Sound of Music, The (film), 229
Spader, James, 474
Spamalot (theater), 539, 544–47, 548–52, 553, 554, 565
Spiegel, Sam, 292–94, 350–51
Spielberg, Steven, 393, 493, 499, 569, 592
Spinella, Stephen, 520
Spolin, Viola, 29
Spook Show, The (theater), 391–93, 411
SS *Bremen*, 8–9, 592
Stanislavski, Konstantin, 30, 519
Stapleton, Maureen, 231–34, 243–44, 402, 594
Star Is Born, A (film), 423–24
Starr, Kenneth I., 569–70
Stasio, Marilyn, 580
Steel, Dawn, 444, 446, 448
Steinem, Gloria, 150, 161–62, 166, 167, 175, 182, 184, 192
Stephanopoulos, George, 494
Stern, Matthew, 579
Sterritt, David, 382
Steve Allen Show, The (TV), 75–76, 77
Stevens, George, 32
Stevens, Inger, 44, 45
Stevens, Norma, 115n, 544
Stevenson, Juliet, 462
Stiller, Jerry, 385
Stoddard, Brandon, 360
Stone, Oliver, 426
Stone, Peter, 373–74, 539
Stoppard, Tom, 411, 461
  and *Innocent Blood*, 349
  and *The Real Thing*, 375, 377–79, 384
  and tributes to Nichols, 538, 592
Stradling, Harry, 173
Strand, Mark, 490
Strasberg, Lee:
  influence on Nichols of, 44–45, 46, 57, 58, 126, 127, 344
  and Method acting, 42, 532
  Nichols's attendance at classes of, 43, 47, 48, 49, 96
  Nichols's network of classmates with, 123, 210, 435

Strathairn, David, 365

Streamers (theater), 314–20, 322, 323, 366, 385, 387
    awards for, 328
    homosexuality as theme in, 316, 483
    in New Haven, 315–16, 318, 319, 343
    Nichols's appraisal of, 314
    Nichols's work with actors in, 316–17, 319–20, 325
    opening of, 320
    reviews of, 318, 319, 320
    as turning point, 326, 335, 418
    violence in, 317–18, 320

Streep, Meryl, 384–85, 412, 413, 427, 436, 491, 544
    and *Angels in America*, 516, 523, 524, 529, 531, 533, 535, 536, 538
    and *Betrayal*, 350, 375, 453
    and *The French Lieutenant's Woman*, 339, 350, 360, 375
    and *Heartburn*, 372, 375, 397, 398–99, 400–403, 410
    and *Hope Springs*, 568
    and *A Little Night Music*, 566
    and Nichols's death and memorial, 592, 593
    Nichols working with, 366–68, 370, 371, 383, 398, 401, 402–3, 518–19, 520–21, 533
    and *Postcards from the Edge*, 424, 445, 446–48
    and *Primary Colors*, 489, 493
    at Public Theater, 338
    and *The Real Thing*, 375
    and *The Remains of the Day*, 453, 460–61
    and *The Seagull*, 508–9, 517–21
    and *Silkwood*, 360–69, 371, 382, 383
    and *Sophie's Choice*, 338–39, 361, 362, 375, 400
    and tributes to Nichols, 502, 538, 569, 593

Streetcar Named Desire, A (theater):
    influence of, on Nichols, 24–25, 32, 121–22, 172, 173, 572
    and Kazan, 24–25, 537, 572
    and repertory, 384
    Stradling as cinematographer for, 173

Streisand, Barbra, 398, 500, 582
Strick, Wesley, 472, 473
Strouse, Charles, 89, 325, 327
Sturges, Preston, 228, 418
Styne, Jule, 104
Styron, Rose, 129, 277, 284, 299, 300, 432, 505
Styron, William, 129, 291, 299, 338, 339, 432, 505
Sundance Festival, 442
Sunshine, Norman, 445
Surtees, Robert:
    awards of, 212, 229
    and *Ben-Hur*, 212
    and *Bogart Slept Here*, 304
    and *The Graduate*, 208, 212–13, 216, 217, 229, 257, 285, 304
Susskind, David, 102
Sweet, Jeffrey, 52
Sylbert, Anthea, 264, 306

Sylbert, Richard:
    and *Carnal Knowledge*, 264, 281
    and *Catch-22*, 239, 241–42, 245
    and *The Fortune*, 296, 298–99, 303
    and *The Graduate*, 206, 208, 211, 213, 257
    and *Who's Afraid of Virginia Woolf?*, 175–76, 181, 208

Take Her, She's Mine (theater), 123
Tallman, Frank, 244
Tandy, Jessica, 24, 331–33, 593
Tanen, Ned, 330
Tate, Sharon, 278
Taubman, Howard, 101, 102, 145
Taxi Driver (film), 304
Taylor, Elizabeth:
    and Burton, 113, 114, 153, 174–75, 177–78, 241
    and *Cleopatra*, 113, 174
    death of, 574
    Nichols working with, 175, 177–79, 180, 182, 183, 185–87, 192
    personal traits of, 113, 207
    and *A Place in the Sun*, 32, 172
    and *Who's Afraid of Virginia Woolf?*, 32, 153, 168, 170, 172, 173–75, 176–87, 189, 192, 195, 213, 348
Taylor, Juliet, 398, 429, 524–25, 526
Taylor, Laurette, 24
Teachout, Terry, 580
Tharp, Twyla, 482
That Was the Week That Was (TV), 140, 150
Thomas, Marlo, 404, 406
Thompson, Emma, 458–59, 592
    and *Angels in America*, 523, 524, 529, 533, 535
    Nichols working with, 459, 510, 513–14, 521
    and *Primary Colors*, 489, 492–93, 495, 497, 509
    and *Remains of the Day*, 460, 461
    and *Wit*, 510, 511–12, 513–14, 516
Thompson, Sada, 321
Thorns, The (TV), 426–27
Thornton, Billy Bob, 494, 499
Three Sisters (theater), 384
Tichler, Rosemarie, 517–18, 520
Tomlin, Lily, 586
Tonight at 8:30, 30–31
Tonight Show (TV), 428
Toobin, Jeffrey, 507
Toobin, Jerome, 47
Towne, Robert, 278
Town Hall, New York, 88, 90
Travolta, John, 494, 495–96, 497
Troobnick, Eugene, 39
True Confessions (theater), 261–62
    see also *Carnal Knowledge*
Truffaut, François, 155, 172, 256
Tucci, Maria, 225, 336
Tune, Tommy, 341, 355, 356, 372, 373–74
Turan, Kenneth, 548

Turman, Lawrence, 142–43, 152, 196, 197
20th Century Fox, 426, 429, 442, 567
Twiggy (Lesley Lawson), 374
Twilight Zone (TV), 439
Tynan, Kenneth, 104

Ullmann, Liv, 320
Uncle Vanya (theater), 280, 286–89, 290, 291, 333, 424
United Artists, 478–79, 485
Universal Studios:
    and *Charlie Wilson's War*, 556, 559
    and *Melvin and Howard*, 330–31
    and *Primary Colors*, 492, 494, 498
    and *The Public Eye*, 142, 152, 158
    and *An Unmarried Woman*, 334
University of Chicago, 26–34, 36–37, 38, 137
Unmarried Woman, An (film), 334
U.S. Film Festival, 442

Vadim, Roger, 176
Valenti, Jack, 194
Vanderbilt, Gloria, 100
Van Devere, Trish, 280, 283
Van Doren, Charles, 93
Van Dyke, Dick, 89
Village Vanguard, New York, 70–72, 79
Visconti, Luchino, 264
Voight, Jon, 242, 247

Wade, Kevin, 416, 427
Wag the Dog (film), 497
Waiting for Godot (theater), 65, 424–25, 436–41, 479
Walken, Christopher, 385, 387, 389, 419, 517, 521, 593
Wallace, George, 167
Wallace, Mike, 83
Wallach, Eli, 147, 148
Walters, Barbara, 196
Walton, Tony, 284, 463
    and *The Knack*, 144–45
    Nichols's friendship with, 105, 144, 150, 458, 584
    set designs by, 144, 201, 317, 341, 376–77, 458, 465
    and *Uncle Vanya*, 288
Warner, Jack, and *Who's Afraid of Virginia Woolf?*, 152–53, 157, 168, 173–74, 176, 177, 187, 189–90, 191–92, 194
Warner Bros.:
    and *Bogart Slept Here*, 304, 306, 313
    and Calley, 278, 304, 306, 340
    and *Farragut North*, 560–61
    and Geffen, 313
    and *Who's Afraid of Virginia Woolf?*, 153, 157, 168, 172–73, 177, 183, 189, 192, 193–94, 207
Waterston, Sam, 352
Watkin, David, 244–45, 252
Watt, Douglas, 74

Watts, Richard, 135
Wayne, John, 251–52
"We Are Family" (song), 483
Weaver, Fritz, 283
Weaver, Sigourney, 385, 428–29, 431, 443
Webb, Charles, 142, 143, 196, 197
Weiner, Matthew, 567, 569, 587
Weinstein, Harvey and Bob, 442
Weir, Peter, 471
Weiss, Hedy, 439
Weisz, Rachel, 583
Welch, Bo, 476, 481, 483, 504
Welch, Raquel, 263
Welles, Orson, 242–43, 249–50
Welsh, Kenneth, 377, 404–5
Wexler, Haskell, 157, 168, 173–75, 179–80, 182, 183–84, 185
WFMT (radio), Nichols as DJ at, 40, 42
What Planet Are You From? (film), 501–2, 503–6, 507, 508, 539
Who's Afraid of Virginia Woolf? (film), 166–69, 170–87, 193–98, 296, 366, 451, 459
    and Albee, 121, 153, 157, 171, 181, 192, 347
    awards and honors for, 203, 208
    and Burton, 153, 170, 171, 174, 175, 177–78, 180–81, 182–87, 189, 192, 195, 348
    casting of, 152–53, 157, 168, 176–77, 343
    and censorship, 157–58, 182, 189–90, 191–92, 194, 262
    and filming, 156–57, 172–74, 175, 179–87, 211
    and Lehman, 152–53, 157–58, 166, 168, 170–78, 182–84, 186
    premiere of, 194, 198
    rehearsals for, 177–79, 209
    reviews of, 194–95, 203
    success of, 195–96, 203, 207
    and Taylor, 32, 153, 168, 170, 172, 173–75, 176–87, 189, 192, 195, 213, 348
    themes of, 121, 174, 350, 539
    and Warner, *see* Warner, Jack; Warner Bros.
Who's Afraid of Virginia Woolf? (theater), 301, 343–48
Wick, Douglas, 421
    and *What Planet Are You From?*, 501, 504
    and *Wolf*, 471–72, 476
    and *Working Girl*, 427, 428, 429, 430, 441, 443
Wieseltier, Leon, 396
Wiest, Dianne, 482
Wilde, Oscar, 483
Wilder, Billy, 156, 172, 181, 478, 547
Wilding, Michael, 168
Williams, Robin:
    and *The Birdcage*, 479–80, 481, 482, 484–85, 486, 526
    and *Good Morning, Vietnam*, 438
    and *Mrs. Doubtfire*, 479
    and *Waiting for Godot*, 425, 436–37, 438–39, 440
Williams, Tennessee, 24, 60, 100, 108, 223

Williamson, Nicol, 286–89
Willimon, Beau, 560–62
Willingham, Calder, 196
Willis, Bruce, 452
Wilson, Charlie, 555–56, 558, 559
Wilson, Edmund, 23, 103, 111, 118, 230, 238, 353
Wilson, Elizabeth, 210, 220, 223, 227, 337–38
Wilson, Lanford, 353
Wilson, Patrick, 526, 530, 533, 538
Winer, Linda, 441–42, 521
Winfrey, Oprah, 569, 592
Winsten, Archer, 292
Winters, Shelley, 167
Wintour, Anna, 592
Wise, Greg, 458
Wise, Robert, 359
Wit (film), 509–13, 514, 516–17, 523, 537, 540
Witherspoon, Reese, 524
Wittrock, Finn, 575–76, 577, 579
Wolf (film), 461, 462, 471–77, 526, 569
Wolfe, George C., 423–24, 522
Wolsky, Albert, 563
Woodward, Bob, 422
Woodward, Joanne, 235
Woodward, Jonathan M., 511–13

Working Girl (film), 417, 424, 426–31, 432, 446, 467
  awards for, 443
  casting of, 428–29, 449
  filming of, 427–28, 429–31, 445
  limited success of, 442, 452
  marketing of, 442–43
  public response to, 441, 459, 462
  reviews of, 441–42
  screenplay for, 341, 416, 426
World News Tonight (TV), 570
World of Jules Feiffer, The (musical), 113, 116–17, 143
Wranovics, Fred, 52
Wright, Jeffrey, 524, 535, 538
Wright, Max, 352
Wurtzel, Stuart, 511
Wyler, William, 176, 269

Yeston, Maury, 355–56, 413
"You Don't Know Me" (song), 446

Zeffirelli, Franco, 192
Zinnemann, Fred, 156, 213, 323, 369
Zollo, Fred, 385, 386, 388, 464
Zolotow, Sam, 152
Zorich, Louis, 65, 162
Zuckerman, Henry, 14

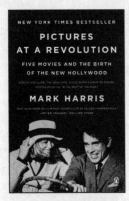

PICTURES AT A REVOLUTION
Five Movies and the Birth of the New Hollywood

In the mid-1960s, westerns, war movies, and blockbuster musicals like *Mary Poppins* swept the box office. But by the Oscar ceremonies of 1968, the tastes of American moviegoers had radically changed. Films like *Bonnie and Clyde*, *The Graduate*, *Guess Who's Coming to Dinner*, and *In the Heat of the Night* signaled a change in Hollywood—and America. As an entire industry advanced and struggled, the landscape of filmmaking was transformed beyond all recognition.

FIVE CAME BACK
A Story of Hollywood and the Second World War

During World War II, the U.S. government farmed out its war propaganda effort to Hollywood, allowing five major directors—John Ford, George Stevens, John Huston, William Wyler, and Frank Capra—the freedom to film in combat zones as never before. They were on the scene at almost every major moment of America's war. *Five Came Back* is the product of five years of scrupulous archival research, and provides a revelatory new understanding of Hollywood's role in the war through the life and work of these men.

PENGUIN BOOKS